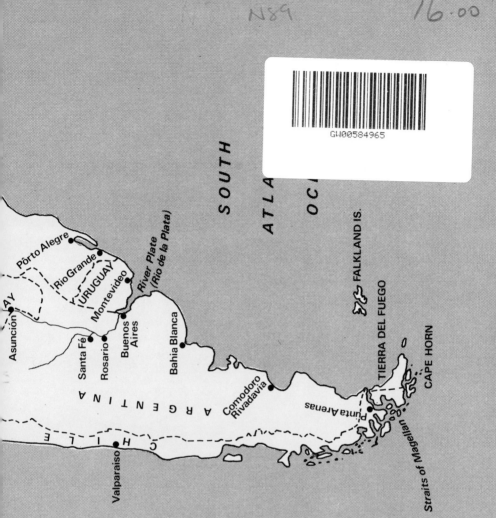

SOUTH AMERICA

SOUTH ATLANTIC
SEAWAY

1966 EUGENIO C 30,567 tons
With only one exception the largest ship built for the River Plate trade.

SOUTH ATLANTIC SEAWAY

*An illustrated history
of the passenger lines and liners
from Europe to
Brazil, Uruguay and Argentina*

by

N.R.P. BONSOR

BROOKSIDE PUBLICATIONS

JERSEY CHANNEL ISLANDS

ISBN 0 905824 06 7

© N.R.P. Bonsor 1983

Set in Times and printed and bound in Great Britain by The Garden City Press Limited, Letchworth, Hertfordshire SG6 1JS
for Brookside Publications, Brookside, Petit Port, St. Brelade, Jersey, Channel Islands.

UK, British Commonwealth and European Distributors:
PATRICK STEPHENS LIMITED, Bar Hill, Cambridge, CB3 8EL.

CONTENTS

Note: Dates in brackets indicate when an already existing line started a South American steamship service.

SUMMARY

Lines	Number of chapters
Italian	22
British	17
French	11
German	5
Portuguese	4
Spanish	3
Dutch	3
Austrian	2
Argentinian	2
Polish	1
Panamanian	1
	71

LIST OF ILLUSTRATIONS

INTRODUCTION

With 40 years of intensive research in connection with the first and second editions of NORTH ATLANTIC SEAWAY behind me, I could perhaps be forgiven for having then decided to have a good rest.

I confess that this was what I had in mind but, like so many good intentions, it was short-lived. Another project quickly beckoned and I was not idle for long. This volume is the result.

Some years previously, I had undertaken a little preliminary research on transatlantic lines running to the West Indies, Central America and South America, and at one time thought that eventually I might write a history of the entire subject. The idea perforce went into cold storage as NORTH ATLANTIC SEAWAY expanded. Moreover, the subject was a vast one and, if covered thoroughly, would need almost as many pages as the eventual 2,000 page, five volume, second edition of 'NAS', finally completed in 1980. From every point of view, this was now too big a job for me to attempt, but I soon realised that a satisfactory compromise might be to start work on a history of the multi-passenger lines and liners which run and used to run (sadly, the only survivor is the Costa Line) from Europe to Brazil, Uruguay and Argentina.

I decided to adopt the same general format as in NORTH ATLANTIC SEAWAY, and it was fortunate that more than 30 of the 250 or more lines described in that book ran services from Europe to South America for short or long periods, so that there was already a substantial groundwork on which to build. It is strange that no comprehensive book has hitherto been published on this very interesting subject, although there have been a few books and articles on some of the individual lines.

Not unnaturally, the title I have used for this new book is SOUTH ATLANTIC SEAWAY, which would, of course, be misleading without the subtitle: 'An illustrated history of the passenger lines and liners from Europe to Brazil, Uruguay and Argentina.'

For reasons of space, there have been some minor omissions, including several short-lived British and Italian lines as well as lines whose ships were restricted to 12 passengers. In addition there were two or more lines between Europe, Australia and/or New Zealand whose steamers called, usually on the homeward voyage, at a port or ports on the east coast of South America. A few of these omissions are dealt with briefly in Appendix A.

When writing NORTH ATLANTIC SEAWAY I was in the fortunate position of being able to spend the equivalent of several months at the Newspaper Library at Colindale, North London, where to quote only one example, I studied virtually every daily issue of the *New York Herald* or *New York Herald-Tribune* from 1845 to 1960 with eminently satisfactory results. Moreover, through the courtesy of a friend, I made considerable use of the official schedules of sailings actually undertaken by all the North Atlantic passenger conference lines from 1898 onwards. I have not been so fortunate in the case of SOUTH ATLANTIC SEAWAY, but I acknowledge with gratitude the co-operation of the Guildhall Library in the City of London, the National Maritime Museum at Greenwich, the Newspaper Library at Colindale, H.M. Customs' Library and the Jersey Public Library. In addition, many friends have been extremely helpful and it is no exaggeration to say that without their encouragement and assistance it would not have been possible to produce this new book in its desired format.

It is too much to hope that the book is without some blemishes, and I shall much appreciate receiving comments and suggestions from readers.

ACKNOWLEDGEMENTS

My first words of thanks must unquestionably go to Roy Anderson, author of *White Star*, who, as was the case with *North Atlantic Seaway*, has edited virtually the entire manuscript. In addition to making quite a number of corrections, he has been responsible for innumerable alterations, thereby making a vast difference to the quality of the text.

There seems to be no satisfactory alternative but to place the numerous other kind helpers in alphabetical order, and I sincerely hope that there are no omissions. I am greatly indebted to all the following:

The late Contre-Amiral M. Adam, CVO, CBE (Messageries Maritimes, Société Générale de Transports Maritimes, Chargeurs Réunis and other lines, and many rare photographs); the late Dr. Herbert Bischoff (much information about the German lines and many photographs; joint author of the three volume *Die Schiffe der Hamburg–Amerika Linie*); P.C. Brandwijk of Maassluis (books and photographs); Frank C. Braynard of Sea Cliff, New York (books); David Burrell (helpful advice and the names and addresses of other experts); Nereo Castelli of Italy (name of the pioneer South American steamer of Lloyd Austriaco and much Italian information); the late Dr. F. de' Rossi of Naples (information about the principal Italian lines and many photographs); the late Tomaso Gropallo of Italy (help with various Italian lines; author of *Navi a Vapore ed Armamenti Italiani*); R.M.B.H. Hackman (a great many launching dates); Professor E.K. Haviland of Baltimore (launching dates and the exact number of passengers permitted on a great many Lamport & Holt ships – a most valuable contribution); J.H. Isherwood (much worthwhile advice, and much assistance from his monthly articles in *Sea Breezes*); Professor John H. Kemble of California (Pacific Steam Navigation Company and Ybarra Line); Arnold Kludas (author of *Great Passenger Ships of the World* (5 volumes); *Die Schiffe der Hamburg–Süd* and joint author of *Die Schiffe der Hamburg–Amerika Linie* (3 volumes); A. Lagendijk of Holland (author of *Passagierschepen op Afrika en Latijns Amerika*; W.A. Laxon of New Zealand (Lamport & Holt Line); Lt. Commander John M. Maber, RN (Royal Mail Steam Packet Company); Dr. W. Moore McLean of Florida (a wide variety of information); F.G.E. Moll of Holland (Holland America Line, Royal Holland Lloyd and Rotterdam South America Line; also a number of photographs); Wilton J. Oldham (books and magazines); Dr. Lamberto Radogna of Naples (much information about Italian lines); John Raper (numerous launching dates); Tom Rayner (photographs); Armand Rensonnet (translation from German); Captain E.E. Sigwart, RFA (Retd) (many rare photographs); Eugene W. Smith (author of *Passenger Ships of the World*); C.E.C. Townsend (dimensions and detailed activities of many early steamships); World Ship Society – Michael Crowdy, founder and chairman; Graeme Somner, Harold Appleyard, Kevin O'Donoghue and P.L. White (ship details) and J.L. Loughran (funnels and houseflags), all of whom have supplied a great deal of extremely helpful information.

Sincere thanks are due to the Costa Line for photographs of their two principal ships, and to Skyfotos for permission to reproduce the MS ALHENA.

There are three important last-minute additions: Fred M. Walker (launching dates) and Captain Altino Magalhães Gomes of Lisbon, who has enabled me to rewrite Chapter 4 (Companhia de Navagação a Vapor Luso-Brasileira) and has supplied the Portuguese name of the Anglo-Luso-Brazilian Royal Mail Steam Navigation Company (Chapter 11). Also Luis Miguel Correia for much additional information regarding the Companhia Nacional de Navegação and Companhia Colonial de Navegação.

To all the foregoing I again express my very real thanks.

It is very good news that Patrick Stephens Limited are again acting as distributors, and that Ray Hedley of The Garden City Press Limited is again in charge of production.

Noel R.P. Bonsor,
Damaris,
Petit Port,
Corbiere,
Jersey,
Channel Islands.
1983.

BIBLIOGRAPHY

ADAM, Contre-Amiral M. *Compagnie des Chargeurs Réunis, Sea Breezes* October 1956

ADAM, Contre-Amiral M. *Story of the Messageries Maritimes, Sea Breezes* February 1957

ADAM, Contre-Amiral M. *Société Générale de Transports Maritimes, Sea Breezes*

BUSHELL, T.A. *Royal Mail 1839–1939* London, 1939

DUNN, Laurence *Passenger Liners* Southampton, 1961

DUNNETT, Alastair M. *The Donaldson Line 1854–1954* Glasgow, 1960

GIBBS, C.R.V. *British Passenger Liners of the Five Oceans* London, 1963

GROPALLO, Tomaso *Navi a Vapore ed Armamenti Italiani*

HEATON, P.M. *The Lamport & Holt Fleet, Sea Breezes* June 1977

HEATON, P.M. *Booth Line's Rise and Progress, Sea Breezes* January 1979

ISHERWOOD, J.H. *Steamers of the Past* (monthly article in *Sea Breezes* for upwards of 30 years).

JOHN, A.H. *A Liverpool Merchant House* London, 1959

KLUDAS, Arnold *Great Passenger Ships of the World* (5 volumes) Cambridge, 1975

KLUDAS, Arnold *Die Schiffe der Hamburg–Süd* Oldenburg and Hamburg, 1976

KLUDAS, Arnold and BISCHOFF, Herbert *Die Schiffe der Hamburg–Amerika Linie* (3 volumes) Herford, Germany, 1979

LAGENDIJK, A. *Passagiersschepen op Afrika en Latijns Amerika*

LYON, David John *The Denuy List* (Parts 1 and 2) National Maritime Museum, Greenwich, London

MABER, John *North Star to Southern Cross* Prescot, Merseyside 1967

MONDADORI, Grafiche A *Il Lloyd Triestino* Verona, 1938

OGLIARI, Francisco and RADOGNA, Lamberto *Trasporti Marittimi di Linea* (3 volumes) Milan, 1975

SMITH, Eugene W. *Passenger Ships of the World – Past and Present* Boston, Mass, 1978

STEVENS, Edward F. *One Hundred Years of Houlders* London

WARDLE, Arthur C. *Steam Conquers the Pacific* London, 1940

EXPLANATORY NOTES
Abbreviations used in Fleet Lists

EXAMPLES

1865[1] DOURO[2]
 2,824[3]. 99,48 x 12,25[4]. (326.4 x 40.2)[5]. C[6]17–2[8]. I[10]–S[11]–I(2)[12]–12[13].
 Caird & Co, Greenock[14].
1960[1] ARLANZA[2] (II) (M/S)
 20,363[3]. 164,58 [178,00] x 23,86[4]. (540.0 [584.0] x 78.3)[5]. 1[7]–1[8]–C[9].
 2S[11]–2SC.SA[12]–17½[13].

1. DATE
 Year of maiden voyage on South Atlantic.
 Dates in brackets indicate that the ship had been in previous employment – not necessarily for the same owners or under the same name.
2. NAME OF SHIP
 Where (c) (chartered) follows the name, this should not necessarily be used in the literal sense. In some cases ships so noted were 'managed', 'loaded on the berth', etc.
 In the numbering of ships, chartered vessels are distinguished by 'a', 'b', etc.
 (M/S) after the name indicates motorship.
3. GROSS TONNAGE
 Note: Gross tonnage is the cubic capacity of the permanently enclosed space of the ship (i.e. hull, superstructure and deckhouses, less exemptions, calculated on the basis of 100 cubic feet being equal to one gross ton.
 It is not generally known that there are a good many exemptions when calculating gross tonnage, the following being some of the most important: the wheelhouse, chartroom and navigating aid spaces; all the shelter deck space; the sheltered passenger spaces when glassed in but not furnished; water ballast tanks if not for any other use; storage spaces for safety equipment; cable lockers; the double bottom spaces; the washing rooms and toilets for the crew as well as their galley and bakery. From the foregoing, it will be evident that the inclusion or omission of these items can make a very considerable difference to the gross tonnage of a ship.
 It frequently happened that the gross tonnage of a ship altered many times during her lifetime. As far as possible, the figures for new ships are those quoted by *Lloyd's Register* at the time of completion and for second-hand ships at the time of being

commissioned by the company in question. Changes of tonnage are often mentioned. Anomalies frequently exist between the tonnage quoted by *Lloyd's Register* and the owning line.

Gross tonnage is used almost exclusively except in the case of some ships built before 1854, when what is now known as 'old measurement' was used, this being the tons burthen of a ship plus the engine room tonnage. A number of pre-1854 ships were never remeasured.

4. DIMENSIONS
Length between perpendiculars (BP) in metres and hundredths of metres multiplied by ('x') beam. Length overall (OA) where shown is in square brackets.

5. DIMENSIONS
Length between perpendiculars (BP) in feet and tenths of feet multiplied by ('x') beam. Length overall (OA) where shown is in square brackets.

6. TYPE OF BOW
C – Clipper
S – Straight
This information is normally omitted after about 1900.

7. NUMBER OF FUNNELS

8. NUMBER OF MASTS

9. CRUISER STERN
When the number of funnels and masts is followed by 'C', this indicates that the ship had a cruiser stern.

10. CONSTRUCTION
W – Wood
I – Iron
S – Steel
Where this information is omitted – usually after about 1900 – the ship was built of steel.

11. PROPULSION
P – Paddle
S – Single-screw
2S – Twin-screw
3S – Triple-screw
4S – Quadruple-screw

12. ENGINES
B – Beam
C – Compound
D – Diagonal
DE – Diesel electric
G – Geared

H – Horizontal
I – Inverted
O – Oscillating
Q – Quadruple-expansion
SL – Side lever
ST – Steam turbines (direct acting)
ST(SR) – Steam turbines (single-reduction)
ST(DR) – Steam turbines (double-reduction)
T – Triple-expansion
TE – Turbo-electric
T&ST – Combination of triple-expansion reciprocating engines and steam turbines
VT – Vertical trunk
2SC.DA – Two stroke double-acting engines (motor-ships)
4SC.DA – Four stroke double-acting engines (motor-ships)
2SC.SA – Two stroke single-acting engines (motor-ships)
4SC.SA – Four stroke single acting engines (motor-ships)

The number immediately following I, C, T or Q, indicates the number of cylinders – eg I(2), C2, T6, Q8. Thus, a twin-screw ship shown as Q8 had two sets of four-cylinder quadruple-expansion engines. Steam reciprocating engines not shown as C, T or Q are single-expansion.

13. SERVICE SPEED (in knots)
14. BUILDER
Engine-builders are normally mentioned when they differed from the builders of the hull.

SHIP'S ACTIVITIES
1983 (5/1) – 1983 (5 January)
MV – Maiden voyage
FV – First voyage (ie on that particular route or for that particular company)
LV – Last voyage
RV – Round vovage

The number in brackets following the loss of or an accident to a ship indicates the number of fatal casualties.

Some ships appear in two or more fleet lists, not necessarily under the same name.

Date of sale and renaming or scrapping of a ship was not necessarily the actual date when the ship was renamed or scrapped.

METRES AND FEET
Generally speaking, dimensions in feet are taken from *Lloyd's Register* and metric equivalents obtained by means of a conversion table.

CURRENCY CONVERSIONS
Conversions of other currencies into sterling have been made at the rates in effect at the date in question.
GUINEAS
One guinea = £1.05.
HOUSEFLAGS
Houseflags have been divided into five different shapes, as follow:
(1) Flag – rectangular.
(2) Burgee – As (1) except for a 'swallow-tail' at fly.
(3) Pennant – triangular.
(4) Long Pennant – as (3) but longer.
(5) Swallow-tailed pennant – as (3) but with a 'swallow-tail' at fly.
Note: Unless otherwise stated, the houseflags described at the end of the fleet lists are flags.
CHANGES OF NAME OF PORTS

Old Name	Present Name
BAHIA	SALVADOR
CEARA	FORTALEZA
MANAOS	MANAUS
MARANHAM	SÃO LUIZ
PARA	BELEM
PERNAMBUCO	RECIFE

SÃO VICENTE Portuguese)   ST. VINCENT (English version)
RIO DE LA PLATA (Spanish) RIVER PLATE (English version)

Chapter 1

(1851–1932)

ROYAL MAIL STEAM PACKET COMPANY

1932–69

ROYAL MAIL LINES LIMITED

(British)

The ROYAL MAIL STEAM PACKET COMPANY was granted a Royal Charter by Queen Victoria on 26 September 1839, its first mail contract being signed by the Admiralty on 20 March 1840, less than a year after one received by the company now known as Cunard.

Responsibility for the formation of Royal Mail must be credited to a Scot, James MacQueen, who had lived for many years in the West Indies and knew all the principal islands intimately. In July 1837 he submitted to the British Government detailed proposals for a steamship line between England and the West Indies, followed two months later by a much more ambitious 'General Plan' for world-wide services. The successful transatlantic voyages of the steamers SIRIUS and GREAT WESTERN to New York in 1838 increased MacQueen's enthusiasm even further, and early in 1839 he succeeded in persuading the West India Committee, a London association of West Indian merchants and planters, to support a scheme for a steamship service to the West Indies, subject to a substantial Government subsidy. The first directors' meeting of the ROYAL MAIL STEAM PACKET COMPANY was held on 24 July 1839.

The mail contract was worth £240,000 a year and called for fortnightly sailings to Barbados, Grenada, the Danish Virgin Islands, Haiti, Cuba and Mexico, with a wide variety of connecting services to the other islands and to ports on the American mainland. Southampton was chosen as the British terminal, a major factor being that the London & Southampton Railway was opened throughout on 11 May 1841. However, the Admiralty insisted until September 1843 on a call at Falmouth out and home to load and off-load the mails.

To cover the entire range of services, 14 wooden paddle steamers of about 1,800 tons old measurement, or 1,285 tons gross [1], were ordered from nine builders, none of whom supplied the engines. Two sets were ordered from Acramans, Morgan & Co of Bristol, who went into

1

liquidation soon afterwards, and it is believed that the actual suppliers were Maudslay, Sons & Field of London [2]. In addition, three small wooden schooners, the LARNE, LEE and LIFFEY, were laid down for local services in the West Indies, and two second-hand wooden paddle steamers were bought for a similar purpose.

The Company's nominal capital was £1,500,000, of which £900,000 was paid up – enough to take care of the total cost of the fleet, about £800,000.

Two of the schooners sailed from Blackwall, London, on 3 December 1841, the steamer FORTH from Southampton on 17 December, the SOLWAY, TWEED and CLYDE from the same port a day later and the THAMES from Gravesend on 29 December. These preliminary sailings enabled the ships to take up their stations in the West Indies in preparation for the first mail sailing by the TAY on 31 December 1841 from Southampton and 3 January 1842 from Falmouth. The second mail sailing was taken by the DEE from Southampton on 14 January, fortnightly departures taking place on the same days of each subsequent month except that Sunday sailings were postponed to the Monday. All the newly-built steamers were named after rivers, those not already mentioned being the MEDINA, MEDWAY, TRENT, TEVIOT, ISIS, AVON and SEVERN. Unfortunately, the ISIS was lost in 1842, the SOLWAY in 1843, the TWEED in 1847 and the FORTH in 1849.

In addition, the 1,775 ton wooden paddle steamer GREAT WESTERN was bought in 1847 from the Great Western Steam Ship Company, for whom she had been running between Bristol or Liverpool and New York since 1838. Her first RMSP sailings were to the West Indies.

An important innovation was the fitting of feathering paddle-wheel floats to the THAMES in April 1850, and she achieved an average speed of 10.4 knots over the measured mile at Stokes Bay, off the Hampshire coast near Spithead, an improvement of no less than two knots. She was the first steamer to cross the Atlantic with feathering paddles and some of her consorts were similarly treated.

On 5 July 1850 an additional contract was signed for a monthly service between Southampton and Rio de Janeiro via Lisbon, Madeira, St. Vincent (São Vicente, Cape Verde Islands), Pernambuco and Bahia. In fact, James MacQueen had proposed such a service as long previously as 1840, but at that time the Admiralty wisely turned down the suggestion in the knowledge that Royal Mail would have their resources stretched to the utmost by their West Indies commitments.

It was arranged for a small feeder steamer to run between Rio de Janeiro, Santos, Montevideo and Buenos Aires, since traffic to and from Uruguay and Argentina was not considered likely to compare with that to and from Brazil and, furthermore, the River Plate ports had few, if

2

any, facilities for berthing steamers and much of the river was extremely shallow.

The steamer selected was a 232 ton wooden screw ship taken over on the stocks of R. Menzies at Leith, named ESK and sailed from Southampton on 10 November 1850 for Lisbon, Madeira, St. Vincent, Pernambuco, Bahia, Rio de Janeiro, Montevideo and Buenos Aires, where she arrived on 12 January 1851 in 63 days from Southampton. She was notable as the forerunner of the first regular steamship service to South America, the first steamer to wear the Royal Mail houseflag in Brazilian, Uruguayan or Argentinian waters and the first screw steamer to carry the British mails. She had accommodation for 29 passengers and a crew of 22.

The new service was opened by the 1,285 ton TEVIOT, which sailed from Southampton on 9 January 1851 with 45 passengers. She was due to arrive at Rio in 28 days 19 hours from Southampton, and adhered almost exactly to this schedule. The TEVIOT was followed on 10 February by her sister ship TAY and a month later by another sister, the MEDWAY. The latter only made one South American voyage at this time, her successor being the 1,295 ton SEVERN. The MEDWAY was taken up as a Crimean War transport in 1854 as, in the following year, was the GREAT WESTERN, which had joined the Brazilian service in 1853 and made nine round voyages in it. She did not re-enter Royal Mail service after the war, and was scrapped at Vauxhall, London.

The 1,295 ton THAMES replaced the SEVERN in December 1853, while the SOLENT, built in 1853 by T. & J. White of Cowes, Isle of Wight, made two voyages to Brazil in 1855, followed by the AVON, a

1853 SOLENT 1,804 tons
A 'composite' ship which made two voyages to Brazil.

3

product of William Patterson of Bristol, builder of the GREAT WESTERN. The SOLENT was unusual in that she was a composite ship – that is to say, her sides were of wood but she had iron frames.

Five much larger wooden paddle steamers had been built for the West Indies trade in 1851 – the 2,900 ton ORINOCO, MAGDALENA and PARANA and the 2,300 ton AMAZON and DEMERARA. The AMAZON became infamous on 4 January 1852, during her maiden voyage, when she was destroyed by fire in the Bay of Biscay with the loss of 105 lives. She was replaced by the purchase of the 2,402 ton ARABIA from Cunard who, in turn, replaced her by a similar ship of the same name. Both were two-funnelled two masted wooden paddle steamers, the RMSP newcomer being renamed LA PLATA. For the first eight years of her Royal Mail service she plied between Southampton and the West Indies. But on 24 November 1860 she caught fire at Southampton and it seemed likely that she would become a complete loss. However, thanks largely to the efforts of the crew of the P&O TAGUS she was saved and made many voyages from Southampton to South America between 1865 and 1871, after the withdrawal of the MAGDALENA and PARANA. The former served as a Crimean War transport and ran to Brazil between 1860 and 1864, as did the PARANA between 1863 and 1865. The DEMERARA never entered Royal Mail service because she stranded in the River Avon when under tow from her builders to the Bristol Channel and beyond and was badly strained. She was rebuilt as a sailing ship.

Royal Mail had been established in the Brazil trade for little more than two years when they were confronted by serious competition from a

1852 LA PLATA 2,402 tons
Laid down as Cunard ARABIA. Ran to South America for several years.

4

Liverpool concern, the South American & General Steam Navigation Company (Chapter 2), whose pioneer iron screw steamer, the 1,100 ton BRASILEIRA, sailed from Liverpool on 24 August 1853 for Rio de Janeiro. However, their last sailing took place only 14 months later as their ships were taken up as Crimean War transports and the service was never reinstated.

Hitherto the RMSP mail contracts had insisted on the building of wooden ships. The burning of the AMAZON, however, resulted in a change of heart by the Admiralty and the appearance in 1854 of the 3,467 ton iron paddle steamer ATRATO, by far the largest and best Royal Mail unit to date. She ran exclusively to the West Indies, but it is worth noting that she entered service almost two years before Cunard's first iron mail paddle steamer, the 3,300 ton PERSIA, and that when sold in 1870 she was converted to single-screw.

The last wooden paddler to be built for Royal Mail was the 1,963 ton TAMAR in 1854, which after serving as a Crimean War transport replaced the GREAT WESTERN on 9 October 1855. The 1,603 ton iron paddler TYNE, also completed in 1854, entered the South American trade on 9 August 1856. She stranded on the Dorset coast on 13 January 1857 in fog, but was successfully refloated and re-entered service on 9 October 1857.

The first iron screw steamer to be built for Royal Mail was the 819 ton WYE, launched in 1853 for service in the West Indies. She was followed on the Company's books by the 2,293 ton ONEIDA, completed in 1855 for the Canada Ocean Steam Ship Company, but more noteworthy as one of the fleet of the ill-fated European & Australian Royal Mail Company, from whom she was bought with a consort, the TASMA-NIAN. The ONEIDA made many South American voyages, the first on 10 October 1859, but the TASMANIAN made only one.

The new mail contract which came into operation in 1863 no longer debarred the use of iron screw mail steamers, and in consequence the 2,824 ton DOURO and the 2,738 ton RHONE were laid down for the South American trade and entered service in 1865, at almost the same time as the LA PLATA (ex-ARABIA), the last wooden paddler to run to South America. They had accommodation for 253 first, 30 second and 30 third class passengers. The RHONE was later transferred to the West Indies trade and wrecked on 29 October 1867 in the Virgin Islands during a hurricane, as were the feeder steamers DERWENT and WYE. The RHONE was replaced in 1868 by the 3,025 ton NEVA, bought on the stocks from Norddeutscher Lloyd.

For many years, Royal mail had a serious competitor in the French Messageries Imperiales, better-known by its 1871 change of name to Messageries Maritimes, whose service to Brazil, with a feeder steamer to the River Plate, started in 1860 with iron paddle steamers, converted in 1872 to single-screw, but whose first screw steamer was introduced as early as 1861. It seems surprising that in the early days many Royal Mail passengers as well as those of other lines preferred paddle steamers to screw.

The Royal Mail service functioned for 18 years with Rio de Janeiro as its terminal, but the 398 ton iron paddle steamer PRINCE soon superseded the ESK as the feeder vessel to River Plate ports, followed by the 539 ton wooden paddle CAMILLA in 1853 and the 1,039 ton iron paddle MERSEY in 1859. It was not until 9 July 1869 that the DOURO inaugurated a through service from Southampton to Montevideo and Buenos Aires. The feeder steamer with withdrawn.

In 1870 Royal Mail commissioned the 3,108 ton iron screw ELBE, notable as the first of the fleet to be fitted with compound engines, their exhaust steam passing into a second cylinder and, thus, doing further useful work. In this way coal consumption was greatly reduced, which meant that extra space was available for cargo. To begin with, the ELBE ran to the West Indies, but was transferred to the South American service in 1886.

The 3,300 ton MOSELLE, TAGUS and BOYNE were completed in 1871. The MOSELLE ran exclusively to the West Indies and the BOYNE to South America, but the TAGUS was detailed to the West Indies line until 1876, when she was rammed and sunk at Colon by the RMSP SEVERN. She was refloated, repaired and on 9 September 1876 sailed from Southampton for Brazil, Uruguay and Argentina. The BOYNE had a short life as she was wrecked near Brest on 12 August 1875.

The South American service was increased from monthly to fortnightly on 21 August 1872, the first augmented sailing being taken by the EBRO. After two more sailings the appointed departure date became the 24th of the month (or the 25th when the 24th fell on a Sunday). The premier service still sailed on the 9th (or 10th).

The most interesting trio of ships ever owned by RMSP, and introduced at this time, were built in 1865–6 for the Panama, New Zealand and Australian Royal Mail Company by Randolph, Elder & Co as the 1,509 ton RAKAIA; by Charles Lungley & Co of Deptford Green, London, as the 1,591 ton KAIKOURA; and by J. & W. Dudgeon & Co of Cubitt Town, London, as the 1,504 ton RUAHINE. All three had approximately similar dimensions and passenger capacity, which was 100 first class, 40 second and 65 third. But it was in the propelling machinery where, for experimental purposes, there was a vast difference. The RAKAIA (renamed EBRO when acquired by Royal Mail in 1872) had four-cylinder compound engines, a favourite arrangement by Randolph

Elder at that time; the KAIKOURA (renamed TIBER) had two-cylinder single-expansion engines, which were compounded by Day, Summers & Co of Southampton in 1872; and the RUAHINE (renamed LIFFEY) was a twin-screw steamer. Each screw was driven by a two-cylinder engine, each cylinder consisting of a high-pressure section and an outer annular low pressure section. She was converted to single-screw and fitted with compound engines by Day Summers in 1872, her mean speed at the subsequent trials being 13.227 knots compared with 12.374 knots on 8 August 1865. She had stowage for 300 tons more cargo than hitherto, and consumed 20 tons of coal a day instead of 34 [3]. This was undoubtedly one of the very few examples (if not the only one) of an ocean-going ship being converted from twin to single-screw.

In 1873–4 the 2,540 ton LEOPOLD II and the 2,564 ton SANTIAGO of the short-lived Ryde Line (Chapter 23) each made two round voyages from London, Antwerp and Southampton to South America. They were bought by Royal Mail in 1874, renamed MINHO and MONDEGO respectively, and again ran from Southampton to the River Plate.

Royal Mail was subjected to serious competition from another British line in 1868, when the Pacific Steam Navigation Company (Chapter 19) started a passenger and cargo service between Liverpool, Rio de Janeiro, Montevideo, the Straits of Magellan and Valparaiso. By January 1873 a weekly service was being maintained, for which 22 steamers were built or building. However, the service was reduced to fortnightly in March 1874, by which time a severe slump meant that 11 ships had to be disposed of or laid up. Two, the 3,805 ton CORCOVADO and PUNO, were sold in 1875 to become the RMSP DON and PARA. They were the largest units

1875 DON 3,805 tons
Built as PSN CORCOVADO but bought by RMSP in 1875.

7

in the Royal Mail fleet, and both were detailed to the West Indies service. The DON made at least one River Plate voyage in 1885, although no trace has been found of any similar voyages by the PARA.

A new South American mail contract had come into operation on 1 January 1875, payment being made for the first time according to the weight of the mails carried. The subsidy for the West Indian services was considerably reduced to £86,750. From 1876 onwards the South American steamers made occasional calls at Vigo, and later these became a regular feature.

By 1876 Royal Mail had competitors on the South American route in the form of three French lines – Messageries Maritimes, Société Générale de Transports Maritimes and Chargeurs Réunis – and two German lines – Hamburg–Süd and Norddeutscher Lloyd – in addition to the British-owned Pacific Steam Navigation Company, Donaldson and Allan lines.

More purchases resulted in the 2,900 ton TAMAR (ex-VANCOUVER) and TRENT (ex-VASCO DE GAMA) being bought in 1878 from the China Transport Steamship Company, and the 3,240 ton LA PLATA (II) (ex-NORFOLK) from Wigram's Australian line in 1882. Royal Mail was quite capable of holding its own.

An outbreak of yellow fever in Brazil in November 1878 obliged the Company to comply with quarantine regulations by amending its sailing schedule. To begin with, the second sailing from Southampton left on the 27th of the month, calling at Cherbourg, Carril, Vigo, Montevideo and Buenos Aires, omitting calls at Brazilian ports. From July 1879 to 30 April 1880 there were three sailings a month – on the 9th to Cherbourg, Lisbon, St. Vincent, Pernambuco, Bahia, Rio de Janeiro and Santos; on the 24th to Lisbon, Pernambuco, Maceio, Bahia, Rio de Janeiro and Santos; and on the 30th to Carril, Vigo, Lisbon, Montevideo and Buenos Aires.

The DOURO, commissioned in 1865, was always a very popular ship and could number among her passengers, in 1872, Emperor Dom Pedro II of Brazil and the Empress. Unfortunately, the Spanish steamer YRURAC BAT collided with and sank the DOURO on 1 April 1882 off Cape Finisterre with the loss of 17 lives.

Four additional intermediate steamers of about 2,500 tons – the GUADIANA, DERWENT, HUMBER and DART – were commissioned between 1875 and 1882. A diversion came when the GUADIANA sailed from Southampton on 1 May 1884 but instead of returning from Santos and Rio de Janeiro by her outward route, proceeded via Barbados and St. Thomas to New York, thence direct to London. The DERWENT followed and, again at monthly intervals, the MINHO and DART, but the latter foundered on 11 September 1884

8

after striking the Zapato Rock near Santos. Worse was to follow as the HUMBER, having sailed from Southampton for Brazil on 1 December 1884 and reached New York safely, left there on 15 February 1885 and went missing with her complement of 66. The MONDEGO took the 1 April 1885 sailing from Southampton but returned there by the direct route from Brazil as the Company had already decided to discontinue the Brazil – New York – London detour. In consequence, the GUADIANA, which had completed three triangular voyages, would also have returned direct had she not been wrecked on the Peredes Rocks off Abrolhos, Brazil, on 20 June 1885[4].

A notable quartet of steel single-screw steamers appeared in 1889–90 as the 5,350 ton ATRATO (II) and MAGDALENA (II) and the 5,600 ton THAMES (II) and CLYDE (II). All products of R. Napier & Sons of

1890 THAMES 5,621 tons
Sister ships ATRATO, MAGDALENA and CLYDE, of which ATRATO ran to the West Indies apart from her maiden voyage to South America.

Glasgow, they had a pleasing appearance with clipper bows, two funnels and three masts. Although subsequently transferred to the West Indies service, the ATRATO made her maiden voyage, starting on 17 January 1889, to Buenos Aires. The other three were built for the South Atlantic trade and, in consequence, had provision for 330 instead of 26 third class passengers.

The next newcomers apart from five feeder steamers built for service in the West Indies, were the 5,900 ton NILE and DANUBE, completed in 1893 by J. & G. Thomson of Clydebank. Detailed to the South American trade, they closely resembled their immediate predecessors apart from having straight stems. Three smaller ships, the 3,445 ton LA PLATA (III), MINHO (II) and EBRO (II) were products of Napier in 1896 for the carriage of emigrants to South America, but were not long

9

retained by Royal Mail. The LA PLATA became the Booth Line CLEMENT in 1900, while the other two were sold British in 1903, and in 1905 became the Compagnie Générale Transatlantique MONTRÉAL and QUÉBEC. The TAGUS, TAMAR and TRENT had been sold in 1897.

The DANUBE and the West Indies service ORINOCO attended Queen Victoria's diamond jubilee Naval Review at Spithead on 26 June 1897. This was the occasion when the TURBINIA stole the show by racing up and down the closed lines at a speed of almost 35 knots, and succeeded in persuading the Admiralty to start ordering ships propelled by Parsons' steam turbines.

An interesting event of 1901 was the substitution of a yellow funnel for the former black. For a short time, also, the steamers' hulls were painted white, but soon reverted to black owing to the high cost of keeping them spick and span.

A turning point in Royal Mail history was the appointment in January 1903 of Owen Cosby Philipps (the future Lord Kylsant) to the board. So great was his influence that on 25 March of the same year he became the Company's chairman.

By this time, there were twin-screw liners of over 20,000 tons in service on the North Atlantic, and of over 12,000 tons running to South Africa, Australia and New Zealand, whereas the largest Royal Mail unit was the 5,891 ton single-screw DANUBE. Prompt steps were taken to remedy this state of affairs, but first of all the Company commissioned the 2,650 ton cargo steamers CARONI, CONWAY and CATALINA in 1904 for the West Indies trade and the 4,000 ton PARANA (II), PARDO and POTARO for the South American. A feature of the latter trio was the large amount of refrigerated space for carrying homeward cargoes of Argentine meat. Outwards, provision was made for a large number of emigrants from Spain and Portugal.

It was decided to give the forthcoming group of passenger liners names beginning with 'A'. Owing to the close friendship that already existed between the Company's chairman and Lord Pirrie of Harland & Wolff of Belfast, all but one came from his firm. The first was the 9,588 ton twin-screw ARAGON, which was launched on 23 February 1905. Propelled by two sets of quadruple-expansion engines, she had a service speed of 15 knots, and accommodation for 305 first, 66 second and 632 third class passengers, features of the first class being her spacious public rooms and the greatly-improved cabin arrangements. For the first time, there were suites as well as single-berth rooms, all with an electric fan. Her maiden voyage from Southampton started on 14 July 1905 for La Rochelle–Pallice, Coruña, Vigo, and Leixões, Lisbon, Madeira, Pernambuco, Bahia, Rio de Janeiro, Santos, Montevideo and Buenos Aires.

1905 ARAGON 9,588 tons
The first RMSP 'A' steamer and their first twin-screw.

Four more ships – the 10,037 ton AMAZON (II), the 10,537 ton ARAGUAYA, the 11,073 ton AVON (III) and the 12,015 ton ASTURIAS – followed in 1906–08, the ARAGUAYA being a product of Workman, Clark & Company Limited of Belfast. The maiden voyage of the ASTURIAS, starting on 24 January 1908, took place from London to Australia, Royal Mail having acquired the Pacific Steam Navigation Company's Australian fleet and connection in 1906, but they withdrew within three years. Apart from a second voyage to Australia, all further peacetime sailings of the ASTURIAS were to South America. She was the first of the fleet to be fitted with a passenger lift.

Although the 'A' steamers had refrigerated holds, the Argentine meat trade had increased to such an extent that five intermediate type 'D' steamers were placed in service in 1911–2 – the 11,500 ton twin-screw DESEADO, DEMERARA (II), DESNA, DARRO and DRINA, which could carry 40,000 carcasses of meat and had accommodation for 95 first, 38 intermediate and 800 third class passengers.

The 14,930 ton ARLANZA was launched on 23 November 1911, her propelling machinery differing from her predecessors' in having triple-screws driven by the well-known Harland & Wolff combination of triple-expansion engines and a low-pressure turbine.

The six 'A' steamers in service by 1912 were insufficient to provide an accelerated weekly service to South America so Royal Mail chartered the 10,328 ton VANDYCK from their associated company, Lamport & Holt, for two round voyages without change of name, and also the 10,660 ton VAUBAN, which retained her name for a time, but from April 1913 until returned to her owners in the following December was temporarily renamed ALCALA.

11

Three more 'A' steamers completed the series – the 15,620 ton ANDES, launched on 8 May 1913, the ALCANTARA, launched on 20 October 1913 and the ALMANZORA, launched on 19 November 1914. Eight of the nine ships were in commission before the outbreak of World War I in August 1914, and were fully capable of maintaining a weekly service to South America. The ANDES, in fact, was laid down and launched for the allied Pacific Steam Navigation Company.

Meanwhile, a number of ships were sold, including the NILE in 1911 to the Pacific Mail Steamship Company, the ATRATO in 1912 to the Viking Cruising Company, who renamed her THE VIKING, the CLYDE for scrapping in 1913 and the THAMES to become a blockship at Scapa Flow in 1914.

All the 'A' steamers except the AMAZON were taken up by the British Government during the early days of the war. The ARAGON was torpedoed and sunk on 30 December 1917 outside Alexandria with 2,500 troops on board, of whom 610 were lost, after she had entered the port and had then been instructed to leave. The AMAZON was torpedoed and sunk by German submarine U.52 about 30 miles from Malin Head on 15 February 1918, fortunately without loss of life, and it was a further consolation that the U.52 was sunk shortly afterwards by one of the destroyers which came to the rescue.

The ARLANZA, ANDES and ALCANTARA served as armed merchant cruisers. The last-named intercepted the German raider GREIF with fatal results to herself, but two other ships, including the ANDES, came on the scene in time to make sure that the German was also sunk. The ASTURIAS was torpedoed off Start Point on 21 March 1917 while serving as a hospital ship. Forty-four lives were lost, but she remained afloat and after being beached was later taken to Plymouth, where she was declared a constructive total loss. After the war, Royal Mail bought her back and she was rebuilt as the cruising liner ARCADIAN. The 'D' ship DRINA was torpedoed and sunk near Milford Haven on 1 March 1917.

Another war victim was the West Indies service itself [5], for which the 8,500 ton ESSEQUIBO and EBRO were launched on 6 July and 8 September 1914. The former sailed from London on 18 November 1914 and the latter from Newport, Monmouth, on 28 April 1915, becoming an armed merchant cruiser upon return to Britain. The last sailing of the service was taken by the MAGDALENA on 25 August 1915 from London and despite the fact that Royal Mail had been established for the express purpose of running to the West Indies it was never reinstated.

The 8,422 ton single-screw BRECKNOCKSHIRE was launched by Harland & Wolff on 12 September 1916 for the Far East service of the Shire Line, but was handed over to Royal Mail upon completion and sailed from Liverpool on 24 January 1917 on her maiden voyage to Rio de Janeiro. Only a few days later, on 15 February, she was intercepted by the German raider MOEWE, captured and sunk. The BRECKNOCK-SHIRE had accommodation for 12 first class passengers and 400 third.

Owing to their exceptional cargo-carrying ability, the DESEADO, DEMERARA, DESNA and DARRO had continued running to South America during the war, and in consequence the Liverpool – River Plate service returned to normal immediately after the Armistice of 11 November 1918, although with four ships instead of five.

1915 ALMANZORA 15,551 tons
Launched November 1914 and completed as armed merchant cruiser. Entered River Plate service in 1920.

The 'A' steamer service was not so fortunate as only five of the nine ships were still available. Of these, the ALMANZORA had been commissioned as an armed merchant cruiser in September 1915, and sailed to South America for the first time on 14 January 1920. The ANDES sailed to the River Plate on 4 November 1919 and the AVON on 14 November. The ARLANZA was not ready to follow until 27 July 1920 and the ARAGUAYA on 29 October 1920. The last-named did not remain much more than a year in the service as from December 1921 she was employed almost exclusively on cruising.

Chairman of Royal Mail since 1903, Sir Owen Philipps, as he had become, received a Barony in February 1923 and chose the title of Baron Kylsant of Carmarthen and Amroth.

One reason why Royal Mail did not at once add new passenger tonnage for their South American lines was their decision to start a passenger and cargo service in January 1921 between Hamburg, Southampton, Cherbourg and New York, which to some extent replaced the pre-war service from Southampton to New York via the West Indies, which had been introduced in 1905[5]. They had also founded RMSP

Meat Transports Limited in December 1914 in order to increase their refrigerated space from Buenos Aires, but owing to the war, when shipbuilders were occupied to the utmost on Government orders, the first of the ships, the NAVASOTA, was not placed in service until March 1918; others followed at intervals. In addition, a service by 'LOCH' motorships carrying 12 passengers was started in 1922 jointly with the Holland America Line to North Pacific coast ports and proved very successful.

In 1924 orders were placed with Harland & Wolff for two large passenger motorships and the first, the 22,071 ton ASTURIAS (II), was launched on 7 July 1925, her maiden voyage starting from Southampton on 27 February 1926 for South America. She was the largest motorship afloat and had what was at that time an unusual appearance with two broad stumpy funnels with horizontal tops, two masts and a cruiser stern. Her passenger complement was 408 first, 200 second and 674 third class. The second ship, the 22,181 ton ALCANTARA (II), was launched on 23 September 1926, and left her home port for South America on 4 March 1927.

The AVON was sold in 1930 for scrapping, the ARAGUAYA, for long confined to cruising, was sold to the Yugoslav Lloyd to become the KRALJICA MARIJA and the cruising liner ARCADIAN (ex-ASTURIAS (I)) was laid up. Meanwhile, the ANDES (I) had been taken in hand by Harland & Wolff, converted to burn oil fuel and reappeared in 1930 as the white-hulled cruising liner ATLANTIS.

An important event, hitherto unrecorded in this chapter, had taken place on 5 July 1904 with the granting of a supplementary Royal Charter, which allowed Royal Mail for the first time to purchase an interest in other lines. A long string of acquisitions resulted during ensuing years, starting with the Pacific Steam Navigation Company's share of the Orient – Pacific Line in 1906, followed by a controlling interest in the Shire Line (1907), Forward Line (1908), Pacific Steam Navigation Company (1910), Glen Line and Lamport & Holt (1911), Union-Castle Line (1912), Nelson Line (1913) and MacIver Line (1919). Then came a pause until towards the end of 1926, when the famous White Star Line was bought from the International Mercantile Marine Company. By 1930 the Royal Mail fleet had a total tonnage of 400,000, while the associated lines (all except the Forward Line retaining their separate identities) reached a further 1,600,000, making a staggering grand total of two million tons.

It was out of the question to integrate the whole into one colossal concern as had once been Lord Kylsant's intention. Not only was the parent company having difficulty in repaying Government loans, but the price paid for White Star was greatly in excess of its true value, the Blue Star Line (Chapter 62) was capturing quite a large portion of Royal

1929 HIGHLAND CHIEFTAIN 14,141 tons
As running for Royal Mail from 1932.

Mail's South American business and the world depression of the late 1920s and early 1930s was the final blow from which there was no hope of recovery. The Royal Mail Steam Packet Company went into liquidation.

A new company, ROYAL MAIL LINES LIMITED, was formed on 4 August 1932 and took over the Royal Mail fleet in its entirety, together with RMSP Meat Transports Limited, the Nelson Steam Navigation Company Limited and David MacIver & Company Limited, but the remaining Kylsant companies regained their independence. Lord Essendon became the first chairman of the new concern.

The multi-passenger ships coming into Royal Mail Lines' possession were the ALCANTARA, ASTURIAS, ALMANZORA, ARLANZA, the cruising liner ATLANTIS and the ex-Nelson Line motorships HIGHLAND PATRIOT, HIGHLAND MONARCH, HIGHLAND CHIEFTAIN, HIGHLAND BRIGADE and HIGHLAND PRINCESS (Chapter 49). The 'HIGHLAND' ships continued to run between London and Buenos Aires.

The popular ALCANTARA and ASTURIAS had excellent accommodation but their speed of 16 knots did not compare with a number of foreign liners and they suffered from vibration. The ASTURIAS, therefore, was sent to Harland & Wolff at Belfast in May 1934, by which time trade was improving, and fitted with two sets of single-reduction geared turbines, her funnels were lengthened by 4½ metres (15 feet), and three metres (10 feet) were added at the bow and she returned to service in October 1934 two knots faster. The ALCANTARA received similar treatment and returned to service on 4 May 1935. The ARLANZA, by then 26 years old, arrived at Southampton for the last time on 6 September 1938 and was subsequently scrapped at Rosyth.

The centenary of Royal Mail's original Royal Charter on 26 September 1939 was due to be celebrated by the departure on that day of the 25,689

15

ALCANTARA
1927 Built as motorship 22,181 tons
1935 Geared turbine steamer 22,209 tons
1948 Dummy funnel removed 22,608 tons

16

ton ANDES (II) from Southampton on her maiden voyage to Buenos Aires. Unfortunately, World War II broke out at the beginning of the month and, instead, she was requisitioned as a transport, her first job being to bring a large contingent of Canadian troops to England. Soon afterwards, she made a round the world voyage from Liverpool via the Panama Canal, Wellington, Karachi and the Suez Canal to England in the record time of 72 days. She travelled 165,000 miles during the war and carried a total of 109,000 troops.

The ALCANTARA and ASTURIAS also survived the war, but not without many anxious moments. The ALCANTARA became an armed merchant cruiser, her appearance, like that of her sister ship, being considerably changed by the removal of her forward dummy funnel and of her mainmast. On 28 July 1940 she came upon the raider THOR near Trinidad Island, but the German ship managed to escape owing to one of her shells exploding in the ALCANTARA's engine room. The ASTURIAS became a troopship and was torpedoed in July 1943 about 400 miles from Freetown, to which she was towed and then abandoned for about 18 months. After that she was towed to Gibraltar and later to Belfast, repaired and ended her active career carrying emigrants to Australia. She was scrapped in 1957.

The ANDES carried the exiled Norwegian Government back to Oslo in May 1945. She was released from British Government service in 1947 and reconditioned by Harland & Wolff, her new passenger complement being 324 first class and 204 second. She was a twin-screw ship, propelled by single-reduction geared turbines, her service speed being 20 knots. Her first commercial voyage to the River Plate started from Southampton on 22 January 1948. Apart from the Costa Line EUGENIO C,

1939 ANDES 25,689 tons
Largest British liner in the River Plate trade.

she is believed to have been the only ship on the South Atlantic to be fitted with Denny-Brown stabilisers.

When reconditioned after the war the ALCANTARA's passenger complement became 220 first class, 185 cabin and 462 third; her tonnage had increased to 22,608. She was still a one-funnelled ship, but her mainmast had been reinstated. She joined the ANDES on the Southampton – Buenos Aires service on 8 October 1948 and was scrapped in 1958, by which time, also, changed conditions in Argentina coupled with severe air competition and the forthcoming completion of three new Royal Mail ships made further employment of the ANDES in the South American trade unprofitable. She was converted into a cruising liner in 1959–60, carrying 480 one-class passengers and remained in this role until sold to Belgian shipbreakers in 1971.

The HIGHLAND MONARCH, HIGHLAND CHIEFTAIN, HIGHLAND BRIGADE and HIGHLAND PRINCESS served as troopships during World War II, the HIGHLAND PATRIOT being torpedoed and sunk in the Atlantic on 1 October 1940. After the war, on 18 January 1946, the HIGHLAND BRIGADE was badly damaged by a mine near Singapore.

1949 MAGDALENA 17,547 tons
Became a total loss on homeward maiden voyage.

The 17,547 ton twin-screw turbine steamer MAGDALENA (III) was completed by Harland & Wolff in 1949 to replace the HIGHLAND PATRIOT in the London – Buenos Aires service. She had a speed of 17 knots and accommodation for 133 first and 346 third class passengers. Unfortunately, she stranded near Rio de Janeiro on 25 April 1949 during her maiden homeward voyage, and although refloated a day later broke in two when under tow and became a total loss. Ports of call served by the 'HIGHLAND' steamers at this time were Vigo, Leixões, Lisbon, Las Palmas, Rio de Janeiro, Santos and Montevideo on the voyage from London to Buenos Aires.

18

The HIGHLAND CHIEFTAIN was sold in 1959 and became the whaling depot ship CALPEAN STAR. She sustained rudder damage in the Atlantic in March 1960 and after being repaired at Montevideo left there on 1 June for the UK with a cargo of blubber and whale by-products. While still in the entrance channel an explosion in a sea-water valve caused the engine room to be flooded and all power cut off. She lay beside the channel partly submerged and became a total loss. Later in 1959 the HIGHLAND BRIGADE and HIGHLAND PRINCESS were bought by the Greek shipowner Latsis and renamed HENRIETTA and MARIETTA. The former, as the MARIANNA, was scrapped in 1965, but at the time of writing the latter is still listed as the Chinese GUANG HUA. The last of the group to remain in Royal Mail service was the HIGHLAND MONARCH, which was scrapped in 1960.

1960 ARAGON (II) 20,362 tons
Sister ship of AMAZON (II) and ARLANZA (II).

The 20,350 ton twin-screw motorships AMAZON (III), ARAGON (II) and ARLANZA (II) were built by Harland & Wolff in 1960. Fitted with accommodation for 107 first, 82 cabin and 275 third class passengers, they were built to replace the 'HIGHLAND' ships on the London to River Plate route, indicating the final abandonment of the Southampton service already deserted by the ASTURIAS (II), ALCANTARA (II) and ANDES (II). Unfortunately, the AMAZON was withdrawn in 1968 owing to a ban on the import of meat from Argentina following an outbreak of foot and mouth disease. She was sold to an associated company, Shaw, Savill & Albion, to become the AKAROA, running between Southampton, Australia and New Zealand. The ARAGON and ARLANZA followed her to the same owners a year later, becoming the ARANDA and ARAWA. Here again they were but a limited success, and in 1971–2 were converted into very peculiar-looking car transports under foreign ownership. All three have since been scrapped.

19

Royal Mail Lines Limited are no longer involved in the passenger business. In fact, their activities as a whole are minute in comparison with their one-time greatness – a state of affairs for which the jet aeroplane must be held responsible.

[1] Old measurement was the tons burthen of a ship plus the engine-room tonnage. It seems that the modern reckoning of gross tonnage came into operation in 1854, but that most of the early Royal Mail ships were not remeasured. Gross tonnage is shown almost exclusively in the fleet lists.
[2] T.A. Bushell, *Royal Mail 1839–1939*.
[3] *Shipping & Mercantile Gazette* 11/10/1872.
[4] N.R.P. Bonsor, *North Atlantic Seaway*, Volume 3, Pages 1160–2.
[5] N.R.P. Bonsor, *North Atlantic Seaway*, Volume 3, Pages 1334–9.

1. (1851) TEVIOT
   1,285. 64,61 x 10,18. (212.0 x 33.4). C–1–3. W–P–SL2–10. (I–100). Robert Duncan, Greenock (engines Caird & Co, Greenock). 1841 (4/10) launched. 1842 (15/2) MV Southampton–West Indies. 1851 (9/1) Southampton–Lisbon–Madeira–St. Vincent–Pernambuco–Bahia–Rio de Janeiro. 1853 (9/4) LV ditto (10 RV). 1857 resumed ditto (3 RV). 1864 scrapped at St. Thomas, Virgin Islands.
2. (1851) TAY
   1,285. 64,61 x 10,18. (212.0 x 33.4). C–1–3. W–P–SL2–10. (I–100). Charles Wood, Dumbarton (engines Caird & Co, Greenock). 1841 (6/7) launched. 1841 (31/12) MV Southampton–West Indies. 1851 (10/2) FV Southampton–Lisbon–Madeira–St. Vincent–Pernambuco–Bahia–Rio de Janeiro. 1853 (9/11) LV ditto (12 RV). 1854 lengthened forward and aft by J. & R. White, Cowes. 1855 (9/8) resumed Southampton–Rio de Janeiro (4 RV). 1856 (31/8) lost on Mexican coast near Vera Cruz.
3. (1851) MEDWAY
   1,285. 64,61 x 10,18. (212.0 x 33.4). C–1–3. W–P–SL2–10. (I–100). William Pitcher, Northfleet, London (engines Maudslay, Sons & Field, London). 1841 (7/7) launched. 1842 (31/1) MV London–West Indies. 1851 (10/3) FV Southampton–Lisbon–Madeira–St. Vincent–Pernambuco–Bahia–Rio de Janeiro (1RV). 1854 Crimean War transport. 1857 (9/2) resumed Southampton–Rio de Janeiro. 1858 LV ditto. 1862 scrapped.
4. (1851) SEVERN
   1,295. 65,52 x 10,27. (215.0 x 33.7). C–1–3. W–P–SL2–10.

(I–100). Wm. Patterson, Bristol (engines Maudslay, Sons & Field, London). 1842 (28/1) launched. 1851 (9/6) FV Southampton–Lisbon–Madeira–St. Vincent–Pernambuco–Bahia–Rio de Janeiro. 1854 (10/11) LV ditto (14 RV). 1861 scrapped.

5. (1853) GREAT WESTERN
   1,775. 64,61 x 10,76. (212.0 x 35.3). C–1–4. W–P–SL2–10. (I–128; 11–20). Wm. Patterson, Bristol (engines Maudslay, Sons & Field, London). 1837 (19/7) launched for Great Western SS Co. 1838 (8/4) MV Bristol–New York. 1839–40 tonnage increased from 1,340 to 1,775. 1847 GREAT WESTERN (RMSP). 1847 (2/6) FV Southampton–West Indies. 1853 (9/7) FV Southampton–Rio de Janeiro. 1855 (9/7) LV ditto (9 RV). 1855 Crimean War transport. 1856 scrapped at Vauxhall, London.

6. (1853) THAMES
   1,295. 64,61 x 10,06. (212.0 x 33.0). C–1–3. W–P–SL2–10. (I–100). William Pitcher, Northfleet, London (engines Maudslay, Sons & Field, London). 1841 (20/5) launched. 1850 fitted with feathering paddle wheels; the first transatlantic liner so fitted. 1853 (9/12) FV Southampton–Lisbon–Madeira–St. Vincent–Pernambuco–Bahia–Rio de Janeiro (4 RV). 1865 scrapped.

7. (1855) SOLENT
   1,804. 97,83 x 10,67. (321 x 35.0). C–2–3. W–P–SL2–10. T. & J. White, Cowes (engines Miller, Ravenshill & Co, London). 1853 (8/6) launched. 1853 (3/10) MV Southampton–West Indies. 1855 (9/2) FV Southampton–Lisbon–Madeira–St. Vincent–Pernambuco–Bahia–Rio de Janeiro (2 RV). 1869 scrapped at St. Thomas, Virgin Islands.

8. (1855) AVON (I)
   1,892. 75,50 x 10,50. (247.7 x 34.5). C–1–2. W–P–SL2–10. (I–100). Wm. Patterson, Bristol (engines Maudslay, Sons & Field, London). 1842 (28/1) launched. 1852 dimensions increased from 65,52 x 10,15 metres (215.0 x 33.3 feet); former tonnage 1,295. 1855 (9/3) FV Southampton–Lisbon–Madeira–St. Vincent–Pernambuco–Bahia–Rio de Janeiro. 1859 (9/12) LV ditto (19 RV). 1862 (21/11) torn from moorings at Colon during gale and stranded. 1864 scrapped.

9. (1855) TAMAR (I)
   1,963. 87,62 x 10,27. (287.5 x 33.7). C–2–3. W–P–?–10. William Pitcher, Northfleet, London. 1854 (31/1) launched. 1854 Crimean War transport. 1855 (9/10) FV Southampton–Brazil. 1859 (10/4) LV ditto. 1871 scrapped at Southampton.

10. (1856) TYNE
    2,179. 90,21 x 11,03. (296.0 x 36.2). C–2–3. I–P–02–10. Miller &

Ravenhill, Low Walker-on-Tyne. 1854 (16/10) launched. 1856 (9/8) FV Southampton–Brazil. 1857 (13/1) stranded in fog on Dorset coast; refloated. 1857 (9/10) resumed Southampton–Brazil. 1862 (10/11) LV ditto. 1883 scrapped.

11. (1859) TASMANIAN
2,445. 105,45 x 11,89. (346.0 x 39.0). C–2–3. I–S–I (2)–11. Laurence Hill, Port Glasgow. Laid down as MELBOURNE but changed to AFRICAN. 1858 launched for European & Australian as TASMANIAN. 1859 ditto (RMSP). 1859 (9/7) FV Southampton–Brazil (1 RV). 1871 compound engines. 1878 (27/5) wrecked during RMSP voyage Jamaica–St. Thomas.

12. (1859) ONEIDA
2,317. 93,50 x 11,85. (306.8 x 38.9). C–1–3. I–S–2VT–10. John Scott & Sons, Greenock. 1855 (20/3) launched for Canada Ocean SS Co. 1855 (Jun) Crimean War transport. 1858 ONEIDA (RMSP). 1859 (10/10) FV Southampton–Brazil. 1871 (9/9) LV ditto. 1874 sold; engines removed; ran as a sailing ship.

13. (1860) MAGDALENA (I)
2,943. 81,07 x 11,61. (266.0 x 38.1). C–2–3. W–P–SL2–10. (I–80). William Pitcher, Northfleet, London (engines Robert Napier, Glasgow. 1851 (12/7) launched. 1854 Crimean War transport. 1860 (9/3) FV Southampton–Brazil. 1861 sailed as transport to Canada after TRENT affair. 1864 (9/12) LV Southampton–Brazil. 1866 scrapped at Vauxhall, London.

14. (1862) PARANA (I)
2,250. 92,96 x 12,80. (305.0 x 42.0). C–2–3. W–P–SL2–11. Wigram & Sons, Southampton (engines Caird & Co, Greenock). 1851 (15/7) launched. 1852 lengthened from 81,07 metres (266.00 feet). 1860 (27/6) FV for Galway Line (c), Galway–New York (3 RV). 1862 (9/5) FV Southampton–Brazil. 1865 (10/4) LV ditto. 1868 hulked at St. Thomas. 1876 scrapped.

15. (1865) LA PLATA (I)
2,402. 86,62 x 12,50. (284.2 x 41.0). C–2–2. W–P–SL2–12. (I–116; II–20). R. Steele & Co, Greenock (engines Robert Napier, Glasgow). 1851 (24/12) launched for Cunard as ARABIA. 1852 LA PLATA (RMSP). 1852 (17/8) MV Southampton–West Indies. 1860 (24/11) caught fire at Southampton; ship saved mainly by crew of P&O TAGUS. 1865 (9/5) FV Southampton–Brazil. 1871 (9/6) LV ditto. 1871 sold to Wm. Denny & Bros in part payment for BOYNE. 1874 scrapped.

16. 1865 DOURO
2,824. 99,48 x 12,25. (326.4 x 40.2). C–1–2. I–S–I(2)–12. (I–253;

II–30; III–30). Caird & Co, Greenock. 1864 (3/12) launched. 1865 (10/7) MV Southampton–Lisbon–Madeira–St. Vincent–Pernambuco–Bahia–Rio de Janeiro. 1869 (9/7) ditto plus Montevideo and Buenos Aires. 1872 had as passengers Dom Pedro II, Emperor of Brazil, and the Empress. 1879 C2 by Day, Summers & Co, Southampton. 1882 (1/4) sunk in collision with Spanish ss YRURAC BAT off Cape Finisterre (23).

17. 1865 RHONE

2,738. 98,44 x 12,22 (323.0 x 40.1). C–1–2. I–S–?–12. (I–253; II–30; III–30). Millwall Iron Works, London. 1865 (11/2) launched. 1865 (9/10) MV Southampton–Lisbon–Madeira–St. Vincent–Pernambuco–Bahia–Rio de Janeiro. 1867 (29/10) wrecked during hurricane in Virgin Islands (123).

18. (1871) NEVA

3,025. 106,09 x 19,31. (348.1 x 40.4). C–1–2. I–S–I(2)–13. (I–272; II–55; III–42). Caird & Co, Greenock. Laid down as RHEIN (Norddeutscher Lloyd) and bought on stocks to replace RHONE. 1868 (10/2) launched as NEVA. 1868 (2/7) MV Southampton–West Indies. 1871 (10/8) FV Southampton–Brazil. 1891 scrapped.

19. 1872 BOYNE

3,318. 113,38 x 12,37. (372.0 x 40.6). C–1–2. I–S–C2–12. Wm. Denny & Bros, Dumbarton. 1871 (18/8) launched. 1872 (9/3) MV Southampton–Rio de Janeiro–Montevideo–Buenos Aires. 1875 (12/8) wrecked in dense fog near Brest. (0).

20. (1872) EBRO (I)

1,509. 83,20 x 10,39. (273.0 x 34.1). C–1–2. I–S–C4–11. (I–100; II–60; III–60). Randolph, Elder & Co, Glasgow. 1866 (31/1) launched as RAKAIA (Panama, New Zealand & Australian RM Co). 1871 EBRO (RMSP). 1872 (21/8) FV Antwerp–Southampton–Brazil. 1881 BALDOMERO YGLESIAS (Cia Trasatlántica Española). 1898 scrapped.

21. (1872) TIBER

1,591. 82,02 x 10,39. (272.4 x 34.1). C–1–2. I–S–C2–11. (I–100; II–40; III–65). Charles Lungley, Deptford Green, London. 1865 launched as KAIKOURA (Panama, New Zealand & Australian RM Co). 1872 TIBER (RMSP); compound engines by Day, Summers & Co, Southampton for single-expansion ones. 1872 (21/9) FV Southampton–Rio de Janeiro–Montevideo–Buenos Aires. 1882 (10/2) wrecked off Puerto Plata when trading in the West Indies. (0).

22. (1872) LIFFEY

1,504. 87,81 x 10,36. (288.1 x 34.0). C–1–2. I–S–C2–11. (I;100;

II–40; III–65). J. & W. Dudgeon, London. 1865 (March) launched with single-expansion engines as the twin-screw RUAHINE (Panama, New Zealand & Australian RM Co). 1872 LIFFEY (RMSP) single-screw compound engines by Day, Summers & Co, Southampton. 1872 (21/10) FV Southampton–Buenos Aires. 1874 (27/8) wrecked at Point J. Ignacio, Uruguay.

23. (1874) MINHO (I)
2,540. 106,79 x 11,21). (350.4 x 36.8). S–1–2. I–S–C2–11. (I–80; II–30; III–500). Barclay, Curle & Co, Glasgow. 1872 (17/10) launched as LEOPOLD II (Ryde). 1873 (10/6) MV London–Antwerp–Falmouth–Rio de Janeiro–Montevideo–Buenos Aires. 1874 MINHO (RMSP) 1874 (25/5) FV Southampton–Brazil. 1884 (7/7) FV Southampton–Lisbon–Rio de Janeiro–New York–London. 1885 (2/3) LV ditto. 1887 ASLAN (Turkish). 1901 (1/4) wrecked near Yembo, Red Sea. (180).

24. (1874) MONDEGO (I)
2,564. 106,85 x 11,21. (350.6 x 36.8). S–1–2. I–S–C2–11. (I–80; II–30; III–500). Tod & McGregor, Glasgow. 1872 (30/12) launched as SANTIAGO (Ryde). 1873 (10/8) MV London–Antwerp–Falmouth–Rio de Janeiro–Montevideo–Buenos Aires. 1874 MONDEGO (RMSP). 1874 (24/10) FV Southampton–Brazil. 1885 (1/4) sailed Southampton–Brazil with intention of returning to London via New York; instead returned direct to Southampton. 1888 MONDEGO (Br). 1891 (15/9) wrecked at St. Mary's, NF.

25. 1875 GUADIANA
2,504. 101,22 x 11,06. (332.1 x 36.3). 1–3. I–S–C2–11. London & Glasgow Co, Glasgow. 1874 (Aug) launched. 1875 (24/9) MV Southampton–Brazil. 1884 (1/5) FV Southampton–Rio de Janeiro–Santos–New York–London. 1885 (1/5) sailed ditto. 1885 (20/6) wrecked on Peredes Rocks off Abrolhos, Brazil.

26. (1876) TAGUS
3,298. 109,11 x 12,53. (358.0 x 41.1). C–2–2. I–S–C2–12. John Elder & Co, Glasgow. 1871 (21/1) launched. 1871 MV Southampton–West Indies. 1876 rammed and sunk by SEVERN (RMSP) at Colon; refloated; repaired. 1876 (9/9) FV Southampton–Brazil–Montevideo–Buenos Aires. 1890 (4/10) FV Rotterdam–London–Southampton–Montevideo–Buenos Aires. 1897 scrapped.

27. (1879) TAMAR (II)
2,923. 106,55 x 11,28. (349.6 x 37.0). S–1–3. I–S–C2–12. (I–122; II–23). Henderson, Coulborn & Co, Renfrew. 1873 (10/11) launched as VANCOUVER (China Transport SS Co). 1878

TAMAR (RMSP). 1879 (24/3) FV Southampton–S. America. 1897 scrapped in Holland.

28. (1879) TRENT

2,912. 106,49 x 11,28. (349.4 x 37.0). S–1–3. I–S–C2–12. (I–122; II–23). Henderson, Coulborn & Co, Renfrew. 1873 (May) launched as VASCO DE (sic) GAMA (China Transport SS Co). 1878 TRENT (RMSP). 1879 (24/9) FV Southampton–S. America. 1897 LUIGI (G.B. Lavarello, Genoa). 1898 scrapped at Genoa.

29. 1880 DERWENT

2,471. 100,30 x 10,97 (329.1 x 36.0). C–1–3. I–S–C2–11. R. Thompson Junr, Sunderland (engines North Eastern Marine Engineering Co, Sunderland). 1879 (Oct) launched. 1880 MV Southampton–Brazil. 1884 (2/6) FV Southampton–Rio de Janeiro–Santos–New York–London. 1885 (2/2) LV ditto (3 RV). 1902 LILIA (Fr). 1904 DERWENT (Hong Kong). 1930 scrapped at Hong Kong.

30. 1880 AVON (II)

2,162. 86,34 x 10,73. (283.3 x 35.2). C–1–3. I–S–C2–11. J. Laing, Sunderland. 1880 (10/1) launched. 1880 MV Southampton–S. America. 1903 AVON (Br). 1908 ditto (Ellerman). 1916 (19/4) sunk in collision in R. Mersey off New Brighton.

31. (1881) HUMBER

2,371. 100,58 x 10,91. (330.0 x 35.8). C–1–3. I–S–C2–12. London & Glasgow Co, Glasgow. 1880 (Jan) launched. 1881 (27/11) FV Southampton–Brazil. 1884 (1/12) FV Southampton–Rio de Janeiro–Santos–New York. 1885 (15/2) sailed New York–London; went missing (66).

32. (1882) LA PLATA (II)

3,240. 101,31 x 12,22. (332.4 x 40.1). C–1–3. I–S–C2–12. R. & H. Green, London. 1879 (21/6) launched as NORFOLK (Wigram). 1882 LA PLATA (RMSP). 1882 (9/10) FV Southampton–S. America. 1893 ORIENTA (Clubs Yachting Association, London). 1895 NORSE KING (Norse King SS Co (Br)). 1896 C2 became Q4. 1897 ALBION (Br). 1898 ARGONAUT (Co-operating Cruising Co (Lunn's), London).

33. 1883 DART

2,641. 97,53 x 11,67. (320.0 x 38.3). C–1–3. I–S–C2–11. Raylton Dixon & Co, Middlesbrough (engines T. Richardson & Sons, Hartlepool). 1882 (Nov) launched. 1883 (27/11) MV London–Southampton–Brazil. 1884 (1/8) sailed Southampton–Brazil *en route* to New York and London. 1884 (11/9) foundered after striking Zapata Rock, Santos.

25

34. (1885) DON

3,805. 118,10 x 13,13. (387.5 x 43.1). C–1–3. I–S–C2–12. (I–60; II–90; III–325). Laird Bros, Birkenhead. 1872 (Sep) launched for PSN as CORCOVADO. 1873 (19/2) MV Liverpool–Rio de Janeiro–Montevideo–Valparaiso. 1875 DON (RMSP). 1875 FV Southampton–West Indies. 1885 (24/9) FV Southampton–Rio de Janeiro–Montevideo–Buenos Aires. 1901 scrapped.

35. (1886) ELBE

3,108. 106,67 x 12,25. (350.0 x 40.2). C–2–2. I–S–C2–12. John Elder & Co, Glasgow. 1869 (20/11) launched. 1870 MV Southampton–West Indies. 1886 (24/2) FV Southampton–Brazil–Montevideo–Buenos Aires. 1902 (9/3) Southampton–Azores and return to embark passengers ex ETRURIA (Cunard) after engine breakdown. 1902 scrapped.

36. 1889 ATRATO

5,347. 128,37 x 15,24. (421.2 x 50.0). C–2–3. S–S–T3–15. (I–221; II–32; III–26. R. Napier & Sons, Glasgow. 1888 (22/9) launched for West Indies service. 1889 (17/1) MV Southampton–Brazil–Montevideo–Buenos Aires. 1889 (2nd and subsequently) Southampton–West Indies. 1912 THE VIKING. (Viking Crusing Co). 1914 VIKNOR (armed merchant cruiser). 1915 (13/1) in communication with Malin Head signal station; disappeared without trace (probably sunk by German mine). (284).

37. 1889 MAGDALENA (II)

5,373. 128,37 x 15,24. (421.2 x 50.0). C–2–3. S–S–T3–15. (I–174; II–44; III–330). R. Napier & Sons, Glasgow. 1889 (2/5) launched. 1889 (2/8) Southampton–Naval Review at Spithead. 1889 (Aug) MV Southampton–Brazil–Montevideo–Buenos Aires. 1910 (Jun) stranded at Cartagena (Colombia); refloated after 4 days. 1915 British troopship. 1921 scrapped.

38. 1890 THAMES (II)

5,621. 132,98 x 15,30. (436.3 x 50.2). C–2–3. S–S–T3–15. (I–174; II–44; III–330). R. Napier & Sons, Glasgow. 1889 (10/12) launched. 1890 (24/4) MV Southampton–Brazil–Montevideo–Buenos Aires. 1914 blockship at Scapa Flow.

39. 1890 CLYDE

5,618. 132,98 x 15,30. (436.3 x 50.2). C–2–3. S–S–T3–15. (I–174; II–44; III–330). R. Napier & Sons, Glasgow. 1890 (5/4) launched. 1890 (31/7) MV Southampton–Brazil–Montevideo–Buenos Aires. 1913 scrapped on Firth of Forth.

40. 1893 NILE

5,855. 128,01 x 15,85. (420.0 x 52.0). S–2–3. S–S–T3–15. J. & G. Thomson, Glasgow. 1893 (21/3) launched. 1893 (19/10) MV

Southampton–Brazil–Montevideo–Buenos Aires. 1900 Boer War transport. 1911 NILE (Pacific Mail). 1915 NILE (China Mail). 1925 scrapped at San Francisco.

41. 1894 DANUBE

5,891. 128,01 x 15,85. (420.0 x 52.0). S–2–3. S–S–T3–15. J. & G. Thomson, Glasgow. 1893 (16/5) launched. 1894 (2/6) MV Southampton–Brazil–Montevideo–Buenos Aires. 1917 British troopship. 1920 scrapped.

42. 1896 LA PLATA (III)

3,445. 105,36 x 13,44. (345.7 x 44.1). S–1–2. S–S–T3–12. (I–135; III–600). R. Napier & Sons, Glasgow. 1896 (28/5) launched. 1896 (27/8) MV Southampton–Brazil–Montevideo–Buenos Aires. 1900 CLEMENT (Booth). 1914 FRESHFIELD (Br). 1918 (5/8) torpedoed and sunk by German submarine.

43. 1896 MINHO (II)

3,445. 105,36 x 13,44. (345.7 x 44.1). S–1–2. S–S–T3–12. (I–135; III–600). R. Napier & Sons, Glasgow. 1896 (14/7) launched. 1896 (22/10) MV Southampton–Brazil–Montevideo–Buenos Aires. 1899 Boer War transport. 1903 HALIFAX (Br). 1905 MONTRÉAL (CGT) (III–800). 1917 (24/3) torpedoed and sunk by German submarine U.46, 77 miles NE of Cape Ortegal, Spain.

44. 1896 EBRO (II)

3,445. 105,36 x 13,44. (345.7 x 44.1). S–1–2. S–S–T3–12. (I–135; III–600). R. Napier & Sons, Glasgow. 1896 (22/9) launched. 1896 (18/12) MV Southampton–Brazil–Montevideo–Buenos Aires. 1899 Boer War transport. 1903 QUEBEC (Br). 1905 QUÉBEC (CGT) (III–800). 1917 (24/1) sunk at mouth of R. Gironde by mine laid by German submarine UC.21.

45. 1904 PARANA (II)

4,575. 114,38 x 14,72. (375.3 x 48.3). 1–2. S–T3–12. Workman, Clark & Co Ltd, Belfast. 1904 (28/4) launched. 1904 (Jun) MV Southampton–Buenos Aires. 1933 scrapped.

46. 1904 PARDO

4,538. 114,29 x 14,72. (375.0 x 48.3). 1–2. S–T3–12. Harland & Wolff, Belfast. 1904 (30/6) launched. 1904 (14/10) MV London–Rosario. 1934 scrapped.

47. 1904 POTARO

4,378. 114,29 x 14,72. (375.0 x 48.3). 1–2. S–T3–12. Harland & Wolff, Belfast. 1904 (14/9) launched. 1904 (26/12) MV London–Buenos Aires. 1915 (10/1) captured by German merchant cruiser KRONPRINZ WILHELM. 1915 (6/2) scuttled by ditto.

48. 1905 ARAGON (I)

9,588. 156,41 x 18,41. (513.2 x 60.4). 1–2. 2S–Q8–15. (I–305;

II–66; III–632). Harland & Wolff, Belfast. 1905 (23/2) launched. 1905 (14/7) MV Southampton–Buenos Aires. 1915 (Apr) troopship to Dardanelles. 1917 (30/12) torpedoed and sunk near Alexandria (610).

49. 1906 AMAZON (I)
10,037. 156,41 x 18,41. (512.2 x 60.4). 1–2. 2S–Q8–15. (I–300; II–70; III–500). Harland & Wolff, Belfast. 1906 (24/2) launched. 1906 (15/6) MV Southampton–Buenos Aires. 1918 (15/2) torpedoed and sunk by German submarine U.52, 30 miles from Malin Head (0).

50. 1906 ARAGUAYA
10,537. 157,02 x 18,68. (515.2 x 61.3). 1–2. 2S–Q8–15. (I–300; II–100; III–800). Workman, Clark & Co Ltd, Belfast. 1906 (6/7) launched. 1906 (12/10) MV Southampton–Buenos Aires. 1917–19 British hospital ship. 1919 (15/11) arr Belfast for overhaul. 1920 (29/10) resumed Southampton–Buenos Aires. 1921 (19/12) FV Hamburg–Southampton–New York (6 RV). 1927 cruise ship. 1930 KRALJICA MARIJA (Yugoslav Lloyd). 1940 SAVOIE (CGT). 1942 (8/11) sunk near Casablanca during American landings.

51. 1907 AVON (III)
11,073. 158,58 x 19.00. (520.3 x 62.3). 1–2. 2S–Q8–15. (I–300; II–140; III–1,200). Harland & Wolff, Belfast. 1907 (2/3) launched. 1907 (28/6) MV Southampton–Buenos Aires. 1914–15 troopship. 1916 (14/3) armed merchant cruiser; renamed AVOCA. 1919 reverted to AVON (RMSP). 1930 scrapped.

52. (1908) ASTURIAS (I)
12,015. 158,58 x 19,00. (520.3 x 62.3). 1–2. 2S–Q8–15. (I–300; II–140; III–1,200). Harland & Wolff, Belfast. 1907 (26/9) launched. 1908 (24/1) MV London–Suez Canal–Australia (1 RV). 1908 (15/5) FV Southampton–Buenos Aires. 1909 resumed London–Suez Canal–Australia (1 RV). 1914 (1/8) requisitioned as British hospital ship. 1917 (20/3) torpedoed near Start Point (45); beached; refloated; towed to Plymouth. 1923 rebuilt by Harland & Wolff as cruise liner ARCADIAN (RMSP); converted to oil fuel. 1930 (autumn) laid up. 1933 scrapped.

53. 1912 DESEADO
11,475. 152,60 x 19,00 (500.7 x 62.3). 1–2. 2S–Q8–13. (I–95; intermediate 38; III–800). Harland & Wolff, Belfast. 1911 (26/10) launched. 1912 (5/12) MV Liverpool–Buenos Aires. 1934 scrapped.

53a. (1912) VANDYCK (c)
10,328. 150,87 x 18,56. (495.0 x 60.9). 1–2. 2S–Q8–14. (I–280;

II–130; III–200). Workman, Clark & Co Ltd, Belfast. 1911 (1/6) launched for Lamport & Holt, Liverpool–S. America. 1912 (15/11) FV for RMSP (c), Southampton–Brazil–Montevideo–Buenos Aires (2 RV); returned to Lamport & Holt and ran New York–S. America. 1914 (28/10) captured and sunk by German cruiser KARLSRUHE in S. Atlantic.

53b. (1912) VAUBAN (c)
(1913) ALCALA (c)
10,660. 151,02 x 18,53. (495.5 x 60.8). 1–2. 2S–Q8–14. (I–280; II–130; III–200). Workman, Clark & Co Ltd, Belfast. 1912 (20/1) launched for Lamport & Holt, Liverpool–S. America. 1912 (4/10) FV for RMSP (c), Southampton–Buenos Aires (3 RV). 1913 ALCALA (RMSP) (c). 1913 (4/4) FV Southampton–Buenos Aires. 1913 (28/11) LV ditto. 1913 (28/12) FV Buenos Aires–New York as VAUBAN (Lamport & Holt). 1932 scrapped at Inverkeithing.

54. 1912 ARLANZA (I)
14,930. 173,81 x 19,90. (570.3 x 65.3). 1–2. 3S–T8&ST–16. (I–400; II–230; III–760). Harland & Wolff, Belfast. 1911 (23/11) launched. 1912 (Sep) MV Southampton–Buenos Aires. 1915 (Apr) armed merchant cruiser. 1915 (22/10) damaged by mine in White Sea. 1920 (27/7) resumed Southampton–Buenos Aires. Later converted to oil fuel. 1938 scrapped at Rosyth.

55. 1912 DESNA
11,466. 152,60 x 19,00 (500.7 x 62.3). 1–2. 2S–Q8–13. (I–95; intermediate 38; III–800). Harland & Wolff, Belfast. 1912 (2/3) launched. 1912 (July) MV Liverpool–Buenos Aires. 1933 scrapped.

56. 1912 DEMERARA
11,484. 152,60 x 19,00. (500.7 x 62.3). 1–2. 2S–Q8–13. (I–95; intermediate 38; III–800). Harland & Wolff, Belfast. 1911 (21/12) launched. 1912 (Aug) MV Liverpool–Buenos Aires. 1917 (1/7) torpedoed by German submarine off La Rochelle; beached; re-entered service. 1933 scrapped in Japan.

57. 1912 DARRO
11,493. 152,60 x 19,00. (500.7 x 62.3). 1–2. 2S–Q8–13. (I–95; intermediate 38; III–800). Harland & Wolff, Belfast. 1912 (16/5) launched. 1912 (Oct) MV Liverpool–Buenos Aires. 1933 scrapped. (Wholly-owned by RMSP, but first registered in name of Imperial Direct Line Ltd).

58. 1912 DRINA
11,483. 152,60 x 19,00. (500.7 x 62.3). 1–2. 2S–Q8–13. (I–95; intermediate 38; III–800). Harland & Wolff, Belfast. 1912 (29/6)

launched. 1912 (Dec) MV Liverpool–Buenos Aires. 1914 (1/8) requisitioned as a hospital ship but soon resumed normal duties. 1917 (1/3) torpedoed and sunk by German submarine near Milford Haven (13). (Wholly-owned by RMSP, but first registered in name of Elder Line Ltd).

59. (1913) ANDES (I)
   15,620. 173,81 x 20,51. (570.3 x 67.3). 1–2. 3S–T8&ST–16. (I–380; II–250; III–700). Harland & Wolff, Belfast. 1913 (8/5) launched. 1913 (26/9) MV Southampton–Valparaiso for PSN. 1914 (30/1) FV for RMSP, Southampton–Buenos Aires. 1915 (Apr) auxiliary cruiser (10th Cruiser Squadron). 1916 (29/2) assisted ALCANTARA in sinking of German auxiliary cruiser GREIF; ALCANTARA also sunk. 1919 (23/10) left Belfast after overhaul. 1919 (4/11) resumed Southampton–Buenos Aires. 1930 converted by Harland & Wolff to cruise liner; oil fuel; white hull; renamed ATLANTIS (RMSP); 15,135 tons; (I–450). 1939 hospital ship. 1946 emigrant carrier to Australia and New Zealand. 1952 scrapped at Faslane.

60. 1914 ALCANTARA (I)
   15,831. 173,72 x 20,42. (570.0 x 67.0). 1–2. 3S–T8&ST–16. (I–400; II–230; III–760). Harland & Wolff, Glasgow. 1913 (30/10) launched. 1914 (19/6) MV Southampton–Buenos Aires. 1915 (Apr) armed merchant cruiser. 1916 (29/2) sunk in engagement with German auxiliary cruiser GREIF, which was also sunk. (69).

60a. 1917 BRECKNOCKSHIRE (c)
   8,422. 143,31 x 18,38. (470.2 x 60.3). 1–4. S–Q4–14. (I–12; III–400). Harland & Wolff, Belfast. 1916 (12/9) launched for Shire Line (Far East service). 1917 (24/1) MV for RMSP (c), Liverpool–Rio de Janeiro. 1917 (15/2) intercepted by German raider MOEWE; sunk after capture.

61. (1920) ALMANZORA
   15,551. 173,72 x 20,42. (570.0 x 67.3). 1–2. 3S–T8&ST–16. (I–400; II–230; III–760). Harland & Wolff, Belfast. 1914 (19/11) launched. 1915 (Sep) armed merchant cruiser. 1918 (23/12) arr Belfast for overhaul. 1920 (14/1) FV Southampton–Buenos Aires. Later converted to oil fuel. 1939 troopship. 1947 scrapped at Blyth.

62. 1926 ASTURIAS (II) (M/S)
   22,071. 192,16 [199,63] x 23,92. (630.5 [655.0] x 78.5). 2–2–C. 2S–4SC.DA–16. (I–408; II–200; III–674). Harland & Wolff, Belfast. 1925 (7/7) launched. 1926 (26/2) MV Southampton–Buenos Aires. 1934 (May–Oct) Geared turbines (SR) substituted by Harland & Wolff for diesel engines; lengthened to 195,21

[202,98] metres (640.5 [666.0] feet); 22,048 tons. (I–330; II–220; III; 768); two funnels of increased height; 18 knots. 1934 (Oct) resumed Southampton–Buenos Aires. 1939 troopship; forward dummy funnel and mainmast removed. 1943 (Jly) torpedoed by Italian submarine CAGNI 400 miles from Freetown, to where towed and abandoned for 1½ years; bought by British Admiralty; towed to Gibraltar and later to Belfast. 1947 troop transport. 1949 carried emigrants to Australia (Royal Mail (C)). 1957 scrapped at Faslane.

63. 1927 ALCANTARA (II) (M/S)
22,181. 192,16 [199,63] x 23,92. (630.5 [655.0] x 78.5). 2–2–C. 2S–4SC.DA–16. (I–432; II–200; III–674). Harland & Wolff, Belfast. 1926 (23/9) launched. 1927 (4/3) MV Southampton–Buenos Aires. 1934–5 Geared turbines (SR) substituted by Harland & Wolff for diesel engines; lengthened to 195,21 [202,98] metres (640.5[666.0] feet); 22,209 tons. (I–330; II–220; III–768); two funnels of increased height; 18 knots. 1935 (4/5) resumed Southampton–Buenos Aires. 1939 armed merchant cruiser; forward dummy funnel and mainmast removed. 1940 (28/7) damaged in contest with German auxiliary cruiser THOR: put into Rio de Janeiro. 1943–4 fitted at Birkenhead as troop transport. 1947–8 refitted by Harland & Wolff; 22,608 tons; (I–220; cabin 185; tourist 462); 1–2–C. 1948 (8/10) resumed Southampton–Buenos Aires. 1958 (Jun) KAISHO MARU (Jap). 1958 (30/9) arr Osaka; scrapped.

64. (1932) HIGHLAND BRIGADE (M/S)
14,131. 159,52 [165,89] x 21,15. (523.4 [544.3] x 69.4). 2–2–C. 2S–4SC.DA–15. (I–150; intermediate 70; III–500). Harland & Wolff, Belfast. 1928 (1/11) launched for Nelson. 1929 (May) MV London–S. America. 1932 HIGHLAND BRIGADE (Royal Mail). 1932 (23/7) FV London–S. America. 1940 British transport. 1946 (18/1) damaged by mine at Singapore. 1959 HENRIETTA (J. S. Latsis (Greek)). 1960 MARIANNA (ditto). 1965 (29/6) arrived at Kaohsiung for demolition.

65. (1932) HIGHLAND PATRIOT (M/S)
14,157. 159,52 [166,04] x 21,15. (523.4 [544.8] x 69.4). 2–2–C. 2S–4SC.DA–15. (I–150; intermediate 70; III–500). Harland & Wolff, Belfast. 1931 (10/12) launched for Nelson. 1932 (28/5) MV London–S. America. 1932 HIGHLAND PATRIOT (Royal Mail). 1932 (6/8) FV London–S. America. 1940 (1/10) torpedoed and sunk by German submarine in Atlantic.

66. (1932) HIGHLAND MONARCH (M/S)
14,137. 159,52 [166,04] x 21,15. (523.4 [544.8] x 69.4. 2–2–C.

31

2S–4SC.DA–15. (I–150; intermediate 70; III–500. Harland & Wolff, Belfast. 1928 (3/5) launched for Nelson. 1928 (18/10) MV London–S. America. 1932 HIGHLAND MONARCH (Royal Mail). 1932 (20/8) FV London–S. America. 1960 scrapped at Dalmuir.

67. (1932) HIGHLAND CHIEFTAIN (M/S)
14,141. 159,52 [166,04] x 21,15. (523.4 [544.8] x 69.4. 2–2–C. 2S–4SC.DA–15. (I–150; intermediate 70; III–500). Harland & Wolff, Belfast. 1928 (21/6) launched for Nelson. 1929 (21/2) MV London–S. America. 1932 HIGHLAND CHIEFTAIN (Royal Mail). 1932 (3/9) FV London–S. America. 1959 CALPEAN STAR (Calpe Shipping Co, Gibraltar). 1960 (1/6) wrecked at Montevideo.

68. (1932) HIGHLAND PRINCESS (M/S)
14,157. 159,52 [166,01] x 21,15. (523.4 [544.1] x 69.4). 2–2–C. 2S–4SC.DA–15. (I–150; intermediate 70; III–500). Harland & Wolff, Belfast. 1929 (11/4) launched for Nelson. 1930 (20/3) MV London–S. America. 1932 HIGHLAND PRINCESS (Royal Mail). 1932 (17/9) FV London–S. America. 1959 MARIANNA (Greek). 1960 SLAPY (Czechoslovak). 1960 GUANG HUA (Chinese). 1982 still listed.

69. (1948) ANDES (II)
25,689. 195,21 [204,00] x 25,45. (643.8 [669.3] x 83.5). 1–2–C. 2S–ST(SR)–20. (I–403; II–204). Harland & Wolff, Belfast. 1939 (7/3) launched. 1939 (26/9) scheduled MV Southampton–Buenos Aires but cancelled; became British troopship. 1947 refitted by Harland & Wolff, Belfast; (I–324; II–204). 1948 (22/1) FV Southampton–Buenos Aires. 1960 became cruise liner; (I–480). 1971 scrapped at Ghent.

70. 1949 MAGDALENA (III)
17,547. 167,93 [173,72] x 22,40. (551.0 [570.0] x 73.5). 1–2–C. 2S–ST(DR)–17. (I–133; III–346). Harland & Wolff, Belfast. 1948 (11/5) launched. 1949 (9/3) MV London–Buenos Aires. 1949 (25/4) stranded near Rio de Janeiro. 1949 (26/4) refloated; broke in two when under tow to Rio de Janeiro; total loss.

71. 1960 AMAZON (II) (M/S)
20,368. 164,58 [178,00] x 23,83. (540.0[584.0] x 78.2). 1–1–C. 2S–2SC.SA–17½. (I–107; cabin 82; III–275). Harland & Wolff, Belfast. 1959 (7/7) launched; registered under Welldeck Shipping Co, 1960 (22/1) MV London–Buenos Aires. 1967 18,565 tons. 1968 AKAROA (Shaw, Savill & Albion). 1968 (28/5) FV Southampton–Australia–New Zealand. 1971 AKARITA (Uglands Rederi, Grimstad); rebuilt as car transport. 1972 rebuilding

completed at Rijeka; 10,886 tons. 1981 scrapped at Kaohsiung.
72. 1960 ARAGON (II) (M/S)
    20,362. 164,58 [178,00] x 23,86. (540.0 [584.0] x 78.3). 1–1–C.
    2S.2SC.SA–17½. (I–107; cabin 82; III–275). Harland & Wolff,
    Belfast. 1959 (20/10) launched. 1960 (29/4) MV London–Buenos
    Aires. 1967 18,575 tons. 1969 ARANDA (Shaw, Savill &
    Albion). 1969 (28/3) FV Southampton–Australia–New Zealand.
    1971 HOEGH TRAVELLER (Leif Hoegh & Co, Oslo). 1971
    (12/5) arr Rijeka; rebuilt as car transport. 1972 re-commissioned;
    10,912 tons. 1981 scrapped at Kaohsiung.
73. 1960 ARLANZA (II) (M/S)
    20,362. 164,58 [178,00] x 23,86. (540.0 [584.0] x 78.3). 1–1–C.
    2S–2SC.SA–17½. (I–107; cabin 82; III–275). Harland & Wolff,
    Belfast. 1960 (13/4) launched. 1960 (7/10) MV London–Buenos
    Aires. 1967 18,595 tons. 1969 ARAWA (Shaw, Savill & Albion).
    1969 (28/2) FV Southampton–Australia–New Zealand. 1971
    HOEGH TRANSIT (Leif Hoegh & Co, Oslo). 1971 (1/7) arr
    Rijeka; rebuilt as car transport. 1972 (Jun) renamed HOEGH
    TROTTER; 10,895 tons. Later HUAL TROTTER; later TROT-
    TER. 1981 scrapped at Kaohsiung.

FUNNEL: (a) 1851. Black.
           (b) 1901. Yellow.
FLAG   : White; red saltire with golden crown in centre.

Chapter 2

1853–5

SOUTH AMERICAN & GENERAL STEAM NAVIGATION COMPANY

(British)

Seven years after Isambard Kingdom Brunel's pioneer ocean-going iron screw steamer, the GREAT BRITAIN, entered North Atlantic service, the SOUTH AMERICAN & GENERAL STEAM NAVIGATION COMPANY was founded in Liverpool in 1852 to run the first fleet of iron screw steamers to South America. Orders were placed with John Laird of Birkenhead for the 1,100 ton BRASILEIRA and LUSITANIA and with John Reid & Co of Port Glasgow for a similar ship, the OLINDA [1]. The BRASILEIRA and OLINDA were both launched on 23 April 1853; the LUSITANIA followed on 9 August. In addition, a 500 ton wooden paddle steamer, the ARGENTINA, intended to operate a feeder service between Rio de Janeiro, Montevideo and Buenos Aires, was launched by Laird on 21 May 1853 and sailed for Rio in July, thereby undertaking the Company's first sailing.

It was decided that sailings in the new service would take place on the 24th of each month from Liverpool, which meant that they would not conflict with the Royal Mail Steam Packet Company's monthly departures on the 9th or 10th. The BRASILEIRA was completed in time to open the service on 24 August 1853. Under the command of Captain Green, she encountered a heavy gale in the English Channel, but reached Lisbon in less than five days. She was due to call at St. Vincent (São Vicente) in the Cape Verde Islands, for coal but, weather conditions being unfavourable, she continued to Pernambuco, which she reached on the 12th, making the passage in 19 days 12 hours from Liverpool, including stoppages. She coaled at Bahia and reached Rio de Janeiro on the 19th.

Meanwhile, the ARGENTINA had reached Montevideo some days earlier, on 11 September. After proceeding to Buenos Aires and some 300 miles up the Parana River, she returned to Rio de Janeiro, leaving there on 22 September with the BRASILEIRA's passengers and mails, reaching Montevideo on 27 September and Buenos Aires on the following day, the 36th after the BRASILEIRA's departure from Liverpool. Unfortunately, the ARGENTINA had a very short life as she was wrecked in the River Plate in December 1853 [2].

The BRASILEIRA'S homeward voyage started on 10 October from Rio. She reached Liverpool on 5 November 'having steamed the entire distance with very little assistance from her sails' [3]. Of the 73 days occupied by the round voyage, she was 21 days in port.

The second outward sailing was taken by the OLINDA on 24 September, but the LUSITANIA was not completed in time to sail on 24 October and in her place the Company chartered the 768 ton iron screw LADY EGLINTON [3] from the British & Irish Steam Packet Company. She had recently completed two round voyages between Liverpool, Quebec and Montreal under charter to the Canadian Steam Navigation Company. She duly sailed from Liverpool on 24 October via Lisbon, St. Vincent, Pernambuco, Bahia and Rio de Janeiro to Montevideo, arriving back at Lisbon on 6 January 1854 with 11 passengers and leaving two days later for Liverpool.

The LUSITANIA sailed from Liverpool on 24 November for Lisbon, St. Vincent (for coal), Pernambuco, Bahia and Rio de Janeiro. It seems that owing to the loss of the feeder steamer ARGENTINA she continued to Montevideo and Buenos Aires, leaving the latter on 31 December and reaching Liverpool on 10 February 1854.

The BRASILEIRA sailed from Liverpool on 25 December 1853, but then a second disaster befell the Company on 26 January 1854, when the OLINDA was wrecked near Holyhead a few hours after the start of her second voyage. Fortunately, there was no loss of life. The 1,530 ton BAHIANA was launched on 31 January, but several months elapsed before she was ready to take up her station.

The LUSITANIA sailed in February 1854 and the BRASILEIRA in March, but neither ship proceeded beyond Rio de Janeiro in order to cause a minimum amount of disruption to the sailing schedule. Meanwhile, the 500 ton iron screw LA PLATA was launched by John Laird on 16 February 1854 and sailed for Rio de Janeiro early in March to undertake the feeder service so unexpectedly terminated by the loss of the ARGENTINA [4]. She was quickly joined by a second feeder steamer, the MENAI, which left Liverpool on 10 April [5].

There was no sailing from Liverpool on 24 April, but the LUSITANIA left on 24 May. The June sailing was omitted because the BRASILEIRA had to undergo repairs, but the BAHIANA was nearly ready and actually started her maiden voyage on 1 July.

The following announcement was made in September 1854:

'Mails to Brazil. An additional line of contract mail steamers has been established to Brazil via Liverpool, calling at Lisbon, Madeira, Bahia and Pernambuco. The mails will be made up in London on the 23rd of every month. When the 23rd of the month falls on a Sunday, the mails will be made up on the day following' [6].

In fact, there was a slight error in the announcement as, after calling at Madeira, the steamers proceeded to Pernambuco, Bahia and Rio de Janeiro. The BAHIANA's second sailing started on 24 September, and she had the distinction of opening the mail service.

Following the loss of the OLINDA, two further steamers were ordered – the 1,700 ton IMPERADOR and IMPERATRIZ, which were launched by Laird on 13 July and 7 October 1854, respectively. The maiden voyage of the IMPERADOR started on 24 October and was both the second and the last of the mail sailings as by the time she returned to Liverpool on 4 January 1855 the BRASILEIRA and LUSITANIA had been sold to the Messageries Imperiales [7] and the BAHIANA and IMPERATRIZ taken up as Crimean War transports. The IMPERADOR followed suit a few days later.

The 630 ton paddle steamer PAMPERO, ordered as a further feeder steamer, was for a time advertised as taking the 24 November 1854 sailing in place of the BRASILEIRA, but this was later postponed and eventually cancelled outright.

Thus, the Company undertook a total of 12 sailings to South America by iron screw steamers, and deserved a full measure of praise for being the pioneer in this connection. Rather surprisingly, the surviving ships were sold after the Crimean War and the service was never resumed. Perhaps this was just as well, however, as no fewer than eight other concerns established lines of iron screw steamers to Brazil between 1854 and 1859 and not one of them remained in operation for more than a year or two.

[1] *The Albion* (Liverpool) 25/4/1853.
[2] *British Press & Jersey Times* 14/2/1854 and 21/3/1854.
[3] *The Albion* (Liverpool) 3/10/1853.
[4] C.R.V. Gibbs: *British Passenger Liners of the Five Oceans* (Putnam, London 1963).
[5] *British Press & Jersey Times* 28/4/1854. (N.B. The LA PLATA returned from South America in 1855, calling at Lisbon on 19 February and sailing again on the 21st for Liverpool).
[6] *British Press & Jersey Times* 19/9/1854.
[7] *The Times* 25/10/1854.

1. 1853 BRASILEIRA
   1,100. 70,10 x 8,84 (230.0 x 29.0). C–1–3. I–S–?–9. (I; II). John
   Laird, Birkenhead. 1853 (23/4) launched. 1853 (24/8) MV
   Liverpool–Lisbon–St. Vincent–Pernambuco–Bahia (for coal)–
   Rio de Janeiro (arr 19/9). 1853 (25/12) 2nd voyage Liverpool–
   Lisbon–St. Vincent–Pernambuco–Bahia–Rio de Janeiro. 1854
   (24/3) 3rd voyage ditto. 1854 (24/7) 4th voyage ditto. 1854 (8/9)
   dep Rio de Janeiro. 1854 (11/10) arr Liverpool. 1854 sold to
   Messageries Imperiales; became Crimean war transport.
2. 1853 OLINDA
   1,100. 70,10 x 8,84. (230.0 x 29.0). C–1–3. I–S–?–9. (I; II). John
   Reid & Co, Port Glasgow. 1853 (23/4) launched. 1853 (24/9) MV
   Liverpool–Lisbon–St. Vincent–Pernambuco–Bahia–Rio de
   Janeiro. 1854 (26/1) wrecked near Holyhead at start of 2nd
   voyage. (0).
2a. (1853) LADY EGLINTON (c)
   768. 58,51 x 8,53. (192 x 28). C–1–3. I–S–?–9. Robert Napier,
   Glasgow. 1853 launched for British & Irish. 1853 (16/6) FV for
   Canadian SN Co (c), Liverpool–Quebec–Montreal (2 RV). 1853
   (24/10) FV Liverpool–Lisbon–St Vincent–Pernambuco–Bahia–
   Rio de Janeiro–Montevideo (1 RV). 1854 became Crimean War
   transport. 1891–2 scrapped.
3. 1853 LUSITANIA
   1,100. 70,10 x 8,84. (230.0 x 29.0). C–1–3. I–S–?–9. (I; II). John
   Laird, Birkenhead. 1853 (9/8) launched. 1853 (24/11) MV
   Liverpool–Lisbon–St. Vincent–Pernambuco–Bahia–Rio de
   Janeiro–Montevideo–Buenos Aires (dep 31/12)–Montevideo–
   Rio de Janeiro (dep 1854 (10/1))–Bahia–Pernambuco–St. Vin-
   cent–Lisbon–Liverpool. 1854 (24/2) 2nd voyage Liverpool–Lis-
   bon–St. Vincent–Pernambuco–Bahia–Rio de Janeiro (dep 30/3)–
   Bahia–Pernambuco–St. Vincent–Madeira–Lisbon–Liverpool (arr
   30/4). 1854 (24/5) 3rd voyage Liverpool–Lisbon–Pernambuco–
   Bahia–Rio de Janeiro (dep 8/7)–Bahia–Pernambuco–Madeira–
   Lisbon–Liverpool (arr 5/8). 1854 (24/8) 4th voyage Liverpool–
   Lisbon–Madeira–Pernambuco–Bahia–Rio de Janeiro (dep 1/10)–
   Bahia–Pernambuco–Madeira–Lisbon–Liverpool (arr 31/10). 1854
   HYDASPE (Messageries Imperiales) became Crimean War
   transport. 1864 (25/10) wrecked in the Riouw Straits, Singapore.
4. 1854 BAHIANA
   1,530. 74,97 x 10,67. (246.0 x 35.0). C–1–3. I–S–?–10. (I; II).
   John Laird, Liverpool. 1854 (31/1) launched. 1854 (1/7) MV
   Liverpool–Lisbon–St. Vincent–Pernambuco (arr 23/7)–Bahia–
   Rio de Janeiro (dep 9/8)–Bahia–Pernambuco–Madeira–Lisbon–

Liverpool (arr 9/9). 1854 (24/9) 2nd voyage (1st mail sailing) Liverpool–Lisbon–Madeira–Pernambuco–Bahia–Rio de Janeiro (dep 1/11)–Bahia–Pernambuco–Madeira–Lisbon–Liverpool (arr 2/12). 1854 (Dec) fitted for the conveyance of troops to the Crimea. 1855 SIMOIS (Messageries Imperiales). 1875 scrapped at La Ciotat.

5. 1854 IMPERADOR
   1,700. 80,77 x 11,12. (265.0 x 36.5). C–1–3. I–S–D2–10. (I–160; II; III). John Laird, Liverpool. 1854 (13/7) launched. 1854 (24/10) MV Liverpool–Lisbon–Madeira–Pernambuco–Bahia–Rio de Janeiro (dep 1/12)–Bahia–Pernambuco–Madeira–Lisbon–Liverpool (arr 1855 (4/1). 1855 (10/1) being fitted at Liverpool for conveyance of troops to the Crimea. 1862 TAMPICO (CGT). 1870 GUADELOUPE (CGT). 1889 SORRENTO (Norwegian). 1890 (Aug) foundered in North Sea.

– —— IMPERATRIZ
   1,700. 80,77 x 11,15. (265.0 x 36.6). C–1–3. I–S–D2–10. (I–160; II; III). John Laird, Liverpool. 1854 (7/10) launched. 1854 (7/12) ordered to proceed to Cork to embark 1,000 rank and file for the Crimea. 1862 VERA CRUZ (CGT). 1869 MARTINIQUE (CGT). 1892 scrapped.

FUNNEL: Black.
FLAG   : A blue saltire on red.

Chapter 3

(1853–8)

COMPAGNIE DE NAVIGATION MIXTE

(French)

The COMPAGNIE DE NAVIGATION MIXTE, founded in 1850 by Louis Arnaud, of Lyons, France, and the brothers Auguste and Félix Touache, of Marseilles, began operations on 28 February 1852 with a steamship service between Marseilles and Algiers.

At that time the only line of steamers running from Europe to Brazil was the Royal Mail Steam Packet Company (Chapter 1), whose first sailing from Southampton to Rio de Janeiro had taken place in the previous year. But in April 1853 the French company decided to introduce its own service from Marseilles to Brazil, and placed orders with Forges & Chantiers de la Méditerranée of La Seyne, Toulon, for two 2,000 ton iron single-screw steamers, the FRANCE and BRÉSIL.

Not content with awaiting the completion of these two vessels, however, the Compagnie Mixte despatched the 738 ton L'AVENIR from Marseilles for Barcelona, Malaga, Lisbon, Las Palmas, Gorée, Pernambuco and Rio de Janeiro on 25 November 1853, by which time a second British line, the South American & General (Chapter 2) was in operation. The L'AVENIR had engine trouble and did not reach Rio de Janeiro until 9 February 1854. The homeward voyage took 57 days, but a second arrival at Rio took place on 6 August, after a voyage of 42 days, which was also the duration of the homeward leg [1].

Instead of the FRANCE and BRÉSIL joining the service in 1854, as intended, they were taken up by the French Government as Crimean War transports. They and the two ships which followed them had engines driven by a combination of steam and ether vapour.

The South Atlantic service, suspended after the L'AVENIR's second sailing, was resumed on 26 August 1856, when the FRANCE left Marseilles for Rio de Janeiro, followed by the BRÉSIL on 25 September, but disaster came only two days later when the FRANCE was destroyed by fire at Bahia, caused by her unorthodox combination of propellents.

A third steamer, the AMÉRIQUE, was launched at La Seyne on 17 January 1857 and started her maiden voyage to Brazil later that year. By then, however, the Company had realised that the service was unprofitable. The AMÉRIQUE was sold to Messageries Imperiales, the predecessors of Messageries Maritimes, on 28 April 1858, while the

BRÉSIL and a fourth unit, the VILLE DE LYON, were transferred to the Compagnie Mixte's Mediterranean services. Like the others, the latest newcomer relied on the aforementioned mixture of propellents, the danger of which was emphasised by the fact that they were responsible for her destruction by fire in 1868.

In 1969 the COMPAGNIE DE NAVIGATION MIXTE joined forces with the Mediterranean services of COMPAGNIE GÉNÉRALE TRANSATLANTIQUE to become the COMPAGNIE GÉNÉRALE TRANSMÉDITERRANÉENNE.

[1] *Courier du Brésil* 24/12/1854.

1. (1853) L'AVENIR
   738. Forges & Chantiers de la Méditerranée, La Seyne. 1853 (25/11) FV Marseilles–Barcelona–Malaga–Lisbon–Las Palmas–Gorée–Pernambuco–Rio de Janeiro (arr 1854 (9/2). Second voyage, arr Rio de Janeiro 1854 (6/8). 1880 scrapped at Genoa.
2. (1856) FRANCE
   2,000. Forges & Chantiers de la Méditerranée, La Seyne. 1854 (May) launched. 1855 Crimean War transport. 1856 (26/8) FV Marseilles–Brazil. 1856 (28/9) destroyed by fire at Bahia.
3. (1856) BRÉSIL
   2,000. Forges & Chantiers de la Méditerranée, La Seyne. 1854 (Aug) launched. 1855 Crimean War transport. 1856 (25/9) FV Marseilles–Brazil. 1868 lost.
4. 1857 AMÉRIQUE
   1,697. Forges & Chantiers de la Méditerranée, La Seyne. 1857 (17/1) launched. 1857 MV Marseilles–Brazil. 1858 (28/4) AMÉRIQUE (Messageries Imperiales). 1871 ditto (Messageries Maritimes). 1875 scrapped at La Ciotat.
– —— VILLE DE LYON
   2,200. Forges & Chantiers de la Méditerranée, La Seyne. 1856 launched for Brazil service, but ran for Compagnie Mixte in Mediterranean. 1868 16/6) destroyed by fire off Cape Spartivento.

Chapter 4

1854–7

COMPANHIA DE NAVEGAÇÃO A VAPOR LUSO–BRASILEIRA

(Portuguese)

The COMPANHIA DE NAVEGAÇÃO A VAPOR LUSO–BRASILEIRA was founded in Oporto, Portugal, on 30 December 1852 to run from Lisbon to Brazil.

The 1,534 ton DONNA MARIA SEGUNDA, so named after the Queen of Portugal, was ordered from Richard & Henry Green of Blackwall, London, and was a wooden screw steamer, with sides and bottom protected by copper sheeting. She had an oscillating engine built by Miller & Ravenhill of London, capable of a speed of about nine knots. Accommodation was provided for 80 first class, 76 second and 250 steerage passengers.

The DONNA MARIA SEGUNDA was launched on 17 September 1853, and sailed from London via Plymouth for Lisbon on 28 April 1854, arriving there on 6 May and starting her maiden voyage on 7 June for Madeira, São Vicente (St. Vincent), Pernambuco, Bahia and Rio de Janeiro, which she reached on 1 July, leaving again on the 16th and arriving at Lisbon on 10 August with 199 passengers. She made one more round voyage in 1854, four in 1855 and one in 1856. On one at least of the 1855 voyages she proceeded from Brazil to Uruguay and Argentina, sailing from Buenos Aires on 7 April, Montevideo on the 12th, Rio de Janeiro on the 28th, Bahia on 3 May, Pernambuco on the 5th, St. Vincent on the 15th, Madeira on the 22nd and reached Lisbon on the 25th.

A second 1856 voyage started from Lisbon on 24 May with a complement of 327 passengers, but she had engine trouble before reaching St. Vincent, where her passengers were landed and transferred in due course to her sister ship. She returned light to Lisbon, arriving there on 20 July, this being her last activity for the line.

The 1,512 ton DOM PEDRO SEGUNDO, named after Donna Maria II's brother, the Emperor of Brazil, was built by William Pitcher of Northfleet, London, and like her predecessor was a wooden screw steamer fitted with copper sheeting, her horizontal engines being built by Miller, Ravenhill & Salkeld of London. Passenger figures were much the same as those of her consort.

The DOM PEDRO SEGUNDO was launched on 26 August 1854, sailing from London via Plymouth and Oporto to Lisbon, which she

41

reached on 14 May 1855, leaving again on 30 May via the usual ports to Rio de Janeiro with 158 passengers. She made a second round voyage in 1855 and three in 1856, on the second of which she reached Lisbon with 327 passengers. She only made one voyage in 1857.

A proportion of the Company's capital was held in Brazil, and at a general meeting of the Brazilian shareholders on 1 March 1857 it was decided that the Company should close down. It was announced in Oporto on 2 May 1857 that the ships would be sold. The DOM PEDRO SEGUNDO sailed from Lisbon for London with cargo on 23 September 1857. A year later she became the British SIR WILLIAM PEEL, and in 1866 the CRESCENT CITY of S.B. Guion.

The DONNA MARIA SEGUNDA was sold by auction in Lisbon, and it is believed that she became the British steamer LIVERPOOL, which sailed from Lisbon for Liverpool in ballast on 11 November 1859.

The failure of the Company was partly due to its inability to obtain a subsidy, but more especially because of the lack of dockyards and even marine engineers in Portugal at that time, to say nothing of the need to import large quantities of coal. From the point of view of gross revenue the Company was an undoubted success.

The COMPANHIA DE NAVEGAÇÃO A VAPOR LUSO–BRA-SILEIRA was notable as the first non-British steamship line to run a service to and from Brazil.

1. 1854 DONNA MARIA SEGUNDA
   1,534. 74,36 x 11,28. (244.0 x 37.0). C–1–3. W–S–0(1)–9. (I–80; II–76; III–250). Richard & Henry Green, Blackwall, London (engines Miller & Ravenhill, London). 1853 (17/9) launched. 1854 (28/4) MV London–Plymouth–Lisbon (arr 6/5; dep 7/6)–Madeira–St. Vincent–Pernambuco–Bahia–Rio de Janeiro (arr 1/7; dep 16/7)–Lisbon (arr 10/8). 1855 4 RV. 1856 (24/5) Lisbon–Madeira–St. Vincent (engine trouble; passengers disembarked). 1856 (20/7) ship arrived light at Lisbon. 1859 (11/11) believed to have sailed as the British steamer LIVERPOOL from Lisbon for Liverpool in ballast.

2. 1855 DOM PEDRO SEGUNDO
   1,512. 75,46 x 10,70. (247.6 x 35.1). C–1–3. W–S–H2–9. (I–88; II–70; III–250). Wm. Pitcher, Northfleet, London (engines Miller, Ravenhill & Salkeld, London). 1854 (26/8) launched. 1855 MV London–Plymouth–Oporto–Lisbon (arr 14/5; dep 30/5)–Madeira–St. Vincent–Pernambuco–Bahia–Rio de Janeiro. 1855 2nd RV ditto. 1856 3 RV. 1857 1 RV. 1857 (May) sold. 1857 (23/9) sailed Lisbon–London. 1858 SIR WILLIAM PEEL (Br). 1866 CRESCENT CITY (S.B. Guion (Br)).

Chapter 5

1856

COMPAGNIE FRANCO – AMÉRICAINE

(French)

Following on the heels of the Compagnie de Navigation Mixte (Chapter 3), which was the first French line to introduce a steamship service to Brazil, GAUTHIER FRÈRES & COMPAGNIE, of Paris and Lyons, formed the COMPAGNIE FRANCO – AMÉRICAINE to run a service from Havre to Brazil as well as another to New York, and acquired a fleet of eight iron screw steamers, six of which were built by John Laird of Birkenhead and the other two in France.

The South American service was due to start on 22 February 1856, by which time the Compagnie de Navigation Mixte had achieved only two sailings, but was delayed until 26 February, when the Laird-built CADIX, which had been launched as the CADIZ for the short-lived Linea de Vapores Correos Españoles Trasatlánticos, left Havre for Lisbon, Pernambuco, Bahia and Rio de Janeiro. She was followed by two of the other Laird ships, the LYONNAIS on 5 April (postponed from 22 March) and the FRANC–COMTOIS on 7 May (postponed from 22 April), these delays being due to the late arrival of the ships from Birkenhead. They had been launched on 9 and 10 January 1856, respectively, and the FRANC–COMTOIS attained 11 knots during her trials in April [1]. The CADIX made two more round voyages and the other ships one more each.

On 1 October, shortly after the completion of her second voyage to Brazil, the LYONNAIS sailed from Havre for New York, in place of the BARCELONE, which was not ready after a late arrival from the USA. The LYONNAIS was in collision with the American bark ADRIATIC on 2 November, a few hours after the start of her homeward voyage. She was abandoned on the following day and six days later the survivors were rescued by the German bark ELISE. Owing largely to exposure to the cold, there were 120 fatal casualties.

The BARCELONE sailed from Havre on 26 October 1856 for Lisbon, Tenerife, Bahia and Rio de Janeiro, her passenger complement from Lisbon being no greater than 15, and this was probably the reason why no subsequent sailings to South America by the Company have been traced.

Instead of being detailed to the New York service, as originally intended, the French-built JACQUART and FRANÇOIS ARAGO took part in a third service between Havre, Havana and New Orleans, which was no more successful than the other two.

There were 11 completed round voyages to New York in addition to the eight to Brazil. Four of the six Laird ships were sold to the P&O, and the other survivor, the VIGO, went to the Inman Line.

[1] *The Albion* (Liverpool) 21/3/1856.

1. 1856 CADIX
   1,600. 82,90 x 11,21. (272.0 x 36.8). C-1-3. I-S-H2-10. (I-80; II-40; III). John Laird, Birkenhead (engines G. Rennie & Son, London). 1855 (30/8) launched as CADIZ (Linea de Vapores Correos Españoles Trasatlánticos. 1855 CADIX (Cie Franco-Américaine). 1856 (26/2) MV Havre-Brazil (3 RV). 1857 (9/2) FV Havre-Liverpool (for repairs) – New York. (1 RV). 1858 ELLORA (P&O). 1877 ELLORA (Austrialian); engines removed. 1887 renamed CADIZ. 1890 ditto (Norwegian). 1899 (Sep) hulked.

2. 1856 LYONNAIS
   1,605. 82,90 x 11,21. (272.0 x 36.8). C-1-3. I-S-H2-10. (I-80; II-40; III). John Laird, Birkenhead (engines G. Rennie & Son, London). 1856 (9/1) launched. 1856 (1/4) arr Havre from Liverpool. 1856 (5/4) MV Havre-Brazil (2 RV). 1856 (1/10) FV Havre-New York. 1856 (2/11) collided with American bark ADRIATIC. 1856 (3/11) abandoned; sank (120).

3. 1856 FRANC-COMTOIS
   1,600. 82,90 x 11,21. (272.0 x 36.8). C-1-3. I-S-H2-10. (I-80; II-40; III). John Laird, Birkenhead (engines Fawcett & Co, Liverpool). 1856 (10/1) launched. 1856 (7/5) MV Havre-Brazil (2 RV). 1858 ORISSA (P&O). 1878 ORISSA (J. Matheson & Co, Hong Kong); converted to sail.

4. 1856 BARCELONE
   1,603. 82,90 x 11,21. (272.0 x 36.8). C-1-3. I-S-H2-10. (I-80; II-40; III). John Laird, Birkenhead (engines Fawcett, Preston & Co, Liverpool). 1855 (1/9) launched as BARCELONA (Linea de Vapores Correos Españoles Trasatlánticos). 1855 bought by Cie Franco-Américaine; renamed BARCELONE. 1856 (3/2) MV Havre-New York (4 RV). 1856 (26/10) FV Havre-Lisbon-Tenerife-Bahia-Rio de Janeiro (1 RV). 1858 BEHAR (P&O). 1874 NIIGATA MARU (Jap). 1898 scrapped.

Chapter 6

(1856–7)

UNION LINE

(1853). Union Steam Collier Company
1856. Union Steam Ship Company Limited

(British)

The UNION STEAM COLLIER COMPANY was founded in October 1853, the original intention being to name it the Southampton Steam Shipping Company. Its principal object was to carry coal from South Wales to Southampton for the benefit of steamship lines calling at or making this Hampshire port their terminal.

The 336 ton UNION, the 491 ton BRITON, the 550 ton SAXON and the 531 ton NORMAN and DANE were ordered from London builders – the UNION, NORMAN and DANE from C. Lungley of Rotherhithe, and the other two from J. D'A. Samuda of Poplar. The UNION, BRITON and SAXON had their engines aft, but the NORMAN and DANE were fitted with amidships machinery. The UNION made one voyage from Cardiff to Southampton with coal in June 1854, but she and her consorts were subsequently employed in carrying materials to and from Turkey and the Crimean War. So great was the demand that a sixth ship, the 551 ton CELT was built.

When the war ended there was no longer the same need to transport coal from South Wales to Southampton so it was decided to start a new line to Brazil in competition with the Royal Mail Steam Packet Company (Chapter 1). The first sailing was taken by the NORMAN, which left Southampton on 23 September 1856. The UNION followed on 23 October, carrying passengers and cargo.

The Company's title was no longer appropriate as the ships were not carrying cargoes of coal, and on 5 December 1856 it was amended to UNION STEAM SHIP COMPANY LIMITED.

The DANE had been unable to sail in November 1856, but the CELT left Southampton on 24 December for the Brazils and had proceeded some distance across the Bay of Biscay when it was considered advisable to return on account of engine trouble. She reached Cowes Roads on 29 December and put to sea again on the 31st after the necessary repairs had been made. Having for the second time proceeded some hundreds of miles, the CELT was found to be making water, and as it could not be kept under it was decided to return to Southampton for a detailed examination to take place. It was rumoured that the NORMAN was being sent round from Liverpool for the CELT's cargo [1].

The NORMAN duly left Southampton on 23 January 1857 with about 200 tons of cargo, but an advertisement of 11 February [2] stated that the ships would in future sail from Liverpool each month, starting with the DANE on 15 March. She would be followed by the CELT on 1 May. In fact, the DANE did not sail until 21 March and was succeeded by the CELT, whose sailing was postponed until 17 May, when she left with a full cargo and a Post Office mail.

It had been announced from early days that the steamers would carry cabin passengers at a fare of 20 guineas, but in February 1857 it was stated that first class fares were 30 guineas to Pernambuco and 32 guineas to Bahia, while a few third class passengers would be taken at £10 and £12, respectively [3].

The sailing of the CELT on 17 May 1857 was the last of the line to South America and future prospects appeared dim until the British Admiralty invited tenders for a mail service to Cape Colony. The Union Company submitted an application and was informed on 4 September that it had been accepted. Only 11 days later the DANE sailed from Southampton for Table Bay, thus establishing a service which placed the former collier company among the ranks of the world's great mail steam packet companies, and which on 8 March 1900 became part of the renowned Union Castle Mail Steamship Company Limited.

[1] *The Times* 6/1/1857.
[2] *The Times* 11/2/1857.
[3] *The Times* 11/3/1857.

1. (1856) NORMAN
   531. 52,11 x 7,52. (171.0 x 24.7). C–1–3. I–S–?–7. C. Lungley, Rotherhithe, London. 1854 launched. 1854 (3/12) MV South-ampton–Constantinople–Balaklava. 1856 (23/9 FV South-ampton–Rio de Janeiro. 1857 (23/1) 2nd voyage ditto. 1864 sold to G. Lungley, Southampton.
2. (1856) UNION
   336. 48,00 x 6,40. (157.6 x 21.0). C–1–3. W&I–S–?–7. (composite ship; engines aft). C. Lungley, Rotherhithe. 1854 launched. 1854 (Jun) MV Cardiff–Southampton with cargo of coal. 1854 (Jly) FV Southampton–Constantinople. 1856 (23/10) FV Southampton–Rio de Janeiro (1 RV). 1858 UNION (P&O). 1863 sold in Chinese waters.

3. (1856) CELT
   551. 55,67 x 7,74. (179.4 x 25.4). C–1–3. I–S–?–7. C. Lungley,
   Rotherhithe. 1856 (24/12) sailed Southampton–Pernambuco–
   Bahia–Rio de Janeiro. Returned to Cowes Roads on 1856 (29/12)
   owing to engine trouble. Sailed again 1856 (31/12), but after
   proceeding some hundreds of miles returned to Southampton
   owing to a leak. 1857 (17/5) Liverpool–Brazil (2nd RV). 1864
   GOTHENBURG (Dutch). 1875 CELT (Newcastle owners).
4. (1857) DANE
   531. 54,00 x 7,19. (177.2 x 24.6). C–1–3. I–S–?–7. C. Lungley,
   Rotherhithe. 1854 launched. 1855 MV as Crimean War transport.
   1857 (21/3) FV Liverpool–Brazil (1 RV). 1857 (15/9) FV
   Southampton–Table Bay. 1865 (4/12) wrecked at Algoa Bay.

Total 6 RV.

Chapter 7

1856–7

COMPAGNIA TRANSATLANTICA

(Italian)

The first Italian ocean-going steamship company, the COMPAGNIA TRANSATLANTICA, was founded in Genoa in October 1852 with a capital of 10 million Lire (£400,000) in 2,000 shares of 500 lire each. Its aim was to establish passenger and cargo services from Genoa to both North and South America. At a later date the Company was awarded a subsidy of 50,000 lire (£2,000) for each voyage undertaken from Genoa to Rio de Janeiro, with a feeder service from there to the River Plate. The services were to be maintained by steamers of not less than 1,500 tons and 250 horse-power; the duration of voyages to Brazil was not to exceed 38 days. The Company was required to carry mail free of charge, as well as diplomatic and consular officials. The ships were to fly the flag of the Kingdom of Sardinia, and could be requisitioned by the Government in the event of war.

To begin with, the 1,685 ton iron screw steamers VITTORIO EMANUELE and CONTE DI CAVOUR were ordered from C. J. Mare & Co of Blackwall, London, their engines to be supplied by Maudslay, Sons & Field of London. They were completed early in 1855, but were immediately chartered by the French Government as Crimean War transports. Before the second pair, the 1,985 ton GENOVA and TORINO, was built by the same firm the Company's capital was increased from 10 million to 18 million lire. They were launched on 12 April and 20 June 1856, respectively, and an article describing the GENOVA's trials confirmed that both the South American and North American services were still contemplated, the former being almost ready to start [1].

The 610 ton iron screw SARDEGNA was chartered from Raffaele Rubattino, a well-known Genoese shipowner, who at the time was also chairman of the Compagnia Transatlantica. She was despatched from Genoa on 11 October 1856 to take up her station at Rio de Janeiro as the feeder ship responsible for sailings thence to Buenos Aires.

The GENOVA opened the service proper by leaving Genoa on 20 October, later departures being advertised for the 20th of each month for St. Vincent (for coal), Pernambuco (22 days), Bahia (25 days) and Rio de Janeiro (30 days). The GENOVA had accommodation for 48 first class,

36 second and 174 steerage passengers, but only managed to attract a total of 71. She reached Rio in 38 days, the time allowed by the contract, and arrived back at Genoa on 31 December.

The second sailing was taken on 21 November 1856 by the TORINO and the third a month later by another feeder steamer, the 800 ton ITALIA, bought from Raffaele Rubattino to take the place of the SARDEGNA, which was evidently too small and too slow. The ITALIA extended her voyage from Rio de Janeiro to Buenos Aires in place of the SARDEGNA, which sailed from Rio on 7 February 1857, reaching Genoa on 2 April with 24 passengers after a voyage of 54 days.

The GENOVA started her second voyage from Genoa on 20 January 1857, by which time it had been decided not to take any further steps in connection with the New York line. Instead, the CONTE DI CAVOUR,

1857 CONTE DI CAVOUR 1,685 tons
Made two round voyages from Genoa to Rio de Janeiro.

which had completed her Crimean transport service some time previously, took the 20 February sailing from Genoa to Rio de Janeiro. Next to sail was the VITTORIO EMANUELE on 20 March, followed by the GENOVA in April, the CONTE DI CAVOUR in June, the TORINO in July and, finally, the VITTORIO EMANUELE started her second voyage on 20 August, her passage time to Rio de Janeiro being 36 days. She sailed again on 1 October via Bahia, Pernambuco, St. Vincent and Marseilles, reaching Genoa on 18 November with 69 passengers and 200 tons of cargo.

This, apart from a homeward voyage by the feeder steamer ITALIA, was the completion of the service, which had attracted disappointingly small numbers of passengers and not over much cargo.

[1] *The Times* 22/9/1856.

a. (1856) SARDEGNA
610. 44,15 x 6,46. (144.9 x 21.2). C–1–3. I–S–?–8. Greenock. 1854 (Jan) launched. 1856 SARDEGNA (Cia Trasatlantica (c)). 1856 (11/10) FV Genoa–Rio de Janeiro; acted as feeder steamer Rio de Janeiro–Buenos Aires. 1857 (7/2) dep Rio de Janeiro for Genoa (passage 54 days).

1. 1856 GENOVA
1,985. 80,77 x 11,58. (265.0 x 38.0). C–1–3. I–S–?–10. (I–48; II–36; III–174). C.J. Mare & Co, Blackwall, London (engines Maudslay, Sons & Field, London). 1856 (12/4) launched. 1856 (20/10) MV Genoa–St. Vincent–Pernambuco–Bahia–Rio de Janeiro (arr 27/11)–Genoa (arr 31/12). 1857 (20/1) 2nd voyage ditto. 1857 (20/4) LV ditto (3 RV). 1859 (30/11) destroyed by fire at Malaga when employed by Spanish Govt. as troop transport Spain–Morocco.

2. 1856 TORINO
1,985. 80,77 x 11,58. (265.0 x 38.0). C–1–3. I–S–?–10. (I–48; II–36; III–174). C.J. Mare & Co, Blackwall, London (engines Maudslay, Sons & Field, London). 1856 (20/6) launched. 1856 (21/11) MV Genoa–St. Vincent–Pernambuco–Bahia–Rio de Janeiro. 1857 (20/7) LV ditto (2 RV). 1859 chartered by Spanish Govt. as hospital ship. 1860 (19/8) set on fire by French fleet and foundered.

3. (1856) ITALIA (c)
800. 45,15 x 7,80. (148.2 x 25.6). C–1–3. I–S–?–9. Chester Graham, Blackwall, London. 1856 (20/12) FV for Cia Transatlantica (c), Genoa–St. Vincent–Pernambuco–Bahia–Rio de Janeiro; continued to Buenos Aires as feeder steamer in replacement of SARDEGNA. 1857 returned to Rubattino.

4. (1857) CONTE DI CAVOUR
1,685. 74,67 x 10,67. (245.0 x 35.0). C–1–3. I–S–?–10. (I–48; II–36; III–155). C.J. Mare & Co, Blackwall, London (engines Maudslay, Sons & Field, London). 1854 (Dec) launched. 1855 chartered by French Govt. as Crimean War transport. 1857 (20/2) FV Genoa–St. Vincent–Pernambuco–Bahia–Rio de Janeiro. 1857 (20/6) LV ditto (2 RV). 1860 AMERIGO VESPUCCI (Italian Navy – school ship); later FLAVIO GIOIA. 1900 scrapped.

5. (1857) VITTORIO EMANUELE
1,685.74,67 x 10,67. (245.0 x 35.0). C–1–3. I–S–?–10. (I–48; II–36; III–155. C.J. Mare & Co, Blackwall, London (engines Maudslay, Sons & Field, London). 1854 (21/11) launched. 1855 chartered by French Govt. as Crimean War transport. 1857 (20/3)

FV Genoa–St. Vincent–Pernambuco–Bahia–Rio de Janeiro. 1857 (20/8) LV ditto (2 RV) 1857 (18/11) arr Genoa from Rio de Janeiro–Bahia–Pernambuco–St. Vincent and Marseilles. 1860 VOLTURNO (Italian Naval transport). 1873 (12-13/2) wrecked near Cape Linaro.

Chapter 8

1856–8

HAMBURG BRASILIANISCHE PACKETSCHIFFAHRT GESELLSCHAFT

(Hamburg Brazilian Steam Navigation Company)

(German)

It was advertised that the HAMBURG BRAZILIAN STEAM NAVIGATION COMPANY (HAMBURG BRASILIANISCHE PACKETSCHIFFAHRT GESELLSCHAFT) steamers TEUTONIA, PETROPOLIS and another (not named) would sail monthly from Southampton for Lisbon, Pernambuco, Bahia and Rio de Janeiro, starting in November or December 1856. [1] As was only to be expected, voyages would originate at Hamburg.

A later announcement stated that the 2,000 ton iron screw steamer PETROPOLIS was launched by Caird & Co of Greenock on 30 October 1856 and was a sister ship of the TEUTONIA, which was taking in her coals before proceeding to Southampton and Hamburg. It was mentioned that the ships could carry sufficient coal for the entire voyage to Rio de Janeiro, and thus avoid the inconvenience and delay of obtaining a fresh supply at Lisbon or St. Vincent, which was the normal procedure at that time. The two ships were contracted for early in February 1856 for delivery in February and May 1857, and it was believed that such an early completion was unprecedented. It was added that Petropolis was a town in Brazil, and that the figurehead of the steamer was a well-executed bust of the Brazilian Emperor, Dom Pedro II. [2]

The service was opened by the TEUTONIA, which sailed from Hamburg on 20 December 1856 and from Southampton four days later. She left the English port with 60 passengers and 600 tons of cargo.

The PETROPOLIS left Southampton on 25 February 1857 with about 70 passengers and 900 tons of cargo. A second voyage was started by the TEUTONIA from Hamburg and Southampton in March, and was followed from the same ports by the GOLDEN FLEECE of the European & American Steam Shipping Company (Chapter 9) on 20 and 24 April. It had been arranged for the two companies to run a joint service but, in fact, there were only two more European & American sailings, both from Antwerp to Brazil via Southampton and Lisbon.

The third Hamburg line's ship was launched by Caird & Co on (

October 1857 as the PRINZESSIN VON JOINVILLE, and was expected to be ready to sail from Hamburg on 20 December. However, there was a delay and although it was announced on 24 February 1858 that she would be leaving the Clyde for Hamburg during the following week to take her place as a consort to the TEUTONIA and PETROPO- LIS, [3] her South American departure was in fact cancelled. Furth- ermore, no trace has been found of sailings later than 25 October 1857 from Southampton by the TEUTONIA and 26 November by the PETROPOLIS.

Eight of the first nine steamship lines from Europe to South America closed down within a year or two, and it is evident that in those early days it was virtually impossible to run a viable service without a mail subsidy. Even so, the TEUTONIA left Southampton on 25 October 1857 with 196 passengers, specie and jewellery valued at £40,000 and nearly 1,000 tons of merchandise 'supposed to be the most valuable cargo ever yet exported in one steamer to the Brazils!'. [4] It does seem, however, that if the Company had been able to persevere a bit longer it might have been able to turn the financial corner.

The TEUTONIA and PETROPOLIS were sold to the Hamburg American Line in 1858. No further trace has been found of the steamer PRINZESSIN VON JOINVILLE, which was presumably sold and renamed. Historically, the Princesse de Joinville (or Prinzessin von Joinville) was the wife of a son of King Louis Phillipe of France. It is stated in an encyclopaedia under 'Joinville' that 'Doña Francisca or Joinville is a small town in Brazil'. The Prince and Princess were forced into exile in 1848 and came to England. The implication is that subsequently one or both of them were active in a Brazilian promotion of some importance – hence the name of the ship.

[1] *The Times* 17/9/1856.
[2] *Greenock Advertiser* 31/10/1856.
[3] *North British Daily Mail* 24/2/1858.
[4] *The Times* 26/10/1857.

1. 1856 TEUTONIA
    2,693. 86,00 x 12,00. (282.1 x 39.4). C–1–3. I–S–I(2)–10. (I–50; II–136; III–310). Caird & Co, Greenock. 1856 (4/8) launched. 1856 (20/12) MV Hamburg–Southampton–Lisbon–Pernambuco– Bahia–Rio de Janeiro. 1857 (20/10) LV ditto. 1858 (21/10) TEUTONIA (Hapag). 1877 TEUTONIA (Dominion). 1883 ditto (Br). 1884 REGINA (Italian). 1889 PIEMONTESE (ditto). 1890 CITTÀ DI SAVONA (ditto). 1891 MENTANA (ditto). 1894 scrapped in Italy.

2. 1857 PETROPOLIS
   2,405. 86,00 x 12,00. (282.1 x 39.4). C–1–3. I–S–I(2)–10. (I–50;
   II–136; III–310). Caird & Co, Greenock. 1856 (30/10) launched.
   1857 (20/2) MV Hamburg–Southampton–Lisbon–Pernambuco–
   Bahia–Rio de Janeiro. 1857 (20/11) LV ditto. 1858 (21/10)
   BAVARIA (Hapag). 1876 ditto (Dominion). 1877 (6/2) destroyed by fire at sea on voyage New Orleans–Liverpool (0).
–. —— PRINZESSIN VON JOINVILLE
   2,500. 86,00 x 12,00. (282.1 x 39.4). C–1–3. I–S–I(2)–10. Caird &
   Co, Greenock. 1857 (6/10) launched for Hamburg Brasilianische,
   but did not run for them.

Chapter 9

1857

EUROPEAN & AMERICAN STEAM SHIPPING COMPANY

(British)

The EUROPEAN & AMERICAN STEAM SHIPPING COMPANY came into existence in 1857 with the purchase of eight iron screw steamers from the General Screw Steam Shipping Company, which were paid for with shares in the new concern. [1] It was devised and managed by T.R. Croskey, American Consul at Southampton. Four of the ships – the 2,768 ton GOLDEN FLEECE, the 2,243 ton HYDASPES, the 2,260 ton CALCUTTA and the 2,260 ton LADY JOCELYN – were earmarked for a service to South America, and the remainder – the QUEEN OF THE SOUTH, INDIANA, ARGO and JASON – were placed in a fortnightly service between Bremen, Southampton and New York.

The GOLDEN FLEECE sailed from Hamburg on 20 April 1857 via Southampton for Rio de Janeiro, Bahia and Pernambuco in a joint service with the TEUTONIA and PETROPOLIS of the Hamburg Brasilianische Packetschiffahrt Gesellschaft (Chapter 8), and was followed by the HYDASPES and CALCUTTA, although they sailed instead from Antwerp via Southampton on 30 May and 30 June, respectively. The LADY JOCELYN was intended to sail for South America a month later but, in fact, left Southampton on 8 August for Calcutta as she had been taken up by the East India Company as an Indian Mutiny transport. The other three ships were similarly chartered as soon as they returned to Southampton from South America.

Unfortunately, the Company lost no less than £11,602 on the three Brazilian voyages, while a further £899 was lost on 11 voyages undertaken to New York. Worse still, the value of the fleet was shown on the balance sheet as £564,623, [2] whereas the fleet was eventually sold for only £250,000 to J.O. Lever, [3] independently of his interests in the Galway Line. In one respect only, the European & American Company had not done so badly as the total of seven steamers chartered to the East India Company made them a profit of £17,000 for the conveyance of 199 officers, 5,560 men and various munitions to India, [2] with prospects of full cargoes being obtained and paid for in connection with the homeward voyages to England.

55

The European & American service was never reinstated. Instead, Lever made over three of the ships to the Anglo–Luso–Brazilian Steam Navigation Company (Chapter 11) to sail under the Portuguese flag between Milford Haven or Liverpool, Portugal and Brazil, but this proved to be only a temporary arrangement and the ships were soon reacquired by Lever. Four others made a few voyages for his ill-fated Galway Line (one of them was lost in the process), and finally he sold seven ships to the East India & London Shipping Company in 1861 to sail direct between London, Madras and Calcutta. This service was no more successful than its predecessors.

[1] *New York Daily Tribune* 27/1/1857.
[2] *The Times* 4/2/1858.
[3] *The Times* 4/9/1858.

1. (1857) GOLDEN FLEECE
   2,768*. 77,41 x 11,89. (254.0 x 39.0). C–1–3. I–S–D2–9. C.J. Mare & Co, West Ham, London (engines Maudslay, Sons & Field, London). 1853 (17/11) launched for General Screw. 1857 GOLDEN FLEECE (European & American). 1857 (20/4) FV Hamburg–Southampton (24/4)–Brazil. 1860 ditto (Galway Line (c) (1 RV)). 1869 foundered in Penarth Roads.
2. (1857) HYDASPES
   2,243*. 75,12 x 11,37 (246.5 x 37.3). C–1–3. I–S–D2–9. C.J. Mare & Co, Poplar, London (engines Maudslay, Sons & Field, London). 1852 (16/10) launched for General Screw. 1855 increased from 2 to 3 decks; previous tonnage 1871*. 1857 HYDASPES (European & American). 1857 (30/5) Antwerp–Southampton (4/6)–Brazil (1 RV). 1861 HYDASPES (East India & London). 1868 ditto (sailing ship). 1880 sunk in collision.
3. (1857) CALCUTTA
   2,260*. 74,51 x 11,61 (244.5 x 38.1). C–1–3. I–S–D2–9. C.J. Mare & Co, West Ham, London (engines Maudslay, Sons & Field, London). 1852 launched for General Screw. 1857 increased from 2 to 3 decks; previous tonnage 1,802*. 1857 CALCUTTA (European & American. 1857 (30/6) FV Antwerp–Southampton (4/7) Brazil. (1 RV). 1857 Indian Mutiny transport. 1859 PORTUGAL (Anglo–Luso–Brazilian (Portuguese)). 1861 CALCUTTA (East Indian & London); 2,124 GT. 1868 DARLING DOWNS (sailing ship). 1887 sunk in collision.
–.—— LADY JOCELYN
   2,042*. 72,74 x 11,64. (238.7 x 38.2). C–1–3. I–S–D2–9. C.J.

Mare & Co, West Ham, London (engines Maudslay, Sons & Field, London). 1851 (24/12) launched for General Screw. 1857 increased from 2 to 3 decks; previous tonnage 1,825*. 1857 LADY JOCELYN (European & American), but voyage cancelled. 1857 Indian Mutiny transport. 1859 BRAZIL (Anglo–Luso–Brazilian). 1861 LADY JOCELYN (East India & London). 1868 ditto (Shaw Savill); engines removed. Later meat hulk in West India Dock, London. 1922 scrapped in Holland.

* Burthen plus engine-room.

Chapter 10

1858–80

FRÈRES QUESNEL

(French)

In 1858 the FRÈRES QUESNEL (Quesnel Brothers) of Havre acquired a 466 ton auxiliary sailing ship, which had been launched at Glasgow in 1856, renamed her JEAN BAPTISTE and placed her in service between Havre and Brazil, together with a much larger auxiliary, the 1,331 ton MONTEZUMA.

The JEAN BAPTISTE was found to be too small for the transatlantic trade and was sold at Marseilles in 1861, after which the MONTEZUMA carried on alone until joined in 1864 by the three-masted FÉNELON, built at Honfleur and supplied with an engine of 370 horse-power by a Havre firm.

The 954 ton LA FONTAINE was added in 1865, and the 1,250 ton MERCURY and FRANCOIS I in 1867, all from the same builders as before.

1871 HENRI IV 1,590 tons
Sold in 1872 to Chargeurs Réunis, who retained her name.

After this spate of new building there came a lull until 1871, when the 1,590 ton iron screw HENRI IV was commissioned. A product of Chantiers & Ateliers de la Méditerranée of La Seyne, she was fitted with compound engines giving her a service speed of 10 knots. The 2,131 ton LOUIS XIV, built by the Chantiers de l'Ocean at Havre, followed in 1872.

The surprising sequel was that both these ships were bought in 1872 by the newly-founded Compagnie des Chargeurs Réunis (Chapter 28) and kept in the same service.

There seem to be three possible reasons for this sudden change of ownership – that the brothers had gone ahead too quickly and found it necessary to get some ready money, or that Chargeurs Réunis, seeing the possibilities of the route, decided to make the brothers a tempting offer for the ships, or perhaps that the brothers had learned of an intended rival service and thought it prudent to sell out before being forced out.

The fact that Frères Quesnel commissioned the 1,318 ton SULLY, built in 1874 by the Forges & Chantiers de la Méditerranée at Havre, suggests that the second of these possibilities may have been the correct one.

In 1880 the SULLY was also sold to Chargeurs Réunis. Frères Quesnel went into liquidation soon afterwards, and it looks very much as if Chargeurs were the cause of their downfall.

1. (1858) JEAN BAPTISTE
    466. Auxiliary steamer built at Glasgow. 1861 sold at Marseilles.
2. 1858 MONTEZUMA
    1,331. Auxiliary steamer.
3. 1864 FÉNELON
    Three masts. Built at Honfleur. 370 HP engine built at Havre.
4. 1865 LA FONTAINE
    954. Built at Honfleur; engined at Havre.
5. 1867 MERCURY
    1,250. Built at Honfleur; engined at Havre.
6. 1867 FRANCOIS I
    1,250. Built at Honfleur; engined at Havre.
7. 1871 HENRI IV
    1,590. 75,43 x 10,97. (247.5 x 36.0). 1–3. I–S–C2–10. Forges & Chantiers de la Méditerranée, La Seyne. 1872 HENRI IV (Chargeurs Réunis). 1886 ditto (Bossière (Fr)). 1890 (11/7) wrecked at mouth of R. Loire.
8. 1872 LOUIS XIV
    2,131. 107,89 x 10,06. (354.0 x 33.0). 1–3. I–S–C2–10. Chantiers

de l'Occan, Havre. 1872 BELGRANO (Chargeurs Réunis). 1894 scrapped.

9. 1874 SULLY

1,278. 75,28 x 9,14. (247.0 x 30.0). S–1–3. I–S–C2–10. Forges & Chantiers de la Méditerranée, Havre. 1874 (19/3) launched. 1880 SULLY (Chargeurs Réunis). 1891 SULLY (Br). 1900 (5/4) wrecked on Horns Reef, Jutland.

Chapter 11

1859–60

REAL COMPANHIA DE NAVAGAÇÃO A VAPOR ANGLO–LUSO–BRASILEIRA

(Anglo–Luso–Brazilian Royal Mail Steam Navigation Company)

(Portuguese)

It was announced in September 1859 [1] that J.O. Lever, well-known for his activities concerning the ill-fated Galway Line, had bought the remains of the former fleet of the General Screw Steam Shipping Company, which had passed into the hands of the European & American Steam Shipping Company in 1857 (Chapter 9).

A new line of Royal Mail steamships was envisaged to undertake a monthly service between Milford Haven, Lisbon, St. Vincent, Pernambuco, Bahia and Rio de Janeiro under the title of REAL COMPANHIA DE NAVEGAÇÃO A VAPOR ANGLO–LUSO–BRASILEIRA (Anglo–Luso–Brazilian Royal Mail Steam Navigation Company), and the ships were to fly the Portuguese flag. The president was the Infante Dom Luiz (later King Luiz I of Portugal). There were three British directors in London in addition to the Portuguese directors.

The 2,221 ton THE MILFORD HAVEN (ex-QUEEN OF THE SOUTH) sailed from the port of that name on 1 October 1859 after Mr. Lever had presided at a banquet celebrating the opening of the new line, observing that the vessel's new name was a compliment to her port of departure. The 2,261 ton PORTUGUAL (ex-CALCUTTA) sailed on 1 November and the 2,242 ton BRAZIL (ex-LADY JOCELYN) on 24 December. The BRAZIL was unavailable for her second sailing arranged for 24 March, and a consort, the 2,667 ton JASON, was chartered to take her place. [2]

It was stated in May 1860 that at the request of many influential merchants in the Brazilian trade the ships would in future sail from Liverpool on the 24th of each month as Milford Haven had been found inconvenient. [3] Unfortunately, this produced but little more success, and after a handful of further sailings the service closed down. The three ships regained their original names and their British nationality under the ownership of Lever. Together with their four consorts they were sold in 1861 to the East India & London Shipping Company Limited, which ran them for a time from London direct to Madras and Calcutta.

[1] *The Times* 3/9/1859.
[2] *The Times* 16/5/1860.
[3] *The Times* 21/3/1860.

1. (1859) THE MILFORD HAVEN

2,221*. 74,06 x 11,98. (243.6 x 39.3). C–1–3. I–S–D2–9. C.J. Mare & Co, West Ham, London (engines Maudslay, Sons & Field, London). 1851 (29/10) launched as QUEEN OF THE SOUTH for General Screw (1,850 tons). 1857 QUEEN OF THE SOUTH (European & American). 1857 Indian Mutiny transport. 1859 THE MILFORD HAVEN (Anglo–Luso–Brazilian) (Portuguese). 1859 (1/10) FV Milford Haven–Lisbon–St. Vincent–Pernambuco–Bahia–Rio de Janeiro. 1861 QUEEN OF THE SOUTH (East India & London). 1872 MALTA (Br); sailing ship. 1885 (24/11) wrecked near Sandy Hook, USA.

2. (1859) PORTUGAL

2,260*. 74,51 x 11,61. (244.5 x 38.1). C–1–3. I–S–D2–9. C.J. Mare & Co, West Ham, London (engines Maudslay, Sons & Field, London. 1852 launched as CALCUTTA for General Screw. 1857 increased from 2 to 3 decks; previous tonnage 1,802*. 1857 CALCUTTA (European & American). 1857 Indian Mutiny transport. 1859 PORTUGAL (Anglo–Luso–Brazilian) (Portuguese). 1859 (1/11) FV Milford Haven–Lisbon–St. Vincent–Pernambuco–Bahia–Rio de Janeiro. 1861 CALCUTTA (East India & London). 1868 DARLING DOWNS (sailing ship). 1887 sunk in collision.

3. (1859) BRAZIL

2,042*. 72,74 x 11,64. (238.7 x 38.2). C–1–3. I–S–D2–9. C.J. Mare & Co, West Ham, London (engines Maudslay, Sons & Field, London). 1851 (24/12) launched as LADY JOCELYN for General Screw. 1857 increased from 2 to 3 decks; previous tonnage 1,825*. 1857 LADY JOCELYN (European & American) but voyage cancelled. 1857 Indian Mutiny transport. 1859 BRAZIL (Anglo–Luso–Brazilian) (Portuguese). 1859 (24/12) FV Milford Haven–Lisbon–St. Vincent–Pernambuco–Bahia–Rio de Janeiro. 1861 LADY JOCELYN (East India & London). 1868 ditto (Shaw Savill); engines removed. Later meat hulk in West India Dock, London. 1922 scrapped in Holland.

3a. (1860) JASON

2,667*. 77,41 x 11,89. (254.0 x 39.0). C–1–3. I–S–D2–9. C.J. Mare & Co, London (engines Watt & Co, London). 1853 (6/8) launched for General Screw. 1857 JASON (European & Amer-

62

ican). 1858 Indian Mutiny transport. 1859 (20/8) FV for Galway Line (c), Galway–New York (2 RV). 1860 (24/3) FV Milford Haven–Lisbon–Brazil for Anglo–Luso–Brazilian (c) (1 RV). 1861 JASON (East India & London. 1862 (27/12) wrecked north of Madras.

* Burthen plus engine-room.

Chapter 12

(1860–1912)
(1962–1972)

MESSAGERIES MARITIMES

1853 Compagnie des Services Maritimes des Messageries Imperiales
1871 Compagnie des Messageries Maritimes

(French)

The well-known COMPAGNIE DES MESSAGERIES MARITIMES, so named for more than a century, can be traced back to 1851, when Messageries Nationales, a road transport company serving the principal towns of France, acquired the steamship line between France and the Levant, hitherto run by the French Government. In 1852 it was considered desirable for the Company's marine activities to be taken over by an allied concern, the COMPAGNIE DES SERVICES MARITIMES DES MESSAGERIES NATIONALES, whose name was amended on 28 February 1853 to COMPAGNIE DES SERVICES MARITIMES DES MESSAGERIES IMPERIALES. On 1 August 1871, after the fall of the French Empire, the name was shortened to COMPAGNIE DES MESSAGERIES MARITIMES.

It was evident from the first that a considerable number of ships would have to be built, and in order to undertake this task with efficiency combined with value for money the Company bought the Benet Shipyard at La Ciotat, situated half-way between Marseilles and Toulon and only a few miles from the Forges & Chantiers de la Méditerranée yard at La Seyne.

By 1857 the Company was running services from Marseilles to many parts of the Eastern Mediterranean as well as to Algiers, Oran, Bona and Tunis and, on 19 September 1857, a new contract was obtained for a mail service to Brazil, with a feeder service from there to the River Plate, which was too shallow for the mail steamers to reach Montevideo and Buenos Aires. Sailings were intended to alternate from Marsailles and Bordeaux, but rather surprisingly all took place from Bordeaux.

The 1,945 ton iron paddle steamer GUIENNE, a product of La Ciotat, undertook the pioneer sailing from Bordeaux on 25 May 1860 for Rio de Janeiro via St. Vincent, Cape Verde Islands, for coal. She was followed by the slightly larger NAVARRE and ESTRAMADURE, built at La Seyne, and the 2,470 ton BÉARN from La Ciotat. The 800 ton paddle steamers SAINTONGE and AUNIS were completed in France for the

64

1860 NAVARRE 2,100 tons
As built as a paddle steamer.

1872 RIO GRANDE 2,735 tons
The former paddle steamer NAVARRE after conversion to single screw.

feeder service from Rio de Janeiro to Santos and the two River Plate ports. From 1866 the mail steamers called for coal at Dakar instead of St. Vincent.

The 2,188 ton iron screw steamer PROVENCE, under construction at La Ciotat in 1860, was hurriedly renamed IMPÉRATRICE when it became known that Impératrice Eugénie (the Empress Eugénie) was to attend her launching on 10 September 1860. The maiden voyage took place from Bordeaux to Rio de Janeiro, but the IMPÉRATRICE did not remain long on the transatlantic service as she sailed from Suez for India and Indo-China on 27 October 1862, thus pioneering the final stage of a new mail service from Marseilles to Alexandria and then overland to Suez. The opening of the Suez Canal in November 1869 enabled through sailings from Marseilles to Indo-China to be substituted for the three-stage journey.

The 3,260 ton iron screw steamer GIRDONDE was launched for the South American trade on 31 January 1869. A two-funnelled ship with clipper bow, she was to have been followed by the 3,350 ton AMAZONE and URUGUAY but, instead, they were completed for the new Marseilles–Indo-China run. The former retained her name, but the latter became the SINDH.

These two ships were replaced on the transatlantic service by the 3,717 ton SÉNÉGAL, launched on 18 September 1870, and a sister ship, the NIGER, launched on 24 December 1871. The 3,910 ton ORENOQUE followed in 1874.

In 1872 the three surviving South American paddle steamers were converted to single-screw, given an extra deck and emerged with tonnage increased to around 2,700. In addition, the GUIENNE was renamed GAMBIE, the NAVARRE became the RIO GRANDE and the ESTRAMADURE became the MENDOZA. The fourth of the group, the BÉARN, had been wrecked on the Brazilian coast on 27 February 1865, and unfortunately the GAMBIE was wrecked at Bahia in 1873. The RIO GRANDE was lit by electricity in 1888 with 100 bulbs, each of 10 candle power.

The 3,900 ton EQUATEUR and PARANA, completed in 1876, and the CONGO of 1878 were sister ships of the NIGER class. The PARANA had a very short life as she was wrecked off Bahia on 7 October 1877. Her place was taken by the 2,788 ton HOOGLY, built in 1867 for the Indo-China service, and badly damaged by fire at Marseilles on 6 January 1876, when she had to be scuttled.

The feeder steamers SAINTONGE and AUNIS were scrapped in 1880 and 1882, respectively, owing to the fact that conditions in the River Plate had improved sufficiently for the transatlantic mail steamers to proceed through to Montevideo and Buenos Aires.

The 3,650 ton cargo steamers TROIS ILES, MÈDOC, MATAPAN, CORDOUAN and ORTEGAL were commissioned by Messageries in 1884–5 for a monthly service between Bordeaux, Brazil and the River Plate, the first three being built at La Seyne and the last two at La Ciotat. They had a speed of 12 knots.

The 5,335 ton PORTUGAL, launched at La Ciotat on 27 July 1886, [1] was notable as the first long-distance steel steamer to be built by the Company. She was propelled by triple-expansion engines giving her a service speed of 16 knots, and had accommodation for 125 first, 90 second and 700 third class passengers. Her maiden voyage from Bordeaux to Brazil and Argentina started on 5 August 1887.

An interesting ship joined the service a year later – the 3,718 ton NERTHE, launched in 1874 as the LESSING of the short-lived Adler Linie service from Hamburg to New York, in which she made a few voyages before she and her sister ships were taken over by the Hamburg American Line. Originally a single-funnelled ship, she was rebuilt in 1882 with two funnels and continued to run between Hamburg and New York until bought by Messageries.

1889 BRÉSIL 5,809 tons
Completing at La Seyne. Lifeboats still to be fitted.

Two more newcomers appeared in 1889 – the 5,540 ton LA PLATA and the 5,809 ton BRÉSIL, both slightly enlarged versions of the PORTUGAL.

The 5,543 ton ERNEST SIMONS was launched for the Indo-China service on 24 September 1893, but her maiden voyage starting on 5 August 1894 took place to South America. Her second and following voyages were to the Far East.

The 6,000 ton CHILI and CORDILLÈRE, slightly larger versions of LA PLATA and BRÉSIL, were completed for the South American trade

67

in 1895–6, but four years elapsed before the next ship was built. This was the 6,479 ton ATLANTIQUE of 1900, notable as the first twin-screw steamer on the run, her propelling machinery consisting of two sets of triple-expansion engines, giving her a service speed of 16 knots. Her South American consorts for the next three years were the CORDIL-LÈRE, CHILI, BRÈSIL and LA PLATA, but after the last two had been transferred in 1903 to an Australian mail service which Messageries had been running for the past two decades, two more twin-screw steamers were introduced in 1904 to replace them. These were the 6,300 ton LAOS and INDUS, built for the Far East Line in 1896–7, and were renamed AMAZONE and MAGELLAN before transfer to Bordeaux. They had an attractive appearance with two funnels and two masts, and were notable not only as the Company's first long-distance twin-screw liners but also as the first to dispense with yards.

Another addition in 1906 was the ESMERALDA, an ageing Messageries emigrant ship, but in 1910 the Company made a considerable stride by laying down the 12,989 ton twin-screw BUENOS AYRES, the largest ship planned for the River Plate trade. On 27 May of the same year, however, the newly-established Société d'Etudes de Navigation, founded by the French shipowners Cyprien Fabre, Fraissinet and the Société Générale de Transports Maritimes, in conjunction with two French banks, submitted a request to the French authorities to be allowed to undertake all the mail services then maintained by Messageries Maritimes. After the authorities had private discussions with both Messageries and the Société d'Etudes, contracts were signed on 11 July 1911 whereby Messageries were allowed to retain all their mail services except that to South America, which was to be transferred to the Société d'Etudes. The latter were required to build four 18 knot passenger liners and six slower ships in order to maintain a fortnightly mail service and a fortnightly intermediate one between Bordeaux and Buenos Aires. On 8 February 1912 the Société d'Etudes changed its name to Compagnie de Navigation Sud Atlantique (Chapter 56).

The Messageries CHILI, CORDILLÈRE, ATLANTIQUE, AMA-ZONE and MAGELLAN were transferred to the Far East line, and the BUENOS AYRES joined them in the same trade under the name PAUL LECAT.

*   *   *

In 1962, exactly 50 years after the withdrawal of Messageries Maritimes' South American service, their successors, Compagnie de Navigation Sud Atlantique, themselves withdrew, as did Chargeurs Réunis, the latter's managers since April 1916. It was arranged that

1952 LOUIS LUMIÈRE 12,358 tons
Built for Chargeurs Réunis, but sold to Messageries in 1962. (Note latter's new funnel).

Messageries should replace them, and they acquired from Chargeurs the 12,358 ton LOUIS LUMIÈRE, which sailed on 13 November 1962 from Havre for Vigo, Madeira, Rio de Janeiro, Santos, Montevideo and Buenos Aires. She was a twin-screw motorship with accommodation for 109 first class and 266 second class passengers. The 12,021 ton Chargeurs CLAUDE BERNARD had been running to the Far East since 1954 and in 1962 was sold to East Germany to become the J. G. FICHTE, while the 11,968 ton LAVOISIER had become the Italian cruising liner RIVIERA PRIMA a year previously.

Additionally, Messageries bought from the Compagnie de Navigation Sud Atlantique the 12,006 ton twin-screw motorship CHARLES TELLIER and the 12,003 ton LAËNNEC, both built by the Ateliers &

1962 LAËNNEC 12,003 tons
Bought by Messageries from Cie Sud Atlantique. Made one voyage only with black funnel.

69

Chantiers de la Loire, of St. Nazaire, in 1952. They sailed from Havre for Buenos Aires on 4 December and 26 December 1962, respectively. These three ships maintained a regular service until the closing weeks of 1966, when they were replaced by the 17,986 ton twin-screw motorship PASTEUR, which sailed from Havre on 24 December for the River Plate. The LOUIS LUMIÈRE, CHARLES TELLIER and LAËNNEC were sold. The two last-named became pilgrim ships, and the BELLE ABETO (ex-LAËNNEC) sank at Sasebo on 31 July 1976 after sustaining serious fire damage.

1966 PASTEUR 17,986 tons
Ran for six years from Havre to Buenos Aires.

The PASTEUR sailed as a lone ship for six years, but like so many other passenger liners during the 1970s was unable to compete with air competition. In 1973 she became the CHIDAMBARAM of the Shipping Corporation of India. The South American passenger service closed down.

On 21 December 1972 the Compagnie Générale Transatlantique and Messageries Maritimes were merged by an official decree to become the COMPAGNIE GÉNÉRALE MARITIME.

[1] The PORTUGAL was intended to be launched on 25 July 1886, but stuck two-thirds of the way down the slipway.

1. 1860 GUIENNE
   (1872) GAMBIE
       1,945. 99,97 x 11,89. (328.0 x 39.0). C–1–2. I–P–?–10. Messageries Imperiales, La Ciotat. 1859 (15/10) launched. 1860 (25/5) MV Bordeaux–St. Vincent (for coal)–Rio de Janeiro. 1872

converted to single-screw; extra deck fitted; 2,700 tons; engines C3; renamed GAMBIE. 1873 (13/4) wrecked at Bahia.

2. 1860 NAVARRE
(1872) RIO GRANDE
   2,100. 99,97 x 11,89. (328.0 x 39.0). C–1–2. I–P–?–10. Forges & Chantiers de la Méditerranée, La Seyne. 1859 (15/11) launched. 1860 (25/6) MV Bordeaux–St. Vincent–Rio de Janeiro. 1872 converted to single-screw; extra deck fitted; 2,735 tons; engines C3; renamed RIO GRANDE. 1888 electric light fitted (100 bulbs each of 10 candle power). 1892 scrapped at Marseilles.

3. 1860 ESTRAMADURE
(1872) MENDOZA
   2,132. 99,97 x 11,89. (328.0 x 39.0). C–1–2. I–P–?–10. Forges & Chantiers de la Méditerranée, La Seyne. 1860 (25/1) launched. 1860 (25/7) MV Bordeaux–St. Vincent–Rio de Janeiro. 1872 converted to single-screw; extra deck fitted; 2,735 tons; engines C3; renamed MENDOZA. 1872 (21/12) rescued crew of GERMANY (Allan Line) at entrance to R. Gironde. 1888 transferred to Indian Ocean service. 1891 scrapped.

4. 1860 BÉARN
   2,470. 101,19 x 11,58. (332.0 x 38.0). C–1–2. I–P–?–10. Messageries Imperiales, La Ciotat. 1860 (11/6) launched. 1860 (25/9) MV Bordeaux–St. Vincent–Rio de Janeiro. 1865 (27/2) wrecked on Brazilian coast on voyage from Bordeaux.

5. 1861 IMPÉRATRICE
   2,188. 100,88 x 11,58. (331.0 x 38.0). C–1–3. I–S–V2–12. (I–36; II–30; III–21). Messageries Imperiales, La Ciotat. Laid down as PROVENCE (paddle); changed on stocks to screw). 1860 (10/9) launched as IMPÉRATRICE by Impératrice Eugénie. 1861 MV Bordeaux–St. Vincent (for coal)–Rio de Janeiro. 1862 (27/10) FV Marseilles–Suez Canal–Indo-China. 1871 renamed PROVENCE. 1881 (28/12) rammed and sunk at Constantinople (Istanbul) by Russian steamer ASOW.

6. 1862 ERYMANTHE
   1,513. 105,08 x 10,00. (344.8 x 32.8). C–1–2. I–S–C3–12. Messageries Imperiales, La Ciotat, 1862 (17/2) launched. 1862 MV Bordeaux–Rio de Janeiro. 1888 lengthened; triple-expansion engines. 1895 sold at Marseilles; resold to Cie de Navigation Mixte. 1898 (19/11) collided with ss BERRY off Carro; beached; broke her back.

7. 1869 GIRONDE
   3,260. 118,24 x 12,19. (388.3 x 40.0). C–2–3. I–S–C3–12. Messageries Imperiales, La Ciotat. 1869 (31/1) launched for

Indo-China line. 1869 MV Bordeaux–S. America. 1875 (20/12) collided with and sank LOUISIANE (CGT) off Pauillac. 1887 triple-expansion engines; funnels reduced to one. 1906 scrapped at Saigon.

— — AMAZONE
3,350 tons. Laid down for South American service but launched 1869 (May)for Marseilles–Indo-China.

— — URUGUAY
3,373 tons. Laid down for South American service but launched 1869 (25/7) as SINDH for Marseilles–Indo-China.

8. 1871 SÉNÉGAL
3,717. 119,59 x 12,19. (392.4 x 40.0). 1–3. I–S–C2–13. Messageries Imperiales, La Ciotat. 1870 (18/9) launched. 1871 MV Bordeaux–S. America. 1888 (Jun) FV Marseilles–Egypt–Syria. 1913 scrapped after damage from a mine at Smyrna.

9. 1872 NIGER
3,726. 120,17 x 12,10. (394.3 x 39.7). 1–3. I–S–C2–12. Messageries Maritimes, La Ciotat. 1871 (24/12) launched. 1872 MV Bordeaux–S. America. 1913 stranded at Tschemieh; refloated; scrapped.

10. 1874 ORÉNOQUE
3,910. 119,87 x 12,10. (393.7 x 39.7). 1–3. I–S–C2–12. Messageries Maritimes, La Ciotat. 1874 (22/2) launched. 1874 MV Bordeaux–S. America. 1925 scrapped at Saigon.

11. 1876 EQUATEUR
3,914. 120,26 x 12,10. (394.6 x 39.7). S–1–3. I–S–C2–12. Messageries Maritimes, La Ciotat. 1875 (20/6) launched. 1876 MV Bordeaux–S. America. 1887 triple-expansion engines. 1922 scrapped at Marseilles.

12. 1876 PARANA
3,928. 120,26 x 12,10. (394.6 x 39.7). S–1–3. I–S–C2–12. Messageries Maritimes, La Ciotat. 1876 (5/3) launched. 1876 MV Bordeaux–S. America. 1877 (7/10) wrecked off Bahia.

13. (1877) HOOGLY
2,788. 115,20 x 11,89. (378.0 x 39.0). C–2–3. I–S–C2–12. (I–100; II–37; III–36). Messageries Imperiales, La Ciotat. 1867 (17/3) launched for Indo-China service. 1876 (6/1) serious fire at Marseilles; scuttled; refloated. 1877 FV Bordeaux–S. America (as replacement for PARANA). 1878 (19/11) wrecked near Montevideo.

14. 1878 CONGO
3,897. 120,26 x 12,10. (394.6 x 39.7). S–1–3. I–S–C2–12. Messageries Maritimes, La Ciotat. 1878 (17/3) launched. 1878

MV Bordeaux–S. America. 1888 (5/8) sailed Bordeaux–S. America (passengers to Brazil included Emperor Dom Pedro, Empress and Prince). 1889 transferred to Indo-China service. 1913 scrapped in Italy.

15. 1887 PORTUGAL
    5,336. 134,98 x 13,98. (442.9 x 45.9). S–2–3. S–S–T3–16. (I–125; II–90; III–700). Messageries Maritimes, La Ciotat. 1886 (27/7) launched. 1887 (5/8) MV Bordeaux–S. America. 1899 FV Marseilles–Alexandria. Later masts reduced to two. 1916 (17/3) torpedoed and sunk by German submarine U.33 near Batum, Black Sea (90).

16. 1888 GUADALQUIVIR
    2,598. 101,95 x 11,49. (334.5 x 37.7). 1–2. S–S–T3–12. (I–31; III). Messageries Maritimes, La Ciotat. 1888 (1/3) launched. 1888 MV Bordeaux–S. America. 1903 (28/4) bomb explosion at Salonica caused a serious fire; towed to Marseilles by OCEANIEN (MM); scrapped.

17. (1888) NERTHE
    3,718. 114,32 x 12,20. (375.1 x 40.0). S–2–2. I–S–C2–13. (I–180; III–800). A. Stephen & Sons, Glasgow. 1874 (20/2) launched as LESSING (Adler Linie). 1875 LESSING (Hapag). 1882 rebuilt; funnels increased to two. 1888 NERTHE (MM). 1888 (20/8) FV Bordeaux–S. America. 1888 (Oct) towed ORTEGAL (MM) Lisbon–Bordeaux (lost propeller). 1893 FV London–Marseilles–Constantinople. 1894 FV Marseilles–Madagascar. 1897 scrapped at Marseilles.

18. 1888 GUADIANA
    2,614. 101,98 x 11,49. (334.6 x 37.7). 1–2. S–S–T3–12. (I–31; III). Forges & Chantiers de la Méditerranée, Graville. 1888 (23/8) launched. 1888 MV Bordeaux–S. America. 1922 scrapped in Italy.

19. 1889 DORDOGNE
    3,723. 113,19 x 13,10. (371.4 x 43.0). 1–2. S–S–T3–12. (I–31; III). Forges & Chantiers de la Méditerranée, Graville. 1888 (5/12) launched. 1889 (30/3) MV Bordeux–S. America. 1896 (29/4) FV Marseilles–Shanghai. 1911 scrapped in Italy.

20. 1889 BRÉSIL
    5,809. 141,38 x 11,14. (463.9 x 46.4). S–2–3. S–S–T3–16. (I–132; II–90; III–745). Forges & Chantiers de la Méditerranée, La Seyne. 1888 (7/11) launched. 1889 MV Bordeaux–Brazil–Argentina. 1903 renamed DUMBEA (MM – Australian service). 1938 scrapped at La Seyne.

21. 1889 LA PLATA
    5,540. 141,00 x 13,98. (462.6 x 45.9). S–2–3. S–S–T3–16. (I–132;

II–90; III–/45). Messageries Maritimes, La Ciotat. 1888 (18/6) launcned. 1889 (5/4) MV Bordeaux–Brazil–Argentina. 1903 renamed NERA (MM – Australian service). 1923 scrapped in Italy.

22. 1889 DOURO
2,697. 102,98 x 11,61. (337.9 x 38.1). 1–2. S–S–T3–12. (I–31; III). Forges & Chantiers de la Méditerranée, Graville. 1889 (16/2) launched. 1889 MV Bordeaux–S. America. 1910 (12/5) wrecked on coast of Madagascar.

23. 1889 CHARENTE
3,775. 113,19 x 13,10. (371.4 x 43.0). 1–2. S–S–T3–12. (I–31; III). Forges & Chantiers de la Méditerranée, Graville. 1889 (3/3) launched. 1889 (17/5) MV Havre–S. America. 1911 scrapped.

24. 1889 ADOUR
3,923. 112,98 x 13,10. (370.7 x 43.0). 1–2. S–S–T3–12. (I–31; III). Forges & Chantiers de la Méditerranée, La Seyne. 1889 (11/4) launched. 1889 (11/9) MV Bordeaux–S. America. 1909 transferred to Madagascar coastal service. 1912 wrecked on Madagascar coast.

25. 1894 ERNEST SIMONS
5,543. 134,98 x 14,35. (442.9 x 47.1). S–2–3. S–S–T3–15. (I–103; II–78; III–79), Messageries Maritimes, La Ciotat. 1893 (24/9) launched for MM Indo-China service. 1894 (5/8) MV Bordeaux–S. America (1 RV). 1894 (23/12) FV Marseilles–Far East. 1917 (3/4) torpedoed and sunk on voyage Marseilles–Port Said.

26. 1895 CHILI
6,097. 141,00 x 14,50. (462.6 x 47.6). S–2–2. S–S–T3–15. (I–129; II–149; III–689). Messageries Maritimes, La Ciotat. 1894 (14/10) launched. 1895 (5/8) MV Bordeaux–S. America. 1903 (23–24/4) capsized and sank in port at Bordeaux. 1903 (6/7) refloated; reconditioned. 1912 FV Marseilles–Far East. 1927 scrapped at La Spezia.

27. 1896 CORDILLÈRE
6,022. 141,00 x 14,50. (462.6 x 47.6). S–2–2. S–S–T3–15. (I–129; II–149; III–869). Messageries Maritimes, La Ciotat. 1895 (12/10) launched. 1896 (5/8) MV Bordeaux–S. America. 1912 FV Marseilles–Far East. 1925 scrapped at La Seyne.

28. 1900 ATLANTIQUE
6,479. 142,91 x 15,42. (468.9 x 50.6). S–2–2. S–2S–T6–16. (I–249; II–86; III–396). Messageries Maritimes, La Ciotat. 1899 (5/11) launched. 1900 (4/5) MV Bordeaux–S. America. 1912 (22/9) FV for Sud Atlantique (c), Bordeaux–S. America. 1912 FV Marseilles–Far East. 1918 (9/5) torpedoed in Mediterranean; reached

Bizerta, where temporarily repaired. 1921 rebuilt at La Ciotat with extra promenade deck; 7,357 tons (I–134; II–75; III–87); renamed ANGKOR. 1921 (28/10) FV Marseilles–Far East. 1933 (Dec) sold; scrapped.

29. (1903) MAGELLAN
   6,357. 136,00 x 15,48. (446.2 x 50.8). 2–2. 2S–T6–17. (I–148; II–71; III–818). Messageries Maritimes, La Ciotat. 1897 (29/8) launched as INDUS (MM – Far East service). 1903 (11/11) FV Bordeaux–S. America. 1912 returned to Far East service. 1916 (11/12) torpedoed and sunk by German submarine U.62 south of Pantellaria.

30. (1904) AMAZONE
   6,337. 134,98 x 15,48. (442.9 x 50.8). 2–2. 2S–T6–17. (I–148; II–71; III–818). Messageries Maritimes, La Ciotat. 1896 (8/11) launched as LAOS (MM – Far East service). 1904 (24/12) FV Bordeaux–S. America. 1912 returned to Far East service. 1932 scrapped.

31. (1906) ESMERALDA
   3,785. 121,36 x 12,10. (398.2 x 39.7). 1–3. I–S–C2–13. Messageries Maritimes, La Ciotat. 1872 (1/12) launched as IRAOUADDY (MM – Far East service). 1906 ESMERALDA (MM – emigrant ship). 1906 (21/9) FV Bordeaux–S. America. 1908 scrapped in Italy.

— — BUENOS AYRES
   Laid down at La Ciotat for Bordeaux–S. America service, but owing to its pending closure was launched on 1911 (19/3) as PAUL LECAT (12,989 tons); 155,00 x 18,80 (508.5 x 61.7); Far East Service. 2S–Q8–16. (I–205; II–84; III–107).

32. (1962) LOUIS LUMIÈRE (M/S)
   12,358. 157,14 [164,21] x 19,62. (515.6 [538.8] x 64.4). 1–2–C. 2S–2SC.SA–17. (I–109; II–266). Ateliers & Chantiers de St. Nazaire. 1951 (28/11) launched for Chargeurs Réunis. 1952 (18/10) MV Havre–S. America. 1962 LOUIS LUMIÈRE (Messageries Maritimes). 1962 (13/11) FV Havre–S. America. 1967 MEI ABETO (Cie de Navigacion Abeto (Panamanian).

33. (1962) CHARLES TELLIER (M/S)
   12,006. 157,14 [163,97] x 19,62. (515.6 [538.0] x 64.4. 1–2–C. 2S–2SC.SA–17. (I–92; III–326). Ateliers & Chantiers de la Loire, St. Nazaire. 1951 (2/12) launched for Sud Atlantique. 1952 (2/8) MV Bordeaux–S. America. 1962 (3/11) CHARLES TELLIER (Messageries Maritimes). 1962 (4/12) FV Havre–S. America. 1967 LE HAVRE ABETO (Panamanian); became a pilgrim ship.

34. (1962) LAËNNEC (M/S)
   12,003. 157,14 [163,97] x 19,62. (515.6 [538.0] x 64.4). 1–2–C.
   2S–2SC.SA–17. (I–94; III–230). Ateliers & Chantiers de la Loire,
   St. Nazaire. 1951 (25/2) launched for Sud Atlantique. 1952 (16/1)
   MV Havre–S. America. 1962 (20/9) LAËNNEC (Messageries
   Maritimes). 1962 (26/12) FV Havre–S. America. 1966 BELLE
   ABETO (Panamanian); became a pilgrim ship. 1976 (30/7)
   severe fire damage at Sasebo. 1976 (31/7) sank in the harbour.
35. 1966 PASTEUR (M/S)
   17,986. 159,97 [174,00] x 24,38. (524.9 [570.9] x 80.0). 1–2–C.
   2S–2SC.SA–20. (I–163; tourist 256). Ateliers & Chantiers de
   Dunkerque, Dunkirk. Laid down as AUSTRALIEN (Messageries Maritimes). 1966 (2/6) launched as PASTEUR (ditto).
   1966 (24/12) MV Havre–S. America. 1972 LV Hamburg–
   Southampton–Havre–River Plate. 1973 CHIDAMBARAM
   (Shipping Corporation of India); (I–154; dormitories, 1,526).

FUNNEL: (a) 1860. Black.
        (b) 1962 (approx). White with narrow black top; reproduc-
        tion of the houseflag on the white.
FLAG: (a) 1860. White with red triangles at the four corners; large
        black 'MI' on the white.
        (b) 1871. White with red triangles at the four corners; large
        black 'MM' on the white.

Chapter 13

(1863–1921)

LAMPORT & HOLT LINE

1865. Liverpool, Brazil & River Plate Steam
Navigation Company Limited

(British)

The firm of LAMPORT & HOLT was founded by William James Lamport and George Holt in Liverpool in 1845. The senior partner, Lamport, not only became a famous shipowner but was born on a famous day, 18 June 1815, the occasion of the Battle of Waterloo. George Holt was born in 1824.

For many years the LAMPORT & HOLT LINE fleet consisted entirely of wooden sailing ships, of which the first was the 335 ton CHRISTABEL launched at Workington on 17 September 1845. Although this pioneer was sold within a year, the business grew rapidly, and by 1850 no fewer than 14 ships were in commission. Four were added in that one year. The fleet sailed to many parts of the world, including North and South America, South Africa and India.

It was not until 1857 that Lamport & Holt bought their first steamer, the 189 ton ZULU, but they retained her for less than 12 months, probably because she was too small for long voyages. It was four years before they acquired a second steamer, as there is no doubt that W.J. Lamport, like many of his contemporaries, was diffident about going wholeheartedly into steam. But in 1861–2 the 1,290 ton MEMNON was delivered by Scott & Co of Greenock, and the 1,372 ton COPERNICUS (I) by A. Leslie & Co of Hebburn-on-Tyne, although it is interesting to see that three sailing ships were added simultaneously. The two steamers went tramping to various parts, but for some considerable time relations and friends of W.J. Lamport had been trying without success to persuade him to start a first class steamship line. At long last he agreed and decided on the Brazil and River Plate trade, for which his nearest serious competitor was the Royal Mail Steam Packet Company, whose steamers sailed from Southampton and not from Liverpool.

In 1862, therefore, the 1,500 ton iron screw steamer KEPLER was ordered from A. Leslie & Co, who in the next 20 years were to supply the firm with not far short of 40 new ships – a truly remarkable record! Alfred Holt, a younger brother of George, took a great interest in the

KEPLER and, in fact, sailed in her on her maiden voyage from Liverpool on 18 July 1863 for Lisbon, Brazil and the River Plate. He later founded the company which became known as the Blue Funnel Line.

A further sailing ship, the CHRISTABEL (II) was delivered more or less simultaneously with the KEPLER, and seven more appeared between then and 1867, but after that no further sail was acquired and, on the contrary, the existing ships were disposed of one by one. The last was sold in 1873.

1873 GALILEO 2,267 tons
Registered to carry 92 passengers.

Meanwhile, the KEPLER started her third voyage in April 1864, followed by the 1,585 ton GALILEO (I), which sailed on her maiden voyage from Liverpool to the River Plate on 20 July. The KEPLER left again on 20 August and the MEMNON, already mentioned, her first to South America on 20 September in place of the COPERNICUS, also mentioned.

An interesting second-hand ship reached Lamport & Holt in 1864. She had been launched on 23 May 1853 by John Laird of Birkenhead for the African Steamship Company as the 1,339 ton CHARITY, but was bought before completion by the Canadian Steam Navigation Company, the pioneer line to Canada. After four round voyages from Liverpool, she was taken up as a Crimean War transport and a year later became the LA CUBANA. Lamport & Holt renamed her HERSCHEL, and retained her services for seven years.

Thus, the Lamport steamship fleet, like their sailing ships, had grown fast, and partly for this reason and partly because no fewer than five new steamers were due to be delivered in 1866, all by Leslie, it was decided to form a limited liability company entitled the LIVERPOOL, BRAZIL & RIVER PLATE STEAM NAVIGATION COMPANY LIMITED, and do away with the previous traditional arrangement under which each vessel was divided into 64 shares. The new concern started to function on 18 December 1865, and Lamport & Holt were appointed managers.

Additions to the fleet in 1866–7 were the HUMBOLDT, CASSINI, LA PLATA, FLAMSTEED, LAPLACE, DONATI, COPERNICUS (II) and TYCHO BRAHE, allowing the Company to run steamers from London, Antwerp and Glasgow as well as from Liverpool. A mystery ship was the 1,778 ton LA PLATA, which from time to time was scheduled to sail from Liverpool, but no evidence has been found that she actually did so for several years. One possible explanation is that she was a reserve ship and was sometimes detailed to the South American run at the last minute. She did, however, sail from Liverpool for South America on 1 October 1872 and 1 January 1883.

Two sister ships of the 1,808 ton TYCHO BRAHE, the HIPPARCHUS and PASCAL (I), were delivered by Leslie in 1868 and 1870, followed in the latter year by the 2,170 ton BIELA and the 2,162 ton OLBERS. Another 1870 acquisition was the CITY OF RIO DE JANEIRO of the London, Belgium, Brazil & River Plate Steamship Company (Chapter 18). She only made one L&H voyage before being rebuilt and renamed TENIERS.

In 1869 Lamport & Holt began carrying cargoes of coffee from Brazil to New York. The ships so employed either returned to South America or proceeded to the United Kingdom, usually with cargoes of cotton.

A Lamport & Holt advertisement of 30 March 1868 stated: 'Liverpool, Brazil & River Plate steamers, under postal contract with the Government of Brazil.' [1] While on 27 July 1868 there was a further statement: 'One of these steamers monthly may call at Paranagua if required by the Brazilian Government.' [2] An appreciably more important announcement was made from 3 August 1868 onwards: 'The steamer of the 20th of each month is under contract with Her Majesty's Postmaster-General.' [3] The Portuguese arrangements were considerably extended by 1873 and read: 'On 1st, 10th, 12th and 20th of each month under postal contract with the Government of Brazil.' [4]

The KEPLER was lengthened from 82,29 to 97,68 metres (270.0 to 320.5 feet) in 1871, thereby making her the largest unit of the fleet with a tonnage of 2,258. At the same time, compound engines superseded the single-expansion set fitted initially. Meanwhile, the 993 ton CASSINI, which had been built to run between Liverpool and Pernambuco, was sold and her place was taken by the 1,249 ton GASSENDI.

A consort of the CITY OF RIO DE JANEIRO, the CITY OF LIMERICK, became the T. & J. Harrison WARRIOR in 1870, and two years later made some L&H voyages under that name. She, too, had some alterations and reappeared in 1874 as the L&H VANDYCK (I).

No fewer than 12 new ships were built for L&H between 1873 and 1875. Of these, Gourlay of Dundee were responsible for the 1,007 ton MALAGA, which after a voyage or two was renamed MEMLING, the Whitehaven Shipbuilding Company produced the 1,002 ton MARALDI, Inglis of Glasgow the 1,048 ton LALANDE, Iliff Mounsey of Sunderland the 1,708 ton RUBENS, Hall Russell of Aberdeen the 1,488 ton THALES and the 1,520 ton ARCHIMEDES (I), and William Hamilton of Port Glasgow the 1,308 ton DELAMBRE. A Leslie & Co were responsible for the remaining five – the 2,267 ton GALILEO (II), the 2,280 ton LEIBNITZ, the 1,131 ton CERVANTES, the 2,605 ton MASKELYNE and the 2,611 ton HEVELIUS. The last-named was the largest ship built for L&H up to that time. In fact, she was not exceeded in size until the 2,687 ton CAXTON was received second-hand in 1885 and the 2,743 ton DRYDEN was delivered by Leslie during the same year.

It is evident that most of the L&H steamers up to World War I had accommodation for first and third class passengers; they also carried a doctor and stewardess. The *Underwriter Registry for Iron Vessels* for 1874–84 inclusive listed in the case of British vessels with Board of Trade passenger certificates, the number of passengers allowed and the initial and terminal date of the certificate. The period of validity varied from a couple of months to a couple of years, and a given ship sometimes appeared as having a passenger certificate and sometimes not. The reasons for this are not clear, but no case has been found where a particular ship is listed with a varying passenger capacity. In many cases, the number of passengers permitted is shown in the accompanying fleet list.

In 1874 the Company had received a severe blow by the death of W.J. Lamport. In due course, Walter Holland and Charles W. Jones joined the partnership.

Following the withdrawal of the Ryde Line service in 1874 (Chapter 23), Lamport & Holt were responsible for forming the Société de Navigation Royale Belge Sud-Américaine in Antwerp, and in 1877–8 no fewer than eight ships were transferred to it – the COPERNICUS (II), the pioneer KEPLER, the TYCHO BRAHE, HIPPARCHUS, PASCAL (I), TENIERS, ROSSE and HORROX.

In 1885 R. & W. Hawthorn of Newcastle amalgamated with A. Leslie & Co to become R. & W. Hawthorn, Leslie & Company Limited of Hebburn-on-Tyne, their first completion for L&H being the 2,769 ton CHAUCER of 1886. Oswald, Mordaunt & Co of Southampton were responsible for the 2,846 ton SIDDONS in 1886 and were also the builders of the 3,230 ton COPERNICUS (III), which entered the fleet in

1888, although she had been built a year previously as the LILIAN for other Liverpool owners.

By 1895 over 70 ocean-going steamers had been built for L&H and, judging by the experience of many other lines, it was only to be expected that there would have been some casualties. The first took place as early as 1873 when the FLAMSTEED (I) was sunk in collision with H.M.S. BELLEROPHON. Just over a year later, on 28 February 1875, the MARALDI was wrecked near Pernambuco. Subsequent disasters took place on 9 April 1881 when the NEWTON was wrecked near Madeira; while on 13 May 1882 the PLINY was wrecked at Long Branch, New Jersey, when carrying coffee from Brazil to New York; in February 1883 the COPERNICUS (II) was wrecked on voyage from Liverpool to Brazil; on 21 January 1889 the MEMLING was wrecked on the coast of Morocco; on 1 March 1892 the PLATO broke her main shaft during the early stages of a voyage from Liverpool to Brazil and foundered south of the Scilly Isles; on 22 June 1895 the BESSEL was sunk in collision with the Wilson Line steamer HERO near the Royal Sovereign Lightship; and on 28 September 1895 the DALTON was wrecked on the Isle of Islay on voyage from New York to Glasgow. During the same period, 21 ships had been sold for further service and all told a total of 18 had been or were to be scrapped, including the pioneer KEPLER, which survived until 1903. It should be added that seven more ships commissioned before 1895 were lost subsequently. Three were wrecked, one foundered and three were lost in collision.

The 2,585 ton HOMER and the 4,978 ton CAVOUR were completed by Sir Raylton Dixon of Middlesbrough in 1895, and in the same year D. & W. Henderson Ltd of Glasgow were responsible for the 3,335 ton HORACE, the 4,637 ton CANOVA (II) and the 4,635 ton CER-VANTES (II). In 1896 the 3,338 ton VIRGIL came from Henderson, as did the largest ship so far, the 5,366 ton CANNING.

The maiden voyages of the CANOVA, CAVOUR, CERVANTES and CANNING all took place to Rio de Janeiro, the Straits of Magellan and Valparaiso, but no evidence has been found that any of them called at a River Plate port or ports. There were, in fact, some earlier and later sailings to Chile, and all went well until October 1888, when the COPERNICUS (III) went missing between Sandy Point (in the Straits of Magellan) and Valparaiso. This disaster was followed by the FLAM-STEED (II), built in 1892, being wrecked on the Chilean coast on 26 March 1893 and the CHANTREY, of 1890, near Valparaiso on 17 October 1896. In all probability these disasters were largely responsible for the withdrawal of the extended service.

George Holt died in 1896. A nephew, George H. Melly, had already joined the partnership, to which Arthur Cook was added.

The first of five 'R' class chips, the 5,855 ton RAPHAEL, was delivered by Henderson in 1898, and like her successors was built specially for the carriage of live cattle from Argentina to the United Kingdom. Sir Raylton Dixon was responsible for the 4,501 ton ROMNEY, but the other three, the 4,667 ton REMBRANDT, the 6,511 ton RAEBURN and the 6,540 ton ROSETTI were products of Henderson. There appears to have been a change of plan in the case of the RAEBURN, which has been omitted from the fleet list as her maiden voyage took place to Montreal, from where she proceeded to Cape Town. She subsequently had a varied career, and it is by no means certain that she ever ran to South America.

Two 4,000 ton 'C' class ships, the CAMOENS (II) and CALDERON (II), came from Workman, Clark & Co Ltd of Belfast in 1900, and the 'T' class THESPIS, TERENCE, TITIAN and TINTORETTO put in an appearance in 1901–02, the last two from Workman Clark and the others from Dixon and Henderson, respectively.

The 3,900 ton EVANGELINE and LOYALIST were commissioned by Furness, Withy & Co Ltd in 1901–02 for their London–Halifax–St. John, New Brunswick, service and had accommodation for 70 first class, 24 second and 48 third class passengers. Found to be too large for the requirements of the trade, they were sold in 1902 to Lamport & Holt as the TENNYSON and BYRON for service between New York, Rio de Janeiro, Santos, Montevideo and Buenos Aires, and proved an instant success. So much so that the 7,542 ton passenger liner VELASQUEZ was delivered by Sir Raylton Dixon in 1906 for similar activities, the VERDI by Workman Clark in 1907 and the 8,615 ton VOLTAIRE by D. & W. Henderson in the latter year. The first three voyages of the VELASQUEZ were from Liverpool to the River Plate, but she subsequently ran between the latter and New York, and unfortunately stranded near Santos on 16 October 1908 during fog. She became a total loss, but there were no casualties. She was replaced by the 10,117 ton single-screw VASARI, which was already under construction and was launched by Sir Raylton Dixon on 8 December 1908. Her passenger complement was 200 first class, 48 second and 70 third. By this time, the TENNYSON and BYRON did not as a rule proceed south of Santos.

Mention must be made of the 7,063 ton VERONESE, launched on 14 November 1905, which had a good deal in common with the VELAS-QUEZ, VOLTAIRE and VERDI, but ran extensively from British ports to the River Plate whereas the VERDI's maiden voyage took place from Liverpool to New York, after which she confined her activities between New York and the River Plate. For this reason she has been omitted from the fleet list.

The VERONESE was wrecked on 16 January 1913 near Leixões with a loss of 43 lives. When she left Vigo a few hours previously she was stated to have 142 passengers on board.

The last of the Belgian-flag ships of the Société de Navigation Royale Belge Sud-Américaine's service between Antwerp and Buenos Aires were tranferred back to Lamport & Holt in 1908.

A large batch of ships was acquired or built between 1911 and 1915 – namely, the 4,189 ton SIDDONS (II), the 4,186 ton SPENSER (II), the 5,839 ton DRYDEN (II), the 5,364 ton ARCHIMEDES (II), the 4,770 ton EUCLID (II), the 5,587 ton PASCAL (II), the 5,623 ton PHIDIAS (II), the 4,936 ton STRABO (II), the 5,613 ton PLUTARCH, the 4,979 ton SOCRATES, the 6,293 ton HERSCHEL (III) and the 6,278 ton HOLBEIN (II).

In view of the success of the New York–Buenos Aires venture, it was decided to augment the rather limited passenger accommodation of the Liverpool–River Plate ships by means of three twin-screw passenger steamers superior to any yet built for the Company. Orders were placed with Workman Clark for the VANDYCK, VAUBAN and VESTRIS, each of over 10,000 tons, and the first-named was launched on 1 June 1911.

In 1911 the firm of Lamport & Holt became a public company under the title LAMPORT & HOLT LIMITED, continuing as managers of the ships, which were still registered under the description Liverpool, Brazil & River Plate Steam Navigation Company Limited. George H. Melly and Arthur Cook became joint managing directors, but not for long as later in 1911 the Company came under the control of the Royal Mail Steam Packet Company (Chapter 1), whose chairman Owen Cosby Philipps, the future Lord Kylsant, also took over the chairmanship of Lamport & Holt which, however, retained its separate existence.

The arrival of the VANDYCK at Liverpool on 25 September 1911 from her Belfast builders did not at all please Royal Mail, who had ordered five 11,500 ton 'D' class steamers to carry large numbers of passengers between Liverpool and the River Plate, and up to 40,000 carcasses of meat back to Liverpool. The first of these, the DESEADO, was launched on 26 October 1911, but the VANDYCK had already sailed from Liverpool on 5 October for Vigo, Lisbon, Rio de Janeiro, Montevideo and Buenos Aires. At the conclusion of her fifth round voyage, however, she was chartered by Royal Mail and sailed from Southampton for the River Plate on 15 November 1912 on the first of two round voyages. After that she was detailed to the L&H New York–River Plate service, to which the VESTRIS also went after making only one voyage from Liverpool to Buenos Aires.

The VAUBAN left Liverpool on 4 May 1912 on her L&H maiden voyage to South America, but her third outward voyage started from

83

Southampton on 4 October under charter to Royal Mail and she made three round voyages under their auspices as the VAUBAN. Furthermore, as the seventh of Royal Mail's eight 'A' steamers required to run an accelerated weekly service was not due until the autumn of 1913, the VAUBAN was retained, renamed ALCALA and, painted in Royal Mail colours, left Southampton on 4 April 1913. Her last outward voyage started from Southampton on 28 November 1913, and upon arrival at Buenos Aires she reverted to the name VAUBAN, sailing again on 28 December for New York. She and the other 'V' ships added calls at Trinidad and Barbados.

When World War I broke out in August 1914 the Lamport & Holt fleet consisted of 36 ships of a total tonnage of nearly 200,000. Of these, 11 were lost, the first being the CERVANTES, which was torpedoed and sunk on 8 October 1914 by the German light cruiser KARLSRUHE, which also accounted for the VANDYCK (II) on 26 October. The next casualty was the HORACE, which was captured and sunk by the German raider MOEWE on 9 February 1916, as was the VOLTAIRE on 2 December 1916. A fortnight later, on 17 December, the PASCAL was torpedoed and sunk off the Casquets. The TERENCE met the same fate on 28 April 1917 in the vicinity of Fastnet, as did the VERDI on 22 August 1917 off the Irish coast. The TITIAN was sunk near Malta on 26 August, the CANOVA was sunk off the Irish coast on 24 December 1917 and on 6 January 1918 the SPENSER (II) met her end in the Irish Sea. Finally, the 7,307 ton MEMLING, delivered to the Company in 1915 was torpedoed off Brest on 3 October 1917, but managed to reach port. However, she was so badly damaged that she had to be scrapped.

Thus, the VANDYCK, VOLTAIRE and VERDI of the New York–River Plate service all became war casualties, but the VAUBAN, VESTRIS and VASARI survived, as did the TENNYSON and BYRON, which were sold in 1922. The three 'V's each made six or seven voyages for Cunard from Liverpool to New York between 1919 and 1921, continuing thence to the River Plate under L&H auspices and returning to Liverpool with cargoes of frozen meat, a trade in which L&H had been engaged since 1886. The two old-timers were more than replaced by the 13,233 ton VANDYCK (III), launched on 24 February 1921 and the 13,248 ton VOLTAIRE (II), launched on 14 August 1923.

Unfortunately, the VESTRIS foundered on 12 November 1928 300 miles from Hampton Roads, USA, with a loss of 112 passengers and crew. This disaster naturally gave rise to a lot of adverse publicity, and coupled with the effects of an increasing trade depression it was decided in 1930 to withdraw the New York–South American service. The VANDYCK, VOLTAIRE and VAUBAN were laid up in England.

The VAUBAN was scrapped in 1932, in which year the VOLTAIRE

84

1912 VESTRIS 10,494 tons
Foundered off USA coast in 1928 with heavy casualties.

was detailed to make a series of short pleasure cruises. They were sufficiently successful for her to be joined by the VANDYCK in 1933, and this became a regular feature of the pair – painted white – until the outbreak of World War II in 1939. The VANDYCK then became an auxiliary cruiser and was sunk off Norway on 10 June 1940 during an air attack. The VOLTAIRE was sunk by the German raider THOR on 18 April 1941, five days after leaving Trinidad.

After the collapse of the Kylsant empire in the early 1930s, Lamport & Holt went into liquidation. In 1934 the Liverpool, Brazil & River Plate Steam Navigation Company Limited took over their assets, and its name was changed to LAMPORT & HOLT LINE LIMITED. In June 1944, L&H came under the control of the Vestey group, to which the Booth Steamship Company (Chapter 16) was added in 1946. Both lines retained their offices, staff and ships, but from time to time there was considerable interchange of tonnage.

In 1974 the Vestey group took over Oceanic House, former headquarters of the White Star Line, in James Street, Liverpool, renamed it Albion House and formed a new company, Blue Star Ship Management Limited, which became responsible for the management of all ships operated by Lamport & Holt, Booth and Blue Star. A year later, both Lamport & Holt and Booth moved their head offices to Albion House. This was quite an upheaval for Lamport & Holt, in particular, as they had been situated in the Royal Liver Building, Liverpool, since 1912.

The VANDYCK and VOLTAIRE were the last multi-passenger ships owned by Lamport & Holt, and subsequent ships have been limited to 12 passengers or to cargo only.

The Blue Star Line has gone from strength to strength, but unfortunately the same cannot be said about Lamport & Holt, who at the time of writing own no more than two or three dry cargo ships, managed by Blue Star Ship Management Limited.

[1] *The Times* 30/3/1868.
[2] *The Times* 27/7/1868.
[3] *The Times* 3/8/1868.
[4] *The Times* 3/1/1873.

1. 1863 KEPLER
   1,500. 82,29 x 9,93. (270.0 x 32.6). 1–2. I–S–I(2)–9. (113 passengers). A. Leslie & Co, Hebburn-on-Tyne. 1863 (Apr) launched. 1863 (18/7) MV Liverpool–S. America. 1871 lengthened to 97,68 metres (320.5 feet); 2,258 tons; C2 replaced I(2). 1903 scrapped.
2. 1864 GALILEO (I)
   1,585. 82,47 x 9,48. (270.6 x 33.1). 1–2. I–S–I(2)–9. A. Leslie & Co, Hebburn-on-Tyne. 1864 (7/4) launched. 1864 (20/7) MV Liverpool–Bahia–River Plate. 1873 JUAN (Br). 1898 (26/8) sailed Hong Kong–Kiaochow; went missing.
3. (1864) MEMNON
   1,290. 77,29 x 9,93. (253.6 x 32.6). 1–2. I–S–I(2)–9. Scott & Co, Greenock. 1861 (28/3) launched. 1864 (20/9) FV Liverpool–Pernambuco (several S. American voyages). 1872 C2 by Fawcett, Preston & Co, Liverpool. 1888 MEMNON (Ocean SS Co (Alfred Holt)). 1899 hulked.
4. (1864) HERSCHEL (I)
   1,339. 74,06 x 9,14. (243.0 x 30.0). C–1–3. I–S–?–9. (I&II–100; III). John Laird, Birkenhead. 1853 (23/5) launched as CHARITY (African SS Co); purchased by Canadian SN Co. 1854–5 Crimean War transport. 1856 LA CUBANA. 1864 HERSCHEL (Lamport & Holt). 1864 (20/10) FV Liverpool–Pernambuco–Bahia–Rio de Janeiro–Montevideo–Buenos Aires. 1872 HERSCHEL (R.M. Sloman & Co, Hamburg). 1874 PALMERSTON (German four-masted barque. 1894 FEDERICO (It). 1899 (approx) scrapped.
5. 1864 NEWTON (I)
   1,324. 76,04 x 9,54. (249.5 x 31.3). 1–2. I–S–I(2)–9. Macnab & Co, Greenock. 1864 (18/10) launched. 1864 (16/12) MV Liverpool–Bahia–Rio de Janeiro–Montevideo–Buenos Aires. 1870 C2 replaced I(2). 1881 (9/4) wrecked on Madeira during voyage Rio de Janeiro–London.
6. 1865 PTOLEMY
   1,115. 78,39 x 9,51. (257.2 x 31.2). 1–2. I–S–I(2)–9. (68

passengers). A. Leslie & Co, Hebburn-on-Tyne. 1864 (21/7) launched. 1865 (10/6) MV Liverpool–S. America. 1874 C2 by G. Forrester & Co, Liverpool. 1899 scrapped.

7. 1865 HALLEY
1,347. 81,62 x 9,78. (267.8 x 32.1). 1–2. I–S–I(2)–9. (64 passengers). A. Leslie & Co, Hebburn-on-Tyne. 1865 (13/9) launched. 1865 (23/12) MV Liverpool–Bahia–Rio de Janeiro–Montevideo–Buenos Aires. 1874 C2 by G. Forrester & Co, Liverpool. 1895 scrapped at Preston.

8. 1866 HUMBOLDT
1,638. 81,74 x 9,78. (268.2 x 32.1). 1–2. I–S–I(2)–9. (59 passengers). A. Leslie & Co, Hebburn-on-Tyne. 1866 launched. 1866 (28/4) MV Liverpool–River Plate. 1880 C2 replaced I(2). 1894 CAMOCIM (Brazilian). 1917 scrapped.

9. 1866 CASSINI
993. 66,98 x 8,53. (219.8 x 28.0). 1–2. I–S–I(2)–9. A. Leslie & Co, Hebburn-on-Tyne. 1866 launched. 1866 FV Liverpool–Pernambuco. 1871 CASSINI (Br). 1873 C2 by R. & W. Hawthorn, Newcastle. 1881 PALMARIA (NGI (It)). 1909 scrapped at Palermo.

10. 1866 LA PLATA
1,778. 90,91 x 9,78. (298.3 x 32.1). 1–2. I–S–I(2)–9. A. Leslie & Co, Hebburn-on-Tyne. 1866 launched. 1872 (or earlier) FV Liverpool–River Plate. 1875 LA PLATA (Br); C4 replaced I(2). 1886 (3/7) wrecked near Thisted.

11. 1866 FLAMSTEED (I)
1,376. 83,81 x 9,75. (275.0 x 32.0). 1–2. I–S–I(2)–9. (72 passengers). A. Leslie & Co, Hebburn-on-Tyne. 1866 launched. 1866 (22/9) MV Liverpool–River Plate. 1873 (24/11) sunk in collision with H.M.S. BELLEROPHON during voyage from Liverpool–S. America.

12. 1866 LAPLACE
1,410. 78,45 x 9,51. (257.4 x 31.2). 1–2. I–S–I(2)–9. (64 passengers). A. Leslie & Co, Hebburn-on-Tyne. 1866 launched. 1866 (15/12) MV Liverpool–Bahia–Rio de Janeiro–Santos. 1874 C2 by Fawcett, Preston & Co, Liverpool. 1894 CAPIBARIBE (Brazilian). 1917 scrapped.

13. 1867 DONATI
1,392. 78,51 x 9,48. (257.6 x 31.1). 1–2. I–S–I(2)–9. (60 passengers. A. Leslie & Co, Hebburn-on-Tyne. 1866 launched. 1867 (9/2) MV Liverpool–Bahia–Rio de Janeiro–Santos. 1874 C2 by Fawcett, Preston & Co, Liverpool. 1891 DONATI (Br). 1892 (10/12) sailed New York–Oporto; went missing.

14. 1867 COPERNICUS (II)
    1,629. 84,33 x 9,87. (276.7 x 32.4). 1–2. I–S–I(2)–9. (66
    passengers). A. Leslie & Co, Hebburn-on-Tyne. 1866 launched.
    1867 (30/3) MV Liverpool–R. Plate. 1874 C2 by R. Stephenson &
    Co, Newcastle. 1883 (26/2) wrecked at Ponta de Pedras on
    voyage Liverpool–Brazil. (0).
15. 1867 TYCHO BRAHE
    1,808. 88,69 x 10,54. (291.0 x 34.6). 1–2. I–S–I(2)–9. (80
    passengers). A. Leslie & Co, Hebburn-on-Tyne. 1867 launched.
    1867 (26/9) MV Liverpool–R. Plate. 1892 PALAIS ROYAL
    (Br). 1894 TAIF (Turkish) 1908 (30/10) sunk in collision with ss
    BAGDAD at Constantinople.
16. 1868 HIPPARCHUS
    1,863. 88,60 x 10,51. (290.7 x 34.5). 1–2. I–S–I(2)–9. (118
    passengers). A. Leslie & Co, Hebburn-on-Tyne. 1867 launched.
    1868 (25/1) MV Liverpool–R. Plate. 1895 hulked.
17. 1870 PASCAL (I)
    1,876. 91,70 x 10,18. (300.9 x 33.4). 1–2. I–S–C2–10. (78
    passengers). A. Leslie & Co, Hebburn-on-Tyne (engines R.
    Stephenson & Co, Newcastle). 1869 (13/12), launched. 1870
    (20/4) MV Liverpool–Rio de Janeiro–Montevideo–Buenos Aires.
    1897 scrapped at Genoa.
18. 1870 BIELA
    2,170. 96,31 x 10,63. (316.0 x 34.9). 1–2. I–S–C2–10. (102
    passengers). A. Leslie & Co, Hebburn-on-Tyne (engines R.
    Stephenson & Co, Newcastle). 1870 launched. 1870 (20/5) MV
    Liverpool–R. Plate. 1900 (1/10) sunk in collision with ss EAGLE
    POINT off Nantucket.
19. (1870) CITY OF RIO DE JANEIRO
    (1873) TENIERS
    1,803. 83,20 x 10,12. (273.0 x 33.2). C–1–3. I–S–C2–10. Ran-
    dolph, Elder & Co, Glasgow. 1868 launched as CITY OF RIO
    DE JANEIRO (London, Belgium, Brazil & R. Plate SS Co;
    1,597 tons. 1870 ditto (Lamport & Holt). 1870 (20/10) FV
    Liverpool–R. Plate. 1873 TENIERS (Lamport & Holt); (I–100;
    III). 1878 (20/6) LV (?) Liverpool–London–Rio de Janeiro. 1878
    wore Belgian flag. 1892 scrapped at Sunderland.
20. 1870 OLBERS
    2,162. 96,43 x 10,63. (316.4 x 34.9). 1–2. I–S–C2–10. (95
    passengers). A. Leslie & Co, Hebburn-on-Tyne (engines R.
    Stephenson & Co, Newcastle). 1870 launched. 1870 (29/10) MV
    Liverpool–Rio de Janeiro–Montevideo–Buenos Aires. 1901
    scrapped at Genoa.

21. 1871 CAMOENS (I)
    1,053. 75,98 x 8,93. (249.3 x 29.3). 1–2. I–S–C2–10. A. Leslie &
    Co, Hebburn-on-Tyne (engines R. Stephenson & Co, Newcas-
    tle). 1871 (Jan) launched. 1871 (12/4) MV Liverpool–Bahia–Rio
    de Janeiro–Paranagua–Santa Catharina–Rio Grande do Sol. 1887
    CAMOENS (Br). 1888 ORETO (NGI (It)). 1914 LOGUDORO
    (It). 1923 scrapped in Italy.
22. 1871 CALDERON (I)
    1,054, 75,95 x 8,93. (249.2 x 29.3). 1–2. I–S–C2–10. A. Leslie &
    Co, Hebburn-on-Tyne (engines R. Stephenson & Co, Newcas-
    tle). 1871 (Feb) launched. 1871 (2/5) MV Liverpool–Bahia–Rio
    de Janeiro–Santos. 1887 ARLINDO (Brazilian). 1900
    CAMINHA (ditto). 1904 SANTA MARIA (ditto).
23. 1872 GASSENDI
    1,249. 72,56 x 9,23. (238.1 x 30.3). 1–2. I–S–C2–10. Hall, Russell
    & Co, Aberdeen. 1872 (Apr) launched. 1872 (19/7) MV
    Liverpool–Pernambuco. 1885 GASSENDI (Br). 1891 MADON-
    NA DELLA COSTA (It). 1894 (6/7) destroyed by fire at
    Santos.
24. (1872) WARRIOR
    (1874) VANDYCK (I)
    1,686. 80,67 x 9,81. (264.7 x 32.2). C–1–3. I–S–C2–10. Randolph,
    Elder & Co, Glasgow. 1867 launched as CITY OF LIMERICK
    (London, Belgium, Brazil & R. Plate SS Co); 1,339 tons. 1870
    WARRIOR (T. & J. Harrison). 1872 ditto (Lamport & Holt).
    1872 (12/9) FV Liverpool–Bahia–Rio de Janeiro–Santos. VAN-
    DYCK (Lamport & Holt); (I–100; III). 1874 (10/4) FV Liver-
    pool–R. Plate. 1892 coal hulk at Rio de Janeiro.
25. 1873 GALILEO (II)
    2,267. 104,60 x 10,70. (343.2 x 35.1). 1–2. I–S–C2–10. (92
    passengers). A. Leslie & Co, Hebburn-on-Tyne (engines Mauds-
    lay, Sons & Field, London). 1872 (Oct). 1873 (3/4) MV
    Liverpool–R. Plate. 1899 scrapped.
26. 1873 MALAGA
    (1873) MEMLING
    1,007. 67,05 x 9,20. (220.0 x 30.2). 1–2. I–S–C2–10. (8 passen-
    gers). Gourlay & Co, Dundee. 1872 (Sep) launched as MALA-
    GA (Br). 1873 (10/4) MV for Lamport & Holt. 1873 MEMLING
    (ditto). 1873 (10/12) FV Liverpool–R. Plate. 1885 MEMLING
    (Br). 1889 (21/1) wrecked near Cape Blanco, Morocco.
27. 1873 MARALDI
    1,002. 67,69 x 8,62. (222.1 x 28.3) 1–2. I–S–C2–10. Whitehaven
    Shipbuilding Co, Whitehaven. 1872 (14/11) launched. 1873 (1/5)

MV Liverpool–Bahia–Rio de Janeiro. 1875 (28/2) wrecked near Pernambuco.

28. 1873 LEIBNITZ
2,280. 104,38 x 10,63. (342.5 x 34.9). 1–2. I–S–C2–10. (78 passengers). A. Leslie & Co, Hebburn-on-Tyne (engines Maudslay, Sons & Field, London). 1873 (25/8) launched. 1873 MV Liverpool–R. Plate. 1896 scrapped.

29. 1873 LALANDE
1,048. 67,29 x 9,29. (220.8 x 30.5). 1–2. I–S–C2–10. (12 passengers). Inglis & Co, Glasgow. 1872 (Dec) launched. 1873 (7/7) MV Liverpool–Pernambuco. 1886 LALANDE (Br). 1892 PHOENIX (Greek). 1896 CASTELLACCIO (It). 1909 BERSAGLIERE (It). 1924 scrapped.

30. 1873 RUBENS
1,708. 82,29 x 9,90. (270.0 x 32.5). 1–2. I–S–C2–10. Iliff, Mounsey & Co, Sunderland. 1872 (Sept) launched. 1873 (10/9) MV Liverpool–Bahia–Rio de Janeiro–Santos. 1909 sold; hulked.

31. 1873 THALES
1,488. 68,88 x 9,54. (226.0 x 31.3). 1–2. I–S–C2–10. (56 passengers). Hall, Russell & Co, Aberdeen. 1873 (11/8) launched. 1873 (10/10) MV Liverpool–Montevideo–Buenos Aires–Rosario. 1891 JULES COUDERT (Fr). 1898 scrapped at Genoa.

32. 1874 CERVANTES (I)
1,131. 76,59 x 9,02. (251.3 x 29.6). 1–2. I–S–C2–10. (74 passengers). A. Leslie & Co, Hebburn-on-Tyne (engines Thompson, Boyd & Co, Newcastle). 1874 launched. 1874 (23/5) MV Liverpool–Bahia–Rio de Janeiro. 1884 CAMILLO (Brazilian). 1895 NORTE-SUL (ditto). 1897 (Aug) sank at Rio Grande del Norte.

33. 1874 DELAMBRE
1,308. 71,22 x 9,51. (233.7 x 31.2). 1–2. I–S–C2–10. Wm. Hamilton & Co, Port Glasgow. 1873 (11/9) launched. 1874 (12/8) MV Liverpool–Bahia–Rio de Janeiro–Santos. 1896 DELAMBRE (Br). 1897 scrapped.

34. 1875 ARCHIMEDES (I)
1,520. 82,50 x 9,78. (270.7 x 32.1). 1–2. I–S–C2–10. (58 passengers). Hall, Russell & Co, Aberdeen. 1874 (29/7) launched. 1875 (9/1) MV Liverpool–S. America. 1888 (Nov) collision in R. Plate with MILTON (Lamport & Holt); serious damage. 1893 HELENE (Fr). 1902 RICONOSCENZA (It). 1904 (8/3) wrecked at Montana.

35. 1875 MASKELYNE
   2,605. 106,82 x 11,24. (350.5 x 36.9). 1–2. I–S–C2–10. (137
   passengers). A. Leslie & Co, Hebburn-on-Tyne (engines R.
   Stephenson & Co, Newcastle). 1874 launched. 1875 (20/1) MV
   Liverpool–S. America. 1903 (31/1) foundered in North
   Atlantic.
36. 1875 HEVELIUS
   2,611. 106,61 x 11,28. (349.8 x 37.0). 1–2. I–S–C2–10. (129
   passengers). A. Leslie & Co, Hebburn-on-Tyne (engines R.
   Stephenson & Co, Newcastle). 1874 launched. 1895 (3/3) MV
   Liverpool–S. America. 1903 scrapped.
37. 1876 ROSSE
   1,685. 86,19 x 10,15. (282.8 x 33.3). 1–2. I–S–C2–10. A. Leslie &
   Co, Hebburn-on-Tyne (engines R. Stephenson & Co, Newcastle). 1875 launched. 1876 (10/7) MV Liverpool–Montevideo–
   Buenos Aires–Rosario. 1898 ROSSE (Brazilian). 1902 scrapped
   at Hamburg.
38. 1876 CANOVA (I)
   1,120. 77,72 x 8,99. (255.0 x 29.5). 1–2. I–S–C2–10. A. Leslie &
   Co, Hebburn-on-Tyne (engines Thompson & Co, Newcastle).
   1876 (23/9) launched. 1876 (4/11) MV Liverpool–Bahia. 1883
   CANOVA (Brazilian).
39. 1877 EUCLID (I)
   1,545. 84,21 x 9,96. (276.3 x 32.7). 1–2. I–S–C2–10. (63
   passengers). Hall, Russell & Co, Aberdeen. 1877 (Jly) launched.
   1877 (10/11) MV Liverpool–R. Plate. 1898 EUCLID (Brazilian).
   1903 scrapped.
40. 1878 HORROX
   1,711. 85,64 x 10,30. (281.0 x 33.8). 1–2. I–S–C2–10. T.R.
   Oswald, Southampton. 1877 (16/6) launched. 1878 (20/3) MV
   Liverpool–London–S. America. 1903 scrapped at Naples.
41. 1878 PLINY
   1,671. 87,90 x 10,15. (288.4 x 33.3). 1–2. I–S–C2–10. (46
   passengers). Barrow Shipbuilding Co, Barrow. 1878 (4/3)
   launched. 1882 (13/5) wrecked at Long Branch, New
   Jersey.
42. 1878 BESSEL
   1,911. 93,53 x 10,27. (306.9 x 33.7). 1–2. I–S–C2–10. (48
   passengers). A. Leslie & Co, Hebburn-on-Tyne (engines R.
   Stephenson & Co, Newcastle). 1878 launched. 1878 MV London
   (?)–S. America. 1895 (22/6) sunk in collision with Wilson Line
   HERO near Royal Sovereign Lightship on voyage London–
   Santos (0).

43. 1878 PLATO

1,684. 88,39 x 10,15. (290.0 x 33.3). 1–2. I–S–C2–10. (56 passengers). A. Leslie & Co, Hebburn-on-Tyne (engines R. Stephenson & Co, Newcastle). 1878 (10/1) launched. 1878 (15/10) MV Liverpool–R. Plate. 1892 (29/2) broke main shaft during voyage Liverpool–Brazil. 1892 (1/3) foundered 150 miles S. of Scilly Isles.

44. (1878) SIRIUS

2,169. 96,37 x 10,63. (316.2 x 34.9). 1–2. I–S–C2–10. (105 passengers). A. Leslie & Co, Hebburn-on-Tyne (engines R. Stephenson & Co, Newcastle). 1869 launched for Star Navigation, Liverpool. 1878 SIRIUS (Lamport & Holt). 1878 (25/10) FV Liverpool–S. America. 1899 scrapped at Genoa.

45. 1878 LASSELL

1,955. 94,48 x 10,42. (310.0 x 34.2). 1–2. I–S–C2–10. (50 passengers). A. Leslie & Co, Hebburn-on-Tyne (engines R. Stephenson & Co, Newcastle). 1878 launched. 1878 (21/11) MV Liverpool–R. Plate. 1900 LASSELL (USA), 1920 ditto (Moroccan). 1920 SIRENE (Algerian). 1924 scrapped in Italy.

46. 1879 HERSCHEL (II)

1,947. 94,79 x 10,48. (311.0 x 34.4) 1–2. I–S–C2–10. (48 passengers). A. Leslie & Co, Hebburn-on-Tyne (engines R. Stephenson & Co, Newcastle). 1879 (21/5) launched. 1879 MV Liverpool–R. Plate. 1901 (17/11) collided with ss ARDEOLA in Mersey; severe damage. 1902 scrapped at Rotterdam.

47. 1880 NASMYTH

1,991. 96,09 x 10,51. (315.3 x 34.5). 1–2. I–S–C2–10. (50 passengers). A. Leslie & Co, Hebburn-on-Tyne (engines R. Stephenson & Co, Newcastle). 1880 launched. 1880 (30/4) MV Liverpool–Rio de Janeiro. 1902 scrapped at Genoa.

48. 1881 DALTON

2,030. 96.12 x 10,63. (315.4 x 34.9). 1–2. I–S–C2–10. (56 passengers). A. Leslie & Co, Hebburn-on-Tyne (engines R. Stephenson & Co, Newcastle). 1881 launched. 1881 (19/2) MV Liverpool–R. Plate. 1895 (28/9) wrecked on Isle of Islay on voyage New York–Clyde (0).

49. 1881 STRABO (I)

1,959. 88,39 x 10,76. (290.0 x 35.3). 1–2. I–S–C2–10. (50 passengers). Barrow Shipbuilding Co, Barrow. 1881 (2/4) launched. 1881 (26/5) MV Liverpool–R. Plate. 1905 scrapped at Genoa.

50. 1881 HANDEL
    1,977. 88,39 x 11,03. (290.0 x 36.2). 1–2. I–S–C2–10. (56 passengers). A. Leslie & Co, Hebburn-on-Tyne (engines R. Stephenson & Co, Newcastle). 1881 (30/7) launched. 1881 (27/9) MV Liverpool–R. Plate. 1902 GUASCO (It). 1911 scrapped in Italy.
51. 1881 MOZART
    1,994. 88,57 x 11,03. (290.6 x 36.2). 1–2. I–S–C2–10. (56 passengers). A. Leslie & Co, Hebburn-on-Tyne (engines R. Stephenson & Co, Newcastle). 1881 launched. 1881 (19/12) MV Liverpool–R. Plate. 1902 scrapped at Rotterdam.
52. 1882 HOGARTH (I)
    2,053. 90,03 x 11,03. (295.4 x 36.2). 1–2. I–S–C2–10. (50 passengers). A. Leslie & Co, Hebburn-on-Tyne (engines R. Stephenson & Co, Newcastle). 1882 launched. 1882 (11/9) MV Liverpool–R. Plate. 1904 ATTILIO (Brazilian). 1902 scrapped at Rio de Janeiro.
53. 1882 HOLBEIN (I)
    2,050. 90,12 x 11,03. (295.7 x 36.2). 1–2. I–S–C2–10. (50 passengers). A. Leslie & Co, Hebburn-on-Tyne (engines R. Stephenson & Co, Newcastle). 1882 launched. 1882 (11/11) MV Liverpool–R. Plate. 1901 TAMBRE (Spanish). 1930 scrapped.
54. 1882 FLAXMAN
    2,168. 91,22 x 11,00. (299.3 x 36.1). 1–2. I–S–C2–10. (50 passengers). Oswald, Mordaunt & Co, Southampton. 1882 (26/8) launched. 1882 (18/12) MV Liverpool–R. Plate. 1903 CANOE (Brazilian). 1906 JAGUARIBE (Brazilian). 1932 (24/8) foundered off Brazilian coast.
55. 1883 BUFFON
    2,304. 92,04 x 11,37. (302.0 x 37.3). 1–2. I–S–C2–10. (84 passengers). A. Leslie & Co, Hebburn-on-Tyne (engines R. Stephenson & Co, Newcastle. 1883 launched. 1883 (17/7) MV Liverpool–R. Plate. 1908 TIJUCA (Brazilian). 1917 (20/5) torpedoed and sunk by German submarine near Ushant.
56. 1883 CUVIER
    2,299. 92,04 x 11,34. (302.0 x 37.2). 1–2. I–S–C2–10. (80 passengers). A. Leslie & Co, Hebburn-on-Tyne (engines R. Stephenson & Co, Newcastle). 1883 (Oct) launched. 1883 (3/11) MV Liverpool–R. Plate. 1900 (9/3) sunk in collision with ss DOVRE off East Goodwin lightship (26).
57. 1885 GARRICK
    2,561. 97,83 x 11,52. (321.0 x 37.8). 1–2. I–S–C2–10. A. Leslie &

Co, Hebburn-on-Tyne (engines R. & W. Hawthorn, Newcastle).
1885 launched. 1885 (13/4) MV Liverpool–R. Plate. 1906
FRIDTJOF NANSEN (Norwegian whaling ship). 1906 (10/11)
wrecked at South Georgia.

58. (1885) CAXTON

2,624. 94,66 x 11,82. (310.6 x 38.8. 1–2. I–S–C2–10. Oswald,
Mordaunt & Co, Southampton. 1883 launched as TEST (Br).
1885 CAXTON (Lamport & Holt). 1885 (26/6) FV Liverpool–R.
Plate. 1895 MENDOTA (T. Hogan & Sons). 1900 ANGIOLINA
(It). 1905 CITTA DI NEW YORK (It). 1907 COSTANZA (It).
1917 (14/8) torpedoed and sunk by German submarine in North
Sea.

59. 1885 SPENSER (I)

2,564. 95,09 x 11,79. (312.0 x 38.7). 1–2. S–S–C2–10. Oswald,
Mordaunt & Co, Southampton. 1885 (14/9) launched. 1885 (5/12)
MV Liverpool–R. Plate. 1895 MANITOU (T. Hogan & Sons).
1899 IDA (It). 1909 scrapped in Italy.

60. 1885 DRYDEN (I)

2,716. 94,66 x 11.82. (310.6 x 38.8). 1–2. I–S–C2–10. A. Leslie &
Co, Hebburn-on-Tyne (engines R. & W. Hawthorn, Newcastle).
1885 launched. 1885 (21/12) MV Liverpool–R. Plate. 1895
MENEMSHA (T. Hogan & Sons. 1898 IRIS (US Navy). 1928
scrapped at San Francisco.

61. 1886 SIDDONS (I)

2,860. 96,92 x 11,28 (318.0 x 37.0). 1–2. I–S–C2–10. Oswald,
Mordaunt & Co, Southampton. 1886 (19/6) launched. 1886 (12/9)
MV Liverpool–R. Plate. 1894 SIDDONS (Br). 1896 (18/4) sunk
in collision with ss CRAIGEARB off Norderney on voyage
Odessa–Hamburg (0).

62. 1886 CHAUCER

2,769. 96,60 x 11,98. (315.0 x 39.3). 1–2. I–S–T3–11. R. & W.
Hawthorn, Leslie & Co, Hebburn-on-Tyne. 1886 launched. 1886
(7/12) MV Liverpool–R. Plate. 1913 scrapped at Dunkirk.

63. (1888) COPERNICUS (III)

3,153. 101,00 x 12,83. (331.4 x 42.1). 1–2. I–S–C2–10. Oswald,
Mordaunt & Co, Southampton. 1887 launched as LILIAN (Br).
1888 COPERNICUS (Lamport & Holt). 1888 (20/1) FV Liverpool–Santa Fé. 1895 (16/10) sailed Sandy Point–Valparaiso; went
missing.

64. 1888 MILTON

2,679. 94,48 x 11,95. (310.0 x 39.2). 1–2. S–S–T3–11. D. & W.
Henderson Ltd, Glasgow. 1888 launched. 1888 (2/10) MV
Liverpool–R. Plate. 1888 (Nov) collision in R. Plate with

ARCHIMEDES (Lamport & Holt); minor damage. 1911 (15/6) wrecked near Cabo Espichel, Portugal.

65. 1888 NEWTON (II)

2,540. 95,21 x 11,95. (312.4 x 39.2). 1–2. S–S–T3–11. R. & W. Hawthorn, Leslie & Co, Hebburn-on-Tyne. 1888 (6/10) launched. 1888 (24/11) MV Liverpool–Rosario. 1910 scrapped at Antwerp.

66. (1889) WORDSWORTH

3,339. 111,85 x 11,92. (367.0 x 39.1). 1–2. I–S–C4–10. A. Leslie & Co, Hebburn-on-Tyne (engines R. Stephenson & Co, Newcastle). 1882 launched as CAPELLA (Star Navigation Co (Br). 1889 WORDSWORTH (Lamport & Holt). 1889 (4/9) FV Liverpool–Antwerp–River Plate. 1902 (4/8) wrecked near Bahia on voyage New York–Brazil.

67. (1890) COLERIDGE

2,610. 107,49 x 11,28. (352.7 x 37.0). 1–2. I–S–C2–10. A. Leslie & Co, Hebburn-on-Tyne (engines R. Stephenson & Co, Newcastle). 1875 launched as MIRA (Star Navigation (Br)). 1889 COLERIDGE (Lamport & Holt). 1890 (7/3) FV Liverpool–Antwerp–River Plate. 1890 T3 by D. Rollo & Son, Liverpool. 1904 scrapped at Marseilles.

68. 1890 CHANTREY

2,788. 98,84 x 12,86. (324.3 x 42.2). 1–2. S–S–T3–11. R. & W. Hawthorn, Leslie & Co, Hebburn-on-Tyne. 1890 (24/1) launched. 1890 (3/4) MV Middlesbrough–Buenos Aires. 1896 (17/10) wrecked near Valparaiso.

69. 1890 PHIDIAS (I)

2,822. 98,75 x 12,86. (324.0 x 42.2). 1–2. S–S–T3–11. R. & W. Hawthorn, Leslie & Co, Hebburn-on-Tyne. 1890 (10/3)launched. 1890 (17/5) MV Middlesbrough–Buenos Aires. 1911 TUPY (Brazilian). 1918 (21/9) wrecked near Agadir.

70. 1892 FLAMSTEED (II)

3,381. 105,15 x 13,34. (345.0 x 43.8). 1–2. S–S–T3–11. R. & W. Hawthorn, Leslie & Co, Hebburn-on-Tyne. 1892 (14/1) launched. 1892 (15/4) MV Liverpool–Rosario. 1893 (26/3) wrecked on Chilean coast.

71. 1895 HOMER

2,585. 94,54 x 12,80. (310.2 x 42.0). 1–2. S–S–T3–11. Sir Raylton Dixon & Co, Middlesbrough (engines N.E. Marine Engineering Co, Newcastle). 1894 (27/11) launched. 1895 (14/2) MV Liverpool–R. Plate. 1914 ODILA (Spanish). 1915 SOLBAKKEN (Norwegian). 1917 (4/2) torpedoed and sunk by German submarine near Cape Finisterre.

72. 1895 CANOVA (II)
    4,640. 124,96 x 14,66. (410.0 x 48.1). 1–2. S–S–T3–11. D. & W.
    Henderson Ltd, Glasgow. 1894 (27/12) launched. 1895 (26/2) MV
    Liverpool–Bahia–Rio de Janeiro–Valparaiso. 1917 (24/12) torpe-
    doed and sunk by German submarine off Irish coast.
73. 1895 CERVANTES (II)
    4,640. 124,96 x 14,66. (410.0 x 48.1). 1–2. S–S–T3–11. D. & W.
    Henderson Ltd, Glasgow. 1895 (11/4) launched. 1895 (25/5) MV
    Liverpool–Rio de Janeiro–Valparaiso. 1914 (8/10) sunk by
    German cruiser KARLSRUHE.
74. 1895 CAVOUR
    4,920. 124,99 x 15,63. (410.1 x 51.3). 1–2. S–S–T3–11. Sir Raylton
    Dixon & Co, Middlesbrough (engines N.E. Marine Engineering
    Co, Newcastle). 1895 (24/6) launched. 1895 (22/9) MV Liver-
    pool–Rio de Janeiro–Valparaiso. 1929 scrapped at Danzig.
75. 1895 HORACE
    3,335. 106,67 x 13,95. (350.0 x 45.8). 1–2. S–S–T3–11. D. & W.
    Henderson Ltd, Glasgow. 1895 (19/10) launched. 1895 (15/12)
    MV Liverpool–Buenos Aires. 1916 (9/2) sunk by German raider
    MOEWE in South Atlantic.
76. 1896 VIRGIL
    3,338. 106,67 x 13,95. (350.0 x 45.8). 1–2. S–S–T3–11. D. & W.
    Henderson Ltd, Glasgow. 1896 (2/4) launched. 1896 (17/5) MV
    Liverpool–Montevideo–Buenos Aires. 1924 scrapped in Ger-
    many.
77. 1896 CANNING
    5,366. 129,59 x 15,88. (425.2 x 52.1) 1–2. S–S–T3–11. D. & W.
    Henderson Ltd, Glasgow. 1896 (13/7) launched. 1896 (21/9) MV
    Liverpool–Rio de Janeiro–Valparaiso. 1914 H.M.S. CANNING
    (balloon ship). 1919 resumed for Lamport & Holt. 1921
    OKEANIS (Greek). 1924 ARENZANO (It). 1925 scrapped.
78. 1898 SALLUST
    3,628. 108,07 x 14,35. (354.6 x 47.1). 1–2. S–S–T3–11. Sir Raylton
    Dixon & Co, Middlesbrough (engines N.E. Marine Engineering
    Co, Newcastle). 1897 (14/8) launched. 1898 (5/3) MV Liverpool–
    Bahia–Rio de Janeiro. 1924 scrapped at Hamburg.
79. 1898 RAPHAEL
    4,699. 115,81 x 15,30. (380.0 x 50.2). 1–2. S–S–T3–11. D. & W.
    Henderson Ltd, Glasgow. 1898 (15/10) launched. 1898 (3/12) MV
    Liverpool–Buenos Aires. 1930 scrapped at Morecambe.
80. 1899 ROMNEY
    4,501. 115,81 x 15,30. (380.0 x 50.2). 1–2. S–S–T3–11. Sir Raylton
    Dixon & Co, Middlesbrough (engines T. Richardson & Sons,

Hartlepool). 1898 (19/10) launched. 1899 (7/2) MV Liverpool–
Buenos Aires. 1926 scrapped at Copenhagen.

81. 1899 REMBRANDT
4,667. 115,81 x 15,30. (380.0 x 50.2). 1–2. S–S–T3–11. D. & W.
Henderson Ltd, Glasgow. 1899 (29/3) launched. 1899 (22/5) MV
Liverpool–Buenos Aires. 1922 scrapped in Germany.

82. 1900 CALDERON (II)
4,083. 115,20 x 14,47. (378.0 x 47.5). 1–2. S–T3–11. Workman,
Clark & Co. Ltd, Belfast. 1900 (17/5) launched. 1900 (21/7) MV
Liverpool–Rio de Janeiro–Santos. 1912 (23/1) during voyage
Glasgow–Santos collided with ss MUSKETEER in R. Mersey;
broke in two.

83. 1900 ROSETTI
6,508. 123,56 x 15,91. (405.4 x 52.2) 1–2. S–T3–11. D. & W.
Henderson Ltd, Glasgow. 1900 (30/7) launched. 1900 (19/9) MV
Liverpool–Rio de Janeiro. 1929 scrapped at Danzig.

84. 1900 CAMOENS (II)
4,070. 115,20 x 14,47. (378.0 x 47.5). 1–2. S–T3–11. Workman,
Clark & Co Ltd, Belfast. 1900 (23/8) launched. 1900 (6/10) MV
Liverpool–Montevideo–Rosario. 1924 scrapped at Genoa.

85. 1902 THESPIS
4,343. 118,86 x 15,27. (390.0 x 50.1). 1–2. S–T3–11. Sir Raylton
Dixon & Co, Middlesbrough (engines Richardsons, Westgarth &
Co, Hartlepool). 1901 (29/10) launched. 1902 (11/1) MV Liverpool–Bahia–Rio de Janeiro. 1930 scrapped at Blyth.

86. 1902 TERENCE
4,309. 118,92 x 15,30. (390.2 x 50.2). 1–2. S–T3–11. D. & W.
Henderson Ltd, Glasgow. 1902 (22/4) launched. 1902 (10/6) MV
Clyde–Rio de Janeiro. 1917 (28/4) torpedoed and sunk by
German submarine near Fastnet.

87. 1902 TITIAN
4,170. 118,86 x 15,33. (390.0 x 50.3). 1–2. S–T3–11. Workman,
Clark & Co, Ltd, Belfast. 1902 (9/5) launched. 1902 (20/6) MV
Clyde–Rio de Janeiro. 1917 (26/8 torpedoed and sunk near
Malta.

88. 1902 TINTORETTO
4,181. 118,86 x 15,33. (390.0 x 50.3). 1–2. S–T3–11. Workman,
Clark & Co Ltd, Belfast. 1902 (5/7) launched. 1902 (6/9) MV
Liverpool–Rio de Janeiro–Santos. 1930 scrapped at Savona.

89. 1906 VERONESE
7,063. 141,72 x 18,04. (465.0 x 59.2). 1–2. S–T3–12. Workman,
Clark & Co Ltd, Belfast. 1905 (14/11) launched. 1906 (28/1) MV
Liverpool–Buenos Aires. 1906 (21/6) 2nd voyage Clyde–Buenos

Aires. 1906 (10/11) 3rd voyage ditto. 1913 (16/1) wrecked near Leixões on voyage Liverpool–Buenos Aires (43).

90. 1906 VELASQUEZ

7,542. 141,87 x 18,07. (465.5 x 59.3). 1–2. S–T3–12. Sir Raylton Dixon & Co, Middlesbrough (engines Richarsons, Westgarth & Co, Middlesbrough). 1905 (9/12) launched. 1906 (18/3) MV Liverpool–Buenos Aires. 1906 (2/8) 2nd voyage Clyde–Buenos Aires. 1906 (15/12) 3rd voyage Liverpool–Buenos Aires. Later voyages, Buenos Aires–New York. 1908 (16/10) wrecked on Sebastian Island, Brazil, Buenos Aires–New York.

91. 1907 VOLTAIRE

8,406. 147,91 x 17,74. (485.3 x 58.2). 1–2. S–T3–12. (I–60). D. & W. Henderson Ltd, Glasgow. 1907 (31/1) launched. 1907 (28/3) MV Middlesbrough–Liverpool (31/3)–Buenos Aires. 1907 (10/8) 2nd voyage Liverpool–Buenos Aires. 1970 (6/10) FV Buenos Aires–New York. Subsequent voyages ditto. 1916 (2/12) sunk by German raider MOEWE 600 miles W. of Fastnet.

92. 1911 VANDYCK (II)

10,328. 150,87 x 18,56. (495.0 x 60.9). 1–2. 2S–Q8–14. (I–280; II–130; III–200). Workman, Clark & Co Ltd, Belfast. 1911 (1/6) launched. 1911 (5/10) MV Liverpool–Buenos Aires (5 RV). 1912 (15/11) FV for RMSP (c), Southampton–Buenos Aires (2 RV). 1913 (29/3); FV Southampton–New York for Lamport & Holt; subsequently ran New York–Buenos Aires. 1914 (28/10) captured and sunk by German cruiser KARLSRUHE in South Atlantic.

93. 1912 VAUBAN

10,660. 151,02 x 18,53. (495.5 x 60.8). 1–2. 2S–Q8–15. (I–280; II–130; III–200). Workman, Clark & Co Ltd, Belfast. 1912 (20/1) launched. 1912 (4/5) MV Liverpool–Buenos Aires (2 RV). 1912 (4/10) FV for RMSP (c), Southampton–Buenos Aires (3 RV). 1913 ALCALA (RMSP (c)). 1913 (4/4) FV Southampton–Buenos Aires. 1913 (28/11) LV ditto. 1913 (28/12) FV Buenos Aires–New York as VAUBAN (Lamport & Holt). 1919–21 Buenos Aires–Liverpool (6 one-way voyages). 1932 scrapped at Inverkeithing.

94. (1912) ARCHIMEDES (II)

5,364. 132,12 x 16,52. (433.5 x 54.2). 1–2. S–T3–11. Russell & Co, Port Glasgow (engines D. Rowan & Co, Glasgow). 1911 launched as DEN OF AIRLIE (Br). 1912 ARCHIMEDES (Lamport & Holt). 1912 (28/5) FV Liverpool–R. Plate. 1932 BENMACDHUI (Br). 1941 (10/2) damaged by German air attack off Great Yarmouth. 1941 (21/12) sunk by mine off Spurn Head.

95. (1912) SIDDONS (II)

4,189. 117,40 x 15,54. (385.2 x 51.0). 1–4. S–T3–11. Sir W.G. Armstrong, Whitworth & Co Ltd, Walker-on-Tyne (engines N.E. Marine Engineering Co Ltd, Newcastle). 1910 (Jan) launched as TREMONT (Br). 1912 SIDDONS (Lamport & Holt). 1912 (1/6) FV Liverpool–S. America. 1923 CAMBRIAN MAID (Br). 1931 scrapped at Blyth.

96. (1912) EUCLID (II)

4,770. 125,02 x 15,85. (410.2 x 52.0). 1–2. S–T3–11. Northumberland Shipbuilding Co, Howdon-on-Tyne (engines Earle's Co Ltd, Hull). 1911 launched as HORLEY (Br). 1912 EUCLID (Lamport & Holt). 1912 (12/7) FV Clyde–Santos. 1931 BENVANNOCH (Br). 1936 MARIE MOLLER (Br). 1937 (22/3) severe fire damage off Holyhead. 1937 scrapped at Troon.

97. (1912) SPENSER (II)

4,186. 117,40 x 15,54. (385.2 x 51.0). 1–4. S–T3–11. Sir W.G. Armstrong, Whitworth & Co Ltd, Walker-on-Tyne (engines N.E. Marine Engineering Co Ltd, Newcastle). 1910 (Mar) launched as TRIPOLI (Br). 1912 SPENSER (Lamport & Holt). 1912 (24/7) FV Liverpool–R. Plate. 1918 (6/1) torpedoed and sunk by German submarine off Bardsey Island.

98. 1912 VESTRIS

10,494. 151,02 x 18,53. (495.5 x 60.8). 1–2. 2S–Q8–15. (I–280; II–130; III–200). Workman, Clark & Co Ltd, Belfast. 1912 (16/5) launched. 1912 (19/9) MV Liverpool–Buenos Aires. 1912 (26/10) FV Buenos Aires–New York. 1919–21 Buenos Aires–Liverpool (6 one-way voyages). 1928 (12/11) foundered 300 miles from Hampton Roads, USA (112).

99. 1912 DRYDEN (II)

5,839. 129,35 x 16,15. (424.4 x 53.0). 1–2. S–T3–11. Wm. Hamilton & Co, Port Glasgow (engines D. Rowan & Co, Glasgow). Laid down as BOLTON CASTLE (Br). Bought on stocks as DRYDEN (Lamport & Holt). 1912 (Sep) launched. 1912 (27/10) MV Liverpool–S. America. 1932 PANAGIOTIS TH. COUMANTAROS (Greek). 1940 EUGENIA (Greek). 1940 (16/5) sunk by German air attack off Ostend.

100. 1913 PASCAL (II)

5,587. 126,52 x 17,07. (415.4 x 56.0). 1–2. S–T3–11. A. McMillan & Son, Dumbarton (engines D. Rowan & Co, Glasgow). 1912 (24/12) launched. 1913 (19/4) MV Liverpool–Bahia–Santos. 1916 (17/12) torpedoed and sunk by German submarine off the Casquets.

101. 1913 PHIDIAS (II)

5,623. 126,55 x 17,07. (415.5 x 56.0). 1–2. S–T3–11. A. McMillan & Son, Dumbarton (engines D. Rowan & Co, Glasgow). 1913 (3/4) launched. 1913 (31/5) MV Liverpool–S. America. 1941 (8/6) torpedoed and sunk by German submarine near the Azores.

102. 1913 SOCRATES

4,979. 123,53 x 15,91. (405.3 x 52.2). 1–2. S–T3–11. Russell & Co, Port Glasgow (engines Rankin & Blackmore, Greenock). 1913 (2/9) launched. 1913 (8/11) MV Liverpool–R. Plate. 1930 P. MARGARONIS (Greek). 1940 (8/3) torpedoed and sunk by German submarine near Lands End.

103. 1913 STRABO (II)

4,920. 122,15 x 15,88. (400.8 x 52.1). 1–2. S–T3–11. A. McMillan & Son, Dumbarton (engines D. Rowan & Co, Glasgow). 1913 (Sep) launched. 1913 (27/11) MV Liverpool–S. America. 1932 PAULINE (Greek). 1934 PAVLINA (Greek). 1935 BRIGHT-VEGA (Br). 1936 SHOU SING. 1938 YAMAYURI MARU (Jap). 1944 (24/1) bombed and sunk by USA off Bougainville.

104. 1914 PLUTARCH

5,613, 129,07 x 17,07. (423.5 x 56.0). 1–2. S–T3–11. Russell & Co, Port Glasgow (engines J.G. Kincaid & Co, Greenock). 1913 (13/11) launched. 1914 MV Liverpool–S. America. 1931 DUR-MITOR (Yugoslavian) 1940 (21/10) captured by German raider ATLANTIS near Sundra Strait. 1941 (Feb) recaptured by H.M.S. SHROPSHIRE at Mogadishu. 1943 RADWINTER (Br). 1946 DURMITOR (Yugoslavian). 1963 scrapped at Split.

105. 1914 HERSCHEL (III)

6,293. 132,58 x 16,82. (435.0 x 55.2). 1–2. S–Q4–12. D. & W. Henderson Ltd, Glasgow. 1914 (23/4) launched. 1914 (4/10) MV Liverpool–Buenos Aires. 1934 scrapped in Italy.

106. 1915 HOLBEIN (II)

6,278. 132,82 x 16,82. (435.8 x 55.2). 1–2. S–Q4–12. D. & W. Henderson Ltd, Glasgow. 1914 (3/11) launched. 1915 MV Liverpool–S. America. 1935 scrapped in Italy.

107. (1919) VASARI

10,117. 148,12 x 18,07. (486.0 x 59.3). 1–2. S–Q4–14. (I–200; II–48; III–70). Sir Raylton Dixon & Co, Middlesbrough. 1908 (8/12) launched. 1909 (24/4) MV River Tees–Plymouth–New York (arr 9/5; dep 20/5)–Buenos Aires. 1919 FV Buenos Aires–Liverpool. 1921 LV ditto (7 one-way voyages). 1928 ARCTIC QUEEN (Br. cargo steamer). 1935 PISTCHEVALA INDUSTRIA (USSR). 1960 removed from *Lloyd's Register*.

108. 1921 HOGARTH (II)

      8,109. 134,80 x 16,88. (442.3 x 55.4). 1–2. S–ST(SR)–14.
(III–230). D. & W. Henderson Ltd, Glasgow (engines Harland &
Wolff, Belfast). 1933 scrapped at Port Glasgow.

FUNNEL: Blue with broad white band surmounted by broad black top.
FLAG: Horizontal red-white-red stripes. L+H in black on the white.

Chapter 14

1864–83

LAVARELLO LINE

1864. Captain Giovanni Battista Lavarello
1871. G. B. Lavarello & Co

(Italian)

Captain GIOVANNI BATTISTA LAVARELLO opened an office in Genoa in 1863, and placed an order almost at once with Giacomo Westermann of Sestri Ponente for the 663 ton wooden screw clipper BUENOS AIRES, which started her maiden voyage from Genoa to Montevideo and Buenos Aires on 4 January 1864. When using her engines alone her speed was a modest five knots, but with a full spread of canvas and a favourable wind the passage to Buenos Aires was said to be completed in about 30 days. However, her second voyage started from Genoa on 9 October 1864, her third on 16 August 1865 and her fourth on 16 June 1866 – all of which makes the 30 day claim highly suspect.

Encouraged by the apparent success of the BUENOS AIRES, Alessandro Cerruti fu Antonio (Chapter 15) started a parallel service in November 1865, and towards the end of 1867 introduced an iron screw steamer, followed a year or so later by a second-hand one of similar construction.

Captain Lavarello decided to commission a second ship, the 721 ton wooden screw clipper MONTEVIDEO, which left Genoa on 19 November 1867. She was followed in 1869–70 by the 798 ton LIGURIA and the 837 ton AQUILA, it being announced that the three would undertake a monthly service between Genoa and Buenos Aires. The pioneer BUENOS AIRES was detailed to make a connection from Buenos Aires to Valparaiso, Chile, and Callao, Peru, via Cape Horn.

Further competition came from the Società Italo Platense (Chapter 22), which started operations between Genoa and Buenos Aires in June 1870 with the first of three 1,790 ton iron screw steamers built in England.

Not to be outdone, Captain Lavarello ordered from Wigham Richardson of Walker-on-Tyne the 1,865 ton iron screw steamer ESPRESSO, which was launched on 27 September 1870 and started her maiden voyage from Genoa on 23 February 1871 for Marseilles, Cadiz, Tenerife (for coal), Montevideo and Buenos Aires. She had a modern appearance

102

with a straight stem, a single funnel and four masts. Her compound engines gave her a speed in excess of 11 knots – hence her name – enabling her in all truth to complete the voyage to Montevideo in about 30 days. Her passenger complement was 34 first class and 900 steerage.

One full-powered modern steamer was insufficient to meet the Italo Platense competition, however, and on 2 December 1871 the firm of G.B. LAVARELLO & CO was registered in Genoa with a capital of four million lire (£160,000), the directors being Captain Lavarello and Matteo Bruzzo, treasurer of the Genoa municipality. With the aid of a bond issue of 3½ million lire, orders were placed with Wigham Richardson for the 2,200 ton EUROPA, SUD AMERICA and NORD AMERICA of an improved ESPRESSO class. Their service speed was 12 knots, and they could accommodate 50 first class, 50 second and 800 steerage passengers. They were commissioned in 1872–3, their usual itinerary being Genoa, Gibraltar, Cadiz, St. Vincent (for coal). Montevideo and Buenos Aires, although from time to time they proceeded on to Rosario to load cereals for the homeward voyage. The name ESPRESSO was no longer particularly appropriate, so this vessel was renamed COLOMBO in 1874 in honour of Italy's most famous sailor, Christopher Columbus.

One of the first results of these acquisitions was that the engines of the BUENOS AIRES and MONTEVIDEO were removed, but the outcome was fatal as the BUENOS AIRES was sunk in collision with the British steamer MARATHON and the MONTEVIDEO wrecked near the Cape of Good Hope on 9 January 1874.

In 1876 the engines of the LIGURIA and AQUILA were also discarded, but infinitely more important from Lavarello's point of view was that the Italo Platense service was withdrawn during the same year and their three ships sold. Moreover, Cerruti had died in 1872 and although his two surviving ships were taken over by Sivori & Schiaffino of Genoa, the service was continued with decreasing success until 1878, when it was abandoned.

Captain Lavarello himself died in December 1881 at the age of 57, and was replaced on the board of G.B. Lavarello & Co by his sons Enrico and Pietro. But by this time the Company was in financial difficulties, which were aggravated by the loss of the NORD AMERICA on the Spanish coast on 2 January 1883. Only a few weeks later, on 28 February, G. B. Lavarello & Co went into liquidation. Matteo Bruzzo one of the liquidators, was responsible almost at once for setting up the firm of M. BRUZZO & CO (Chapter 34), and in due course the Lavarello Brothers founded the SOCIETÀ DI NAVIGAZIONE A VAPORE FRATELLI LAVARELLO (Chapter 39). There was a further change in 1884 when the well-known LA VELOCE LINEA DI NAVIGAZIONE A VA-

PORE (Chapter 35) was formed and acquired, *inter alia*, three of Captain Lavarello's ships.

1. 1864 BUENOS AIRES
663. 44,00 x 8,80. (144.4 x 28.9). C–1–3. W–S–?–5. (I; III–200/300). Giacomo Westermann, Sestri Ponente. 1863 launched. 1864 (4/1) MV Genoa–Montevideo–Buenos Aires. 1864. (9/10) 2nd voyage ditto. 1865 (16/8) 3rd voyage ditto, 1866 (16/6) 4th voyage ditto. 1870 ran in connecting service, Buenos Aires–Valparaiso–Callao. 1873 engines removed. 1873 (6/7) sunk in collision with ss MARATHON (Br) on voyage Chile–Buenos Aires.

2. 1867 MONTEVIDEO
721. C–1–3. W–S–?–7. Giacomo Westermann, Sestri Ponente. 1867 launched. 1867 (19/11) MV Genoa–Montevideo–Buenos Aires. 1868 (25/6) 2nd voyage ditto. 1873 engines removed. 1874 (9/1) wrecked near Cape of Good Hope.

3. 1869 LIGURIA
798. C–1–3. W.S–?–7. Giacomo Westermann, Sestri Ponente. 1869 launched. 1869 (27/11) MV Genoa–Montevideo–Buenos Aires. 1876 engines removed. 1876 AUSONIA (Italian sailing ship); wrecked in Red Sea.

4. 1870 AQUILA
837. C–1–3. W–S–?–7. Giacomo Westermann, Sestri Ponente. 1870 launched. 1870 (27/8) MV Genoa–Montevideo–Buenos Aires–Genoa (arr 1870 (15/12). 1876 engines removed; sold at Malaga.

5. 1871 ESPRESSO
(1874) COLOMBO
1,865. 91,09 x 10,82. (298.9 x 35.5). S–1–4. I–S–C2–11. (I–34; III–900). Wigham Richardson & Co, Walker-on-Tyne. 1870 (27/9) launched as ESPRESSO. 1871 (23/2) MV Genoa–Marseilles–Cadiz–Tenerife–Montevideo–Buenos Aires. 1874 COLOMBO (Lavarello). 1883 ditto (M. Bruzzo & Co). 1884 NAPOLI (La Veloce; 2,009 tons. 1893 (5/12) abandoned off Brazilian coast. (See La Veloce (35)).

6. 1872 EUROPA
2,226. 95,46 x 10,79. (313.2 x 35.4). S–1–4. I–S–C2–12. (I–75; II–52; III–750). Wigham Richarson & Co, Walker-on-Tyne. 1872 (27/2) launched. 1872 MV Genoa–Gibraltar–Cadiz–St. Vincent (for coal)–Montevideo–Buenos Aires. 1883 EUROPA (M. Bruzzo & Co). 1884 ditto (La Veloce). 1884 (18/6) FV Genoa–S. America. 1893 scrapped. (See La Veloce (35)).

7. 1872 SUD AMERICA
2,246. 95,70 x 10,76. (314.0 x 35.3). S–1–4. I–S–C2–12. (I–75; II–52; III–750). Wigham Richardson & Co, Walker-on-Tyne. 1872 (12/6) launched. 1872 MV Genoa–Gibraltar–Cadiz–St. Vincent (for coal)–Montevideo–Buenos Aires. 1883 SUD AMERICA (M. Bruzzo & Co). 1884 ditto (La Veloce). 1888 (13/9) sunk in collision with ss FRANCE (SGTM collier) at Las Palmas (See La Veloce (35)).
8. 1873 NORD AMERICA
2,175. 95,79 x 10,82. (314.3 x 35.5). S–1–4. I–S–C2–12. (I–50; II–50; III–800). Wigham Richardson & Co, Walker-on-Tyne (engines R. & W. Hawthorn, Newcastle). 1872 (23/11) launched. 1873 (10/4) MV Genoa–Gibraltar–Cadiz–St. Vincent (for coal)– Montevideo–Buenos Aires. 1883 (2/1) wrecked on Spanish coast.

Chapter 15

1865–72

LINEA NAZIONALE DI NAVIGAZIONE A VAPORE

(CERRUTI LINE)

(Italian)

ALESSANDRO CERRUTI FU ANTONIO of Genoa watched the activities of the Compagnia Transatlantica (Chapter 7) and of Captain Giovanni Battista Lavarello (Chapter 14) with increasing interest. The latter had sent the 663 ton wooden screw clipper BUENOS AIRES on her maiden voyage from Genoa to Montevideo and Buenos Aires in January 1864, and almost at once Cerruti decided to inaugurate his own South American line, which he advertised as the LINEA NAZIONALE DI NAVIGAZIONE A VAPORE (or sometimes as the Linea di Navigazione a Vapore Nazionale).

An order was placed with Agostino Briasco of Sestri Ponente, Italy, for the 680 ton CLEMENTINA (I), a wooden screw clipper, whose length of 57 metres (187 feet) was apparently 13 metres (43 feet) greater than that of the BUENOS AIRES. She was supplied by Ansaldo of Sampierdarena with an engine of 145 horse-power, giving her a speed of seven knots, again appreciably more than that of her rival. A limited number of first class berths and about 250 steerage were fitted. The CLEMENTINA was launched on 15 July 1865 and sailed from Genoa on 5 December for Montevideo and Buenos Aires.

Cerruti decided almost at once that the CLEMENTINA was sufficiently successful to justify ordering a consort from the same builder. The 792 ton AGNESE had a length of 71 metres (230 feet), and a vertical two-cylinder engine, giving her a speed of about eight knots on a daily consumption of 15 tons of coal. First class accommodation in the poop was provided for 43 passengers, who occupied porthole cabins on either side of the dining saloon. The 50 second class berths were at the forward end, with accommodation for 250 steerage in the 'tween decks.

The AGNESE's maiden voyage started from Genoa on 2 November 1866, but only a few weeks later, on 12 December, the CLEMENTINA was destroyed by fire at her berth in Genoa when loading for a further voyage.

At this stage, Cerruti stole a march on Lavarello by deciding to replace the CLEMENTINA (I) by an iron screw CLEMENTINA (II). There were very few facilities in Italy at that time for building in iron, so Cerruti went to Palmer Brothers of Jarrow-on-Tyne for a 1,384 ton ship, which had a speed of nearly 10 knots and accommodation for 50 first class, 60 second and 250 steerage passengers. She was ready in time to sail from Genoa on 2 November 1867. The somewhat larger ISABELLA was completed by Wigham Richardson & Co of Walker-on-Tyne in 1869 and followed her predecessor to Montevideo and Buenos Aires.

Cerruti died in 1872 and the CLEMENTINA (II) and ISABELLA were taken over by Sivori & Schiaffino of Genoa, who arranged for them to continue in the South American trade without change of name. By this time, however, Lavarello had commissioned the 1,865 ton iron screw ESPRESSO, and three larger ships of similar construction were on the way. Sivori & Schiaffino, having come to the conclusion that they were not in a position to acquire ships to meet this new competition, continued with decreasing success until 1878, when the CLEMENTINA and ISABELLA were sold and renamed CENTRO AMERICA and RIO DE LA PLATA. They were put up for auction a few years later, to become the CENISIO and RIGHI. After a spell with two British firms the CENISIO became the Portuguese ELISA in 1891 and the Brazilian CRUZEIRO in 1895, only to be wrecked during the same year. The RIGHI was acquired by a Hull owner in 1888. She was wrecked near Drontheim (Trondheim) on 9 September 1894.

1. 1865 CLEMENTINA (I)
    680. 57,00 x 9,00. (187.0 x 29.5). C–1–3. W–S–?–7. (I; III–250). Agostino Briasco, Sestri Ponente (engines Ansaldo, Sampierdarena). 1865 (15/7) launched. 1865 (5/12) MV Genoa–Montevideo–Buenos Aires. 1866 (12/12) destroyed by fire in port at Genoa.
2. 1866 AGNESE
    792. 71,00 x 9,75. (230.0 x 32.0). C–1–3. W–S–V2–8. (I–43; II–50; III–240). Agostino Briasco, Sestri Ponente (engines Ansaldo, Sampierdarena). 1866 (27/6) launched. 1866 (2/11) MV Genoa–Montevideo–Buenos Aires. 1873 engines removed.
3. 1867 CLEMENTINA (II)
    1,384. 66,37 x 11,00. (217.8 x 36.1). 1–2. I–S–I(2)–10. (I–50; II–60; III–250). Palmer Bros & Co, Jarrow-on-Tyne. 1867 (30/7) launched. 1867 (2/11) MV Genoa–Montevideo–Buenos Aires. 1874 CLEMENTINA (Sivori & Schiaffino (Italian)). 1878 CENTRO AMERICA (Italian). 1889 CENISIO (F. Stumore & Co, London); new compound engines. 1890 CENISIO (Christ-

opher Furness). 1891 ELISA (Portuguese). 1895 CRUZEIRO (Brazilian). 1895 (Dec) wrecked near Aracaju, Brazil.
4. 1869 ISABELIA
1,391. 77,20 x 11,03. (253.3 x 36.2). 1–2. I–S–I(2)–10. Wigham Richardson & Co, Walker-on-Tyne (engines R. & W. Hawthorn, Newcastle). 1869 (Sep) launched for Cerruti. 1869 MV Genoa–Montevideo–Buenos Aires. 1874 ISABELLA (Sivori & Schiaffino (It)). 1878 RIO DE LA PLATA (It). 1888 RIGHI (R. Jameson & Co, Hull). 1894 ditto (Bryson & Jameson & Co, Hull). 1894 (9/9) wrecked near Drontheim (Trondheim) while on passage to Soroka, White Sea.

Chapter 16

1866–1963

BOOTH LINE

(1863) Alfred Booth & Company
1881 Booth Steamship Company Limited
1901 Booth Steamship Company (1901) Limited
1901 Booth Steamship Company Limited

(British)

Alfred Booth, born in Liverpool in 1834, took up temporary residence in the United States in 1857 and three years later entered into partnership in New York with an American named Walden in a firm of importers, which adopted the style of Walden & Booth. In 1863 Walden retired owing to ill health, and Alfred Booth was joined by his younger brother, Charles, the name of the firm being changed to Booth & Company. An office was also opened in Liverpool under the name ALFRED BOOTH & COMPANY.

In a matter of months it was decided to start a steamship line from Liverpool to the North Brazilian ports of Ceara, Maranham and Para, at that time served solely by sailing ships, and in 1865 an order was placed with the Liverpool shipbuilders Hart & Sinnot for two iron screw steamers, the 1,106 ton AUGUSTINE and the 1,090 ton JEROME, each with accommodation for 25 first class and 50 steerage passengers. The AUGUSTINE left Liverpool on 15 February 1866 on her maiden voyage to Lisbon, Ceara, Maranham and Para, and was followed by the JEROME in May.

Two years later the 1,168 ton AMBROSE was ordered from A. Leslie & Co of Hebburn-on-Tyne, and was placed in service in 1869. More or less simultaneously, R. Singlehurst & Co of Liverpool, who had been running sailing ships to Brazil for many years, commissioned three iron screw steamers newly-built by T. Royden & Sons of Liverpool for a service known as the Red Cross Line (Chapter 20), which ran parallel with that of the Booth Line.

Thus, serious competition existed between the two firms, but common sense soon prevailed, and in 1870 it was agreed that each concern should be responsible for a fortnightly sailing.

The 915 ton BERNARD was built for Booth by Royden in 1870, and owing to the loss of one of the Red Cross ships at this time two further

1,500 tonners were laid down for them by the same builders. The result was a total of four ships for Booth, four for Red Cross as well as a further two for the Maranham Steamship Company of Liverpool, a newly-founded concern which agreed to confine its activities to a direct service between Liverpool and Maranham.

The 1,171 ton MIRFIELD, built in 1871 by Scott of Greenock, was bought second-hand by Booth in 1880 and in due course renamed BASIL.

Hitherto, as was often the case in those days, the ownership of the Booth ships was divided into 64 shares, of which Alfred Booth & Company invariably held the vast majority, most of the remainder being in the hands of a member of the Holt family, which was connected by marriage and friendship with the Booths. Indeed, Alfred Booth had started his business career as an apprentice in the firm of Lamport & Holt (Chapter 13). In 1881 it was decided to discard the 64 share system, and on 25 June of that year the BOOTH STEAMSHIP COMPANY LIMITED was formed.

The fleet continued to grow. The 1,227 ton BARBARY was bought from David MacIver & Co in 1881 and renamed CLEMENT a year later. The 1,190 ton PACAXO, built in 1882 by the London & Glasgow Company, became the Booth CYRIL in 1884, while in the same year T. Royden & Sons delivered the 1,657 ton LANFRANC, which started her maiden voyage on 19 September. The 1,587 ton LAURIUM, built in 1880, became the GREGORY in 1889, the 1,744 ton PONCA became the JUSTIN in 1890, the 1,612 ton GLOAMIN became the ORIGEN in 1891 and the 1,983 ton RED SEA became the HILARY in 1892. Thus, the Company had commissioned a total of 13 ships by 1892, although the first four were sold between 1889 and 1893. Two new vessels, the 1,947 ton HILDEBRAND and the 1,965 ton HUBERT, were completed in 1893–4 by Hall, Russell & Co of Aberdeen. They shared with the ORIGEN and HILARY the advantages of being built of steel instead of iron, and of having triple-expansion engines instead of compound.

Some items of importance call for belated mention – from about the middle 1870s some ships proceeded 1,000 miles up the Amazon to Manaos. In 1889 or earlier many sailings took place via Hamburg or Havre and some, instead, via Penarth, there to take on coal. In 1880 the twin-screw launch BELEM was built by Christopher Strickland of Liverpool and fitted with engines by J.H. Wilson & Co, for the Booth Line. She took part in mail and passenger traffic on the Amazon. [1] Towards the end of the 1880s, the Booth and Red Cross lines built up fleets of tugs and lighters for service at the principal Brazilian ports of call. It was in 1887 that Alfred Booth retired from active involvement in the business, but remained a director until his death in 1914.

The Company decided in 1895 to order three large cargo steamers, the 2,966 ton DOMINIC, DUNSTAN and POLYCARP, from Barclay Curle of Glasgow, while the HORATIO, catering for bulk cargo shipments to Brazilian ports and the Amazon, was bought second-hand in the same year and entered the Booth fleet without a name change. On occasions there was insufficient homeward cargo for the ships, in which case they proceeded in ballast to Galveston to load cotton. A further ship of similar type was the 3,378 ton LEYDEN, which in 1897 became Booth's BENEDICT.

Two large passenger ships were acquired at this time from the Castle Line – the 3,498 ton GRANTULLY CASTLE and the 3,056 ton WARWICK CASTLE, which in 1896–7 became the AUGUSTINE (II) and JEROME (II).

1896 AUGUSTINE 3,498
Built 1880 as Castle Line GRANTULLY CASTLE.

No fewer than eight ships were sold in 1897–9 – the BASIL, CLEMENT, ANSELM, LANFRANC, CYRIL, GREGORY, JUSTIN and ORIGEN.

In 1898, a year after the Red Cross Line started sailings from Liverpool to Iquitos, Peru, 2,000 miles from the mouth of the Amazon, Booth were instrumental in starting the Booth Iquitos Steamship Company Limited, for which they acquired the 960 ton steamer HUASCAR and the 1,016 ton BOLIVAR.

The 3,200 ton MOURNE and MOUNT SIRION, built by Workman Clark of Belfast in 1895, were bought by Booth in 1898 and renamed BASIL (II) and BERNARD (II). In addition, the 3,445 ton LA PLATA (III), one of three ships built by Royal Mail in 1896 to carry emigrants to South America, was acquired in 1900 and renamed CLEMENT (II).

In 1901 agreement was reached between the Singlehurst family and the

Booth Line for the latter to take over the Red Cross Line. A new title, the BOOTH STEAMSHIP COMPANY (1901) LIMITED, came into use, the combined fleet consisting of 25 ships, of which Red Cross provided 11 of 25,411 tons (average tonnage 2,310). The Booth contribution was 14 of 39,923 tons (average 2,851). Five more ships from the Booth Iquitos Steamship Company and the Red Cross Iquitos Steamship Company were amalgamated into the Iquitos Steamship Company Limited. At about the same time, Booth took over the Maranham Steamship Company, but did not obtain any ships from them.

The 4,594 ton AMBROSE (II) was delivered by Sir Raylton Dixon & Co of Middlesbrough in 1903 and could accommodate 149 first class and 330 third class passengers. A year later the 4,380 HAWARDEN CASTLE of the recently-formed Union–Castle Mail Steamship Company was acquired as the CYRIL (II), followed by the newly-built 3,500 ton BONIFACE, JUSTIN (II) and CUTHBERT, all three with 16 first class berths and 100 third.

By this time, three of the ex-Red Cross ships had been sold – the PARAENSE in 1902, and the LISBONENSE and SOBRALENSE in 1904.

Booth's largest ship to date, the 5,442 ton ANSELM (II), was launched by Workman Clark of Belfast on 10 January 1905 and started her maiden voyage from Liverpool to the Amazon via Havre on 29 March 1905. Misfortune struck later that year, on 5 September, when she collided with and sank the CYRIL (II) in the Amazon – the first loss of a ship during the 39 years of the Company's active existence. For some time its ships had frequently been proceeding from Para to Manaos, a thousand miles up the Amazon.

Three more ships followed the ANSELM in quick succession – the 6,439 ton twin-screw ANTONY from Hawthorn Leslie of Hebburn-on-Tyne in 1907 and the 6,275 ton LANFRANC (II) and the 6,325 ton HILARY (II), both from Caledon of Dundee in 1907–08. All accommodated 200 first class and 350 third class passengers and were the first twin-screw units of the fleet.

A short-term acquisition in 1907 was the Portuguese-owned Andresen Line's DONA MARIA, built by Wigham Richardson in 1887 as the PORT FAIRY. She reverted to this name, but only remained two years with the Company.

In 1907, also, the GREGORY (II) was transferred to the Iquitos Steamship Company, as were the HILDEBRAND and HUBERT in 1908, renamed HUAYNA and ATAHUALPA, respectively. They were incorporated into the Booth fleet in 1911 without further change of name, as was the 2,979 ton MANCO, completed in 1908. Her passenger complement was 62 first class and 92 third.

112

1907 LANFRANC 6,275 tons
In 1917 torpedoed and sunk by German submarine in English Channel.

Eight ex-Red Cross ships remained in the fleet, but all were disposed of – two in 1909, four in 1910 and two, the 2,769 ton CEARENSE of 1891 and the 2,828 ton AMAZONENSE of 1899 in 1911. In addition, the HILARY, JEROME, HORATIO, POLYCARP and AUGUSTINE were sold in 1911–2.

This made room for a batch of new single-screw passenger – cargo steamers – the 3,900 ton FRANCIS and HUBERT (II) (17 first class and 100 third class passengers) in 1910, the 4,400 ton CHRISTOPHER, STEPHEN and DENIS (36 first and 100 third) in 1910–1, and the almost identical PANCRAS and AIDAN in 1911.

Larger than any of her predecessors, the 6,995 ton twin-screw HILDEBRAND (II), launched on 14 February 1911 by Scott's Ship-building & Engineering Company of Greenock, began her maiden voyage two months later from Liverpool via Havre. She accommodated 218 first class and 406 third class passengers.

The 4,383 ton FORT SALISBURY, built for the Bucknall Line in 1895, became the Booth VINCENT. She sailed from Liverpool on 3 March 1913, but was disposed of to Andrew Weir & Co later in the same year.

Two ships were commissioned in 1914, just after the outbreak of World War I. The 3,172 ton MICHAEL sailed in August and the 5,223 ton ALBAN on 13 November 1914, the latter proceeding to New York before continuing to the Amazon.

Sir Raylton Dixon & Co of Middlesbrough launched the 5,220 ton OSWALD on 23 September 1914. She was completed without her passenger accommodation in the following year and requisitioned for Government service. She was torpedoed and sunk by a German submarine on 23 April 1917 about 200 miles south-west of the Fastnet.

113

The 3,550 ton ORIGEN (II) was completed by the Caledon Shipbuilding & Engineering Company of Dundee in 1918, and sailed in convoy from Falmouth on 29 June for Brazil but a German submarine sank her only a day later. One further ship, the POLYCARP (II), was completed during the war.

The HILDEBRAND (II), HILARY (II) and AMBROSE (II) were taken up as armed merchant cruisers soon after the outbreak of hostilities. The AMBROSE was bought outright by the Admiralty in 1915 and converted into a submarine depot ship. The Company was extremely fortunate in the matter of losses until 17 March 1917, when the ANTONY was torpedoed and sunk near the Coninbeg Lightship, and then a long string of disasters followed. The CRISPIN succumbed near Waterford on 29 March, the LANFRANC (II), when serving as a hospital ship and carrying wounded British and German troops, was sunk between Havre and Southampton on 17 April, while the loss of the OSWALD on 23 April has already been mentioned. The PANCRAS was deliberately run ashore on 15 May on passage from Gibraltar to Genoa to avoid a German submarine, which had been shadowing her, and 10 days later the HILARY was torpedoed and sunk in the North Sea. The BONIFACE was torpedoed and sunk near Aran on 8 July 1917, while the BASIL was rammed and sunk by the French steamer MARGAUX during the night of 11 November when sailing without lights from Southampton to Boulogne with a cargo of ammunition, 14 out of 30 lives being lost. Finally, the PANCRAS was torpedoed on 3 May 1918 when in convoy in the Mediterranean, but fortunately the torpedo did not explode and it was possible to tow her to Malta.

Despite all these losses there was no immediate need after the Armistice to acquire new ships as business to and from Brazil was at a low ebb. In fact, the passenger liner ANSELM was sold to Argentine owners in 1922, while the DOMINIC and DUNSTAN were sold in 1923 for further trading, as were the BENEDICT and MICHAEL in 1924.

The 4,870 ton cargo steamers BASIL and BONIFACE were delivered by Hawthorn Leslie in 1928 and a similar ship, the BENEDICT, by Cammell Laird in 1930. The Company had decided to concentrate on both passenger liners and purely cargo ships, which meant a gradual phasing out of the once numerous passenger–cargo ships.

Meanwhile, the passenger–cargo steamers often sailed outwards from Liverpool and the Continent to North Brazil and the Amazon, then did one or more round voyages between Brazil and New York before returning to the United Kingdom via Brazil. Booth Line sailings between New York and Brazil had, in fact, been in operation for quite a long time, but do not come within the scope of this chapter.

Since the sale of the ANSELM in 1922 the only passenger liner in the fleet was the HILDEBRAND (II), dating from 1911. An order was accordingly placed with Cammell Laird for the 7,403 ton single-screw HILARY (III), which could accommodate 80 first and 250 third class passengers. She was launched on 17 April 1931 and sailed from Liverpool on her maiden voyage in August for Oporto, Lisbon, Madeira, Para and Manaos. A year later, the HILDEBRAND was laid up and was scrapped in 1934.

No fewer than nine passenger–cargo steamers were sold between 1930 and 1936 – the JUSTIN, CUTHBERT, FRANCIS, DENIS, PANCRAS, HUBERT, STEPHEN, ALBAN and AIDAN, thus disposing of the last of the type.

The 5,000 ton cargo steamers CLEMENT and CRISPIN were built by Cammell Laird in 1934 and the DUNSTAN (II) was bought second-hand.

The 5,954 ton ANSELM (III) joined the HILARY in time to start her maiden voyage from Liverpool to Manaos on 31 December 1935. A single-screw ship driven by single-reduction geared turbines, she was a product of Wm. Denny & Brothers of Dumbarton.

At the outbreak of World War II in September 1939 the fleet consisted of nine ships, including the HILARY and ANSELM. Five were lost by enemy action, the first being the CLEMENT, which was sunk off the Brazilian coast by the German pocket battleship ADMIRAL GRAF SPEE on 30 September 1939. As is well-known, the German ship was scuttled off Montevideo in December 1939, four days after the Battle of the River Plate. The second loss was of the World War I POLYCARP near Ushant on 2 June 1940. The CRISPIN, in service as an auxiliary cruiser, was torpedoed and sunk in the North Atlantic on 3 February 1941, while the DUNSTAN was bombed and sunk by German aircraft on 6 April 1941 off the north-west coast of Scotland. Finally, the ANSELM, serving as a troopship, was torpedoed and sunk on 5 July 1941 in the North Atlantic.

The HILARY had an exciting wartime career and survived despite being struck amidships by an enemy torpedo which failed to explode. She was returned to the Company in 1945.

When the war ended the Booth fleet consisted only of the passenger steamer HILARY and the cargo steamers BASIL, BONIFACE and BENEDICT. The directors decided that the task of rebuilding an adequate fleet was one that they could not contemplate, but at an opportune moment the Vestey Group, then best-known in connection with the Blue Star Line, made an offer for the Booth Steamship Company Limited, together with their shipping activities in Brazil, New York and Liverpool. The offer was accepted, but the Booth Line retained their offices, their staff ashore and afloat and their fleet of ships, which soon began to carry on their black funnels a replica of the houseflag on either side – a white rectangle with a red saltire surmounted by a large blue 'B'.

One of the first steps necessary after the war was the reconditioning of the HILARY, whose passenger accommodation was amended to 93 first class and 138 tourist. And although the subsequent activities of the Booth Line are concerned largely with cargo ships, three more passenger ships were built or acquired. The 7,735 ton HILDEBRAND (III) was launched by Cammel Laird on 20 July 1951, a single-screw ship driven by double-reduction geared turbines. She was followed by the 7,905 ton HUBERT (III), which was launched by Cammel Laird on 31 August 1954 and left Liverpool on her maiden voyage to the Amazon on 11 February 1955. She, too, was driven by a set of double-reduction geared turbines and had accommodation for 74 first class and 96 tourist passengers.

1951 HILDEBRAND 7,735 tons
Wrecked in fog near Lisbon in 1957.

In 1956 intermediate calls by the passenger steamers were introduced at Trinidad and Barbados.

On 25 September 1957 the HILDEBRAND, outward bound from Liverpool to the Amazon was approaching Lisbon in dense fog when she stranded near Cascais. For a month or more strenuous efforts were made to refloat her but to no avail. There were no casualties.

The HILARY (III) was bought by Thos W. Ward in 1959 and scrapped at Inverkeithing, leaving the HUBERT as the only passenger ship. However, in 1961 the 10,868 ton twin-screw motorship THYSVILLE (ex-BAUDOUINVILLE), built by John Cockerill of Hoboken, Antwerp, in 1950 for service between Antwerp and the Belgian Congo, was acquired and rebuilt to carry 135 first class and 101 tourist passengers. She was renamed ANSELM (IV), and was considerably larger than any predecessor in the fleet.

Unfortunately, the air lines in all parts of the world were securing the cream of the passenger traffic, and it was decided only two years after her acquisition that the ANSELM was superfluous. She was, therefore, passed to the Blue Star Line in 1963 for service between London, Brazil and the River Plate as the IBERIA STAR, but they, too, soon found her surplus to requirements and in 1965 she became the AUSTRALASIA of the Austasia Line, another Vestey Group concern.

It was decided in 1964 that Booth would sever their connection with the passenger business. This must have been a sad blow for both the sea and shore personnel, but judging by the actions of so many other companies it was seemingly unavoidable. In consequence, the HUBERT (III) was taken over by the Austasia Line as the MALAYSIA.

However, the Booth Line, now well over 100 years old, is still running a service between Liverpool, Trinidad, Barbados, North Brazil and the River Amazon with semi-container ships. The first of these was the BENEDICT (III), followed by the BONIFACE (III), both launched in 1978 and managed by Blue Star Management Limited.

Practically all the Booth Line steamers were named after people connected with the early Christian church.

[1] Liverpool *Daily Post* 20/5/1880.

1. 1866 AUGUSTINE (I)
   1,106. 65,06 x 9,02. (213.5 x 29.6). 1–2. I–S–C2–10. (I–25; III–50). Hart & Sinnot, Liverpool (engines J. Taylor & Co, Birkenhead). 1865 (4/11) launched. 1866 (15/2) MV Liverpool–Lisbon–Ceara–Maranham–R. Amazon. 1892 AUGUSTINE (Maltese). 1906 (2/3) wrecked at Benghazi.
2. 1866 JEROME (I)
   1,090. 65,15 x 9,05. (213.8 x 29.7). 1–2. I–S–C2–10. (I–25; III–50). Hart & Sinnot, Liverpool (engines J. Taylor & Co, Birkenhead). 1865 (17/3) launched. 1866 (May) MV Liverpool–R. Amazon. 1890 MURCIA (Br). 1898 scrapped at Garston.
3. 1869 AMBROSE (I)
   1,168. 73,75 x 9,02. (242.0 x 29.6). 1–2. I–S–C2–10. A. Leslie & Co, Hebburn-on-Tyne (engines Fawcett, Preston & Co, Liverpool). 1869 launched. 1869 MV Liverpool–R. Amazon. 1893 AMBROSE (Br). 1898 coal hulk in R. Thames.
4. 1871 BERNARD (I)
   915. 72,29 x 7,98 (237.2 x 26.2). 1–2. I–S–C2–10. T. Royden & Sons, Liverpool (engines Fawcett, Preston & Co, Liverpool). 1870 (Oct) launched. 1871 MV Liverpool–R. Amazon. 1889 sold to USA. 1897 (19/10) wrecked at Port Morant, Jamaica.

5. (1880) MIRFIELD
   (1882) BASIL (I)
   1,171. 67,47 x 9,26. (221.4 x 30.4). 1–2. I–S–C2–10. Scott & Co,
   Greenock (engines Greenock Foundry Co). 1871 (1/12) launched
   as MIRFIELD (Br). 1880 MIRFIELD (Booth). 1880 FV
   Liverpool–R. Amazon. 1882 BASIL (Booth). 1882 (2/1) FV
   Liverpool–Para. 1897 SALINAS (Empreza Navegação Gran
   Para). 1904 (Oct) wrecked at Maranham.
6. (1881) BARBARY
   (1882) CLEMENT (I)
   1,227. 70,22 x 9,48. (230.4 x 31.1). 1–2. I–S–C2–10. Laird Bros,
   Birkenhead (engines Westgarth, English & Co, Middlesbrough).
   1877 (Feb) launched as BARBARY (David MacIver & Co). 1881
   BARBARY (Booth). 1881 FV Liverpool–R. Amazon. 1882
   CLEMENT (Booth). 1882 (24/11) FV Liverpool–R. Amazon.
   1897 MARAJO (Empreza Navegação Gran Para). 1912 hulked.
7. 1883 ANSELM (I)
   1,562. 82,60 x 10,30. (271.0 x 33.8). 1–2. I–S–C2–10. A. Leslie &
   Co, Hebburn-on-Tyne (engines R. Stephenson & Co, Newcastle). 1882 launched. 1883 (8/1) MV Liverpool–R. Amazon. 1898
   sold. 1908 scrapped at New York.
8. 1884 LANFRANC (I)
   1,657. 85,61 x 10,39. (280.9 x 34.1). 1–2. I–S–C2–10. T. Royden
   & Sons, Liverpool (engines G. Forrester & Co, Liverpool). 1884
   launched. 1884 (19/9) MV Liverpool–R. Amazon. 1898 OLYM-
   PIA (Br. Honduras). 1914 PLAN DE GUADELOUPE (USA).
   1919 ST. CHARLES (USA). 1923 scrapped.
9. (1884) CYRIL (I)
   1,190. 77,72 x 9,54. (255.0 x 31.3). 1–2. I–S–C2–10. London &
   Glasgow Engineering & Iron Shipbuilding Co, Glasgow. 1882
   (13/9) launched as PACAXO. 1884 CYRIL (Booth). 1884 (18/3)
   FV Liverpool–R. Amazon. 1897 BRAGANCA (Empreza Navegação Gran Para). 1925 (28/12) wrecked at Aracari.
10. (1889) GREGORY (I)
    1,587. 78,94 x 9,84. (259.0 x 32.3). 1–2. I–S–C2–10. Schlesinger,
    Davis & Co, Wallsend-on-Tyne (engines R. & W. Hawthorn,
    Newcastle). 1879 (2/8) launched as LAURIUM (Fr). 1889
    GREGORY (Booth). 1889 (9/4) FV Liverpool–Hamburg–R.
    Amazon. 1897 GUAJARA (Empreza Navegação Gran Para).
    1930 scrapped.
11. (1890) JUSTIN (I)
    1,744. 84,73 x 10,48. (278.0 x 34.4). 1–2. I–S–C2–10. A. Hall &
    Co, Aberdeen (engines Fawcett, Preston & Co, Liverpool). 1880

(3/11) launched as PONCA (Mediterranean & New York). 1890
JUSTIN (Booth). 1890 (11/6 FV Liverpool–Hamburg–R. Ama-
zon. 1898 JUSTIN (Fr). 1905 (28/7) wrecked at Le Conquet,
Brest.

12. (1891) ORIGEN (I)
1,612. 76,37 x 10,54. (250.6 x 34.6). S–1–2. S–S–T3–11. Hall,
Russell & Co, Aberdeen. 1886 (Apr) launched as GLOAMIN
(Br). 1891 ORIGEN (Booth). 1891 (11/5) FV Liverpool–
Hamburg–Havre–R. Amazon. 1899 ORIGEN (Norwegian). 1915
(13/11) sailed from Philadelphia for Copenhagen; went
missing.

13. (1892) HILARY (I)
1,983. 83,81 x 11,34. (275.0 x 37.2). S–1–2. S–S–T3–11. W.B.
Thompson & Co, Dundee. 1889 (30/5) launched as RED SEA
(Dundee, Perth & London). 1892 HILARY (Booth), 1892
(17/10) FV Penarth–New York–R. Amazon. 1892 (23/12) FV
Ceara–Liverpool. 1893 (23/1) FV Liverpool–Penarth–R. Amazon. 1911 MISUMI MARU (Jap). 1916 TORYU MARU (Jap).
1945 (2/5) torpedoed and sunk off South Korea.

14. 1893 HILDEBRAND (I)
1,947. 79,33 x 11,03. (260.3 x 36.2). 1–2. S–S–T3–11. Hall,
Russell & Co, Aberdeen. 1893 (30/5) launched. 1893 (12/7) MV
Liverpool–Havre–R. Amazon. 1908 HUAYNA (Iquitos SS Co).
1911 HUAYNA (Booth). 1917 sold to Admiralty for use as a 'Q'
ship. 1919 MANUEL CARSI (Spanish). 1921 (19/5) foundered
off Cape Torinana.

15. 1894 HUBERT (I)
1,965. 79,67 x 11,03. (261.4 x 36.2). S–1–2. S–S–T3–11. Hall,
Russell & Co, Aberdeen. 1894 (21/3) launched. 1894 (18/5) MV
Liverpool–Hamburg–Havre–R. Amazon. 1908 ATAHUALPA
(Iquitos). 1911 ditto (Booth). 1919 CITY OF ALGIERS (Fran-
co–British). 1927 (29/11) foundered off Catania.

16. (1895) HORATIO†
3,212. 100,88 x 12,25. (331.0 x 40.2). C–1–2. S–S–T3–11.
Edwards Shipbuilding Co, Howdon-on-Tyne (engines T.
Richardson & Sons, Hartlepool). 1892 (14/5) launched as
HORSLEY TOWER (F. Stumore & Co). 1893 HORATIO
(Wilson). 1895 HORATIO (Booth). 1895 (17/4) FV Liverpool–
R. Amazon. 1911 HORATIO (Br). 1916 (11/3) destroyed by fire
at Leith Harbour, South Georgia.

17. 1895 DOMINIC†
2,966. 98,14 x 12,89. (322.0 x 42.3). 1–2. S–S–T3–11. Barclay,
Curle & Co, Glasgow. 1895 (10/10) launched. 1895 (22/11) MV

119

Liverpool–Penarth–R. Amazon. 1923 TAXIARCHIS (Greek). 1931 NAZIM (Turkish). 1952 scrapped at Grays, Essex.

18. 1896 DUNSTAN†

2,966. 98,14 x 12,89. (322.0 x 42.3). 1–2. S–S–T3–11. Barclay, Curle & Co, Glasgow. 1895 (16/12) launched. 1896 (15/2) MV Liverpool–Hamburg–Havre–R. Amazon. 1923 DESPINA (Greek). 1923 (12/9) sunk in collision with ss SAXICAVA near Gibraltar.

19. 1896 POLYCARP (I)†

2,966. 98,14 x 12,89. (322.0 x 42.3). 1–2. S–S–T3–11. Barclay, Curle & Co, Glasgow. 1896 (28/2) launched. 1896 (24/3) MV Liverpool–Hamburg–Havre–R. Amazon. 1912 AUGUSTA (Swedish). 1918 BIA (ditto). 1922 FALCO (ditto). 1935 BOSILJ-KA (Yugoslavian). 1942 (19/6) torpedoed and sunk by German submarine near New Orleans.

20. (1896) AUGUSTINE (II)

3,498. 109,59 x 13,34. (359.6 x 43.8). 1–2. I–S–T3–13. (I–120; II–100; III–160). Barclay, Curle & Co, Glasgow. 1879 (Nov) launched as GRANTULLY CASTLE (Castle). 1895 AUGUS-TINE (Booth). 1896 (10/1) FV Liverpool–Havre–R. Amazon. 1912 scrapped at Falmouth.

21. (1897) JEROME (II)

3,056. 106,33 x 12.00. (348.9 x 39.4). 1–2. I–S–T3–12. (I–133; III–205). Robert Napier & Sons, Glasgow. 1877 (Aug) launched as WARWICK CASTLE (Castle). 1891 T3 replaced C2. 1897 JEROME (Booth). 1897 (20/10) FV Liverpool–R. Amazon. 1911 KERASOUNDE (Turkish). 1924 KIRESSON (ditto). 1926 scrapped.

22. (1897) BENEDICT†

3,378. 105,15 x 13,25. (345.0 x 43.5). 1–2.S–S–T3–11. Raylton Dixon & Co, Middlesbrough (engines T. Richardson & Sons, Hartlepool). 1894 (19/4) launched as LEYDEN (Br). 1897 BENEDICT (Booth). 1897 FV Liverpool–R. Amazon. 1916 (28/2) escaped from German submarine attack. 1924 sold. 1932 scrapped in Italy.

23. (1899) BERNARD (II)

3,282. 102,10 x 13,31. (335.0 x 43.7). 1–2. S–T3–12. Workman, Clark & Co Ltd, Belfast. 1895 (12/2) launched as MOUNT SIRION (Br). 1898 BERNARD (Booth). 1899 (9/2) FV Liver-pool–R. Amazon. 1911 REDBARN (Br). 1911 LORDOS BYRON (Greek). 1911 (5/11) foundered off the Casquets.

24. (1899) BASIL (II)

3,200. 103,00 x 13,31. (338.0 x 43.7). 1–2. S–T3–12. Workman,

Clark & Co Ltd, Belfast. 1895 (19/9) launched as MOURNE (Br). 1898 BASIL (Booth). 1899 (29/3) FV Penarth–R. Amazon. 1917 (11/11) sunk in collision with MARGAUX (Fr) in English Channel.

25. (1899) GREGORY (II)

2,030. 80,77 x 12,19. (265.0 x 40.0). 1–2. S–T3–11. Palmers Co Ltd, Jarrow-on-Tyne. 1891 launched as CRESSWELL (Br). 1899 GREGORY (Booth). 1899 (8/12) FV Liverpool–R. Amazon. 1907 transferred to Iquitos SS Co. 1920 (22/11) wrecked on Tutoia Bar, Brazil.

26. (1900) CLEMENT (II)

3,445. 105,36 x 13,44. (345.7 x 44.1). 1–2. S–T3–12. (I–135; III–600). R. Napier & Sons, Glasgow. 1896 (28/5) launched as LA PLATA (RMSP). 1900 CLEMENT (Booth). 1900 (13/12) FV Liverpool–Hamburg–R. Amazon. 1914 FRESHFIELD (Br). 1918 (5/8) torpedoed and sunk by German submarine.

27. (1901) LISBONENSE

1,508. 82,11 x 10,12. (269.4 x 33.2). 1–2. I–S–C2–10. T. Royden & Sons, Liverpool. (engines J. Jack & Co, Liverpool) 1871 (Jan) launched. 1871 MV Liverpool–R. Amazon. 1901 LISBONENSE (Booth). 1904 QUIMSTAN (Br).

28. (1901) PARAENSE

1,520. 82,35 x 10,06. (270. 2 x 33.0). 1–2. I–S–C2–10. T. Royden & Sons, Liverpool (engines J. Jack, Rollo & Co, Liverpool. 1871 (May) launched. 1871 MV Liverpool–R. Amazon. 1901 PARAENSE (Booth). 1902 ROSINA (Br). 1926 scrapped.

29. (1901) SOBRALENSE

1,982. 83,84 x 10,42. (275.1 x 34.2). 1–2. I–S–T4–11. Barrow Shipbuilding Co, Barrow. 1884 (9/8) launched. 1884 (4/10) MV Liverpool–R. Amazon. 1901 SOBRALENSE (Booth). 1904 sold. 1905 (12/5) sunk by mine off Port Arthur.

30. (1901) MARANHENSE

2,767. 95,58 x 12,83. (313.6 x 42.1). 1–2. S–S–T3–11. Caird & Co. Ltd, Greenock. 1890 (28/3) launched as GULF OF LIONS. 1899 MARANHENSE (Red Cross). 1899 (20/5) FV Liverpool–Hamburg–R. Amazon. 1901 MARANHENSE (Booth). 1910 scrapped at Garston.

31. (1901) FLUMINENSE

2,150. 92,04 x 11,70. (302.0 x 38.4). C–1–2. S–S–T3–11. Palmers Co Ltd, Jarrow-on-Tyne. 1891 launched as IL PRINCIPE DI NAPOLI (Italo-Britannica). 1895 FLUMINENSE (Red Cross). 1895 (9/2) FV Liverpool–R. Amazon. 1901 FLUMINENSE (Booth). 1909 AMAZONIA (Brazilian). 1928 scrapped in Italy.

32. (1901) MADEIRENSE
    2,700. 101,19 x 12,19. (332.0 x 40.0). S–1–2. S–S–T3–12. (I–40;
    III–464). Bonn & Mees, Rotterdam (engines Nederlandsche
    Stoomboot Maatschappij, Fijenoord). 1891 (Aug) launched as
    DUBBELDAM (Holland America). 1895 MADEIRENSE (Red
    Cross). 1895 (17/12) FV Liverpool–Hamburg–R. Amazon. 1901
    MADEIRENSE (Booth). 1910 MADEIRENSE (Norwegian).
    1912 (30/7) foundered near Bahamas Islands.
33. (1901) CAMETENSE
    2,150. 92,04 x 11,70. (302.0 x 38.4). 1–2. S–T3–11. Palmers Co
    Ltd, Jarrow-on-Tyne. 1891 (22/9) launched as CARLO POERIO
    (Italo-Britannica). 1894 CAMETENSE (Red Cross). 1894 (Jly)
    FV Liverpool–Havre–R. Amazon. 1901 CAMETENSE (Booth).
    1909 TONG HONG (Penang). 1919 (27/7) torpedoed and sunk in
    Mediterranean by enemy submarine.
34. (1901) OBIDENSE
    2,380. 91,43 x 11,31. (300.0 x 37.1). 1–2. S–T3–11. T. Royden &
    Sons, Liverpool (engines Fawcett, Preston & Co, Liverpool).
    1890 launched. 1891 (5/2) MV Liverpool–R. Amazon. 1901
    OBIDENSE (Booth). 1914 CUNEO (Norwegian). 1915 (1/1)
    wrecked on Shipwash.
35. (1901) CEARENSE
    2,769. 96,92 x 12,31. (318.0 x 40.4). 1–2. S–T3–11. Naval
    Construction & Armament Co Ltd, Barrow. 1891 (27/6) launched
    as WEST INDIAN (West India & Pacific; later Frederick
    Leyland & Co Ltd). 1900 CEARENSE (Red Cross). 1901 (29/1)
    FV Liverpool–R. Amazon. 1901 CEARENSE (Booth). 1911
    CEARENSE (USA). 1913 (13/9) wrecked off March Point,
    Nelson River, Hudson Bay.
36. (1901) GRANGENSE
    2,162. 92,04 x 11,70. (302.0 x 38.4). 1–2. S–T3–11. Palmers Co.
    Ltd, Jarrow-on-Tyne. 1891 (20/10) launched as RUGGIERO
    SETTIMO (Italo-Britannica). 1892 GRANGENSE (Red Cross).
    1894 (10/8) FV Liverpool–R. Amazon. 1901 GRANGENSE
    (Booth). 1910 ON TEMMOUZ (Turkish). 1915 (7/3) sunk in
    Black Sea by Russian Navy.
37. (1901) AMAZONENSE
    2,828. 95,09 x 12,45. (312.0 x 40.9). 1–2. S–T3–11. D.J. Dunlop
    & Co, Port Glasgow. 1899 (27/4) launched. 1899 (8/7) MV
    Liverpool–Hamburg–Havre–R. Amazon. 1901 AMAZONENSE
    (Booth). 1911 sold.
38. 1903 AMBROSE (II)
    4,594. 114,35 x 14,56. (375.2 x 47.8). 1–2. S–T3–14. (I–149;

III–330). Sir Raylton Dixon & Co, Middlesbrough (engines N.E. Marine Engineering Co Ltd, Newcastle). 1903 (31/3) launched. 1903 (7/10) MV Liverpool–R. Amazon. 1914 armed merchant cruiser (10th Cruiser Squadron). 1915 H.M.S. AMBROSE (submarine depot ship). 1938 H.M.S. COCHRANE. 1946 scrapped.

39. (1904) CYRIL (II)
4,380. 116,00 x 14,69. (380.6 x 48.2). 1–2. I–S–T3–14. (I–160; II–90; III). John Elder & Co, Glasgow. 1883 (Jan) launched as HAWARDEN CASTLE (Castle). 1904 CYRIL (Booth) 1904 (21/1) FV Liverpool–R. Amazon. 1905 (5/9) sunk in collision with ANSEIM (Booth) in R. Amazon. (0).

40. 1904 BONIFACE
3,506. 108,20 x 14,84. (355.0 x 48.7). 1–2. S–T3–12. (I–16; III–100). Barclay, Curle & Co Ltd, Glasgow. 1904 (28/7) launched. 1904 (31/8) MV Liverpool–R. Amazon. 1917 (23/8) torpedoed and sunk by German submarine off Aran Islands (1).

41. 1904 JUSTIN (II)
3,498. 108,20 x 14,84. (355.0 x 48.7). 1–2. S–T3–11. (I–16; III–100). Barclay, Curle & Co Ltd, Glasgow. 1904 (8/9) launched. 1904 (12/10) MV Liverpool–R. Amazon. 1930 scrapped.

42. 1905 ANSELM (II)
5,442. 122,03 x 15,27. (400.4 x 50.1). 1–2. S–T3–14. Workman, Clark & Co Ltd, Belfast. 1905 (10/1) launched. 1905 (29/3) MV Liverpool–Havre–R. Amazon. 1905 (5/9) collided with and sank CYRIL (Booth) in R. Amazon. 1922 COMODORO RIVADA-VIA (Argentinian). 1944 RIO SANTA CRUZ (Argentine Govt.). 1959 scrapped at Rio de Janeiro.

43. 1906 CUTHBERT
3,563. 108,23 x 15,02. (355.1 x 49.3). 1–2. S–T3–11. (I–16; III–100). R. & W. Hawthorn, Leslie & Co, Hebburn-on-Tyne. 1906 (12/2) launched. 1906 (22/4) MV Cardiff–R. Amazon. 1931 scrapped in Italy.

44. 1907 CRISPIN
3,694. 138,71 x 15,02. (455.1 x 49.3). 1–2. S–T3–11. (I–17; III–100). Sir Raylton Dixon & Co, Middlesbrough (engines N.E. Marine Engineering Co Ltd, Sunderland). 1907 (7/10) launched. 1907 (16/12) MV London–Cardiff–R. Amazon. 1917 (29/3) torpedoed and sunk by German submarine near Waterford (8).

45. 1907 ANTONY
6,439. 127,55 x 15,94. (418.5 x 52.3). 1–2. 2S–T6–14. (I–200;

III–350). R. & W. Hawthorn, Leslie & Co, Hebburn-on-Tyne. 1906 (17/11) launched. 1907 (18/3) MV Liverpool–Havre–R. Amazon. 1917 (17/3) torpedoed and sunk by German submarine 20 miles from Coninbeg Lightship (55).

46. 1907 LANFRANC (II)
6,275. 127,55 x 15,91. (418.5 x 52.2). 1–2. 2S–T6–14. (I–200; III–350). Caledon Shipbuilding & Engineering Co Ltd, Dundee. 1906 (18/10) launched. 1907 (18/2) MV Liverpool–Havre–R. Amazon. 1917 (17/4) torpedoed and sunk by German submarine between Havre and Southampton when serving as hospital ship (34).

47. (1907) PORT FAIRY
2,581. 100,57 x 11,67. (330.0 x 38.3). 1–3. S–T3–11. (I–50; III–700). Wigham Richardson & Co, Walker-on-Tyne. 1887 (18/10) launched as PORT FAIRY (Br). 1892 DONA MARIA (Andresen (Portuguese)). 1907 PORT FAIRY (Booth). 1907 (17/8) FV Liverpool–R. Amazon. 1909 ITALIAN (Ellerman). 1913 scrapped at Preston.

48. 1908 HILARY (II)
6,325. 127,55 x 15,91. (418.5 x 52.2). 1–2. 2S–T6–14. (I–210; III–372). Caledon Shipbuilding & Engineering Co Ltd, Dundee. 1908 (31/3) launched. 1908 (8/8) MV Liverpool–Havre–R. Amazon. 1914 armed merchant cruiser (10th Cruiser Squadron). 1917 (25/5) torpedoed and sunk by German submarine U.88 40 miles from Lerwick.

49. 1910 FRANCIS
3,963. 108,20 x 14,93. (355.0 x 49.0). 1–2. S–T3–11. (I–17; III–100). Barclay, Curle & Co Ltd, Glasgow. 1909 (11/12) launched. 1910 (23/2) MV Liverpool–London–Havre–R. Amazon. 1931 ROSALIE MOLLER (Moller). 1941 (8/10) bombed and sunk at Suez.

50. 1910 HUBERT (II)
3,930. 108,20 x 14,93. (355.0 x 49.0). 1–2. S–T3–11. (I–17; III–100). Barclay, Curle & Co Ltd, Glasgow. 1910 (26/2) launched. 1910 (1/5) MV Liverpool–London–Havre–R. Amazon. 1934 scrapped.

51. 1910 CHRISTOPHER
4,416. 109,72 x 15,24. (360.0 x 50.0). 1–2. S–T3–11. (I–32; III–100). Tyne Iron Shipbuilding Co, Howdon-on-Tyne (engines N.E. Marine Engineering Co Ltd, Newcastle). 1909 (27/12) launched as KADUNA (Elder Dempster). 1910 CHRIST-OPHER (Booth). 1910 (31/5) MV Liverpool–London–R. Amazon–New York (dep 16/8)–R. Amazon. 1914 OBUASI (Elder

Dempster). 1917 (8/7) torpedoed and sunk by German submarine 300 miles W. of Fastnet.

52. 1910 STEPHEN
4,435. 114,75 x 15,33 (376.5 x 50.3). 1–2. S–T3–11. (I–34; III–100). R. & W. Hawthorn, Leslie & Co Ltd, Hebburn-on-Tyne (engines N.E. Marine Engineering Co Ltd, Newcastle). 1910 (20/9) launched. 1910 (29/12) MV Liverpool–Penarth–London–Pera. 1934 scrapped.

53. 1911 DENIS
4,435. 114,72 x 15,33. (376.4 x 50.3). 1–2. S–T3–11. (I–36; III–100). R. & W. Hawthorn, Leslie & Co Ltd, Hebburn-on-Tyne (engines N.E. Marine Engineering Co Ltd, Newcastle). 1911 (15/2) launched. 1911 (27/5) MV Liverpool–London–R. Amazon. 1932 scrapped in Italy.

54. 1911 PANCRAS
4,436. 114,75 x 15,33. (376.5 x 50.3). 1–2. S–T3–11. (I–46; III–100). R. & W. Hawthorn, Leslie & Co. Ltd, Hebburn-on-Tyne (engines N.E. Marine Engineering Co Ltd, Newcastle). 1911 (29/4) launched. 1911 (4/10) MV Liverpool–Para. 1917 (15/5) beached near Adra, Spain, to avoid a German submarine; refloated. 1918 (3/5) torpedoed in the Mediterranean; towed to Malta. 1932 scrapped in Italy.

55. 1911 AIDAN
4,545. 114,56 x 15,33. (375.9 x 50.3). 1–2. S–T3–11. (I–46; III–100). Tyne Iron Shipbuilding Co, Howdon-on-Tyne. 1911 (27/7) launched. 1911 (5/12) MV Liverpool–R. Amazon–New York–Liverpool. 1936 scrapped at Savona.

56. 1911 HILDEBRAND (II)
6,995. 134,19 x 16,49. (440.3 x 54.1). 1–2. 2S–Q8–14. (I–218; III–406). Scott's Shipbuilding & Engineering Co Ltd, Greenock. 1911 (14/2) launched. 1911 (19/4) MV Liverpool–Havre–R. Amazon. 1914 armed merchant cruiser (10th Cruiser Squadron). 1932 laid up. 1934 scrapped.

57. (1911) MANCO
2,979. 91,52 x 13,77. (300.3 x 45.2). 1–2. S–T3–12. (I–62; III–92). Scott's Shipbuilding & Engineering Co Ltd, Greenock. 1907 (27/11) launched for Iquitos SS Co. 1908 (15/2) MV Liverpool–Hamburg–Iquitos. 1911 MANCO (Booth). 1914–8 British fleet auxiliary. 1921 MORAZAN (Standard Fruit Co). 1944 (8/9) as EKKAI MARU (Jap) bombed and sunk by Allied aircraft in the Philippines.

58. (1913) VINCENT
4,383. 109,72 x 14,32. (360.0 x 47.0). 1–2. S–T3–13. (I–60; III).

Sir W.G. Armstrong, Mitchell & Co Ltd, Walker-on-Tyne. 1894 (27/12) launched as FORT SALISBURY (Bucknall). 1913 VINCENT (Booth). 1913 (5/3) FV Liverpool–R. Amazon. 1913 GUJARAT (Andrew Weir). 1919 GORJISTAN (Bombay). 1928 scrapped.

59. 1914 MICHAEL
   3,172. 91,70 x 13,95. (300.9 x 45.8). 1–2. S–T3–12. Sir Raylton Dixon & Co, Middlesbrough (engines N.E. Marine Engineering Co Ltd, Newcastle). 1914 (12/3) launched. 1914 (Aug) MV Liverpool–R. Amazon. 1924 CHARLES SCHIAFFINO (Algiers). 1929 (1/2) wrecked near Cape Villano.

60. 1914 ALBAN
   5,223. 114,35 x 15,75. (375.2 x 51.7). 1–2. S–T3–13. Caledon Shipbuilding & Engineering Co, Dundee. 1914 (11/3) launched. 1914 (13/11) Liverpool–New York–R. Amazon. 1935 ZENA (It).

— — OSWALD
   5,220. 114,29 x 15,69. (375.0 x 51,5). 1–2. S–T3–11. Sir Raylton Dixon & Co Ltd, Middlesbrough (engines N.E. Marine Engineering Co Ltd, Newcastle). 1914 (23/9) launched. 1915 completed without passenger accommodation; requisitioned. 1917 (23/4) torpedoed and sunk by German submarine 200 miles SW of Fastnet (1).

61. 1918 ORIGEN (II)
   3,550. 103,80 x 14,23. (340.6 x 46.7). 1–2. S–T3–12. Caledon Shipbuilding & Engineering Co Ltd, Dundee. 1918 (29/6) MV Falmouth for Brazil in convoy. 1918 (30/6) torpedoed and sunk by German submarine.

62. 1918 POLYCARP (II)
   3,577. 103,83 x 14,26. (340.7 x 46.8). 1–2. S–T3–11. Barclay, Curle & Co Ltd, Glasgow. 1918 (9/2) launched. 1940 (2/6) torpedoed and sunk by German submarine near Ushant (0).

63. 1931 HILARY (III)
   7,403. 129,29 x 17,13. (424.2 x 56.2). 1–2. S–T3 & ST (DR)–15. (I–80; III–250). Cammell, Laird & Co Ltd, Birkenhead. 1931 (17/4) launched. 1931 (14/8) MV Liverpool–Para–Manaos. 1941 (Jan) ocean boarding vessel; subsequently various other duties. 1945 (Jan) returned to Booth. 1945 resumed Liverpool–R. Amazon; (I–93; tourist 138). 1959 scrapped at Inverkeithing.

64. 1935 ANSELM (III)
   5,954. 125,66 x 16,97. (412.3 x 55.7). 1–2. S–ST(SR)–14. Wm. Denny & Bros, Dumbarton. 1935 (15/10) launched. 1935 (31/12) MV Liverpool–R. Amazon. 1941 (5/7) torpedoed and sunk by German submarine N. of Azores when service as troopship.

65. 1951 HILDEBRAND (III)
   7,735. 128,16 [133,80] x 18,38. (420.5 [439.0] x 60.3). 1–1.
   S–ST(DR)–15. Cammell, Laird & Co Ltd, Birkenhead. 1951
   (20/7) launched. 1951 (28/12) MV Liverpool–R. Amazon. 1957
   (25/9) wrecked during fog at Cascais, near Lisbon (0); later broke
   her back.
66. 1955 HUBERT (III)
   7,905. 128,16 [133,80] x 18,38. (420.5 [439.0] x 60.3). 1–1.
   S–ST(DR)–15. (I–74; tourist 96). Cammell, Laird & Co Ltd,
   Birkenhead. 1954 (31/8) launched. 1955 (11/2) MV Liverpool–R.
   Amazon. 1964 MALAYSIA (Austasia).
67. (1961) ANSELM (IV) (M/S)
   10,868. 145,99 [153,91] x 19,74. (479.0 [505.0] x 64.8). 1–2.
   2S–2SC.DA–17. (one class 348). SA John Cockerill, Hoboken
   (engines Burmeister & Wain, Copenhagen). 1950 (4/3) launched
   as BAUDOUINVILLE (Cie Maritime Belge). 1950 (19/9) MV
   Antwerp–Matadi. 1957 THYSVILLE (ditto). 1961 ANSELM
   (Booth); (I–135; tourist 101). 1961 (16/6) FV Liverpool–R.
   Amazon. 1963 IBERIA STAR (Blue Star). 1965 AUSTRALA-
   SIA (Austasia); ran Singapore–Melbourne. 1973 scrapped at
   Kaohsiung.

† Cargo steamer.

FUNNEL: 1866. Black.
         1947. Black with replica of houseflag on each side (white
               rectangle with red saltire surmounted by large 'B').
FLAG: 1866. A red saltire on white with blue 'B' in centre.
         1947. Ditto, but a larger 'B'.
         1950. Ditto, but a still larger 'B'.

Chapter 17

(1867–1962)

SOCIÉTÉ GÉNÉRALE DE TRANSPORTS MARITIMES

(French)

The SOCIÉTÉ GÉNÉRALE DE TRANSPORTS MARITIMES was founded at Marseilles on 18 March 1865 with a capital of 20 million francs (£800,000) to run a fleet of steamers between Marseilles, Sete and Algeria, but no more than two years later had begun a service to Brazil. It was the fifth French concern to enter this field, but two of its predecessors had already packed up. Both had made Marseilles their French terminal and as this was the home port selected by SGTM it can at least be said that it had no direct competition, for the remaining French lines had chosen Bordeaux and Havre.

The SGTM service opened on 15 September 1867 with the departure for Rio de Janeiro of the 1,966 ton iron screw BOURGOGNE, built two years previously by J. Laing & Sons of Sunderland as the UITENHAGE. Additionally, the 536 ton paddle steamer WASP, built at Liverpool in 1864, had been bought, renamed VILLE DE BUENOS AYRES and already despatched to Rio to act as a feeder steamer between there, Montevideo and Buenos Aires.

The second sailing was taken in October 1867 by the 2,303 ton POITOU, newly-built by Malcolmson Brothers of Waterford, Ireland, followed in November by the 2,588 ton SAVOIE and in December by the 1,371 ton PICARDIE. The SAVOIE was a product of John Laird of Birkenhead, and launched in 1854 as the CRISTOBAL COLON, while the PICARDIE came from Laing, who launched her in 1865 as the French steamer ALBANY.

When the first South Atlantic steamship line entered the River Plate trade in 1851, it did so by means of a feeder steamer from Rio de Janeiro, port facilities at Montevideo and Buenos Aires being more or less non-existent, and the river itself badly in need of dredging. However, conditions were much improved by 1868, and in that year the SGTM ships proceeded through to both River Plate ports. In consequence, the VILLE DE BUENOS AYRES was sold.

The 3,811 ton LA FRANCE was completed by the Chantiers & Ateliers de la Méditerranée at La Seyne in 1871, and was not only appreciably larger than her predecessors but enabled SGTM to keep a steamer in reserve. The 2,209 ton BRETAGNE (I) of 1876 enabled the PICARDIE to be sold. The newcomer was extensively employed on the South Atlantic, but also ran when required on one of SGTM's Mediterranean lines.

The 4,134 ton NAVARRE and BÉARN were completely by the Barrow Shipbuilding Company in 1881–2. Unfortunately, the NAVARRE was wrecked at Marseilles within a few months, but was replaced by the 3,874 ton PROVENCE (I), which was delivered from La Seyne in 1884 and differed from her predecessors by having three masts instead of two.

In 1890 the 3,161 ton emigrant carrier AQUITAINE was bought on the stocks at Sunderland, and orders were placed at La Seyne for the ESPAGNE, ITALIE, FRANCE and ALGÉRIE, each of about 4,000 tons, the first two having three masts and the second pair two. They were completed at intervals between 1891 and 1901, and allowed the POITOU, LA FRANCE and BOURGOGNE to be scrapped. In addition, the SAVOIE was sold for further service.

Two interesting emigrant carriers were bought in August 1895 – the 3,870 ton BRITISH PRINCE and BRITISH PRINCESS which, the property of British Shipowners, had been running for the American Line's British-flag fleet between Liverpool and Philadelphia. They were renamed LES ANDES and LES ALPES.

1896 LES ALPES 3,864 tons
Built in 1883 for British Shipowners as BRITISH PRINCESS.

The 3,000 ton cargo steamers MONT BLANC, MONT CENIS and MONT ROSE were acquired by SGTM between 1899 and 1902. The MONT BLANC was sold in 1905 and became notorious on 6 December 1917 when, carrying munitions, she collided in the harbour of Halifax, Nova Scotia, with the Norwegian steamer IMO. She exploded and devastated the town, several thousand people being killed and wounded. The exact number will never be known.

1901 NIVERNAIS 2,565 tons
Built in 1882 as Nederland Line's SUMATRA.

Next came four second-hand purchases – the Nederland Line SUMATRA, LOMBOK and BURGOMEISTER DEN TEX and the Rotterdam Lloyd SOEMBING. They were renamed NIVERNAIS, ORLÉANAIS, ILE DE FRANCE and POITOU (II), respectively. At a later date, the ILE DE FRANCE became the first French cruising yacht, but had previously made a few South American voyages.

The first twin-screw steamer laid down by SGTM, the 4,933 ton CORDOBA, was sold on the stocks to Lloyd Italiano – presumably at a profit – in 1905 at a time when the Italian line was about to start operations on both North and South Atlantic and was in need of additional tonnage. In her place, SGTM commissioned two similar ships in 1906, the 4,471 ton twin-screw FORMOSA and PAMPA.

SGTM were having difficulties with the Spanish Government over the carriage of emigrants to South America, and to show their willingness to co-operate founded the COMPAGNIE DE NAVIGATION FRANCE–AMÉRIQUE (Chapter 53) in 1907, to which they transferred the PROVENCE, ESPAGNE and LES ALPES. The two last-named were soon replaced by the AQUITAINE and ITALIE.

The twin-screw PLATA of 1907 was, like the FORMOSA and PAMPA, built by the London & Glasgow Shipbuilding Company of Glasgow, but her tonnage had risen to 5,577 and her dimensions were slightly greater. The 6,248 ton PARANA was delivered from La Seyne in 1908.

Three more disasters have to be recorded – the BRETAGNE (I) was wrecked at Bahia on 12 September 1903, the POITOU (II) was wrecked on the Uruguayan coast on 7 May 1907 and the ORLÉANAIS was badly damaged in collision with the CGT VILLE D'ALGER at Marseilles in

1909 and was scrapped. Two other ships, LES ANDES and LES ALPES, were also scrapped at about this time.

The two final passenger ships to be built for SGTM before World War I were the 7,384 ton SALTA and the 7,168 ton VALDIVIA, completed in 1911, enabling four sailings a month to be run from Marseilles to South America. Both were chartered by the British Government as hospital ships soon after the war broke out, and on 10 April 1917 the SALTA sank after striking a mine in a French minefield outside Havre.

1907 PAMPA 4,471 tons
Torpedoed and sunk by German submarine in the Mediterranean in 1918.

SGTM suffered very severely during World War I. First victim was the FRANCE, which was sunk by gunfire from the German submarine U.38 on 7 November 1915 when on voyage from Salonica to Marseilles. The ALGÉRIE was sunk by a German submarine in December 1916, as were the PARANA on 24 August 1917, the NIVERNAIS on 10 June 1918 and the PAMPA on 27 August 1918.

In 1915 SGTM bought the Compagnie Mixte's cargo steamers VEGA, ASTER, MIRA and RIGEL, of which the VEGA and MIRA were lost in 1916. Two more cargo steamers call for mention – the MONT AGEL, homeward bound from Santos, was captured by the German auxiliary cruiser KRONPRINZ WILHELM on 5 December 1914 and was sunk after the crew had been transferred to the Hapag steamer OTAVI, which landed them at Las Palmas. And the MONT VISO was lost on 29 June 1917.

The ITALIE returned to SGTM from France–Amérique in 1916 and the ESPAGNE in 1919. Together with the FORMOSA, PLATA and, in particular, the VALDIVIA they performed valuable service to South America, the first resumed voyage of the last-named starting from Marseilles on 20 July 1920.

131

1912 VALDIVIA 7,168 tons
Served for a time as a British hospital ship.

SGTM wasted no time in ordering two new passenger liners from Swan, Hunter & Wigham Richardson of Tyneside. They were the 8,285 ton MENDOZA, launched on 6 February 1920, and the 8,604 ton ALSINA, launched on 9 May 1921. Twin-screw ships with two funnels, two masts and cruiser sterns, they were propelled by double-reduction geared turbines, their service speed being 15 knots.

The Société was helped somewhat to recoup its war losses by being allotted the ex-German East Africa Line steamer PRINZREGENT of 6,375 tons, which was renamed CORDOBA. She was fitted to carry a large complement of emigrants, but despite the fact that she had only been in service from 1903–14, the Italian authorities, mindful of the

1919 CORDOBA 6,375 tons
Built 1903 as German East Africa Line PRINZREGENT.

several Italian lines running to South America, made difficulties about granting her a licence, with the result that she was transferred to France–Amérique in 1925 and ran for them until scrapped at Savona in May 1932. SGTM also received seven or more cargo steamers, which were placed in service between Marseilles and West African ports. The cargo steamers MONT AGEL (II) and MONT VISO (II) were completed in 1920–1 at Greenock and Middlesbrough, respectively.

The 4,282 ton single-screw GUARUJA and IPANEMA were built at La Seyne in 1921 and within a year or so were transferred to France–Amérique. They were unusual in that their propelling machinery consisted of two Ljunstrom turbines connected to two electric motors, and when both systems were in operation their service speed was 13 knots. With the turbines only in use the speed was no more than 10 knots. As speed was of greater importance southbound than northbound, the arrangement should, in theory, have proved advantageous, but it can hardly have proved so in practice as SGTM did not repeat it.

The last of the Compagnie de Navigation France–Amérique ships, the IPANEMA, was seized by the Italians in 1942 and renamed VILLA-ROSA. She was scuttled by the Germans at Naples in September 1943, but later refloated by Italy, repaired and re-entered service as the Italian TAURINIA. France–Amérique, which had been an off-shoot of SGTM since its inception in 1907, was allowed to fade out.

In 1926 the Ateliers & Chantiers de la Loire of St. Nazaire delivered the 9,331 ton FLORIDA of enlarged and improved MENDOZA type. She had an unfortunate accident on 1 April 1931 when, in the Mediterranean east of Gibraltar, she saw in the distance the aircraft carrier H.M.S. GLORIOUS escorted by a group of destroyers. Without warning a patch of fog obliterated the ships and the FLORIDA was struck by the carrier on the portside forward of the bridge. Her 500 passengers, among whom there were a number of casualties, were transferred to the GLORIOUS, and later were put on board the GOUVERNEUR GÉNÉNRAL LAFÉRIERRE, specially diverted from her customary Oran–Marseilles voyage. The FLORIDA was towed to Malaga by two of the destroyers, patched up and then returned to Marseilles to be reconditioned.

The 10,816 ton CAMPANA, launched by Swan Hunter in 1929, by which time the AQUITAINE had been scrapped, was an improved version of the FLORIDA, with accommodation for 120 first class and 1,040 third class passengers.

During the period preceding World War II, the CAMPANA, FLORIDA, ALSINA and MENDOZA sailed twice a month, on the 6th and 19th from Genoa and one day later from Marseilles, for Dakar, Rio

133

de Janeiro, Santos, Montevideo and Buenos Aires, the voyage from Marseilles to Rio taking 15 days and to Buenos Aires 19.

SGTM lost two of their principal South American passenger ships during World War II – the MENDOZA was torpedoed and sunk in the South Atlantic on 1 November 1942, and the ALSINA was sunk by Allied air attack at Bougie on 13 November 1942. After the war, SGTM received three 'LIBERTY' ships and placed orders in 1950–1 for the cargo steamers MONT AGEL (III) and MONT VISO (III), replacing the earlier ships of these names, which had been World War II casualties.

The CAMPANA was laid up at Buenos Aires in 1940, and in 1943 was seized by Argentina and renamed RIO JACHAL. She reverted to SGTM in 1946 under her original name, was reconditioned and resumed service between Marseilles and the River Plate. The FLORIDA was rebuilt in 1948 and reappeared with one funnel instead of two. Both she and the CAMPANA were sold to Chargeurs Réunis in 1951.

Orders were placed with Swan, Hunter & Wigham Richardson for the 15,719 ton PROVENCE (II) and with Chantiers & Ateliers de St. Nazaire for the 16,355 ton BRETAGNE (II) which, commissioned in 1951–2, were propelled by two sets of single-reduction geared turbines giving them a service speed of 18 knots. Passenger figures differed somewhat, those of the PROVENCE being 157 first class, 167 tourist,

FLORIDA 9,331 tons
As built 1926.

As rebuilt 1948.

134

508 third and 470 fourth. In other words, 508 third class were carried in cabins and 470 in dormitories. Unfortunately, their SGTM service lasted only a decade as they were very expensive to run, and by that time jet aircraft were securing the cream of the passenger traffic. Starting in April 1961, the PROVENCE operated a joint service with the Costa FEDERICO C and ANDREA C. In 1965 she was bought by Costa and became the ENRICO C.

The activities of the BRETAGNE were considerably shorter and more tragic as she was chartered to the Chandris Line in 1960, bought by them a year later and in 1962 renamed BRITTANY. On 8 April 1963 she was destroyed by fire while undergoing engine repairs at Piraeus, and scrapped at La Spezia in 1964. Thus the SGTM passenger service came to an abrupt end.

1951 PROVENCE 15,719 tons
In 1965 became Costa Line ENRICO C.

1. (1867) BOURGOGNE
   1,966. 96,98 x 9,69. (318.2 x 31.8). 1–3. I–S–I(2)–10. J. Laing & Sons, Sunderland. 1865 (11/1) launched as UITENHAGE. 1867 BOURGOGNE (SGTM). 1867 (15/9) FV Marseilles–Rio de Janeiro. 1868 FV Marseilles–Buenos Aires. 1870s compound engines by Forges & Chantiers de la Méditerranée, La Seyne. 1896 scrapped at Marseilles.
2. 1867 POITOU (I)
   2,303. 99,00 x 10.60. (324.8 x 34.8). 1–2. I–S–I(2)–10. Malcolmson Brothers, Waterford. 1867 launched. 1867 (Oct) MV Marseilles–Rio de Janeiro. 1868 FV Marseilles–Buenos Aires. 1870s C2 replaced I(2). 1893 scrapped.

3. (1867) SAVOIE

2,588. 102,86 x 11,46. (337.5 x 37.6). 1–2. I–S–I(2)–10. John Laird, Birkenhead. 1854 launched as CRISTOBAL COLON. 1867 SAVOIE (SGTM). 1867 (Nov) FV Marseilles–Rio de Janeiro. 1868 FV Marseilles–Buenos Aires. 1871 C2 replaced I(2). 1891 SAVOIA (Italian). 1892 scrapped.

4. (1867) PICARDIE

1,371. 92,96 x 9,75. (305.0 x 32.0). C–1–3. I–S–I(2)–10. (I–28; II–55; III–356). J. Laing & Sons, Sunderland. 1865 (11/1) launched as ALBANY (Fr). 1867 PICARDIE (SGTM). 1867 (Dec) FV Marseilles–Rio de Janeiro. 1868 FV Marseilles–Buenos Aires. 1876 PICARDIE (Valery (Fr)). 1881 ditto (CGT). 1883 (18/1) foundered off Newfoundland after taken in tow by LABRADOR (CGT).

5. 1871 LA FRANCE

3,811. 129,84 x 10,97. (426.0 x 36.0). 2–2. I–S–C2–11. Forges & Chantiers de la Méditerranée, La Seyne. 1870 (Nov) launched. 1871 MV Marseilles–S. America. 1887 triple-expansion engines. 1895 scrapped at Marseilles.

6. 1876 BRETAGNE (I)

2,209. 88,00 x 11,89. (288.7 x 39.0). 1–3. I–S–C2–11. Forges & Chantiers de la Méditerranée, La Seyne. 1876 (21/12) launched. 1877 MV Marseilles–S. America. 1903 (12/9) wrecked at Bahia (0).

7. 1881 NAVARRE

4,134. 121,57 x 12,25. (398.9 x 40.2). 1–2. I–S–C2–14. Barrow Shipbuilding Co, Barrow. 1881 (16/7) launched. 1881 (17/11) MV Marseilles–S. America. 1882 (14/11) wrecked at Marseilles.

8. 1882 BÉARN

4,134. 121,57 x 12,25. (398.9 x 40.2). 1–2. I–S–C2–14. Barrow Shipbuilding Co, Barrow. 1881 (25/10) launched. 1882 (15/5) MV Marseilles–S. America. 1901 scrapped at Marseilles.

9. 1884 PROVENCE (I)

3,874. 117,98 x 12,89. (387.1 x 42.3). 1–3. S&I–S–C2–14. Forges & Chantiers de la Méditerranée, La Seyne. 1884 (1/4) launched. 1884 (20/7) MV Marseilles–S. America. 1907 PROVENCE (France–Amérique). 1918 (13/4) torpedoed off Spanish coast on voyage Buenos Aires–Marseilles; foundered at Palamos; later refloated and returned to France–Amérique service. 1927 scrapped at La Seyne.

10. 1891 AQUITAINE

3,161. 106,82 x 12,98. (350.5 x 42.6). 1–2. S–S–T3–13. Sunderland Shipbuilding Co, Sunderland. 1890 (27/10) launched. 1891

(Feb) MV Marseilles–Genoa–Barcelona–Montevideo–Buenos Aires. 1908 AQUITAINE (France–Amérique). 1915–8 served as ammunition depot ship at Salonica. 1927 scrapped at La Seyne.

11. 1891 ESPAGNE

3,952. 121,54 x 12,77. (398.8 x 41.9). 1–3. S–S–T3–14. (I–17; II–88; III–1,204). Forges & Chantiers de la Méditerranée, La Seyne. 1891 (8/3) launched. 1891 (8/8) MV Genoa–Marseilles–S. America. 1907 ESPAGNE (France–Amérique). 1919 ditto (SGTM). 1934 scrapped in Italy.

12. 1895 ITALIE

3,966. 121,73 x 12,80. (399.4 x 42.0). 1–3. S–S–T3–14. (I–17; II–88; III–1,204). Forges & Chantiers de la Méditerranée, La Seyne. Laid down as SAVOIE. 1894 (18/9) launched as ITALIE. 1895 (29/4) MV Marseilles–S. America, 1908 ITALIE (France–Amérique). 1916 ditto (SGTM). 1929 scrapped in Italy.

13. (1895) LES ANDES

3,871. 128,04 x 12,86. (420.1 x 42.2). 1–4. S–S–C2–12. (I; II; III–1,200). Harland & Wolff, Belfast. 1882 (4/2) launched as BRITISH PRINCE (British Shipowners). 1882 (12/4) MV for American Line (c), Liverpool–Philadelphia. 1895 LES ANDES (SGTM). 1895 (20/11) FV Marseilles–S. America. 1908 (Jun) scrapped at Marseilles.

14. (1896) LES ALPES

3,864. 128,04 x 12,86. (420.1 x 42.2). 1–4. S–S–C2–12. (I; II; III–1,200). Harland & Wolff, Belfast. 1882 (Dec) launched as BRITISH PRINCESS (British Shipowners). 1883 (28/4) MV for American Line (c), Liverpool–Philadelphia. 1896 LES ALPES (SGTM). 1896 (24/3) FV Marseilles–S. America. 1907 LES ALPES (France–Amérique). 1910 scrapped at Marseilles.

15. 1897 FRANCE

4,025. 121,06 x 12,80. (397.2 x 42.0). 1–2. S–S–T3–14. Forges & Chantiers de la Méditerranée, La Seyne. 1896 (1/9) launched. 1897 (20/3) MV Marseilles–S. America. 1915 (7/11) sunk on voyage Salonica–Marseilles by gunfire of German submarine U.38.

16. 1901 ALGÉRIE

4,035. 121,00 x 12,80. (397.0 x 42.0). 1–2. S–T3–14. Forges & Chantiers de la Méditerranée, Havre. 1901 (21/3) launched. 1901 (21/8) MV Marseilles–S. America. 1916 (4/12) sunk by German submarine UC.22 in Mediterranean.

17. (1901) NIVERNAIS

2,565. 99,20 x 11,31. (325.5 x 37.1). 1–3. I–S–C2–12. John Elder & Co, Glasgow. 1882 (Aug) launched as SUMATRA (Neder-

137

land). 1901 NIVERNAIS (SGTM). 1901 (25/11) FV Marseilles–
Genoa–S. America. 1918 (10/6) torpedoed and sunk by German
submarine in Mediterranean (18 Men; 7,000 sheep lost).

18. (1903) ORLÉANAIS

2,602. 99,20 x 11,31. (325.5 x 37.1). 1–3. I–S–C2–12. John Elder
& Co, Glasgow. 1882 (1/8) launched as PRINSES WILHELM-
INA (Nederland). 1896 LOMBOK (Nederland). 1903
ORLÉANAIS (SGTM). 1903 (2/11) FV Marseilles–S. America.
1909 (27/2) in collision with VILLE D'ALGER (CGT) at
Marseilles; scrapped.

19. (1903) POITOU (II)

2,679. 97,40 x 11,18. (319.6 x 36.7). 1–2. I–S–C2–12. Koninklijke
Maatschappij de Schelde, Flushing. 1883 launched as BATAVIA
(Rotterdam Lloyd). 1893 rebuilt; C2 became Q4; renamed
SOEMBING (Rotterdam Lloyd). 1903 POITOU (SGTM). 1903
(30/12) FV Genoa–Marseilles–S. America. 1907 (7/5) wrecked on
coast of Uruguay (20).

20. (1904) ILE DE FRANCE

3,488. 106,67 x 12,00. (350.0 x 39.4). 1–2. I–S–C2–12. John Elder
& Co, Glasgow. 1882 (1/5) launched as INSULINDE (Neder-
land). 1890 BURGOMEISTER DEN TEX (Nederland). 1903
ILE DE FRANCE (SGTM). 1904 (20/4) FV Marseilles–S.
America. Later served mainly as a cruising yacht – the first
French one. 1914 URGUITO (Spanish). 1914 scrapped at
Glasgow.

—— —— CORDOBA

4,933. D. & W. Henderson, Glasgow. 1905 sold on stocks to
Lloyd Italiano (Chapter 50); renamed CORDOVA.

21. 1906 FORMOSA

4,471. 124,35 x 14,44. (408.0 x 47.4). 1–2. 2S–T6–13. (I–57; II–70;
III–44). London & Glasgow Shipbuilding Co, Glasgow. 1906
(31/5) launched. 1906 (5/9) MV Marseilles–Genoa (19/9)–S.
America. 1927 (25/10) went to rescue of PRINCIPESSA
MAFALDA (It). 1929 scrapped in Italy.

22. 1907 PAMPA

4,471. 124,35 x 14,44. (408.0 x 47.4). 1–2. 2S–T6–16. (I–57; II–70;
III–44). London & Glasgow Shipbuilding Co, Glasgow. 1906
(16/8) launched. 1907 (19/2) MV (Marseilles)–Genoa–S. America. 1914 French hospital ship; later troopship. 1918 (27/8)
torpedoed and sunk by German submarine when bound Bizerta–
Salonica.

23. 1907 PLATA

5,577. 128,01 x 15,30. (420.0 x 50.2). 1–2. 2S–T6–15. (I–57; II–76;

III–44). London & Glasgow Shipbuilding Co, Glasgow, 1907 (Jly) launched. 1907 (29/10) MV (Marseilles)–Genoa–S. America. 1931 BEOGRAD (Yugoslavian).

24. 1908 PARANA
6,238. 128,01 x 15,24. (420.0 x 50.0). 1–2. 2S–T6–15. (I–57; II–70; III–44). Forges & Chantiers de la Méditerranée, La Seyne. 1908 (29/2) launched. 1908 MV Marseilles–Genoa (19/8)–S. America. 1917 (24/8) torpedoed by German submarine in Mediterranean. 1917 (25/8) sank when under tow.

25. 1911 SALTA
7,384. 136,85 x 16,15. (449.0 x 53.0). 2–2. 2S–T6–16. (I–60; II–80; III–79). Forges & Chantiers de la Méditerranée, La Seyne. 1911 (13/3) launched. 1911 (29/7) MV Marseilles–Genoa–S. America. 1914 British hospital ship (c). 1917 sank after striking mine near Havre (86).

26. 1912 VALDIVIA
7,168. 141,05 x 16,55. (462.8 x 54.3). 2–2. 2S–T6–16. (I–60; II–80; III–79. Chantiers & Ateliers de Provence, Port Bouc. 1911 (27/8) launched. 1912 (19/3) MV Genoa–S. America. 1913 (13/1) FV for Cie Sud Atlantique (c), Bordeaux–S. America. 1913 (25/9) returned to SGTM. 1914 British hospital ship (c). 1920 (20/7) resumed Marseilles–S. America. 1933 scrapped at Genoa.

27. (1919) CORDOBA
6,375. 127,10 x 15,30, (417.0 x 50.2). 1–2. 2S–T6–14. (I–115; II–84; III–80). Blohm & Voss, Hamburg. 1903 (10/1) launched as PRINZREGENT (German East Africa). 1919 CORDOBA (SGTM). 1919 FV Marseilles–S. America. 1925 CORDOBA (France–Amérique). 1932 scrapped at Savona.

28. 1920 MENDOZA
8,199. 137,30 x 17,80. (450.5 x 58.4). 2–2–C. 2S–ST(DR)–15. (I–74; II–128; III–46). Swan, Hunter & Wigham Richardson, Wallsend-on-Tyne. 1920 (6/2) launched. 1920 MV Marseilles–S. America. 1942 (1/11) sunk by German submarine U.178, 100 miles east of Durban.

29. 1921 ALSINA
8,404. 137,30 x 17,80. (450.5 x 58.4). 2–2–C. 2S–ST(DR)–15 (I–74; II–128; III–48). Swan, Hunter & Wigham Richardson, Wallsend-on-Tyne. 1921 (9/5) launched. 1921 MV Marseilles–S. America. 1942 (13/11) sunk by Allied air attack at Bougie. 1943 refloated. 1953 sold for scrap.

30. 1921 GUARUJA
4,282. 110,39 x 13,98. (362.2 x 45.9). 1–2. S–ST&TE–13). Forges & Chantiers de la Méditerranée, La Seyne. 1921

launched. 1921 MV Marseilles–S. America. 1923 GUARUJA (France–Amérique). 1938 (2/1) stranded near Almeria; broke her back.

31. 1921 IPANEMA

4,282. 109,78 x 13,98. (360.2 x 45.9). 1–2. S–ST&TE–13. Forges & Chantiers de la Méditerranée, La Seyne. 1921 launched. 1921 MV Marseilles–S. America. 1923 IPANEMA (France–Amérique). 1942 seized by Italy; renamed VILLAROSA. 1943 (Sep) scuttled by Germans at Naples, 1946 refloated by Italians; repaired; re-entered service as TAURINIA (It).

32. 1926 FLORIDA

9,331. 143,00 [149,46] x 18,44. (469.2 [490.4] x 60.5). 2–2–C. 2S–ST(DR)–16. Ateliers & Chantiers de la Loire, St. Nazaire. 1926 (14/1) launched. 1926 (16/11) MV Marseilles–S. America. 1931 (1/4) collision near Gibraltar with H.M.S. GLORIOUS (aircraft carrier) during sudden fog (33). Two British destroyers towed FLORIDA to Malaga, where patched up; repaired at Marseilles. 1942 (13/11) bombed and sunk by Axis aircraft at Bone. 1944 (15/5) refloated; reconditioned at Toulon. 1948 funnels reduced from 2 to 1; (I–59; II–108; III–112). 1951 FLORIDA (Chargeurs Réunis). 1955 ASCANIA (Grimaldi Siosa Lines). 1968 scrapped in Italy.

33. 1929 CAMPANA

10,816. 155,44 [163,54] x 20,42. (509.1 [536.6] x 67.0). 2–2–C. 2S–ST(SR)–17. (I–107; II–96; economic 56; III–230; IV–816). Swan, Hunter & Wigham Richardson, Walker-on-Tyne (engines Parsons Marine Steam Turbine Co, Newcastle). 1929 (11/6) launched. 1929 (14/10) MV Marseilles–Genoa–S. America. 1940 laid up at Buenos Aires. 1943 RIO JACHAL (Argentina). 1946 CAMPANA (SGTM). 1951 ditto (Chargeurs Réunis). 1955 IRPINIA (Siosa); 12,279 tons; converted to motorship. 1975 (29/11) left Barcelona for demolition at La Spezia.

34. 1951 PROVENCE (II)

15,719. 168,94 [176,77] x 22,31. (554.3 [580.0] x 73.2). 1–2–C. 2S–ST(SR)–18. (I–148; tourist 167; III–436; IV–736). Swan, Hunter & Wigham Richardson, Walker-on-Tyne (engines Parsons Marine Steam Turbine Co, Newcastle). 1950 (15/8) launched. 1951 (30/3) MV Marseilles–S. America. 1954 (18/2) collision in R. Plate with SAXONSEA (Liberian tanker); PROVENCE patched up at Buenos Aires; reconditioned at Marseilles. 1955 (26/3) resumed Marseilles–S. America. 1961 (5/4) FV for Costa (c), Genoa–Marseilles–Barcelona–Lisbon–Madeira–Recife–Rio de Janeiro–Santos–Montevideo–Buenos

Aires. 1965 ENRICO C (Costa); 13,607 tons; (I–218; tourist 980). 1966 FV Genoa–Buenos Aires. 1983 still undertakes occasional Genoa–Buenos Aires voyages, but principally employed in cruising.

35. 1952 BRETAGNE (II)

16,355. 169,12 [176,77] x 22,28. (554.9 [580.0] x 73.1). 1–2–C. 2S–ST(SR)–18. (I–149; tourist 167; III–606; IV–368). Chantiers & Ateliers de St. Nazaire. 1951 (20/7) launched. 1952 (14/2) MV Marseilles–S. America. 1960 chartered to Chandris Line; (I–150; tourist 1,050). 1961 BRETAGNE (Chandris). 1961 (22/9) FV Southampton–Australia. 1962 BRITTANY (Chandris). 1963 (8/4) destroyed by fire at Piraeus when undergoing repair. 1964 (31/3) arrived at La Spezia; scrapped.

FUNNEL: Black with broad red band.
FLAG: 1867. Four triangles – blue at top; red at bottom; white at sides. Large 'S' and 'G' on white.

           1910 (approx). Four triangles as before. Black 'S' on blue; black 'G' on red; blue 'T' and 'M' on white.

Chapter 18

1867–70

LONDON, BELGIUM, BRAZIL & RIVER PLATE MAIL STEAMSHIP COMPANY

(British)

The 1,250 ton single-screw CITY OF LIMERICK, which had accommodation for about 100 first class passengers, sailed from Gravesend, London, on 31 August 1867, reached St. Vincent (São Vicente) on 11 September and, after coaling, proceeded to Rio de Janeiro, Montevideo and Buenos Aires. She was owned by Messrs Tait, 'the eminent army contractors of Limerick and Leeds', [1], but no name of the line was mentioned in early advertisements. In those days, this was by no means unusual.

A slightly larger ship, the CITY OF BUENOS AYRES, left Gravesend on 14 November, and after a further voyage by the CITY OF LIMERICK advertisements appeared in the name of the LONDON, BELGIUM, BRAZIL & RIVER PLATE STEAMSHIP COMPANY [2]. Two additional steamers were mentioned – the CITY OF RIO DE JANEIRO and the CITY OF BRUSSELS. The latter sailed from the Victoria Docks, London, on 14 March 1868 for Antwerp, Falmouth – for the embarkation of British passengers – and South America. The agents were Alex. Howden & Co of 19 Birchin Lane, London, EC.

The last of the quartet, the CITY OF RIO DE JANEIRO, sailed from London on 13 September 1868, subsequent sailings taking place on the 28th of each month from London, 1st from Antwerp and 3rd from Falmouth. The name of the company was amended to LONDON, BELGIUM, BRAZIL & RIVER PLATE MAIL STEAMSHIP COMPANY [3], after it obtained a contract to carry the Belgian mails from Antwerp to South America.

Sailings continued with commendable regularity until 28 July 1870, when the CITY OF BUENOS AYRES left London for Antwerp, Falmouth and the usual ports under the command of Captain James. A day or two later, the CITY OF LIMERICK was announced as loading, but instead of her sailing on 28 August the 1,400 ton LACYDON was substituted. The agents were Alex. Howden & Co, as before, and the ports of call were unchanged, but the LONDON, BELGIUM, BRAZIL & RIVER PLATE MAIL STEAMSHIP COMPANY went into liquidation and a new line, the RYDE LINE (Chapter 23) took over.

[1] *Illustrated London News* 23/11/1867.
[2] *The Times* 30/1/1868.
[3] *The Times* 6/6/1868.

1. 1867 CITY OF LIMERICK
  1,339. 80,67 x 9,81. (264.7 x 32.2). C–1–3. I–S–C2–10. (1–100).
  Randolph, Elder & Co, Glasgow. 1867 launched. 1867 (31/8) MV
  London–St. Vincent (for coal)–Rio de Janeiro–Montevideo–
  Buenos Aires. 1868 (13/4) FV London–Antwerp–Falmouth–St.
  Vincent–S. America. 1870 WARRIOR (T. & J. Harrison;. 1872
  ditto (Lamport & Holt). 1873 VANDYCK (Lamport & Holt);
  1,686 tons; 1892 hulked at Rio de Janeiro.
2. 1867 CITY OF BUENOS AYRES
  1,712. 91,31 x 9,90. (299.6 x 32.5). C–1–3. I–S–I(2)–10. (I–100).
  Richardson, Duck & Co, Stockton. 1867 (Jly) launched. 1867
  (14/11) MV London–St. Vincent (for coal)–Rio de Janeiro–
  Montevideo–Buenos Aires. 1868 (13/5) FV London–Antwerp–
  Falmouth–St. Vincent–S. America. 1872 CALIPSO (Lloyd
  Austriaco); 1,712 tons; engines compounded by G. Forrester &
  Co, Liverpool.
3. 1868 CITY OF BRUSSELS
  1,600. 83,20 x 10,12. (273.0 x 33.2). C–1–3. I–S–C2–10. (I–100).
  Randolph, Elder & Co, Glasgow. 1868 (10/2) launched. 1868
  (14/3) MV London–Antwerp–Falmouth–St. Vincent (for coal)–
  Rio de Janeiro–Montevideo–Buenos Aires.
4. 1868 CITY OF RIO DE JANEIRO
  1,597. 83,20 x 10,12. (273.0 x 33.2). C–1–3. I–S–C2–10. (I–100).
  Randolph, Elder & Co, Glasgow. 1868 launched. 1868 (13/9) MV
  London–Antwerp–Falmouth–St. Vincent (for coal)–Rio de
  Janeiro–Montevideo–Buenos Aires. 1873 TENIERS (Lamport &
  Holt); 1,803 tons; 1878 wore Belgian flag but owners unchanged.
  1892 scrapped at Sunderland.

Chapter 19

(1868–1939)

PACIFIC STEAM NAVIGATION COMPANY

(British)

The PACIFIC STEAM NAVIGATION COMPANY was founded on 6 September 1838 with a capital of £250,000 and headquarters at 5 Barge Yard, Bucklersbury, London, EC. This was some months before the start of the Royal Mail Steam Packet Company (Chapter 1), although their Royal Charter was granted by Queen Victoria on 26 September 1839 whereas the PSN charter was not received until 17 February 1840.

To begin with PSN ran a service from Valparaiso to Callao, and in due course Valparaiso – Callao – Panama. But what made them eligible for the present chapter was, however, the introduction in the late 1860s of regular sailings from Liverpool to Rio de Janeiro, Montevideo, the Straits of Magellan and Valparaiso.

The foundation of the Pacific Steam Navigation Company was due almost entirely to an American, William Wheelwright, who was born at Newburyport, Massachusetts, on 18 March 1798. He settled at Guayaquil, Ecuador, in 1833 but moved to Valparaiso, Chile, where he founded a line of sailing ships, although his real ambition was to start a steamship service between Chile, Peru and Panama. Meanwhile, in August 1835, the Chilean Government granted him exclusive rights to establish steamship lines between ports and rivers in Chile for a period of 10 years provided he placed in service two or more steamers of at least 300 tons each within two years.

Wheelwright proceeded via Peru, where he received promises of full support, and Panama to New York, where he hoped to raise the necessary capital. However, he was disappointed and left for Britain where, in London, Liverpool and Glasgow, he met with full success.

Progress was not particularly brisk, but orders were placed in October 1839 with Curling & Young, of Limehouse, London, for two wooden paddle steamers of 700 tons, the CHILE and PERU. The former sailed from Gravesend via Falmouth for Rio de Janeiro on 24 June 1840, while the PERU left Gravesend via Plymouth on 10 July. They sailed in company on 30 August from Rio via the Straits of Magellan for Valparaiso. Both countries, Chile and Peru, had extended the time limit for the start of sailings.

The two ships were placed in service between Valparaiso and Callao, with stops at a number of ports *en route* and all went well until May 1841, when the CHILE reached Valparaiso in a sinking condition after striking a reef. However, she was back in commission before the end of the year, and a monthly service was maintained by the two ships until 1852.

On 29 August 1845 PSN was awarded a mail contract valued at £20,000 a year for five years for a monthly service between Panama, Callao and Valparaiso.

During the next 20 years more than a dozen newly-built PSN steamers sailed from Liverpool for Valparaiso via the Straits of Magellan to take part in the Valparaiso–Panama service or in Chilean coastal activities, but although it is believed that all of them called at Rio de Janeiro or Montevideo, or both, on the way out they cannot really be considered to have undertaken a service to Brazil or the River Plate to make them eligible for inclusion in the accompanying detailed fleet list. They certainly merit brief mention, however, and for the record they were: 1845 ECUADOR (323 tons), 1846 NEW GRENADA (649), 1849 BOLIVIA (773), 1851 SANTIAGO (1,000), 1851 LIMA (1,150), 1852 BOGOTA (1,150), 1852 QUITO (I) (1,150), 1853 VALDIVIA (573),

1864 QUITO 1,800 tons
Paddle steamer built for Valparaiso – Panama service.

1856 INCA (290), 1856 VALPARAISO (1,060), 1858 CALLAO (1,062), 1862 PERU (II) (1,307), 1863 CHILE (II) (1,672), 1864 QUITO (II) and 1864 PAYTA (1,800). All were iron paddle steamers except the VALDIVIA, which was a wooden screw vessel.

The first really successful compound engine fitted to an ocean-going steamer was supplied to the 1,060 ton VALPARAISO in 1856, and not only were subsequent units of the PSN fleet similarly treated but the LIMA and others were sent back to England for conversion. It is a remarkable fact that the VALPARAISO's consumption of coal for the round voyage from Valparaiso to Panama was 640 tons compared with the 1,150 tons required by her predecessors. The importance of this

145

saving cannot be overestimated as one of the Company's biggest headaches was the maintenance of adequate supplies of coal on the West Coast.

John Elder was the man very largely responsible for the compound engine. In 1852 he joined the firm of Randolph, Elliott & Co of Glasgow, which became Randolph, Elder & Co, and from 1860 ships as well as engines were built by them. In 1868 John Elder became the sole owner but unfortunately, having changed the name of the firm to John Elder & Co, he died in September of the following year at the early age of 45.

A significant event in the PSN story was the appointment of a new board of directors in 1845 following the loss in five years of no less than £72,000 of the Company's capital, and more or less simultaneously their headquarters were transferred from London to Liverpool. Ten years later, in 1855, the Panama Railroad was opened from Atlantic to Pacific, thus enabling PSN to issue through bills of lading and through passage tickets between Europe and the west coast of South America. Furthermore, a supplementary Charter granted in 1859 authorised an increase of the Company's capital to £500,000.

The high rates and fares charged by the Panama Railroad were a considerable bone of contention. The railroad's superintendent, Colonel A. J. Center, travelled to Callao in 1866 to discuss the matter with George Petrie of PSN. A provisional agreement was made that one-third of the through revenue should go to the railroad, and similar proportions to RMSP for the journey from England to Panama and to PSN for the section from Panama to the west coast destination. When Colonel Center reported to the railroad directors in New York they were adamant that their proportion should be a great deal higher, and would not change their minds even when told that PSN had indicated that, failing a satisfactory agreement, they would build a fleet of steamers for an express line between the west coast and England via the Straits of Magellan, thereby eliminating the railroad.

So PSN applied for and received a supplementary Charter in 1867, authorising them to run a through steamship service between England and Chile, and it also permitted an increase of the Company's capital to £2,000,000. The railroad soon had every reason to regret their decision.

The 1,600 ton iron paddle steamers PACIFIC, SANTIAGO, PANAMA and LIMENA, which had been completed in 1865 by Randolph, Elder & Co for the Valparaiso–Panama route, were selected to open the new PSN service. Imposing looking vessels with two funnels, two masts and clipper bows, they were fitted with compound engines giving them a service speed of upwards of 10 knots. The PACIFIC sailed from Valparaiso on 13 May 1868 as the pioneer and called at Montevideo, Rio de Janeiro, St. Vincent, Lisbon and St. Nazaire *en route* to Liverpool, from which she sailed again on 15 July. Her three sisters followed. It may be mentioned that the Royal Mail Steam Packet Company's mail steamers only proceeded as far as Brazil, with a feeder steamer thence to the River Plate, until July 1869. Improvements in the port facilities at Montevideo and Buenos Aires were among the reasons for the introduction of a through service, but the appearance of PSN on the scenes was undoubtedly partly responsible.

Four iron screw ships, the 2,800 ton MAGELLAN, PATAGONIA, ARAUCANIA and CORDILLERA were completed for the new PSN service in 1869, the first by Randolph, Elder & Co and the other three by its successor firm, John Elder & Co. All had compound engines giving a service speed of 12 knots. The MAGELLAN's maiden voyage started from Liverpool on 13 March 1869 for Rio de Janeiro, Montevideo and Valparaiso. The PATAGONIA sailed on 13 May, and from then onwards a monthly service was in operation, the regular sailing day from Liverpool being the 13th. It would appear that people were not superstitious in those days!

By 1870 the service had been increased from monthly to fortnightly, but to begin with some of the sailings were taken by chartered steamers such as the GALATEA, which made three round voyages (see Ryde Line, Chapter 23). Normal sailing days were the 13th and 29th. A call at Pauillac (Bordeaux) was substituted for St. Nazaire.

The 3,832 ton JOHN ELDER, which started her maiden voyage on 13 December 1870, was completed after the death of her builder, whose name was allotted to her as an exceptional reward for the great services he had rendered PSN by the introduction of the compound engine. She had a length of 116,39 metres (381.9 feet) – that is to say, 6,8 metres (22.3 feet) greater than that of the MAGELLAN, but her passenger accommodation was less – 72 first, 92 second and 265 third class. Her immediate successors, the GARONNE (by Napier), LUSITANIA (by Laird) and CHIMBORAZO of 1871 and CUZCO of 1872 were approximately similar. It would seem that they were underpowered in comparison with the smaller MAGELLAN class and in 1872 the JOHN ELDER was lengthened by 7,47 metres (24.5 feet), thereby increasing her tonnage to 4,151. In addition, both her passenger accommodation and boiler power were increased and she was given a second funnel. None of her consorts were similarly treated.

The 4,000 ton ACONCAGUA, SORATA, ILLIMANI and COTO-PAXI were completed by Elder in 1872–3 with engines of increased power, their dimensions being approximately similar to those of the lengthened JOHN ELDER, but they had only one funnel.

A weekly service was started by the SORATA on 8 January 1873, and to make this possible there were further additions during the year of the

1873 SORATA 4,014 tons
In addition to South American voyages ran London – Australia for six years.

3,805 ton CORCOVADO and PUNO by Laird and the GALICIA by Napier.

A smaller ship, the 3,525 ton TACORA, had started her maiden voyage from Liverpool on 4 October 1872 and was wrecked 24 days later at Cape Santa Maria, Montevideo. She had sailed one day before the White Star REPUBLIC (Chapter 27), which was breaking PSN's virtual monopoly of the west coast of South America service, and it was said that she was racing the intruder.

There were also two newcomers each with two funnels in 1873 – the 4,218 ton POTOSI by Elder and the 4,219 ton BRITANNIA by Laird, as well as the single funnel VALPARAISO which, rather surprisingly, was about the same size as the TACORA.

The 3,805 ton CORCOVADO's maiden voyage started from Liverpool on 19 February 1873, and it is interesting to see that she left Lisbon at 7.30 am on 26 February and arrived at Rio de Janeiro at 2.50 am on 11 March, which was stated to give 12 days 18 hours steaming time after deducting a stoppage of 1 hour 20 minutes for discharging the pilot during fog off Lisbon. The distance run by the ship was 4,247 nautical miles, equal to 13.88 knots. [1] It should, however, be added that no apparent allowance was made for difference of time between the two ports. Working on the assumption that this was three hours, these should be added to the total duration, this reducing the average speed to 13.74 knots.

William Wheelwright left the west coast of South America in 1873 for London, where he died soon afterwards, on 26 September. His coffin was carried across the North Atlantic and he was buried in his native Newburyport. Four years later a statue was unveiled in his memory in the Plaza Aduana, Valparaiso, the ceremony being attended by several thousand people.

148

1873 POTOSI 4,218 tons
One of four ships built 1873–74 with two funnels.

The weekly service lasted only until February 1874 when, by agreement with the Post Office, it reverted to fortnightly. The time taken between the start of a steamer's round voyage and that of her next was 17 weeks or longer, and that meant that allowing for eventualities upwards of 17 steamers were required to maintain a weekly service. By October 1874 there were 21 ships as two final units came from Elder in 1874 – the 4,688 ton LIGURIA and the 4,702 ton IBERIA, whose maiden voyage started on 21 October. Both had two funnels, and the latter's accommodation consisted of 140 first class, 50 second and 800 third. Apart from one Inman and two White Star units they were the largest passenger liners in the world.

The Company's capital had been increased to £3,000,000 and provisionally to £4,000,000 to pay for the fleet of new ships, but when the weekly service was reduced to fortnightly in 1874 this meant that 10 or 11 ships would suffice instead of 21, and that the Company had been guilty of some serious miscalculations. Moreover, laying up 11 ships cost the Company well over £1,000 a week.

In 1875 PSN were fortunate in selling the 3,805 ton CORCOVADO and PUNO to Royal Mail, who renamed then DON and PARA, respectively. Even more important, PSN was approached by Anderson, Anderson & Co, of London, in February 1877 concerning a possible charter of two or more ships in order to start a steamship service to Australia. In the event, it was agreed that four ships should inaugurate a monthly Orient Line service from London via Plymouth to Cape Town and Australia, returning via Suez, under satisfactory financial arrangements and an option to purchase. The ships chosen were the LUSITANIA, CHIMBORAZO, CUZCO and GARONNE, the service being opened by the first-named on 28 June 1877. All four ships were bought by the Orient Line in 1878.

149

Despite this dispersal of tonnage, PSN still had some spare ships and the MAGELLAN, PATAGONIA, ARAUCANIA and CORDILLERA, the four Elder products of 1869, were despatched from Liverpool to the River Plate in 1877. Some time later they were fitted with refrigeration plant in order to participate in the Argentine – Europe meat trade.

In 1879 the JOHN ELDER joined the Australian service, and took the first sailing of what had become joint Orient Steam Navigation Company Limited and Pacific Steam Navigation Company fortnightly sailings. Orient Line contributions were the 5,386 ton ORIENT plus the four PSN steamers bought in the previous year. In addition, PSN supplied the ACONCAGUA, SORATA, COTOPAXI, POTOSI, IBERIA and LIGURIA.

The ILLIMANI was wrecked on Mocha Island, Chile, in July 1879. Happily, in the following October a newly-built iron screw steamer for the west coast service, the 2,160 ton MENDOZA, attracted much attention as the first British merchant ship to be lit by electricity, beating by three months the conversion to electricity of the four year old Inman Line CITY OF BERLIN.

In 1885 the French port of call was changed from Bordeaux to La Rochelle–Pallice.

From 1884 onwards the Australian service steamers proceeded outwards as well as homewards via the Suez Canal. The 6,000 ton steel single-screw steamers ORIZABA and OROYA (I) were completed in 1886–7, and were the first straight-stemmed units in the fleet. They had two funnels and four masts, and were placed in the Australian service. They were followed in 1889 by the 5,850 ton OROTAVA and ORUBA (I), which were originally intended for the South American trade but instead ran to Australia. By 1890 all the PSN fleet except the new 'O' ships and those bought by Orient had resumed their service to South America.

The VALPARAISO was wrecked at Vigo on 28 February 1887, and the COTOPAXI foundered in the Straits of Magellan in April 1889 as the result of a collision with the German steamer OLYMPIA. She was beached when on the point of sinking, and the collision damage was patched up. She was refloated with considerable difficulty, proceeded on her voyage and was nearing the Pacific when she struck an unknown rock. She sank within a few minutes, but by good fortune the 200 passengers and crew were saved. A further loss took place on 16 January 1892 when the JOHN ELDER was wrecked on the coast of Chile. The BRITANNIA stranded at Rio de Janeiro on 4 September 1895. She was refloated and sold. On 1 October 1894 the PATAGONIA, also, was wrecked on the coast of Chile.

The 3,600 ton cargo steamers MAGELLAN (II), INCA, SARMIEN-TO and ANTISANA were completed in 1893 in addition to the 4,821 ton ORELLANA and the 4,803 ton ORCANA, which were products of Harland & Wolff of Belfast and had accommodation for 70 first and 675 third class passengers. They were detailed to the Valpariso service, in which they remained for 12 years before being sold to the Hamburg American Line.

A trio of 5,300 ton twin-screw ships came from the Belfast firm – the ORISSA and OROPESA (I) in 1895 and the ORAVIA in 1897. All three ran between Liverpool and Valparaiso, but the 7,945 ton ORTONA appeared in 1899 for the Australian service.

In 1902 the joint Australian service became known as the Orient–Pacific Line, by which time the Orient Steam Navigation Company had themselves placed six ships in commission.

1903 ORITA 9,239 tons
Proceeded via Panama Canal after 1927.

At the end of 1902 the PSN fleet consisted of 47 steamers of a total tonnage of 162,813, these figures including, of course, the numerous ships employed on local services on the west coast of South America. By the end of 1903 the only survivor of the fleet of 22 ships built for the Liverpool–Valparaiso service between 1869 and 1874 was the 'CUZCO, which ran for Orient until 1905 without change of name. Of the remainder, the MAGELLAN (I) was scrapped in 1893, the SORATA in 1895, the POTOSI in 1897 and the IBERIA and LIGURIA in 1903. In addition, the ACONCAGUA was sold in 1895, the ARAUCANIA in 1897 and the GALICIA in 1898. The last-named became the GASPESIA of the short-lived Canadian Steamship Company.

The 5,550 ton MEXICO and CALIFORNIA were built by Caird & Co

151

of Greenock in 1902, and the 5,981 ton PANAMA and the 5,967 ton VICTORIA by Fairfield of Glasgow. Fitted with accommodation for 130 first class passengers, they were intended for the coastal trade but made a number of Liverpool–Valparaiso voyages. The VICTORIA's first activities were as a Boer War transport.

The 9,239 ton twin-screw ORITA was completed by Harland & Wolff in 1903 for the Liverpool–Valparaiso service, followed in 1906 by the 8,000 ton ORIANA from Barclay Curle and the ORTEGA and ORONSA from the Belfast firm. The passenger complement of the last two was 150 first, 130 second and 800 third class.

Abandonment of the call at St. Vincent in 1904 enabled ships to put in from time to time at additional ports in Brazil. The new itinerary included some or all of the following: La Pallice, Coruña, Vigo, Lisbon, Pernambuco, Bahia, Rio de Janeiro, Montevideo, Buenos Aires, Port Stanley (Falkland Islands), Punta Arenas, Coronel and Talcahuano *en route* to Valparaiso.

The ORIZABA stranded near Freemantle on 17 February 1905, and was sold for a small sum. In the following year PSN disposed of its share of the Orient–Pacific Line to Royal Mail, together with the OROYA, OROTAVA, ORUBA and ORTONA, and RMSP themselves withdrew within three years.

The ORISSA was in port at Valparaiso in August 1906 during the earthquake, and took on board numerous refugees. A year later, the first class accommodation of the ORISSA, OROPESA and ORAVIA was thoroughly modernised.

It was not until they commissioned the 9,588 ton ARAGON in 1905 that RMSP introduced twin-screw ships. PSN had anticipated this move as long previously as 1895 and, moreover, their twin-screw ORITA of 1903 was not greatly inferior to the ARAGON. The 11,546 ton ORCOMA, completed by Wm. Beardmore & Co Ltd of Glasgow in 1908, certainly compared well with the latest RMSP ships, the AMA-

1908 ORCOMA 11,546 tons
Made one post-World War I voyage via Straits of Magellan.

ZON, ARAGUAYA and AVON, and she was somewhat faster. She had accommodation for 250 first class, 200 second, 100 intermediate and 500 third class passengers, and was often referred to as 'the electric ship' on account of her lifts, fires, ovens, dish washers, laundry and other electrical gadgets.

The two lines were undoubtedly competing with one another for the traffic between England, France, Spain, Portugal, Rio de Janeiro and the River Plate, so it is hardly surprising that the RMSP chairman, Owen Cosby Philipps (the future Lord Kylsant), cast covetous eyes on PSN, with which his company had been closely connected since the first days of services from England to Panama, and Panama to Valparaiso. In 1910 talks took place between the two companies and in due course it was arranged that Royal Mail should take over PSN. However, the latter retained its name, and Thomas Rome continued as chairman of the Court of Directors. Royal mail had changed their funnel from black to yellow in 1901, and PSN followed suit.

The ORAVIA was wrecked on 16 November 1912 on Seal Rocks, Falkland Islands, when on voyage from Liverpool to Montevideo, the Straits of Magellan and Valparaiso. It seems that there were occasional PSN calls at the Falkland Islands.

As a friendly gesture, the 15,620 ton ANDES, laid down by Harland & Wolff for RMSP, was handed over to PSN and made her maiden voyage under their flag from Southampton to Valparaiso, starting on 26 September 1913, although she subsequently sailed for Royal Mail. She was a triple-screw ship driven by the well-known Harland & Wolff combination of triple-expansion engines and a low-pressure turbine, and could accommodate 400 first, 230 second and 760 third class passengers.

The 15,507 ton ORDUÑA was delivered by Harland & Wolff in time to leave Liverpool on 19 February 1914 on her maiden voyage to Valparaiso, but two sister ships, the ORBITA and ORCA, were not launched until 7 July 1914 and 15 January 1918, respectively. The latter, which differed from the others by having a cruiser stern, was then without her passenger accommodation. The ORBITA became an auxiliary cruiser in 1915, whereas after two voyages to Valparaiso the ORDUÑA was chartered to the Cunard Line, for whom she ran regularly until the end of 1919. The ORDUÑA and ORBITA were six metres (20 feet) shorter than the ANDES and had a smaller passenger complement – 240 first, 180 second and 700 third class.

The fact that the Panama Canal was not opened until the war year of 1914 meant that its immediate effect on PSN was minimal, but for some years previously they had felt extremely anxious about its effect on their service via the Straits of Magellan, and the lucrative passenger business which had been built up from Britain, France, Spain and even Brazil and

1914 ORDUÑA 15,507 tons
Showing the black funnel as painted in 1914.

the River Plate to the west coast of South America. A delegation was sent to Panama to report upon the situation. Completion of the Transandine Railway in 1910 was, of course, another serious problem.

Three of the Liverpool–Straits of Magellan–Valparaiso ships were lost during the war. The OROPESA (I) was taken up as an auxiliary cruiser of the 10th Cruiser Squadron in November 1914 and in December 1915 became the CHAMPAGNE of the French Navy although she retained her British crew. She was torpedoed and sunk by a German submarine in the Irish Sea on 15 October 1917 with the loss of 56 lives. The ORONSA was torpedoed and sunk off Bardsey Island on 28 April 1918 and two months later, on 25 June, the ORISSA was sunk 21 miles south-west of Skerryvore. In September 1914 the ORTEGA, homeward bound from Valparaiso, had been chased by the German cruiser DRESDEN. The British ship managed to reach the uncharted Nelson Strait and escaped by taking a dangerous 100 mile passage. The MEXICO and CALIFORNIA were victims of German submarines in 1917; the PANAMA became a hospital ship. Principal survivors of the war were the ORDUÑA, ORBITA, ORCOMA, ORITA, ORTEGA and ORIANA, plus the cargo steamer ORCA.

After the Armistice of November 1918 some of the fleet continued to run via the Straits of Magellan, but the remainder opened a service via the Panama Canal. The ANDES sailed exclusively for Royal Mail betweeen Southampton and Buenos Aires.

The ORBITA and ORCOMA both received thorough refits, and the former was ready to sail from Liverpool on 26 September 1919 for Rio de Janeiro, Montevideo and Valparaiso. She was followed on the same route by the ORIANA on 20 October, and by the ORCOMA on 6 November, but on nearly all subsequent voyages the latter proceeded via Panama.

The 14,118 ton OROPESA (II) was launched by Cammel Laird of Birkenhead on 9 December 1919, and sailed on her maiden voyage from

154

Liverpool to Valparaiso via the Straits on 16 September, 1920.

Royal Mail decided to start a service between Hamburg, Southampton, Cherbourg and New York in 1921, and as it was evident by that time that conditions did not justify their continuance on either the Straits or the Panama Canal route, the ORBITA, OROPESA and ORDUÑA were chartered for the new service.

The 7,814 ton MILTIADES and the 7,848 ton MARATHON, both launched in 1903, were bought from the Aberdeen Line in 1921 and renamed ORCANA (II) and ORUBA (II). The latter sailed from Liverpool on 26 May 1921 for Rio de Janeiro, Montevideo, Valparaiso, Panama Canal and back to Liverpool, and undertook a second voyage by the same route, after which she was laid up. The ORCANA started a similar voyage on 11 August 1921 and was scheduled for a second on 1 December 1921, but it was cancelled. These two ships proved expensive to operate, and after being laid up at Liverpool and Dartmouth were scrapped in 1923–4.

The local services on the west coast of South America had, unfortunately, to be discontinued in 1922 owing to the introduction of the Chilean Cabotage (coastal trade) Law. This serious set-back was partly made up for by the introduction of a passenger and mail service from New York to Valparaiso via the Panama Canal by the 8,500 ton EBRO and ESSEQUIBO, formerly of Royal Mail. This remained in operation until 1930, when the pair was laid up in the River Dart.

A final 'O' steamer, the 12,257 ton OROYA (II) was launched by Harland & Wolff on 16 December 1920, but her completion was deliberately delayed and she did not enter service until 1923. She ran exclusively via the Panama Canal.

Following the addition of the ORCA's passenger accommodation at the end of 1922, she was bought by Royal Mail and entered the New York service in place of the OROPESA, which was returned to PSN and made numerous voyages via the Straits until 1926, after which she was detailed to the Panama Canal route. She had been converted to oil fuel in 1924. The ORCOMA had been similarly converted a year previously, when also she was extensively modernised. She continued to run via Panama.

Royal Mail withdrew their New York service shortly before taking over the White Star Line on 1 January 1927. The ORDUÑA and ORBITA reverted to PSN, and both were converted to burn oil. The ORDUÑA normally proceeded out and home via Panama apart from an annual tour out via the east coast and home via the west, but the ORBITA was detailed exclusively to the Panama route. The ORTEGA and ORIANA were scrapped in 1927.

A 17,702 ton quadruple-screw motorship was launched for PSN on 23

1931 REINA DEL PACIFICO 17,702 tons
Made an annual voyage from Liverpool round South America.

September 1930 by Harland & Wolff of Glasgow, and was such an advance on her predecessors that instead of being given an 'O' name she was called REINA DEL PACIFICO ('Queen of the Pacific'). Her passenger complement was 280 first, 162 second and 446 third class. Her maiden voyage started on 9 April 1931 from Liverpool for Valparaiso via the Panama Canal, and this was her normal route, but once a year she made a tour round South America, out via Panama, Valparaiso and the Straits of Magellan, and home via the east coast.

Following the 'REINA's debut, the OROYA (II) was laid up at Dartmouth until 1939, when she was towed to La Spezia and scrapped. The OROPESA (II) was also consigned to Dartmouth in 1931, but re-entered service in 1937. The ORITA was scrapped in 1932 and the ORCOMA in 1933, leaving only the REINA DEL PACIFICO, ORDUÑA, ORBITA and OROPESA.

All four served as troopships during World War II, and the OROPESA was torpedoed and sunk by German submarine U.96 about 100 miles from Bloody Foreland on 16 January 1941 with the loss of 113 lives. The ORDUÑA was retained as a troopship until 1950 and was scrapped a year later. The ORBITA was scrapped in 1950.

The REINA DEL PACIFICO went to Belfast in 1946 for reconditioning. Unfortunately, her return to service was delayed by a severe engine-room explosion on 11 September 1947 during her subsequent trials, resulting in 23 deaths. She resumed service between Liverpool, the Panama Canal and Valparaiso in 1948.

The 20,234 ton twin-screw REINA DEL MAR ('Queen of the Sea')

156

was launched at Belfast on 7 June 1955, and left Liverpool on 3 May 1956 on the first of numerous voyages to the Panama Canal and Valparaiso. Unlike the REINA DEL PACIFICO, she was provided with double-reduction geared turbines, which gave her a service speed of 18 knots – slightly less than that of her consort, which was scrapped at Newport, Monmouth, in 1958.

By the start of the 1960s practically all ocean-going steamship companies were feeling the effects of air competition. PSN was no exception, and in 1963 the REINA DEL MAR was withdrawn from South American service. Instead, she was chartered to the Travel Savings Association as a cruise liner. A year later she was rebuilt as such and placed under Union-Castle Line management, receiving their hull and funnel colours. Sold to Union-Castle in 1973, she was scrapped at Kaohsiung two years later.

The Pacific Steam Navigation Company is no longer involved in the passenger business, but acts as managers for a handful or so of freighters.

[1] *Liverpool Journal of Commerce* 14/4/1873.

1. (1868) PACIFIC
    1,631. 81,50 x 12,25. (267.4 x 40.2). C–2–2. I–P–C2–10. Randolph, Elder & Co, Glasgow. 1865 (28/1) launched. 1868 (13/5) FV Valparaiso–Montevideo–Rio de Janeiro–St. Vincent–Lisbon–St. Nazaire–Liverpool. 1868 (15/7) FV Liverpool–St. Nazaire–Lisbon–St. Vincent–Rio de Janeiro–Montevideo–Straits of Magellan–Valparaiso. 1870 (approx) hulked.
2. (1868) SANTIAGO
    1,619. 81,38 x 12,25. (267.0 x 40.2). C–2–2. I–P–C2–10. Randolph, Elder & Co, Glasgow. 1865 (27/5) launched. 1868 FV Valparaiso–Montevideo–Rio de Janeiro–Liverpool. 1869 (23/1) wrecked in Straits of Magellan when homeward bound (2).
3. (1868) PANAMA
    1,642. 81,38 x 12,22. (267.0 x 40.1). C–2–2. I–P–C2–10. Randolph, Elder & Co, Glasgow. 1866 (17/3) launched. 1880 (approx) hulked.
4. (1868) LIMENA
    1,622. 81,44 x 12,25. (267.2 x 40.2). C–2–2. I–P–C2–10. Randolph, Elder & Co, Glasgow. 1865 launched. 1874 (approx) sold to Peruvian Government.
5. 1869 MAGELLAN
    2,856. 109,59 x 12,50. (359.6 x 41.0). C–1–3. I–S–C2–12. (I–145; II–75; III–300). Randolph, Elder & Co, Glasgow. 1868 (30/12)

launched. 1869 (13/3) MV Liverpool–Rio de Janeiro–Montevideo–Valparaiso. 1869 (20/8) 2nd voyage ditto. 1877 MV Liverpool–R. Plate. 1890 sold. 1893 scrapped in England.

6. 1869 PATAGONIA
2,866. 107,59 x 12,50. (353.0 x 41.0). C–1–3. I–S–C2–12. (I–145; II–75; III–300). John Elder & Co, Glasgow. 1869 (1/3) launched. 1869 (13/5) MV Liverpool–Rio de Janeiro–Montevideo–Valparaiso. 1877 FV Liverpool–R. Plate. 1880 (4/5) FV for White Star (c), Liverpool–New York (1 RV). 1890 T3 replaced C2. 1894 (1/10) wrecked on Chilean coast.

7. 1869 ARAUCANIA
2,877. 108,13 x 12,50. (354.8 x 41.0). C–1–3. I–S–C2–12. (I–145; II–75; III–300). John Elder & Co, Glasgow. 1869 (29/4) launched. 1869 (13/7) MV Liverpool–Rio de Janeiro–Montevideo–Valparaiso. 1877 FV Liverpool–R. Plate. 1890 T3 replaced C2. 1897 sold.

8. 1869 CORDILLERA
2,860. 107,65 x 12,50. (353.2 x 41.0). C–1–3. I–S–C2–12. (I–145; II–75; III–300). John Elder & Co, Glasgow. 1869 (26/6) launched. 1869 (13/10) MV Liverpool–Rio de Janeiro–Montevideo–Valparaiso. 1877 FV Liverpool–R. Plate. 1884 (20/9) wrecked in Straits of Magellan.

9. 1870 JOHN ELDER
3,832. 116,39 x 12,68. (381.9 x 41.6). C–1–3. I–S–C2–12. John Elder & Co, Glasgow. 1870 (29/8) launched. 1870 (13/12) MV Liverpool–Rio de Janeiro–Montevideo–Valparaiso. 1872 lengthened to 123,86 metres (406.4 feet); 4,151 tons; 2 funnels. 1879 FV London–Cape Town–Australia. 1886 (3/11) resumed Straits of Magellan service. 1892 (16/1) wrecked on Chilean coast.

10. 1871 GARONNE
3,871. 116,45 x 12,62. (382.1 x 41.4). C–1–3. I–S–C2–12. (I–72; II–92; III–265). R. Napier & Sons, Glasgow. 1871 (Apr) launched. 1871 (29/6) MV Liverpool–Rio de Janeiro–Montevideo–Valparaiso. 1877 FV London–Cape Town–Australia. 1878 GARONNE (Orient). 1897 sold. 1898 bought by US Govt. 1901 (Jan) wrecked.

11. 1871 LUSITANIA
3,825. 115,78 x 12,59. (379.9 x 41.3). C–1–3. I–S–C2–12. (I–72; II–92; III–265). Laird Bros, Birkenhead. 1871 (Jun) launched. 1871 (29/9) MV Liverpool–Rio de Janeiro–Montevideo–Valparaiso. 1877 (28/6) FV (London)–Plymouth–Cape Town–Australia. 1878 LUSITANIA (Orient). 1886 T3 replaced C2. 1900 LUSITANIA (Elder Dempster). 1900 (Jul) resold to PSN. 1901 (Feb)

repurchased by Elder Dempster. 1901 (26/6) wrecked near Cape Race (0).

12. 1871 CHIMBORAZO
3,847. 117,03 x 12,59. (384.0; x 41.3). C–1–3. I–S–C2–12. (I–72; II–92; III–265). John Elder & Co, Glasgow. 1871 (21/6) launched. 1871 (13/10) MV Liverpool–Rio de Janeiro–Montevideo–Valparaiso. 1877 FV London–Cape Town–Australia. 1878 CHIMBORAZO (Orient). 1895 CLEOPATRA (Br). 1897 scrapped.

13. 1872 CUZCO
3,845. 117,09 x 12,62. (384.2 x 41.4). C–1–3. I–S–C2–12. (I–72; II–92; III–265). John Elder & Co, Glasgow. 1871 (18/10) launched. 1872 (13/1) MV Liverpool–Rio de Janeiro–Montevideo–Valparaiso. 1877 FV London–Cape Town–Australia. 1878 CUZCO (Orient). 1905 scrapped in Italy.

14. 1872 ACONCAGUA
4,105. 123,37 x 12,62. (404.8 x 41.4). C–1–3. I–S–C2–12. (I–126; II–40; III–800). John Elder & Co, Glasgow. 1872 (6/6) launched. 1872 (28/9) MV Liverpool–Rio de Janeiro–Montevideo–Valparaiso. 1880 FV London–Cape Town–Australia. 1883 (24/10) resumed Liverpool–Rio de Janeiro–Montevideo–Valparaiso. 1895 EGYPTE (Fr).

15. 1872 TACORA
3,525. 114,47 x 12,59. (375.6 x 41.3). C–1–3. I–S–C2–12. (I–60; II–90; III–335). John Elder & Co, Glasgow. 1872 (23/5) launched. 1872 (4/10) MV Liverpool–Lisbon–Rio de Janeiro. 1872 (28/10) wrecked during MV at Cape Santa Maria, Montevideo.

16. 1873 SORATA
4,014. 122,31 x 13,84. (401.3 x 42.8). C–1–3. I–S–C2–12. (I–140; II–50; III–800). John Elder & Co, Glasgow. 1872 (2/10) launched. 1873 (8/1) MV Liverpool–Rio de Janeiro–Montevideo–Valparaiso. 1880 FV London–Cape Town–Australia. 1886 (22/9) resumed Liverpool–Rio de Janeiro–Montevideo–Valparaiso. 1895 scrapped at Tranmere.

17. 1873 CORCOVADO
3,805. 118,10 x 13,13. (387.5 x 43.1). C–1–3. I–S–C2–12. (I–60; II–90; III–325. Laird Bros, Birkenhead. 1872 (Sep) launched. 1873 (19/2) MV Liverpool–Rio de Janeiro–Montevideo–Valparaiso. 1875 DON (RMSP). 1901 scrapped.

18. 1873 ILLIMANI
4,022. 122,61 x 13,04 (402.3 x 42.8). C–1–3. I–S–C2–12. (I–140; II–50; III–800). John Elder & Co, Glasgow. 1872 (16/12) launched. 1873 (26/3) MV Liverpool–Rio de Janeiro–Monte-

video–Valparaiso. 1879 (18/7) wrecked on Mocha Island, Chile.

19. 1873 GALICIA
3,829. 116,85 x 13,10. (383.4 x 43.0). C–1–3. I–S–C2–12. (I–60; II–90; III–325). R. Napier & Sons, Glasgow. 1873 (14/1) launched. 1873 (23/4) MV Liverpool–Rio de Janeiro–Montevideo–Valparaiso. 1898 GASPESIA (Canadian SS Co). 1900 scrapped in Italy.

20. 1873 PUNO
3,805. 118,10 x 13,13. (387.5 x 43.1). C–1–3. I–S–C2–12. (I–60; II–90; III–325). Laird Bros, Birkenhead. 1873 (Mar) launched. 1873 (14/5) MV Liverpool–Rio de Janeiro–Montevideo–Valparaiso. 1875 PARA (RMSP). 1903 scrapped.

21. 1873 COTOPAXI
4,022. 122,58 x 13,04. (402.2 x 42.8). C–1–3. I–S–C2–12. (I–136; II–41; III–800). John Elder & Co, Glasgow. 1873 (15/3) launched. 1873 (18/6) MV Liverpool–Rio de Janeiro–Montevideo–Valparaiso. 1880 FV London–Cape Town–Australia. 1883 resumed Liverpool–Rio de Janeiro–Montevideo–Valparaiso. 1889 (6/3) LV Liverpool–Rio de Janeiro–Montevideo. 1889 (15/4) foundered in Straits of Magellan after striking uncharted rock. (0).

22. 1873 POTOSI
4,218. 128,49 x 13,34. (421.6 x 43.8). C–2–3. I–S–C2–13. (I–136; II–41; III–800). John Elder & Co, Glasgow. 1873 (14/5) launched. 1873 (6/8) MV Liverpool–Rio de Janeiro–Montevideo–Valapariso. 1880 FV London–Cape Town–Australia. 1889 (19/10) resumed Liverpool–Rio de Janeiro–Montevideo–Valparaiso. 1897 scrapped at Genoa.

23. 1873 BRITANNIA
4,129. 125,39 x 13,34. (411.4 x 43.8). C–2–3. I–S–C2–13. (I–138; II–41; III–570). Laird Bros, Birkenhead. 1873 (27/5) launched. 1873 (27/8) MV Liverpool–Rio de Janeiro–Montevideo–Valparaiso. 1885 auxiliary cruiser during Russian war scare. 1895 (4/9) stranded at Rio de Janeiro; refloated; sold. 1901 scrapped at Preston.

24. 1873 VALPARAISO
3,575. 115,57 x 12,74. (379.2 x 41.8). C–1–3. I–S–C2–12. (I–116; II–50; III–800). John Elder & Co, Glasgow. 1873 (30/7) launched. 1873 (8/10) MV Liverpool–Rio de Janeiro–Montevideo–Valparaiso. 1887 (28/2) wrecked at Vigo.

25. 1874 LIGURIA
4,688. 132,09 x 13,71. (433.4 x 45.0). C–2–3. I–S–C3–13. (I–100;

II–150; III–340). John Elder & Co, Glasgow. 1874 (Feb) launched. 1874 (9/9) MV Liverpool–Rio de Janeiro–Montevideo–Valparaiso. 1880 FV London–Cape Town–Australia. 1890 (17/9) resumed Liverpool–Rio de Janeiro–Montevideo–Valparaiso. 1893 T3 replaced C3. 1903 scrapped.

26. 1874 IBERIA

4,702. 132,12 x 13,71. (433.5 x 45.0). C–2–3. I–S–C3–13. (I–140; II–50; III–800). John Elder & Co, Glasgow. 1873 (6/12) launched. 1874 (21/10) MV Liverpool–Rio de Janeiro–Monte-video–Valparaiso. 1880 (12/5) FV London–Cape Town–Austra-lia. 1882 troopship during Egyptian Expedition. 1890 (11/6) resumed Liverpool–Rio de Janeiro–Montevideo–Valparaiso. 1893 T3 replaced C3. 1903 scrapped in Italy.

27. 1893 ORELLANA

4,821. 121,18 x 14,50. (397.6 x 47.6). S–1–4. S–T3–13. (I–70; III–675). Harland & Wolff, Belfast. 1892 (7/12) launched. 1893 (12/4) MV Liverpool–Rio de Janeiro–Montevideo–Valparaiso. 1905 ALLEMANNIA (Hapag). 1906 KOWNO (Russian Amer-ican). 1907 ALLEMANNIA (Hapag). 1916 OWASCO (US). 1917 (10/12) torpedoed by German submarine near Alicante; beached; refloated; scrapped.

28. 1893 ORCANA (I)

4,803. 121,21 x 14,50. (397.7 x 47.6). S–1–4. S–T3–13. (I–70; III–675). Harland & Wolff, Belfast. 1893 (7/3) launched. 1893 (19/7) MV Liverpool–Rio de Janeiro–Montevideo–Valparaiso. 1905 ALBINGIA (Hapag). 1906 GRODNO (Russian Amer-ican). 1907 ALBINGIA (Hapag). 1916 ARGONAUT (US). 1918 (5/6) torpedoed and sunk by German submarine U.82 off Bishop Rock.

29. 1895 OROPESA (I)

5,303. 128,31 x 14,87. (421.0 x 48.8). S–1–2. 2S–T6–15. Harland & Wolff, Belfast. 1894 (29/11) launched. 1895 (28/2) MV Liverpool–Rio de Janeiro–Montevideo–Valparaiso. 1907 accom-modation modernised. 1914 (Nov) auxiliary cruiser (10th Cruiser Squadron). 1915 (Dec) CHAMPAGNE (French Navy – British crew). 1917 (15/10) torpedoed and sunk by German submarine in Irish Sea (56).

30. 1895 ORISSA

5,317. 128,31 x 14,87. (421.0 x 48.8). S–1–2. 2S–T6–15. Harland & Wolff, Belfast. 1894 (15/12) launched. 1895 (11/4) MV Liverpool–Rio de Janeiro–Montevideo–Valparaiso. 1906 (Aug) at Valparaiso during earthquake; took on board numerous refugees. 1907 accommodation modernised. 1918 (25/6) torpedoed and sunk by German submarine 21 miles SW of Skerryvore (6).

31. 1897 ORAVIA
 5,321. 128,31 x 14,87. (421.0 x 48.8). 1–2. 2S–T6–15. Harland & Wolff, Belfast. 1896 (5/12) launched. 1897 (1/7) MV Liverpool–Rio de Janeiro–Montevideo–Valparaiso. 1907 accommodation modernised. 1912 (16/11) wrecked on Seal Rocks, Falkland Islands, on voyage Liverpool–Montevideo–Valparaiso (0).

32. 1902 MEXICO
 5,549. 122,18 x 15,94. (400.9 x 52.3). 1–2. 2S–T6–15. (I–130). Caird & Co, Greenock. 1902 (22/3) launched. 1902 (30/7) MV London–Montevideo–Valparaiso; usually ran on Pacific coast. 1917 (23/3) torpedoed and sunk by German submarine.

33. 1902 CALIFORNIA
 5,547. 121,98 x 15,94. (400.3 x 52.3). 1–2. 2S–T6–15. (I–130). Caird & Co, Greenock. 1902 (21/6) launched. 1902 (2/10) MV Liverpool–Montevideo–Valparaiso; usually ran on Pacific coast. 1917 (Oct) torpedoed and sunk by German submarine off Cape Vilano (4).

34. 1902 PANAMA
 5,981. 122,28 x 15,94. (401.2 x 52.3). 1–2. 2S–T6–15. (I–130). Fairfield Co Ltd, Glasgow. 1902 (8/3) launched. 1902 (May) MV Liverpool–Montevideo–Valparaiso. 1915 British hospital ship. 1920 ditto; renamed MAINE. 1948 scrapped.

35. 1903 VICTORIA
 5,967. 122,34 x 15,94. (401.4 x 52.3). 1–2. 2S–T6–15. (I–130). Fairfield Co Ltd, Glasgow. 1902 (21/6) launched. 1903 (5/3) MV Liverpool–Montevideo–Valparaiso. 1923 scrapped in Holland.

36. 1903 ORITA
 9,239. 147,94 x 17,74. (485.4 x 58.2). 1–2. 2S–Q8–15. Harland & Wolff, Belfast. 1902 (15/11) launched. 1903 (8/4) MV Liverpool–Rio de Janeiro–Montevideo–Valparaiso. 1919 (10/2) FV Liverpool–Panama Canal–Valparaiso. 1927 (22/9) LV Liverpool–Rio de Janeiro–Montevideo–Valparaiso. 1932 scrapped.

37. 1906 ORIANA
 8,066. 141,93 x 17,13. (465.7 x 56.2). 1–2. 2S–Q8–15. (I–160; II–150; III–550). Barclay, Curle & Co Ltd, Glasgow. 1906 (26/4) launched. 1906 (21/6) MV Liverpool–Rio de Janeiro–Montevideo–Valparaiso. 1919 (17/10) resumed ditto. 1922 (31/8) LV Liverpool–Rio de Janeiro–Montevideo–Valparaiso. 1926 (5/8) LV Liverpool–Panama Canal–Valparaiso. 1927 scrapped.

38. 1906 ORTEGA
 7,970. 141,81 x 17,16. (465.3 x 56.3). 1–2. 2S–Q8–15. (I–150;

II–130; III–800). Harland & Wolff, Belfast. 1906 (22/3) launched. 1906 (19/7) MV Liverpool–Rio de Janeiro–Montevideo–Valparaiso. 1914 (Sep) chased by German cruiser DRESDEN when homeward bound from Valparaiso; reached uncharted Nelson Strait and escaped by a dangerous 100 mile passage. 1918 carried American troops to France. 1919 (31/1) FV Liverpool–Panama Canal–Valparaiso. 1924 (4/12) LV Liverpool–Rio de Janeiro–Montevideo–Valparaiso. 1927 (3/3) LV Liverpool–Panama Canal–Valparaiso. 1927 scrapped at Briton Ferry.

39. 1906 ORONSA
   7,970. 141,81 x 17,16. (465.3 x 56.3). 1–2. 2S–Q8–15. (I–150; II–130; III–800). Harland & Wolff, Belfast. 1906 (26/5) launched. 1906 (13/9) MV Liverpool–Pernambuco–Montevideo–Valparaiso. 1918 (28/4) torpedoed and sunk by German submarine off Bardsey Island (4).

40. 1908 ORCOMA
   11,546. 155,92 x 18,96. (511.6 x 62.2). 1–2. 2S–Q8–16. (I–250; II–200; intermediate 100; III–600). W. Beardmore & Co Ltd, Glasgow. 1908 (2/4) launched. 1908 (27/8) MV Liverpool–Rio de Janeiro–Montevideo–Valparaiso. 1915 auxiliary cruiser. 1919 (6/11) resumed Liverpool–Montevideo–Valparaiso; subsequent voyages via Panama Canal. 1923 modernised; converted to oil fuel. 1933 (May) arrived Liverpool for the last time. 1933 scrapped at Blyth.

41. 1913 ANDES
   15,620. 173,81 x 20,51. (570.3 x 67.3). 1–2. 3S–T8&ST–16. (I–380; II–250; III–700). Harland & Wolff, Belfast. 1913 (8/5) launched for RMSP. 1913 (26/9) MV for PSN, Southampton–Buenos Aires–Valparaiso. 1914 (30/1) FV for RMSP, Southampton–Buenos Aires. 1915 auxiliary cruiser (10th Cruiser Squadron). 1916 (29/2) assisted RMSP ALCANTARA in sinking German auxiliary cruiser GREIF; ALCANTARA also sunk. 1919 (4/11) resumed Southampton–Buenos Aires for RMSP. 1930 ATLANTIS (RMSP cruise liner); 15,135 tons; (I–450). 1952 scrapped at Faslane.

42. 1914 ORDUÑA
   15,507. 167,65 x 20,51. (550.3 x 67.3). 1–2. 3S–T8&ST–14. (I–240; II–180; III–700). Harland & Wolff, Belfast. 1913 (2/10) launched. 1914 (19/2) MV Liverpool–Rio de Janeiro–Montevideo–Valparaiso (2 RV). 1914 (1/11) FV for Cunard (c), Liverpool–New York. 1919 (13/12) LV ditto. 1920 (1/4) resumed Liverpool–Rio de Janeiro–Montevideo–Valparaiso. 1921 (28/5) FV Hamburg–Southampton–New York for RMSP (c). 1923 (1/1)

ORDUÑA (RMSP), 1926 converted by builders to oil fuel; (I–234; II–186; III–483). 1927 ORDUÑA (PSN). 1927 resumed Liverpool–Rio de Janeiro–Montevideo–Valparaiso. 1927 (7/4) Liverpool–Panama Canal–Valparaiso. 1930 (7/1) LV Liverpool–Rio de Janeiro–Montevideo–Valparaiso; subsequently Liverpool–Panama Canal–Valparaiso. 1941–50 troopship. 1951 scrapped at Dalmuir.

43. (1919) ORBITA

15,495. 167,65 x 20,51. (550.3 x 67.3). 1–2. 3S–T8&ST–14. (I–190; II–221; III–476). Harland & Wolff, Belfast. 1914 (7/7) launched. 1915 auxiliary cruiser; later troopship. 1919 (26/9) FV Liverpool–Rio de Janeiro–Montevideo–Valparaiso. 1921 (30/4) FV Hamburg–Southampton–New York for RMSP (c). 1923 (1/1) ORBITA (RMSP). 1926 converted by builders to oil fuel. 1926 ORBITA (PSN). 1926 (4/11) Liverpool–Panama Canal–Valparaiso. 1940 troopship. 1950 scrapped at Newport, Mon.

44. 1920 OROPESA (II)

14,118. 161,53 x 20,20. (530.0 x 66.3). 1–2–C. 2S–ST(DR)–14. (I–141; II–131; III–360). Cammell, Laird & Co Ltd, Birkenhead. 1919 (9/12) launched. 1920 (16/9) MV Liverpool–Rio de Janeiro–Montevideo–Valparaiso. 1921 (14/5) FV Hamburg–Southampton–New York for RMSP (c). 1922 (30/11) resumed Liverpool–Rio de Janeiro–Montevideo–Valparaiso. 1924 converted to oil fuel. 1926 (7/10) LV Liverpool–Rio de Janeiro–Montevideo–Valparaiso; subsequently Liverpool–Panama Canal–Valparaiso. 1931 laid up at Dartmouth. 1937 resumed Liverpool–Panama Canal–Valparaiso. 1939 troopship. 1941 (16/1) torpedoed and sunk by German submarine U.96, 100 miles from Bloody Foreland (113).

— 1923 OROYA (II)

12,257. 160,03 x 19,14. (525.3 x 62.8). 1–2–C. 2S–ST(SR)–14. (I–150; II–123; III–450). Harland & Wolff, Belfast. 1920 (16/12) launched; laid up before completion. 1923 (26/4) MV Liverpool–Panama Canal–Valparaiso; she ran to South America exclusively by this route. 1931 (8/9) laid up at Dartmouth. 1939 towed to La Spezia, where scrapped.

45. (1921) ORUBA (II)

7,848. 153,57 x 16,79. (504.1 x 55.1). C–2–2. 2S–T6–15. Alexander Stephen & Sons Ltd, Glasgow. 1903 (18/11) launched as MARATHON (Aberdeen); 6,795 tons, 1912 lengthened from 138,43 metres (454. 2 feet); dummy second funnel added. (I–90; III–150). 1921 ORUBA (PSN). 1921 (26/5) FV Liverpool–Rio de Janeiro–Montevideo–Valparaiso–Panama Canal–Liverpool. 1921

(6/10) ditto (2 RV). 1922 laid up at Liverpool. 1924 (Apr) laid up at Dartmouth. 1924 scrapped.

46. (1921) ORCANA (II)

7,814. 153,63 x 16,79 (504.3 x 55.1). C–2–2. 2S–T6–15. Alexander Stephen & Sons Ltd, Glasgow. 1903 (11/8) launched as MILTIADES (Aberdeen); 6,793 tons. 1912 lengthened from 138,64 metres (454.9 feet); dummy second funnel added. (I–90; III–150). 1921 ORCANA (PSN). 1921 (11/8) FV Liverpool–Rio de Janeiro–Montevideo–Valpariso–Panama Canal–Newport News–Liverpool. 1921 (1/2) 2nd voyage scheduled but cancelled. 1922 laid up at Liverpool. 1923 laid up at Dartmouth. 1923 towed to Holland; scrapped.

47. 1931 REINA DEL PACIFICO

17,702. 168,02 [175,03] x 23,25. (551.3 [574.3] x 76.3). 2–2–C. 4S–4SC.SA–18. (I–280; II–162; III–446). Harland & Wolff, Glasgow. 1930 (23/9) launched. 1931 (9/4) MV Liverpool–Panama Canal–Valparaiso. 1932 (19/1) FV Liverpool–Rio de Janeiro–Montevideo–Valparaiso (annual tour round South America). 1939 (Aug) troopship. 1946 reconditioned by Harland & Wolff. 1947 (11/9) engine room explosion during trials (23). 1948 resumed Liverpool–Panama Canal–Valparaiso. 1958 scrapped at Newport, Mon.

— 1956 REINA DEL MAR

20,234. 170,68 [183,11] x 23,89. (560.0 [600.8] x 78.4). 1–1–C. 2S–ST(DR)–18. (I–207; cabin 216; tourist 343). Harland & Wolff, Belfast. 1955 (7/6) launched. 1956 (3/5) MV Liverpool–Panama Canal–Valparaiso. 1963 chartered to Travel Savings Association. 1964 rebuilt as cruise liner; Union Castle Line management and colours. 1973 sold to Union Castle. 1975 (30/7) arr Kaohsiung; scrapped. (Note: REINA DEL MAR did not run via River Plate and Straits of Magellan).

FUNNEL: 1868. Black.
          1914. Yellow.
FLAG: White with blue cross; gold and red crown in centre; red 'PSNC" in four corners.

Chapter 20

(1869–1901)

RED CROSS LINE

(R. Singlehurst & Co)

(British)

The Liverpool firm of R. Singlehurst & Co had been running sailing ships from Liverpool to North Brazil under the description RED CROSS LINE for many years before 1866, when Alfred Booth & Company (Chapter 16) inaugurated the first steamship line from Liverpool to Ceara, Maranham and Para. Not to be outdone, Singlehurst placed orders with T. Royden & Sons of Liverpool for the 1,300 ton iron screw compound-engined steamers PARAENSE, MARANHENSE and CEARENSE, whose maiden voyages started from Liverpool on 5 June, 13 July and 12 August 1869, respectively, under the Red Cross Line flag.

This meant that the two lines were in direct competition with one another, and had they followed the examples of many similarly situated concerns, before and since, one or both might well have gone under. But wisdom prevailed, and it was arranged in 1870 that each company should operate a fortnightly service. Steps were taken to see that sailings did not conflict.

The PARAENSE was wrecked at Ceara on 4 May 1870, with the result that orders were placed with Roydens for the 1,500 ton LISBONENSE and PARAENSE (II), which were delivered in 1871. By that time, Booth had commissioned two further ships, making a total of eight for the two lines, plus two more for Hugh Evans & Company's newly-established Maranham Steamship Company, which soon agreed to concentrate its sailings on the Liverpool–Maranham (São Luiz) trade. In return, Red Cross and Booth discontinued their Maranham call.

At an early date the Red Cross ships began to put in at Havre in addition to Lisbon, where numerous Portuguese emigrants were embarked. Some voyages were extended to Manaos, 1,000 miles up the Amazon.

An appreciably larger ship, the 1,865 ton AMAZONENSE (I) was completed by Oswald, Mordaunt & Co of Southampton in 1879, but wrecked on 16 April 1881 near St. David's Head, outward bound for Para. Five second-hand ships followed her into the fleet – the 1,109 ton THERESINA, which was allowed to retain her name, in 1879; the 1,517 ton AMAZONENSE (II) (ex-HINDOSTAN) in 1881; the 1,480 ton MARANHENSE (II) (ex-BLODWEN) in 1882, the first of the name having been sold in 1880; and the 1,509 ton MANAUENSE (ex-BOWEN) and the 1,470 ton PORTUENSE (ex-GLENAPP ex-ABDIEL) in 1883. This meant that the Company now had a fleet of eight ocean-going ships, but a joint Red Cross and Booth service started in 1882 between Manaos, Para and New York and this partly accounted for the additions.

The 1,982 ton SOBRALENSE, first unit of the fleet to have triple-expansion engines instead of compound, was launched by the Barrow Shipbuilding Company of Barrow in May 1884 and started her maiden voyage from Liverpool to the Amazon on 4 October 1884.

The 420 ton GRANGENSE (I) was built in 1887 for service in the Amazon, but sold to a Brazilian company in 1890. Laird Bros of Birkenhead launched on 26 August 1880 the 300 ton paddle steamer THERESINENSE for river purposes. A rudder was fitted at each end, and she had superior accommodation for passengers, with deckhouses fore and aft and a wooden awning above. [1]

1891 OBIDENSE 2,380 tons
Taken over by Booth Line in 1901.

The PORTUENSE foundered near Angada on 23 April 1890, bound from Baltimore to Para, but the 2,380 ton OBIDENSE was already almost at the launching stage by T. Royden & Sons, and was notable as the first ship in the fleet to be built of steel. Her maiden voyage from Liverpool, Havre and Lisbon to the Amazon started on 5 February 1891.

The 2,150 ton RUGGIERO SETTIMO, CARLO POERIO and IL PRINCIPE DI NAPOLI, all launched by Palmers of Jarrow-on-Tyne for the Italo-Britannica Royal Italian Mail Steam Navigation Co Ltd, of London, in 1891, were bought by Red Cross and became the

GRANGENSE (II) in 1892, the CAMETENSE in 1894 and the FLUMINENSE in 1895.

Two further ships were acquired in 1895 – the 2,700 ton DUBBEL-DAM and DIDAM of the Holland America Line (Chapter 41), laid down in 1890 for their newly-established service from Holland to the River Plate, which through no fault of the company had to be withdrawn before the ships were completed. They ran for a time between Holland and New York, and when acquired by Red Cross were renamed MADEIRENSE and SANTARENSE. Unfortunately, the latter was sunk in collision with the British barque DUNDONALD on 17 June 1896.

The 2,767 ton GULF OF LIONS, built by Caird & Co of Greenock,

1895 MADEIRENSE 2,700 tons
Built 1891 as Holland America DUBBELDAM.

was acquired in 1899 and renamed MARANHENSE (III). During the same year the 2,828 ton AMAZONENSE (III) was launched by D.J. Dunlop & Co of Port Glasgow and less than three months later, on 8 July, sailed on her maiden voyage from Liverpool to the Amazon via Hamburg and Havre. She was the largest ship to be laid down for the Company.

The 2,769 ton WEST INDIAN, built in 1891 for the West India & Pacific Line and taken over by Frederick Leyland & Co Ltd, became the Red Cross CEARENSE (II) in 1900 and sailed for them for the first time on 29 January 1901.

Thus, no fewer than eight new or second-hand ships were commissioned by Red Cross between 1894 and 1900. During this time, five were sold for further service – the MARANHENSE (II) in 1895, the AMAZONENSE (II) in 1896, the THERESINA and MANAUENSE in 1898 and the pioneer CEARENSE in 1899. They were all considerably smaller than the ships which replaced them.

An important event of 1898 was the starting of a service from Liverpool to Iquitos, in Peru, 2,000 miles from the mouth of the

Amazon. Two newly-built steamers, the HARMONY and PARIS, were acquired for the service and renamed NAPO and UCAYALI, and were joined a year later by the JAVARY, formerly the HARLECH. The Booth Line introduced a similar service at approximately the same time.

In 1901 agreement was reached between the Red Cross Line owners, the Singlehurst family, and the Booth Line for the two concerns to be amalgamated under the style of BOOTH STEAMSHIP COMPANY (1901) LIMITED (Chapter 16). Nevertheless, the Singlehursts retained an important interest in the line for a good many years.

All told, Red Cross had commissioned 21 transatlantic steamships, of which 11 of 25,411 tons were incorporated into the new concern. The Booth contribution was 14 ships of 39,923 tons.

1] Liverpool *Daily Post*, 27/8/1880.

1. 1869 PARAENSE (I)
1,330. 82,08 x 9,29. (269.3 x 30.5). 1–3. I–S–C2–10. T. Royden & Sons, Liverpool (engines Fawcett, Preston & Co, Liverpool). 1869 (Mar) launched. 1869 (5/6) MV Liverpool–R. Amazon. 1870 (4/5) wrecked at Ceara on voyage Liverpool–Maranham (0).

2. 1869 MARANHENSE (I)
1,334. 82,08 x 9,29. (269.3 x 30.5). 1–3. I–S–C2–10. T. Royden & Sons, Liverpool (engines Fawcett, Preston & Co, Liverpool). 1869 (Jul) launched. 1869 (13/7) MV Liverpool–R. Amazon. 1880 CAMILIA (Italian). 1887 EUROPA (Italian). 1898 SHARKI (Turkish). 1912 scrapped.

3. 1869 CEARENSE (I)
1,381. 82,11 x 9,29. (269.4 x 30.5). 1–2. I–S–C2–10. T. Royden & Sons, Liverpool (engines Fawcett, Preston & Co, Liverpool). 1869 (Jun) launched. 1869 (12/8) MV Liverpool–R. Amazon. 1899 PICNIC (Italian). 1902 scrapped at Palermo.

. 1871 LISBONENSE
1,508. 82,11 x 10,12. (269.4 x 33.2). 1–2. I–S–C2–10. T. Royden & Sons, Liverpool (engines J. Jack & Co, Liverpool). 1871 (Jan) launched. 1871 MV Liverpool–R. Amazon. 1888 triple-expansion engines. 1901 LISBONENSE (Booth (16)); q.v.

. 1871 PARAENSE (II)
1,520. 82,35 x 10,06. (270.2 x 33.0). 1–2. I–S–C2–10. T. Royden & Sons, Liverpool (engines J. Jack, Rollo & Co, Liverpool). 1871 (May) launched. 1871 MV Liverpool–R. Amazon. 1901 PARA-ENSE (Booth (16)); q.v.

6. 1879 AMAZONENSE (I)
   1,865. 87,38 x 10,57. (286.7 x 34.7). 1–3. I–S–C2–10. (I–50).
   Oswald, Mordaunt & Co, Southampton. 1879 (Jan) launched.
   1879 (18/5) MV Liverpool–R. Amazon. 1881 (16/4) wrecked near
   St. David's Head on voyage Liverpool–Para (1).
7. (1879) THERESINA
   1,109. 73,08 x 9,38. (239.8 x 30.8). 1–2. I–S–C2–10. Raylton
   Dixon & Co, Middlesbrough (engines Fawcett & Preston,
   Liverpool). 1876 (Sep) launched as THERESINA (Br). 1879
   THERESINA (Red Cross). 1879 (19/12) FV Liverpool–R.
   Amazon. 1898 CITY OF BRUSSELS (Br). 1925 (31/10) wrecked
   at Zuetina.
8. (1881) AMAZONENSE (II)
   1,517. 88,39 x 10,73. (290.0 x 35.2). 1–2. I–S–C2–10. Wigham
   Richardson & Co, Walker-on-Tyne (engines C.D. Holmes & Co,
   Hull). 1869 (Feb) launched as HINDOSTAN (Br). 1881 AMA-
   ZONENSE (Red Cross). 1881 (15/4) FV Liverpool–R. Amazon.
   1896 SAINT AUGUSTIN (Fr). 1897 scrapped at Marseilles.
9. (1882) MARANHENSE (II)
   1,480. 76,56 x 10,21. (251.2 x 33.5). 1–2. I–S–C2–10. Sunderland
   Shipbuilding Co, Sunderland (engines J. Dickinson, Sunderland).
   1880 (30/11) launched as BLODWEN (Br). 1882
   MARANHENSE (Red Cross). 1882 (10/11) FV Liverpool–R.
   Amazon. 1895 SAINT ANTOINE (Fr). 1925 scrapped at
   Inverkeithing.
10. (1883) PORTUENSE
    1,470. 84,39 x 9,17. (276.9 x 30.1). 1–2. I–S–C2–10. Aitken &
    Mansel, Glasgow (engines J. & J. Thomson, Glasgow). 187?
    (Apr) launched as ABDIEL (Br). 1880 GLENAPP (ditto). 188?
    PORTUENSE (Red Cross). 1883 (19/10) FV Liverpool–Ham-
    burg–R. Amazon. 1890 (28/8) foundered near Angada on voyage
    Baltimore–Para.
11. (1884) MANAUENSE
    1,509. 85,67 x 9,78. (281.1 x 32.1). 1–2. I–S–C2–10. J. Reid & Co
    Port Glasgow (engines Walker, Henderson & Co, Glasgow)
    1874 (Dec) launched as BOWEN (Eastern & Australian (Br))
    1884 MANAUENSE (Red Cross). 1884 (5/7) FV Liverpool–R
    Amazon. 1898 sold. 1900 MEXICO (Mexican). 1903 (16/12
    wrecked at Muroran.
12. 1884 SOBRALENSE
    1,982. 83,84 x 10,42. (275.1 x 34.2). 1–2. I–S–T3–11. Barrow
    Shipbuilding Co, Barrow. 1884 (9/8) launched. 1884 (4/10) MV
    Liverpool–R. Amazon. 1901 SOBRALENSE (Booth (16)); q.v

13. 1891 OBIDENSE
    2,380. 91,43 x 11,31. (300.0 x 37.1). 1–2. S–S–T3–11. T. Royden
    & Sons, Liverpool (engines Fawcett, Preston & Co, Liverpool).
    1890 (27/9) launched. 1891 (5/2) MV Liverpool–Havre–Lisbon–
    R. Amazon. 1901 OBIDENSE (Booth (16)); q.v.
14. (1894) GRANGENSE (II)
    2,162. 92,04 x 11,70. (302.0 x 38.4). 1–2. S–S–T3–11. Palmers Co.
    Ltd, Jarrow-on-Tyne. 1891 (20/10) launched as RUGGIERO
    SETTIMO (Italo-Britannica). 1894 GRANGENSE (Red Cross).
    1894 (10/8) FV Liverpool–Hamburg–R. Amazon. 1901
    GRANGENSE (Booth (16)); q.v.
15. (1894) CAMETENSE
    2,150. 92,04 x 11,70. (302.0 x 38.4). 1–2. S–S–T3–11. Palmers Co
    Ltd, Jarrow-on-Tyne. 1891 (22/9) launched as CARLO POERIO
    (Italo-Britannica). 1894 CAMETENSE (Red Cross). 1894 (Jly)
    FV Liverpool–Havre–R. Amazon. 1901 CAMETENSE (Booth
    (16)); q.v.
16. (1895) FLUMINENSE
    2,150. 92,04 x 11,70. (302.0 x 38.4). C–1–2. S–S–T3–11. Palmers
    Co Ltd, Jarrow-on-Tyne. 1891 launched as IL PRINCIPE DI
    NAPOLI (Italo-Britannica). 1894 FLUMINENSE (Red Cross).
    1895 (9/2) FV Liverpool–R. Amazon. 1901 FLUMINENSE
    (Booth (16)); q.v.
17. (1895) MADEIRENSE
    2,700. 101,19 x 12,19. (332.0 x 40.0). S–1–2. S–S–T3–12. (I–40;
    III–464) Bonn & Mees, Rotterdam (engines Nederlandsche
    Stoomboot Maatschappij, Fijenoord). 1891 (Aug) launched as
    DUBBELDAM (Holland America). 1895 MADEIRENSE (Red
    Cross). 1895 (17/12) FV Liverpool–Hamburg–R. Amazon. 1901
    MADEIRENSE (Booth (16)); q.v.
18. (1895) SANTARENSE
    2,751. 101,46 x 12,16. (332.9 x 39.9). S–1–2. S–S–T3–12. (I–44;
    III–464). Nederlandsche Stoomboot Maatschappij, Fijenoord
    (Rotterdam). 1891 (Feb) launched as DIDAM (Holland Amer-
    ica). 1895 SANTARENSE (Red Cross). 1895 (19/12) FV
    Liverpool–Penarth–R. Amazon. 1896 (17/6) sunk in collision
    with barque DUNDONALD (Br).
19. (1899) MARANHENSE (III)
    2,767. 95,58 x 12,83. (313.6 x 42.1). 1–2. S–S–T3–11. Caird & Co
    Ltd, Greenock. 1890 (28/3) launched as GULF OF LIONS. 1899
    MARANHENSE (Red Cross). 1899 (20/5) FV Liverpool–
    Hamburg–R. Amazon. 1901 MARANHENSE (Booth (16));
    q.v.

20. 1899 AMAZONENSE (III)

2,828. 95,09 x 12,46. (312.0 x 40.9). 1–2. S–S–T3–11. D.J. Dunlop & Co, Port Glasgow. 1899 (27/4) launched. 1899 (8/7) MV Liverpool–Hamburg–Havre–R. Amazon. 1901 AMAZONENSE (Booth (16)); q.v.

21. (1901) CEARENSE (II)

2,769. 96,92 x 12,31. (318.0 x 40.4). 1–2. S–S–T3–11. Naval Construction & Armament Co Ltd, Barrow. 1891 (27/6) launched as WEST INDIAN (West India & Pacific; later Frederick Leyland & Co Ltd). 1900 CEARENSE (Red Cross). 1901 (29/1) FV Liverpool–R. Amazon. 1901 CEARENSE (Booth (16)); q.v.

FUNNEL: Black with broad white band containing a red cross.
FLAG: White with small red cross.

Chapter 21

1869–71

HAMBURG – BRASILIANISCHE DAMPFSCHIFFAHRTS GESELLSCHAFT

(HBDG)

(German)

The HAMBURG – BRASILIANISCHE DAMPFSCHIFFAHRTS GESELLSCHAFT was founded during 1869 after two Tyneside firms got together with Hamburg shipbroker, August Bolten. It was nominally a German company, but it is evident that the majority of the capital was provided by the two British concerns – shipbuilders C. Mitchell & Co and shipowners Watts Milburn & Co, and in consequence there were frequent changes of flag in a rather complicated situation.

The 961 ton SANTOS was launched by Mitchell for Watts Milburn on 10 April 1869, but on 2 June was transferred to HBDG under the German flag, sailing from Hamburg for Brazil 13 days later. In the following year, however, she was returned to Watts Milburn and wore the British flag while continuing to run to Brazil.

The second HBDG steamer was launched for Watts Milburn as the BRAZILIAN and chartered to the German concern, but in March 1870 the spelling of her name was changed to BRASILIEN, and still under charter she assumed the German flag.

A third steamer, laid down as the CRITERION, was launched in September 1870 as the British-flag RIO. She was acquired by HBDG, but continued to fly the red ensign.

Despite all these comings and goings, the service prospered. It was decided, however, to form a fully-fledged German company, the title chosen being HAMBURG – SÜDAMERIKANISCHEN DAMPF-SCHIFFAHRTS GESELLSCHAFT (Chapter 26), in which a German bank was the majority shareholder, followed by August Bolten, with the Mitchell and Watts Milburn companies as British supporters and nine Hamburg firms as a small German contingent.

1. 1869 SANTOS (Ger)
   (1870) SANTOS (Br)
   > 961. 68,51 x 8,50. (224.8 x 27.9). S–1–2. I–S–?–10. C. Mitchell & Co, Walker-on-Tyne (engines T. Clark & Co, Newcastle). 1869

(10/4) launched for Watts Milburn & Co, Newcastle. 1869 (2/6) transferred to HBDG. 1869 (15/6) MV Hamburg–Brazil. 1870 SANTOS (Br). 1872 SANTOS (Hamburg–Süd). 1873 ST. PAULI (Ger). 1877 (30/10) wrecked.

1a. 1869 BRAZILIAN (Br) (c)
   (1870) BRASILIEN (Ger) (c)
   1,315. 73,14 x 9,87. (240.0 x 32.4). S–1–2. I–S–?–10). C. Mitchell & Co, Walker-on-Tyne (engines Thompson, Boyd & Co, Newcastle). 1869 (Jun) launched as BRAZILIAN (Br). 1869 chartered to HBDG. 1870 (3/3) BRASILIEN (Ger) (c). 1872 BRASILIEN (Hamburg–Süd). 1873 BRAZILIAN (Watts, Milburn & Co). 1912 removed from *Lloyd's Register*.

2. 1869 RIO (Br)
   1,688. 80,77 x 9,14. (265.0 x 30.0). S–1–2. I–S–C2–10. (I–26; III–52). C. Mitchell & Co, Walker-on-Tyne (engines T. Clark & Co, Newcastle). 1869 keel laid as CRITERION (Watts, Milburn & Co). 1870 (Sep) launched as RIO (Br). 1870 MV Hamburg–Brazil (HBDG) (Br). 1871 RIO (Hamburg–Süd). 1901 scrapped.

Chapter 22

1870–6

SOCIETÀ ITALO PLATENSE

(Italian)

Fourth of the important Italian stteamship lines running to South America was the SOCIETÀ ITALO PLATENSE, founded in 1868 by Captain Antonio Oneto, who, although born in Italy had by that time settled in Buenos Aires. With the financial assistance of some 150 Italians resident in Argentina, a sum of 800,000 pesos (£160,000) was eventually accumulated – sufficient to order three steamers from J. & W. Dudgeon of Cubitt Town, London.

The pioneer, the ITALO PLATENSE, was launched on 30 December 1869 and was the first Italian steamer that could be said to rival those running for French lines from Marseilles to South America. She had a tonnage of 1,695, one funnel, two masts, a clipper bow and a speed of about 10 knots. She could accommodate 40 first class passengers, 45 second and 500 steerage. The first class had a spacious saloon, which included a piano, cabins with four berths, a bath room, a stall for a cow, an ice-room, a bakery and passengers were supplied with bread and fresh meat throughout the voyage. The three ships cost a total of £125,000 and flew the Italian flag.

The ITALO PLATENSE sailed from Genoa on 16 June 1870 for Marseilles, Gibraltar, Tenerife (for coal), Rio de Janeiro, Montevideo and Buenos Aires, which she reached in 38 days from Genoa. Sailing again from the River Plate on 28 July, she reached Genoa on 4 September, also in 38 days, which was an average crossing at the time.

The LA PAMPA, launched on 22 April 1870, started her maiden voyage from Genoa in March 1871, while the PO, under the command of an Argentinian, Captain Pedro de Gelindez, joined the line on 1 April 1871 and steamed from Gibraltar to Rio de Janeiro in 17 days 8 hours.

Although Italo Platense met with initial success, the French Société Générale de Transports Maritimes commissioned a much larger ship, while the Lavarello management (Chapter 14) were able to raise sufficient capital to build a new fleet. Captain Oneto was unable to withstand this competition, and his three steamers were laid up in Genoa before being sold by auction in April 1876 for little more than half their original cost.

1. 1870 ITALO PLATENSE

    1,695. 82,29 x 10,36. (270.0 x 34.0). C–1–2. I–S–C4–10. (I–40; II–45; III–500). J. & W. Dudgeon, Cubitt Town, London. 1869 (30/12) launched. 1870 (16/6) MV Genoa–Marseilles–Gibraltar–Tenerife–Rio de Janeiro–Montevideo–Buenos Aires (dep 28/7)–Genoa (arr 4/9). 1876 L'ITALIA (Piaggio) (Italian). 1885 (19/6) foundered off Mollendo (Peru) (57).

2. 1870 LA PAMPA

    1,698. 82,29 x 10,36. (270.0 x 34.0). S–1–2. I–S–C4–10. (I–40; II–45; III–500). J. & W. Dudgeon, Cubitt Town, London. 1870 (2/4) launched. 1870 (2/11) MV Genoa–Gibraltar–Tenerife–Rio de Janeiro–Montevideo–Buenos Aires. 1876 LA PAMPA (Fr).

3. 1871 PO

    1,700. 82,29 x 10,36. (270.0 x 34.0). S–1–2. I–S–C4–10. (I–40; II–45; III–500). J. & W. Dudgeon, Cubitt Town, London. 1870 (Jun) launched. 1871 (1/4) MV Genoa–Gibraltar–Tenerife–Rio de Janeiro–Montevideo–Buenos Aires. 1876 SANTIAGO. 1890 removed from *Lloyd's Register*.

Chapter 23

1870–4

RYDE LINE

(British)

The RYDE LINE can be said to have started where the London, Belgium, Brazil & River Plate Mail Steamship Company (Chapter 18) left off. An advertised sailing by the latter company's steamer CITY OF LIMERICK from London on 28 August 1870 was, in fact, taken by the 1,400 ton LACYDON, whose owners were not mentioned but eventually transpired to be the RYDE LINE. Ports of call were as before – Antwerp, Falmouth, St. Vincent, Rio de Janeiro, Montevideo and Buenos Aires, and the agents were again Alex. Howden & Co of 19 Birchin Lane, London, EC.

It is evident that the new concern was making every effort to acquire the Belgian mail contract held by its predecessors. This was achieved, and advertisements from January 1871 onwards stated 'Under contract with the Belgian Government'. Not long afterwards the Company began to be referred to as the RYDE LINE.

The LACYDON was succeeded by the 2,000 ton BORNEO, the 1,412 ton ARIADNE, the 1,886 ton BONITA, the 1,160 ton MENDOZA, the 1,717 ton EVORA and the 2,001 ton GALATEA, all except the BORNEO and MENDOZA undertaking further sailings. The GALATEA, only recently running for the Pacific Steam Navigation Company, left London on 26 July 1872, Antwerp on 1 August and Falmouth on 3 August. Advertisements stated she was 'highly recommended and complete with every comfort for cabin passengers'. The EVORA was wrecked near Montevideo on 24 April 1872.

The 2,540 ton LEOPOLD II was launched by Barclay, Curle & Co of Glasgow on 17 October 1872 for the Ryde Line, and was followed on 30 December by the 2,564 ton SANTIAGO, the last steamer to be built by the well-known firm of Tod & McGregor of Glasgow. Trials of the LEOPOLD II took place on the Clyde in February 1873 and a speed of 14¼ knots was attained. She had accommodation for 80 first class, 30 second and 500 steerage passengers.

Advertisements in April 1873 stated that starting in the following June the LEOPOLD II, SANTIAGO, ANTWERPEN or BRABANT would be despatched from the Millwall Docks, London, on the 10th of each month, calling at Lisbon, Rio de Janeiro and the River Plate, receiving

1873 LEOPOLD II 2,540 tons
Made two voyages London via Antwerp to Buenos Aires.

the Belgian mails at Antwerp and embarking passengers and specie at Falmouth.

The LEOPOLD II sailed as scheduled on 10 June, but the SANTIAGO was not ready before 10 August, and the July sailing was taken by the 1,348 ton RICHARD COBDEN. It was at this time that fortnightly instead of monthly sailings were announced, the LACYDON, ARIADNE and BONITA all being involved in London departures on the 26th of the month. However, the ANTWERPEN was not launched until 26 June 1873, and the BRABANT until 6 October, and in consequence they were not ready to take the 10 October and 10 December sailings.

Advertisements in January 1874 stated that the SANTIAGO would sail from Southampton (instead of Falmouth) on 17 January, having left London and Antwerp a few days previously, for Lisbon, Rio de Janeiro, the River Plate and Valparaiso, fares to Rio being £30, the River Plate £35 and Valparaiso £75. She would be followed by the ANTWERPEN on 17 February, BRABANT on 17 March and LEOPOLD II on 17 April. However, it transpires that the ANTWERPEN and BRABANT were still not even ready to leave their builder's yard, and before doing so became the P&O KHIVA and KASHGAR.

Nor did the LEOPOLD II sail again as such, and on 25 May 1874 left Southampton for South America as the Royal Mail Steam Packet Company's MINHO. The SANTIAGO duly sailed from Southampton on 17 January for the Ryde Line, but her next departure was on 24 October 1874 as the RMSP MONDEGO.

The 1,343 ton RHONE took the place of the ANTWERPEN in February 1874, and the CHARLES HOWARD substituted for the

178

BRABANT in March. After this, the fortnightly service reverted to monthly, sailings being taken by the LACYDON, ARIADNE, RICHARD COBDEN, RHONE and GALATEA on the 26th of each month from London, 1st from Antwerp and 3rd from Southampton. They no longer proceeded beyond Buenos Aires. This state of affairs continued until 26 August 1874, when the ARIADNE left London on what turned out to be the Company's last voyage.

Some clue to the Ryde Line's decision to withdraw from the service may be gained from the SANTIAGO's departure from Southampton on 17 January 1874 with what was described as a large cargo but only 16 passengers. Bearing in mind the considerable passenger capacity of the new ships, this disappointing total was probably one of several reasons for the withdrawal.

1. (1870) LACYDON
   1,400. 77.72 x 9,81 (255.0 x 32.2). 1–2. I–S–I(2)–10. Pile & Co, Sunderland (engines R. & W. Hawthorn, Newcastle). 1869 (Jly) launched. 1870 (28/8) FV London–Antwerp–Falmouth–St. Vincent–Rio de Janeiro–Montevideo–Buenos Aires. 1874 (26/7) LV London–Antwerp–Southampton–Lisbon–Rio de Janeiro–Montevideo–Buenos Aires (11 RV). 1875 CADIZ (J. Hall Junr & Co, London).

2. (1870) ARIADNE
   1,412. 77,41 x 9,81. (254.0 x 32.2). 1–2. I–S–I(2)–10. Pile & Co, Sunderland (engines R. & W. Hawthorn, Newcastle). 1869 (Oct) launched. 1870 (27/11) FV London–Antwerp–Falmouth–St. Vincent–Rio de Janeiro–Montevideo–Buenos Aires. 1874 (26/8) LV London–Antwerp–Southampton–Lisbon–Rio de Janeiro–Montevideo–Buenos Aires (12 RV). 1875 GIBRALTAR (J. Hall Junr & Co, London).

3. (1871) BONITA
   1,886. 89,91 x 11,24. (295.0 x 36.9). 1–2. I–S–C2–10. Backhouse & Dixon, Middlesbrough (engines T. Richardson & Sons, Hartlepool). 1870 (Aug) launched. 1871 (27/1) FV London–Antwerp–Falmouth–St. Vincent–Rio de Janeiro–Montevideo–Buenos Aires (10 RV). 1874 (18/5) wrecked on Vigo Island.

4. (1871) EVORA
   1,717. 83,81 x 10,06. (275.0 x 33.0). 1–2. I–S–C2–10. Pile & Co, Sunderland (engines R. & W. Hawthorn, Newcastle). 1871 (Jan) launched. 1871 (26/6) FV London–Antwerp–Falmouth–St. Vincent–Rio de Janeiro–Montevideo–Buenos Aires. 1872 (24/4) wrecked near Montevideo.

5. (1872) GALATEA

2,001. 88,26 x 10,79. (289.6 x 35.4). 1–2. I–S–C2–11. Pile & Co, Sunderland (engines R. & W. Hawthorn, Newcastle). 1870 (Nov) launched. 1871 (23/3) MV Liverpool–Rio de Janeiro–Montevideo–Valparaiso for PSN (c) (3 RV). 1872 (26/7) FV London–Antwerp–Falmouth–Rio de Janeiro–Montevideo–Buenos Aires for Ryde (5 RV). 1881 (Jan) FV Glasgow–Liverpool–Bombay for Anchor (c). 1883–4 BORGHESE (Raeburn & Verel, Glasgow). 1899 (29/12) foundered near Cape Finisterre.

6. (1873) RHONE

1,343. 76,07 x 9,17. (249.6 x 30.1). 1–2. I–S–C2–10. Pile & Co, Sunderland. 1868 (Feb) launched. 1871 C2 by Millwall Dock Engineering Works replaced I(2). 1873 (22/2) FV London–Antwerp–Falmouth–St. Vincent–Rio de Janeiro–Montevideo–Buenos Aires (4 RV). 1879 RHONE (Westcott & Laurance). 1898 sold to Belgium.

7. 1873 LEOPOLD II

2,540. 106,79 x 11,21. (350.4 x 36.8). S–1–2. I–S–C2–11. (I–80; II–30; III–500). Barclay, Curle & Co, Glasgow. 1872 (17/10) launched. 1873 (10/6) MV London–Antwerp–Falmouth–Rio de Janeiro–Buenos Aires (2 RV). 1874 MINHO (RMSP). 1874 (25/5) FV Southampton–Brazil. 1884 (1/7) FV Southampton–Lisbon–Rio de Janeiro–Santos–New York–London. 1885 (2/3) LV ditto. 1887 ASLAN (Turkish). 1901 (1/4) wrecked near Yembo, Red Sea (180).

8. (1873) RICHARD COBDEN

1,348. 75,89 x 9,17. (249.0 x 30.1). 1–2. I–S–C2–10. Pile & Co, Sunderland. 1868 (Mar) launched. 1871 C2 by Millwall Dock Engineering Works replaced I(2). 1873 (10/7) FV London–Antwerp–Falmouth–Rio de Janeiro–Montevideo–Buenos Aires. 1874 (26/5) LV London–Antwerp–Southampton–Rio de Janeiro–River Plate–Valparaiso (2 RV). 1876 VIDAL SALA (Spanish). 1886 LYS (Belgian). 1889 SCIENCE (Westcott & Laurance). 1899 (26/3) sunk in collission near Cape St. Vincent.

9. 1873 SANTIAGO

2,564. 106,85 x 11,21. (350.6 x 36.8). S–1–2. I–S–C2–11. (I–80; II–30; III–500). Tod & McGregor, Glasgow. 1872 (30/12) launched. 1873 (10/8) MV London–Antwerp–Falmouth–Rio de Janeiro–Montevideo–Buenos Aires. 1874 (10/1) LV London–Antwerp–Southampton (17/1)–Rio de Janeiro–River Plate–Valparaiso (2 RV). 1874 MONDEGO (RMSP). 1874 (24/10) FV Southampton–Brazil. 1888 MONDEGO (Br). 1891 (15/9) wrecked at St. Mary's, NF.

10. (1873) CHARLES HOWARD

      1,304. 75,89 x 9,17. (249.0 x 30.1). 1–2. I–S–C2–10. Pile & Co, Sunderland. 1866 (Nov) launched. 1873 C2 by Kincaid & Co, Glasgow, replaced I(2). 1873 (26/10) FV London–Antwerp–Falmouth–Rio de Janeiro–Montevideo–Buenos Aires. 1874 (10/3) LV London–Antwerp–Southampton–Rio de Janeiro–River Plate–Valparaiso (2 RV). 1874 CHARLES HOWARD (Sunderland (Br)). 1890 MINERAL (refitted to carry petroleum in bulk). 1894 experimentally fired by oil.

— ––– ANTWERPEN

      2,600. James Laing, Sunderland. 1873 (26/6) launched for Ryde Line but did not run for them. Completed as KHIVA (P&O).

— ––– BRABANT

      3,600. James Laing, Sunderland. 1873 (6/10) launched for Ryde Line but did not run for them. Completed as KASHGAR (P&O).

Note: In addition, the 2,000 ton BORNEO and the 1,160 ton MENDOZA were each responsible for one round voyage.

Chapter 24

1870–89

DONALDSON LINE
(British)

The firm of DONALDSON BROTHERS was founded in 1855 by John and William Falconer Donaldson, who three years later acquired their first sailing ship, the 299 ton wooden barque JOAN TAYLOR, which was placed in service between the Clyde, Brazil and the River Plate. From this small beginning grew the Clyde Line of Packets, carried on in 1866 by no fewer than 16 sailing ships, of which six were owned by the firm and the remainder chartered.

It was announced in January 1870 that Donaldson Brothers would shortly be inaugurating a line of steamers between Glasgow, Montevideo and Buenos Aires [1], the first unit, the 1,350 ton iron screw ASTARTE, being launched on 11 August 1870 and a sister ship, the MARINA, on 25 October. The centenary history of the Donaldson Line states that these steamers were built for the Canadian trade, but the January statement proves otherwise.

The ASTARTE undertook the first steamship sailing of the DONALDSON LINE from Glasgow on 18 October 1870 to South American ports [2], the MARINA left in December [3] and further departures took place at intervals of about two months.

The 2,001 ton COLINA started her maiden voyage from Glasgow to Montevideo and Buenos Aires on 27 February 1873, but the Company was finding only a limited demand for passages and freight to and from South America during the spring and summer months, and in May 1874 she was chartered to the Red Star Line for four round voyages between Antwerp and New York, after which she reverted to the South Atlantic. A sister ship, the CYBELE, undertook her maiden voyage for Red Star in March 1874, but entered Donaldson service to South America on 25 September of the same year.

The MARINA was sold to the Brazil Steamship Company of Liverpool in 1873. A year later, the ASTARTE made a voyage to Canada under the auspices of J. & R. Young & Co of Glasgow, and the Company's South American sailings were but few during that summer, as was also the case during the spring and summer of 1876, when the ASTARTE sailed for Donaldson to Halifax, Nova Scotia, and the COLINA was responsible for two more Young sailings to Quebec and Montreal.

182

The Allan Line (Chapter 30) started a service from Glasgow to Montevideo and Buenos Aires in November 1876, and subsequently arranged regular sailings thereto during the autumn and winter months. It was probably as a result of this competition that the CYBELE, ASTARTE and COLINA sailed to South America throughout 1877, but the ASTARTE was wrecked off the Uruguayan coast on 18 February 1878.

The Donaldson Line's decision to inaugurate a fortnightly service from Glasgow to Quebec and Montreal in April 1878 by the new 2,035 ton EIRENE, assisted by the COLINA and CYBELE, was made because Canadian prospects during the spring and summer were much better than those to South America, but it seems clear that they would have been quite justified in starting the service as a retaliation for the Allan Line's entry into the South American trade.

The EIRENE started a round voyage to the River Plate in October 1878, but this was her first and last to that destination. The 2,193 ton ERL KING had already been chartered for two South Atlantic voyages, followed by two to Canada and she sailed again for Buenos Aires in December 1878.

The EIRENE was wrecked at Belle Isle in September 1879 and the CYBELE on Anticosti Island in August 1880. They were replaced by the 2,150 ton CYNTHIA and TITANIA in 1880, and the 2,544 ton CONCORDIA was added in 1881. By this time there were some Donaldson Line winter sailings to Baltimore as well as departures for South America between the months of October and February. This state of affairs continued for some years longer, but in 1887 there were few if any Donaldson steamship sailings to South America. There were, however, two in December 1888, and two by chartered steamers early in 1889, after which the service was withdrawn and the Company's steamship activities were confined to the Glasgow–Quebec–Montreal and Glasgow–Halifax–Baltimore trades. The last of their sailing ships was wrecked in 1892.

Withdrawal of the Donaldson Line's South American service can be attributed to competition from the Allan Line, but the tables were turned in 1913, when Donaldson re-entered the South American trade by the purchase of the Allan Line service which had become cargo only. The Donaldson South American Line was formed in 1919, four 7,000 ton freighters being built for it. This new concern continued in business until 1941, when its ships were taken over by the parent company, which itself closed down in 1967 after an active career of 112 years.

[1] *Glasgow Herald* 22/1/1870
[2] Ibid 19/10/1870
[3] Ibid 18/12/1870

1. 1870 ASTARTE
    1,360. 73,48 x 9,87. (241.1 x 32.4). S–1–2. I–S–C2–10. (I; III).
    Barclay & Curle, Glasgow. 1870 (11/8) launched. 1870 (18/10)
    MV Glasgow–Montevideo–Buenos Aires. 1878 (18/2) wrecked
    off coast of Uruguay.
2. 1870 MARINA
    1,358. 73,38 x 9,93. (240.8 x 32.6). S–1–2. I–S–C2–10. (I; III).
    Barclay & Curle, Glasgow. 1870 (25/10) launched. 1870 (Dec)
    MV Glasgow–Montevideo–Buenos Aires. 1873 MARINA (Bra-
    zil SS Co (Br)). 1875 MARIA (Rocco Piaggio (Italian)), 1885
    PARAGUAY (NGI). 1930 TORERO (Italian); scrapped.
3. 1873 COLINA
    2,001. 97,31 x 10,60. (319.3 x 34.8). S–1–2. I–S–C2–10. (I–14;
    III–250). Barclay & Curle, Glasgow. 1872 (31/10) launched. 1873
    (27/2) MV Glasgow–Montevideo–Buenos Aires. 1874 (13/5) FV
    for Red Star (c), Antwerp–New York. 1874 (17/12) resumed
    Glasgow–Montevideo–Buenos Aires. 1895 COLINA (Edward
    Watson (Br)). 1898 scrapped at Genoa.
4. (1874) CYBELE
    1,980. 97,40 x 10,54. (319.6 x 34.6). S–1–2. I–S–C2–10. (I–16;
    III–284). A. Stephen & Sons, Glasgow. 1874 (21/1) launched.
    1874 (12/3) MV for Red Star (c), Antwerp–New York. 1874
    (25/9) FV for Donaldson, Glasgow–Montevideo–Buenos Aires.
    1878 (19/5) FV Glasgow–Quebec–Montreal. 1880 (13/8) wrecked
    on Anticosti Island (0).
4a. (1878) ERL KING (c)
    2,193. 93,14 x 10,39. (305.6 x 34.1). C–1–3. I–S–C2–10. (I–40; II
    and III–400). A. & J. Inglis, Glasgow. 1865 (9/9) launched for
    Robertson & Co, London. 1874 lengthened; compound engines.
    1878 FV Glasgow–Montevideo–Buenos Aires for Donaldson (c).
    1891 (15/12) wrecked on Long Reef, Key West, Florida.
5. (1878) EIRENE
    2,035. 97,83 x 10,79. (321.0 x 35.4). S–1–2. I–S–C2–10. (I; III).
    D. & W. Henderson Ltd, Glasgow. 1878 (22/2) launched. 1878
    (20/4) MV Glasgow–Quebec–Montreal. 1878 (4/10) FV Glas-
    gow–Montevideo–Buenos Aires (1 RV). 1879 (30/9) wrecked at
    Belle Isle (0).

FUNNEL: 1870. Red with white band under black top.
           1878 (?) Black with white band.
FLAG: Red-white-blue vertical stripes with large blue 'D' on the
         white.

SOCIETÀ ROCCO PIAGGIO & FIGLI

(Italian)

Last of the wooden screw clippers built in Italy for service to South America was the ESTER (I) of the SOCIETÀ ROCCO PIAGGIO & FIGLI [1] of Genoa. She had a tonnage of 807, was built in 1870 by Agostino Briasco of Sestri Ponente and was fitted with a 70 horse-power engine capable of propelling her at a speed of five or six knots.

In 1874 the 1,390 ton iron screw steamer BEETHOVEN, launched at Sunderland in May 1870 by W. Watson, was placed in service by Rocco Piaggio as the COLUMBIA, and Westermann of Sestri Ponente supplied the 1,500 ton ESTER (II), also of iron screw construction. The ESTER (I) was renamed PAMPA, and was destroyed by fire at Santos in 1880 when on voyage from South America to Italy.

The COLUMBIA and ESTER (II) provided a service about every three months from Genoa via the Canaries to Montevideo and Buenos Aires, outward voyages occupying up to 40 days, and homeward ones slightly longer as they were usually made via Santos and Rio de Janeiro.

By this time G. B. Lavarello & Co (Chapter 14) were running four iron screw steamers, the largest of them having a tonnage of 2,246, while in 1870 the Società Italo Platense (Chapter 22) commissioned two of their three 1,700 ton ships, all of which were put up for auction in 1876. Rocco Piaggio managed to acquire the ITALO PLATENSE, which was renamed L'ITALIA, having a year previously bought the 1,358 ton MARINA, completed in 1870 for the Donaldson Line, and renamed her MARIA.

The L'ITALIA was placed in service to South America, and was joined on 10 December 1878 by the 2,822 ton UMBERTO I, built by A. McMillan & Son of Dumbarton. She was fitted with compound engines, which gave her a service speed of 14 knots, and could accommodate 98 first class, 80 second and 800 steerage passengers. She was able to steam from Genoa to Montevideo in approximately 22 days.

Rocco Piaggio went again to McMillan for the 3,577 ton REGINA MARGHERITA, which was launched in July 1884 and started her maiden voyage from Genoa on 1 December for Barcelona, St. Vincent, Montevideo, where she arrived on 17 December, and Buenos Aires. She

1884 REGINA MARGHERITA 3,577 tons
An outstanding Rocco Piaggio ship, shown as running later with NGI funnels.

was undoubtedly the best looking unit of the Italian mercantile marine with her two funnels, two masts and clipper bow, and with the exception of the La Veloce NORD AMERICA was the fastest, her service speed being 16 knots. Her passenger accommodation was unsurpassed, and consisted of 250 first and second class berths and 1,200 steerage. The dining saloon extended from porthole to porthole on the principal deck aft, and could be divided in two by a heavy velvet curtain when second class was being carried. A music room and ladies' room were situated on the upper deck. A special feature was that the public rooms of all classes were lit by electricity.

In July 1883 an agreement was reached between the Società Rocco Piaggio & Figli and the Società Italiano di Trasporti Marittimi Raggio & Co (Chapter 31) for a joint fast line from Naples and Genoa to the River Plate, sailings to be fortnightly. To begin with the principal Rocco Piaggio participants were the UMBERTO I and L'ITALIA, while Raggio supplied the 4,150 ton SIRIO, whose maiden voyage started simultaneously with the start of the agreement. Two sister ships of the latter, the ORIONE and PERSEO, followed early in 1884 and finally the Rocco Piaggio REGINA MARGHERITA.

With the commissioning of this fine ship, the L'ITALIA was despatched from Genoa to Montevideo and thence to Valparaiso and Callao via the Straits of Magellan. Unfortunately, she foundered on 19 June 1885 after striking an uncharted rock off Mollendo on the homeward stage of her first voyage. She sank almost immediately with a death roll of 57.

Two more Rocco Piaggio steamers call for mention – the 1,105 ton CARMELA, built in 1880 as the COREBO TREZO, acquired by them in 1883, but taken over by a Genoese bank a year later, and the 2,655 ton

186

ADRIA, acquired in 1884 and built as long previously as 1855 as the Cunard Line ETNA.

The Navigazione Generale Italiana (Chapter 36) started a South American service in November 1884. This may or may not have been decided on in preparation for taking over Raggio & Co in January 1885 and Rocco Piaggio in July of the same year. With the REGINA MARGHERITA and UMBERTO I of the latter owners and the SIRIO, ORIONE and PERSEO of the former, NGI had a ready-made express service and took full advantage of it. It is hardly an exaggeration to say that the events of 1885 were largely responsible for NGI being the premier Italian steamship company for many years prior to the formation of Italia Flotte Riuniti Cosulich – Lloyd Sabaudo – NGI in January 1932.

[1] Figli = Sons.

1. 1870 ESTER (I)
   807. 70 h.p. C–1–3. W–S–?–5½. Briasco, Sestri Ponente. 1870 launched. 1870 (Oct) MV Genoa–Naples–Rio de Janeiro–Montevideo–Buenos Aires–Rosario–Asuncion–Parana. 1874 PAMPA (Rocco Piaggio). 1880 destroyed by fire at Rio de Janeiro.

2. (1874) COLUMBIA
   1,390. W. Watson, Sunderland. 1870 (May) launched as BEETH-OVEN. 1874 COLUMBIA (Rocco Piaggio). 1880 (5/7) sunk in collision near Bahia.

3. 1874 ESTER (II)
   1,500. 61,96 x 9,78. (203.3 x 32.1). I–S–C2–10. Westermann, Sestri Ponente. 1874 FV Genoa–Montevideo–Buenos Aires. 1882 omitted from Register.

4. (1875) MARIA
   1,358. 73,38 x 9,93. (240.8 x 32.6). S–1–2. I–S–C2–10. (III–820). Barclay & Curle, Glasgow. 1870 (25/10) launched as MARINA (Donaldson). 1870 (Dec) MV Glasgow–Montevideo–Buenos Aires. 1873 MARINA (Brazil SS Co). 1875 MARIA (Rocco Piaggio). 1875 MARIA (NGI). 1885 PARAGUAY (NGI). 1930 TORERO (Italian); scrapped.

5. (1876) L'ITALIA
   1,695. 82,29 x 10,36. (270.0 x 34.0). C–1–2. I–S–C4–10. (I–40; II–50; III–500). J. & W. Dudgeon, London. 1869 (30/12) launched as ITALO PLATENSE (Italo Platense). 1870 (16/6) MV Genoa–Rio de Janeiro–Montevideo–Buenos Aires. 1876 L'ITALIA (Rocco Piaggio). 1876 (17/11) FV Genoa–Monte-

video–Buenos Aires. 1885 (Mar) FV Genoa–Montevideo–Straits of Magellan–Valparaiso–Callao. 1885 (19/6) foundered off Mollendo (57).

6. (1883) CARMELA

1,105. 67,14 x 9,87. (220.3 x 32.4). I–S–C2–10. (III–400). A. McMillan & Son, Dumbarton (engines M. Paul & Co, Dumbarton). 1880 (23/2) launched as COREBO TREZO. 1883 CARMELA (Rocco Piaggio). 1884 ditto (Banco di Sconto, Genoa), 1885 PARANA (NGI). 1885 (25/12) FV Genoa–Montevideo–Buenos Aires. 1902 scrapped.

7. 1878 UMBERTO I

2,822. 109,72 x 11,58. (360.0 x 38.0). C–1–2. I–S–C2–13. (I–98; II–80; III–800). A. McMillan & Son, Dumbarton. 1878 (15/8) launched. 1878 (10/12) MV Genoa–Montevideo–Buenos Aires. 1885 UMBERTO I (NGI). 1885 (18/7) FV Genoa–Montevideo–Buenos Aires. 1894 ran in NGI Egyptian line. 1910 UMBERTO I (Soc. Nazionale di Servizi Marittimi). 1917 (14/8) sunk by gunfire from German submarine UC.35 off Gallinara Island.

8. (1884) ADRIA

2,655. 106,49 x 11,46. (349.4 x 37.6). C–1–3. I–S–C2–10. Caird & Co, Greenock. 1854 (26/8) launched as ETNA (Cunard). 1855 Crimean war troopship. 1856 (5/2) FV Havre–New York. 1860 ETNA (Inman). 1871 lengthened from 92,96 metres (305.0 feet) by Laird Bros, Birkenhead; C2 replaced GB2; renamed CITY OF BRISTOL (Inman). 1881 MEXICO (Spanish). 1882 MESSICO (Italian). 1883 SEMPIONE (Italian). 1884 ADRIA (Rocco Piaggio). 1884 (1/6) FV Genoa–Montevideo–Buenos Aires. 1885 ADRIA (NGI). 1896 scrapped in Italy.

9. 1884 REGINA MARGHERITA

3,577. 120,69 x 12,80. (396.0 x 42.0). C–2–2. I–S–C2–16. (I & II–250; III–1,200. A. McMillan & Son, Dumbarton. 1884 (Jly) launched. 1884 (1/12) MV Genoa–Barcelona–St. Vincent–Montevideo (arr 17/12)–Buenos Aires. 1885 REGINA MARGHERITA (NGI). 1896 T3 by Ansaldo, Genoa; 17 knots. 1898 ran in NGI Egyptian Line. 1910 REGINA MARGHERITA (Soc. Nazionale di Servizi Marittimi). 1913 (11/2) capsized at Genoa while under repair; scrapped.

Chapter 26

1872–1964

HAMBURG – SÜDAMERIKANISCHEN DAMPFSCHIFFAHRTS GESELLSCHAFT
(HAMBURG – SÜD)

(Hamburg South American Line)

(German)

The HAMBURG SÜDAMERIKANISCHEN DAMPFSCHIF-FAHRTS GESELLSCHAFT (or Hamburg South American Line) can be said to have started in 1871 where the Hamburg–Brasilianische Dampfschiffahrts Gesellschaft (Chapter 21) left off. This concern had been founded in 1869 by two Tyneside firms – shipbuilders C. Mitchell & Co and shipowners Watts, Milburn & Co – in conjunction with the Hamburg shipbroker August Bolten. All three were involved in the formation of Hamburg–Süd, but the Commerz & Disconto Bank of Hamburg, holding 3,260 of the 5,000 shares, was the largest shareholder. August Bolten's firm acquired 840, and the remainder were divided between the two British concerns and nine from Hamburg. Registration of the company took place on 29 November 1871, the chairman being Heinrich Amsinck, whose family were connected with Hamburg–Süd for over 100 years.

Hamburg–Brasilianische had been operating the iron screw steamers SANTOS, BRASILIEN (formerly BRAZILIAN) and RIO, of which the last-named, a ship of 1,685 tons, was bought by Hamburg–Süd on 27 December 1871 and sailed from Hamburg for Rio de Janeiro, Santos and Bahia in January 1872, followed by the 961 ton SANTOS and the 1,315 ton BRASILIEN. The latter was sold to Watts, Milburn & Co in 1873 and reverted to the name BRAZILIAN, while the SANTOS was sold to a Hamburg firm during the same year to become the ST. PAULI.

Meanwhile, the 1,983 ton BAHIA was delivered by J. Laing of Sunderland in time to sail on 6 May 1872 for Brazil and Buenos Aires, this being the line's first sailing to the River Plate. The 2,438 ton BUENOS AIRES was launched by the same builders on 18 October 1872, followed by the 2,114 ton ARGENTINA on 30 December and the 2,238 ton MONTEVIDEO in February 1873, both built by C. Michell & Co. The final addition of 1873 was the 2,247 ton VALPARAISO, a

189

product of Reiherstieg of Hamburg and the first of the fleet to be built in Germany.

After this came a pause as the 3,000 ton HOHENZOLLERN of Norddeutscher Lloyd (Chapter 29), launched in May 1873 for a new line from Bremen to the River Plate but detailed temporarily to other services owing to the worldwide depression, was despatched from Bremen for South America on 1 March 1876, succeeded by two sister ships, the SALIER and HABSBURG, at monthly intervals. They were much larger ships than any possessed by Hamburg–Süd, this handicap being overcome by chartering the 2,876 ton GERMANIA and the 3,408 ton GOETHE from the Hamburg American Line, who must have been delighted to come to arrangements with Hamburg–Süd as, with business in the doldrums, they would otherwise have been laid up. Unfortunately, the GERMANIA was wrecked at Bahia on 10 August 1876 and the GOETHE, which was larger and probably superior to any of the NDL ships, was wrecked off Lobos Island, at the mouth of the River Plate on 23 December 1876. This was her first or second voyage to South America but it is not known when the GERMANIA entered the service. It is possible that other Hapag ships were chartered by Hamburg–Süd. Despite the fact that it was not until 1895 that Hamburg–Süd possessed any ships as large as the HOHENZOLLERN group, and, moreover, that by then NDL had commissioned several larger ships which from time to time ran to South America, it seems that they and Hamburg–Süd had come to an amicable arrangement.

In 1877–8 C. Mitchell & Co delivered to Hamburg–Süd the 2,273 ton SANTOS (II), the 1,644 ton HAMBURG, which sailed direct to the Plate without calling at Brazil, and the 1,693 ton PARANAGUA. The last two had accommodation for 20 first class and 100 steerage passengers, but the first class of most of the earlier ships consisted of 30 berths and the steerage figure varied between 150 and 200.

The pioneer RIO was lengthened in 1880 by 6,00 metres (about 20 feet), bringing her more in line with the new ships of the fleet. In 1882, for the first time, some of the steamers extended their voyages to Rosario, so the next newcomer, the 1,824 ton ROSARIO, built in 1881, by Blohm & Voss of Hamburg, was aptly named. In 1881–4 C. Mitchell & Co supplied the CORRIENTES and CEARA, Reiherstieg was responsible for the PETROPOLIS, PERNAMBUCO and LISSABON, Sir W.G. Armstrong, Mitchell & Co (successors to C. Mitchell & Co) the URUGUAY and Blohm & Voss the DESTERRO.

Between 1886 and 1890 a huge batch of 14 ships was built of steel (two of them of steel and iron), and had three-cylinder triple-expansion engines instead of two-cylinder compound. They were the BAHIA (II), TIJUCA, OLINDA and ITAPARICA by Armstrong Mitchell, the

CAMPINAS, CURITYBA, BELGRANO, SAN NICOLAS, PARA-
GUASSU and PATAGONIA by Reiherstieg and the PORTO
ALEGRE, MONTEVIDEO (II), CINTRA and AMAZONAS by
Blohm & Voss. Their tonnage varied between 2,156 and 2,975, and the
first class capacity of all but three was 40 – the exceptions catered for 56.
Steerage capacity varied between 230 and 280.

Another large group of 11 ships varying in size between 2,601 and
3,834 tons was commissioned between 1892 and 1896 – the RIO (II),
BUENOS AIRES (II), ROSARIO (II), MENDOZA, CORRIENTES
(II), ARGENTINA (II), DESTERRO (II), GUAHYBA, PARA-
NAGUA (II), TAQUARY and MACEIO. Half of them had accommodation for 20 first class and the remainder for 12. Steerage numbers
varied considerably, but the last four ships could accommodate 300.
Blohm & Voss built five of the ships, Reiherstieg three, Sir Raylton
Dixon of Middlesbrough two and Edwards of Howdon-on-Tyne one. In
addition, three 2,400 ton steamers carrying cargo and 12 first class
passengers were built.

All this added up to a total of 44 ships, of which, as already stated, two
of the pioneers had been sold almost immediately. Of the remainder, one
was sold to the Hansa Line, five to the Deutsche Levante, three to
Woermann, two to the Hamburg American Line and three to miscel-
laneous buyers. In addition, the CORRIENTES was wrecked on 29
April 1890, the BUENOS AIRES on 21 July 1890, the DESTERRO was
sunk in collision on 24 March 1892 and the URUGUAY was wrecked on
30 September 1895. This left 24 ships still in the fleet in 1896.

There was a serious outbreak of cholera at Hamburg in 1892, and for a
time Hamburg–Süd ships terminated at Rotterdam instead of Hamburg.
From the later 1870s onwards there were numerous cases of yellow fever
in Brazil.

It was not until 1892 that a passage was cut through the bar off Rio
Grande do Sol, thereby giving access to several South Brazilian ports
including Porto Alegre, which was reached by lighters hauled by a
tug.

The year 1895 saw the commissioning of two appreciably larger ships –
the Blohm & Voss 4,663 ton ASUNCION and the 4,871 ton TUCU-
MAN, which were single-screw vessels with a speed of 11 knots, and
were the first of the fleet to be fitted with quadruple-expansion engines.
Passenger figures were 24 first class and 440 steerage. The 4,871 ton
CORDOBA by Reiherstieg and the 4,724 ton SÃO PAULO by Blohm
& Voss followed in 1896, the 4,792 ton PETROPOLIS (II) and
BELGRANO (II) by Reiherstieg and the 4,788 ton PERNAMBUCO
(II) and 4,739 ton SAN NICOLAS (II) by Blohm & Voss in 1897, the
4,817 ton BAHIA (III) by Reiherstieg in 1898, the 4,855 ton SANTOS

(III) by Reiherstieg and the 4,801 ton TIJUCA (II) by Blohm & Voss in 1899.

Two slightly smaller ships, the 4,010 ton ANTONINA (II) and the 4,004 ton PELOTAS (II) were completed in 1898 and chartered to Italia (Chapter 48) in 1901, the former retaining her name but the latter became the LA PLATA. They ran for Italia until sold to the Hamburg American Line in 1904.

Antonio Delfino was appointed the Hamburg–Süd representative for the River Plate area in 1894. He served the Company long and well, so much so that in 1922 one of the Company's steamers was named after him.

From 1894 Hamburg–Süd came to a satisfactory working arrangement with the A. C. de Freitas Line, which had been running a cargo service to the east coast of South America by steamers carrying a handful or two of passengers. However, in 1899, for some inexplicable reason, this arrangement was allowed to lapse. Intense competition sprang up and the Hamburg American Line took advantage of the situation by buying 14 de Freitas steamers. It was announced on 15 November 1900 that Hamburg–Süd had come to terms with Hapag concerning services from Germany to Brazil and the River Plate – Hamburg–Süd to have a two-thirds interest and Hapag one third.

1900 CAP VERDE 5,909 tons
Sister ship of CAP FRIO and CAP ROCA.

Owing to a considerable increase in the number of emigrants to Brazil, Uruguay and Argentina, and also to a two-way demand for first class passenger accommodation, Hamburg–Süd decided to build three greatly-improved liners of the 'CAP' class. The first two were the 5,732 ton CAP FRIO and the 5,786 ton CAP ROCA by Reiherstieg, their maiden voyages starting from Hamburg on 2 March and 26 June 1900, closely followed by the 5,909 ton CAP VERDE by the Flensburger Schiffsbau of

Flensburg. They were single-screw ships whose quadruple-expansion engines gave them a speed of 12 knots. They could cater for 80 first class passengers and 500 steerage.

The 4,494 ton SANTA FÉ and the 4,395 ton ENTRERIOS were delivered in 1902 by C.S. Swan & Hunter of Tyneside and Sir James Laing & Sons, of Sunderland, respectively, to help cope not only with increasing cargo commitments, but more especially with the growing requirements of emigrants, of which each ship could carry 800. They had no first class.

Two more 'CAP' ships, the 7,523 ton CAP BLANCO by Reiherstieg and the 7,818 ton CAP ORTEGAL by Blohm & Voss, were commissioned in 1904 and were a great improvement on their predecessors. In the first place, they were twin-screw ships with two sets of triple-expansion engines giving them a service speed of 13 knots, while their first class passenger accommodation was considerably more extensive – 164 in the case of the CAP ORTEGAL. Further, they catered not only for steerage (fourth class) in dormitory accommodation but also for third class in cabins.

The 9,467 ton CAP VILANO and the 9,832 ton CAP ARCONA (I) were completed by Blohm & Voss in 1906–07. Their service speed was increased to 15 knots by two sets of quadruple-expansion engines instead of the triple-expansion machinery of the immediate predecessors.

But Hamburg–Süd were not neglecting their intermediate ships, and in 1905–06 J.C. Tecklenborg of Geestemünde delivered the 4,556 ton RIO GRANDE, the 4,613 ton RIO NEGRO and the 4,588 ton RIO PARDO. They were single-screw ships with triple-expansion engines, a speed of 12 knots and had accommodation for 50 first class and 230 steerage passengers.

A series of emigrant ships appeared in 1905–08 – the 4,924 ton SANTA CRUZ by Swan, Hunter & Wigham Richardson of Tyneside, the 4,752 ton SANTA RITA by Reiherstieg, the 4,247 ton SANTA CATHARINA and the 4,238 ton SANTA LUCIA by J.C. Tecklenborg, the 7,401 ton SANTA MARIA by Flensburger and the 7,415 ton SANTA ELENA by Blohm & Voss. All were single-screw ships with a speed of 11 knots, catering only for cargo and steerage passengers, the numbers carried varying between 500 and, in the case of the last two, 1,200.

The 14,503 ton CAP FINISTERRE, launched by Blohm & Voss on 8 August 1911 and despatched from Hamburg for Buenos Aires on 2 December 1911, was by far the best ship commissioned to date by Hamburg–Süd. She had a service speed of 17 knots, and could cater for 297 first, 222 second and 870 steerage passengers, and in this connection was the first ship of the line to call any of her secondary accommodation second class. Moreover, it seems that she was the first to have the

1911 CAP FINISTERRE 14,503 tons
Later saw much service as Japanese TAIYO MARU.

Company's distinctive white funnels with red tops, but this may not have taken place for a year or two.

It was announced in 1912 that Hamburg–Süd's capital was being increased from 15 million to 25 million marks. Four services were being run in conjunction with Hapag – to Northern, Central and Southern Brazil and also to the River Plate. A further service from New York to Brazil is beyond the scope of this volume. In view of the vast number of ships commissioned since the turn of the century, it may be mentioned that 20 vessels were sold between 1897 and 1907.

Four twin-screw ships of a new type were placed in service in 1912–13 – the 9,349 ton BAHIA BLANCA and 9,959 ton BAHIA CASTILLO by Reiherstieg, and the 9,180 ton BUENOS AIRES (III) and the 9,791 ton BAHIA LAURA by Bremer Vulkan of Vegesack. They had a service speed of 13 knots and could accommodate 200 second class and 2,500 steerage passengers.

The 18,710 ton three funnelled CAP TRAFALGAR was launched by AG Vulcan of Hamburg on 31 July 1913 and started her maiden voyage from Hamburg for Buenos Aires on 10 March 1914. Her speed of 17 knots was much the same as that of the CAP FINISTERRE, but she was a triple-screw ship driven by a combination of triple-expansion engines and a low-pressure steam turbine on a similar system to that adopted by Harland & Wolff. She was appreciably larger than any competitor on the South Atlantic and her passenger accommodation was outstanding. Her first class capacity was 400, second class 275 and steerage 900.

The CAP FRIO had been wrecked on 30 August 1908 near Rio de Janeiro during a tropical storm, and the MENDOZA was wrecked on 10 July 1914 off the Argentinian coast when on voyage from Rio Gallegos to Buenos Aires. It must also be mentioned that the 20,576 ton CAP POLONIO was launched by Blohm & Voss on 25 March 1914. At this time Hamburg–Süd owned 56 ocean-going steamers of 325,031 tons, plus

194

the partly-completed CAP POLONIO and three cargo steamers in course of construction, totalling a further 34,140 tons.

The CAP BLANCO was sold to Hapag on 10 August 1914 and was renamed PRINZ HUBERTUS. The CAP ORTEGAL sheltered at Tenerife soon after war broke out, and was intended to become the Hapag PRINZ WILHELM, but the sale never went through.

The CAP TRAFALGAR was at Buenos Aires at the beginning of August 1914. She sailed for Montevideo on the 18th to take on a supply of coal, and on the 23rd had a rendezvous with the German EBER, from which the CAP TRAFALGAR received her armament of two 4.1 inch guns and three one-pounders as well as additional officers and crew. She also discarded her third funnel, which was a dummy. On 13 September she reached the Brazilian-owned Trinidad Island, where there were colliers in readiness to replenish her coal.

1914 CAP TRAFALGAR 18,710 tons
Sunk in 1914 by British merchant cruiser CARMANIA.

On the following day a large liner was seen approaching, so the CAP TRAFALGAR left the colliers and went to meet her. She turned out to be the 19,524 ton British armed merchant cruiser CARMANIA, belonging to the Cunard Line. In the scrap that followed, the German ship was sunk after 1 hour 40 minutes. She had given a good account of herself as the CARMANIA was on fire in her upperworks and it took some time to extinguish the blaze. In addition, smoke could be seen in the far distance from what looked suspiciously like a German cruiser, so the CARMANIA steamed southwards at full speed, changing her course to the east when night fell, and leaving it to the German colliers to pick up survivors from the stricken ship.

Two other Hamburg–Süd steamers were sunk by the British Navy

195

during the war. On 14 August 1914 the SANTA CATHARINA, when on voyage from New York to Santos, was captured by H.M.S. GLASGOW. Six days later the British cruiser decided to sink her as it was considered impossible to extinguish a serious fire in her bunkers. And on 18 October 1915 the PERNAMBUCO was torpedoed and sunk in the Baltic by the submarine E.9.

Some 15 Hamburg–Süd transatlantic steamers were safely in harbour at Hamburg when the war started, and subsequently, at least one ship sailed home through the allied blockade. About 20 ships took refuge in Spain, Portugal, Brazil, Argentina and Chile. Many were seized when Brazil and Portugal entered the war, and the remainder were surrendered after the war, as were those in port at Hamburg.

The most important of the surrendered ships was the 20,576 ton triple-screw CAP POLONIO, which arrived at Southend on 18 April 1919. After an overhaul she made a voyage under Union Castle colours from Plymouth to Cape Town lasting 29 days. Upon return to Plymouth her engines received attention in Devonport Dockyard, she was painted in P&O colours and made one round voyage to Bombay which was just as unsatisfactory, speedwise, as had been her South African one. On 20 July 1921 she was sold to Hamburg–Süd.

The 5,668 ton JACOBY was launched for Hamburg–Süd on 13 April 1918 by G. Seebeck of Wesermünde. She was completed in 1920 as the ARGENTINA and sailed on 30 December of that year on her maiden voyage from Hamburg for the River Plate. She was the first sizeable post-war vessel to be owned by Hamburg–Süd and could accommodate 585 steerage passengers.

The next newcomer was the 7,322 ton ESPAÑA, launched by Howaldtswerke of Kiel on 15 October 1921. She was a single-screw ship fitted with triple-expansion engines giving her a service speed of 12 knots. Passenger statistics were 200 third class and 675 fourth. Her maiden voyage from Hamburg for the River Plate started on 21 January 1922.

1919 CAP POLONIO 20,576 tons
Surrendered to Britain and made one voyage for Union-Castle and one for P&O.

After her purchase in July 1921 the CAP POLONIO was sent to Blohm & Voss to have her speed capabilities corrected to the scheduled 17 knots. Her passenger figures were 356 first class, 250 second and 949 third. Her first voyage from Hamburg to the River Plate started on 16 February 1922 and was in the nature of a cruise as was much of her subsequent activity as she did not fit in at all well with her smaller and less luxurious consorts.

The 7,271 ton LA CORUÑA, a sister ship of the ESPAÑA, was completed by Reiherstieg in time to start her maiden voyage from Hamburg to the River Plate on 18 February 1922, and was followed by the 7,309 ton VIGO on 29 April.

But in between these last two came the 13,589 ton twin-screw ANTONIO DELFINO, built by AG Vulcan of Hamburg, her passenger complement being 184 first, 334 second and 1,350 steerage. A sister ship, the 13,615 ton CAP NORTE, was launched on 8 May 1922 and was ready for her maiden voyage to the River Plate by 14 September 1922.

The 13,625 ton twin-screw motorship MONTE SARMIENTO and the 13,750 ton MONTE OLIVIA were launched by Blohm & Voss in 1924. They were the first of five sister ships, had a service speed of 14 knots and accommodation for 1,300 third and 1,150 fourth class passengers. Their maiden voyages started on 15 November 1924 and 23 April 1925.

1927 CAP ARCONA 27,561 tons
Bombed and destroyed in Bay of Lubeck in May 1945 with 5,000 fatal casualties.

At last, on 19 November 1927, a ship superior to the CAP POLONIO left Hamburg for Buenos Aires – the 27,561 ton CAP ARCONA (II), which also had three funnels but, unlike her consort, had a cruiser stern. She had twin-screws and her single-reduction geared turbines gave her a speed of 20 knots. Built by Blohm & Voss, she could accommodate 575 first, 275 second and 465 third class passengers. Among her many amenities was a full-sized tennis court at the after end of the promenade

197

1931 MONTE ROSA 13,882 tons
Last of five sister ships built by Blohm & Voss.

deck, but the protective netting considerably detracted from her appearance. The lifeboats, painted brown, were slung in pairs. She could proceed from Hamburg to Rio de Janeiro in 12 days and to Buenos Aires in 15.

The three final ships of the 'MONTE' class were the 13,913 ton MONTE CERVANTES, the 13,870 ton MONTE PASCOAL and the 13,882 ton MONTE ROSA, one commissioned in 1928 and two in 1931, all being products of Blohm & Voss. An interesting sign of the times was that their top class was called tourist instead of third.

All three were extensively used for cruising. Unfortunately, the MONTE CERVANTES became a total loss as the result of striking an uncharted rock off Tierra del Fuego on 22 January 1930. She capsized two days later, and sank in deep water when raised many years later, in 1954.

Owing to the worldwide depression, the CAP POLONIO was laid up in 1931. Two years later she became an exhibition ship in Hamburg and was finally scrapped at Bremerhaven in 1935.

Intense rivalry had existed between Norddeutscher Lloyd (Chapter 29) and the Hamburg American Line (Chapter 47) for several decades. It was announced in 1930 that an alliance, known as the Hapag–Lloyd Union, had been entered into. All services were to be jointly operated, and all costs, profits and losses pooled, but neither company was to lose its separate identity. In 1931 Hamburg–Süd signed a 10 year agreement with Hapag-Lloyd for the three concerns to pool their South American traffic. A noticeable result was that in the following year the Hamburg–Süd ANTONIO DELFINO and CAP NORTE were chartered to NDL, and renamed SIERRA NEVADA and SIERRA SALVADA.

However, the Hapag–Lloyd Union was considerably amended in 1934, and it was decided, *inter alia*, that the services to the east coast of South

198

America would be withdrawn from the Union. It was announced in November 1934 that Hamburg–Süd were to have a monopoly of the German services to Brazil and the River Plate. One of the first moves was the return to Hamburg–Süd of the ANTONIO DELFINO and CAP NORTE under their original names. In addition, the 8,753 ton NDL passenger steamer MADRID (ex-SIERRA NEVADA) was acquired by Hamburg–Süd in 1934, while nine NDL freighters were chartered to them in 1934–5 and bought by them within a year or two. Most were sunk or badly damaged during World War II. It may be added that the other three NDL 'SIERRA' ships were not taken over by Hamburg–Süd.

At the end of 1934 Hamburg–Süd chartered the 11,590 ton Hamburg American motorship GENERAL OSORIO, the 11,251 ton single-screw GENERAL SAN MARTIN and the 11,254 ton single-screw GENERAL ARTIGAS, all of which they bought in 1935, when also they chartered the 8,109 ton SACHSEN – later bought and renamed LA PLATA. She had accommodation for 20 first class passengers. In addition, they chartered and in due course bought 11 purely cargo steamers. Of these 15 ex-Hapag ships only the GENERAL SAN MARTIN survived the war, and she was seized by Britain at Copenhagen on 8 October 1945.

When World War II started in September 1939, Hamburg–Süd possessed an ocean-going fleet of 52 ships of 402,732 tons, while four ships were under construction totalling a further 25,000 tons.

During the war eight Hamburg–Süd passenger ships were destroyed by Allied bombing. From every point of view the worst of these losses was that of the CAP ARCONA, which became an accommodation ship at Gotenhafen (Gdynia) in 1940. In 1945 she made three voyages to East Germany and thereby was able to evacuate 25,000 people to West Germany. On 3 May she was bombed and destroyed in the Bay of Lubeck when carrying a large number of refugees, of whom about 5,000 were lost. After the war, all the ships which had survived were seized by the Allies.

Under the terms of the Treaty of Potsdam it was not permissible for Hamburg–Süd to start rebuilding its fleet until 1950, by which time amendments made it possible to place firm orders with shipbuilders.

The 6,962 ton single-screw motorship SANTA URSULA was launched by Howaldtswerke of Hamburg on 16 December 1950, and sailed on 5 April 1951 on her maiden voyage to the River Plate. She had accommodation for 24 first class passengers. Three sister ships, the SANTA ELENA, SANTA CATARINA and SANTA ISABEL were completed by the same builders in 1951–2. The SANTA CATARINA had a facelift by her builders in 1959 and was renamed CAP SALINAS.

The 8,996 ton single-screw motorship SANTA TERESA and a sister ship, the SANTA INÉS were delivered by Howaldtswerke in time to

1951 SANTA ELENA 6,971 tons
Sister ships SANTA URSULA, SANTA CATARINA and SANTA ISABEL. (24–26 first class passengers).

start their maiden voyages from Hamburg for the River Plate on 28 January and 26 March 1953. Their service speed was 14 knots compared with the 13 of their predecessors, and they catered for 28 first class. Rather surprisingly, these two ships were sold in 1961 whereas the first batch of four remained intact until 1964. The SANTA ISABEL became the Hamburg–Süd training ship in 1962 and was sold in 1968.

By the 1960s the effects of air competition were being felt by all passenger shipowners and although Hamburg–Süd built many more cargo ships and a handful carrying up to 12 passengers, they were involved in no more multi-passenger ships after commissioning the six 'SANTA' ships already dealt with.

1. (1872) RIO (I)
   1,688. 80,77 x 9,14. (265.0 x 30.0). S–1–2. I–S–C2–11. (I–26; III–52). C. Mitchell & Co, Walker-on-Tyne (engines T. Clark & Co, Newcastle). 1870 (Sep) launched as RIO (Br). 1871 RIO (Hamburg–Süd). 1872 FV Hamburg–Brazil. 1880 lengthened 6,0 metres (20 feet). 1897 sold. 1901 scrapped.
2. (1872) SANTOS (I)
   961. 68,51 x 8,50. (224.8 x 27.9). S–1–2. I–S–?–10. C. Mitchell & Co, Walker-on-Tyne (engines T. Clark & Co, Newcastle. 1869 (10/4) launched as SANTOS (Br). 1872 SANTOS (Hamburg–Süd). 1872 FV Hamburg–Brazil. 1873 ST. PAULI (Ger). 1877 (30/10) wrecked.
3. (1872) BRASILIEN
   1,315. 73,14 x 9,87. (240.0 x 32.4). S–1–2. I–S–?–10. C. Mitchell & Co, Walker-on-Tyne. 1869 (Jun) launched as BRAZILIAN

(Br). 1872 BRASILIEN (Hamburg–Süd). 1872 FV Hamburg–
Brazil. 1873 BRAZILIAN (Br). 1894 MURVET (Turkish). 1912
removed from *Lloyd's Register*.

4. 1872 BAHIA (I)

1,983. 92,13 x 10,70. (302.3 x 35.1). S–1–2. I–S–C2–10. (I–40;
III–160). J. Laing, Sunderland (engines Thompson, Boyd & Co,
Newcastle). 1871 (3/8) launched. 1872 (6/5) MV Hamburg–
Buenos Aires. 1885 C2 became T3. 1887 CREMON (Hansa).
1892 CREMON (Hapag). 1894 DALMATIA (Hapag). 1900
FIDES (It). 1916 scrapped at Genoa.

5. 1873 BUENOS AIRES (I)

2,438. 100,32 x 11,06. (339.0 x 36.3). C–2–2. I–S–C2–10. (I–30;
III–200). J. Laing, Sunderland (engines Humphreys, Tennant &
Dykes, London). Bought on the stocks. 1872 (18/10) launched.
1873 MV Hamburg–Brazil. 1890 (21/7) wrecked on Rosa Island.

6. 1873 ARGENTINA (I)

2,114. 91,43 x 11,03. (300.0 x 36.2). S–1–2. I–S–C2–10. (I–30;
III–200). C. Mitchell & Co, Walker-on-Tyne (engines Thompson, Boyd & Co, Newcastle). 1872 (30/12) launched. 1873 MV
Hamburg–Brazil. 1894 TINOS (Deutsche Levante. 1909 scrapped in Germany.

7. 1873 MONTEVIDEO (I)

2,238. 94,48 x 10,97. (310.0 x 36.0). I–S–C2–10. (I–30; III–100).
C. Mitchell & Co, Walker-on-Tyne (engines Thompson, Boyd &
Co, Newcastle). 1873 (Feb) launched. 1873 MV Hamburg–
Brazil. 1888 APENRADE (Danish). 1890 BANKOKU MARU
(Jap. 1908 (8/8) sank off Japanese coast.

8. 1873 VALPARAISO

2,247. 91,43 x 10,97. (300.0 x 36.0). S–1–2. I–S–C2–10. (I–30;
III–150). Reiherstieg, Hamburg. 1873 (May) launched. 1873
(19/11) MV Hamburg–Brazil. 1893 VALPARAISO (Br). 1902
DON MATIAS (Chilean). 1908 (23/7) sunk in collision off coast
of Chile.

8a. (1876) GERMANIA (c)

2,876. 100,60 x 11,90. (330.0 x 39.0). S–1–2. I–S–C2–11. (I–150;
II–70; III–150). Caird & Co, Greenock. 1870 (24/12) launched as
GERMANIA (Hapag). 1871 (4/5) MV Hamburg–New York.
1876 FV Hamburg–S. America for Hamburg–Süd (c). 1876 (10/8)
wrecked at Bahia.

8b. (1876) GOETHE (c)

3,408. 114,52 x 12,22. (375.8 x 40.1). S–2–2. I–S–C2–13. (I–90;
II–100; III–800). R. Napier & Sons, Glasgow. 1873 (28/4)
launched as GOETHE (Adler). 1875 ditto (Hapag). 1876 (May)

FV Hamburg–Plymouth–New York (1 RV). 1876 FV Hamburg–
S. America for Hamburg–Süd (c). 1876 (23/12) wrecked off
Lobos Island at mouth of R. Plate.

9. 1877 SANTOS (II)
2,273. 95,37 x 11.00. (312.9 x 36.1). S–1–2. I–S–C2–10. (I–30;
III–160). C. Mitchell & Co, Walker-on-Tyne (engines Thompson, Boyd & Co, Newcastle). 1877 (28/4) launched. 1877 (19/7)
MV Hamburg–Buenos Aires. 1897 VENUS (Danish). 1913
scrapped at Philadelphia.

10. 1878 HAMBURG
1,644. 82,08 x 10,30. (269.3 x 33.8). S–1–2. I–S–C2–10. (I–20;
III–100). C. Mitchell & Co, Walker-on-Tyne (engines Wallsend
Slipway Co Ltd). 1878 (Aug) launched. 1878 (25/10) MV
Hamburg–Buenos Aires. 1892 NAXOS Deutsche Levante. 1902
KHALIF (Deutsche–Ost–Afrika). 1905 scrapped at Stavanger.

11. 1878 PARANAGUA (I)
1,653. 82,20 x 10,30. (269.7 x 33.8). S–1–2. I–S–C2–10. (I–20;
III–100). C. Mitchell & Co, Walker-on-Tyne (engines Wallsend
Slipway Co Ltd). 1878 (Oct) launched. 1878 (26/11) MV
Hamburg–Buenos Aires. 1892 EURIPOS (Deutsche Levante).
1893 (24/8) collided with ROUMELIA (Br) in Sea of Marmara.
1893 (25/8) sank.

12. 1881 ROSARIO (I)
1,824. 82,29 x 10,36. (270.0 x 34.0). S–1–2, I–S–C2–10. (I–20;
III–300). Blohm & Voss, Hamburg. 1881 (16/4) launched. 1881
(1/10) MV Hamburg–Buenos Aires. 1892 ANDROS (Deutsche
Levante). 1911 VARAZZE (It). 1916 (2/10) wrecked on Welsh
coast.

13. 1881 CORRIENTES (I)
1,939. 86,86 x 10,79. (285.0 x 35.4). S–1–2. I–S–C2–10. (I–30;
III–260). C. Mitchell & Co, Walker-on-Tyne (engines Wallsend
Slipway Co Ltd). 1881 (Sep) launched. 1881 (18/11) MV
Hamburg–Brazil. 1890 (29/4) wrecked near Montevideo.

14. 1882 PETROPOLIS (I)
1,989. 86,86 x 10,85. (285.0 x 35.6). S–1–2. I–S–C2–10. (I–30;
III–260). Reiherstieg, Hamburg. 1882 (19/1) launched. 1882
(14/3) MV Hamburg–Buenos Aires. 1894 PETROPOLIS (Ger).
1896 PERGAMON (Ger). 1908 HOURRIET (Turkish). 1911
severe fire damage; scrapped.

15. 1883 CEARA
1,990. 86,86 x 11,09. (285.0 x 36.4). S–1–2. I–S–C2–10. (I–30;
III–250). C. Mitchell & Co, Walker-on-Tyne (engines Wallsend
Slipway Co Ltd). 1882 (Oct) launched. 1883 (4/2) MV Hamburg–

Buenos Aires. 1894 MILOS (Deutsche Levante). 1894 (Dec) went missing between Gibraltar and Hamburg.

16. 1883 PERNAMBUCO (I)

2,027. 86,86 x 11,00. (285.0 x 36.1). S–1–2. I–S–C2–10. (I–30; III–260). Reiherstieg, Hamburg. 1883 (Mar) launched. 1883 (2/6) MV Hamburg–R. Plate. 1894 KURT WOERMANN (Woermann). 1894 (22/12) wrecked on the Gold Coast.

17. 1883 LISSABON

2,000. 86,86 x 11,00 (285.0 x 36.0). S–1–2. I–S–C2–10. (I–30; III–260). Reiherstieg, Hamburg. 1883 (18/9) launched. 1883 (20/12) MV Hamburg–R. Plate. 1896 MELITA BOHLEN (Woermann). 1907 scrapped at Rotterdam.

18. 1884 URUGUAY

1,982. 86,86 x 11,00. (285.0 x 36.0). S–1–2. I–S–C2–10. (I–30; III–260). Sir W.G. Armstrong, Mitchell & Co, Walker-on-Tyne (engines Wallsend Slipway Co Ltd). 1883 (Dec) launched. 1884 (15/2) MV Hamburg–R. Plate. 1895 (30/9) wrecked at Cape Frio.

19. 1885 DESTERRO (I)

2,011. 86,86 x 11,00. (285.0 x 36.0). S–1–2. I–S–C2–10. (I–20; III–284). Blohm & Voss, Hamburg. 1885 (25/2) launched. 1885 (3/6) MV Hamburg–R. Plate. 1892 (24/3) sunk in collision with INDRA (Br) near Terschelling Island.

20. 1886 BAHIA (II)

2,156. 93,69 x 11.00. (307.4 x 36.1). S–1–2. S&I–S–T3–11. (I–40; III–280). Sir W.G. Armstrong, Mitchell & Co, Walker-on-Tyne (engines Wallsend Slipway Co Ltd). 1886 (Jly) launched. 1886 (22/9) MV Hamburg–R. Plate. 1897 LAUENBURG (Ger). 1903 MOBILE (Munson (US)). 1918 SIDI MABROUCK (Fr). 1930 scrapped.

21. 1886 TIJUCA (I)

2,165. 94,18 x 11,12. (309.0 x 36.5). S–1–2. S–S–T3–11. (I–40; III–280). Sir W.G. Armstrong, Mitchell & Co, Walker-on-Tyne (engines Wallsend Slipway Co Ltd. 1886 (8/8) launched. 1886 (5/11) MV Hamburg–Brazil. 1896 VALDIVIA (Hapag). 1907 boiler explosion 100 miles S. of Cape Hatteras (7). 1908 TOM. G. CORPI (Ger). 1909 FLANDRE (SGTM (Fr)). 1927 scrapped at La Seyne.

22. 1886 CAMPINAS

2,194. 94,18 x 11,06. (309.0 x 36.3). S–1–2. S&I–S–T3–11. (I–40; III–280). Reiherstieg, Hamburg. 1886 (25/9) launched. 1886 (5/12) MV Hamburg–Brazil. 1896 VALENCIA (Hapag). 1904 (23/12) wrecked at Jeremie, Haiti.

23. 1887 OLINDA
    2,376. 94,18 x 12,19. (309.0 x 40.0). S–1–2. S–S–T3–11. (I–40; III–280). Sir W.G. Armstrong, Mitchell & Co, Walker-on-Tyne (engines Wallsend Slipway Co Ltd). 1887 (17/8) launched. 1887 (21/10) MV Hamburg–R. Plate. 1897 OLINDA (Ger). 1903 OLINDA (USA). 1923 scrapped in USA.
24. 1887 CURITYBA
    2,363. 94,18 x 12,19. (309.0 x 40.0). S–1–2. S–S–T3–11. Reiherstieg, Hamburg. 1887 (Aug) launched. 1887 (18/10) MV Hamburg–Brazil. 1897 CURITYBA (Ger). 1903 ditto (USA). 1914 LIBERIA (Br). 1915 (1/9) wrecked on West African coast.
25. 1888 BELGRANO (I)
    2,488. 97,83 x 12.13. (321.0 x 39.8). S–1–2. S–S–T3–11. (I–40; III–250). Reiherstieg, Hamburg. 1888 (Mar) launched. 1888 (15/6) MV Hamburg–R. Plate. 1896 ADOLPH WOERMANN (Woermann). 1906 FRIEDA WOERMANN (ditto). 1914 interned at Bahia. 1917 seized by Brazil; renamed MACAPA. 1934 scrapped in Spain.
26. 1888 SAN NICOLAS (I)
    2,515. 98,17 x 12,10. (322.1 x 39.7). S–1–2. S&I–S–T3–11. (I–40; III–250). Reiherstieg, Hamburg. 1888 (Aug) launched. 1888 (28/10) MV Hamburg–R. Plate. 1896 LOTHAR (Woermann). 1898 (28/5) wrecked at Cape Palmas, Liberia.
27. 1888 PORTO ALGEGRE
    2,499. 97,83 x 12,16. (321.0 x 39.9). S–1–2. S–S–T3–11. (I–56; III–244). Blohm & Voss, Hamburg. 1888 (5/6) launched. 1888 (23/11) MV Hamburg–R. Plate. 1898 PERA (Deutsche Levante). 1913 MISURATA (It). 1917 (3/5) torpedoed and sunk by German submarine UC.73 in North Atlantic.
28. 1889 MONTEVIDEO (II)
    2,574. 98,14 x 12,19. (322.0 x 40.0). S–1–2. S–S–T3–11. (I–56; III–244). Blohm & Voss, Hamburg. 1888 (8/8) launched. 1889 (18/1) MV Hamburg–Brazil. 1898 HELENE WOERMANN (Woermann). 1907 LOME (Hamburg). 1914 (Aug) took refuge at Duala, Cameroons; sunk by British but later refloated. 1915 MONTEVIDEO (Br). 1918 AFRICSHORE (Br). 1923 SACARIA (Turkish). 1934 SAKARYA (ditto). 1943 (19/5) foundered near Fethiye, Turkey.
29. 1889 CINTRA
    2,506. 98,14 x 12,13. (322.0 x 39.8). S–1–2. S–S–T3–11. (I–56; III–244). Blohm & Voss, Hamburg. 1889 (16/3) launched. 1889 (11/6) MV Hamburg–Brazil. 1899 STAMBUL (Deutsche Levante). 1910 ditto (NDL). 1912 CORNIGLIANO (It). 1916

(23/5) torpedoed and sunk by German submarine U.34 in Mediterranean.

30. 1890 ITAPARICA

2,543. 99,36 x 12,19. (326.0 x 40.0). S–1–2. S–S–T3–12. (I–40; III–246). Sir W.G. Armstrong, Mitchell & Co, Walker-on-Tyne (engines Wallsend Slipway Co Ltd). 1889 (21/10) launched. 1890 (8/1) MV Hamburg–Brazil. 1901 CHUBUT (Hamburg–Süd (Argentinian flag). 1904 ITAPARICA (Hamburg–Süd). 1905 VIRGINIA (Hapag). 1914 interned at Cartagena, Colombia. 1916 JASON (USA). 1920 URALKER (Sp). 1923 scrapped at Wilhelmshaven.

31. 1890 PARAGUASSU

2,541. 100,58 x 12,68. (330.0 x 41.6). S–1–2. S–S–T3–12. (I–40; III–246). Reiherstieg, Hamburg. 1890 (15/2) launched. 1890 (19/6) MV Hamburg–Brazil. 1901 COMODORO RIVADAVIA (Argentinian). 1903 (25/2) wrecked on coast of Patagonia.

32. 1890 AMAZONAS

2,950. 99,26 x 12,59. (325.7 x 41.3). S–1–2. S–S–T3–12. (I–40; III–230). Blohm & Voss, Hamburg. 1890 (26/7) launched. 1890 (11/11) MV Hamburg–Brazil. 1903 RIO GALLEGOS (Argentinian). 1904 AMAZONAS (Hamburg–Süd). 1905 VENETIA (Hapag). 1915 (25/9) torpedoed by British submarine off Borkum; beached; constructive total loss. (See Hapag (47)).

33. 1890 PATAGONIA

2,975. 100,58 x 12,68. (330.0 x 41.6). S–1–2. S–S–T3–12. (I–40; III–230). Reiheistieg, Hamburg. 1890 (6/9) launched. 1890 (19/12) MV Hamburg–R. Plate. 1903 FV Genoa–R. Plate. 1904 PATAGONIA (Hapag). 1914 interned at Bahia Blanca. 1920 sailed Bahia Blanca–Hamburg. 1921 PATAGONIA (Br). 1923 VALDIVIA (Chilean). 1933 (4/10) wrecked on Chilean coast.

34. (1892) RIO (II)

3,187. 100,88 x 12,25. (331.0 x 40.2). C–1–2. S–S–T3–11. (I–20; III). Edwards Shipbuilding Co, Howdon-on-Tyne (engines Wallsend Slipway Co Ltd). 1892 (14/3) launched as BRANKSOME TOWER (F. Stumore & Co). 1892 RIO (Hamburg–Süd). 1892 (20/7) MV Hamburg–R. Plate. 1902 SERIPHOS (Deutsche Levante). 1916 (3/9) seized by British Navy. 1917 HUNTSGULF (Br). 1919 JUGOSLAVEN PRVI (Yugoslavian). 1927 scrapped at Inverkeithing.

35. 1893 BUENOS AIRES (II)

3,184. 96,27 x 12,19. (315.9 x 40.0). S–1–2. S–S–T3–11. (I–20; III). Blohm & Voss, Hamburg. 1893 (2/3) launched. 1893 (11/5)

MV Hamburg–R. Plate. 1902 ASCAN WOERMANN (Woermann). 1908 (9/1) wrecked at Grant Bassam, Ivory Coast.

36. 1893 ROSARIO (II)
3,184. 96,27 x 12,19. (315.9 x 40.0). S–1–2. S–S–T3–11. (I–20; III). Blohm & Voss, Hamburg. 1893 (15/4) launched. 1893 (22/6) MV Hamburg–R. Plate. 1904 ERICH WOERMANN (Woermann). 1907 TOGO (Hapag). 1914 (Aug) took shelter at St. Vincent. 1916 seized by Portugal; renamed BRAVA. 1918 (3/9) torpedoed and sunk by German submarine UB.125 near Trevose Head, Cornwall.

37. 1894 MENDOZA
3,797. 103,00 x 12,80. (338.0 x 42.0). S–1–2. S–S–T3–11. (I–20; III–120). Reiherstieg, Hamburg. 1894 (Sep) launched. 1894 (20/11) MV Hamburg–R. Plate. 1914 (10/7) wrecked on Argentinian coast on voyage from Rio Gallegos to Buenos Aires.

38. 1894 CORRIENTES (II)
3,720. 104,23 x 12,80. (342.0 x 42.0). S–1–2. S–S–T3–11. (I–12; III–144). Blohm & Voss, Hamburg. 1894 (27/9) launched. 1894 (29/11) MV Hamburg–Brazil. 1914 (4/8) sheltered at Maranhão. 1914 (Aug) support ship for German light cruiser DRESDEN. 1914 (14/8) interned at Pernambuco. 1917 seized by Brazil; renamed GUARATUBA. 1936 scrapped at Rio de Janeiro.

39. 1895 ARGENTINA (II)
3,791. 104,23 x 12,80. (342.0 x 42.0). S–1–2. S–S–T3–11. (I–12; III–130. Reiherstieg, Hamburg. 1894 (Dec) launched. 1895 (8/3) MV Hamburg–Brazil. 1907 PRESIDENTE MITRE (Argentinian). 1923 TARAPACA (Chilean). 1941 AVILES (Argentinian). 1956 scrapped at Buenos Aires.

40. 1895 DESTERRO (II)
2,543. 91,43 x 11,58. (300.0 x 38.0). S–1–2. S–S–T3–10. (I–10; III–228). Blohm & Voss, Hamburg. 1894 (11/12) launched. 1895 (25/3) MV Hamburg–Brazil. 1917 UHLENHORST (Ger). 1919 surrendered to Britain. 1921 FRICKA (Ger). 1931 SELONIJA (Latvian). 1932 (19/4) foundered in Bay of Biscay.

41. 1895 GUAHYBA
2,756. 91,43 x 12,50. (300.0 x 41.0). S–1–2. S–S–T3–10. (I–20; III–300). Blohm & Voss, Hamburg. 1895 (8/6) launched. 1895 (16/8) MV Hamburg–Brazil. 1914 (Aug) sheltered at Madeira. 1916 (Feb) seized by Portugal; renamed PORT SANTO. 1918 (29/3) lost.

42. 1895 PARANAGUA (II)
2,803. 91,43 x 12,50. (300.0 x 41.0). S–1–2. S–S–T3–10. (I–20; III–300). Reiherstieg, Hamburg. 1895 (31/7) launched. 1895

(23/10) MV Hamburg–Brazil. 1917 HARVESTEHUDE (Ger). 1919 surrendered to Britain. 1922 PARANAGUA (Danzig). 1925 HARALD (Ger). 1927 OLAF A (Italian). 1928 CESAREA (Tunis). 1928 PRADO (Tunis). 1932 EL MEDINA (Tunis). 1934 scrapped at La Spezia.

43. 1895 ASUNCION
4,663. 114,29 x 14,02. (375.0 x 46.0). S–1–2. S–S–Q4–11. (I–24; III–440). Blohm & Voss, Hamburg. 1895 (4/9) launched. 1895 (31/10) MV Hamburg–Brazil. 1914 (Aug) sheltered at Santos; later became support ship to German light cruiser KARLS-RUHE, which sank about 400 miles east of Trinidad after an internal explosion; proceeded to Para with some of the crew. 1917 (June) seized by Brazil at Para; renamed CAMPOS. 1943 (23/10) torpedoed and sunk by German submarine U.170 in mid Atlantic.

44. 1895 TUCUMAN
4,661. 114,29 x 14,02. (375.0 x 46.0). S–1–2. S–S–Q4–11. (I–24; III–440). Blohm & Voss, Hamburg. 1895 (17/10) launched. 1895 (1/12) MV Hamburg–Brazil. 1914 (Aug) sheltered at Punta Arenas. 1919 sailed to Hamburg. 1921 surrendered to Britain. 1921 (13/7) resold to Hamburg–Süd. 1927 scrapped in England.

45. 1896 CORDOBA
4,871. 114,29 x 14,02. (375.0 x 46.0). S–1–2. S–S–Q4–11. (I–24; III–400). Reiherstieg, Hamburg. 1895 (28/10) launched. 1896 (Jan) MV Hamburg–Brazil. 1919 surrendered to Britain; name unchanged. 1920 (22/5) destroyed by fire near Island of Socotra.

46. 1896 TAQUARY
2,788. 91,43 x 12,59. (300.0 x 41.3). S–1–2. S–S–T3–10. (I–12; III–300). Sir Raylton Dixon & Co, Middlesbrough (engines T. Richardson & Sons, Hartlepool). 1896 (1/5) launched. 1896 (15/8) MV Hamburg–Brazil. 1904 CAMARONES (Argentinian). 1922 BUENOS AIRES (Argentinian). 1946 (27/8) wrecked near Rio Grande do Sul.

47. 1896 MACEIO
2,786. 91,43 x 12,50. (300.0 x 41.0). S–1–2. S–S–T3–10. (I–12; III–300). Sir Raylton Dixon & Co, Middlesbrough, (engines T. Richardson & Sons, Hartlepool). 1896 (13/7) launched. 1896 (2/10) MV Hamburg–R. Plate. 1904 PRESIDENTE ROCA (Argentinian). 1909 (18/2) caught fire and sank off coast of Patagonia.

48. 1896 SÃO PAULO
4,724. 114,29 x 14,02. (375.0 x 46.0). S–1–2. S–S–Q4–11. (I–28; III–440). Blohm & Voss, Hamburg. 1896 (3/10) launched. 1896

(6/12) MV Hamburg–R. Plate. 1914 (Aug) SPERRBRECHER 8 (German Navy). 1915 (14/1) sunk by mine in North Sea.

49. 1897 PETROPOLIS (II)
4,792. 114,29 x 14,02. (375.0 x 46.0). S–1–2. S–S–Q4–11. (I–28; III–440). Reiherstieg, Hamburg. 1897 (10/4) launched. 1897 (2/7) MV Hamburg–R. Plate. 1914 (Aug) sheltered at Madeira. 1916 (Feb) seized by Portugal; renamed MADEIRA. 1918 (7/10) torpedoed and sunk by German submarine UB.105 near Island of San Pietro, Italy.

50. 1897 PERNAMBUCO (II)
4,788. 114,29 x 14,02. (375.0 x 46.0). S–1–2. S–S–Q4–11. (I–28; III–440). Blohm & Voss, Hamburg. 1897 (13/5) launched. 1897 (15/7) MV Hamburg–Brazil. 1915 (18/10) torpedoed and sunk by British submarine E.9 in the Baltic.

51. 1897 BELGRANO (II)
4,792. 114,78 x 14,11. (376.6 x 46.3). S–1–2. S–S–Q4–11. (I–30; III–440). Reiherstieg, Hamburg. 1897 (Jly) launched. 1897 (22/10) MV Hamburg–R. Plate. 1914 (Aug) sheltered at Coruña. 1919 (Jun) surrendered to France. 1932 scrapped at La Seyne.

52. 1897 SAN NICOLAS (II)
4,739. 114,53 x 14,11. (375.8 x 46.3). S–1–2. S–S–Q4–11. (I–28; III–400). Blohm & Voss, Hamburg. 1897 (25/9) launched. 1897 (21/11) MV Hamburg–R. Plate. 1914 (Aug) sheltered at Pernambuco. 1917 (Jun) seized br Brazil; renamed ALFENAS. 1923 CAMPOS SALLES (Brazilian). 1962 scrapped in Brazil.

53. 1898 BAHIA (III)
4,817. 114,50 x 14,20. (375.7 x 46.6). S–1–2. S–S–Q4–11. (I–40; III–450). Reiherstieg, Hamburg. 1898 (19/3) launched. 1898 (30/6) MV Hamburg–Brazil. 1914 (Aug) sheltered at Montevideo. 1917 (1/9) seized by Uruguay; renamed PAYSANDU. 1927 scrapped at Copenhagen.

54. 1898 ANTONINA (II)
4,010. 110,10 x 13,60. (361.3 x 44.6). S–1–2. S–S–T3–12. (I–52; III–330). Blohm & Voss, Hamburg. 1898 (18/6) launched. 1898 (25/8) MV Hamburg–Brazil. 1901 (17/4) FV for Italia (c), Genoa–R. Plate. 1904 ANTONINA (Hapag). 1905 (4/9) FV Hamburg–Para. 1914 (Aug) interned at Tampico. 1920 towed to Hamburg. 1922 HAIMON (Roland). 1925 ditto (NDL). 1927 ANCONA (ditto). 1928 PIRANGY (Brazilian). 1961 scrapped in Brazil.

55. 1898 PELOTAS (II)
4,004. 110,10 x 13,60. (361.3 x 44.6). S–1–2. S–S–T3–12. (I–54; III–330). Reiherstieg, Hamburg. 1898 (15/6) launched. 1898

(11/9) MV Hamburg–Brazil. 1901 (27/3) FV as LA PLATA for Italia (c), Genoa–R. Plate. 1904 LA PLATA (Hapag). 1904 (28/5) FV Genoa–Buenos Aires. 1914 (Aug) laid up at Hamburg. 1919 surrendered to Britain. 1921 resold to Germany. 1923 GUINE (Companhia Colonial de Navegação). 1930 (22/8) wrecked at Bolama.

56. 1899 SANTOS (III)
   4,855. 114,47 x 14,20. (375.6 x 46.6). S–1–2. S–S–Q4–12. (I–50; III–400). Reiherstieg, Hamburg. 1898 (7/12) launched. 1899 (16/3) MV Hamburg–Brazil. 1914 (Aug) sheltered at Pernambuco. 1917 (Jun) seized by Brazil; name unchanged. 1961 scrapped in Brazil.

57. 1899 TIJUCA (II)
   4,801. 114,47 x 14,11. (375.6 x 46.3). S–1–2. S–S–Q4–12. (I–50; III–400). Blohm & Voss, Hamburg. 1899 (5/7) launched. 1899 (23/8) MV Hamburg–Brazil. 1914 (Aug) sheltered at Pernambuco. 1917 (Jun) seized by Brazil; renamed BAEPENDY. 1942 (16/8) torpedoed and sunk by German submarine U.507 off Brazilian coast.

58. 1900 CAP FRIO
   5,732. 125,39 x 14,72. (411.4 x 48.3). 1–2. S–Q4–12. (I–80; III–500). Reiherstieg, Hamburg. 1899 (23/11) launched. 1900 (2/3) MV Hamburg–R. Plate. 1908 (30/8) wrecked near Bahia during a tropical storm.

59. 1900 CAP ROCA
   5,786. 125,39 x 14,72. (411.4 x 48.3). 1–2. S–Q4–12. (I–80; III–500). Reiherstieg, Hamburg. 1900 (7/4) launched. 1900 (26/6) MV Hamburg–R. Plate. 1914 (Aug) sheltered at Rio de Janeiro. 1917 (Jun) seized by Brazil; renamed ITU. 1926 ALMIRANTE ALEXANDRINO (Lloyd Brasileiro). 1966 scrapped in Brazil.

60. 1900 CAP VERDE
   (1922) MADEIRA
   5,909. 125,11 x 14,72. (410.5) x 48.3). 1–2. S–Q4–12. (I–87; III–500). Flensburger Schiffsbau, Flensburg. 1900 (8/5) launched. 1900 (5/8) MV Hamburg–Buenos Aires. 1919 surrendered to Britain. 1922 MADEIRA (Hamburg–Süd). 1925 RAUL SOARES (Lloyd Brasileiro). 1965 scrapped at Rio de Janeiro.

61. 1902 SANTA FÉ
   4,494. 118,40 x 14,56. (388.5 x 47.8). 1–2. S–T3–11. (III–800). C.S. Swan & Hunter, Wallsend-on-Tyne (engines Wallsend Slipway Co Ltd). 1901 (11/12) launched. 1902 (11/2) MV Hamburg–R. Plate. 1919 surrendered to Britain. 1922 SANTA

FÉ (Hamburg–Süd). 1922 (23/2) resumed Hamburg–S. America. 1932 scrapped at Danzig.

62. 1902 ENTRERIOS
4,395. 118,46 x 14,56. (388.7 x 47.8). 1–2. S–T3–11. (III–800). Sir James Laing & Sons, Sunderland (engines Wallsend Slipway Co Ltd). 1902 (8/2) launched. 1902 (24/5) MV Hamburg–R. Plate. 1914 (Aug) at Hamburg. 1915 (17/9) wrecked on Swedish coast.

63. 1904 CAP BLANCO
7,523. 134,25 x 15,97. (440.5 x 52.4). 1–2. 2S–T6–13. (I–140; III–90; IV–350). Reiherstieg, Hamburg. 1903 (28/11) launched. 1904 (6/4) MV Hamburg–R. Plate. 1914 (10/8) PRINZ HUBERTUS (Hapag). 1919 surrendered to Britain. 1919 (23/11) gutted by fire in R. Thames. 1920 partially dismantled at Falmouth; later towed to Hamburg for completion of demolition.

64. 1904 CAP ORTEGAL
7,818. 134,34 x 15,97. (440.8 x 52.4). 1–2. 2S–T6–13. (I–164; III–96; IV–338). Blohm & Voss, Hamburg. 1903 (30/12) launched. 1904 (6/5) MV Hamburg–R. Plate. 1914 (Aug) sheltered at Tenerife. 1914 (Aug) intended to become PRINZ WILHELM (Hapag) but sale did not go through. 1919 surrendered to France. 1922 CHAMBORD (Messageries Maritimes. 1932 scrapped at La Seyne.

65. 1905 RIO GRANDE
4,556. 110,08 x 14,23. (361.2 x 46.7). J.C. Tecklenborg, Geestemünde. 1904 (24/11) launched. 1905 (28/2) MV Hamburg–Brazil. 1914 (Aug) sheltered at Para. 1917 (Jun) seized by Brazil; renamed BENEVENTE. 1926 DUQUE DE JANEIRO (Lloyd Brasileiro). 1963 scrapped in Brazil.

66. 1905 RIO NEGRO
4,613. 110,08 x 14,23. (361.2 x 46.7). 1–2. S–T3–12. (I–50; III–230). J.C. Tecklenborg, Geestemünde. 1905 (20/2) launched. 1905 (29/4) MV Hamburg–Brazil. 1914 (Aug) sheltered at Para; later became support ship to German light cruiser KARLSRUHE, which sank about 400 miles E. of Trinidad after an internal explosion; RIO NEGRO sailed to Germany. 1919 surrendered to Britain. 1921 CITY OF PALERMO (Ellerman). 1933 scrapped in Italy.

67. 1905 SANTA CRUZ
4,924. 119,44 x 15,30. (391.9 x 50.2). 1–2. S–T3–11. (III–850). Swan, Hunter & Wigham Richardson, Wallsend-on-Tyne (engines Wallsend Slipway Co Ltd). 1905 (17/6) launched. 1905 (14/9) MV Hamburg–R. Plate. 1914 (Aug) at Hamburg. 1919

surrendered to Britain. 1921 MERTON HALL (Ellerman's Hall). 1926 CITY OF SALFORD (Ellerman). 1933 scrapped.

68. 1905 SANTA RITA

4,752. 119,47 x 15,30. (392.0 x 50.2). 1–2. S–T3–11. (III–850). Reiherstieg, Hamburg. 1905 (21/10) launched. 1905 (1/12) MV Hamburg–R. Plate. 1914 (Aug) sheltered at Valparaiso. 1920 (Sep) left Valparaiso under tow. 1921 surrendered to Britain. 1922 BILBAO (Hamburg–Süd – cargo steamer). 1932 scrapped at Hamburg.

69. (1906) RIO PARDO

4,588. 110,05 x 14,23. (361.1 x 46.7). 1–2. S–T3–12. (I–50; III–230). J.C. Tecklenborg, Geestemünde. 1905 (20/5) launched; sold to Hapag and renamed DALMATIA. 1905 (1/9) MV Hamburg–Brazil. 1906 RIO PARDO (Hamburg–Süd). 1914 (Aug) at Hamburg. 1919 surrendered to Britain. 1921 CITY OF ALEXANDRIA (Ellerman). 1933 scrapped at Cobh.

70. 1906 CAP VILANO

9,467. 145,00 x 16,85. (475.7 x 55.3). 1–2. 2S–Q8–15. (I–200; III–98; IV–302). Blohm & Voss, Hamburg. 1906 (7/4) launched. 1906 (25/8) MV Hamburg–Buenos Aires. 1914 (Aug) sheltered at Pernambuco. 1917 (Jun) seized by Brazil; renamed SOBRAL. 1923–4 GÉNÉRAL METZINGER (Messageries Maritimes). 1940 (11/6) sunk by German bomber in Havre roads. 1950 refloated; scrapped.

71. 1907 SANTA CATHARINA

4,247. 106,67 x 14,38. (350.0 x 47.2). 1–2. S–T3–11. (III–500). J.C. Tecklenborg, Geestemünde. 1907 (19/1) launched. 1907 (24/3) MV Hamburg–R. Plate. 1914 (14/8) captured by British cruiser GLASGOW and taken to Abrolhos Island, Brazil. 1914 (20/8) sunk by gunfire from GLASGOW after a serious fire in her bunkers.

72. 1907 SANTA LUCIA

4,238. 106,73 x 14,38. (350.2 x 47.2). 1–2. S–T3–11. (III–500). J.C. Tecklenborg, Geestemünde. 1907 (10/4) launched. 1907 (1/6) MV Hamburg–Brazil. 1914 (Aug) sheltered at Bahia. 1917 (Jun) seized by Brazil; renamed JOAZEIRO. 1955 scrapped at Rio de Janeiro.

73. 1907 CAP ARCONA (I)

9,832. 147,27 x 16,91. (483.2 x 55.5). 1–2. 2S–Q8–15. (I–244; III–110; IV–404). Blohm & Voss, Hamburg. 1907 (25/4) launched. 1907 (15/9) MV Hamburg–Buenos Aires. 1914 (Aug) sheltered at Villagarcia, Spain. 1919 surrendered to France. 1921 ANGERS (Messageries Maritimes). 1939 scrapped.

74. 1908 SANTA MARIA
   7,401. 129,87 x 16,85. (426.1 x 55.3). 1–2. S–Q4–11. (III–1,200),
   Flensburger Schiffsbau, Flensburg. 1907 (5/11) launched. 1908
   (5/1) MV Hamburg–R. Plate. 1914 (Aug) sheltered at Caleta
   Buena, Chile. 1920 towed to Hamburg. 1922 surrendered to
   Britain but remained at Hamburg. 1922 VILLAGARCIA (Hamburg–Süd). 1932 scrapped at Kiel.
75. 1908 SANTA ELENA (I)
   7,415. 131,33 x 16,70. (430.9 x 54.8). 1–2. S–Q4–11. (III–1,200).
   Blohm & Voss, Hamburg. 1907 (16/11) launched. 1908 (7/1) MV
   Antwerp–River Plate. 1914 (Aug) át Hamburg. 1919 surrendered
   to Britain. 1920 transferred to France. 1922 LINOIS (Chargeurs
   Réunis). 1942 ORVIETO (Italian). 1943 seized by Germans at
   Genoa. 1944 (Aug) scuttled at Marseilles. 1945 refloated;
   scrapped.
76. 1911 CAP FINISTERRE
   14,503. 170,68 x 19,90. (560.0 x 65.3). 2–2. 2S–Q8–17. (I–297;
   II–222; III–870). Blohm & Voss, Hamburg. 1911 (8/8) launched.
   1911 (2/12) MV Hamburg–Buenos Aires. 1914 (Aug) at Ham-
   burg. 1919 surrendered to USA. 1919 transferred to Britain. 1921
   TAIYO MARU (Toyo Kisen Kaisha). 1926 ditto (Nippon Yusen
   Kaisha). 1942 (8/5) torpedoed and sunk by US submarine
   GRENADIER in China Sea.
77. 1912 BAHIA BLANCA
   9,349. 149,92 x 18,07. (491.9 x 59.3). 1–2. 2S–T6–13. (II–108;
   III–2,300). Reiherstieg, Hamburg. 1911 (30/12) launched. 1912
   (14/3) MV Hamburg–R. Plate. 1914 (Aug) sheltered at Buenos
   Aires. 1918 sold to Argentina; name unchanged. 1935 UMBRIA
   (It). 1940 (Jun) scuttled at Port Sudan; later refloated and
   scrapped.
78. 1912 BUENOS AIRES (III)
   9,180. 149,34 x 17,98. (490.0 x 59.0). 1–2. 2S–T6–13. (II–110;
   III–2,200). Bremer Vulkan, Vegesack. 1912 (2/4) launched. 1912
   (21/5) MV Hamburg–Buenos Aires. 1914 (Aug) at Hamburg.
   1919 surrendered to France. 1922 CEPHÉE (Messageries Maritimes). 1936 scrapped at Blyth.
79. 1913 BAHIA CASTILLO
   9,959. 149,83 x 18,00. (491.6 x 59.1). 1–2. 2S–T6–13. (II–200;
   III–2,500). Reiherstieg, Hamburg. 1913 (4/1) launched. 1913
   (11/4) MV Hamburg–Buenos Aires. 1914 (Aug) at Hamburg.
   1919 surrendered to Britain. 1922 GENERAL SAN MARTIN;
   later GENERAL BELGRANO (Hugo Stinnes); 10,121
   tons; (cabin 142; III–540). 1926 GENERAL BELGRANO

(Hapag). 1926 FV Hamburg–Buenos Aires. 1933 scrapped at Hamburg.
80. 1913 BAHIA LAURA
9,791. 149,89 x 18,04. (491.8 x 59.2). 1–2. 2S–T6–13. (II–200; III–2,500). Bremer Vulkan, Vegesack. 1913 (29/4) launched. 1913 (11/7) MV Hamburg–Buenos Aires. 1914 (Aug) sheltered at Pernambuco. 1917 (Jun) seized by Brazil; renamed CAXIAS. 1923 RUY BARBOSA (Lloyd Brasileiro). 1934 (31/7) wrecked near Leixões.
81. 1914 CAP TRAFALGAR
18,710. 186,83 x 22,00 (613.0 x 72.2). 3–2. 3S–T8&ST–17. (I–400; II–275; III–900). AG Vulcan, Hamburg. 1913 (31/7) launched. 1914 (10/3) MV Hamburg–Buenos Aires. 1914 (18/8) sailed Buenos Aires–Montevideo for coal. 1914 (23/8) rendezvous with German gunboat EBER, which handed over guns and ammunition; third funnel removed. 1914 (13/9) at Trinidad Island (Brazil). 1914 (14/9) gun duel with British auxiliary cruiser CARMANIA. CAP TRAFALGAR sank; CARMANIA proceeded to Gibraltar for repairs.
82. 1920 ARGENTINA (III)
5,668. 111,36 x 15,60. (365.4 x 51.2). 1–2. S–T3–11. (III–600). G. Seebeck AG, Wesermünde. 1918 (13/4) launched as JACOBY (Hamburg–Süd). 1920 completed as ARGENTINA (ditto). 1920 (30/12) MV Hamburg–R. Plate. 1928 passenger accommodation removed. 1932 scrapped at Hamburg.
83. 1922 ESPAÑA
7,322. 125,97 x 16,82. (413.3 x 55.2). 1–2. S–T3–12. (III–200; IV–675). Howaldtswerke, Kiel. 1921 (15/10) launched. 1922 (21/1) MV Hamburg–R. Plate. 1945 (May) taken as prize at Sandefjord. 1946 GENERAL BAGRATION (USSR). 1973 FUJI MARU No. 3 (Jap). 1974 scrapped at Kaohsiung.
84. (1922) CAP POLONIO
20,576. 194,39 x 22,06. (637.8 x 72.4). 3–2. 3S–T8&ST–17. (I–356; II–250; III–950). Blohm & Voss. Hamburg. 1914 (25/3) launched. 1919 surrendered to Britain; chartered to Union Castle; later P&O. 1921 (20/7) sold to Hamburg–Süd. 1922 (16/2) FV Hamburg–Buenos Aires. 1931 laid up at Hamburg. 1935 scrapped at Bremerhaven.
85. 1922 LA CORUÑA
7,271. 126,18 x 16,82. (414.0 x 55.2). 1–2. S–T3–12. (III–146; IV–438). Reiherstieg, Hamburg. 1921 (16/9) launched. 1922 (18/2) MV Hamburg–R. Plate. 1939 (Sep) sheltered at Rio de Janeiro. 1940 (9/2) sailed for Germany. 1940 (13/3) intercepted

by British auxiliary cruiser MALOJA to E. of Iceland; scuttled to avoid capture.

86. 1922 ANTONIO DELFINO
13,589. 152,24 x 19,50. (499.5 x 64.0). 1–2–C. 2S–T6–13. (I–184; II–334; III–1,350). AG Vulcan, Hamburg. 1921 (10/11) launched. 1922 (16/3) MV Hamburg–R. Plate. 1932 (2/8) LV Buenos Aires–Bremen. 1932 SIERRA NEVADA (NDL (c)). 1934 ANTONIO DELFINO (Hamburg–Süd). 1939 (Sep) proceeded from Bahia to Germany. 1940 accommodation ship at Kiel. 1943 ditto at Gotenhafen (Gdynia). 1945 (May) seized by Britain at Copenhagen. 1946 EMPIRE HALLADALE (Anchor Line (c)). 1956 scrapped at Dalmuir.

87. 1922 VIGO
7,309. 125,97 x 16,79. (413.3 x 55.1). 1–2. S–T3–12. (III–190; IV–680). Howaldtswerke, Kiel. 1922 (20/1) launched. 1922 (29/4) MV Hamburg–Brazil. 1939 (Sep) at Hamburg; became SPERR-BRECHER X (German Navy). 1944 (7/3) sunk by mine off Norderney.

88. 1922 CAP NORTE
13,615. 15,224 x 19,50. (499.5 x 64.0). 1–2–C. 2S–T6–13. (I–184; II–334; III–1,350). AG Vulcan, Hamburg. 1922 (8/5) launched. 1922 (14/9) MV Hamburg–R. Plate. 1932 (1/7) LV Buenos Aires–Hamburg. 1932 SIERRA SALVADA (NDL (c)). 1934 CAP NORTE (Hamburg–Süd). 1939 (9/10) captured by British cruiser BELFAST when blockade-running from Pernambuco–Hamburg. 1940 EMPIRE TROOPER (British India (c)). 1955 caught fire in shipbreakers' yard at Inverkeithing and sank; later raised and scrapped.

89. 1924 MONTE SARMIENTO (M/S)
13,625. 152,57 x 20,05 (500.6 x 65.8). 2–2–C. 2S–4SC.SA–14. (III–1,300; IV–1,150). Blohm & Voss, Hamburg. 1924 (31/7) launched. 1924 (15/11) MV Hamburg–Buenos Aires. 1939 (Sep) at Hamburg. 1939 (Dec) accommodation ship at Kiel. 1942 (26/2) sunk at Kiel by Allied bomber. 1943 refloated; towed to Hamburg and scrapped.

90. 1925 MONTE OLIVIA (M/S)
13,750. 152,57 x 20.05. (500.6 x 65.8). 2–2–C. 2S–4SC.SA–14. (III–1,350; IV–1,150). Blohm & Voss, Hamburg. 1924 (28/10) launched. 1925 (23/4) MV Hamburg–Buenos Aires. 1939 (19/10) reached Hamburg after blockade-running from Santos. 1945 (3/4) sunk at Kiel by Allied bomber. 1946–8 scrapped.

91. 1927 CAP ARCONA (II)
27,561. 196,15 x 25,78. (643.6 x 84.6). 3–2–C. 2S–ST(SR)–20.

(I–575; II–275; III–465). Blohm & Voss, Hamburg. 1927 (14/5) launched. 1927 (19/11) MV Hamburg–Buenos Aires. 1939 (Sep) at Hamburg. 1940 accommodation ship at Gotenhafen (Gdynia). 1945 three voyages and evacuated 25,000 people from East to West Germany. 1945 (3/5) bombed and destroyed in Bay of Lubeck (5,000).

92. 1928 MONTE CERVANTES (M/S)
13,913. 152,57 x 20,05. (500.6 x 65.8). 2–2–C. 2S–43C.SA–14. (tourist 1,354; III–1,138). Blohm & Voss, Hamburg. 1927 (25/8) launched. 1928 (7/1) MV Hamburg–Buenos Aires; extensively employed as a cruise ship. 1930 (22/1) struck an uncharted rock off Tierra del Fuego; passengers took to the boats; ship stuck fast on a reef. 1930 (24/1) capsized (1). 1954 raised but sank in deep water.

93. 1931 MONTE PASCOAL (M/S)
13,870. 152,48 x 20,02. (500.3 x 65.7). 2–2–C. 2S–4SC.SA–14. (tourist 1,372; III–1,036). Blohn & Voss, Hamburg. 1930 (17/9) launched. 1931 (26/1) MV Hamburg–Buenos Aires; extensively employed as a cruise ship. 1939 (14/10) reached Hamburg from Buenos Aires. 1940 accommodation ship at Wilhelmshaven. 1944 (3/2) burnt and sunk by Allied bomber. 1944 (12/5) refloated. 1946 (31/12) sunk by British in the Skagerrak after being filled with chemicals.

94. 1931 MONTE ROSA (M/S)
13,882. 152,48 x 20,02. (500.3 x 65.7). 2–2–C. 2S–4SC.SA–14. (tourist 1,372; III–1,036). Blohm & Voss, Hamburg. 1930 (4/12) launched. 1931 MV Hamburg–Buenos Aires; extensively employed as a cruise ship. 1940 (11/1) accommodation ship at Stettin. 1945 (16/2) damaged by mine and towed to Gotenhafen (Gdynia); after repairs towed to Copenhagen with 5,000 refugees on board. 1945 British war prize. 1946 EMPIRE WINDRUSH (New Zealand Line (c)). 1954 (28/3) caught fire in Mediterranean after an explosion (4); ship abandoned. 1954 (29/3) sank after an attempt to tow her to Gibraltar.

95. (1934) MADRID
8,753. 133,95 x 17,28. (439.5 x 56.7). 2–2. 2S–T6–14. (cabin 221; tourist 209; III–302). AG Vulcan, Stettin. 1922 (2/5) launched as SIERRA NEVADA (NDL). 1922 (16/9) MV Bremen–New York (2 RV). 1922 FV Bremen–S. America. 1925 MADRID (NDL). 1934 ditto (Hamburg–Süd). 1934 FV Hamburg–S. America. 1941 (9/12) sunk by British air attack off Den Helder, Holland.

96. (1934) GENERAL SAN MARTIN (c)
(1935) GENERAL SAN MARTIN
11,251. 144,34 x 18,50. (473.6 x 60.7). 1–2. S–ST(DR)–13. (cabin

215

169; III–650). Howaldtswerke, Kiel. 1922 (12/8) launched as THURINGIA (Hapag). 1923 (22/1) MV Hamburg–New York. 1930 GENERAL SAN MARTIN (Hapag). 1930 (6/3) FV Hamburg–R. Plate. 1934 GENERAL SAN MARTIN (Hamburg–Süd (c)). 1935 GENERAL SAN MARTIN (Hamburg–Süd). 1935 (27/7) FV Hamburg–Buenos Aires. 1945 11 voyages with 30,000 evacuees from East to West Germany. 1945 (8/10) seized by Britain at Copenhagen. 1946 EMPIRE DEBEN (Shaw Savill (c)). 1949 scrapped at Newport, Mon.

97. (1934) GENERAL OSORIO (M/S) (c)
(1935) GENERAL OSORIO (c)
11,590. 151,93 x 20,11. (498.5 x 66.0). 2–2–C. 2S–2SC.DA–14. (cabin 228; III–752). Bremer Vulkan, Vegesack. 1929 (20/3) launched for Hapag. 1929 (29/6) MV Hamburg–R. Plate. 1934 GENERAL OSORIO (Hamburg–Süd (c)). 1935 GENERAL OSORIO (Hamburg–Süd). 1935 (16/8) FV Hamburg–Buenos Aires. 1940 accommodation ship at Kiel. 1944 (24/7) damaged by Allied air attack at Kiel. 1944 temporarily repaired. 1945 (9/4) sunk by Allied air attack at Kiel. 1947 refloated; scrapped in Britain.

98. (1934) GENERAL ARTIGAS (c)
(1935) GENERAL ARTIGAS
11,254. 144,34 x 18,50. (473.6 x 60.7). 1–2. S–ST(DR)–13. (cabin 169; III–650). Howaldtswerke, Kiel. 1923 (19/1) launched as WESTPHALIA (Hapag). 1923 (21/6) MV Hamburg–New York. 1930 GENERAL ARTIGAS (Hapag). 1934 GENERAL ARTIGAS (Hamburg–Süd (c)). 1935 GENERAL ARTIGAS (Hamburg–Süd). 1935 (26/7) FV Buenos Aires–Hamburg. 1935 (2/9) FV Hamburg–Buenos Aires. 1940 accommodation ship at Hamburg. 1943 (25/7) burnt out in British air attack on Hamburg. 1946 scrapped.

99. (1935) SACHSEN (c)
(1936) SACHSEN
(1937) LA PLATA
8,109. 142,79 x 17,83. (468.5 x 58.5). 1–4. S–T3–13. (I–20). Bremer Vulkan, Vegesack. 1922 (3/6) launched for Hapag. 1922 (16/9) MV Hamburg–River Plate. 1935 SACHSEN (Hamburg–Süd (c)). 1936 SACHSEN (Hamburg–Süd). 1937 LA PLATA (Hamburg–Süd). 1939 sheltered at Vigo. 1940 (Dec) returned to Germany. 1943 (4/10) badly damaged by Allied air attack at Bodö, Norway; beached. 1949 scrapped.

100. 1951 SANTA URSULA (M/S)
6,962. 136,30 x 18,68. (447.2 x 61.3). 1–2–C. S–2SC.SA–13.

(I–24). Howaldtswerke, Hamburg. 1950 (16/12) launched. 1951
(5/4) MV Hamburg–R. Plate. 1964 ANGOL (Chilean). 1969
BRIGHT SKY (Greek). 1971 BRIGHT SKY (Panamanian).
101. 1951 SANTA ELENA (M/S) (II)
    6,971. 136,30 x 18,68. (447.2 x 61.3). 1–2–C. S–2SC.SA–13.
    (I–24). Howaldtswerke, Hamburg. 1951 (17/2) launched. 1951
    (25/5) MV Hamburg–R. Plate. 1964 AUSTRAC (Chilean). 1967
    (2/1) sank at Santos after serious fire damage.
102. 1951 SANTA CATARINA (M/S)
    (1959) CAP SALINAS
    6,997. 136,30 x 18,65. (447.2 x 61.2). 1–2–C. S–2SC.SA–13.
    (I–26). Howaldtswerke, Hamburg. 1951 (28/7) launched. 1951
    (30/10) MV Hamburg–R. Plate. 1959 CAP SALINAS (Ham-
    burg–Süd). 1965 KALIMNOS (Greek). 1975 POPI II (Panama-
    nian).
103. 1952 SANTA ISABEL (M/S)
    6,982. 136,30 x 18,65. (447.2 x 61.2). 1–2–C. S–2SC.SA–13.
    (I–26). Howaldtswerke, Hamburg. 1951 (10/11 launched. 1952
    (1/2) MV Hamburg–R. Plate. 1962 became Hamburg–Süd
    training ship. 1968 SANTA ISABEL (Uruguayan). 1972 ditto
    (German). 1972 BARING (Panamanian).
104. 1953 SANTA TERESA (M/S)
    8,996. 144,22 x 18,68. (473.2 x 61.3). 1–2–C. S–2SC.SA–14.
    (I–28). Howaldtswerke, Hamburg. 1952 (Oct) launched. 1953
    (28/1) MV Hamburg–R. Plate. 1961 RUSTOM (Bangladesh).
105. 1953 SANTA INÉS (M/S)
    8,995. 144,22 x 18,71. (473.2 x 61.4). 1–2–C. S–2SC.SA–14.
    (I–28). Howaldtswerke, Hamburg. 1953 (Jan) launched. 1953
    (26/3) MV Hamburg–R. Plate. 1961 OCEAN ENERGY (Pakis-
    tan).

FUNNEL: (a) 1872. Black.
        (b) 1900. ('CAP' liners only) Buff.
        (c) 1911. White; red top.
FLAG: Four triangles – white at top ('H') and bottom ('G');
        red 'S' and 'D' at left and right sides. [Black letters as
        shown].

Chapter 27

1872–4

WHITE STAR LINE

(British)

Fresh from its dramatic entry into the North Atlantic passenger trade between Liverpool and New York, the OCEANIC STEAM NAVIGATION COMPANY LIMITED, invariably known as the WHITE STAR LINE, extended its operations to the South American trade, too, only a year later.

The Oceanic Company had been founded on 6 September 1869 by Thomas Henry Ismay and others with a capital of £400,000. But Ismay, who had bought the name and flag of the original White Star Line of sailing packets to Australia in 1867, had for some time been running sailing ships to the west coast of South America and elsewhere and knew the potential of this new business.

For the New York line Harland & Wolff of Belfast had built the 3,707 ton OCEANIC, ATLANTIC, BALTIC and REPUBLIC, as well as two slightly larger ships, the ADRIATIC and CELTIC, while the 2,000 ton TROPIC and ASIATIC and the 2,650 ton GAELIC and BELGIC were bought on the stocks. All were commissioned in 1871–3, but only five ships were required to maintain a weekly service to New York, and it transpired that Ismay was setting out to break the Pacific Steam Navigation Company's virtual monopoly of the steam traffic to Chile and Peru via the Straits of Magellan.

The REPUBLIC was selected to open the service and sailed from Liverpool on 5 October 1872 for Lisbon, Rio de Janeiro (reached in the record or near record time of 13 days 21½ hours from Lisbon), Montevideo, Sandy Point, Valparaiso and Callao. The 3,525 ton PSN steamer TACORA, which left Liverpool on her maiden voyage only a day before the REPUBLIC, was wrecked on 28 October at Cape Santa Maria, near Montevideo, and it was said at the time that her loss was due to her racing the White Star ship.

Second of the White Star sailings was taken by the TROPIC, which left Liverpool on 5 November 1872, and called at Vigo in addition to the other ports of her predecessor. She arrived back at Liverpool on 10 April 1873, having already made one voyage to South America under charter to Lamport & Holt (Chapter 13).

Launched at Belfast on 4 October 1872, the GAELIC began her

218

maiden voyage to South America on 29 January 1873. She was followed on 25 February by the ASIATIC, which, also, had already made one voyage to South America under charter to Lamport & Holt.

The BELGIC's maiden voyage began on 16 April 1873 via Lisbon, Rio de Janeiro and, presumably, Montevideo *en route* to Valparaiso. But her speed must have been a disappointment as she took nearly 30 days from Lisbon to Rio de Janeiro – appreciably more than double the REPUBLIC's time.

White Star arranged a few further sailings, some by chartered steamers, and then withdrew from the steamship trade to South America. This was not altogether surprising as, owing to a serious depression, even PSN reduced their sailings from weekly to fortnightly in 1874, and there would undoubtedly have been occasions when, but for their mail contract, they would gladly have reverted to monthly.

The GAELIC and BELGIC made some voyages from both Liverpool and London to New York before being chartered to the Occidental & Oriental Steamship Company to run between San Francisco and Hong Kong via Japan. The TROPIC and ASIATIC were sold, while the REPUBLIC's services were required on the Liverpool – New York run following the disastrous loss of the ATLANTIC near Halifax. [1]

[1] N.R.P. Bonsor, *North Atlantic Seaway*, Volume 2, pages 732–71.

1. (1872) REPUBLIC
    3,707. 128,01 x 12,46. (420.0 x 40.9). S–1–4. I–S–C2–14. (I–166; III–1,000). Harland & Wolff, Belfast (engines G. Forrester & Co, Liverpool). 1871 (4/7) launched. 1872 (1/2) MV Liverpool–New York. 1872 (5/10) FV Liverpool–Lisbon–Rio de Janeiro–Montevideo–Straits of Magellan–Valparaiso (1 RV). 1889 MAASDAM (Holland America); triple-expansion engines. 1902 VITTORIA (Italian). 1902 CITTÀ DI NAPOLI (La Veloce); III–1,424. 1910 scrapped at Genoa.
Note: Subsequent sailings by the TROPIC, GAELIC, ASIATIC, BELGIC, etc, offered limited accommodation for passengers.

FUNNEL: Buff; black top.
FLAG: Red swallow-tailed pennant with white star.

Chapter 28

1872–1962

COMPAGNIE DES CHARGEURS RÉUNIS

(French)

The sixth and certainly not the least successful French line to be established in the transatlantic trade to Brazil was the COMPAGNIE DES CHARGEURS RÉUNIS, which like two of its predecessors was based on Havre. It started operations on 16 October 1872 with the 2,131 ton iron screw steamer BELGRANO, the former LOUIS XIV of Frères Quesnel (Chapter 10), and was followed by the 1,590 ton HENRI IV, acquired under that name from the same owners, who went into liquidation a few years later.

1872 BELGRANO 2,131 tons
Made the first Chargeurs Réunis voyage to Brazil.

To begin with, these ships and their successors proceeded no further than Brazil, the state of the River Plate and the port facilities at Montevideo and Buenos Aires being singularly unsatisfactory and, moreover, opportunities for trade with Argentina and Uruguay being much more limited than with the principal Brazilian ports. However, sailings were extended to the Plate in 1878, by which time the 1,435 ton VILLE DE BAHIA, VILLE DE SANTOS and VILLE DE RIO JANEIRO as well as the appreciably larger SAN MARTIN, MORENO,

220

RIVADAVIA and PORTENA had been commissioned, all products of the Forges & Chantiers de la Méditerranée, four at La Seyne and three at Graville (Havre).

The 1,971 ton MORENO had a very short life as she was wrecked on 15 October 1874 when leaving Rio de Janeiro, while the 2,258 ton RIVADAVIA was wrecked in dense fog on 20 August 1880 near Cape Villano.

In preparation for the 1878 extension of the line to Montevideo and Buenos Aires, the BELGRANO and PORTENA were fitted for the carriage of frozen meat from the Argentine, and during the same year the 3,021 ton PAMPA and the 2,999 ton DOM PEDRO became the first of the Company's ships to be completed with these facilities, a sure sign that the experiment was successful.

Two second-hand ships, the 1,278 ton SULLY and the 1,561 ton COMTE D'EU, were bought in 1880–1 to make provision for the extended service. The former came from Quesnel and the latter was formerly the POWHATAN, pioneer unit of the Mediterranean & New York Steamship Company.

But further ships were urgently required and orders were placed at La Seyne for the 2,100 ton VILLE DE SAN NICHOLAS, VILLE DE ROSARIO, VILLE DE MONTEVIDEO, VILLE DE BUENOS AYRES and VILLE DE PERNAMBUCO, which were placed in service in 1881–2. In addition, the 3,360 ton PARANA, the 3,376 ton URUGUAY and the 3,366 ton RIO NEGRO were launched in 1882–3, the last two by the Ateliers & Chantiers de la Loire at St. Nazaire.

Meanwhile, the 2,350 ton VILLE DE PARA and VILLE DE CEARA were launched by Schlesinger, Davis & Co of Wallsend-on-Tyne on 1 June and 1 August 1882, and were chartered to the Société Postale Française de l'Atlantique, in which Chargeurs Réunis had an interest, and which proposed to run a regular service between Havre, Quebec and Montreal as well as one from Quebec, Halifax and the West Indies to Brazil [1]. In fact, the VILLE DE PARA made one voyage from Havre to Quebec, Halifax and Rio de Janeiro, a voyage from Rio to Halifax and back and then returned to Havre before being handed back to Chargeurs and employed by them between Havre and South America. The VILLE DE CEARA's early activities were much the same except that after proceeding from Havre to Quebec, Halifax and Rio de Janeiro she returned at once to Havre via Halifax and Boston. The COMTE D'EU was chartered from Chargeurs by the same company for four round voyages between Rio de Janeiro, St. Thomas (Virgin Islands) and Halifax, and two further steamers each chartered from another line made one or two trips on this route.

The Société Postale had originally advertised three additional ships,

1883 VILLE DE VICTORIA 2,482 tons
Rammed and sunk in 1886 in River Tagus by H.M.S. SULTAN, whose anchors had
parted.

the VILLE DE MONTRÉAL, VILLE D'HALIFAX and VILLE DE QUÉBEC, which together with the company's other assets were taken over by Chargeurs Réunis and placed in service as the VILLE DE MARANHAO, VILLE DE VICTORIA and VILLE DE MACEIO, respectively, all being built by the Ateliers & Chantiers de la Loire at Nantes.

During the 1880s four more of the Company's ships were lost – on 11 October 1884 the VILLE DE PARA sank after hitting an unchartered rock when approaching Las Palmas; on 24 December 1886, when moored in the River Tagus, the VILLE DE VICTORIA sank after being rammed by H.M.S. SULTAN; on 7 May 1887 the VILLE DE RIO JANEIRO sank off Barfleur after colliding with the CGT LA CHAMPAGNE; and on 4 September 1889 the SAN MARTIN was wrecked near Montevideo. Unfortunately, she and at least nine other ships of the fleet had less serious mishaps, the most common being fractured propeller shafts, this happening on 12 or more occasions, three of them concerning the PAMPA. This unlucky ship also survived three collisions, while the BELGRANO and SAN MARTIN each survived collisions which resulted in the sinking of the other ship involved.

The 2,900 ton cargo steamers ENTRE RIOS, CORDOBA and

222

1888 PARAGUAY 3,551 tons
Had accommodation for 60 first class passengers.

SANTA FÉ entered the South American trade in 1887, while a much more important ship, the 3,551 ton PARAGUAY, was completed by the Ateliers & Chantiers de la Loire in time to start her maiden voyage to Buenos Aires on 1 October 1888. Accommodation was provided in the after part of the ship for 60 first class passengers, a greater number of that class than carried by any predecessor.

Further losses had taken place on the South American service – the PARANA stranded in fog near Cape Frio on 15 May 1892 and broke in two, and the DOM PEDRO foundered on 27 May 1895 after striking a rock off the Spanish coast.

In the years that followed, Chargeurs Réunis expanded its activities with services to West and South Africa, Madagascar and the Far East. A round-the-world service was opened in 1905 from European ports to the Suez Canal, China, Japan, Hawaii, west coast ports of North America, Straits of Magellan, Montevideo and back. The 8,200 ton twin-screw MALTE and CEYLAN and the 8,500 ton OUESSANT and CORSE were built for the service, but were soon replaced by freighters and the service itself was withdrawn after about six years. The quartet had accommodation for 60 first and 72 second class passengers. The CORSE was sold to the Compagnie Générale Transatlantique in 1910 and renamed NIAGARA, while the others were detailed to the South American service from Havre in 1909 after being fitted to carry frozen meat.

In December 1913 the Compagnie de Navigation Sud Atlantique, which had started operations in the previous year, was placed under the management of the Compagnie Générale Transatlantique and this arrangement lasted until April 1916 when, without prior notice being

223

given, Chargeurs Réunis were substituted as managers. It appears that this came about by their having acquired a large batch of Sud Atlantique shares from the Crédit Français.

Two more 'ISLE' ships, the 9,591 ton BELLE ISLE and the 9,588 ton AURIGNY, were launched for the South American service on 23 March 1917 at Graville and on 23 May 1917 at La Seyne. Their tonnage was, thus, considerably greater than that of the MALTE, and they had accommodation for 74 first, 32 second and 78 third class passengers. Six slightly larger ships – the FORMOSE, DÉSIRADE, LIPARI, EUBÉE, GROIX and HOEDIC – were launched in 1921–2, two by the Chantiers de France, Dunkirk, three at La Seyne and the sixth, the LIPARI, by the Ateliers & Chantiers de la Loire. All were twin-screw and all except the last-named, which had geared turbines, were propelled by two sets of triple-expansion engines. They could accommodate 100 first, 40 second and 85 third class passengers.

The HOEDIC capsized at her berth at Havre on 5 June 1928. She was refloated on 30 November and refitted at Rotterdam, her accommodation being increased to 309 first, 88 second and 42 third class. In addition, she was converted to burn oil fuel, but when she re-entered service in 1930 she was put on the West African run as the FOUCAULD.

The first of the Company's motorships was the 11,700 ton dead-weight twin-screw cargo ship CAMRANH, which sailed from Havre to South America in January 1925, although subsequent voyages were to Indo-China. In 1927 she was taken in hand by her builders and fitted with accommodation for 179 first, 94 second and 90 third class passengers, thereby increasing her tonnage to 10,192 gross. She was renamed BRAZZA and detailed to the West African service. She was the second and last Chargeurs Réunis ship to have two funnels.

By agreement with the Polish Government a cargo and emigrant service was established in 1928 by Chargeurs Réunis between Gdynia, Brazil and Argentina. As a result, the MALTE and OUESSANT were fitted with extensive third class accommodation, were renamed KRAKUS and SWIATOVID and the service was started by the former on 7 September 1928. It was withdrawn in 1931, but it is interesting to note that the Gdynia–America Line started a South American service in 1936 (Chapter 66).

The 10,123 ton KERGUÉLEN and JAMAIQUE were allotted to the South American service in 1928, having been bought from the Compagnie Sud Atlantique as the MEDUANA and MOSELLA. Built by Swan, Hunter & Wigham Richardson in 1921–2, they were very similar to the AURIGNY and BELLE ISLE.

On 31 May 1930 the French aviator Mermoz, flying a hydroplane, succeeded in making the first air crossing of the South Atlantic. Within a

1928 JAMAIQUE 10,123 tons
Built 1922 as Cie Sud Atlantique MOSELLA.

short time transatlantic air crossings became almost everyday events, and by 5 January 1936 the mail service between Paris, Brazil and the River Plate discontinued using steamers, the air trip from Paris to Buenos Aires then taking 3½ days.

At the outbreak of World War II in September 1939, Chargeurs Réunis and Sud Atlantique were running a joint service by the Chargeurs ships FORMOSE, GROIX, BELLE ISLE, LIPARI, JAMAIQUE and KERQUÉLEN, which sailed from Hamburg, Antwerp, Havre and sometimes Bordeaux to Lisbon, Rio de Janeiro, Santos, Montevideo and Buenos Aires. The Bordeaux call was made to augment the Sud Atlantique share of the service, in which the 29,000 ton PASTEUR was due to take her place on 14 September 1939. There was no sign of the MASSILIA, which seems to have been laid up. A few ships called additionally at Casablanca, Pernambuco and Bahia. Fares to Rio and Santos were 7,010 francs first class and 5,080 francs second, and to Buenos Aires 7,720 francs first and 5,580 francs second.

Of the passenger ships, the HOEDIC was sunk by a German bomber at La Pallice on 20 June 1940, the KERQUÉLEN was seized by the Germans at Bordeaux on 6 August 1940 and did not return to Chargeurs service until 1948, the AURIGNY was seriously damaged by fire at Buenos Aires on 21 December 1941, the LIPARI was lost at Casablanca on 8 November 1942, the FORMOSE was seized by the Argentine Government on 28 July 1942, but was returned to Chargeurs in 1946 and the BELLE ISLE was destroyed by fire at Toulon on 24 November 1943 as the result of an air raid.

First post-war buildings for the South American service were the 12,000 ton twin-screw motorships LAVOISIER and CLAUDE BERNARD launched within a day of each other in October 1948 by Ateliers

1950 CLAUDE BERNARD 12,021 tons
Sailed to River Plate for four years.

& Chantiers de la Loire at St. Nazaire. The CLAUDE BERNARD left Havre on 18 March 1950 on her maiden voyage for South America, but was transferred to the Marseilles–Far East run in May 1954. The LAVOISIER's maiden voyage to Buenos Aires did not start until 19 September 1950. A further ship, the 12,358 ton LOUIS LUMIÈRE followed on 18 October 1952. She could accommodate 109 first and 266 second class passengers. Two similar ships, the LAËNNEC and CHARLES TELLIER, were built for Sud Atlantique's share of the joint service to replace the 29,000 ton PASTEUR, which never entered the South American trade, and the MASSILIA, scrapped after being scuttled by the Germans at Marseilles.

In 1961 the LAVOISIER was sold and became the Italian cruising liner RIVIERA PRIMA. A year later, both the Chargeurs Réunis and

1952 LOUIS LUMIÈRE 12,358 tons
Sold to Messageries Maritimes in 1962 without change of name.

226

the Sud Atlantique's services were taken over by Messageries Maritimes, who bought the Chargeurs LOUIS LUMIÈRE and the Sud Atlantique LAËNNEC and CHARLES TELLIER, which they ran from Havre to Brazil and the River Plate (Chapter 12).

[1] N.R.P. Bonsor, *North Atlantic Seaway*, Volume 3, Page 1140.
[2] N.R.P. Bonsor, *North Atlantic Seaway*, Volume 3, Page 1138.

1. (1872) BELGRANO
   2,131. 107,89 x 10,06. (354.0 x 33.0). 1–3. I–S–C2–10. Chantiers de l'Ocean, Havre. 1872 launched as LOUIS XIV (Quesnel) (Fr). 1872 BELGRANO (Chargeurs Réunis). 1872 (16/10) MV of line, Havre–S. America. 1889 (17/1) collided with SS ROMULUS near Dover, latter sank. 1894 scrapped.

2. (1872) HENRI IV
   1,590. 75,43 x 10,97. (247.5 x 36.0). 1–3. I–S–C2–10. Forges & Chantiers de la Méditerranée, La Seyne. 1871 launched as HENRI IV (Quesnel (Fr)). 1872 HENRI IV (Chargeurs Réunis). 1872 FV Havre–S. America. 1886 HENRI IV (Bossière (Fr)). 1890 (11/7) wrecked at mouth of R. Loire.

3. 1873 VILLE DE BAHIA
   1,435. 89,00 x 9,75. (292.0 x 32.0). 1–3. I–S–C2–10. Forges & Chantiers de la Méditerranée, La Seyne. 1872 (14/11) launched. 1873 (16/1) MV Havre–S. America. 1890 VILLE DE BAHIA (Fr). 1898 GÉNÉRAL GALLIENI (Fr). 1909 scrapped.

4. 1873 VILLE DE SANTOS
   1,435. 89,00 x 9,75. (292.0 x 32.0). 1–3. I–S–C2–10. Forges & Chantiers de la Méditerranée, La Seyne. 1873 launched. 1873 (16/3) MV Havre–S. America. 1890 VULKAN (Norwegian); later VULCAN (Japanese).

5. 1873 SAN MARTIN
   2,214. 94,48 x 10,48. (310.0 x 34.4). S–1–3. I–S–C2–10. Forges & Chantiers de la Méditerranée, Havre. 1873 (27/4) launched. 1873 MV Havre–S. America. 1889 (5/9) wrecked near Montevideo. (0).

6. 1873 MORENO
   1,971. 91,13 x 10,36. (299.0 x 34.0). S–1–3. I–S–C2–10. Forges & Chantiers de la Méditerranée, La Seyne. 1873 launched. 1873 MV Havre–S. America. 1874 (15/10) wrecked near Rio de Janeiro.

7. 1873 RIVADAVIA
   2,258. 94,48 x 10,48. (310.0 x 34.4). S–1–3. I–S–C2–10. Forges &

Chantiers de la Méditerranée, Havre. 1873 launched. 1873 (18/9) MV Havre–S. America. 1880 (20/8) wrecked near Cape Villano.

8. 1873 VILLE DE RIO JANEIRO
   1,435. 84,42 x 9,66. (277.0 x 31.7). 1–3. I–S–C2–10. Forges & Chantiers de la Méditerranée, La Seyne. 1873 launched. 1873 (16/12) MV Havre–S. America. 1887 (7/5) sunk in collision with LA CHAMPAGNE (CGT) off Barfleur.

9. 1876 PORTENA
   2,321. 101,49 x 10,36. (333.0 x 34.0). S–1–2. I–S–C2–10. Forges & Chantiers de la Méditerranée, Havre. 1875 (30/9) launched. 1876 MV Havre–S. America. 1896 CONTRE-AMIRAL CAUBET (French cable ship). 1916 VIGO (US).

10. 1878 PAMPA
    3,021. 100,48 x 12,00. (329.7 x 39.4). S–1–2. I–S–C2–10. Forges & Chantiers de la Méditerranée, La Seyne. 1878 (14/4) launched. 1878 MV Havre–S. America. 1905 scrapped.

11. 1879 DOM PEDRO
    2,999. 100,48 x 12,00. (329.7 x 39.4). S–1–2. I–S–C2–10. Forges & Chantiers de la Méditerranée, Havre. 1878 (12/10) launched. 1879 MV Havre–S. America. 1895 (27/5) struck Fraquina Reef near Carril (Villagarcia); boilers exploded (87).

12. (1880) SULLY
    1,278. 75,28 x 9,14. (247.0 x 30.0). S–1–3. I–S–C2–10. Forges & Chantiers de la Méditerranée, Havre. 1874 (19/3) launched for Quesnel (Fr). 1880 (Nov) SULLY (Chargeurs Réunis). 1880 (2/12) FV Havre–S. America. 1891 SULLY (Br). 1900 (5/4) wrecked on Horns Reef, Jutland.

13. (1881) COMTE D'EU
    1,561. 81,53 x 9,81. (267.5 x 32.2). 1–2. I–S–C2–10. T. Royden & Sons, Liverpool. 1878 (Jan) launched as POWHATAN (Mediterranean & New York). 1881 COMTE D'EU (Chargeurs Réunis). 1881 (Oct) FV Havre–S. America. 1887 IBO (Portuguese). 1889 NICTHEROY (Brazilian). 1906 (Apr) wrecked near Para.

14. 1881 VILLE DE ROSARIO
    2,111. 93,08 x 11,00. (305.4 x 36.1). 1–2. I–S–C2–12. Forges & Chantiers de la Méditerranée, La Seyne. 1881 launched. 1881 (16/10) MV Havre–S. America. 1898 VILLE DE CONSTAN-TINE (Cie des Bateaux à Vapeur du Nord). 1917 URRUGNE (Chargeurs Français) 1923 scrapped.

15. 1881 VILLE DE SAN NICHOLAS
    2,112. 93,08 x 11,00. (305.4 x 36.1). 1–2. I–S–C2–12. Forges & Chantiers de la Méditerranée, La Seyne. 1881 (18/8) launched.

1881 (21/11) MV Havre–S. America. 1905 NEUQUEN (Argentina). 1923 ITABIRA (Brazilian). 1927 (11/12) sunk in collision at Bahia.

16. 1882 VILLE DE MONTEVIDEO

2,111. 93,08 x 11,00. (305.4 x 36.1). 1–2. I–S–C2–12. Forges & Chantiers de la Méditerranée, La Seyne. 1881 (21/9) launched. 1882 (13/1) MV Havre–S. America. 1898 VILLE DE LORIENT (Cie des Bateaux à Vapeur du Nord). 1914 scrapped in Italy.

17. 1882 VILLE DE BUENOS AYRES

2,108. 93,08 x 11,00. (305.4 x 36.1). 1–2. I–S–C2–12. Forges & Chantiers de la Méditerranée, La Seyne. 1881 launched. 1882 (16/2) MV Havre–S. America. 1898 VILLE DE ROCHEFORT (Cie des Bateaux à Vapeur du Nord). 1910 (14/10) sunk, in collision with PEVERIL (Br) at entrance to R. Loire.

18. 1882 VILLE DE PERNAMBUCO

2,158. 93,08 x 11,00. (305.4 x 36.1). 1–2. I–S–C2–12. Forges & Chantiers de la Méditerranée, La Seyne. 1882 (10/1) launched. 1882 (2/4) MV Havre–S. America. 1905 VILLE DE PERNAMBUCO (Messageries Maritimes). 1907 scrapped at Marseilles.

19. 1882 PARANA

3,360. 105,76 x 12,19. (347.0 x 40.0). S–1–2. I–S–C2–13. Forges & Chantiers de la Méditerranée, La Seyne. 1882 (19/3) launched. 1882 (30/6) MV Havre–S. America. 1892 (15/5) stranded near Cape Frio. 1892 (19/5) broke in two.

20. (1883) VILLE DE CEARA

2,342. 86,86 x 11,37. (285.0 x 37.3). S–1–2. I–S–C2–12. Schlesinger, Davis & Co, Wallsend-on-Tyne. 1882 (1/8) launched. 1882 (20/10) MV for Société Postale (c), Havre–Quebec–Halifax–Rio de Janeiro–Halifax–Boston–Havre; subsequently Havre–S. America for Chargeurs Réunis. 1896 MOZAFFARI (Bombay & Persia SN Co). 1910 (19/1) wrecked at mouth of Mozambique harbour.

21. (1883) VILLE DE PARA

2,356. 86,86 x 11,37. (285.0 x 37.3). S–1–2. I–S–C2–12. Schlesinger, Davis & Co, Wallsend-on-Tyne. 1882 (1/6) launched. 1882 (24/8) MV for Société Postale (c), Havre–Quebec–Halifax–Rio de Janeiro–Halifax–Boston–Rio de Janeiro–Havre; subsequently Havre–S. America for Chargeurs Réunis. 1884 (11/10) foundered at Las Palmas after striking an uncharted rock.

22. 1883 VILLE DE MARANHAO

2,548. 97,37 x 11,40. (319.5 x 37.4). 1–2. S&I–S–T3–13. Ateliers & Chantiers de la Loire, Nantes. Laid down as VILLE DE MONTRÉAL. 1882 (Nov) launched as VILLE DE

MARANHAO. 1883 (17/6) MV Havre–S. America. 1889 transferred to west coast of Africa service. 1906 scrapped.

23. 1883 URUGUAY
   3,376. 106,00 x 12,28. (347.8 x 40.3). S–1–2. I–S–C2–13. Ateliers & Chantiers de la Loire, St. Nazaire. 1882 (29/9) launched. 1883 (4/7) MV Havre–S. America. 1889 transferred to West African service. 1897 triple-expansion engines. 1901 (4/3) wrecked near Cotonou, Dahomey.

24. 1883 VILLE DE VICTORIA
   2,482. 97,37 x 11,40. (319.5 x 37.4). S–1–2. S&I–S–C2–13. Ateliers & Chantiers de la Loire, Nantes. Laid down as VILLE D'HALIFAX. 1883 (7/4) launched as VILLE DE VICTORIA. 1883 (3/9) MV Havre–S. America. 1886 (24/12) rammed and sunk in R. Tagus by H.M.S. SULTAN, which had parted from her anchors (32).

25. 1883 VILLE DE MACEIO
   2,472. 97,37 x 11,40. (319.5 x 37.4). S–1–2. S&I–S–T3–13. Ateliers & Chantiers de la Loire, Nantes. Laid down as VILLE DE QUÉBEC. 1883 (7/5) launched as VILLE DE MACEIO. 1882 (17/11) MV Havre–S. America. 1889 transferred to west coast of Africa service. 1908 scrapped.

26. 1883 RIO NEGRO
   3,366. 106,00 x 12,28. (347.8 x 40.3). S–1–2. I–S–C2–13. Ateliers & Chantiers de la Loire, St. Nazaire. 1883 (8/5) launched. 1883 (15/12) MV Havre–S. America. 1897 triple-expansion engines, 1906 VALDIVIA (Chile–Argentina Navigation Co). 1906 (3/7) wrecked at Mocha on passage Buenos Aires–Valparaiso.

27. 1888 PARAGUAY
   3,551. 110,00 x 12,28. (360.9 x 40.3). S–1–2. S–S–T3–13. (I–60). Ateliers & Chantiers de la Loire, St. Nazaire. 1888 (24/6) launched. 1888 (1/10) MV Havre–S. America; later transferred to west coast of Africa service. 1908 scrapped.

28. (1909) CEYLAN
   8,223. 147,00 x 16,94. (482.3 x 55.6). 1–2. 2S–T6–15. (I–60; II–72). Swan, Hunter & Wigham Richardson, Wallsend-on-Tyne (engines Wallsend Slipway Co Ltd). 1907 (30/7) launched for round the world service. 1909 (21/2) FV Havre–Buenos Aires; fitted to carry frozen meat. 1914 French transport; later hospital ship. 1929 (31/3) collided in Bay of Biscay with CLODOALD; towed to and beached at La Pallice; repaired. 1934 scrapped.

29. (1909) OUESSANT
   (1928) SWIATOVID
   8,497. 147,88 x 17,10. (485.2 x 56.1). 1–2. 2S–T6–15. (I–60;

230

II–72). Ateliers & Chantiers de la Loire, St. Nazaire. 1908 (3/2) launched for round the world service. 1909 (17/3) FV Dunkirk–Havre–Buenos Aires; fitted to carry frozen meat. 1928 SWIATO-VID (Chargeurs Réunis). 1928 FV Gdynia–Brazil–Argentina. 1934 scrapped.

30. (1909) MALTE
(1928) KRAKUS
8,223. 147,00 x 16,94. (482.3 x 55.6). 1–2. 2S–T6–15. (I–60; II–72). Swan, Hunter & Wigham Richardson, Wallsend-on-Tyne (engines Wallsend Slipway Co Ltd). 1907 (30/5) launched for round the world service. 1909 (20/4) FV Dunkirk–Havre–Buenos Aires; fitted to carry frozen meat. 1914 (13/8)–1915 (25/1) armed merchant cruiser. 1924 (27/11) engine failure in Bay of Biscay; towed to St. Nazaire. 1928 KRAKUS (Chargeurs Réunis). 1928 (7/9) FV Gdynia–Brazil–Argentina. 1934 scrapped.

31. 1918 BELLE ISLE
9,591. 146,00 x 17,68. (479.0 x 58.0). 1–2. 2S–T6–15. (I–74; II–32; III–78). Forges & Chantiers de la Méditérranee, Havre. 1917 (24/3) launched. 1918 (27/9) MV Havre–Brest–S. America. 1942 (24/11) destroyed by fire in dock at Toulon following an air raid.

32. 1918 AURIGNY
9,588. 146,78 x 17,74. (481.6 x 58.2). 1–2. 2S–T6–15. (I–74; II–32; III–78). Forges & Chantiers de la Méditerranée, La Seyne. 1917 (23/5) launched. 1918 MV France–S. America. 1940 interned at Buenos Aires. 1941 (22/12) serious fire at Buenos Aires; repaired by Argentina Government; renamed GENERAL SAN MAR-TIN (cargo only). 1954 (4/9) sailed Buenos Aires–San Antonio, Chile; went missing.

33. 1921 FORMOSE
9,975, 147,00 x 16,94. (482.3 x 55.6). 1–2. 2S–T6–15. (I–100; II–40; III–85). Forges & Chantiers de la Méditerranée, La Seyne. 1921 (12/2) launched. 1921 MV Havre–S. America. 1943 (28/7) seized by Argentina Government at Buenos Aires; renamed RIO TUNUYAN. 1946 returned to Chargeurs Réunis; reverted to FORMOSE. 1953 scrapped at St. Nazaire.

34. 1921 DÉSIRADE
9,645. 147,33 x 17,95. (483.4 x 58.9). 1–2. 2S–T6–15. (I–100; II–40; III–85). Ateliers & Chantiers de France, Dunkirk. 1921 (24/3) launched. 1921 MV Havre–S. America. 1950 scrapped in Belgium.

35. 1922 LIPARI
9,954. 145,84 x 18,04. (478.5 x 59.2). 1–2. 2S–ST(DR)–15.

(I–100; II–40; III–85). Ateliers & Chantiers de la Loire, St. Nazaire. 1921 (Sep) launched. 1922 MV Havre–S. America. 1923 (30/4) foundered near Brest after striking a rock. 1923 (17/5) refloated. 1942 8–11/11) shelled and set on fire at Casablanca during Allied landings; broke her back and sank.

36. 1922 EUBÉE
    9,645. 147,33 x 17,95. (483.4 x 58.9). 1–2. 2S–T6–15. (I–100; II–40; III–85). Ateliers & Chantiers de France, Dunkirk. 1921 (17/12) launched. 1922 MV Havre–S. America. 1936 (14/8) collided with CORINALDO (Donaldson) between Santos and Montevideo. 1936 (16/8) foundered.

37. 1922 GROIX
    9,975. 147,33 x 17,95. (483.4 x 58.9). 1–2. 2S–T6–15. (I–100; II–40; III–75). Forges & Chantiers de la Méditerranée, La Seyne. 1921 (19/12) launched. 1922 (11/10) MV Havre–S. America. 1946 (Aug–1947 (May) refitted by Lorient Dockyard; resumed to S. America but later transferred to Far East service. 1952 scrapped at La Spezia.

38. 1923 HOEDIC
    9,957. 147,33 x 17,95. (483.4 x 58.9). 1–2. 2S–T6–15. (I–100; II–40; III–85). Morges & Chantiers de la Méditerranée, La Seyne. 1922 (21/12) launched. 1923 MV Havre–S. America. 1928 (5/6) capsized in dock at Havre. 1928 (30/11) refloated; refitted at Rotterdam; (I–309; II–88; III–42); renamed FOUCAULD. 1930 (6/1) FV Havre–West Africa. 1940 (20/6) sunk in dock at La Pallice by German bomber.

39. (1928) JAMAIQUE
    10,123. 147,57 x 18,07. 484.2 x 59.3). 1–2. 2S–ST(DR)–15. (I–74; II–32; III–78). Swan, Hunter & Wigham Richardson, Wallsend-on-Tyne (engines Wallsend Slipway Co Ltd). 1921 (3/9) launched as MOSELLA (Cie Sud Atlantique). 1928 JAMAIQUE (Chargeurs Réunis). 1928 (2/6) Hamburg–Antwerp–S. America. 1947–8 refitted by Chantiers de la Loire, St. Nazaire. 1948 (28/1) resumed Bordeaux–S. America, but later transferred to Indo-China line. 1954 scrapped in Belgium.

40. (1928) KERGUELEN
    10,123. 147,57 x 18,07 (484.2 x 59.3). 1–2. 2S–ST(DR)–15. (I–74; II–32; III–78). Swan, Hunter & Wigham Richardson, Wallsend-on-Tyne (engines Wallsend Slipway Co Ltd). 1920 (30/9) launched as MEDUANA (Cie Sud Atlantique). 1928 KERGUELEN (Chargeurs Réunis). 1928 (Jly) FV Hamburg–Antwerp–S. America. 1940 seized by Germans at Bordeaux; renamed WINRICH VON KNIPRODE (German Navy). 1947–8 overhauled at

232

Bordeaux. 1948 (10/6) resumed Bordeaux–S. America, but later transferred to Indo-China line. 1955 scrapped.

41. 1950 CLAUDE BERNARD (M/S)
    12,021. 157,14 [164,21] x 19,62. (515.6 [538.8] x 64.4). 1–2–C. 2S–2SC.SA–16. (I–94, II–230). Ateliers & Chantiers de la Loire, St. Nazaire. 1948 (31/10) launched. 1950 (18/3) MV Havre–S. America. 1954 (31/5) FV Marseilles–Far East. 1962 J.G. FICHTE (East Germany).

42. 1950 LAVOISIER (M/S)
    11,968. 157,14 [164,21] x 19,62. (515.6 [538.8] x 64.4). 1–2–C. 2S–2SC.SA–16. (I–94; II–230). Ateliers & Chantiers de la Loire, St. Nazaire. 1948 (31/10) launched. 1950 (19/9) MV Havre–S. America. 1961 (Jly) RIVIERA PRIMA (Italian cruising liner). 1964 VIKING PRINCESS (Norwegian). 1966 (8/4) engine room fire got out of control; passengers and crew transferred. Liberian NAVIGATOR towed VIKING PRINCESS to Jamaica. She was later towed to Bilbao and scrapped.

43. 1952 LOUIS LUMIÈRE (M/S)
    12,358. 157,14 [164,21] x 19,62. (515.6 [538.8] x 64.4). 1–2–C. 2S–2SC.SA–17. (I–109; II–266). Ateliers & Chantiers de St. Nazaire. 1951 (28/11) launched. 1952 (18/10) MV Havre–S. America. 1962 LOUIS LUMIÈRE (Messageries Maritimes). 1967 MEI ABETO (Ci de Navegacion Abeto (Panamanian)).

FUNNEL: Buff; broad white band with small red stars.
FLAG: White; five red stars arranged two-one-two.

Chapter 29

(1876–1934)

NORDDEUTSCHER LLOYD

(North German Lloyd)
NDL:NGL

(German)

The NORDDEUTSCHER LLOYD, equally well-known as the NORTH GERMAN LLOYD, received its first charter in the Bremen Senate on 18 February 1857, and quickly made a name for itself in the transatlantic passenger business between Bremen and New York. In the years that followed, other routes were opened up to Baltimore, Havana, New Orleans and the West Indies.

NDL was an ambitious company – overly so in the boom which followed the Franco–Prussian War of 1870. Within a period of eight years, 26 new steamers averaging nearly 3,000 tons were commissioned. But by 1874 a serious slump had set in, and at its height in 1875 as many as 19 NDL ships were laid up. The outlook was black, but somehow the Company succeeded in weathering the storm.

Orders had been placed with Earle's Shipbuilding Company of Hull for the 3,100 ton HOHENZOLLERN, HOHENSTAUFEN, SALIER and HABSBURG for a new service from Bremen to Brazil and Argentina. But owing to the slump the Company decided to postpone its start and all four ships made their maiden voyages on other routes. The new inaugural date was fixed for 1 March 1876, when the HOHENZOLLERN sailed from Bremen, followed by the SALIER on 1 April and the HABSBURG in May. The HOHENSTAUFEN, launched on 24 September 1873, did not start her maiden voyage from Bremen to New York until almost a year later, and it was 1881 before she was introduced on the South American run.

Meanwhile, other ships were detailed to the South Atlantic, some for a voyage or two, others more or less regularly – the KRONPRINZ FRIEDRICH WILHELM in 1876, the GRAF BISMARCK in 1877, the BERLIN in 1879, the HANNOVER, FRANKFURT, BALTIMORE and STRASSBURG in 1881, as well as the HOHENSTAUFEN. Also the KÖLN and LEIPZIG in 1883 and the OHIO in 1884.

March 1889 was a red letter month for the South American service, as on the 11th the 4,536 ton MÜNCHEN started her maiden voyage from

1889 KARLSRUHE 5,057 tons
Ran in various NDL services. Her maiden voyage was to the River Plate.

Bremen. She was one of eight steel, triple-expansion-engined ships built by the Fairfield Company of Glasgow within a period of about two years. Six of the eight had a tonnage of over 5,000 and were appreciably longer than the MÜNCHEN and her sister ship DRESDEN. Passenger figures also varied, but the later ships carried 49 first class, 38 second and approximately 1,900 steerage. An outstanding feature of all eight was the interchangeability of the ships between the Company's various routes, although the maiden voyages of no fewer than five besides the MÜNCHEN took place to South America – namely, the KARLSRUHE, STUTTGART, GERA, OLDENBURG and DARMSTADT. This was perhaps hardly surprising as they were considerably larger than any other German steamers running to South America, and NDL justifiably wanted to show them off. The flexibility of the group is well indicated by the fact that the WEIMAR's maiden voyage took place to Baltimore, while subsequently she ran to both New York and Baltimore, Australia, the Far East and between Naples and New York before being detailed to Brazil and Argentina on 23 September 1905.

The 3,870 ton PFALZ and MARK were completed on the Tyne, in 1893 for the Brazil and Argentina service. They, too, had triple-expansion engines and accommodation for 100 first and 700 third class passengers.

It is a remarkable fact that 14 of the steamers built between 1868 and 1875 ended their NDL careers on the South Atlantic service between 1893 and 1899. One of them, the SALIER, was wrecked on the Spanish coast on 7 December 1896 with the appalling loss of 279 lives – her entire complement of passengers and crew.

The 3,603 ton single-screw ROLAND and the 4,700 ton twin-screw WITTEKIND and WILLEHAD were completed in 1893–4 for a new emigrant service to New York known as the 'Roland Line of the

1894 WITTEKIND 4,755 tons
In process of lengthening from 116,85–135,93 metres (355.1–446 feet).

Norddeutscher Lloyd', but in due course all three made a considerable number of voyages to South America. The WITTEKIND was lengthened by 19 metres (62.6 feet) in 1900, but similar action, although originally intended, was not taken with her sister ship.

The Company's first twin-screw steamer, the H.H. MEIER – named after its first chairman – had been acquired in 1892 from the MacIver Line, for whom she was launched as the LUCANIA. The intention was to place her on the South American service, but her first voyage for NDL was to New York and she made only five round voyages to South America. She was sold to the Compañía Trasatlántica Española (chapter 40) in 1901, renamed MANUEL CALVO and remained in their service for about 50 years.

As replacements for ships sold from 1893 onwards, the 3,800 ton single-screw CREFELD, AACHEN, BONN and HALLE entered the South American service in 1895, but all ran extensively on the North Atlantic. They were followed by the 3,200 ton twin-screw MAINZ, COBLENZ and TRIER in 1897–8, of which the last-named was wrecked on the Spanish coast in 1902.

The Company chartered the 5,000 ton ELLEN RICKMERS, MARIA RICKMERS and ELISABETH RICKMERS in 1897–8 for the Bremen–Baltimore service. They were bought outright in 1900, renamed BORKUM, HELGOLAND and NORDERNEY, and carried emigrants

236

to South America. They had accommodation for 18 second class passengers and nearly 1,000 third.

The 4,985 ton single-screw WÜRZBURG, completed in 1901, ran to South America between 1904 and 1914. She took shelter in the Cape Verde Islands after the outbreak of World War I, and was seized by Portugal in 1916. The 6,955 ton twin-screw SCHLESWIG was built for the South Atlantic in 1902, but also made some North Atlantic voyages. Two departures from the fleet at about this time were the PFALZ and MARK of 1893, both going to the Woermann Line.

Of the 1889-built MÜNCHEN and her seven consorts, two were sold in 1902–3, four in 1908 and the last two in 1911. They were superseded by 10 interchangeable twin-screw ships of the 'FELDHERRN' ('Field Marshal') class between 1903 and 1908, but rather surprisingly only one of them, the 7,942 ton SEYDLITZ, was allotted to the South Atlantic and she only made one pre-World War I voyage thereon, in 1913. She had accommodation for 101 first, 105 second and 1,700 third class passengers. One further steamer requires brief mention – the 7,431 ton twin-screw FRANKFURT, which was completed in 1900 and made six South American voyages, the first of which started on 19 September 1908.

The 8,200 ton twin-screw SIERRA NEVADA, SIERRA VEN-TANA, SIERRA CORDOBA and SIERRA SALVADA were completed in 1913 for the South American service, and were a considerable advance on their predecessors. Two were products of AG Vulcan of Stettin and two of Bremer Vulkan of Vegesack, all being propelled by two sets of triple-expansion engines, their service speed being 13 knots. The Stettin ships had accommodation for 115 first class, 74 third and 1,550 fourth and those from Vegesack were approximately similar. The

1913 SIERRA VENTANA 8,262 tons
Arrived Boulogne 31 July 1914 from the River Plate and reached Bremen before the outbreak of war.

237

two first-named started their maiden voyages to Montevideo and Buenos Aires in January 1913 and the other two in February and March.

In theory, the most fortunate of the quartet was the SIERRA VENTANA as she returned to Bremen only a day or two before the outbreak of World War I in August 1914. The other three sheltered in South American ports during the war and were later seized by Brazil (two) and Chile.

After the Armistice on 11 November 1918, NDL was deprived at first of every worthwhile ocean-going steamer, the largest left in its possession being the 800 ton GRÜSSGOTT. But in September 1920 NDL despatched the first of its newly-built ocean-going cargo steamers, the 2,350 ton VEGESACK, to Brazil and the River Plate, a sister ship, the BREMERHAVEN, following in due course. Owing to a gradual relaxation of the rules prohibiting resale to Germany of ex-German ships, the 7,942 ton SEYDLITZ came back into the Company's possession towards the end of 1921. She left Bremen for South America on 11 December 1921, but soon after completing this, the first NDL post-war ocean passenger sailing, was responsible for restarting the New York passenger service.

Meanwhile, the 8,753 ton SIERRA NEVADA (II) was launched on 2 May 1922, the 11,452 ton SIERRA VENTANA (II) on 16 May 1923, the 11,469 ton SIERRA CORDOBA (II) on 26 September 1923 and the 11,430 ton SIERRA MORENA on 3 June 1924. All four were built for the South American trade, but the maiden voyages of the first two were to New York and, in fact, the SIERRA VENTANA over a period of years made no fewer than 21 North Atlantic voyages. The maiden voyage of the SIERRA CORDOBA to the River Plate started on 26 January 1924, and that of the SIERRA MORENA on 25 October 1924. In the

1922 SIERRA NEVADA 8,753 tons
Built for South American service, but first two voyages were to New York.

238

following year the SIERRA NEVADA (II) was renamed MADRID.

Intense and often harmful rivalry had existed between NDL and the Hamburg American Line (Hapag) for several decades. There had been many rumours of the pending fusion of the two concerns, but even so a good deal of surprise was caused in 1930 by the announcement that an alliance, known as the Hapag–Lloyd Union, had been entered into. All services were to be jointly operated, and all costs, profits and losses pooled. Neither company lost its separate identity.

In 1932 the 13,615 ton twin-screw Hamburg–Süd CAP NORTE and the 13,589 ton ANTONIO DELFINO were chartered to NDL, who renamed them SIERRA SALVADA (II) and SIERRA NEVADA (III).

In June 1932 the capital of NDL was reduced from 148,500,000 marks to 49,500,000. There was a further reduction in March 1936 to 11,530,000 marks, but simultaneously new stock valued at 34,360,000 marks was issued in satisfaction of bank debts totalling 2½ times that amount, thereby making the new capital of the Company 45,890,000 marks. It was stated that the losses incurred by NDL were largely due to the devaluation of sterling and the dollar, but an important reason was the boycotting of German ships by Jews in retaliation for their ill-treatment in Germany.

It was decided in April 1934 that the services to the east coast of South America, to Africa and to the Levant would be withdrawn from the Hapag–Lloyd Union, while in November 1934 it was announced that Hamburg–Süd were to have a monopoly of the German services to Brazil and the River Plate. In consequence, the SIERRA SALVADA (II) and SIERRA NEVADA (III) were returned to Hamburg–Süd and reverted to their original names. In addition to the MADRID, which was acquired by Hamburg–Süd in 1934, nine NDL ships were chartered to them in 1934–6 and bought by them within a year or two. But the other 'SIERRA' class ships actually built for NDL did not go to Hamburg–Süd. Instead, the SIERRA MORENA (I) became the NDL cruise ship DER DEUTSCHE and in 1935 was acquired by the Deutsche Arbeitsfront, better-known in the English-speaking world as the 'Strength through Joy' movement, which also acquired the SIERRA CORDOBA (II) during the same year. The SIERRA VENTANA (II) became the SARDEGNA of Italia.

Six of the 10 NDL ships bought by Hamburg–Süd were sunk during World War II, two more were badly damaged and eventually taken over by Britain, and one was filled with poison gas after the war and scuttled in the Skagerrak. The tenth ship, the MÜNSTER, took shelter at Las Palmas in September 1939 and was sold to Spain in 1942.

It became known in April 1970 that a fusion between NDL and Hapag really was imminent. In fact, it took place on 1 September 1970, but was back-dated to 1 January. The name chosen was HAPAG–LLOYD AKTIENGESELLSCHAFT, Hamburg–Bremen.

1. (1876) HOHENZOLLERN
   3,092. 107,59 x 11,91. (353.0 x 39.1). S–1–2. I–S–C2–12. (I–142; III–800). Earle's Shipbuilding Co, Hull. 1873 (24/5) launched. 1873 (7/12) MV Bremen–Southampton–Panama. 1876 (1/3) FV Bremen–S. America (FV of service). 1885 (15/1) LV ditto. 1890 triple-expansion engines. 1899 sold to Hong Kong; converted to barge; scrapped.

2. (1876) SALIER
   3,083. 107,59 x 11,91. (353.0 x 39.1). S–1–2. I–S–C2–12. (I–142; III–800). Earle's Shipbuilding Co, Hull. 1874 (15/6) launched. 1876 (1/4) FV Bremen–S. America. 1880 (10/2) LV ditto. 1890–1 triple-expansion engines. 1895 (10/12) resumed Bremen–S. America. 1896 (7/12) wrecked on north coast of Spain (279).

3. (1876) HABSBURG
   3,094. 107,59 x 11,91. (353.0 x 39.1). S–1–2. I–S–C2–12. (I–142; III–800). Earle's Shipbuilding Co, Hull. 1875 (9/1) launched. 1876 (May) FV Bremen–S. America. 1880 (Jan) LV ditto. 1891 triple-expansion engines. 1895 (10/11) resumed Bremen–S. America. 1896 (10/3) LV ditto. 1898 sold to Italy; when bound thereto stranded near Cadiz. 1899 refloated; scrapped.

4. (1876) KRONPRINZ FRIEDRICH WILHELM
   2,387. 95,18 x 11,91. (312.3 x 39.1). C–1–2. I–S–I(2)–10. (I–105; II–50; III–400). Caird & Co, Greenock. 1870 (13/9) launched for NDL West Indies service. 1875 engines compounded. 1876 FV Bremen–S. America. 1887 quadruple–expansion engines. 1895 resumed Bremen–S. America. 1897 (10/4) LV ditto. 1897 scrapped in Italy.

5. (1877) GRAF BISMARCK
   2,406. 96,46 x 11,91. (316.5 x 39.1). C–1–2. I–S–I(2)–10. (I–105; II–50; III–400). Caird & Co, Greenock. 1870 (9/11) launched for NDL West Indies service. 1877 FV Bremen–S. America. 1879 compound engines. 1896 (10/11) LV Bremen–S. America. 1898 scrapped.

6. (1879) BERLIN
   2,333. 86,86 x 11,88. (285.0 x 39.0). C–1–2. I–S–I(2)–10. (I–84; III–600). Caird & Co, Greenock. 1867 (1/10) launched. 1879 FV Bremen–S. America. 1882 engines compounded. 1894 (3/3) LV Bremen–S. America. 1894 M. BRUZZO (Italian). 1895 scrapped in Italy.

7. (1881) HANNOVER
   2,571. 91,43 x 11,88. (300.0 x 39.0). C–1–2. I–S–I(2)–10. (I–60; III–700). Caird & Co, Greenock. 1869 (28/7) launched for NDL New Orleans service. 1880–1 engines compounded. 1881 (25/7) FV Bremen–S. America. 1894 (27/1) LV ditto. 1894 scrapped in Italy.

8. (1881) FRANKFURT
   2,582. 91,43 x 11,88. (300.0 x 39.0). C–1–2. I–S–I(2)–10. (I–60; III–600). Caird & Co, Greenock. 1869 (18/6) launched for NDL New Orleans service. 1880 engines compounded. 1881 (10/8) FV Bremen–S. America. 1893 (30/9) LV ditto. 1894 FRANKFURT (Br). 1897 scrapped in Italy.

9. (1881) BALTIMORE
   2,321. 86,86 x 11,88. (285.0 x 39.0). C–1–2. I–S–I(2)–10. (I–84; III–600). Caird & Co, Greenock. 1867 (3/8) launched. 1881 engines compounded. 1881 (10/9) FV Bremen–S. America. 1893 (20/12) LV ditto. 1894 scrapped.

10. (1881) HOHENSTAUFEN
    3,098. 107,59 x 11,91. (353.0 x 39.1). S–1–2. I–S–C2–13. (I–142; III–800). Earle's Shipbuilding Co, Hull. 1873 (24/9) launched. 1881 (24/9) FV Bremen–S. America. 1890 triple-expansion engines. 1897 (11/2) LV Bremen–S. America. 1897 scrapped at London.

11. (1881) STRASSBURG
    3,025. 106,67 x 11,89. (350.0 x 39.0). S–1–2. I–S–C2–10. (I–60; II–120; III–900). Caird & Co, Greenock. 1872 (24/5) launched for NDL New Orleans service. 1881 (11/11) FV Bremen–S. America. 1896 (25/1) LV ditto. 1897 scrapped at Genoa.

12. (1883) KÖLN
    2,555. 91,43 x 11,88. (300.0 x 39.0). C–1–2. I–S–I(2)–10. (I–60; III–700). Caird & Co, Greenock. 1870 (11/8) launched for NDL New Orleans service. 1883 (10/2) FV Bremen–S. America. 1884 compound engines. 1895 (23/3) LV Bremen–S. America. 1895 scrapped in Germany.

13. (1883) LEIPZIG
    2,388. 88,46 x 11,88. (290.2 x 39.0). C–1–2. I–S–I(2)–10. (I–84; III–600). Caird & Co, Greenock. 1869 (13/2) launched. 1883 engines compounded. 1883 (25/10) FV Bremen–S. America. 1894 (19/5) LV ditto. 1898 scrapped at Hamburg.

14. (1884) OHIO
    2,394. 88,46 x 11,88. (290.2 x 39.0). C–1–2. I–S–I(2)–10. (I–84; III–600). Caird & Co, Greenock. 1868 (18/12) launched. 1880–1 engines compounded. 1884 (24/3) FV Bremen–S. America. 1893

(25/11) LV ditto. 1894 AMAZZONE (Argentine Govt). 1897 RIO SANTA CRUZ (ditto). 1903 hulked.

15. 1889 MÜNCHEN

4,536. 119,01 x 14,23. (390.5 x 46.7). S–1–2. S–S–T3–13. (I–38; II–20; III–1,763). Fairfield Co. Ltd, Glasgow. 1889 (23/1) launched. 1889 (11/3) MV Bremen–Montevideo–Buenos Aires. 1892 (10/11) LV ditto (6 RV). Ran subsequently Bremen–New York–Baltimore and Bremen–Suez Canal–Australia. 1902 GREGORY MORCH (Russian). 1910 scrapped.

16. 1889 KARLSRUHE

5,057. 126,49 x 14,63. (415.0 x 48.0). S–1–2. S–S–T3–13. (I–44; II–36; III–1,955). Fairfield Co Ltd, Glasgow. 1889 (31/8) launched. 1889 (10/11) MV Bremen–Montevideo–Buenos Aires. Ran subsequently Bremen–New York–Baltimore; Bremen–Suez Canal–Australia and Bremen–Suez Canal–Far East. 1906 (22/9) LV Bremen–S. America (3 RV). 1908 scrapped.

17. (1889) DRESDEN

4,527. 119,01 x 14,23. (390.5 x 46.7). S–1–2. S–S–T3–13. (I–38; II–20; III–1,759). Fairfield Co Ltd, Glasgow. 1888 (1/12) launched. 1889 (30/12) FV Bremen–S. America. Ran subsequently Bremen–Suez Canal–Australia; Bremen–New York and Bremen–Baltimore. 1902 (15/11) LV Bremen–S. America (5 RV). 1903 HELIUS (Houston). 1904 ditto (Union–Castle). 1906 TIRIMUJGHIAN (Turkish Govt). 1914 sunk by Russians in Black Sea.

18. 1890 STUTTGART

5,048. 126,49 x 14,63. (415.0 x 48.0). S–1–2. S–S–T3–13. (I–44; II–36; III–1,955). Fairfield Co. Ltd, Glasgow. 1889 (26/10) launched. 1890 (10/1) MV Bremen–Antwerp–Vigo–Montevideo–Buenos Aires (1 RV). Ran subsequently Bremen–Baltimore; Bremen–New York; Bremen–Suez Canal–Australia; Bremen–Suez Canal–Far East. 1907 (12/1) resumed Bremen–S. America. 1907 (14/12) LV ditto. 1908 scrapped.

19. 1891 GERA

5,005. 126,49 x 14,63. (415.0 x 48.0). S–1–2. S–S–T3–13. (I–49; II–38; III–1,901). Fairfield Co Ltd, Glasgow. 1890 (8/11) launched. 1891 (1/1) MV Bremen–Montevideo–Buenos Aires. Ran subsequently Bremen–New York–Baltimore; Bremen–Suez Canal–Far East; Bremen–Suez Canal–Australia; Genoa–Naples–New York. 1906 (15/12) resumed Bremen–S. America. 1907 (7/9) LV ditto. 1908 VALPARAISO (Lloyd del Pacifico (Italian)). 1917 (14/10) torpedoed and sunk by German submarine off Libya.

20. 1891 OLDENBURG

　　5,006. 126,49 x 14,63. (415.0 x 48.0). S–1–2. S–S–T3–13. (I–49; II–38; III–1,901). Fairfield Co Ltd, Glasgow. 1890 (13/12) launched. 1891 (11/2) MV Bremen–Montevideo–Buenos Aires (1 RV). Ran subsequently Bremen–Baltimore; Bremen–New York; Bremen–Suez Canal–Far East; Bremen–Suez Canal–Australia. 1906 (25/8) resumed Bremen–S. America. 1910 (15/10) LV ditto. 1911 AK–DENIZ (Turkish). 1923 scrapped.

21. 1891 DARMSTADT

　　5,012. 126,49 x 14,63. (415.0 x 48.0). S–1–2. S–S–T3–13. (I–49; II–38; III–1,904). Fairfield Co Ltd, Glasgow. 1890 (27/9) launched. 1891 (10/3) MV Bremen–Montevideo–Buenos Aires (5 RV). Ran subsequently Bremen–New York; Bremen–Suez Canal–Far East; Bremen–Suez Canal–Australia. 1905 (4/11) resumed Bremen–S. America. 1910 (12/11) LV ditto. 1911 KARA DENIZ (Turkish). 1923 scrapped.

22. 1893 PFALZ

　　4,604. 127,19 x 13,19. (417.3 x 43.3). S–1–2. S–S–T3–13. (I–100; III–760). Wigham Richardson & Co, Walker-on-Tyne. 1893 (31/7) launched. 1893 (27/10) MV Bremen–Montevideo–Buenos Aires. 1904 GERTRUD WOERMANN (Woermann). 1904 (19/11) wrecked off Swakopmunde.

23. (1893) ROLAND

　　3,603. 105,15 x 13,34. (345.0 x 43.8). S–1–2. S–S–T3–12. (II–28; III–800). Sir W.G. Armstrong, Mitchell & Co, Walker-on-Tyne. 1893 (1/5) launched. 1893 (9/12) FV Bremen–S. America. 1909 (7/8) LV ditto (16 RV). 1911 BAHRIAHMER (Turkish). 1914 (7/11) sunk by Russian Navy in Black Sea.

24. 1894 MARK

　　3,756. 110,94 x 13,25. (364.0 x 43.5). S–1–2. S–S–T3–13. (I–100; III–760). Armstrong, Mitchell & Co Ltd, Walker-on-Tyne (engines Wigham Richardson & Co, Walker-on-Tyne). 1893 (28/9) launched. 1894 (11/1) MV Bremen–Montevideo–Buenos Aires. 1902 MARKGRAF (Woermann). 1914 (19/8) destroyed by British warship at Tanga, Tanganyika.

25. (1894) H.H. MEIER

　　5,140. 128,31 x 14,63. (421.0 x 48.0). S–1–3. S–2S–T6–13. (I–75; II–300; III–1,000). Sir W.G. Armstrong, Mitchell & Co, Walker-on-Tyne. 1891 (19/10) launched as LUCANIA (MacIver). 1892 H.H. MEIER (NDL). 1894 (23/3) FV Bremen–S. America. 1895 (26/7) LV ditto (5 RV). 1901 MANUEL CALVO (Cia Trasatlantica (Spanish)). 1952 DRAGO (Spanish). 1959 scrapped in Spain.

26. (1894) WILLEHAD
4,761. 116,85 x 14,02. (383.4 x 46.0). S–1–2. S–2S–T6–13.
(II–105; III–1,196). Blohm & Voss, Hamburg. 1894 (21/3)
launched. 1894 (10/11) FV Bremen–S. America. 1903 (23/5) LV
ditto. 1917 (Apr) seized by USA; renamed WYANDOTTE (US
Govt). 1924 scrapped at Baltimore.

27. 1895 CREFELD
3,829. 108,35 x 13,31. (355.5 x 43.7). S–1–2. S–S–T3–13. (II–32;
III–1,013). AG Vulcan, Stettin. 1895 (23/3) launched. 1895 (11/5)
MV Bremen–Rio de Janeiro–Santos. 1901 (30/11) resumed
Bremen–S. America. 1914 (Oct) took refuge at Tenerife. 1918
handed to Spain; renamed ESPAÑA No. 4. 1925 TEIDE (Cia
Trasatlantica). 1932 (10/6) wrecked at Barta, Spanish Guinea.

28. 1895 AACHEN
3,833. 108,29 x 13,31. (355.3 x 43.7). S–1–2. S–S–T3–13. (II–28;
III–1,045). AG Vulcan, Stettin. 1895 launched. 1895 (15/6) MV
Bremen–Montevideo–Buenos Aires. 1897 (Aug) resumed ditto.
1915 (30/7) torpedoed and sunk by British submarine E.1 in
Baltic, when German naval auxiliary.

29. 1895 BONN
3,969. 108,23 x 13,28. (355.1 x 43.6). S–1–2. S–S–T3–13. (II–20;
III–1,043). Germaniawerft, Kiel. 1895 (25/1) launched. 1895 (7/9)
MV Bremen–Montevideo–Buenos Aires. 1901 (Mar) resumed
ditto. 1913 GREGOR (German). 1920 (Feb) stranded in Black
Sea.

30. (1895) WITTEKIND
4,755. 116,85 x 14,02. (383.4 x 46.0). S–1–2. S–2S–T6–13.
(II–174; III–1,366). Blohm & Voss, Hamburg. 1894 (3/2)
launched. 1895 (21/9) FV Bremen–S. America. 1900 lengthened
to 135,93 metres (446.0 feet); tonnage 5,640. 1912 (14/9) LV
Bremen–S. America (33 RV). 1914 (Aug) took refuge at Boston.
1917 (Apr) seized by USA; renamed IROQUOIS (US Govt).
1919 FREEDOM (ditto). 1924 scrapped.

31. 1895 HALLE
3,960. 108,23 x 13,25. (355.1 x 43.5). S–1–2. S–S–T3–13. (II–19;
III–1,071). Germaniawerft, Kiel, 1895 (3/8) launched. 1895 (2/11)
MV Bremen–Montevideo–Buenos Aires. 1899 (Nov) resumed
ditto. 1913 PAWEL (German). 1915 WOUDRICHEM (Dutch).
1919 LLOYD (US), 1923 ditto (Italian). 1924 IRIS (Italian). 1926
scrapped.

32. 1897 MAINZ
3,204. 93,35 x 12,80. (306.3 x 42.0). S–1–2. 2S–T6–13. (II–20;
III–793). J.C. Tecklenborg, Geestemünde. 1897 (15/5) launched.

1897 (May) MV Bremen–Rio de Janeiro–Santos. 1912 LYDIE (Belgian). 1928 scrapped in Holland.

33. 1897 COBLENZ

3,169. 93,26 x 12,80. (306.0 x 42.0). S–1–2. 2S–T6–13. (II–24; III–700). Blohm & Voss, Hamburg. 1897 (18/3) launched. 1897 (Aug) MV Bremen–Rio de Janeiro–Santos. 1917 seized at Manila; renamed SACHEM. 1920 CUBA (Pacific Mail). 1923 (8/9) wrecked in Santa Barbara Channel, California.

34. 1898 TRIER

3,168. 94,05 x 12,83. (308.6 x 42.1). S–1–2. 2S–T6–13. (II–20; III–700). G. Seebeck AG, Bremerhaven. 1898 (5/6) launched. 1898 (10/6) MV Bremen–Rio de Janeiro–Santos. 1902 (6/7) wrecked near Langosteira Point, Spain, on voyage Bremen–Mexico.

35. (1901) NORDERNEY

5,211. 124,96 x 15,39. (410.0 x 50.5). S–1–2. S–Q4–10. (II–19; III–975). Wigham Richardson & Co, Walker-on-Tyne. 1896 (28/3) launched as ELISABETH RICKMERS (Rickmers (Ger)). 1900 NORDERNEY (NDL). 1901 (29/12) Bremen–S. America. 1913 (8/8) LV ditto. 1916 (25/7) lost near Sassnitz.

36. (1902) HELGOLAND

4,888. 124,66 x 15,39. (409.0 x 50.5). S–1–2. S–T3–10. (II–18; III–950). J.L. Thompson & Sons, Sunderland. 1896 (16/1) launched as MARIA RICKMERS (Rickmers (Ger)). 1900 HELGOLAND (NDL). 1902 (19/1) FV Bremen–S. America. 1910 (6/7) LV Buenos Aires–Bremen. 1914 seized by Britain; renamed POLYXENA. 1917 (11/6) torpedoed and sunk by German submarine 57 miles W. of Fastnet.

37. 1902 SCHLESWIG

6,995. 136,91 x 15,94. (449.2 x 52.3). 1–2. 2S–T6–14. (I–227; II–69; III–234). AG Vulcan, Stettin. 1902 launched. 1902 (14/9) MV Bremen–S. America. 1919 allotted to France; renamed GÉNÉRAL DUCHESNE. 1932 scrapped.

38. (1904) WÜRZBURG

4,985. 122,58 x 14,35. (402.2 x 47.1). 1–2. S–T3–12. (II–31; III–1,012). Bremer Vulkan, Vegesack. 1900 (25/9) launched. 1904 (23/4) FV Bremen–S. America. 1914 (30/5) LV ditto. 1916 seized by Portugal in Cape Verde Islands; renamed SÃO VICENTE (Portuguese). 1925 LOANDA (Cia Colonial). 1938 scrapped in Italy.

39. (1904) BORKUM

5,350. 124,66 x 15,39. (409.0 x 50.5). 1–2. S–T3–10. (II–18; III–950). J.L. Thompson & Sons, Sunderland. 1896 (27/2) launched as ELLEN RICKMERS (Rickmers (Ger)). 1900 BORKUM (NDL). 1904 (20/11) FV Bremen–S. America. 1913 (13/4) LV ditto. 1915 seized by Italy; renamed ASTI. 1917 (13/8) torpedoed and sunk by German submarine 220 miles SW of Scilly Isles.

40. (1905) WEIMAR

4,996. 126,49 x 14,63. (415.0 x 48.0). 1–2. S–T3–13. (I–49; II–38; III–1,907). Fairfield Co Ltd, Glasgow. 1891 (9/2) launched. 1891–1905 ran Bremen–Baltimore; Bremen–New York–Baltimore; Bremen–Suez Canal–Australia; Bremen–Suez Canal–Far East; Naples–New York. 1905 (23/9) FV Bremen–S. America. 1908 SANTIAGO (Lloyd del Pacifico (Italian)). 1909 ARMONIA (Chilean). 1917 ditto (Canadian). 1918 (15/3) torpedoed and sunk by German submarine near Porquerolles Island, France.

41. (1908) FRANKFURT

7,431. 131,15 x 16,55. (430.3 x 54.3). 1–2. 2S–T6–13. (II–108; III–1,889). J.C. Tecklenborg, Geestemünde. 1899 (17/12) launched. 1908 (19/9) FV Bremen–S. America (6 RV). 1919 surrendered to Britain; name unchanged. 1922 SARVISTAN (Hong Kong). 1931 scrapped in Japan.

42. (1913) SEYDLITZ

7,942. 137,18 x 16,91. (450.1 x 55.5). 1–2. 2S–T6–14. (I–101; II–105; III–1,700). F. Schichau, Danzig. 1902 (25/10) launched. 1913 (15/3) FV Bremen–S. America (1 RV). 1914 (Aug) took refuge at Bahia Blanca, Argentina; retained by NDL after Armistice; (cabin; III). 1921 (12/11) resumed Bremen–S. America (1 RV). 1933 scrapped at Bremerhaven.

43. 1913 SIERRA NEVADA (I)

8,235. 133,86 x 17,07. (439.2 x 56.0). 1–2. 2S–T6–13. (I–115; III–74; IV–1,550). AG Vulcan, Stettin. 1912 launched. 1913 (4/1) MV Bremen–Antwerp–Montevideo–Buenos Aires. 1914 (Aug) sheltered at Pernambuco. 1917 (Jun) seized by Brazil; renamed BAGÉ. 1943 (31/7) torpedoed and sunk by German submarine off Brazilian coast (48).

44. 1913 SIERRA VENTANA (I)

8,262. 133,95 x 17,07. (439.5 x 56.0). 1–2. 2S–T6–13. (I–120; III–80; IV–1,450). Bremer Vulkan, Vegesack. 1912 (12/10) launched. 1913 (18/1) MV Bremen–Antwerp–Montevideo–Buenos Aires. 1914 (7/7) LV Buenos Aires–Boulogne (arr 31/7)–Bremen. 1920 ALBA (Sud Atlantique). 1926 AMÉRIQUE (Chargeurs Réunis). 1936 scrapped at Blyth.

45. 1913 SIERRA CORDOBA (I)

8,226. 133,83 x 17,07. (439.1 x 56.0). 1–2. 2S–T6–13. (I–115;

III–74); IV–1,550). AG Vulcan, Stettin. 1912 (2/11) launched. 1913 (15/2) MV Bremen–Antwerp–Montevideo–Buenos Aires. 1914 (Aug) sheltered at Callao. 1917 seized by Peru; renamed CALLAO. 1922 RUTH ALEXANDER (Dollar). 1941 (31/12) sunk by Japanese torpedo bombers off Balikpapan.

46. 1913 SIERRA SALVADA (I)
8,250. 133,95 x 17,07. (439.5 x 56.0). 1–2. 2S–T6–13. (I–120; III–80; IV–1,450). Bremer Vulkan, Vegesack. 1912 (5/12) launched. 1913 (1/3) MV Bremen–Antwerp–Montevideo–Buenos Aires. 1917 seized by Brazil; renamed AVARÉ. 1922 (17/6) capsized when leaving Vulkan floating dock (48). 1922 (17/8) refloated; laid up. 1924 PEER GYNT (German); structural alterations; second funnel (dummy) added; painted white. 1926 NEPTUNIA (Sitmar (Italian)). 1927 OCEANA (Hapag). 1945 EMPIRE TARNE (Br). 1946 SIBIR (USSR).

47. (1922) SIERRA NEVADA (II)
(1925) MADRID
8,753. 133,95 x 17,28. (439.5 x 56.7). 2–2. 2S–T6–14. (Cabin 221; III–416). AG Vulcan, Stettin. 1922 (2/5) launched for S. America service. 1922 (16/9) MV Bremen–New York (2 RV). 1922 FV Bremen–S. America. 1925 renamed MADRID (NDL). 1934 MADRID (Hamburg–Süd). 1941 (9/12) sunk by British air attack off Den Helder, Holland.

48. (1924) SIERRA VENTANA (II)
11,452. 149,58 x 18,83. (490.8 x 61.8). 2–2. 2S–T6–14. (cabin 401; III–712). Bremer Vulkan, Vegesack. 1923 (16/5) launched for S. America service. 1923 (8/9) MV Bremen–New York. 1924 FV Bremen–S. America. 1935 SARDEGNA (Italia). 1937 ditto (Lloyd Triestino). 1940 (29/12) torpedoed and sunk by Greek submarine PROTEUS near Saseno, Albania.

49. 1924 SIERRA CORDOBA (II)
11,469. 149,49 x 18,83 (490.5 x 61.8). 2–2. 2S–T6–14. (cabin 160; III–1,143). Bremer Vulkan, Vegesack. 1923 (26/9) launched. 1924 (26/1) MV–Bremen–S. America. 1935 SIERRA CORDOBA (Deutsche Arbeitsfront). 1945 surrendered to Britain. 1946 (13/1) badly damaged by fire. 1948 (18/1) stranded and sank near Esbjerg when under tow Hamburg–Clyde.

50. 1924 SIERRA MORENA
11,430. 149,49 x 18,83. (490.5 x 61.8). 2–2. 2S–T6–14. (I–157; III–1,145). Bremer Vulkan, Vegesack. 1924 (3/6) launched. 1924 (25/10) MV Bremen–S. America. 1934 DER DEUTSCHE (NDL cruise ship). 1935 ditto (Deutsche Arbeitsfront). 1946 ASIA (Russian). 1970 scrapped.

50a. (1932) SIERRA SALVADA (II) (c)
  13,615. 152,24 x 19,50. (499.5 x 64.0). 1–2. 2S–T6–13. (I–184; II–334; III–1,350). AG Vulcan, Hamburg. 1922 (8/5) launched as CAP NORTE (Hamburg–Süd). 1922 (14/9) MV Hamburg–River Plate. 1932 SIERRA SALVADA (NDL) (c). 1932 (6/8) FV Hamburg–Amsterdam–River Plate. 1934 CAP NORTE (Hamburg–Süd). (26); qv.

50b. (1932) SIERRA NEVADA (III) (c)
  13,589. 152,24 x 19,50. (499.5 x 64.0). 1–2. 2S–T6–13. (I–184; II–334; III–1,350). AG Vulcan, Hamburg. 1921 (10/11) launched as ANTONIO DELFINO (Hamburg–Süd). 1922 (16/3) MV Hamburg–R. Plate. 1932 SIERRA NEVADA (NDL) (c). 1932 (3/9) FV Hamburg–R. Plate. 1934 ANTONIO DELFINO (Hamburg–Süd). (26); qv.

FUNNEL: (1876) Black.
  1889 Buff.
FLAG: White; blue key and anchor crossed; oak wreath in centre.

Chapter 30

(1876–1913)

ALLAN LINE

(British)

The ALLAN LINE, popularly known as such from very early days, was founded in Montreal in 1853 as the MONTREAL OCEAN STEAM SHIP COMPANY, and by 1873 had progressed to running a weekly summer service from Liverpool to Quebec and Montreal, another from Glasgow to Quebec and Montreal and a third, at fortnightly intervals, from Liverpool to St. John's (Newfoundland), Halifax and Baltimore.

It has often been said that the Allan Line's entry into the South American trade three years later was in retaliation for the Donaldson Line's entry into the Canadian trade, but as this did not happen until April 1878 it could be said with greater truth that Donaldson (Chapter 24) entered the Canadian trade in retaliation for Allan's entry into the South American.

The 2,911 ton CANADIAN (III), built three years earlier for the Canadian run, was despatched from Glasgow for Montevideo and Buenos Aires on 11 November 1876, followed by the 2,356 ton PHOENICIAN on 5 December and the 2,256 ton WALDENSIAN in January 1877, the two last-mentioned having been built for the Company in the early 1860s as the ST DAVID and ST ANDREW, and in 1873 lengthened, fitted with compound engines and renamed.

There were regular Allan Line sailings from Glasgow to Montevideo and Buenos Aires during subsequent autumns and early winters. First of a series of steamers completed with an eye to the particular requirements of this trade was the 1,925 ton iron single-screw LUCERNE, which was bought on the stocks of Laird Brothers, Birkenhead. Her maiden voyage to South America began on 27 September 1878 but, like four successors which began their careers with a River Plate sailing, a great deal of her life was spent on the North Atlantic, with one or sometimes two South American voyages a year.

The LUCERNE's sailing was followed three weeks later by the departure of the 2,689 ton NESTORIAN, built in 1867, which had considerably more first class accommodation than her predecessors – 115 berths instead of about 30. All carried a considerable number of steerage.

But the sailing on 1 December 1879 was the most epoch-making of any

249

arranged by the Allan Line to the River Plate as it was taken by the 4,005 ton BUENOS AYREAN, the first steamer on the South Atlantic (and also, for that matter, on the North) to be built of steel. She was a product of Wm. Denny & Brothers of Dumbarton, and between 1880 and 1895 made one voyage annually to Montevideo and Buenos Aires. In 1896 quadruple-expansion engines replaced her compound set, and her masts were reduced from three to two.

An Allan Line summer service was successfully started from London to Montreal in 1884, one of the steamers employed being the LUCERNE. In 1886 the experiment was tried of despatching the PHOENICIAN and the 3,613 ton GRECIAN from London to the River Plate, but this was not repeated. The GRECIAN had been completed by Wm. Doxford & Sons, of Sunderland, in 1880 and had already made a voyage from Glasgow to South America. She was chartered in 1882 as a troopship for the Egyptian Expedition.

1887 ROSARIAN 3,077 tons
Made occasional voyages from Glasgow to River Plate.

In 1887, for the first time, the service from Glasgow to South America ran monthly throughout the year instead of seasonally. The 3,100 ton ROSARIAN and MONTE VIDEAN started their maiden voyages in October and November 1887 to the River Plate, and were notable as the first units of the fleet to be fitted with triple-expansion engines. Built of steel by D. & W. Henderson of Glasgow, they had accommodation for 20 first class and 800 steerage passengers. Most of their subsequent activities were on the North Atlantic, but they ran to South America from time to time.

The same builders delivered the 3,204 ton BRAZILIAN in 1890. Her first few voyages were in the Canadian trade and she did not sail to South America until 12 February 1891.

The year 1891 marked the peak of the Allan Line's activities, and for a short time the transatlantic fleet consisted of no fewer than 37 ships, totalling 120,000 tons gross. Eight distinct services were being maintained during the summer months, and no other British transatlantic line, before or since, has provided anything like this variety of passenger services. Unfortunately, this happy state of affairs did not last long as about half the ships in the fleet were at least 20 years old and several were over 30. [1]

Three interesting ships were bought second-hand in 1897, and two of them (but not the ROUMANIAN) ran extensively to Montevideo and Buenos Aires from 1898 and 1899 onwards. These were the 4,162 ton LIVONIAN and the 4,021 ton TURANIAN, built in 1880–2 by Dobie & Co of Glasgow as the steel twin-screw LUDGATE HILL and TOWER HILL of the Twin Screw Line. The TURANIAN stranded on the Cape Verde Islands in November 1899, and although refloated was disposed of to Italian shipbreakers. At the time of their completion they were among the very few ocean-going twin-screw ships in existence.

Seven of the ships already mentioned were sold during the early years of the present century – the CANADIAN and WALDENSIAN in 1903, the PHOENICIAN in 1905, the ROSARIAN, MONTE VIDEAN and BRAZILIAN in 1910 and the BUENOS AYREAN in 1911. All were scrapped except the BRAZILIAN, which saw many more years of service under different names and Brazilian ownership.

For some years past the Company's South American service had been on the decline, and latterly many of the ships taking part were cargo steamers chartered from other companies.

The withdrawal of the Donaldson Line's South American service during the 1880s can be attributed to the competition of the Allan Line, but the tables were turned in 1913, when the goodwill of the Allan Line South American service was sold to the Donaldson Line. Two Allan Line cargo steamers, the ONTARIAN and ORCADIAN, went with the service, and the 31 year old LIVONIAN was another candidate to be taken over. However, the Donaldson Line won an arbitration case, thus enabling her to be excluded from the deal. She did not long survive as in 1914 she was used as a blockship in Dover harbour.

The Allan Line's days, also, were numbered as it had, in fact, been bought by the Canadian Pacific Railway in 1909 and lost its separate identity on 16 July 1917.

[1] N.R.P. Bonsor, *North Atlantic Seaway*, Volume 1, pages 278–325.

1. (1876) CANADIAN
       2,911. 106,64 x 10,85. (349.9 x 35.6). S–1–3. I–S–C2–11.

(I–25; III–850). T. Royden & Sons, Liverpool (engines J. Jack, Rollo & Co, Liverpool. 1872 (Aug) launched. 1873 (23/8) MV Liverpool–Quebec–Montreal. 1876 (11/11) FV Glasgow–S. America (FV of service). 1891 (1/10) LV on N. Atlantic; subsequently S. American service. 1902 (22/9) LV ditto. 1903 scrapped.

2. (1876) PHOENICIAN

2,356. 102,07 x 10,45. (334.9 x 34.3). C–1–3. I–S–C2–11. (I–30; III–350). Barclay & Curle, Glasgow. 1864 (4/6) launched as ST. DAVID (Allan) – 1,516 tons. 82,90 metres (272.0 feet); I(2)–10. 1864 (21/7) MV Liverpool–Quebec–Montreal. 1873 lengthened, compounded and renamed PHOENICIAN. 1876 (5/12) FV Glasgow–S. America. 1888 quadruple-expansion engines. 1888 (9/8) LV on N. Atlantic; subsequently S. American service. 1903 (22/7) LV ditto. 1905 scrapped at Genoa.

3. (1877) WALDENSIAN

2,256. 98,29 x 10,33. (322.5 x 33.9). C–1–3. I–S–C2–11. (I–30; III–350). Barclay & Curle, Glasgow (engines J. & J. Thomson, Glasgow). 1861 (8/8) launched as ST. ANDREW (Allan) – 1,432 tons. 77,11 metres (253.0 feet). I(2)–10. 1861 (28/9) MV Glasgow–Quebec–Montreal. 1873 lengthened, compounded and renamed WALDENSIAN. 1877 (Jan) FV Glasgow–S. America. 1888 triple-expansion engines. 1891 (16/4) LV on N. Atlantic; subsequently S. American service. 1902 (22/11) LV ditto. 1903 scrapped at Genoa.

4. 1878 LUCERNE

1,925. 88,69 x 10,45. (291.0 x 34.3). S–1–3. I–S–C2–11. (I; III). Laird Bros, Birkenhead. 1878 (Mar) launched. 1878 (27/9) MV Glasgow–S. America. 1879–83 1 RV annually to ditto. 1889 onwards mainly S. America. 1898 (19/3) LV Glasgow–St. John's, NF. 1898 sold to A. Harvey & Co, St. John's. 1901 (3/2) wrecked on voyage Ardrossan–St. John's, NF.

5. (1878) NESTORIAN

2,689. 96,82 x 11,73. (317.7 x 39.5). C–1–3. I–S–C2–11. (I–115; III–600). Barclay & Curle, Glasgow. Laid down as ACADIAN. 1866 (11/9) launched as NESTORIAN. 1867 (31/1) MV Liverpool–Portland. 1874–8 laid up. 1878 (17/10) FV Glasgow–S. America (2 RV). 1897 scrapped.

6. 1879 BUENOS AYREAN

4,005. 117,40 x 12,86. (385.2 x 42.2). S–1–3. S–S–C2–12. (I; III). Wm Denny & Bros, Dumbarton. 1879 (2/10) launched. First steel steamer on either S. or N. Atlantic. 1879 (1/12) MV Glasgow–S. America. 1880–95 one Glasgow–S. America RV annually. 1896 quadruple-expansion engines; two masts. 1911 scrapped at Falmouth.

7. (1880) GRECIAN

3,613. 109,87 x 12,22. (360.5 x 40.1). S–1–3. I–S–C2–11. (I–50; II–270; III–500). Wm Doxford & Sons, Sunderland. 1879 (16/10) launched. 1880 (21/4) MV Glasgow–Quebec–Montreal. 1880 (4/12) FV Glasgow–S. America. 1882 troopship for Egyptian Expedition. 1902 (9/2) wrecked near Halifax (0).

8. 1887 ROSARIAN

3,077. 100,58 x 12,83. (330.0 x 42.1). S–1–2. S–S–T3–11. (I–20; III–800). D. & W. Henderson Ltd, Glasgow. 1887 (14/9) launched. 1887 (25/10) MV Glasgow–S. America. 1888 onwards occasional sailings ditto. 1910 scrapped.

9. 1887 MONTE VIDEAN

3,076. 100,58 x 12,83. (330.0 x 42.1). S–1–2. S–S–T3–11. (I–20; III–800). D. & W. Henderson Ltd, Glasgow. 1887 (20/10) launched. 1887 (29/11) MV Glasgow–S. America. 1888 onwards occasional sailings ditto. 1910 scrapped.

10. (1889) AUSTRIAN

2,458. 97,22 x 11,73. (319.0 x 38.5). C–1–3. I–S–T3–11. (I–115; III–600). Barclay & Curle, Glasgow. 1867 (Feb) launched. 1867 (18/7) MV Liverpool–Montreal. 1889 (11/5) FV Glasgow–S. America. 1896–1901 mainly ditto. 1903 (10/4) LV on N. Atlantic, Glasgow–Boston; subsequently Glasgow–S. America. 1904 (9/2) LV ditto. 1905 scrapped.

11. (1891) BRAZILIAN

3,204. 103,62 x 12,80. (340.0 x 42.0). S–1–2. S–S–T3–11. D. & W. Henderson Ltd, Glasgow. 1890 (3/4) launched. 1890 (13/6) MV London–Montreal. 1891 (12/2) FV Glasgow–S. America. 1891 onwards London–Montreal with 1 RV annually to S. America. 1900–10 Glasgow–S. America. 1910 CORCOVADO (Brazilian). 1938 POTENZY (Brazilian).

12. (1898) LIVONIAN

4,162, 128,10 x 14,32. (420.3 x 47.0). S–1–4. S–2S–C4–12. (I–40; III). Dobie & Co, Glasgow (engines J. Howden & Co, Glasgow). 1881 (9/11) launched as LUDGATE HILL (Twin Screw). 1897 LIVONIAN (Allan). 1898 (22/11) FV Glasgow–S. America. 1900 triple-expansion engines. 1913 (17/9) LV Glasgow–S. America. 1914 blockship in Dover harbour. 1933 salvaged; scrapped.

13. (1899) TURANIAN

4,021. 128,13 x 13,74. (420.4 x 45.1). S–1–4. S–2S–C4–12. (I–40; III). Dobie & Co, Glasgow (engines J. Howden & Co, Glasgow). 1880 (28/6) launched as TOWER HILL (Twin Screw). 1897

TURANIAN (Allan). 1899 (22/4) FV Glasgow–S. America. 1899 (Nov) stranded on Cape Verde Islands; salvaged; sold to Italian shipbreakers.

FUNNEL: Red; narrow white band below black top.
FLAG: Red-white-blue vertical stripes; a red long pennant above the flag.

SOCIETÀ ITALIANA DI TRASPORTI MARITTIMI RAGGIO & CO

(Italian)

The SOCIETÀ ITALIANA DI TRASPORTI MARITTIMI RAGGIO & CO was founded on 6 February 1882 by Carlo, Edilio and Armando Raggio and associates in Genoa with a capital of five million lire (£200,000). Its principal aim was to run a fleet of passenger and cargo steamers between Italy and South America.

The Raggio family already owned two 300 ton cargo steamers plus the 2,032 ton passenger and cargo INIZIATIVA, launched by A. Stephen & Sons of Glasgow on 26 July 1881. As her maiden voyage started on 19 October 1881 from Genoa for Montevideo and Buenos Aires, and as she made several more voyages at later dates to the same destinations it seems quite justifiable to regard her as the pioneer unit of the Raggio concern, and to open this chapter in 1881 and not 1882.

Orders were soon placed for seven sister ships of the INIZIATIVA, all having dimensions of approximately 91,43 x 11,28 metres (300.0 x 37.0 feet). They were iron single screw steamers whose compound engines gave them a service speed of about 10 knots, accommodation being provided for 24 first, 24 second and 1,000 steerage passengers.

First to be completed was a product of Raylton Dixon & Co, the SCRIVIA, which sailed from Genoa for Buenos Aires on 11 December 1882, followed by the POLCEVERA, from Blackwood & Gordon of Port Glasgow, on 16 March 1883. However, the third newcomer, the LETIMBRO, never ran to South America for Raggio. Instead, she started her career by a round trip from Cardiff to Genoa, followed by two voyages from Cardiff to Singapore and back (perhaps under charter to the Navigazione Generale Italiana (Chapter 36)). After that she made five trips from South Wales to Italy with coal. Like the remainder of the Raggio fleet, she was then acquired, in January 1885, by NGI, who sent her on a round voyage to Assab and Massowah lasting until July 1885, followed by the first of 30 voyages to New York.

Next Raggio newcomer was another Blackwood & Gordon product, the STURA. She opened her career with four trips from the Clyde or Cardiff to Genoa with coal, then a voyage from Cardiff to Bombay via Suez, three more voyages from Cardiff to Genoa or Naples with coal

1884 STURA 2,245 tons
Made one voyage from Genoa to the River Plate for Raggio, and subsequently ran to New York for NGI.

and, at long last, a first sailing on 16 December 1884 from Genoa for Buenos Aires.

The ENTELLA from the same shipyard, had a good deal in common with the early careers of her two immediate predecessors but eventually sailed from Naples on 23 December 1884 for Buenos Aires, where she arrived on 21 January 1885.

The two final units of the series were the BORMIDA and BISAGNO from Burrell & Sons of Dumbarton. The latter's maiden voyage to Buenos Aires started on 24 January 1885, and there is some doubt as to whether this was a Raggio or NGI sailing. In any event her yard mate sailed for Raggio on 10 December 1884 from Genoa for South America, having been responsible for one or two coal runs.

Much more important than any of the ships hitherto mentioned was the 4,141 ton SIRIO, launched by Napier of Glasgow on 24 March 1883. She sailed thence on 19 June for Genoa, reached on the 27th, her maiden voyage starting from that port on 15 July for Montevideo and Buenos Aires. She was a fine looking vessel with two slender funnels and three masts, her three-cylinder compound engines giving her a service speed of 13 knots. Her first class accommodation, as was still customary on the South Atlantic at the time, was situated aft, a novel feature of her dining saloon being the provision of many small tables. Second class consisted of 40 berths, and she could accommodate 1,200 steerage.

The commissioning of the SIRIO coincided with an agreement between Raggio & Co and the Societa Rocco Piaggio (Chapter 25) for a joint express line from Naples and Genoa to the River Plate, departures to be fortnightly.

Two sister ships of the SIRIO followed, the ORIONE sailing from

256

1883 SIRIO 4,141 tons
Ran for Ragio to the River Plate for two years, followed by a long spell for NGI.

Genoa on 15 January 1884 and the PERSEO on 15 February. A call was made at Las Palmas outwards to the River Plate, Montevideo being reached in 21 days from Genoa. Homewards from Buenos Aires, calls were made at Montevideo, Rio de Janeiro and Cadiz.

The SIRIO, ORIONE and PERSEO were undoubtedly the finest group of Italian ships then running in the South American trade, their principal rivals being the 3,577 ton REGINA MARGHERITA and the 2,822 ton UMBERTO I of Rocco Piaggio, and the 4,826 ton NORD AMERICA and the 3,919 ton MATTEO BRUZZO of M. Bruzzo & Co. (Chapter 34).

The PERSEO took the 30 October 1884 sailing from Genoa and had the misfortune to be delayed by a quarantine of seven weeks owing to an outbreak of cholera on board.

The commissioning of the SIRIO, ORIONE and PERSEO so soon after the completion or ordering of the seven smaller newcomers must be regarded as over ambitious. Not surprisingly, the Società Italiana di Trasporti Marittimi Raggio & Co was unable to continue in existence, and its fleet of 11 ships was sold to the Navigazione Generale Italiana in January 1885. The Company went into liquidation some weeks later, on 14 March.

1. 1881 INIZIATIVA
   2,032. 91,43 x 11,34. (300.0 x 37.2). S–1–2. I–S–C2–10. (I–24; II–24; III–1,000). A. Stephen & Sons, Glasgow. 1881 (26/7) launched. 1881 (19/10) MV Genoa–Montevideo–Buenos Aires (4 RV). 1885 INIZIATIVA (NGI). 1885 (19/5) FV Palermo–New York. 1910 INIZIATIVA (Soc. Nazionale di Servizi Marittimi. 1915 (11/11) sailed Swansea–Italy with coal; went missing.

2. 1882 SCRIVIA
   2,100. 91,49 x 12,28. (300.2 x 40.3). S–1–2. I–S–C2–10. (I–24;
   II–24; III–1,000). Raylton Dixon & Co, Middlesbrough. 1882
   (18/5) launched. 1882 (11/12) MV Genoa–Montevideo–Buenos
   Aires (5 RV). Also Genoa–Singapore (1 RV). 1885 SCRIVIA
   (NGI). 1910 ditto (Soc. Nazionale di Servizi Marittimi. 1925
   scrapped.
3. 1883 POLCEVERA
   2,239. 91,19 x 11,34. (299.2 x 37.2). S–1–2. I–S–C2–10. (I–24;
   II–24; III–1,000). Blackwood & Gordon, Port Glasgow. 1882
   (15/11) launched. 1883 (16/3) MV Genoa–Montevideo–Buenos
   Aires (5 RV). Also 6 voyages S. Wales–Italy with coal. 1885
   POLCEVERA (NGI). 1885 (24/6) FV Palermo–Boston–New
   York. 1910 POLCEVERA (Soc. Nazionale di Servizi Marittimi.
   1913 ditto (Sicilia). 1916 (26/10) torpedoed and sunk by enemy
   submarine off Marettino Island, Sicily (0).
4. (1884) STURA
   2,245. 91,19 x 11,34. (299.2 x 37.2). S–1–2. I–S–C2–10. (I–24;
   II–24; III–1,000). Blackwood & Gordon, Port Glasgow. 1883
   (Sep) launched. 1883 (Dec) 4 RV Clyde or Cardiff–Genoa with
   coal; 1 RV Cardiff–Bombay; 3 RV Cardiff–Italy with coal. 1884
   (16/12) FV Genoa–Montevideo–Buenos Aires. 1885 STURA
   (NGI). 1885 (22/5) FV Messina–Palermo–New York. 1910
   STURA (Soc. Nazionale di Servizi Marittimi). 1913 ditto
   (Sicilia). 1916 (17/5) torpedoed and sunk by enemy submarine off
   Brindisi (6).
5. (1884) ENTELLA
   2,244. 91,19 x 11,34. (299.2 x 37.2). S–1–2. I–S–C2–10. (I–24;
   II–24; III–1,000). Blackwood & Gordon, Port Glasgow. 1883
   (23/5) launched. 1883 (Nov) FV Genoa–Suez Canal–Singapore
   for NGI (c). Subsequently 6 or more RV S. Wales–Italy with
   coal. 1884 (23/12) FV Genoa–Montevideo–Buenos Aires (1 RV).
   1885 ENTELLA (NGI). 1885 (23/7) FV Girgenti–Palermo–New
   York. 1910 ENTELLA (Soc. Nazionale di Servizi Marittimi).
   1913 ditto (Sicilia). 1923 scrapped.
6. (1884) BORMIDA
   2,290. 91,34 x 11,34. (299.7 x 37.2). S–1–2. I–S–C2–10. (I–24;
   II–24; III–1,000). Burrell & Sons, Dumbarton (engines Duncan
   Stewart & Co, Glasgow). 1884 (10/7) launched. 1 RV Newport–
   Genoa with coal. 1884 (10/12) FV Genoa–Montevideo–Buenos
   Aires. 1885 BORMIDA (NGI). 1897 triple-expansion engines.
   1910 BORMIDA (Soc. Nazionale di Servizi Marittimi. 1913 ditto
   (Sitmar). 1928 scrapped.

7. 1885 BISAGNO

    2,290. 91,83 x 11,34. (301.3 x 37.2). S–1–2. I–S–C2–10. (I–24;
II–24; III–1,000). Burrell & Sons, Dumbarton (engines Duncan
Stewart & Co, Glasgow). 1884 (20/9) launched. 1885 (24/1) MV
Genoa–Montevideo–Buenos Aires. 1885 BISAGNO (NGI).
1898 triple-expansion engines. 1898 FV Genoa–Central America
for Regia Marina (c). 1910 BISAGNO (Soc. Nazionale di Servizi
Marittimi). 1913 ditto (Sicilia). 1917 (23/1) stopped by German
submarine U.57 200 miles off W. coast of Ireland. 1917 (26/1)
crew transferred to GAASTERLAND (Dutch) and BISAGNO
was sunk by gunfire.

8. 1883 SIRIO

    4,141. 115,81 x 12,83. (380.0 x 42.1). S–2–3. I–S–C3–14. (I–80;
II–40; III–1,200). Robert Napier & Sons, Glasgow. 1883 (26/3)
launched. 1883 (19/6) sailed Glasgow–Genoa. 1883 (15/7) MV
Genoa–Las Palmas–Montevideo–Buenos Aires. 1885 SIRIO
(NGI). 1885 (21/3) FV Genoa–Las Palmas–Montevideo–Buenos
Aires. 1891 triple-expansion engines; 15 knots. 1906 (4/8)
wrecked near Cape Palos, Spain (442).

9. 1884 ORIONE

    4,161. 115,81 x 12,83. (380.0 x 42.1). S–2–3. I–S–C3–14. (I–80;
II–40; III–1,200). Robert Napier & Sons, Glasgow. 1883 (Jun)
launched. 1884 (15/1) MV Genoa–Las Palmas–Montevideo–
Buenos Aires. 1885 ORIONE (NGI). 1885 (5/3) FV Genoa–Las
Palmas–Montevideo–Buenos Aires. 1891 triple-expansion en-
gines; 15 knots. 1906 modernised; transferred to Marittima
Italiana (Syrian line). 1921 scrapped.

10. 1884 PERSEO

    4,158. 116,00 x 12,80. (380.6 x 42.0). S–2–3. I–S–C3–14. (I–80;
II–40; III–1,200). Robert Napier & Sons, Glasgow. 1883 (16/11)
launched. 1884 (15/2) MV Genoa–Las Palmas–Montevideo–
Buenos Aires. 1885 PERSEO (NGI). 1885 (16/2) FV Genoa–Las
Palmas–Montevideo–Buenos Aires. 1891 triple-expansion engines; 15 knots. 1899 (19–20/12) collision when outward bound
near Alicante with MEUSE (Paquet (Fr)); returned to Genoa for
repairs. 1906 modernised; transferred to Marittima Italiana
(Syrian line). 1908 (12/2) sunk in collision at Naples; salvaged.
1917 (4/5) torpedoed and sunk in Aegean Sea by enemy
submarine (227).

Note: the 2,237 ton LETIMBRO did not run to South America for
Raggio.

Chapter 32

(1882–5)

LLOYD AUSTRIACO

(Austrian Lloyd)

(Austrian)

The LLOYD AUSTRIACO, once well-known throughout the English-speaking world as the AUSTRIAN LLOYD, started steamship operations in 1836 with services based on Trieste and confined to the Adriatic. In due course, its activities were extended to Egypt and other parts of the Mediterranean, and after the opening of the Suez Canal in 1869 the Company's steamers proceeded regularly to India and the Far East. But in October 1881 the Company obtained the approval of the Governor of Vienna for two new lines – one to New York and the other to Brazil and the River Plate, with a subsidy of 26,000 fiorini for each round voyage to the former destination and 38,000 fiorini to the latter. [1]

The 1,964 ton iron screw ACHILLE left Trieste on 25 January 1882 for New York where she arrived on 3 March. [2] Exactly a month after her departure from Trieste a second experimental voyage was made by the 1,533 ton NARENTA to Bari, Catania, Tunis, Barcelona, Gibraltar, St. Vincent, Pernambuco, Rio de Janeiro, Santos, Montevideo and Buenos Aires. [3] She was carrying 8,465 packages of general cargo and 3,200 pieces of timber, but her only passengers were some delegates of the Brünn (Brno?) Chamber of Commerce, who were looking for new markets in South America. The NARENTA was launched on 13 December 1871 as the MARY LAMONT and at a later date was bought by Lloyd Austriaco.

There were no further Lloyd Austriaco sailings on the North Atlantic, but it was decided in 1883 to arrange some sailings to Brazil to coincide with the coffee season. The 1,757 ton iron screw MEMFI sailed from Trieste on 10 July 1883, followed at monthly intervals by the MEDEA, AGLAIA, THISBE, MELPOMENE and POLLUCE, making a total of six round voyages. Outwards, about 6,000 tons of cargo, mostly flour, was carried, and homewards about 9,000 tons of coffee.

In 1884 there were four voyages from Trieste to Brazil, two of them by the MELPOMENE, but in 1885 there was only one by the MEMFI, and after that the service was discontinued – presumably because it did not pay.

Elsewhere, however, the Lloyd Austriaco was a force to be reckoned with. An idea of its importance can be gained by the fact that in 1886, 50 years after its foundation, its fleet consisted of 86 ships totalling 124,341 tons. During that year, 1,526 voyages were undertaken, 230,168 passengers were carried and 592,039 tons of cargo.

The Lloyd Austriaco services were suspended during World War I, and afterwards the Company was reorganised as the LLOYD TRIESTINO under the Italian flag.

[1] *Trasporti Marittimi di Linea,* (Volume 2), (Ogliari and Radogna).
[2] *New York Herald* 4/3/1882.
[3] Signor Nereo Castelli, S. Antonio in Bosco, Italy.

1. (1882) NARENTA
    1,533. 76,04 x 10,27. (249.5 x 33.7). S–1–2. I–S–C2–11. M. Pearse & Co, Stockton (engines Blair & Co, Stockton). 1871 (13/12) launched as MARY LAMONT. 1882 NARENTA (Lloyd Austriaco). 1882 (25/2) FV Trieste–Bari–Catania–Tunis–Barcelona–Gibraltar–St. Vincent–Pernambuco–Rio de Janeiro–Santos–Montevideo–Buenos Aires (1 RV). 1899 TRIESTINO. 1908 no longer in Register.
2. (1883) MEMFI
    1,757. 79,24 x 9,90. (260.0 x 32.5). S–1–3. I–S–C2–11. Lloyd Austriaco, Trieste. 1872 launched. 1883 (10/7) FV Trieste–Fiume–Gibraltar–Lisbon–St. Vincent–Rio de Janeiro–Santos. 1885 (12/3) LV Rio de Janeiro–Trieste (arr 14/4). 1902 MEMFI (Uruguay). 1904 scrapped at Dunkirk.
3. (1883) MEDEA
    1,823. 84,48 x 10,73. (277.2 x 35.2). S–1–2. I–S–C2–12. Lloyd Austriaco, Trieste. 1878 launched. 1883 (10/8) FV Trieste–Lisbon–Pernambuco–Rio de Janeiro. 1908 scrapped at Cadimare.
4. (1883) AGLAIA
    1,898. 86,13 x 10,73. (282.6 x 35.2). S–1–2. I–S–C2–12. Lloyd Austriaco, Trieste. 1879 launched. 1883 (11/9) FV Trieste–Barcelona–Brazil. 1910 scrapped at Trieste.
5. 1883 THISBE
    2,870. 91,43 x 12,86. (300.0 x 42.2). S–1–2. I–S–C2–12. J.L. Thompson & Sons, Sunderland (engines J. Dickinson, Sunderland). 1883 (Apr) launched. 1883 (10/10) MV Trieste–Fiume–Brazil. 1895 (Jun) wrecked.
6. 1883 MELPOMENE
    2,983. 97,74 x 11,98. (320.7 x 39.3). S–1–2. I–S–C2–12. Palmers

Co Ltd, Jarrow-on-Tyne. 1883 (Apr) launched. 1883 (11/11) MV Trieste–Fiume–Brazil. 1884 (28/6) 2nd voyage Trieste–Fiume–Lisbon–Brazil. 1884 (12/9) LV Rio de Janeiro–Trieste (arr 11/10) (3 RV). 1919 MELPOMENE (Lloyd Triestino). 1923 scrapped in Italy.

7. (1883) POLLUCE
2,046. 90,64 x 10,73. (297.4 x 35.2). S–1–2. I–S–C2–11. Lloyd Austriaco, Trieste, 1874 launched. 1883 (10/12) FV Trieste–Brazil. 1908 scrapped at Cadimare.

Chapter 33

1882–1905

FABRE LINE

(Compagnie Française de Navigation à Vapeur
Cyprien Fabre et Compagnie)

(French)

CYPRIEN FABRE & COMPAGNIE, of Marseilles, owners since 1865 of a small fleet of sailing ships, bought their first steamer, the 461 ton PHENICIEN in 1868, but it was not until 1873 that they decided to go in wholeheartedly for steam. A weekly service was introduced between Sete, Marseilles, Oran, Alicante and Valencia in 1877, and five years later a service opened between Marseilles and New York. But Cyprien Fabre, who had founded the COMPAGNIE FRANÇAISE DE NAVIGATION À VAPEUR CYPRIEN FABRE-ET COMPAGNIE on 31 March 1881 with a capital of 15 million francs (£600,000), after gaining a French Government subsidy for building tonnage had more expansive ideas.

He was determined to start a service to South America as well as to North America, and the 1,642 ton DIOLIBAH was despatched from Marseilles for the River Plate on 24 October 1882, Buenos Aires being reached on 1 December. The SCOTIA, one of a quartet of new 2,400 ton steamers built in Britain for the New York run, was detailed to take the second South American sailing on 10 December for Montevideo, Buenos Aires and Rosario. She was followed by the 1,404 ton PATRIA on 25 January 1883, the DIOLIBAH on 13 February and then sailed again herself in March. The 1,892 ton VILLE DE LISBONNE, a chartered steamer belonging to the Compagnie Havraise Péninsulaire, took the April sailing.

The 2,024 ton GERGOVIA, a product of Scott & Co of Greenock and the only passenger steamer to be laid down for Fabre's South American service, started her maiden voyage on 16 March 1884 from Marseilles, but, as a rule, made at least one North Atlantic voyage each year.

The 1,948 ton MAURICE ET RÉUNION was launched by W. Hamilton & Co of Port Glasgow on 18 March 1881 for a service between Marseilles, Mauritius and Réunion, but it seems that the demand was insufficient for the facilities offered, and upon arrival at Marseilles on 14

263

January 1885 she was acquired by Fabre. Her first voyage to South America started on 15 February.

The SCOTIA divided her attention between the North and South Atlantic before being sold in 1887. She had been stranded for a month on Long Island, New York, but was successfully refloated.

The 2,926 ton NEUSTRIA, completed in 1884 by Claparède & Cie of Rouen, made her first round voyage to South America in 1887 and a second in 1895.

1893 OLBIA 2,671 tons
Built 1874 as MARTABAN of the Henderson Line.

Two further second-hand steamers call for mention. The 2,034 ton PICTAVIA (ex-CLARE), acquired by Fabre in January 1890, ran on the South Atlantic from 1 July 1890 until sold in 1899 except for a total of six New York voyages and perhaps one or two to New Orleans. The 2,671 ton OLBIA, launched on 7 November 1873 by Denny of Dumbarton as the Henderson Line MARTABAN, was bought by Fabre in July 1893 and although probably detailed at first to the New Orleans service seems to have made her first River Plate voyage on 10 February 1895. She also made one or two voyages to New York.

Additions continued to be made to the New York fleet, but money was not forthcoming for the South American service and the Company probably had no alternative but to withdraw it in 1905, two years after the irregular service to New Orleans had also closed.

1. (1882) DIOLIBAH
    1,642. 80,64 x 11,06. (264.6 x 36.3). I–S–C2–10. A. McMillan & Son, Dumbarton. 1880 (11/6) launched. 1882 (24/10) FV Marseilles–R. Plate. 1893 triple-expansion engines. 1911 (29/10) sank after collision with SS RIBERA 90 miles from Las Palmas.

264

2. (1882) SCOTIA
2,492. 100,09 x 12,31. (328.4 x 40.4). S–1–3. I–S–C2–11. (I–18; III–1,000). S. & H. Morton & Co, Leith. 1881 (23/11) launched. 1882 (18/4) MV Marseilles–New York. 1882 (10/12) FV Marseilles–R. Plate. 1887 (24/3) stranded on Long Island, NY. 1887 (25/4) refloated; sold; repaired; became MARS (US). 1889 (10/7) wrecked near Los Roques Islands, Venezuela.

3. (1883) PATRIA
1,404. 76,19 x 10,06. (250.0 x 33.0). I–S–C2–10. Raylton Dixon & Co, Middlesbrough (engines T. Richardson & Sons, Hartlepool. 1874 (Aug) launched as COOMASSIE. 1883 (28/1) FV Marseilles–R. Plate. 1882 (11/12) wrecked at Cape Carmel, on passage Syria–Marseilles.

3a. (1883) VILLE DE LISBONNE (c)
1,892. 85,03 x 10,67. (279.0 x 35.0). I–S–C2–10. J. Laing, Sunderland (engines G. Clark, Sunderland). 1880 (23/12) launched for Cie Havraise Péninsulaire. 1883 (15/4) FV for Fabre (c) Marseilles–R. Plate. 1884 (17/2) foundered off Cap de la Hague, France, on voyage Saigon–Rouen (0).

4. 1884 GERGOVIA
2,024. 85,37 x 11,18. (280.1 x 36.7). S–1–2. I–S–C2–10. (I; III–950). Scott & Co, Greenock (engines Greenock Foundry Co). 1883 (17/12) launched. 1884 (16/3) MV Marseilles–R. Plate. 1886–1902 ditto, but 14 RV Marseilles–New York. 1924 scrapped.

5. (1885) MAURICE ET RÉUNION
1,948. 87,78 x 11,03. (288.0 x 36.2). S–1–2. I–S–C2–11. W. Hamilton & Co, Port Glasgow (engines Dunsmuir & Jackson, Glasgow). 1881 (18/5) launched for Marseilles–Mauritius–Réunion service. 1885 MAURICE ET RÉUNION (Fabre). 1885 (15/2) FV Marseilles–R. Plate. 1898 MAURICE ET RÉUNION (Fr). Later VILLE DE CARTHAGE (Fr). 1911 (9/12) abandoned 90 miles from Ushant.

6. (1887) NEUSTRIA
2,926. 100,09 x 12,19. (328.4 x 40.0). S–1–2. I–S–C2–12. (I–18; III–1,100). Claparède & Cie, Rouen. 1883 (19/8) launched. 1884 (21/9) MV Marseilles–New York. 1887 (4/12) FV Marseilles–R. Plate. 1895 (28/10) LV ditto (2 RV). 1898 chartered to repatriate Spanish troops from Cuba. 1908 (27/10) sailed New York–Marseilles; went missing.

7. (1890) PICTAVIA
2,034. 82,41 x 11,70. (270.4 x 38.4). S–1–2. I–S–C2–10. (I; III–900). J. Blumer & Co, Sunderland (engines T. Clark & Co,

Newcastle). 1883 (20/6) launched as CLARE (Br). 1890 (Jan) PICTAVIA (Fabre). 1890 (26/3) FV Marseilles–New York. 1890 (1/7) FV Marseilles–R. Plate. 1899 ASSUNTO (Italian). 1904 (2/2) wrecked at Bereby, Ivory Coast.

8. (1895) OLBIA

2,671. 106,85 x 11,09. (350.6 x 36.4). C–1–3. I–S–Q4–11. (I–30; II–24; III). Wm. Denny & Bros, Dumbarton. 1873 (7/11) launched as MARTABAN (Henderson); compound engines. 1888 Q4 by Denny. 1893 (Jul) OLBIA (Fabre). 1895 (10/2) FV Marseilles–Genoa–S. America. 1906 scrapped at Leghorn.

Note: The BRITANNIA (1882); ALESIA (1882); BURGUNDIA (1883); MASSILIA (1891); PATRIA (II) (1895); GALLIA (ex-CHATEAU YQUEM) (1897); ROMA (1902); GERMANIA (1903) and ships built subsequently did not run on the South Atlantic.

FUNNEL: (a) 1882. Black.
          (b) 1902. Red; white band below black top.
FLAG: White; blue cross.

Chapter 34

1883–4

M. BRUZZO & CO

(Italian)

MATTEO BRUZZO, one of the liquidators of G.B. LAVARELLO & Co (Chapter 14), which he had founded in 1871 with Captain Giovanni Battista Lavarello, decided to remain in business and in partnership with the Marquis Marcello Durazzo and others formed M. BRUZZO & CO in Genoa on 13 June 1883. The new company acquired the three surviving Lavarello steamers – the 2,246 ton SUD AMERICA, the 2,226 ton EUROPA and the 1,865 ton COLOMBO (ex-ESPRESSO).

It has been said that Bruzzo had thoughts of buying the Guion Line record-breaker ALASKA, which in any event was not for sale at that time. Instead, he turned his attention to the 4,423 ton iron screw STIRLING CASTLE, which, built with three-cylinder compound engines by John Elder & Co of Glasgow in 1882 for Thos. Skinner & Co of London, had made a name for herself by steaming home from Shanghai to London via Suez laden with China tea in the then unheard of time of 27 days 23 hours 45 minutes. But this and subsequent voyages cost her owners so dear in respect of fuel that they decided to sell her. About the middle of 1883 Bruzzo stepped in and bought her. He was so proud of his acquisition and her worldwide fame that in addition to naming her NORD AMERICA, he took the unusual course of having on her bows NORD AMERICA STIRLING CASTLE, in a straight line. Immediate arrangements were made for 90 first class, 100 second class and over 1,000 steerage berths to be installed. Her tonnage was increased to 4,826.

At about the same time, the 3,919 ton GOLCONDE, launched by Forges & Chantiers de la Méditerranée of La Seyne for the Compagnie Fraissinet in November 1882, was bought by Matteo Bruzzo and renamed with his own name.

The new company's first sailing was taken by the SUD AMERICA, which left Genoa for Montevideo and Buenos Aires on 3 July 1883, followed by the COLOMBO on 3 August, the EUROPA on 3 September and a second voyage of the SUD AMERICA on 3 October. In view of the time taken to fit her passenger accommodation being longer than expected, the NORD AMERICA was not ready to leave on 3 November, as intended, but got away from Genoa on 13 November,

1883 NORD AMERICA: STIRLING CASTLE 4,826 tons
For many years the fastest steamer to South America.

calling at Marseilles three days later. There seems to have been a good deal of delay in placing the MATTEO BRUZZO in commission as there is no trace of her leaving Genoa before 3 February 1884.

To give the line further prominence, it was called unofficially LA VELOCE LINEA DI NAVIGAZIONE ITALIANA A VAPORE – that is to say, 'The Fast Italian Steamship Line' – in honour of the NORD AMERICA, which on one occasion proceeded from Genoa to Montevideo in 18 days exactly, inclusive of a number of hours spent in coaling at Gibraltar.

Unfortunately, the high cost of buying the NORD AMERICA and MATTEO BRUZZO, the unexpectedly high fuel bills of the former and the necessity to send the COLOMBO to Tyneside in February 1884 for a facelift were too much for Matteo Bruzzo, and on 24 April 1884 a new limited partnership, LA VELOCE LINEA DI NAVIGAZIONE A VAPORE SOCIETÀ IN ACCOMANDITA PER AZIONI, was formed. This, then, was the actual start of the La Veloce Line (Chapter 35), which took over the five Bruzzo ships although nominally that line remained in existence until 1 January 1888.

Matteo Bruzzo himself lived until 30 March 1896, but for some years previously had played no part in running LA VELOCE.

1. (1883) SUD AMERICA
    2,246. 95,70 x 10,76. (314.0 x 35.3). S–1–4. I–S–C2–12. (I–75; II–52; III–750). Wigham Richardson & Co, Walker-on-Tyne.

1872 (12/6) launched for Lavarello. 1883 SUD AMERICA (M. Bruzzo & Co). 1883 (3/7) FV Genoa–S. America. 1884 SUD AMERICA (La Veloce). 1888 (13/9) sunk in collision with ss FRANCE (SGTM collier) (87) at Las Palmas. (See La Veloce (35)).

2. (1883) COLOMBO

1,865. 91,09 x 10,82. (298.9 x 35.5). S–1–4. I–S–C2–11. (I–34; III–900). Wigham Richardson & Co, Walker-on-Tyne. 1870 (27/9) launched as ESPRESSO (Lavarello). 1871 (23/2) MV Genoa–S. America. 1874 COLOMBO (Lavarello). 1883 ditto (M. Bruzzo & Co). 1883 (3/8) FV Genoa–S. America. 1884 NAPOLI (La Veloce); 2,009 tons. 1893 (5/12) abandoned off Brazilian coast.

3. (1883) EUROPA

2,226. 95,46 x 10,79. (313.2 x 35.4). S–1–4. I–S–C2–12. (I–75; II–52; III–750). Wigham Richardson & Co, Walker-on-Tyne. 1872 (27/2) launched for Lavarello. 1883 EUROPA (M. Bruzzo & Co). 1883 (3/9) FV Genoa–S. America. 1884 EUROPA (La Veloce). 1893 scrapped. (See La Veloce (35)).

4. (1883) NORD AMERICA

4,826. 127,58 x 15,24. (418.6 x 50.0). S–2–3. I–S–C3–15. (I–90; II–100; III–1,223). J. Elder & Co, Glasgow. 1882 (21/1) launched as STIRLING CASTLE, 4,423 tons; (Thos. Skinner & Co, London). 1883 NORD AMERICA (M. Bruzzo & Co), but name STIRLING CASTLE also retained. 1883 (13/11) FV Genoa–S. America. 1884 NORD AMERICA (La Veloce – 35); q.v.

5. (1884) MATTEO BRUZZO

3,919. 118,98 x 12,89. (390.4 x 42.3). S–1–2. I&S–S–C2–12. (I–32; II–20; III–1,215. Forges & Chantiers de la Méditeranée, La Seyne. 1882 (Nov) launched as GOLCONDE (Fraissinet). 1883 MATTEO BRUZZO (M. Bruzzo & Co). 1884 (3/2) FV Genoa–S. America. 1884 MATTEO BRUZZO (La Veloce). 1899 CITTÀ DI GENOVA (ditto). 1907 scrapped at Genoa. (See La Veloce (35)).

Chapter 35

1884–1915

LA VELOCE

(Italian)

As earlier chapters show. LA VELOCE NAVIGAZIONE ITALIANA A VAPORE can indirectly be traced back to 1865, when Captain Giovanni Battista Lavarello started a line of auxiliary wooden screw steamers from Genoa to South America, and more particularly to 1883, when his successor, Matteo Bruzzo, decided to operate his South America service under the unofficial title of LA VELOCE LINEA DI NAVIGAZIONE ITALIANA A VAPORE – that is to say, 'The Fast Italian Steamship Line'. This was done in honour of his purchase of the 4,423 ton STIRLING CASTLE, which had become famous for her extremely fast passages in the tea trade from Shanghai to London. She was renamed NORD AMERICA and fitted with accommodation for 90 first class, 100 second and 1,223 steerage passengers, thereby increasing her tonnage to 4,826.

Only a few months later, on 24 April 1884, a new limited partnership was established as LA VELOCE LINEA DI NAVIGAZIONE A VAPORE SOCIETÀ IN ACCOMANDITA PER AZIONI. This was the official start of La Veloce, and it came into being largely because M. Bruzzo & Co had insufficient capital to buy and run the NORD AMERICA and another recent purchase, the MATTEO BRUZZO, let alone acquire further ships. An important advantage of the new arrangement was that the Marquis Marcello Durazzo, who had been associated with M. Bruzzo & Co, acquired a substantial interest in La Veloce and, in fact, became its director in July 1885.

From the Bruzzo fleet, La Veloce also inherited the 2,200 ton EUROPA and SUD AMERICA as well as the 1,865 ton COLOMBO, which was on Tyneside undergoing alterations. She was renamed NAPOLI, her tonnage was increased to 2,009 and she started her first voyage for the new concern on 3 September 1884 from Genoa. The NORD AMERICA was chartered for some months in 1885 by the British Government to carry troops from the Mediterranean to Suakin, Sudan.

The NORD AMERICA continued for a number of years to be the fastest ship on the Italy–South America run, but when the Navigazione Generale Italiana (Chapter 36) started an express service in 1885 with the ex-Piaggio REGINA MARGHERITA and the ex-Raggio SIRIO, ORIONE and PERSEO, as well as a lesser service with other units acquired from these lines, their fleet was, in the aggregate, considerably superior.

La Veloce's new director, Durazzo, was naturally determined that his line should not lag behind, his immediate aim being to build five large and fast ships. He approached the Italian Government with a view to obtaining a substantial subsidy, but without success. However, he was able to buy very advantageously three excellent ships at a total cost of £186,000, namely, the 4,100 ton MEXICO, OAXACA and TAMAULIPAS, which had been built in 1884 by Napier of Glasgow for the Mexico–Liverpool service of the short-lived Compañía Mexicana Trasatlántica of Vera Cruz.

These ships had an attractive appearance with two slim funnels and three masts, were propelled by three-cylinder compound engines giving a service speed of 14 knots, and had accommodation for approximately 100 first class, 100 second and 1,000 steerage passengers. They were taken over at British ports, the first to be delivered being the DUCHESSA DI GENOVA (ex-MEXICO) at Liverpool, her initial sailing from Genoa taking place on 19 November 1887 for Barcelona, Las Palmas (for coal), Montevideo and Buenos Aires, the homeward voyage being made via Rio de Janeiro. The DUCA DI GALLIERA (ex-OAXACA) left Genoa on 29 November, reaching Montevideo in 19 days 3 hours, and finally the VITTORIA (ex-TAMAULIPAS) sailed on 6 December. With the assistance of the NORD AMERICA they were able to make two

1887 DUCA DI GALLIERA 4,304 tons
Built 1884 as OAXACA for Cia Mexicana Trasatlantica.

271

departures each month, and not only did the line become very popular but it thoroughly justified its name.

Payment for the newcomers was made possible by the formation on 30 December 1887 of a joint stock company, LA VELOCE LINEA DI NAVIGAZIONE ITALIANA A VAPORE SOCIETÀ ANONIMA, with a capital of 15 million lire (£600,000). On 1 January 1888 it took over the earlier La Veloce concern and what was left of the firm of M. Bruzzo & Co.

In 1889, in anticipation of the building of some even better ships, a large batch of newly-issued La Veloce shares was bought by two German banks, the Berliner Handelsgesellschaft and the Darmstadter Bank. Like all other lines running to South America, La Veloce was badly hit by the political and financial troubles of 1889–91 in the Argentine and Brazil. The German shareholders were alarmed because the company was running at a loss, and a new Italian president was appointed, with a German as vice-president. Durazzo remained on the board of directors. A year or two later the German became president.

Another line to be seriously hit by events in Argentina and Brazil was the Società di Navigazione a Vapore Fratelli Lavarello (Chapter 38), established by the sons of Captain Giovanni Battista Lavarello after the liquidation of G.B. Lavarello & Co in 1883. It suspended operations on 14 March 1891 and its six surviving ships (two others had already been sold) were bought by La Veloce. The CITTÀ DI GENOVA and ROSARIO retained their names, the GIOVANNI BATTISTA LAVARELLO and ADELAIDE LAVARELLO became the LAS PALMAS and RIO JANEIRO and two ex-Hamburg American Line ships, the MENTANA and CITTÀ DI NAPOLI, became the SUD AMERICA (II) and MONTEVIDEO.

One reason for this purchase was because it had been decided to postpone placing orders for new ships. Although four of those acquired were small, they were modern and between them replaced the SUD AMERICA (I), which had been sunk in collision at Las Palmas on 13 September 1888 with the loss of 87 lives, the NAPOLI (ex-COLOMBO), which was lost off the Brazilian coast in 1893 and the EUROPA, which was scrapped in the same year. More particularly, they were able to maintain a fairly regular cargo and emigrant service to Brazil and, starting on 1 January 1894, four of them were responsible for a new Central America service from Genoa to Marseilles, Barcelona, Tenerife, La Guaira and Colon (Panama). The first sailing was taken by the ROSARIO, followed by the CITTÀ DI GENOVA, LAS PALMAS and RIO JANEIRO.

Despite more than one statement to the contrary by other writers, the only 19th century activities of La Veloce to New York date back to 1892 when, on 24 March, the MATTEO BRUZZO left Leghorn (Livorno) for New York via Messina, Naples and Gibraltar. She reached her destination on 20 April with cargo and 1,080 passengers. Although the voyage was apparently successful, it was not repeated.

Matteo Bruzzo died on 30 March 1896 but had taken no active part in the running of the line for a number of years. In 1896, also, it was decided that La Veloce could no longer postpone building a replacement for the record-breaker NORD AMERICA, then 14 years old.

1897 CENTRO AMERICA 3,474 tons
Built for Central American service but made some South American voyages.

But first of all came two 3,470 ton twin-screw steamers, the CENTRO AMERICA and VENEZUELA, built as their names imply for the Central American line, their speed of 14 knots enabling them to provide a monthly service and fully replace the four ships employed hitherto. Their first class accommodation, unlike that of the other La Veloce ships, was situated amidships and consisted of 138 berths. In addition, they could carry 750 emigrants. Like other ships built by N. Odero fu Alessandro of Sestri Ponente, they were launched fully completed, the CENTRO AMERICA sailing from Genoa on 5 June 1897, only 21 days after being launched. The VENEZUELA left on 3 July 1898.

To replace the ageing NORD AMERICA as the crack ship of the South American line, an order was placed with the same builders for the 4,377 ton SAVOIA, on which work began in May 1896. She was launched fully completed on 26 September 1897, enabling her maiden voyage to start from Genoa for Buenos Aires on 22 October. She was a twin-screw steamer with triple-expansion engines, her service speed being 16 knots, and her passenger complement 80 first class, 40 second and 800 third.

Hard on her heels came the 4,041 ton single-screw CITTÀ DI MILANO and CITTÀ DI TORINO from the same builders. They had a

273

1897 CITTÀ DI MILANO 4,041 tons
Ran on all three services – to River Plate, New York and Central America.

modest speed of 12 knots, and accommodation for 40 first and 1,290 third class passengers, their maiden voyages starting from Genoa on 30 December 1897 and 27 February 1898 for Montevideo, Buenos Aires and Rosario.

In view of this new construction, it was possible to sell the CITTÀ DI GENOVA, ROSARIO, MONTEVIDEO and RIO JANEIRO in 1898–9. Owing to the popularity of the name of the first-mentioned it was decided in 1899 that the MATTEO BRUZZO should be renamed CITTÀ DI GENOVA (II).

The DUCHESSA DI GENOVA, DUCA DI GALLIERA and VITTORIA continued to give good service until January 1899, when the VITTORIA left Genoa on her 55th voyage to South America with about 450 passengers and a considerable cargo. On the morning of the 11th, when in the vicinity of Alicante, it was discovered that she was on fire. Strenuous efforts to extinguish the blaze being of no avail, the ship was beached near Alicante harbour. All her passengers and crew were safely landed, together with her mail and some of the baggage, but not the cargo. In due course, the VITTORIA was refloated, towed back to Genoa and scrapped.

Also in 1899, the NORD AMERICA was chartered by the Russian Government to carry troops from Odessa to Vladivostock via the Suez Canal in connection with the Boxer Rebellion in China. By this time she was well past her prime, so at the completion of these duties she was sent to Palmers on Tyneside. Triple-expansion engines replaced the compound set and as an economy her speed was reduced from 15 to 13½ knots, her funnels were lengthened, her masts reduced from three to two and her accommodation was modified.

In 1899, for the third year running, a financial loss was incurred by the Company, which by now was completely under German control. But in

1900–01 the Banca Commerciale Italiana and the Navigazione Generale Italiana decided to buy almost the entire German shareholding, and on 6 June 1901 a new board of directors was elected. The bank appointed Signor Casanova to represent their interests and Signor Brizzolesi acted for NGI, becoming the administrator of La Veloce, which still retained its independent existence. The Company's title was shortened to LA VELOCE NAVIGAZIONE ITALIANA A VAPORE.

Unfortunately, the SAVOIA as built was not entirely satisfactory, and in 1900 she was sent to the Tyne to be lengthened by 19,7 metres (64.7 feet). Her tonnage became 5,082, and her combined first and second

SAVOIA
1897 The launching 4,377 tons
1900 The lengthened ship 5,082 tons

class accommodation was increased from 120 to 300 berths; her steerage was extended from 800 to 1,000. Speed was not affected, but there is no doubt that with her greatly-improved accommodation her popularity increased by leaps and bounds. It must be admitted, however, that her appearance was completely ruined by the lengthening. A simple remedy would have been to add a dummy second funnel forward of the existing one.

In 1892, the year of the MATTEO BRUZZO's North Atlantic voyage, 43,000 Italian emigrants had left for North America whereas in 1901 the total increased to 125,000. It is not surprising, therefore, that La Veloce –

almost certainly with the approval of NGI – started a service from Genoa and Naples to New York, the first sailing being taken on 15 March 1901 by the DUCHESSA DI GENOVA, other participants that year being the CITTÀ DI TORINO and NORD AMERICA. The last-named took part in the service until 1908, while both the CITTÀ DI TORINO and CITTÀ DI MILANO were employed regularly from 1901–02, respectively, until 1907, after which they were transferred to the Central America line.

Unfavourable conditions affected the Central American line in 1900, and between then and 1903 the CENTRO AMERICA and VENE-ZUELA ran to South America, joining the SAVOIA, DUCHESSA DI GENOVA, DUCA di GALLIERA and, until they were transferred in 1901–02, the CITTÀ DI TORINO and CITTÀ DI MILANO. In 1901 the DUCHESSA DI GENOVA made four round voyages to New York, and in 1903 the DUCA GI GALLIERA made two. Their last South America sailings took place in 1905, and they were scrapped a year later. They had served La Veloce well!

1905 ITALIA 5,018 tons
Ran for six different lines without change of name.

The withdrawal of these two ships was made possible by the completion of the 5,000 ton twin-screw ITALIA, ARGENTINA and BRASILE in 1905–06. Built by Odero of Genoa, Fratelli Orlando of Leghorn and Ligure-Anconetani of Ancona, respectively, they were fitted with two sets of triple-expansion engines giving them a speed of 13 knots, and had accommodation for about 60 first class, 56 second and 1,000 third class passengers. The ITALIA's maiden voyage started from Genoa on 10 August 1905 via Naples to Montevideo and Buenos Aires. The ARGENTINA proceeded to the same destinations, but before entering the South American service the BRASILE began her career

276

with a voyage to New York and made seven more at later intervals. She was the first passenger steamer to be built at Ancona and aroused a great deal of local interest.

The SAVOIA was, of course, still the Company's crack steamer, but was well-supported by the three newcomers, all of which remained in the South American service until 1912.

In December 1908 the NORD AMERICA and SAVOIA, together with La Veloce's North Atlantic emigrant ship CITTÀ DI NAPOLI (II), were sent to Messina as accommodation ships for survivors of the earthquake. The NORD AMERICA was employed subsequently as a cargo steamer, and on 5 December 1910, homeward bound from Buenos Aires to Genoa with a consignment of horses, she stranded on the coast of Morocco. Refloated in due course, she was towed to Genoa, laid up there for some time and then scrapped.

Not content with having gained control of La Veloce in 1901, NGI acquired Italia Società di Navigazione a Vapore (Chapter 48) in 1906 and Lloyd Italiano Società di Navigazione (Chapter 50) in 1910. Sailings of all four were co-ordinated on both North and South Atlantic, and in addition there were many transfers of tonnage between the lines. In exchange for the 9,000 ton AMERICA of its New York line, for example, La Veloce received from NGI the 7,893 ton twin-screw DUCA DI GENOVA, built by the Cantieri Navale Riuniti of La Spezia in 1908, and she joined the South American service.

It will be seen from Chapter 36 (NGI) that an agreement was reached in September 1912 with the Brazilian Government for a direct line from Italy to Brazil. This was started from Genoa on 27 November 1912 by La Veloce's ARGENTINA, tactfully renamed BRASILE for the occasion, the former BRASILE having recently been sold to the Compagnie Générale Transatlantique to become the VENEZUELA. The second sailing was undertaken by the ITALIA, which was transferred from La Veloce to NGI so that all four partners would be represented. La Veloce's UMBRIA, transferred to them earlier in the year by NGI, passed to Italia and was renamed SAN PAULO. It may be added that the Lloyd Italiano CORDOVA was temporarily renamed RIO DE JANEIRO.

The service ceased after the third sailing as the Italian Government stepped in and withdrew the emigration patent. Both the BRASILE, which retained this name, and the ITALIA were transferred to Italia, whose 4,600 ton twin-screw SIENA and BOLOGNA were passed to La Veloce for their Central American line. This meant that the latter's single-screw CITTÀ DI MILANO and CITTÀ DI TORINO were superfluous, and were sold to the Sitmar Line as the ALBANIA and COSTANTINOPOLI.

Following the disposal of the BRASILE and ITALIA, La Veloce's South American line was undertaken by the DUCA DI GENOVA and SAVOIA, the two best ships ever to be detailed to it. However, the SAVOIA's last South American voyage started from Genoa on 16 May 1914, and after that she sailed once or twice to Central America.

The outbreak of World War I in August 1914 was responsible for the DUCA DI GENOVA being despatched from Genoa on 26 September for New York to help in the repatriation of Americans stranded in Europe. She returned to the South American service in November and undertook five more round voyages to Buenos Aires, the last of which terminated at Genoa on 6 October 1915. She then proceeded almost at once to New York, to which she made further voyages in 1916 and 1917 before being taken up by the Italian Government as a troopship. She was torpedoed and sunk by German submarine U.64 near Cape Canet on 6 February 1918.

After Italy entered the war in May 1915, the SAVOIA became first a troop transport and later a support ship. She was laid up at Genoa for a considerable time after the Armistice of November 1918, but made two round voyages to Central America in 1922. She was sold for scrap in the following year.

In 1919 the BOLOGNA was detailed to an extension of the Central American line through the recently-opened Panama Canal to Valparaiso, and was later joined in the same year by the 7,870 ton twin-screw EUROPA, built for the New York service in 1907. She made one Italy–New York voyage in 1920 and two each in 1921 and 1922, after which she was acquired by NGI in exchange for the 6,847 ton single-screw CASERTA (ex-Lloyd Italiano MENDOZA), renamed VENEZUELA.

Thus, the BOLOGNA, VENEZUELA and a wartime cargo steamer, the VITTORIO VENETO, were the only survivors of the once-extensive La Veloce fleet, and not surprisingly the Company was dissolved on 21 September 1924, the three steamers being taken over by NGI. It is strange that the South American service, for long the Company's only activity and probably always regarded by them as the most important, should have been the first to be abandoned.

1. (1884) NORD AMERICA
    4,826, 127,58 x 15,24. (418.6 x 50.0). S–2–3. I–S–C3–15. J. Elder & Co, Glasgow. 1882 (21/1) launched as STIRLING CASTLE; 4,423 tons (Thos. Skinner & Co, London). 1883 NORD AMERICA (M. Bruzzo & Co), but name STIRLING CASTLE also retained at first. (I–90; II–100; III–1,223 fitted). 1883 (13/11) FV Genoa–S. America. 1884 NORD AMERICA (La Veloce).

278

1884 (10/5) FV Genoa–S. America. 1885 chartered by British Govt. for carriage of troops to Suakin, Sudan. 1899 chartered by Russian Govt. for voyage Odessa–Vladivostock as troopship in connection with Boxer Rebellion in China. 1900 rebuilt by Palmers Co Ltd; T3 replaced C3; funnels lengthened; masts reduced from 3 to 2; (II–90; III–1,223). 1901 (27/5) FV Palermo–Naples–New York. 1908 (25/3) LV Genoa–Naples–New York (58 RV). 1908 (Dec) accommodation ship at Messina after earthquake. 1909 cargo steamer. 1910 (6/12) stranded near Cape Spartel; refloated; towed to Genoa. 1911 scrapped.

2. (1884) SUD AMERICA (I)

2,246. 95,70 x 10,76 (314.0 x 35.3). S–1–4. I–S–C2–12. (I–75; II–52; III–750). Wigham Richardson & Co, Walker-on-Tyne. 1872 (12/6) launched for Lavarello. 1872 MV Genoa–S. America. 1883 SUD AMERICA (M. Bruzzo & Co). 1883 (3/7) FV Genoa–S. America. 1884 SUD AMERICA (La Veloce). 1884 (23/5) FV Genoa–S. America. 1888 (13/9) sunk in collision with ss FRANCE (SGTM collier) at Las Palmas (87).

3. (1884) EUROPA

2,226. 95,46 x 10,79. (313.2 x 35.4). S–1–4. I–S–C2–12. (I–75; II–52; III–750). Wigham Richardson & Co, Walker-on-Tyne. 1872 (27/2) launched for Lavarello. 1872 MV Genoa–S. America. 1883 EUROPA (M. Bruzzo & Co). 1883 (3/9) FV Genoa–S. America. 1884 EUROPA (La Veloce). 1884 (18/6) FV Genoa–S. America. 1893 scrapped.

4. (1884) MATTEO BRUZZO
   (1898) CITTÀ DI GENOVA (II)

3,919. 118,98 x 12,89. (390.4 x 42.3). S–1–2. I&S–S–C2–12. (I–32; II–20; III–1,215). Forges & Chantiers de la Méditerranée, La Seyne. 1882 (Nov) launched as GOLCONDE (Fraissinet). 1883 MATTEO BRUZZO (Bruzzo). 1884 (3/2) FV Genoa–S. America. 1884 MATTEO BRUZZO (La Veloce). 1884 (3/7) FV Genoa–S. America. 1899 (1/8) CITTÀ DI GENOVA (La Veloce). 1902–06 Genoa–Naples–New York (8 RV). 1907 scrapped at Genoa.

5. (1884) NAPOLI

2,009. 91,09 x 10,82. (298.9 x 35.5). S–1–4. I–S–C2–11. (I–34; III–900). Wigham Richardson & Co, Walker-on-Tyne. 1870 (27/9) launched as ESPRESSO (Lavarello), 1,865 tons. 1871 (23/2) MV Genoa–S. America. 1874 COLOMBO (Lavarello). 1883 ditto (M. Bruzzo & Co). 1883 (3/8) FV Genoa–S. America. 1884 NAPOLI (La Veloce). 1884 (3/9) FV Genoa–S. America. 1893 (5/12) abandoned off Brazilian coast.

6. (1887) DUCHESSA DI GENOVA
   4,304. 121,91 x 13,41. (400.0 x 44.0). S–2–3. S–S–C3–14. (I–98; II–108; III–784). R. Napier & Sons, Glasgow. 1884 (29/2) launched as MEXICO (Cia Mexicana Trasatlantica). 1887 DUCHESSA DI GENOVA (La Veloce). 1887 (19/11) FV Genoa–S. America. 1901 (15/3) FV Genoa–Naples–New York (4 RV). 1905 (27/9) LV Genoa–S. America. 1906 scrapped.
7. (1887) DUCA DI GALLIERA
   4,304. 121,91 x 13,41. (400.0 x 44.0). S–2–3. S–S–C3–14. (I–98; II–108; III–784). R. Napier & Sons, Glasgow. 1883 (15/12) launched as OAXACA (Cia Mexicana Trasatlantica). 1887 DUCA DI GALLIERA (La Veloce). 1887 (29/11) FV Genoa–S. America. 1903 (21/3) FV Genoa–Naples–New York (2 RV). 1905 (7/9) LV Genoa–S. America. 1906 scrapped at Genoa.
8. (1887) VITTORIA
   4,290. 121,91 x 13,41. (400.0 x 44.0). S–2–3. S–S–C3–14. (I–98; II–108; III–784). R. Napier & Sons, Glasgow. 1883 (19/9) launched as TAMAULIPAS (Cia Mexicana Trasatlantica). 1887 VITTORIA (La Veloce). 1887 (6/12) FV Genoa–S. America. 1899 (11/1) ravaged by fire on voyage Genoa–Buenos Aires; beached at Alicante; towed to Italy; scrapped. (0).
9. (1891) SUD AMERICA (II)
   3,158. 103,60 x 12,20. (339.9 x 40.0). S–2–2. I–S–C2–12. (I–90; II–130; III–520). Caird & Co, Greenock. 1868 (24/6) launched as WESTPHALIA (Hapag). 1868 (16/9) MV Hamburg–New York. 1878 C2 replaced I(2); funnels increased from 1 to 2. 1887 ATLANTICA (Br). 1888 PROVINCIA DI SAN PAULO (Gazzo & Schiaffino (It)). 1889 MENTANA (Fratelli Lavarello). 1889 FV Genoa–S. America. 1891 SUD AMERICA (La Veloce). 1891 (14/1) FV Genoa–S. America. 1901 scrapped at Genoa.
10. (1891) ROSARIO
    1,957. 85,95 x 10,73. (282.0 x 35.2). S–1–2. I–S–T3–12. Wigham Richardson & Co, Walker-on-Tyne. 1887 (17/9) launched for Fratelli Lavarello. 1887 (1/12) MV Genoa–S. America. 1891 ROSARIO (La Veloce). 1891 (29/3) FV Genoa–S. America. 1898 DJURJURA (Cie Mixte (Fr)). 1915 (23/12) sunk in collision.
11. (1891) CITTÀ DI GENOVA (I)
    1,936. 91,43 x 10,76. (300.0 x 35.3). S–1–2. S–S–T3–12. Wigham Richardson & Co, Walker-on-Tyne. 1889 (18/2) launched for Fratelli Lavarello. 1889 (Apr) MV Genoa–S. America. 1891 CITTÀ DI GENOVA (La Veloce). 1891 (12/4) FV Genoa–S. America. 1898 SAVOIE (SGTM (Fr)). 1927 scrapped.

12. (1891) RIO JANEIRO (sic)
    1,916. 91,43 x 10,76. (300.0 x 35.3). S–1–2. S–S–T3–12. Wigham
    Richardson & Co, Walker-on-Tyne. 1888 (4/12) launched as
    ADELAIDE LAVARELLO (Fratelli Lavarello). 1889 (20/2)
    MV Genoa–S. America. 1891 RIO JANEIRO (La Veloce). 1891
    (29/9) FV Genoa–S. America. 1899 ALSACE (SGTM (Fr)).
    1923 scrapped.
13. (1891) LAS PALMAS
    1,861. 82,29 x 10,45. (270.0 x 34.3). S–1–2. S–S–T3–12. Wigham
    Richardson & Co, Walker-on-Tyne. 1886 (16/10) launched as
    GIOVANNI BATTISTA LAVARELLO (Fratelli Lavarello).
    1886 (18/12) FV Genoa–S. America. 1891 LAS PALMAS (La
    Veloce). 1891 (10/10) FV Genoa–S. America. 1905 JONIO
    (NGI). 1915 (4/11) torpedoed and sunk off Algeria.
14. (1891) MONTEVIDEO
    3,142. 103,60 x 12,20. (339.9 x 40.0). S–1–2. I–S–C2–12. (I–90;
    II–130; III–520). Caird & Co, Greenock. 1869 (14/4) launched as
    SILESIA (Hapag). 1869 (23/6) MV Hamburg–New York. 1877
    C2 replaced I(2). 1887 PACIFICA (Br). 1888 CITTÀ DI
    NAPOLI (Solari & Schiaffino (It)). 1889 ditto (Fratelli
    Lavarello). 1891 MONTEVIDEO (La Veloce). 1891 (21/11) FV
    Genoa–S. America. 1899 (2/12) wrecked near Island of Lobos,
    River Plate.
15. 1897 SAVOIA
    4,377. 121,09 x 13,80. (397.3 x 45.3). C–1–2. 2S–T6–16. (I–80;
    II–40; III–800). N. Odero fu Alessandro, Sestri Ponente. 1897
    (26/9) launched. 1897 (22/10) MV Genoa–Barcelona–Las Pal-
    mas–Montevideo–Buenos Aires. 1900 lengthened to 140,80
    metres (462.0 feet); 5,082 tons; (I & II–300; III–1,000). 1900
    (28/9) resumed Genoa–S. America. 1908 (Dec) accommodation
    ship at Messina after earthquake. 1914 (16/5) LV Genoa–S.
    America. 1914 (6/10) FV Genoa–Colon. 1915 troop transport;
    later support ship. 1919 laid up at Genoa. 1922 Genoa–Central
    America (2 RV). 1923 scrapped.
16. 1897 CITTÀ DI MILANO
    4,041. 110,94 x 13,28. (364.0 x 43.6). 1–2. S–T3–12. (I–40;
    III–1,290). N. Odero fu Alessandro, Sestri Ponente. 1897 (17/12)
    launched. 1897 (30/12) MV Genoa–Montevideo–Buenos Aires–
    Rosario. 1902 (3/2) FV Genoa–Naples–New York (26 RV). 1908
    Genoa–La Guaira–Colon. 1914 ALBANIA (Sitmar). 1932 ditto
    (Lloyd Triestino). 1933 scrapped.
17. 1898 CITTÀ DI TORINO
    4,041. 110,69 x 13,28. (363.2 x 43.6). 1–2. S–T3–12. (I–40;

III–1,290). N. Odero fu Alessandro, Sestri Ponente. 1898 (12/2) launched. 1898 (27/2) MV Genoa–Montevideo–Buenos Aires–Rosario. 1901 (23/3) FV Genoa–Naples–New York (30 RV). 1908 Genoa–La Guaira–Colon. 1914 COSTANTINOPOLI (Sitmar). 1932 ditto (Lloyd Triestino). 1933 scrapped.

18. (1899) VENEZUELA
    3,379. 110,54 x 12,65. (362.8 x 41.5). C–1–2. 2S–T6–14. (I–138; III–750). N. Odero fu Alessandro, Sestri Ponente. 1898 (Jun) launched. 1898 (3/7) MV Genoa–La Guaira–Colon. 1899 (Nov) FV Genoa–S. America. 1903 (Jly) returned to Central American line. 1908 VENEZUELA (NGI – Egypt and Syria line). 1909 (21/2) wrecked at Marseilles.

19. (1899) CENTRO AMERICA
    3,474. 109,23 x 12,62. (358.4 x 41.4). C–1–2. 2S–T6–14. (I–138; III–750). N. Odero fu Alessandro, Sestri Ponente. 1897 (15/5) launched. 1897 (5/6) MV Genoa–La Guaira–Colon. 1899 (Jly) engine trouble at Las Palmas; towed by CITTÀ DI MILANO to Genoa. 1899 (8/12) FV Genoa–S. America. 1903 (Jly) returned to Central America service. 1908 SOLUNTO (NGI – Egypt and Syria line). 1911 ditto (Soc. Nazionale di Servizi Marittimi). 1925 scrapped.

20. 1905 ITALIA
    5,018. 119,99 x 14,56. (393.7 x 47.8). 2–2. 2S–T6–13. (I–61; II–56; III–980). N. Odero & Co, Genoa. 1905 (25/6) launched. 1905 (10/8) MV Genoa–Naples–S. America. 1906 (20/3) FV Genoa–Naples–New York (1 RV). 1912 ITALIA (NGI). 1913 ditto (Italia). 1917 ditto (Transoceanica). 1922 ditto (NGI). 1923 ditto (Sitmar). 1932 ditto (Lloyd Triestino. 1944 (6/7) sunk at Arsa (Trieste) by Allied bombers. 1950 refloated; scrapped.

21. 1906 ARGENTINA
    (1912) BRASILE (II)
    4,985. 120,11 x 14,53. (394.1 x 47.7). 2–2. 2S–T6–13. (I–61; II–56; III–950). Fratelli Orlando, Leghorn. 1905 (Jly) launched. 1906 (22/2) MV Genoa–Naples–S. America. 1912 BRASILE (La Veloce). 1912 (Nov) FV Genoa–Naples–Brazil. 1913 BRASILE (Italia). 1917 ditto (Transoceanica). 1921 ditto (NGI). 1922 ditto (Sitmar).

22. (1906) BRASILE (I)
    5,026. 120,17 x 14,56. (394.3 x 47.8). 2–2. 2S–T6–13. (I–58; II–56; III–994). Officine e Cantieri Ligure-Anconetani, Ancona (engines N. Odero & Co, Sestri Ponente). 1905 (29/6) launched for South American service. 1905 (30/12) MV Genoa–Naples–New York. 1906 (22/3) FV Genoa–Naples–S. America. 1908 (8/6) LV

Genoa–Naples–New York (8 RV). 1912 VENEZUELA (CGT). 1920 (7/3) dragged anchor in Casablanca roads and ran ashore. 1920 (5/10) broke her back; scrapped.

23. (1912) DUCA DI GENOVA
   7,893. 145,01 x 16,27. (475.8 x 53.4). 2–2. 2S–Q8–16. (I–66; II–122; III–1,740). Cantieri Navale Riuniti, La Spezia (engines N. Odero & Co, Sestri Ponente). 1907 (8/9) launched for NGI. 1908 (18/10) MV Genoa–Naples–New York. 1912 DUCA DI GENOVA (La Veloce). 1912 (8/12) FV Genoa–Naples–S. America. 1915 (14/8) LV Genoa–Buenos Aires (dep 11/9)–Barcelona–Genoa (arr 6/10). 1915–17 made several Genoa–New York voyages before becoming an Italian troopship. 1918 (6/2) torpedoed and sunk by German submarine U.64 near Cape Canet, Mediterranean France.

24. (1912) UMBRIA
   5,020. 122,32 x 14,20. (401.4 x 46.6). 1–2. S–Q4–14. (I–38; II–49; III–1,016). Fratelli Orlando, Leghorn. 1901 (8/8) launched for NGI. 1902 (19/5) MV Genoa–New York. 1912 UMBRIA (La Veloce). 1912 (1/6) FV Genoa–S. America. 1912 SAN PAULO (Italia). 1913 UMBRIA (Sitmar). 1932 scrapped.

Note: For further information about Nos. 1–5 see Lavarello Line (Chapter 14) and Nos. 9–14 see Fratelli Lavarello (Chapter 38).
   The CITTÀ DI NAPOLI (II) (ex-White Star REPUBLIC (1871)), EUROPA (II), AMERICA and OCEANIA (later STAMPALIA) of La Veloce's North Atlantic Line did not run on the Brazil–River Plate service, nor did the BOLOGNA, SIENA and VENEZUELA (ex-CASERTA) of the Central American line (see text).

FUNNEL: Yellow with red star.
FLAG: White with red cross; St. George on horseback and the dragon in green in top corner near hoist.

Chapter 36

(1884–1931)

NAVIGAZIONE GENERALE ITALIANA

(Navigazione Generale Italiana Società Riunite Florio & Rubattino)

(Italian)

The NAVIGAZIONE GENERALE ITALIANA SOCIETÀ RIUNITE FLORIO & RUBATTINO, created in 1881 by the amalgamation of two long-established companies, I. & V. Florio of Palermo and the Società per la Navigazione a Vapore R. Rubattino of Genoa, entered the South American trade only three years later.

The Rubattino Line, dating from 1838, had begun with Mediterranean services and, spurred on by the opening of the Suez Canal, had extended its sailings to India and the Far East. For a time its co-founder, Raffaele Rubattino, was also head of the ill-fated Compagnia Transatlantica (Chapter 7), which started operations between Italy and South America in 1856. By 1881 the Rubattino fleet had increased to 38 ships with a nett tonnage of 26,918.

The Florio Line also began with Mediterranean sailings, but by 1880, having absorbed along the way the 13 steamers of the liquidated Trinacria Steamship Company of Palermo, introduced in addition a regular service to New York.

But on 2 April 1881 Ignazio Florio, son of the Florio Line's late founder, joined with Raffaele Rubattino in sending a request to the Royal Italian Navy, which administered the Italian merchant marine until 1916, for their two concerns to be allowed to amalgamate. The application was approved by the Lower House on 5 July 1881 and the Upper House on 12 July. King Umberto signed a decree on 23 July authorising the formation of the NAVIGAZIONE GENERALE ITALIANA SOCIETÀ RIUNITE FLORIO & RUBATTINO, which was registered at Genoa on 4 September 1881, but backdated to 1 July 1881. The Company's nominal capital was 100 million lire, of which 35 million (£1,400,000) was paid up. Sadly, Raffaele Rubattino died only a few months later, in 1882.

In addition to running various lines in the Mediterranean, the principal activities of the new concern were the services to New York and to India and the Far East via the Suez Canal. But on 19 November 1884 a significant departure came when the 3,541 ton iron screw steamer

1884 SINGAPORE 3,541 tons
Undertook first NGI voyage to South America.

SINGAPORE (ex-ST. OSYTH) was despatched from Genoa for the River Plate, followed by the 3,650 ton MANILLA (ex-WHAMPOA) on 18 December. These vessels, originally bought by Rubattino in 1878 for the Far East service, were thus responsible for the first NGI sailings to South America, but each made only one round voyage before returning to the Bombay and Far East service.

The third NGI sailing to South America was taken by the 2,041 ton ABISSINIA, also transferred from the Far Eastern line, which left Genoa on 21 January 1885 for Montevideo and Buenos Aires. Ten days after beginning her third voyage on this route in the following November, she stranded on the Moroccan coast between Casablanca and Mogador, and despite all efforts to save her became a total loss.

As already stated in Chapter 31, the fleet of 11 ships of Raggio & Co was taken over by NGI in January 1885. The exact date of the takeover is now known, but only one of its ships sailed from Genoa for South America during that month – the BISAGNO on 24 January – so this may or may not have been an NGI sailing. But as it was also the ship's maiden voyage it has been considered reasonable to credit it to Raggio. The three crack Raggio ships, the 4,150 ton PERSEO, ORIONE and SIRIO, sailed for NGI from Genoa on 16 February, 5 March and 21 March, respectively, followed by the 2,100 ton SCRIVIA on 11 April. Four weeks previously, on 14 March, the Società Italiana di Trasporti Marittimi Raggio & Co went into liquidation.

Further dramatic activities followed in July 1885, when NGI took over the fleet of the Società Rocco Piaggio & Figli [1] (Chapter 25), including the 3,577 ton REGINA MARGHERITA, the 2,822 ton UMBERTO I and the 2,655 ton ADRIA, the last-named built as long previously as 1855 as the Cunard Line ETNA. The other two had been running until

285

the previous January in a joint service with Raggio to the River Plate and the REGINA MARGHERITA, in particular, was a great asset to NGI. She was the fastest Italian transatlantic steamer with the exception of La Veloce's NORD AMERICA, and her first class accommodation was unsurpassed. Her first sailing for NGI started on 2 July 1885 and that of the UMBERTO I on 18 July.

Thus, the REGINA MARGHERITA, UMBERTO I, SIRIO, ORIONE and PERSEO made a very fine quintet and could be relied on to provide a fortnightly express service. In the aggregate, the South American service was weekly as the Company had ample secondary steamers to make this possible. There was a minor change of itinerary as Las Palmas was substituted for St. Vincent as a port of call. Some of the lesser units also called at Rio de Janeiro and Santos.

The 2,840 ton iron screw steamers VINCENZO FLORIO and WASHINGTON were taken from the New York service in 1885 and despatched on a mission to Eritrea. This gave the Company an opportunity for a considerable interchange of ships. On 21 October 1885 the VINCENZO FLORIO sailed from Genoa for Montevideo and Buenos Aires, followed by the WASHINGTON on 5 November.

A cargo and emigrant service was also started at about this time by the PARANA (ex-CARMELA), PARAGUAY and PLATA from Genoa and Naples to Rio de Janeiro, Montevideo, Buenos Aires and Rosario. The 1,358 ton PARAGUAY, in particular, was an interesting ship, built in 1870 as the MARINA of the Donaldson Line's newly-started steam service from Glasgow to South America (Chapter 24). She had changed hands more than once since then and survived until 1930, when she was scrapped as the Italian TORERO. The 1,942 ton PLATA was acquired from Raggio, for whom she ran as the AMEDEO, having been built in 1878 as the Johnston Line LASCELLES.

Three more ships undertook their first South American sailings in 1887. Early that year NGI bought the 2,489 ton LOUDOUN CASTLE, built by J. & G. Thomson of Glasgow in 1876 for T. Skinner & Co. She was renamed MARCO MINGHETTI and after two round voyages on the North Atlantic sailed on 2 October from Genoa for the River Plate. Both she and the VINCENZO FLORIO returned to the New York service in 1900 after a long absence.

Next came the 2,334 ton PO, built in 1880 as the Donaldson Line TITANIA, which sailed from Genoa for Brazil on 10 November 1887, followed in December by the INDIPENDENTE, one of four sister ships of the VINCENZO FLORIO. By a coincidence, two others, the GOTTARDO and ARCHIMEDE, sailed from Genoa for Naples, Montevideo and Buenos Aires on 1 and 15 June 1888.

It has been said that the MANILLA, RAFFAELE RUBATTINO

and DOMENICO BALDUINO, all normally allotted to the eastern line, which from 1895 onwards did not proceed beyond Bombay, ran to South America in 1890 and occasionally at other times when additional tonnage was required. In fact, the MANILLA sailed from Genoa for the River Plate on 31 December 1889 and probably made other voyages to that destination. However, neither the RAFFAELE RUBATTINO nor the DOMENICO BALDUINO sailed to South America in 1890, but may well have done so in an earlier or later year.

An NGI seasonal service was started to New Orleans in 1890. Among the ships so employed were the INIZIATIVA, MARCO MINGHETTI, WASHINGTON and MANILLA. Some of the less important ships had been making extended voyages from the River Plate to Valparaiso and Callao via the Straits of Magellan at intervals of two or three months, but this arrangement was discontinued in 1890.

The SIRIO, ORIONE and PERSEO had always been on the slow side, so they were fitted with triple-expansion engines in 1891 by Ansaldo of Genoa and their service speed increased from 13 to 15 knots. The PERSEO was involved in a collision with the Paquet Line MEUSE near Alicante on 19–20 December 1899. She was patched up at Alicante before returning to Genoa for a refit.

A further ship, the 3,406 ton ARNO, was responsible for a few South American voyages between December 1891 and 1898 when, prior to being turned into a hulk, she became for a time a coal carrier. She had been built in 1872 as the Hamburg American FRISIA.

During the 1890s, despite plenty of demand for accommodation, NGI sailings to New York decreased steadily and severely and, in fact, there were none at all in 1898, a likely explanation being that certain German banks had gained a considerable measure of control over the Company and might understandably have attempted to help Norddeutscher Lloyd (Chapter 29) and the Hamburg American Line (Chapter 47) by reducing Italian competition. The German interest was only temporary, however, and it is significant that NGI sailings to New York increased to 11 in 1899, more or less simultaneously with the withdrawal of the German banks.

But there was another event that may well have played an important part – the death of Ignazio Florio in 1891. This resulted in the ascendency of the Genoese interests, headed by Erasmo Piaggio, who had been been transferred in 1885 to the Genoa headquarters of NGI and had become their director-general at the end of 1894. The Florio family had always been responsible for managing the North American line, whereas the Genoese members of the board had been much more interested in the South American trade.

The late 1890s were difficult times for NGI, and both the North and

South Atlantic lines were badly in need of new tonnage. In particular, the REGINA MARGHERITA was fitted with triple-expansion engines in 1896 by Ansalso of Genoa, whereby her service speed was increased to 17 knots, but in 1898, by which time her former Rocco Piaggio consort, the ADRIA, had finally been scrapped at the ripe old age of 45, she was temporarily transferred to the NGI Egyptian line, which was being hit by the effects of foreign competition.

The vast majority of the share capital of La Veloce Navigazione Italiana a Vapore (Chapter 35) came into the possession of two German banks after the South American financial crisis of 1889. This state of affairs lasted for over 10 years, but in 1900–01 the Banca Commerciale Italiana and NGI brought almost the entire German holding. A new board of directors having a strong NGI influence was appointed on 6 June 1901. And it was probably at NGI's instigation that La Veloce started a passenger service from Genoa and Naples to New York in March 1901. La Veloce retained its separate identity, but ran jointly with NGI to both North and South America.

1902 UMBRIA 5,020 tons
Normally ran to River Plate apart from maiden voyage to New York.

The 4,865 ton LIGURIA, the 4,815 ton LOMBARDIA, the 5,229 ton SICILIA and the 5,255 ton SARDEGNA started their maiden voyages from Genoa and Naples to New York in 1901–02, and although single-screw ships they were a considerable advance on their predecessors in the fleet. They were fitted with triple-expansion engines, and had accommodation for 66 first class (80 in the case of the SARDEGNA), 90 second and over 1,000 third class passengers. The 5,020 ton UMBRIA was built for the South American service, but her maiden voyage starting on 19 May 1902 was to New York, as were three similar voyages in 1903 and one in 1904. She differed from the others in her quadruple-expansion engines – the first Italian-built ship to be so fitted.

For the time being, the UMBRIA's principal consorts were the REGINA MARGHERITA which, having completed her Egyptian duties, undertook another 15 South American sailings, the SIRIO, ORIONE and PERSEO, but the SARDEGNA started her first voyage for the River Plate on 3 August 1905. She was joined on 2 November 1906 by the SICILIA, while the LIGURIA and LOMBARDIA each made one round voyage to Uruguay and Argentina.

The REGINA MARGHERITA's return to the South American service combined with its recent additions enabled the ORIONE and PERSEO to be transferred to the Egyptian line during the early part of 1906. But the SIRIO continued on the South Atlantic, although disaster struck after she sailed from Genoa for Montevideo and Buenos Aires on 4 August 1906 with 695 passengers and a crew of 127. Two days later, when about to enter the Spanish port of Cartagena, her captain decided to take a short cut by steering inside a group of islands instead of proceeding by the normal and safe course outside the islands. The result was that the SIRIO struck some rocks and quickly began to sink, a panic broke out and amid scenes of great disorder she listed and sank by the stern, the death roll being no less than 442.

1883 SIRIO 4,141 tons
Wrecked in 1906 near Cartagena, Spain, with heavy casualties.

The 9,000 ton CAMPANIA, one of three twin-screw cargo steamers bought from the British Shipowners Company in 1906 and subsequently fitted with accommodation for 70 first class and 2,200 steerage passengers, began her NGI career on 30 October 1906 with a voyage from Genoa to the River Plate, followed immediately by another. In 1910 she was chartered to the Northwest Transport Line and later the same year became the CAMPANELLO of the Uranium Line. An eventful career ended on 24 August 1918 when, as the Cunard FLAVIA,

289

she was torpedoed and sunk by German submarine U.107 off Tory Island, Northern Ireland. [2]

Lloyd Sabaudo (Chapter 52) started a rival service in May 1907 between Genoa, Naples and New York, followed in October by one to South America. In July 1907 Sicula Americana (Chapter 57) began operations between Sicily and New York. This new competition had been partly anticipated in 1906 by NGI buying a majority interest in Italia Società di Navigazione a Vapore (Chapter 48), which had been under Hamburg American domination since its foundation in 1899, and had hitherto confined its activities to the South Atlantic. Additionally, on 19 December 1907 NGI acquired a partial interest in Lloyd Italiano, which had been running on North and South Atlantic since 1905.

Although NGI had added eight new or virtually new ships within the space of a few years, the best units of their South American fleet were undoubtedly surpassed by some of those of the British-owned Royal Mail Steam Packet Company (Chapter 1) and Hamburg–Süd (Chapter 26), to say nothing of the aspirations of rival Italian lines. In consequence, NGI placed orders for four 7,800 ton twin-screw ships having a service speed of 16 knots, three being intended for the South Atlantic and one for the North. In the event, six ships were built, the REGINA ELENA, RE VITTORIO and PRINCIPE UMBERTO being allotted to the River Plate line, and the DUCA DEGLI ABRUZZI, DUCA DI GENOVA and DUCA D'AOSTA to New York.

The 'Regal' ships were fitted with three cabins 'di gran lusso' with bedroom, sitting room and bathroom, two cabins 'di lusso' with private bathroom, 13 special cabins for one or two passengers and 28 cabins for two or three passengers, making a total first class capacity of 100, not counting sofa berths. Public rooms consisted of a dining saloon, music room, smoking room, winter garden and children's room. There were 28

1908 REGINA ELENA 7,856 tons
Sister ship of RE VITTORIO and PRINCIPE UMBERTO.

1908 DUCA DEGLI ABRUZZI 7,793 tons
Sister ship of DUCA D'AOSTA and DUCA DI GENOVA.

second class cabins in the poop for a total of 124 passengers, with a dining saloon accommodating 102, a music room and a smoking room. Third class capacity was 900.

The 'Ducal' ships had two cabins 'di lusso' with private bathroom, three special cabins and 27 double cabins, the total first class capacity being 66. Second class consisted of 30 four-berth cabins in the poop, and there was accommodation for 1,200 emigrants.

From the foregoing details it is evident that the South Atlantic service was considered to require a higher grade of luxury than the North Atlantic.

The South American express line's itinerary became Genoa, Barcelona, Dakar, Rio de Janeiro, Santos, Montevideo and Buenos Aires, the call at Las Palmas having been abandoned by the fast ships, which were able to steam from Genoa to Buenos Aires in less than 17 days.

NGI had continued the various subsidised services bequeathed to them by the Florio and Rubattino lines at the time of the 1881 amalgamation, including those in the Mediterranean, Black Sea, Red Sea and further afield to India. But owing to the important growth of the North and South Atlantic business and the greatly-increased competition of foreign lines, it was decided not to apply for renewal of the various agreements with the Italian Government when they expired in 1908. However, in order to allow time for other plans to be made, NGI agreed to continue these services until June 1910, when a new company, Società Nazionale di Servizi Marittimi, came into being and took over no fewer than 65 NGI ships. As a result of this and other sales, the NGI fleet on 31 December 1910 was reduced to 18 units compared with 105 of 288,465 tons registered in its name on 30 June 1910. Subsequently, the Company concentrated entirely on the transatlantic trades.

Among the ships disposed of were the REGINA MARGHERITA, UMBERTO I, VINCENZO FLORIO, WASHINGTON, TEBE (ex-INDIPENDENTE), MEMFI (ex-GOTTARDO), BISAGNO, BORMIDA, GIAVA, PLATA, MARCO MINGHETTI, PO and SCRIVIA. The SINGAPORE was scrapped at Palermo in 1910.

Another important event of 1910 was the purchase by NGI of a controlling interest in Lloyd Italiano in place of their previous minority interest. In consequence, the services of NGI, La Veloce, Italia and Lloyd Italiano were co-ordinated on both North and South Atlantic.

It was decided that two units instead of three would suffice for both NGI and La Veloce's North Atlantic services, so the 8,996 ton twin-screw AMERICA, completed in 1909, was transferred from La Veloce to NGI in exchange for the DUCA DI GENOVA, which was detailed to the South Atlantic. At about the same time, the AMERICA's new consort became the 8,240 ton twin-screw VERONA of Italia, to which was passed the NGI SANNIO, renamed NAPOLI. The AMERICA and VERONA were in sole charge of NGI's New York service from March 1913 to June 1914.

The DUCA DEGLI ABRUZZI, and for that matter the DUCA DI GENOVA, served as an Italian auxiliary cruiser from 5 February 1912 until the following August. She joined the REGINA ELENA, RE VITTORIO and PRINCIPE UMBERTO in the Genoa–South American service on 2 October 1912, followed by the DUCA D'AOSTA on 30 December 1912. Thus, five of the six best ships built for NGI were detailed to the River Plate trade. It was apparently intended that this arrangement should continue indefinitely, but the outbreak of World War I in August 1914 was responsible for both 'DUCA' ships returning to the North Atlantic for a time.

The object behind these changes and others which did not affect NGI was supposed to be to give NGI and its three partners balanced services on both North and South Atlantic, but it cannot be denied that the real result was to make both the NGI North and South Atlantic fleets superior to those of the other members of the group.

In September 1912 NGI concluded on behalf of itself and its three subsidiaries an agreement with the Brazilian Government for a direct emigrant line from Italy to Brazil, a subsidy of 100,000 lire (£4,000) to be paid for each voyage carried out. [3] The new service was started on 27 November 1912 by La Veloce's BRASILE (ex-ARGENTINA), the change of name being considered tactfully necessary. The second sailing was taken by the ex-La Veloce ITALIA, which had been transferred to NGI in order that each of the four partners should be represented. The Lloyd Italiano CORDOVA was renamed RIO DE JANEIRO, while the ex-NGI UMBRIA, transferred to La Veloce earlier in the year, passed to Italia as the SAN PAULO.

However, after the third special sailing in December 1912, the Italian Government withdrew the patent for the direct emigrant line, and the sailings were suspended. The RIO DE JANEIRO reverted to the name CORDOVA and the SAN PAULO to UMBRIA. The BRASILE was passed to Italia but retained her name, as did the ITALIA, which also went to Italia.

By 1913 NGI was again falling behind its international competitors in the size of its ships, and on 30 December of that year an order was placed with Ansaldo of Sestri Ponente for the 20,000 ton GIULIO CESARE, which was to be constructed by Swan, Hunter & Wigham Richardson, builders of the much larger Cunard MAURETANIA, at Wallsend-on-Tyne. A direct order was received by the Italian firm on 30 May 1914 for a second new ship, the DUILIO. Not surprisingly, the outbreak of World War I was responsible for a long delay in the completion of both.

Sicula Americana had by this time become a serious competitor of the NGI group. On 19 August 1917, therefore, NGI founded a new company, Transoceanica Societa Italiana di Navigazione, which absorbed Sicula Americana together with its parent concern, Peirce Brothers, and also took over Italia Società di Navigazione a Vapore.

NGI lost two of their three 'Regal' units during the war – the PRINCIPE UMBERTO was torpedoed and sunk by an enemy submarine off Vallona on 8 June 1916 and the REGINA ELENA met the same fate in the Adriatic on 4 January 1918. In addition, two units of the North Atlantic fleet were torpedoed and sunk – the PALERMO (ex-LAZIO) near San Sebastian on 2 December 1916 and the VERONA near Cape Pellaro on 11 May 1918.

In consequence, NGI became desperately short of tonnage and it was decided on 24 May 1918 to absorb Lloyd Italiano together with its fleet of four, which included the 9,210 ton twin-screw PRINCIPESSA MAFALDA. Permission for the take over was granted on 1 June.

After the war the RE VITTORIO, sole survivor of the 'Regal' class, continued to run to South America and, as was to be expected, was paired with the PRINCIPESSA MAFALDA in a 'di lusso' fast service. The DUCA D'AOSTA and DUCA DEGLI ABRUZZI, which had been running on the North Atlantic since the war, joined them in 1921–2.

There still remained two NGI subsidiaries – Transoceanica and La Veloce. The former was absorbed on 20 August 1921 together with its fleet of 11 ships, and it came as no surprise three years later when La Veloce, whose fleet had dwindled to three ships, was dissolved on 21 September 1924 and its survivors taken over by NGI.

The war had caused serious delays in the completion of the two 20,000 tonners ordered in 1913–14. The British-built ship, the 21,657 ton GIULIO CESARE, was launched on 7 February 1920 and started her maiden voyage on 4 May 1922 from Genoa to Buenos Aires. At that time she was by far the largest unit of the Italian mercantile marine. Her quadruple-screws were driven by single-reduction geared turbines, which gave her a service speed of 19 knots. Accommodation was provided for 256 first, 306 second and 1,800 third class passengers. But after making a second voyage to South America she was transferred to the New York service.

1922 GIULIO CESARE 21,657 tons
Order placed 1913, launched 1920, maiden voyage 1922.

The 24,281 ton DUILIO was launched at Sestri Ponente on 9 January 1916, but was not ready to start her maiden voyage until 29 October 1923, when she left Genoa for Naples and New York. The success of these two ships and the obsolescence of all but one of the others running on either the North or the South Atlantic, prompted NGI to lay down the 32,583 ton ROMA, which was built by Ansaldo, was fitted with four sets of single-reduction geared turbines and entered the New York service on 21 September 1926.

The 32,650 ton AUGUSTUS, launched on 13 December 1926, was similar in appearance to the ROMA, but her quadruple-screws were connected to four six-cylinder oil engines. She was the largest passenger motor liner in the world and never lost that distinction. Like her consort, the AUGUSTUS was a four-class ship, with accommodation for 302 first class, 338 second, 166 intermediate and 1,310 third class passengers. Her maiden voyage started from Genoa on 12 November 1927 for Naples, Rio de Janeiro, Santos, Montevideo and Buenos Aires.

The addition of the AUGUSTUS to the South American service was most opportune as NGI's prestige had suffered a very serious blow on 25 October 1927 by the loss of the PRINCIPESSA MAFALDA when nearing Rio de Janeiro with 971 passengers and a crew of 288. It appears

1927 AUGUSTUS 32,650 tons
World's largest ever passenger motorship.

that about 90 miles from Abrolhos Island her port propeller shaft broke, water entered the boiler room and the boilers burst. The passengers were alarmed at first, but the captain's explanation that the engines had broken down sufficed to reassure them. Later, when it was noticed that the ship was settling down with a slight list to port, panic broke out and hundreds of passengers crowded the decks. During the confusion, boats were lowered and were so overcrowded that two of them capsized when reaching the water. Although the ship remained afloat for 4½ hours before capsizing and sinking, and despite the fact that four British ships, two French and a German were standing by 314 people perished, including the captain. [4]

The GIULIO CESARE had returned to the South Atlantic in the Autumn of 1925, and was joined by the DUILIO in August 1928, simultaneously with the transfer of the AUGUSTUS to the North Atlantic. Two months later the 12,087 ton twin-screw COLOMBO, a former Transoceanica ship which had been running to New York, started her first voyage to the River Plate. By the end of 1929 all the pre-war NGI units had been scrapped, and the passenger fleet was reduced to seven ships. Their aggregate tonnage was, however, no less than 146,658.

La Veloce's Central American service had been extended after World War I through the recently-opened Panama Canal to Valparaiso, the last steamers to be so employed by them being the BOLOGNA and VENEZUELA (ex-CASERTA). This service was continued by NGI, who built the 11,700 ton motorships ORAZIO and VIRGILIO in 1927 to replace the earlier veterans.

The possibility of a merger of NGI with Lloyd Sabaudo (Chapter 52) and Cosulich (Chapter 60), the other two surviving Italian transatlantic lines, was first publically mentioned in 1927. An important step was taken in 1928, when NGI signed a pooling agreement in respect of the two principal North Atlantic ships of each of the three lines. It had a validity of three years from 1 July 1928.

The world depression of the early 1930s hit the Italian transatlantic lines every bit as much as those of other nations. It had already been necessary to place Cosulich under the control of Lloyd Sabaudo, and with the general situation deteriorating still further it became evident that the amalgamation of NGI and Lloyd Sabaudo could not long be delayed. In the autumn of 1931, soon after the expiry of the pooling arrangement, the Banca Commerciale Italiana invited the directorates of the three lines to attend a conference in Milan to discuss their future. Agreement was soon reached, and on 11 November 1931 the Italian Ministry of Communications announced the forthcoming fusion of NGI and Lloyd Sabaudo, with Cosulich included in the same financial group. These arrangements became effective on 2 January 1932 with the formation of ITALIA FLOTTE RIUNITE COSULICH – LLOYD SABAUDO – NGI. The activities of the new concern are dealt with in Chapter 65.

[1] & Fligli = & Sons.
[2] N.R.P. Bonsor, *North Atlantic Seaway*, Volume 4, pages 1405–08 and 1425–29.
[3] Francesco Ogliari and Lamberto Radogna, *Trasporti Marittimi di Linea*.
[4] Charles Hocking, *Dictionary of Disasters at Sea*, Volume 2.

1. (1884) SINGAPORE
   3,541. 118,71 x 12,83. (389.5 x 42.1). C–1–3. I–S–C2–12. (I–18 (later increased); III–1,000). C. Mitchell & Co, Walker-on-Tyne. 1874 (Mar) launched as ST. OSYTH (Br). 1878 SINGAPORE (Rubattino). 1879 (24/4) FV Genoa–Suez Canal–Bombay. 1881 SINGAPORE (NGI). 1884 (19/11) FV Genoa–Montevideo–Buenos Aires. 1885 resumed eastern service, but occasional S. American voyages. 1910 scrapped at Palermo.
2. (1884) MANILLA
   3,650. 121,76 x 12,86. (399.5 x 42.2). C–1–3. I–S–C2–12. (I–60; III–1,250). Palmers Co Ltd, Jarrow-on-Tyne. 1873 (22/10) launched as WHAMPOA (Watts, Milburn & Co (Br)). 1878 MANILLA (Rubattino). 1879 (24/3) FV Genoa–Suez Canal–Bombay. 1881 MANILLA (NGI). 1884 (18/12) FV Genoa–Montevideo–Buenos Aires. 1885 resumed eastern service, but some subsequent S. American voyages. 1899 (11/5) FV Genoa–Naples–New York (7 RV). 1905 sold. 1907 scrapped.

3. (1885) ABISSINIA
  2,041. 101,49 x 10,97. (333.0 x 36.0). 1–2. I–S–C2–12. A. Leslie &
  Co, Hebburn-on-Tyne (engines R. & W. Hawthorn, Newcastle).
  1881 launched. 1882 (1/3) MV Genoa–Bombay–Singapore–Hong
  Kong. 1885 (21/1) FV Genoa–Montevideo–Buenos Aires. 1885
  (21/11) sailed ditto on 3rd voyage. 1885 (1/12) wrecked on coast
  of Morocco between Casablanca and Mogador.
4. (1885) PERSEO
  4,158. 116,00 x 12,80. (380.6 x 42.0). S–2–3. I–S–C3–14. (I–80;
  II–40; III–1,200). Robert Napier & Sons, Glasgow. 1883 (16/11)
  launched for Raggio. 1884 (15/2) MV Genoa–Las Palmas–
  Montevideo–Buenos Aires. 1885 PERSEO (NGI). 1885 (16/2)
  FV Genoa–Las Palmas–Montevideo–Buenos Aires. 1891 triple-
  expansion engines; 15 knots. 1906 modernised; transferred to
  Marittima Italiana (Syrian line). (See Raggio (31)).
5. (1885) ORIONE
  4,161. 115,81 x 12,83. (380.0 x 42.1). S–2–3. I–S–C3–14. (I–80;
  II–40; III–1,200). Robert Napier & Sons, Glasgow. 1883 (Jun)
  launched for Raggio. 1884 (15/1) MV Genoa–Las Palmas–
  Montevideo–Buenos Aires. 1885 ORIONE (NGI). 1885 (5/3) FV
  Genoa–Las Palmas–Montevideo–Buenos Aires. 1891 triple-expansion engines; 15 knots. 1906 modernised; transferred to
  Marittima Italiana (Syrian line). 1921 scrapped. (See Raggio
  (31)).
6. (1885) SIRIO
  4,141. 115,81 x 12,83. (380.0 x 42.1). S–2–3. I–S–C3–14. (I–80;
  II–40; III–1,200). Robert Napier & Sons, Glasgow. 1883 (26/3)
  launched for Raggio. 1883 (19/6) sailed Glasgow–Genoa. 1883
  (15/7) MV Genoa–Las Palmas–Montevideo–Buenos Aires. 1885
  SIRIO (NGI). 1885 (21/3) FV Genoa–Las Palmas–Montevideo–
  Buenos Aires. 1891 triple-expansion engines; 15 knots. 1906 (4/8)
  wrecked near Cape Palos, Spain (442). (See Raggio (31)).
7. (1885) SCRIVIA
  2,100. 91,49 x 12,28. (300.2 x 40.3). S–1–2. I–S–C2–10. (I–24;
  II–24; III–1,000). Raylton Dixon & Co, Middlesbrough. 1882
  (May) launched for Raggio. 1882 (11/12) MV Genoa–Montevideo–Buenos Aires (5 RV). 1885 SCRIVIA (NGI). 1885 (11/4)
  FV Genoa–Montevideo–Buenos Aires. 1910 SCRIVIA (Soc.
  Nazionale di Servizi Marittimi). 1925 scrapped.
8. (1885) REGINA MARGHERITA
  3,577. 120,69 x 12,80. (396.0 x 42.0). C–2–2. I–S–C2–16. (I &
  II–250; III–1,200). A. McMillan & Son, Dumbarton. 1884 (Jly)
  launched for Rocco Piaggio. 1884 (1/12) MV Genoa–Barcelona–

St. Vincent–Montevideo–Buenos Aires. 1885 REGINA MAR-GHERITA (NGI). 1885 (2/7) FV Genoa–Montevideo–Buenos Aires. 1896 engines T3 by Ansaldo, Genoa; 17 knots. 1898 ran in NGI Egyptian line. 1910 REGINA MARGHERITA (Soc. Nazionale di Servizi Marittimi).

9. (1885) UMBERTO I

2,822. 109,72 x 11,58. (360.0 x 38.0). C–1–2. I–S–C2–13. (I–98; II–80; III–800). A. McMillan & Son, Dumbarton. 1878 (15/8) launched for Rocco Piaggio. 1878 (10/12) MV Genoa–Monte-video–Buenos Aires. 1885 UMBERTO I (NGI). 1885 (18/7) FV Genoa–Montevideo–Buenos Aires. 1894 ran in NGI Egyptian line. 1910 UMBERTO I (Soc. Nazionale di Servizi Marittimi).

10. (1885) ADRIA

2,655. 106,49 x 11,46. (349.4 x 37.6). C–1–3. I–S–C2–10. Caird & Co, Greenock. 1854 (26/8) launched as ETNA (Cunard). 1855 Crimean War troopship. 1856 (5/2) FV Havre–New York (2 RV). 1860 ETNA (Inman). 1871 lengthened from 92,96 metres (305.0 feet) by Laird Bros, Birkenhead; C2 replaced GB2; renamed CITY OF BRISTOL (Inman). 1881 MEXICO (Spanish). 1882 MESSICO (Italian). 1883 SEMPIONE (Italian). 1884 ADRIA (Rocco Piaggio (It)). 1885 ADRIA (NGI). 1885 FV Genoa–Montevideo–Buenos Aires. 1896 scrapped in Italy.

11. (1885) BISAGNO

2,290. 91,83 x 11,34. (301.3 x 37.2). S–1–2. I–S–C2–10. (I–24; II–24; III–1,000). Burrell & Sons, Dumbarton (engines Duncan Stewart & Co, Glasgow). 1884 (20/9) launched for Raggio. 1885 (24/1) MV Genoa–Montevideo–Buenos Aires. 1885 BISAGNO (NGI). 1885 (7/10) FV Genoa–Montevideo–Buenos Aires. 1898 triple-expansion engines. 1898 Genoa–Central America (Regia Marina) (c). 1910 BISAGNO (Soc. Nazionale di Servizi Marittimi). (See Raggio (31)).

12. (1885) VINCENZO FLORIO

2,840. 107,31 x 11,61. (352.1 x 38.1). C–1–3. I–S–C2–12. (I–20; II–24; III–500). A. Stephen & Sons, Glasgow. 1880 (29/3) launched for Florio. 1880 (22/5) MV Catania–Messina–Palermo–New York. 1881 VINCENZO FLORIO (NGI). 1885 transport duties to Eritrea. 1885 (21/10) FV Genoa–Montevideo–Buenos Aires. 1900 (21/5) FV Genoa–Naples–New York. 1910 VINCEN-ZO FLORIO (Soc. Nazionale di Servizi Marittimi). 1913 ditto (Sitmar). 1923 scrapped.

13. (1885) WASHINGTON

2,833. 107,31 x 11,61. (352.1 x 38.1). C–1–3. I–S–C2–12. (I–20; II–24; III–500). A. Stephen & Sons, Glasgow. 1880 (26/5)

launched for Florio. 1880 (19/8) MV Palermo–New York. 1881
WASHINGTON (NGI). 1885 transport duties to Eritrea. 1885
(5/11) FV Genoa–Montevideo–Buenos Aires. 1896 triple-expansion engines; masts reduced to two. 1901 (29/4) FV Genoa–
Naples–New York. 1910 WASHINGTON (Soc. Nazionale di
Servizi Marittimi). 1913 ditto (Sitmar). 1916 (23/5) torpedoed and
sunk off Piombino, Italy, by German submarine U.39.

14. (1885) BORMIDA

2,290. 91,34 x 11,34. (299.7 x 37.2). S–1–2. I–S–C2–10. (I–24;
II–24; III–1,000). Burrell & Sons, Dumbarton (engines Duncan
Stewart & Co, Glasgow). 1884 (10/7) launched for Raggio. 1884
(10/12) FV Genoa–Montevideo–Buenos Aires. 1885 BORMIDA
(NGI). 1885 (19/11) FV Genoa–Montevideo–Buenos Aires. 1897
triple-expansion engines. 1910 BORMIDA (Soc. Nazionale di
Servizi Marittimi). 1913 ditto (Sitmar). 1928 scrapped.

15. (1885) GIAVA

2,713. 101,76 x 11,03. (333.9 x 36.2). S–1–2. I–S–C2–11. (I;
III–1,000). A. Leslie & Co, Hebburn-on-Tyne (engines R. & W.
Hawthorn, Newcastle). 1881 (Sep) launched. 1885 (16/12) FV
Genoa–Montevideo–Valparaiso. 1890 (18/2) FV Genoa–Naples–
New York. 1910 GIAVA (Soc. Nazionale di Servizi Marittimi).
1913 ditto (Marittima Italiana). 1916 (27/2) foundered on voyage
Syracuse–Alexandria.

16. (1885) PARANA

1,105. 67,14 x 9,87. (220.3 x 32.4). 1–2. I–S–C2–10. (III–400). A.
McMillan & Son, Dumbarton (engines M. Paul & Co, Dumbar-
ton). 1880 (23/2) launched as COREBO TREZO (Rocco
Piaggio). 1883 CARMELA (Banco di Sconto, Genoa). 1885
PARANA (NGI). 1885 (25/12) FV Genoa–Montevideo–Buenos
Aires. 1902 scrapped.

17. (1886) PARAGUAY

1,358. 73,38 x 9,93. (240.8 x 32.6). S–1–2. I–S–C2–10. (I; III).
Barclay & Curle, Glasgow. 1870 (25/10) launched as MARINA
(Donaldson). 1870 (Dec) MV Glasgow–Montevideo–Buenos
Aires. 1873 MARINA (Brazil SS Co). 1875 MARIA (Rocco
Piaggio (It)). 1885 PARAGUAY (NGI). 1886 (19/10) FV
Naples–River Plate. 1930 TORERO (Italian); scrapped.

18. (1886) BIRMANIA

2,215. 89,00 x 10,97. (292.0 x 36.0). 1–2. I–S–C2–12. Fratelli
Orlando, Leghorn. 1882 (29/1) launched. 1882 (24/6) MV Genoa–
Bombay. 1886 (28/11) FV Naples–Montevideo–Buenos Aires. 1890
NGI Egyptian line. 1916 (21/5) captured by German submarine
U.39. N.E. of Marittimo; explosives placed on board; sunk.

19. (1886) PLATA
    1,942. 91,43 x 10,36. (300.0 x 34.0). C–1–3. I–S–C2–11. Barrow
    Shipbuilding Co. 1878 (17/4) launched as LASCELLES (John-
    ston (Br)). 1883 AMEDEO (Raggio). 1885 PLATA (NGI). 1886
    (2/1) FV Palermo–New York. 1886 (20/12) FV Genoa–R. Plate.
    1894 (26/6) LV Licata–Palermo–New York (20 RV). 1910
    PLATA (Soc. Nazionale di Servizi Marittimi). 1913 ditto
    (Marittima Italiana). 1916 (3/12) torpedoed and sunk by enemy
    submarine near Alexandria (6).
20. (1887) MARCO MINGHETTI
    2,489. 106,88 x 11,21. (350.7 x 36.8). C–1–3. I–S–C2–12. (I–24;
    III–936). J. & G. Thomson, Glasgow. 1876 (Oct) launched as
    LOUDOUN CASTLE (T. Skinner & Co (Br)). 1886 MARCO
    MINGHETTI (NGI). 1887 (19/3) FV Palermo–New York. 1887
    (2/10) FV Genoa–S. America. 1897 triple-expansion engines;
    masts reduced to two. 1900 (21/2) FV Genoa–Naples–New York
    (13 RV). 1905 (23/10) LV Genoa–R. Plate. 1910 MARCO
    MINGHETTI (Soc. Nazionale di Servizi Marittimi). 1913 ditto
    (Sicilia). 1923 scrapped.
21. (1887) PO
    2,334. 100,48 x 11,21. (329.7 x 36.8). S–1–2. I–S–C2–10. D. & W.
    Henderson, Glasgow. 1880 (24/7) launched as TITANIA
    (Donaldson). 1886 (May) stranded on Anticosti Island; refloated;
    sold. 1887 PO (NGI). 1887 (2/10) FV Genoa–S. America. 1910
    PO (Soc. Nazionale di Servizi Marittimi). 1913 ditto (Sicilia).
    1923 scrapped.
22. (1887) INDIPENDENTE
    2,837. 106,67 x 12,19. (350.0 x 40.0). C–1–3. I–S–C2–12. A.
    Stephen & Sons, Glasgow. 1883 (20/6) launched. 1883 (26/8) MV
    Palermo–New York (20 RV). 1887 (Dec) FV Naples–Rio de
    Janeiro. 1903 TEBE (NGI – Egyptian line); masts reduced to
    two. 1910 TEBE (Soc. Nazionale di Servizi Marittimi). 1913 ditto
    (Sicilia). 1929 scrapped at Genoa.
23. (1888) GOTTARDO
    2,837. 106,67 x 12,19. (350.0 x 40.0). C–1–3. I–S–C2–12. A.
    Stephen & Sons, Glasgow. 1883 (18/9) launched. 1884 (7/1) MV
    Palermo–New York. 1888 (1/6) FV Genoa–Rio de Janeiro–
    Montevideo–Buenos Aires. 1903 MEMFI (NGI – Egyptian line.
    1910 MEMFI (Soc. Nazionale di Servizi Marittimi). 1913 ditto
    (Sicilia). 1927 (2/2) stranded on coast of Sardinia; refloated;
    scrapped.
24. (1888) ARCHIMEDE
    2,839. 106,70 x 12,19. (350.1 x 40.0) C–1–3. I–S–C2–12. (I–20;

II–56; III–550). A. Stephen & Sons, Glasgow. Laid down for Florio. 1881 (22/11) launched for NGI. 1882 (7/2) MV Catania–Palermo–New York. 1888 (15/6) FV Naples–Cadiz–Montevideo–Buenos Aires. 1899 (3/3) FV Genoa–Naples–New York. 1903 CAIRO (NGI – Egyptian line). 1905 (5/3) wrecked near Alexandria.

25. (1891) ARNO

3,406. 106,52 x 12,25. (349.5 x 40.2). S–1–2. I–S–C2–12. Caird & Co, Greenock (engines D. Schiattino, Genoa (1882)). Laid down as ALSATIA. 1872 (30/3) launched as FRISIA (Hapag). 1872 (21/8) MV Hamburg–New York. 1888 FRISIA (Br). 1889 TEMERARIO (It). 1890 ARNO (Banco di Genova, Genoa). 1891 ARNO (NGI). 1891 (4/12) FV Genoa–Montevideo–Buenos Aires. 1898 converted to coal carrier. 1901 coal hulk at Genoa. 1902 scrapped in Italy.

26. (1895) SEMPIONE

3,149. 106,85 x 12,01. (350.6 x 39.4). S–1–2. I–S–C2–12. (I–130; III–1,150). W. Denny & Bros, Dumbarton. 1877 (27/6) launched as GERMAN (Union). 1895 SEMPIONE (NGI). 1895 (16/12) FV Naples–R. Plate. 1899 (3/2) FV Genoa–Naples–New York. 1902 coal hulk at Genoa. 1903 scrapped at Genoa.

27. (1902) UMBRIA

5,020. 122,32 x 14,20. (401.4 x 46.6). 1–2. S–Q4–14. (I–66; II–90; III–1,016). Fratelli Orlando, Leghorn. 1901 (8/8) launched. 1902 (19/5) MV Genoa–Naples–New York. 1902 (29/7) FV Genoa–R. Plate. 1912 UMBRIA (La Veloce). 1912 (1/6) FV Genoa–S. America. 1912 SAN PAULO (Italia). 1913 (10/1) FV Genoa–S. America. 1913 UMBRIA (Sitmar). 1932 scrapped.

28. (1905) SARDEGNA

5,255. 127,52 x 14,41. (418.4 x 47.3). 1–2. S–T3–14. (I–80; II–90; III–1,324). Società Escercizio Bacini, Riva Trigoso (engines N. Odero & Co, Sestri Ponente). 1901 (4/5) launched. 1902 (4/1) MV Genoa–Naples–New York. 1905 (6/6) LV ditto. 1905 (3/8) FV Genoa–S. America. 1912 SARDEGNA (Sitmar). 1928 scrapped.

29. (1906) LIGURIA

4,865. 122,83 x 14,20. (403.0 x 46.6). 1–2. S–T3–14. (I–66; II–90; III–1,194). G. Ansaldo & Co, Sestri Ponente. 1901 (15/1) launched. 1901 (16/2) MV Naples–New York. 1906 (17/7) FV Genoa–R. Plate (1 RV). 1909 (21/4) LV Genoa–Naples–New York. 1911 AFFON (Russian). 1928 scrapped.

30. (1906) LOMBARDIA

4,815. 122,83 x 14,20. (403.0 x 46.6). 1–2. S–T3–14. (I–66; II–90;

III–1,194. G. Ansaldo & Co, Sestri Ponente. 1901 (24/4) launched. 1901 (12/6) MV Naples–New York. 1906 (11/10) FV Genoa–Barcelona–R. Plate (1 RV). 1911 (21/3) LV Genoa–Naples–New York. 1911 JEROUSALIM (Russian). 1928 scrapped.

31. (1906) CAMPANIA
   9,001. 143,25 x 17,31. (470.0 x 56.8). 1–4. 2S–T6–13. (I–70; III–2,200). Palmers Co Ltd, Jarrow-on-Tyne. 1901 (29/8) launched as BRITISH EMPIRE (British Shipowners); ran for Phoenix, Antwerp–New York. 1906 CAMPANIA (NGI); passenger accommodation fitted. 1906 (30/10) FV Genoa–Naples–S. America (2 RV). 1907 (7/3) FV Genoa–Naples–New York. 1910 CAMPANIA (Northwest Transport (c)). 1910 CAMPANELLO (Uranium). 1916 FLAVIA (Cunard). 1918 (24/8) torpedoed and sunk by German submarine U.107 off Tory Island, Northern Ireland.

32. (1906) SICILIA
   5,229. 127,49 x 14,41. (418.3 x 47.3). 1–2. S–T3–14. (I–80; II–90; III–1,292). Società Esercizio Bacini, Riva Trigoso (engines N. Odero & Co, Sestri Ponente). 1900 (Nov) launched. 1901 (12/8) MV Genoa–Naples–New York. 1906 (2/11) FV Genoa–S. America. 1912 SICILIA (Sitmar). 1929 scrapped.

33. 1908 REGINA ELENA
   7,856. 145,26 x 16,30. (476.6 x 53.5). 2–2. 2S–Q8–16. (I–100; II–124; III–1,200). Cantieri Ligure–Anconetani, Ancona. 1907 (3/12) launched. 1908 (9/4) MV Genoa–R. Plate. 1916 Italian troop transport. 1918 (4/1) torpedoed and sunk by enemy submarine in Adriatic.

34. 1908 RE VITTORIO
   7,847. 145,29 x 16,24. (476.7 x 53.3). 2–2. 2S–Q8–16. (I–100; II–124; III–1,200). N. Odero & Co, Genoa. 1907 (24/11) launched. 1908 (3/8) MV Genoa–R. Plate. 1916 Italian troop transport. 1918 (4/9) resumed Genoa–R. Plate. 1928 scrapped.

35. 1909 PRINCIPE UMBERTO
   7,833. 145,72 x 16,30. (478.1 x 53.5). 2–2. 2S–Q8–16. (I–100; II–124; III–1,200). Cantieri Navale Riuniti, Palermo. 1908 (31/3) launched. 1909 (13/5) MV Genoa–R. Plate. 1916 Italian troop transport. 1916 (8/6) torpedoed and sunk by enemy submarine off Vallona.

36. (1912) DUCA DEGLI ABRUZZI
   7,793. 145,01 x 16,27. (475.8 x 53.4). 2–2. 2S–Q8–16. (I–66; II–122; III–1,740). Cantieri Navale Riuniti, La Spezia (engines N. Odero & Co, Sestri Ponente). 1907 (5/5) launched. 1908 (4/2)

MV Genoa–Naples–New York. 1911 (22/11) LV Naples–New York. 1912 Italian auxiliary cruiser. 1912 (2/10) FV Genoa–R. Plate. 1914 (11/10) resumed Genoa–Naples–New York. 1922 (23/5) LV ditto; transferred to S. American service. 1929 scrapped.

37. (1912) DUCA D'AOSTA

7,804. 144,77 x 16,24. (475.0 x 53.3). 2–2. 2S–Q8–16. (I–66; II–122; III–1,740. Cantieri Navale Siciliani, Palermo (engines N. Odero & Co, Sestri Ponente). 1908 (29/9) launched. 1909 (9/11) MV Genoa–Naples–New York. 1912 (20/11) LV ditto. 1912 (30/12) FV Genoa–R. Plate. 1914 (7/7) resumed Genoa–Naples–New York. 1921 (20/6) LV ditto; transferred to S. American service. 1929 scrapped.

38. (1918) PRINCIPESSA MAFALDA

9,210. 147,88 x 16,94. (485.2 x 55.6). 2–2. 2S–Q8–16. Società Esercizio Bacini, Riva Trigoso. 1908 (22/10) launched for Lloyd Italiano. 1909 (30/3) MV Genoa–Naples–Buenos Aires. 1914–18 laid up at Taranto, Italy. 1918 PRINCIPESSA MAFALDA (NGI). 1927 (25/10) foundered off Bahia (303).

39. 1922 GIULIO CESARE

21,657. 183,60 x 23,31. (602.4 x 76.5). 2–2–C. 4S–ST(SR)–19. (I–256; II–306; III–1,800). Swan, Hunter & Wigham Richardson, Wallsend-on-Tyne (engines Wallsend Slipway Co Ltd). 1913 (Dec) ordered. 1920 (7/2) launched. 1922 (4/5) MV Genoa–Naples–Buenos Aires (2 RV). 1922 (11/8) FV Genoa–Naples–New York. 1925 resumed Genoa–Naples–Buenos Aires. 1931 (22/10) LV ditto. 1932 GIULIO CESARE (Italia). 1932 (24/3) FV Genoa–Naples–Buenos Aires. 1933 transferred to S. African service. 1937 GIULIO CESARE (Lloyd Triestino). 1944 (11/9) bombed and sunk at Trieste. 1949 refloated; scrapped.

40. (1923) TAORMINA

8,921. 146,90 x 17,77. (482.0 58.3). 1–2. 2S–T6–16. (I–60; III–2,500). D. & W. Henderson, Glasgow. 1908 (15/2) launched for Italia. 1912 TAORMINA (Lloyd Italiano). 1918 ditto (NGI). 1919 (10/6) FV Genoa–New York. 1923 (8/8) LV ditto. 1923 FV Genoa–S. America. 1929 scrapped at Savona.

41. (1924) AMERICA

8,996. 145,23 x 16,97. (476.5 x 55.7). 2–2. 2S–T6–16. (I–30; II–220; III–2,400). Cantieri Navale Riuniti, Muggiano (engines Wallsend Slipway Co Ltd). 1908 (1/11) launched for La Veloce. 1912 AMERICA (NGI). 1912 (23/4) FV Genoa–Naples–New York–Philadelphia. 1924 (Apr) LV Genoa–Naples–Boston. 1924 FV Genoa–Naples–S. America. 1928 scrapped.

42. 1927 AUGUSTUS (M/S)

32,650. 203.07 [216,40] x 25,23. (666.3 [710.0] x 82.8). 2–2. 4S–2SC.DA–19. (I–302; II–338; intermediate 166; III–1,310). G. Ansaldo & Co, Sestri Ponente. World's largest ever passenger motorship. 1926 (13/12) launched. 1927 (12/11) MV Genoa–Naples–Buenos Aires. 1928 FV Genoa–Naples–New York. 1931 (28/12) LV ditto. 1932 (9/1) AUGUSTUS (Italia). (See Italia (65)).

43. (1928) DUILIO

24,281. 183,60 x 23,25. (602.4 x 76.3). 2–2–C. 4S–ST(SR)–19. (I–280; II–670; III–600). G. Ansaldo & Co, Sestri Ponente. 1914 (30/5) keel laid. 1916 (9/1) launched. 1923 (29/10) MV Genoa–Naples–New York. 1928 (Aug) Genoa–Naples–Buenos Aires. 1931 (12/11) LV ditto. 1932 DUILIO (Italia). 1932 (7/1) FV Genoa–Naples–Buenos Aires. 1932 transferred to S. African service. 1937 DUILIO (Lloyd Triestino). 1944 (10/7) bombed and sunk at Trieste. 1948 refloated; scrapped.

44. (1928) COLOMBO

12,087. 157,88 x 19,50. (518.0 x 64.0). 2–2. 2S–Q8–16. Palmers Co Ltd, Jarrow-on-Tyne. 1915 (Oct) launched as SAN GENNARO (Sicula Americana). 1917 completed as ditto (Transoceanica); cargo only; 10,917 tons. 1921 passenger accommodation added in Italy; (I–100; II–700; III–2,000); tonnage 12,087; COLOMBO (NGI). 1921 (23/11) FV Naples–New York. 1928 (18/10) FV Genoa–Naples–Buenos Aires. 1932 COLOMBO (Italia). 1937 COLOMBO (Lloyd Triestino). 1941 (8/4) scuttled at Massaua, Eritrea; later raised. 1949 scrapped.

Note. The RAFFAELE RUBATTINO and DOMENICO BALDUINO are said to have made one or more South American voyages in 1890 but this is not so. The voyages may, however, have taken place earlier or later.

FUNNEL: Black; broad white band.
FLAG: Red and white quarters. A golden lion in upper white; a red cross in lower white.

Chapter 37

(1886–90)

COMPAGNIE FRAISSINET

(French)

Founded at Marseilles in 1836, the COMPAGNIE FRAISSINET was one of the very earliest of the French steamship lines. By 1869 it was running two principal services – the old-established one from Marseilles to Constantinople (Istanbul) and the Black Sea, and one to India, started when the Suez Canal was opened to traffic in November 1869.

It was decided to despatch the 2,703 ton iron screw steamer TIBET on 12 December 1886 from Marseilles for Montevideo and Buenos Aires via Genoa and St. Vincent. The experiment evidently came up to expectations as, after the start of her fourth round voyage, the TIBET was joined by the 2,269 ton LIBAN on 1 November 1887 and the 2,272 ton STAMBOUL on 4 December. The last-mentioned, as her name implies, was transferred from the Company's Constantinople service, the other two having previously run to India. The TIBET was built at La Seyne, but the LIBAN and STAMBOUL came from Clydeside, as did the 2,055 ton AMÉRIQUE, which sailed from Marseilles for Rosario on 8 November 1888.

In August 1889 the Compagnie Fraissinet obtained a mail contract for a service from Marseilles to the west coast of Africa and the Congo, to be shared jointly with the Chargeurs Réunis, and as there were already three French services of long standing in operation to South America as well as two more recent ones, Fraissinet decided to withdraw from this trade, their last sailing being taken by the TIBET on 1 September 1980.

1. (1886) TIBET
    2,703. 101,19 x 12.19. (332.0 x 40.0). S–1–2. I&S–S–C2–12. Forges & Chantiers de la Méditerranée, La Seyne. 1883 (22/9) launched. 1886 (12/12) FV Marseilles–Genoa–Montevideo–Buenos Aires. 1890 (1/9) LV ditto. 1922 scrapped.
2. (1887) LIBAN
    2,269. 91,52 x 11,03. (300.3 x 36.2). S–1–2. I–S–C2–12. R. Napier & Sons, Glasgow. 1882 (Sep) launched. 1887 (1/11) FV Marseilles–Genoa–Montevideo–Buenos Aires. 1890 (1/9) LV ditto. 1903 (7/6) rammed and sunk at Marseilles by INSULAIRE (Fraissinet). (100).

3. (1887) STAMBOUL

     2,272. 91,49 x 11,06 (300.2 x 36.3). S–1–2. I–S–C2–12. A. McMillan & Son, Dumbarton. 1881 (Oct) launched. 1887 (4/12) FV Marseilles–Genoa–Montevideo–Buenos Aires–Rosario. Omitted from *Lloyd's Register* after 1915–16.

4. (1888) AMÉRIQUE

     2,059. 91,43 x 11,12. (300.0 x 36.5). S–1–2. I–S–C2–12. A. McMillan & Son, Dumbarton. 1879 (Nov) launched. 1888 (8/11) FV Marseilles–Genoa–Montevideo–Buenos Aires–Rosario. 1904 (24/3) sunk in collision in Straits of Messina on voyage from Marseilles to Piraeus.

FUNNEL: White; black top.

FLAG: Burgee with red, white and blue horizontal stripes; 'F & CIE' on the white.

Chapter 38

1887–91

FRATELLI LAVARELLO

(Società di Navigazione a Vapore Fratelli Lavarello)

(Italian)

The collapse of G.B. LAVARELLO & Co (Chapter 14) in 1883 was by no means the end of the road for the Lavarello family. Although the three surviving steamers were bought by the late Captain Lavarello's partner, Matteo Bruzzo, Pietro and Enrico Laverello decided to continue the business name and South American activities of their father, and founded the SOCIETÀ DI NAVIGAZIONE A VAPORE FRATELLI LAVARELLO, also in Genoa.

Orders were placed in due course with Wigham Richardson & Co of Walker-on-Tyne, builders of the G.B. Lavarello ships, for the 1,887 ton iron screw steamer GIOVANNI BATTISTA LAVARELLO, which sailed from Genoa on 12 January 1887 on her maiden voyage to Montevideo and Buenos Aires, via St. Vincent for coal. The Uruguayan port was reached in 20 days, and the homeward voyage, completed in 23 days, was made via Santos and Rio de Janeiro.

The sister ships ROSARIO, ADELAIDE LAVARELLO and CITTÀ DI GENOVA, all products of the same builders, followed in 1887–9, while a fifth steamer, the 2,627 ton AQUILA, built of steel and, surprisingly, propelled by twin-screws, was completed in time to start her

1889 ADELAIDE LAVARELLO 1,916 tons
One of six ships built for Fratelli Lavarello.

307

maiden voyage from Genoa on 7 September 1889 with a full complement of 30 first class and 1,100 steerage passengers. She had a service speed of 15 knots compared with the 12 knots of her predecessors, and reached the River Plate in 17 days. It can be assumed that her object was to compete with the NORD AMERICA of La Veloce, successors to M. Bruzzo & Co. However, the AQUILA was very extravagant on coal and within less than two years, having been running at an appreciable loss, she was handed over at Buenos Aires to the Chilean Government, who commissioned her as the transport CASMA.

An even larger and equally fast ship, the 3,794 ton single-screw CITTÀ DI VENEZIA, was ordered from C.S. Swan & Hunter on Tyneside. She left there on 1 December 1890 for Genoa, but never ran for Lavarello, becoming instead the Rotterdam Lloyd SPARTAN.

Fratelli Lavarello also commissioned two second-hand steamers in 1889 – the 3,158 ton MENTANA, built in 1868 as the Hamburg American WESTPHALIA, which was considerably modernised 10 years later and had had two other changes of name, together with the 3,142 ton CITTÀ DI NAPOLI, built in 1869 as the Hapag SILESIA, which had also had two subsequent owners.

The sale of the AQUILA and the CITTÀ DI VENEZIA were obvious signs that the Lavarello brothers were in financial difficulties, but even more significant was the fact that the St. Vincent agents of Cory Brothers, the London firm of coal exporters, refused to fuel the GIOVANNI BATTISTA LAVARELLO when she called there in February 1891. In fact, this was the beginning of the end, and at a meeting of creditors on 14 March of the same year it was decided to place the Society in liquidation. The six surviving steamers were acquired by La Veloce (Chapter 35).

1. 1887 GIOVANNI BATTISTA LAVARELLO
    1,861. 82,29 x 10,45. (270.0 x 34.3). S–1–2. S–S–T3–12. (III–1,100). Wigham Richardson & Co, Walker-on-Tyne. 1886 (16/10) launched. 1886 (2/12) sailed Tyne–Genoa. 1887 (12/1) MV Genoa–St. Vincent (for coal)–Montevideo–Buenos Aires–Santos–Rio de Janeiro–Genoa. 1891 (Feb) refused coal at St. Vincent. 1891 LAS PALMAS (La Veloce). 1891 (10/10) FV Genoa–S. America. 1905 JONIO (NGI). 1915 (4/11) torpedoed and sunk by enemy submarine off Algerian coast.
2. 1887 ROSARIO
    1,957. 85,95 x 10,73. (282.0 x 35.2). S–1–2. I–S–T3–12. (III–1,100) Wigham Richardson & Co, Walker-on-Tyne. 1887 (17/9) launched. 1887 (1/12) MV Genoa–St. Vincent (for coal)–

308

Montevideo–Buenos Aires–Rosario. 1891 ROSARIO (La Veloce). 1891 (29/3) FV Genoa–S. America. 1898 DJURJURA (Cie Mixte (Fr)). 1915 (23/12) sunk in collision.

3. 1889 ADELAIDE LAVARELLO
   1,916. 91,43 x 10,76. (300.0 x 35.3). S–1–2. S–S–T3–12. (III–1,100). Wigham Richardson & Co, Walker-on-Tyne. 1888 (4/12) launched. 1889 (20/2) MV Genoa–St. Vincent (for coal)–Montevideo–Buenos Aires–Rosario. 1891 RIO JANEIRO (La Veloce). 1891 (29/9) FV Genoa–S. America. 1899 ALSACE (SGTM (Fr)). 1923 scrapped.

4. 1889 CITTÀ DI GENOVA
   1,936. 91,43 x 10,76 (300.0 x 35.3). S–1–2. S–S–T3–12. (III–1,100). Wigham Richardson & Co, Walker-on-Tyne. 1889 (18/2) launched. 1889 (Apr) MV Genoa–St. Vincent (for coal)–Montevideo–Buenos Aires. 1891 CITTÀ DI GENOVA (La Veloce). 1891 (12/4) FV Genoa–S. America. 1898 SAVOIE (SGTM (Fr)). 1927 scrapped.

5. 1889 AQUILA
   2,627. 103,47 x 11,95. (339.5 x 39.2). S–1–2. S–2S–T6–15. (I–30; III–1,000). Wigham Richardson & Co, Walker-on-Tyne. 1889 (29/6) launched. 1889 (7/9) MV Genoa–St. Vincent (for coal)–Montevideo–Buenos Aires. 1891 (13/6) LV Genoa–Buenos Aires (9½ RV). 1891 CASMA (Chilean Govt transport). 1905 IRRARAZAVAL (Ecuador Navy auxiliary cruiser).

6. (1889) MENTANA
   3,158. 103,60 x 12,20. (339.9 x 40.0). S–2–2. I–S–C2–12. (I–90; II–130; III–520). Caird & Co, Greenock. 1868 (24/6) launched as WESTPHALIA (Hapag). 1868 (16/9) MV Hamburg–New York. 1878 C2 replaced I (2); funnels increased from one to two. 1887 ATLANTICA (Br). 1888 PROVINCIA DI SAO PAOLO (Gazzo & Schiaffino (Italian)). 1889 MENTANA (Fratelli Lavarello). 1889 (7/3) FV Genoa–S.America. 1891 SUD AMERICA (La Veloce). 1891 (14/1) FV Genoa–S. America. 1901 scrapped at Genoa.

7. (1889) CITTÀ DI NAPOLI
   3,142. 103,60 x 12,20. (339.9 x 40.0). S–1–2. I–S–C2–12. (I–90; II–130; III–520). Caird & Co, Greenock. 1869 (14/4) launched as SILESIA (Hapag). 1869 (23/6) MV Hamburg–New York. 1877 C2 replaced I (2). 1887 PACIFICA (Br). 1888 CITTÀ DI NAPOLI (Solari & Schiaffino) (Italian). 1889 ditto (Fratelli Lavarello). 1889 (Nov) FV Genoa–S. America. 1891 MONTEVIDEO (La Veloce). 1891 (21/11) FV Genoa–S. America. 1899 (2/12) wrecked near Island of Lobos, River Plate.

— —— CITTÀ DI VENEZIA

3,794. 174,93 x 13,50. (377.1 x 44.3). S–1–2. S–S–T3–12. C.S. Swan & Hunter, Wallsend-on-Tyne (engines Wallsend Slipway Co Ltd). 1890 (13/9) launched. 1890 (1/12) sailed R. Tyne–Genoa (arr 10/12); did not run for Lavarello. 1891 SPARTAN (Rotterdam Lloyd). 1896 ANGAMOS (Chilean Government). 1913 scrapped at Valparaiso.

Chapter 39

(1887–91)

COMPAGNIE NATIONALE DE NAVIGATION

(French)

The COMPAGNIE NATIONALE DE NAVIGATION was founded at Marseilles in 1879. A service of steamships was established between Marseilles and French Indo-China and by 1886, when the fleet consisted of eight steamers varying in tonnage between 2,900 and 3,700, some sailings began to New York also.

Finding itself even then with some surplus tonnage, the Company despatched the 3,075 ton CHERIBON from Marseilles on 26 September 1887 for Rio de Janeiro, Montevideo and Buenos Aires. She was, in fact, the ship that had inaugurated the New York service a year previously. She and her successors had accommodation for 24 first, 24 second and 1,600 steerage passengers.

The HINDOUSTAN, which had been bought second-hand in 1886 and was the only unit with a name that did not start with the letter 'C', sailed to South America on 20 October 1888, having been seriously damaged by fire at Marseilles a year previously.

Sailings to South America continued spasmodically for three more years, ships taking part being the CHANDERNAGOR, CANTON CACHAR, and CACHEMIRE, which were also detailed to the North Atlantic from time to time.

During the second half of 1890 there was a financial crisis in Argentina,

1883 CACHAR 3,645 tons
Built for French Indo-China service but sailed to the River Plate in 1888.

311

which resulted in a virtual cessation of immigration. In consequence the South American service was withdrawn, the last sailing being taken by the CACHEMIRE, which left Buenos Aires on 15 November 1891 for Marseilles.

The New York service continued irregularly until 1896, after which the ships ran exclusively between Marseilles, Saigon and Haiphong until 1904 when, at the conclusion of the 25 year period of its statutory existence, the Company went into voluntary liquidation. The surviving ships were bought by Messageries Maritimes and Chargeurs Réunis.

1. (1887) CHERIBON
     3,075. 103,99 x 12,28. (341.2 x 40.3). S–1–2. I–S–C2–11. Wm. Denny & Bros, Dumbarton. 1882 (15/7) launched. 1887 (26/9) FV Marseilles–S. America. 1900 CHERIBON (Chilean). 1902 (11/4) wrecked on Remedios Point, Panama.
2. (1888) HINDOUSTAN
     2,953. 94,69 x 12,25. (310.7 x 40.2). S–1–2. I–S–C2–11. Palmers Co Ltd, Jarrow-on-Tyne. 1881 (23/11) launched as HINDOUSTAN (Fr). 1886 ditto (Cie Nationale). 1887 (24/10) damaged by fire at Marseilles; scuttled. 1887 (10/11) refloated; reconditioned. 1888 (20/10) FV Marseilles–S. America. 1898 HINDOUSTAN (Br). 1901 MUSASHINO MARU (Jap). 1905 (6/2) wrecked on Elliot Island.
3. (1888) CHANDERNAGOR
     3,075. 103,99 x 12,28. (341.2 x 40.3). S–1–2. I–S–C2–11. Wm. Denny & Bros, Dumbarton. 1882 (5/6) launched. 1888 (Nov) FV Marseilles–S. America. 1899 ALEXANDRE III (Fr). 1902 (10/3) sunk in collision with ss ASHMADI (Br) at Jeddah.
4. (1888) CANTON
     3,721. 115,69 x 12,19. (379.6 x 40.0). S–1–2. I–S–C2–11. Forges & Chantiers de la Méditerranée, La Seyne. 1882 (Jun) launched. 1888 (1/12) FV Marseilles–S. America. 1898 PIERRE LE GRAND (Fr). 1899 (17/12) sailed Pera–Marseilles; went missing (45).
5. (1888) CACHAR
     3,645. 104,99 x 12,50. (344.5 x 41.0). S–1–2. I&S–S–C2–11. Forges & Chantiers de la Méditerranée, La Seyne. 1883 (30/10) launched. 1888 (29/12) FV Marseilles–S. America. 1904 CACHAR (Messageries Maritimes). 1914 scrapped at Genoa.
6. (1889) CACHEMIRE
     3,360. 104,99 x 12,50. (344.5 x 41.0). S–1–2. I&S–S–C2–11. Forges & Chantiers de la Méditerranée, La Seyne. 1883 (29/12)

launched. 1889 (20/10) FV Marseilles–S. America. 1891 (15/11)
LV Buenos Aires–Marseilles. 1902 BITHYNIE (Paquet). 1907
scrapped in Italy.
All steamers carried 1–24; II–24; III–1,600.

FUNNEL: Black; broad blue band.
FLAG: White; blue disc centrally in the hoist and red disc centrally
       in the fly; letter 'C' above 'N' in blue between the discs.

Chapter 40

(1887–1932)

COMPAÑÍA TRASATLÁNTICA

(Spanish)

The COMPAÑÍA TRASATLÁNTICA was established in Barcelona on 1 June 1881, but its Spanish activities can be traced back to 1856, when Don Antonio López y López, afterwards the first Marqués de Comillas, founded the firm of A. López in Alicante. To begin with, a service of steamers was run between Alicante, Barcelona and Marseilles, but in September 1861 a mail service was arranged between Spain, Cuba, Puerto Rico and San Domingo, and by 1881 continued expansion was responsible for the formation of a limited company, COMPAÑÍA TRASATLÁNTICA. The head office was transferred to Barcelona and this not only resulted in the transatlantic terminal being changed from Cadiz to Barcelona, with two sailings a month, as before, but also the addition of a third service from Santander and Coruña to Puerto Rico and Havana.

Completely new lines came into operation, one by one, including a mail service between Liverpool, Spain and the Philippine Islands via the Suez Canal, previously in the hands of the Marqués de Campo. Another was from Cadiz to La Guaira, Puerto Cabello, Savanilla, Cartagena and Panama, and there was one from Barcelona to Fernando Po. At the turn of the century, a feeder service between Havana and New York, started in the 1880s, developed into an important through line from Spain to New York, Havana and Vera Cruz. [1]

During the years 1881–3 the 3,460 ton ANTONIO LÓPEZ, the 3,488 ton CATALUÑA and the 3,488 ton CIUDAD DE SANTANDER, all built by Wm. Denny & Bros of Dumbarton, were among the new steamers commissioned. As completed, all three were virtually sister ships except that the first-named was built of steel and the other two of iron. But during the construction of the CATALUÑA and CIUDAD DE SANTANDER it was decided to substitute clipper for straight stems, [2] and thus conform with the ANTONIO LÓPEZ.

As a speculation between William McKinnon, Gray & Daws and Wm. Denny & Bros, the keel of the 5,195 ton JELUNGA was laid on 25 January 1887 and she was launched on 22 August 1887 under that name. She was chartered by the Compañía Trasatlántica, probably before her trials on 27 November, and bought by them soon afterwards to become the pioneer unit of their new service under Spanish Government contract between Barcelona and Buenos Aires. [3] Understandably, she was renamed BUENOS AIRES. She was a steel three-masted single-screw ship, with quadruple-expansion engines giving her a service speed of 15 knots. Her passenger accommodation consisted of 83 first class, 30 second and about 130 steerage berths, her maiden voyage commencing from Barcelona on 28 December 1887 for Tenerife, Montevideo and Buenos Aires. Her fifth and last voyage on this route started from Marseilles on 22 March 1889. Surprisingly, her next voyages were from Liverpool and Barcelona to Manila via the Suez Canal, and there is no evidence that she visited South America again until World War I. From time to time, she proceeded to Havana and Vera Cruz, and later to New York *en route* to these ports. She was refitted by Denny in 1893, when it would seem that her accommodation became 160 first, 40 second and 1,000 steerage, and it may well have been at this time that her masts were reduced from three to two.

Two further Denny ships were ordered by the Compañía Trasatlántica immediately after the commissioning of the BUENOS AIRES – the ALFONSO XIII and REINA MARIA CRISTINA, which were intended for the River Plate service. [4] In fact, the ALFONSO XIII sailed from Marseilles on 22 October 1889 and from Barcelona three days later on her maiden voyage to Buenos Aires, but her normal run was between Barcelona, Havana and Vera Cruz although she made a second trip to South America in 1891. A year previously a near-sister ship, the ALFONSO XII (II), a product of Wigham Richardson of Tyneside, made one round voyage to Montevideo and Buenos Aires and later became a victim of the Spanish–American War. (It may be mentioned in parenthesis that the ALFONSO XII (I), built in 1875, was wrecked in the Canaries in 1885).

In view of the shortness of the BUENOS AIRES' spell in the River Plate trade and the lack of evidence of any South America voyages at all by the REINA MARIA CRISTINA and, despite her name, by the MONTEVIDEO, which, like the BUENOS AIRES, was built as a speculation and bought by the Compañía Trasatlántica, [5] the implication is that the limited volume of traffic then offering to Uruguay and Argentina did not justify the use of such large vessels. Further, it seems evident that the original intention was for the service to take place monthly or even fortnightly, whereas for some years the annual total of round voyages appears to have varied between four and six.

The CIUDAD DE SANTANDER made one or more South American voyages each year from 1889 for five or six years, and would probably have continued at least until the outbreak of the Spanish–American War in 1898 but for the fact that after leaving Barcelona for Montevideo and

Buenos Aires on 2 May 1895, she stranded in fog on Lobos Island, Uruguay, 22 days later. The amidships part of the ship was lying on a stony bottom, whereas she was afloat fore and aft. All passengers, crew and cargo were saved, but the ship became a total loss.

Another unit, the 2,679 ton ESPAÑA, also made a round voyage to South America in 1891. She had been built as long previously as 1873 by Robert Napier & Sons of Glasgow as the Castle Line EDINBURGH CASTLE, was acquired by Lopez in 1880 and was scrapped at Marseilles in 1898.

A more prolific ship than any dealt with so far was the 3,460 ton ANTONIO LÓPEZ, whose South American round voyages numbered 10 or more. However, she was one of five ships lost by Compañía Trasatlántica during the Spanish–American War, which broke out on 21 April 1898. The ANTONIO LÓPEZ sailed from Buenos Aires for Barcelona on 2 January 1898, so this was either her last or last but one voyage from South America. A sister ship, the CATALUÑA, had made one voyage to Buenos Aires in 1892.

Last of the ships known to have run to South America before the war was the 3,084 ton CIUDAD DE CADIZ, launched by Lobnitz, Coulborn & Co of Renfrew in November 1878 for A. López y Cia. She made four round voyages to Buenos Aires in 1893, at least three in 1894 and probably a few more subsequently.

The Cuban Rebellion of 1896 resulted in the shipment of over 200,000 Spanish troops to that island. All available Spanish passenger liners were chartered by the Spanish Government, hence the fact that only one South American voyage by the Company has been recorded during the year. In their turn, they chartered many steamers from foreign lines – mostly British – but four ships were purchased outright, including the British India TARA, which was renamed P. DE SATRÚSTEGUI.

1894 P. DE SATRÚSTEGUI 4,713 tons
For many years a consort of LEON XIII to Argentina.

Similarly, only one sailing to the River Plate has been discovered during the war year of 1898 or the following year.

After the war the P. DE SATRÚSTEGUI made a number of voyages between Liverpool, Barcelona, the Suez Canal and Manila, as did another ex-British India ship, the TAROBA, which had been renamed LEON XIII. Part of their duties at this time included the evacuation of Spanish troops from the Philippine Islands. In due course, the P. DE SATRÚSTEGUI sailed from Liverpool to Barcelona, which she left on 24 November 1899 for Genoa, but when about 40 miles east of Valencia collided with the Wilson Line BASSANO, whose bows were badly crumpled. The Spanish ship suffered only slight damage, returned to Barcelona after calling at Genoa and left again on 27 November for Buenos Aires. The P. DE SATRÚSTEGUI made occasional South American sailings in 1900–01, four or five in both 1902 and 1903 and from 1904–13 maintained a regular monthly service in conjunction with the LEON XIII, whose River Plate sailings in 1901 numbered at least four.

A short-lived service was introduced by the 2,101 ton MEXICO, formerly the British TRENTHAM HALL of 1875, which left Liverpool on 23 March 1900 for the Straits of Magellan and Valparaiso, outwards via Montevideo and homewards via Rio de Janeiro. She was succeeded by the 2,359 ton SAN AGUSTIN, which sailed from Liverpool on 24 May 1900 and arrived back there on 15 September, after an itinerary very much the same as her predecessor's except that she called at Rio de Janeiro on the outward voyage and at Montevideo on the homeward. The MEXICO's second voyage started from Liverpool on 22 July and the SAN AGUSTIN's on 24 September. Both again proceeded to Valparaiso, but the SAN AGUSTIN's steering gear was disabled in Smythe's Channel, Straits of Magellan, during the homeward voyage. She ran ashore, managed to back off but foundered soon afterwards. There were no casualties. A third voyage from Liverpool by the MEXICO did not extend beyond Buenos Aires but also ended in disaster. When making for Vigo on the homeward run she stranded on the Portuguese coast, to become a total loss, but fortunately her entire complement of 580 passengers and crew was saved. No evidence has been found of any subsequent sailings to Valparaiso, nor from Liverpool to the River Plate.

By 1912 more than 20 years had elapsed since the Company had commissioned a new transatlantic steamer. It was something of an event, therefore, when on 26 September 1912 Swan, Hunter & Wigham Richardson of Wallsend-on-Tyne launched the 10,137 ton quadruple-screw REINA VICTORIA EUGENIA, especially as two days later Wm. Denny & Bros launched the 10,348 ton triple-screw INFANTA ISABEL DE BORBON, each of which were built expressly for the River Plate trade. Both had a service speed of 17 knots, but their propelling

1913 REINA VICTORIA EUGENIA 10,137 tons
Sister ship of INFANTA ISABEL DE BORBON. Became ARGENTINA and
URUGUAY after abdication of King Alfonso.

machinery differed considerably. The Tyneside ship had two quadruple-expansion engines driving the two inner shafts and two low-pressure turbines driving the outer shafts, while the Clydeside ship had two triple-expansion engines driving the outer shafts, with a low-pressure turbine driving the inner shaft. In each case, accommodation was provided for 250 first class, 100 second and 75 third class passengers. Their maiden voyages started from Barcelona on 12 March and 4 April 1913, respectively. They had previously called at Genoa, while they subsequently put in at Malaga, Cadiz, Tenerife and Montevideo *en route* to Buenos Aires. Within a few months, the P. DE SATRÚSTEGUI and LEON XIII deserted the Mediterranean and sailed to the River Plate from Bilbao, Santander and Coruña and frequently called at additional ports.

1896 LEON XIII 5,087 tons
Consort of P. DE SATRÚSTEGUI for many years.

The Compañía Trasatlántica's sailing schedule was probably affected less by World War I, between August 1914 and November 1918, than that of any other major line. As it has often been said that the REINA VICTORIA EUGENIA and INFANTA ISABEL DE BORBON made some voyages between Spain and New York or other USA port during the war, the opportunity has been taken to check all their wartime sailings, and there is not the slightest doubt that every one of them took place between Barcelona and the River Plate. [6]

Other wartime items of interest were that the P. DE SATRÚSTEGUI and LEON XIII continued to sail during much or all of the war from Bilbao, Santander and Coruña to Montevideo and Buenos Aires, that the BUENOS AIRES made at least one or two South American voyages, including one from New York to Buenos Aires, and that a 5,617 ton twin-screw steamer whose active career started in 1892 as the Norddeutscher Lloyd H.H. MEIER and continued in 1901 as the Compañía Trasatlántica MANUEL CALVO, sailed from Barcelona for Buenos Aires on 10 October 1917 and may have made other voyages of a similar nature.

Post-war activities of the two crack South American ships, the REINA VICTORIA EUGENIA and INFANTA ISABEL DE BORBON, continued successfully but with an extended itinerary during some of the time – Barcelona, Almeria, Malaga, Cadiz, Tenerife, Rio de Janeiro, Montevideo and Buenos Aires. Owing to the opening of the Panama Canal a new service was introduced from Barcelona to Puerto Rico, La Guaira, Puerto Colombia, Panama Canal and Valparaiso, one of the ships employed being the LEON XIII.

A United States newspaper of 16 April 1931 [7] stated that King Alfonso XIII was at Marseilles, but denied that he had abdicated. Exactly a week later the same newspaper announced that the new republican government of Spain was recognised by the USA. One outcome was that the ALFONSO XIII (III), which never ran to South America, was renamed HABANA in May 1931, while the REINA VICTORIA EUGENIA and INFANTA ISABEL DE BORBON became the ARGENTINA and URUGUAY, respectively. Unfortunately, the two latter were sunk during the Spanish Civil War of 1936–9, and although subsequently refloated were candidates for the scrap heap.

It was announced in Barcelona on 8 May 1932 [8] that the River Plate service would be discontinued because of the inability of the Spanish Government to continue the subsidy. The last but one sailing had already been made by the URUGUAY, which left Buenos Aires for Barcelona on 30 April 1932, and it was reported that a large gathering of Spaniards said farewell to the ARGENTINA when she left Buenos Aires on 2 June

319

for Spain. [9] It was stated that the ships would in future serve Cuba, Central America, Venezuela and Colombia.

In 1939, after the Civil War, the Company's headquarters were transferred from Barcelona to Madrid and its title extended to COMPAÑÍA TRASATLÁNTICA ESPAÑOLA. In fact, this was how it had been known unofficially in Spain for a long time, although in English-speaking countries it was popularly referred to as the SPANISH LINE. Several new passenger ships were built after World War II, and for a time were extensively employed, but not to the River Plate. Unfortunately, the Company has been another victim of the aeroplane and is no longer running a multi-passenger line, the last ship coming within this description being scrapped in December 1974.

[1] N.R.P. Bonsor, *North Atlantic Seaway*, Volume 3, pages 1244–59.
[2] David John Lyon, *The Denny List*, National Maritime Museum. (Part 1, page 224).
[3] David John Lyon, *The Denny List*, National Maritime Museum. (Part II, page 279).
[4] David John Lyon, *The Denny List*, National Maritime Museum. (Part II, page 299).
[5] David John Lyon, *The Denny List*, National Maritime Museum. (Part II, page 306).
[6] It should be noted that the Pinillos Line (Chapter 55) had an INFANTA ISABEL, and she did make some New York voyages.
[7] *New York Herald-Tribune* 16/4/1931.
[8] *New York Herald-Tribune* 8/5/1932.
[9] *New York Herald-Tribune* 3/6/1932.

1. 1888 BUENOS AIRES
     5,195. 125,14 x 14,69. (410.6 x 48.2). 1–3. S–S–Q4–15. (I–83; II–30; III–1,000). Wm. Denny & Bros, Dumbarton. 1887 (25/1) keel laid. 1887 (22/8) launched as JELUNGA (British India and Denny, joint owners). 1887 BUENOS AIRES (Cia Tras). 1887 (28/12) MV Barcelona–Tenerife–Buenos Aires. 1889 (22/3) LV Marseilles–Tenerife–Buenos Aires (dep 29/4)–Marseilles (arr 25/5) (5 RV). Subsequently to Manila via Suez Canal; Havana and Vera Cruz; New York, etc. 1893 refitted by Denny; masts reduced to two; (I–160; II–40; III–1,000). 1917 one or more Barcelona–Buenos Aires voyages. 1932 laid up at Port Mahon, Minorca. 1942 scrapped at Barcelona.
2. (1889) CIUDAD DE SANTANDER
     3,488. 117,09 x 12,86. (384.2 x 42.2). C–1–3. I–S–C2–13. (I–160;

II–70; III–1,000). Wm. Denny & Bros, Dumbarton. 1883 (1/12) launched. 1889 (25/8) FV Marseilles–Buenos Aires. 1895 (2/5) sailed Barcelona for Buenos Aires. 1895 (24/5) wrecked on Lobos Island (0).

3. 1889 ALFONSO XIII
   4,381. 126,30 x 14,69. (414.4 x 48.2). 1–4. S–S–T3–15. Wm. Denny & Bros, Dumbarton. 1889 (24/9) launched. 1889 (22/10) MV Marseilles–Buenos Aires (2 RV). Subsequently to Cuba and Mexico. 1915 (Feb) foundered in the port of Santander.

4. (1890) ALFONSO XII (II)
   5,063. 133,65 x 14,56. (438.5 x 47.8). C–2–4. S–S–T3–15. Wigham Richardson & Co, Walker-on-Tyne. 1888 (29/3) launched. 1888 (25/10) MV Barcelona–Vera Cruz. 1890 (23/2) FV Marseilles–Cadiz–R. Plate (1 RV). 1898 (7/7) destroyed by US fleet at Mariel during Spanish–American War.

5. (1891) ESPAÑA
   2,679. 102,19 x 11,49. (335.3 x 37.7). 1–2. I–S–C2–12. Robert Napier & Sons, Glasgow. 1873 launched as EDINBURGH CASTLE (Castle). 1880 ESPAÑA (A. Lopez y Cia). 1882 ditto (Cia Tras). 1891 FV Marseilles Malaga (dep 4/9)–Montevideo–Buenos Aires (1 RV). 1898 scrapped at Marseilles.

6. (1891) ANTONIO LÓPEZ
   3,460. 117,03 x 12,86. (384.0 x 42.2). C–1–3. S–S–C2–13. (I–156; II–72; III–1,100). Wm. Denny & Bros, Dumbarton. 1881 (8/11) launched. 1891 (8/11) MV Marseilles–Barcelona–Buenos Aires. 1898 (2/1) LV Buenos Aires–Cadiz (21/1)–Barcelona. 1898 (28/6) ran ashore near San Juan, Puerto Rico, to avoid seizure by US warships during Spanish–American War; burnt out.

7. (1892) CATALUÑA
   3,488. 117,09 x 12,86. (384.2 x 42.2). C–1–3. I–S–C2–13. (I–160; II–70; III–1,000). Wm. Denny & Bros, Dumbarton. 1883 (3/10) launched. 1892 (1/1) FV Marseilles–Cadiz–Buenos Aires (1 RV). 1923 (25/6) wrecked in Rio de Oro, West Africa.

8. (1893) CIUDAD DE CADIZ
   3,084. 110,81 x 11,64. (363.6 x 38.2). 1–3. I–S–T3–14. (I–163; II–54; III–200). Lobnitz, Coulborn & Co, Renfrew. 1878 (Nov) launched for A. Lopez y Cia. 1892 CIUDAD DE CADIZ (Cia Trasatlántica). 1893 (1/1) FV Marseilles–Barcelona–Buenos Aires. 1896 (4/1) LV Marseilles–Buenos Aires. Many subsequent voyages to Puerto Rico and Havana. 1924 (10/10) wrecked at San Carlos, Gulf of Guinea.

9. (1899) P. DE SATRÚSTEGUI
   4,713. 124,96 x 14,05. (410.0 x 46.1). 1–2. S–T3–14. (I–118; II–54;

III–500). A. & J. Inglis, Glasgow, 1889 (11/11) launched as TARA (British Indai). 1894 P. DE SATRÚSTEGUI (Cia Trasatlántica). 1894 FV Liverpool–Barcelona–Suez Canal–Manila. 1899 (24/11) FV Barcelona–Genoa–Barcelona (27/11)–Buenos Aires. 1899 (25/11) collision with BASSANO (Wilson) *en route* Barcelona–Genoa; slight damage. 1904–13 regular sailings Genoa–Barcelona–Buenos Aires as consort of LEON XIII. 1913 FV Bilbao–Santander–Coruña–Buenos Aires. Continued this itinerary during much of World War I. 1927 scrapped at Genoa.

10. (1900) MEXICO

2,101. 101,03 x 10,45. (331.5 x 34.3). 1–3. I–S–C2–10. London & Glasgow Co, Glasgow. 1875 launched as TRENTHAM HALL (Sun Shipping Co). 1885 MEXICO (Cia Tras). 1900 (23/3) FV Liverpool–Montevideo–Valparaiso (dep 26/5)–Rio de Janeiro–Liverpool. 1900 (22/7) 2nd voyage Liverpool–Valparaiso. 1900 3rd voyage Liverpool–Cadiz (7/12)–Buenos Aires. 1901 (10/7) wrecked 6 miles south of Vianno do Castello, Portugal (0) on voyage Buenos Aires–Bilbao.

11. (1900) SAN AGUSTIN

2,359. 91,58 x 11,61. (300.5 x 38.1). 1–2. I–S–C2–10. Aitken & Mansel, Glasgow (engines J. & J. Thomson, Glasgow). 1882 launched as ALBANO (Br). 1882 VENEZUELA (Marques de Campo (Spanish)). 1886 SAN AGUSTIN (Cia Tras). 1899 (29/11) FV New York–Cadiz–Barcelona–Marseilles (1 voyage). 1900 (24/5) FV Liverpool–Rio de Janeiro–Valparaiso–Montevideo–Liverpool (arr 15/9). 1900 (24/9) 2nd voyage Liverpool–Montevideo–Valparaiso. 1900 (14/12) foundered in Smythe's Channel, Straits of Magellan, on voyage Valparaiso–Spain–Liverpool.

12. (1901) LEON XIII

5,087. 125,08 x 14,05. (410.4 x 46.1). 1–2. S–T3–14. (I–117; II–58; III–1,000). A. & J. Inglis, Glasgow. 1888 (31/1) launched as TAROBA (British India). 1894 (May) ISLA DE CUBA (Cia Tras). 1896 LEON XIII (Cia Tras). 1901 (2/4) FV Genoa–Cadiz–Buenos Aires. 1904–13 regular sailings Genoa–Barcelona–Buenos Aires as consort of P. DE SATRÚSTEGUI. 1913 FV Bilbao–Santander–Coruña–Montevideo–Buenos Aires. Continued same itinerary during much of World War I. 1931 scrapped in Italy.

13. 1913 REINA VICTORIA EUGENIA
(1931) ARGENTINA

10,137. 146,30 x 18,68. (480.0 x 61.3). 1–2. 4S–Q8&ST–17. (I–250; II–100; III–75). Swan, Hunter & Wigham Richardson,

Wallsend-on-Tyne. 1912 (26/9) launched. 1913 (12/3) MV Barcelona–Buenos Aires. 1931 (May) ARGENTINA (Cia Tras). 1932 (3/5) LV Barcelona–Montevideo–Buenos Aires (dep 2/6)–Barcelona. 1939 (Jan) bombed and sunk by Nationalist air attack when lying at Barcelona during Spanish Civil War. 1939 (8/9) refloated and laid up. 1945 scrapped.

14. 1913 INFANTA ISABEL DE BORBON
    (1931) URUGUAY
    10,348. 146,87 x 18,65. (481.9 x 61.3). 1–2. 3S–T6&ST–17. (I–250; II–100; III–75). Wm. Denny & Bros, Dumbarton. 1912 (28/9) launched. 1913 (4/4) MV Barcelona–Buenos Aires. 1931 (May) URUGUAY (Cia Tras). 1932 (30/4) LV Buenos Aires–Barcelona. 1939 (23/1) bombed and sunk by Nationalist air attack at Barcelona during Spanish Civil War. 1939 (25/7) refloated. 1940 scrapped.

15. (1917) MANUEL CALVO
    5,617. 128,31 x 14,63. (421.0 x 48.0). 1–3. 2S–T6–13. (I–84; II–32; III–1,000). Armstrong, Mitchell & Co, Walker-on-Tyne (engines Hawthorn, Leslie & Co, Newcastle). 1891 (19/10) launched as LUCANIA (MacIver). 1892 H.H. MEIER (NDL). 1901 MANUEL CALVO (Cia Tras). 1917 (10/10) sailed Barcelona–Buenos Aires (may have made other S. American voyages). 1936 laid up at Port Mahon, Minorca. 1939 (Oct) sailed for Cadiz; rebuilt as cargo steamer. 1950 laid up at Santander. 1952 DRAGO (Spanish). 1958 scrapped in Spain.

FUNNEL: Black.
FLAG: Blue; large white ball.

Chapter 41

(1888–90)

NEDERLANDSCHE – AMERIKAANSCHE STOOMVAART MAATSCHAPPIJ
(NASM)

(Holland American Line)

(Dutch)

The NEDERLANDSCHE – AMERIKAANSCHE STOOMVAART MAATSCHAPPIJ owed its origin to a parent concern, Plate, Reuchlin & Co, which was founded on 8 February 1871 and started operations between Rotterdam and New York in October 1872. It soon became apparent, however, that the Company had insufficient capital to continue, let alone increase the service and a joint stock company, NEDERLANDSCHE – AMERIKAANSCHE STOOMVAART MAATSCHAPPIJ (NASM) came into being on 18 April 1873 with a capital of two million guilders (£165,000). In 1897 the alternative of HOLLAND – AMERIKA LIJN was introduced for the Dutch name, although in the English-speaking world the Company had been known from early days as the HOLLAND AMERICA LINE.

In 1888, having considerably expanded its fleet for the services between Rotterdam or Amsterdam and New York, the Company found itself with some surplus tonnage, and turned its attention to the South Atlantic. The 3,063 ton ZAANDAM was despatched from Amsterdam for Brazil, Uruguay and Argentina on 5 December 1888, followed at monthly intervals by the 3,130 ton EDAM and the 2,236 ton SCHIEDAM and in May 1889 by the 2,796 ton LEERDAM. Unfortunately, the last-named sank in the North Sea on 16 December 1889 as the result of a collision with the British steamer GAW-QUAN-SIN, but there were no casualties among her 433 passengers and crew.

Notwithstanding this loss, the South American service was certainly a success, and it was decided early in 1890 to place orders in Holland for the 2,700 ton DIDAM and DUBBELDAM. However, a financial crisis occurred in Argentina during the autumn of that year and brought immigration virtually to a standstill. In consequence, the service was withdrawn after only two years operation, the last sailing being taken by the SCHIEDAM, which left Rotterdam on 15 November 1890, returning from Buenos Aires on 2 January 1891 and reaching Rotterdam on 7

1889 LEERDAM 2,796 tons
Sunk in collision with British steamer GAW-QUAN-SIN in December 1889.

February. Ironically, the DIDAM and DUBBELDAM, found too small to remain permanently in the North Atlantic service, were soon sold to the Red Cross Line to run to ports in the River Amazon (Chapter 20).

In spite of its South American disappointment, the Holland America Line can certainly be regarded as one of the most successful North Atlantic lines, but during the early 1970s it followed the example of a number of other companies by withdrawing its passenger service and concentrating instead on cruising.

1. (1888) ZAANDAM
   3,063. 98,93 x 11,61. (324.6 x 38.1). S–1–2. I–S–C2–10. (I–36; III–524). Nederlandsche Stoomboot Maatschappij, Fijenoord (Rotterdam). 1882 (2/5) launched. 1882 (29/7) MV Amsterdam–New York. 1888 (20/10) LV Amsterdam–New York. 1888 (5/12) FV Amsterdam–S. America. 1890 (25/5) LV ditto. 1897 STYRIA (Austro–Americana). 1902 JULIA LUCKENBACH (Luckenbach (US)). 1913 (3/1) sunk in collision with ss INDRAKUALA (Br) in Chesapeake Bay.

2. (1889) EDAM
   3,130. 100,00 x 12,59. (328.1 x 41.3). S–1–2. S–S–C2–12. (I–36; III–524). Nederlandsche Stoomboot Maatschappij, Fijenoord (Rotterdam). 1883 (29/8) launched. 1883 (27/10) MV Amsterdam–New York. 1889 (5/1) FV Rotterdam–S. America. 1890 (25/6) LV ditto. 1895 (19/9) sunk in collision with ss TURKISTAN (Br) in English Channel (0).

3. (1889) SCHIEDAM
   2,236. 91,74 x 11,98. (301.0 x 39.3). S–1–2. I–S–C2–10. (I–24; III–580). A. McMillan & Son, Dumbarton (engines J. & J. Thomson, Glasgow). 1874 (1/9) launched as SAN MARCOS

(Liverpool & Texas). 1877 SCHIEDAM (c) (NASM). 1880 SCHIEDAM (NASM). 1888 (9/12) LV Amsterdam–New York. 1889 (5/2) FV Amsterdam–S. America. 1890 (15/11) LV Rotterdam–S. America. 1897 MIRAMAR (Cosulich). 1903 scrapped at Genoa.

4. (1889) LEERDAM

2,796. 98,17 x 12,19. (322.1 x 40.0). S–1–2. I–S–C2–10. (I–36; III–500). Nederlandsche Stoomboot Maatschappij, Fijenoord (Rotterdam). 1881 (28/4) launched as NEDERLAND (Dutch). 1882 LEERDAM (NASM). 1889 (19/3) LV Amsterdam–New York. 1889 (7/5) FV Amsterdam–S. America. 1889 (16/12) sunk in collision with ss GAW-QUAN-SIN (Br) in North Sea when on voyage Rotterdam–S. America. (0).

— —— DIDAM

2,751. 101,46 x 12,16. (332.9 x 39.9). S–1–2. S–S–T3–12. (I–44; III–464). Nederlandsche Stoomboot Maatschappij, Fijenoord (Rotterdam). 1891 (Feb) launched for South American service. 1891 (20/5) MV Rotterdam–New York. 1895 SANTARENSE (Red Cross). 1896 (17/6) sunk in collision with British barque DUNDONALD.

— —— DUBBELDAM

2,700. 101,19 x 12,19. (332.0 x 40.0). S–1–2. S–S–T3–12. (I–40; III–464). Bonn & Mees, Rotterdam (engines Nederlandsche Stoomboot Maatschappij). 1891 (Aug) launched for South American service. 1891 (26/8) MV Amsterdam–New York. 1895 MADEIRENSE (Red Cross). 1901 ditto (Booth). 1910 ditto (Norwegian). 1912 (30/7) foundered near Bahamas Is.

FUNNEL: Black; green-white-green bands.
FLAG: Green-white-green horizontal stripes; black 'NASM' on the white.
Note: In 1898 funnel became yellow with green-white-green bands.

Chapter 42

1889–1906

ZINO LINE

(Italian)

The ZINO LINE, founded by Fratelli Zino (Zino Brothers) of Savona, Italy, started operations in 1889 with the 2,473 ton ATTIVITÀ, a single-screw steel steamer built for them by C.S. Swan & Hunter of Wallsend-on-Tyne. She had accommodation for 1,200 steerage passengers, and sailed from Genoa for the River Plate on 26 November 1889.

It had been said that a consort, the AQUILA, was commissioned during the same year, but this ship belonged to Fratelli Lavarello (Chapter 38) and there was no connection.

The ATTIVITÀ evidently paid her way as she was joined in 1894 by the 2,473 ton ALACRITÀ, formerly the COUNSELLOR of the Harrison Line, in 1896 by the 3,296 ton ASSIDUITÀ, formerly the MENTMORE of the Johnston Line, and in 1897 by the 3,369 ton EQUITÀ, formerly the KNIGHT OF ST. JOHN. All these ships, as well as the 4,020 ton LEALTÀ, launched in 1888 as the KNIGHT COMPANION and acquired by Zino in 1900, had accommodation for about 1,200 steerage passengers. To begin with, registration had been in the name of Giuseppe Zino, but before the turn of the century it was transferred to Ottavio Zino.

The ASSIDUITÀ was detailed to the cotton trade in 1900, and caught fire in the North Atlantic on 16 November 1900 on passage from New Orleans to Genoa. She had to be abandoned, her crew being rescued by the British steamer LANARKSHIRE.

The ATTIVITÀ made four round voyages between Genoa, Naples and New York in 1902, while the EQUITÀ made a total of seven between 1902 and 1906.

By 1908 the ATTIVITÀ, ALACRITÀ, EQUITÀ and LEALTÀ had discontinued carrying passengers as they no longer compared in size and amenities with ships in service by other lines. But in that year there was greatly increased emigration to Chile, so Zino decided to form the SOCIETÀ LLOYD DEL PACIFICO, to which the four ships were transferred, the EQUITÀ being renamed CHILE. Other ships were acquired.

The Zino fleet was named after virtues, namely – ALACRITÀ, alacrity; ASSIDUITÀ, assiduity; ATTIVITÀ, activity; EQUITÀ, equity; and LEALTÀ, loyalty.

1. 1889 ATTIVITÀ

   2,473. 94,42 x 11,92. (309.8 x 39.1). 1–2. S–T3–11. (III–1,200). C.S. Swan & Hunter, Wallsend-on-Tyne (engines Wallsend Slipway Co Ltd). 1889 (Oct) launched. 1889 (26/11) MV Genoa–R. Plate. 1902 (9/4) FV Genoa–Naples–New York (4 RV). 1908 ATTIVITÀ (Lloyd del Pacifico). 1911 LIBIA (Italian). 1913 LIBIA (Fabre). 1917 (2/8) torpedoed and sunk by German submarine off Ushant.

2. (1894) ALACRITÀ

   2,244. 94,79 x 10,39. (311.0 x 34.1). 1–2. I–S–C2–10. (III–1,200). Aitken & Mansel, Glasgow (engines J. & J. Thomson, Glasgow). 1877 (17/4) launched as COUNSELLOR (Harrison). 1894 ALACRITÀ (Zino). 1894 (10/10) FV Genoa–R. Plate. 1908 ALACRITÀ (Lloyd del Pacifico). 1921 (17/9) foundered in N. Atlantic.

3. (1896) ASSIDUITÀ

   3,296. 103,50 x 12,25. (339.6 x 40.2). 1–2. I–S–C2–10. (III–1,200). J. Key & Sons, Kinghorn. 1882 (19/2) launched as MENTMORE (Johnston). 1896 ASSIDUITÀ (Zino). 1896 (20/1) FV Genoa–R. Plate. 1900 FV Genoa–New Orleans. 1900 (16/11) caught fire in North Atlantic; abandoned; crew rescued by LANARKSHIRE (Br).

4. (1897) EQUITÀ

   3,369. 100,58 x 13,25. (330.0 x 43.5). 1–2. S–T3–12. (III–1,200). Palmers Co Ltd, Jarrow-on-Tyne. 1885 (15/8) launched as KNIGHT OF ST. JOHN (Br). 1897 EQUITÀ (Zino). 1897 (31/5) FV Genoa–R. Plate. 1902 (14/5) FV Genoa–Naples–New York (7 RV). 1908 CHILE (Lloyd del Pacifico). 1921 (26/10) mined and sunk in Cerigo Channel, Greece.

5. (1900) LEALTA

   4,020. 121,91 x 13,80. (400.0 x 45.3). 1–2. S–T3–12. (III–1,200). Palmers Co Ltd, Jarrow-on-Tyne. 1888 (29/2) launched as KNIGHT COMPANION (Br). 1900 LEALTÀ (Zino). 1900 (29/4) FV Genoa–R. Plate. 1908 LEALTÀ (Lloyd del Pacifico). 1917 (10/8) torpedoed and sunk by enemy submarine near Malta (9).

FUNNEL: Yellow; letter 'Z' in red.
HULL: Grey.

Chapter 43

(1890–1915)

HOULDER LINE

(1856) Houlder Brothers & Company
1898 Houlder Brothers & Company Limited
1899 Houlder Line Limited

(British)

Edwin Savory Houlder, just 21, started business on his own account in Gracechurch Street, London, as a ship and insurance broker in 1849. His early activities were largely in the Australian trade, and before long he was appointed loading broker and often passage broker for an increasing number of sailing ships. He traded as E.S. HOULDER & CO, but by 1856 the business had grown sufficiently to invite his brother Alfred to join him. The firm became HOULDER BROTHERS & COMPANY and soon afterwards moved to larger premises in Leadenhall Street. By 1861 they had branched out into shipowning, and by degrees built up a large fleet of wooden sailing ships. It was not until 1879 that they acquired their first iron ship.

Until the early 1880s, by which time a branch office had been opened in Glasgow, voyages invariably terminated in Australasia, although for some years calls had been made at South African ports. But a dual change came in 1883, when the 2,403 ton iron screw steamer MEATH was chartered to carry frozen meat from the River Plate to Antwerp and London. She and another chartered steamer, the WEXFORD, continued this trade until other ships took their places.

In 1889 Houlder Brothers decided to start their own fleet of steamers and placed an order with Wigham Richardson & Co of Walker-on-Tyne for the 2,356 ton HORNBY GRANGE, a two-funnelled two-masted steel ship with triple-expansion engines giving a service speed of 10 knots. She had 70,000 cubic feet of insulated space, but also catered for passengers, although the number is not known. Her maiden voyage started from London on 9 March 1890 for Montevideo and Buenos Aires, the Company opening an office in the latter port in readiness for her arrival.

Close on her heels came the 2,413 ton OVINGDEAN GRANGE and virtually a sister ship, although built by Sir Raylton Dixon & Co of Middlesbrough. She had been launched nine days before the HORNBY

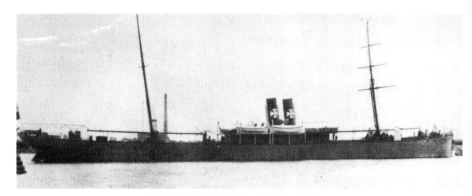

1890 HORNBY GRANGE 2,356 tons
First Houlder Line cargo and passenger steamer.

GRANGE, on 28 November 1889, but her maiden voyage started from London for Rosario on 25 March 1890, a fortnight after her sister sailed.

The 3,424 ton URMSTON GRANGE, accommodating 18 first class passengers, was launched by Workman, Clark & Co Ltd of Belfast on 2 October 1894 and started her maiden voyage to Montevideo and Rosario only a little more than two months later. She reached Montevideo in 23 days from London, the fastest Houlder voyage to date.

Three more steamers, the LANGTON GRANGE, DENTON GRANGE and ELSTREE GRANGE were commissioned for the Australian service, followed by another Workman Clark product for the South American Line, the 4,213 ton ROYSTON GRANGE, which sailed from London for Rosario on 12 January 1898.

It will be seen that the initial letters of these seven steamers make up the words HOULDER. The reason for the suffix GRANGE was that Edwin Savory Houlder lived at The Grange, Sutton, Surrey.

A sister ship of the ROYSTON GRANGE, the BEACON GRANGE, was also built by Workman Clark and as an experiment began her maiden voyage from Glasgow on 24 June 1898.

A limited liability company, HOULDER BROTHERS & COMPANY LIMITED, was formed in 1898, the partners of the earlier concern becoming directors. A further change took place on 16 March 1899 with the formation of HOULDER LINE LIMITED, with a capital of £500,000, to take over the single-ship limited companies which had hitherto been formed for each individual steamer.

The URMSTON GRANGE was the first Houlder steamer to be taken up by the British Government after the outbreak of the Boer War in October 1899, and was not released for over a year. Most of the Company's ships were employed at times by the Government, and carried over 100,000 horses and mules to South Africa.

The Company's general meeting on 29 July 1901 was marked by tragedy when Edwin Savory Houlder collapsed and died of a heart attack. In due course he was succeeded by E. Cayford, who had had many years of experience with the firm.

In 1902 a new subsidiary company, the EMPIRE TRANSPORT COMPANY LIMITED, was formed to take over some of the Houlder activities. The first ship to be registered under the new concern was the 7,557 ton HAVERSHAM GRANGE, built in 1898 as the Furness Withy RAPIDAN and renamed when acquired by Houlders in 1901. During her early days as the RAPIDAN, she collided in the Tyne with the LUCERNE of Liverpool and the BEDFORD of Shields, the bows of all three being considerably damaged. Another second-hand ship, the 4,188 ton THORPE GRANGE, built in 1889 by the London & Glasgow Company as the INDRAMAYO, was bought by Houlder and sailed for them from Liverpool on her first voyage for Rosario on 24 October 1902.

Houlders acted for both sides during the Russo–Japanese War of 1904–05 as 10,000 horses were carried to Japan, while the OVING-DEAN GRANGE carried stores between Vladivostock and Port Arthur. After the war, ships were chartered to repatriate Russian troops from Vladivostock to Odessa. A year later, the HORNBY GRANGE and OVINGDEAN GRANGE were chartered to carry frozen meat to Vladivostock.

In 1911 Furness, Withy & Company Limited acquired a considerable interest in the Houlder Line, and during the same year were largely responsible for the formation of the BRITISH & ARGENTINE STEAM NAVIGATION COMPANY LIMITED, which was run in close association between the two companies and adopted the Houlder funnel colours. Furness Withy provided the second-hand LA BLANCA, EL CORDOBES and EL ARGENTINO, while in 1912–13 five sister ships of 8,300 tons were built – A. Stephen & Sons of Glasgow being responsible

1912 EL URUGUAYO 8,361 tons
British & Argentine Steam Navigation Co – an offshoot of Houlder Line.

331

for the EL URUGUAYO, Irvine's of West Hartlepool for the EL PARAGUAYO and LA CORRENTINA and Palmers Co Ltd of Jarrow for the LA ROSARINA and LA NEGRA. They were all twin-screw ships driven by triple-expansion engines, had a speed of 14 knots and could accommodate 12 first class passengers and 400 steerage.

Reverting to Houlder Line ships proper, the 4,252 ton LYNTON GRANGE and DENBY GRANGE and the 4,499 ton OAKLANDS GRANGE were commissioned in 1912, and the 4,653 ton OLDFIELD GRANGE and the 4,495 ton ROUNTON GRANGE in 1913.

Soon after the outbreak of World War I in August 1914, the URMSTON GRANGE was bought by the Admiralty and sunk as a blockship at Scapa Flow. The LA CORRENTINA was captured and scuttled by the German raider KRONPRINZ WILHELM on 7 October 1914, her passengers and crew being landed at Montevideo by the Norddeutscher Lloyd passenger steamer SIERRA CORDOBA before she passed through the Straits of Magellan and was interned at Callao.

The 5,483 ton BUTESHIRE, built in 1893, was bought in 1915, renamed BOLLINGTON GRANGE and made one or two voyages to the River Plate. She had accommodation for a few first class passengers and a large number of steerage, but whether the latter accommodation was used by Houlder is not known. She was handed over during the same year to FURNESS HOULDER ARGENTINE LINE, which was formed at that time, and renamed CANONESA. Yet another line, the BRITISH EMPIRE STEAM NAVIGATION COMPANY LIMITED had been founded by Furness Withy and Houlders in 1914.

The last Houlder wartime loss was of the DENBY GRANGE, sunk in collision on 24 October 1918 when in convoy.

The pioneer HORNBY GRANGE was sold in 1919 and eventually scrapped at Barcelona in 1928 at the ripe old age of 38. Another veteran, the BEACON GRANGE, was wrecked in September 1921 at Rio Gallegos, Patagonia.

After the Armistice of November 1918 the Furness and Houlder interests went from strength to strength, but there is no great incentive to go into details as the new ships were either purely cargo carriers or at the most catered for a maximum of 12 passengers. Much more recently, bulk carriers, tankers, special service vessels and liquid gas carriers have been added, some under the name of HOULDER BROTHERS & COMPANY LIMITED and others under the name of associated companies such as the Alexander Shipping Co Ltd, Nile Steamship Co Ltd and Ocean Gas Transport Ltd.

1. 1890 HORNBY GRANGE
      2,356. 91,46 x 12,28. (300.1 x 40.3). S–2–2. S–S–T3–10. (I).

Wigham Richardson & Co, Walker-on-Tyne. 1889 (7/12) launched. 1890 (9/3) MV London–Montevideo–Buenos Aires. 1919 AUGUSTINA FORNER (Spanish). 1928 scrapped at Barcelona.

2. 1890 OVINGDEAN GRANGE
   2,413, 90,61 x 12,25. (297.3 x 40.2). S–2–2. S–S–T3–10. (I). Sir Raylton Dixon & Co, Middlesbrough (engines T. Richardson & Sons, Hartlepool). 1889 (28/11) launched. 1890 (25/3) MV London–Rosario. 1906 ROMAN (Russian). 1909 collided with OSTERLEY (Orient) at Port Said. 1916 TAMON MARU (Jap). 1917 went missing.

3. 1894 URMSTON GRANGE
   3,423. 103,62 x 14,17. (340.0 x 46.5). 1–2. S–S–T3–12. (I–18). Workman, Clark & Co Ltd, Belfast. 1894 (2/10) launched. 1894 (15/12) MV London–Montevideo–Rosario. 1906 fitted as cable ship. 1914 (24/4) stranded at Rio Gallegos; refloated and put in at Punta Arenas; temporary repairs at Montevideo; returned to London. 1914 sold to Admiralty; became a blockship at Scapa Flow.

4. 1898 ROYSTON GRANGE
   4,213. 112,77 x 14,50. (370.0 x 47.6). 1–2. S–S–T3–13. (I). Workman, Clark & Co Ltd, Belfast. 1897 (30/6) launched. 1898 (12/1) MV London–Rosario. 1928 scrapped.

5. 1898 BEACON GRANGE
   4,237. 112,77 x 14,50. (370.0 x 47.6). 1–2. S–S–T3–13. (I). Workman, Clark & Co Ltd, Belfast. 1898 (25/1) launched. 1898 (24/6) MV Glasgow–Montevideo–Buenos Aires. 1921 (Sep) wrecked at Rio Gallegos, Patagonia.

6. (1902) HAVERSHAM GRANGE
   7,505. 144,92 x 17,07. (475.5 x 56.0). 1–4. S–T3–13. Furness, Withy & Co Ltd, West Hartlepool (engines N.E. Marine Co Ltd, West Hartlepool). 1898 (22/2) launched as RAPIDAN (Furness Withy). 1901 HAVERSHAM GRANGE (Houlder). 1902 (11/7) FV Barry–Buenos Aires (dep 24/8)–Table Bay). 1902 sold to Empire Transport Co Ltd. 1906 (24/10) on fire during voyage New York–Melbourne; abandoned.

7. (1902) THORPE GRANGE
   4,188. 121,97 x 13,74. (400.2 x 45.1). 1–2. S–T3–12. London & Glasgow Co Ltd, Glasgow. 1889 (3/4) launched as INDRA-MAYO (Br). 1902 THORPE GRANGE (Houlder). 1902 (24/10) FV Liverpool–Rosario. 1930 scrapped.

8. (1911) SUTHERLAND GRANGE
   6,852. 125,39 x 16,06. (411.4 x 52.7). 1–2. S–T3–13. Palmers Co

Ltd, Jarrow-on-Tyne. 1906 (17/11) launched as GUARDIANA (Furness Withy). 1911 SUTHERLAND GRANGE (Houlder). 1911 (6/8) FV Port Talbot–Buenos Aires–Parana.

9. 1912 LYNTON GRANGE
4,252. 115,81 x 14,96. (380.0 x 49.1). 1–2. S–T3–12. Northumberland Shipbuilding Co Ltd, Newcastle (engines Richardsons, Westgarth & Co Ltd, Sunderland). 1912 launched. 1912 (27/7) MV Barry–Buenos Aires.

10. 1912 DENBY GRANGE
4,252. 115,84 x 14,93. (380.1 x 49.0). 1–2. S–T3–12. Northumberland Shipbuilding Co Ltd, Newcastle (engines Richardsons, Westgarth & Co Ltd, Sunderland). 1912 launched. 1912 (15/10) MV Newport–Swansea–Buenos Aires. 1918 (24/10) sunk in collision when in convoy.

11. 1912 OAKLANDS GRANGE
4,488. 117,34 x 15,85. (385.0 x 52.0). 1–2. S–T3–12. Northumberland Shipbuilding Co Ltd, Newcastle (engines Richardsons, Westgarth & Co Ltd, Sunderland). 1912 launched. 1912 (25/12) MV Tyne–Antwerp–River Plate.

12. 1913 OLDFIELD GRANGE
4,653. 117,34 x 15,85. (385.0 x 52.0). 1–2. S–T3–12. Irvine's Shipbuilding & Dry Dock Co Ltd, West Hartlepool (engines Richardsons, Westgarth & Co Ltd, Sunderland).

13. 1913 ROUNTON GRANGE
4,487. 117,34 x 15,85. (385.0 x 52.0). 1–2. S–T3–12. Northumberland Shipbuilding Co Ltd, Newcastle (engines Richardsons, Westgarth & Co Ltd, Sunderland). 1912 (23/12) launched. 1913 (8/4) MV London–Rosario. 1934 ELISE SCHULTE (German). 1942 (10/1) wrecked off Tromso.

14. (1915) BOLLINGTON GRANGE
5,583. 128,01 x 16,46. (420.0 x 54.0). 1–2. S–T3–12. (I–12; III–500). R. & W. Hawthorn, Leslie & Co Ltd, Hebburn-on-Tyne. 1893 (10/10) launched as BUTESHIRE (Br). 1915 BOLLINGTON GRANGE (Houlder). 1916 CANONESA (Furness Houlder). 1919 MAGICSTAR (Blue Star). 1929 scrapped by T. W. Ward Ltd.

BRITISH & ARGENTINE STEAM NAVIGATION COMPANY LIMITED

A. 1912 EL URUGUAYO
  8,361. 134,16 x 17,92. (440.2 x 58.8). 1–2. 2S–T6–14. (I–12; III–400). A. Stephen & Sons, Glasgow. 1911 (5/12) launched. 1912 (30/4) MV Clyde–Buenos Aires. 1937 scrapped at Newport.
B. 1912 EL PARAGUAYO
  8,508. 134,16 x 17,92. (440.2 x 58.8). 1–2. 2S–T6–14. (I–12; III–400). Irvine's Shipbuilding Co, West Hartlepool). 1911 (23/10) launched. 1912 (20/6) MV Newcastle–Bilbao–Montevideo–Buenos Aires. 1936 (12/10) arrived Newport to be scrapped.
C. 1912 LA CORRENTINA
  8,529. 134,16 x 17,92. (440.2 x 58.8). 1–2. 2S–T6–14. (I–12; III–400). Irvine's Shipbuilding Co, West Hartlepool). 1912 (30/5) launched. 1912 (14/12) MV Liverpool–Buenos Aires. 1914 (7/10) captured and scuttled by German auxiliary cruiser KRONPRINZ WILHELM; passengers and crew landed at Montevideo by SIERRA CORDOBA (NDL).
D. 1912 LA ROSARINA
  8,332. 134,16 x 17,92. (440.2 x 58.8). 1–2. 2S–T6–14. (I–12; III–400). Palmers Co Ltd, Jarrow-on-Tyne. 1911 (15/12) launched. 1912 (4/7) MV Tyne–R. Plate. 1937 sold to Japanese breakers. Renamed ROSARINA for voyage to Osaka.
E. 1913 LA NEGRA
  8,312. 134,16 x 17,92. (440.2 x 58.8). 1–2. 2S–T6–14. (I–12; III–400). Palmers Co Ltd, Jarrow-on-Tyne. 1913 (Jan) launched. 1913 (20/4) MV Liverpool–Buenos Aires.

Houlder Line
FUNNEL: Black with broad red band containing a white Maltese cross.

Chapter 44

(1891–1902)

PUGLIA SOCIETÀ DI NAVIGAZIONE

(Italian)

In 1889 the PUGLIA SOCIETÀ DI NAVIGAZIONE of Bari, Italy, decided to enter the passenger and cargo business and placed orders with the Sunderland Shipbuilding Company for the 2,205 ton MESSAPIA, launched on 23 December 1889, and the 2,103 ton CALABRO, launched on 24 March 1890. Both were single-screw steamers with accommodation for 60 first class and 750 steerage passengers.

But despite statements that they were built for the South American trade, the Company seemed in no hurry to employ them on this run. The MESSAPIA, for example, proceeded from Sunderland to Venice in March 1890, and then made a number of voyages to the Black Sea before eventually sailing from Genoa on 2 May 1891 for Naples, St. Vincent, Montevideo, Buenos Aires and Rosario. She had been preceded by the CALABRO, which sailed from Genoa on 11 January 1891 for the same ports.

On 20 October 1900 there was an explosion aboard the MESSAPIA when she was homeward bound about 200 miles from St. Vincent with a large complement of passengers. A severe fire broke out, but thanks largely to the captain's courage she managed to reach St. Vincent, where the passengers were landed and temporary repairs undertaken. It was not until the end of March 1901 that she reached Genoa, but apparently she was not considered to be worth repairing as she was scrapped at Ancona in October 1901.

In replacement, Puglia bought in England the 2,811 ton SIKH of the Mogul Steamship Company and renamed her REGINA ELENA, her first voyage to South America starting on 28 June 1901. She was despatched from Genoa and Naples to New York on 22 April 1902 and from the end of that year onwards – she was sold to the Unione Austriaca (Chapter 54) in 1904 to become the GEORGIA – she was chartered to Ercole Saviotti of Genoa in his capacity of emigrant agent. Apparently, she made four voyages to New York and five to the River Plate under his jurisdiction.

The Italian law of 1901 made it more and more difficult for Italian as well as foreign lines to take part in the emigrant trade from Italy to North and South America, and for this reason the CALABRO was sold in 1904 to the Compagnie Mixte (Chapter 3). Subsequently, Puglia concentrated largely on services in the Adriatic and the Tyrrhenian Sea.

1. (1891) CALABRO
    2,103. 83,81 x 11,64. (275.0 x 38.2). 1–2. S–S–T3–11. (I–60; III–750). Sunderland Shipbuilding Co, Sunderland (engines North Eastern Marine Engineering Co, Newcastle). 1890 (24/3) launched. 1891 (11/1) FV Genoa–Naples–St. Vincent–Montevideo–Buenos Aires–Rosario. 1904 MOULOYA. (Cie Mixte (Fr)). 1930 scrapped.
2. (1891) MESSAPIA
    2,205. 83,81 x 11,64. (275.0 x 38.2). 1–2. S–S–T3–11. (I–60; III–750). Sunderland Shipbuilding Co, Sunderland (engines North Eastern Marine Engineering Co, Newcastle). 1889 (23/12) launched. 1891 (2/5) FV Genoa–Naples–St. Vincent–Montevideo–Buenos Aires–Rosario. 1900 (20/10) explosion and fire when 200 miles from St. Vincent, homeward bound; succeeded in reaching St. Vincent. 1901 (30/3) arrived Genoa after temporary repairs. 1901 MESSAPIA (It). 1901 (Oct) scrapped at Ancona.
3. (1901) REGINA ELENA
    2,811. 102,10 x 12,25. (335.0 x 40.2). 1–2. S–T3–12. (I–25; III–1,200). Wigham Richardson & Co, Walker-on-Tyne. 1889 (16/1) launched as SIKH (Mogul (Br)). 1901 REGINA ELENA (Puglia). 1901 (28/6) FV Genoa–Naples–S. America. 1902 (22/4) FV Genoa–Naples–New York (6 RV). 1904 GEORGIA (Unione Austriaca). 1907 SHINSEI MARU (Jap). 1945 (7/1) bombed and sunk by US aircraft SW of Formosa.

Chapter 45

(1895–7)

PRINCE LINE

(British)

James Knott, founder of the PRINCE LINE, was born at Howdon-on-Tyne on 31 January 1855, entered into business on his own account as a shipbroker at the age of 20, and in 1882 acquired his first steamship, the 832 ton SAXON PRINCE. He formed the PRINCE STEAM SHIPPING COMPANY LIMITED in 1884 with a paid up capital of £52,000. Four new ships were ordered and more followed.

During 1889–91 the Prince Line steamers traded principally between the United Kingdom and the Mediterranean, but the 2,258 ton CIRCASSIAN PRINCE reached New York in ballast on 2 June 1889 and is believed to have been the Company's first direct sailing from the United Kingdom to the United States. In 1890 the ARABIAN PRINCE inaugurated a service between the Mediterranean and New York, while the South American trade was entered in 1894 with cargo sailings from Antwerp and London direct to the River Plate.

The 3,272 ton TARTAR PRINCE was launched by Short Brothers of Sunderland in January 1895, and was despatched from London on 26 September on her maiden voyage to Montevideo, Rosario and Buenos Aires. Yacht-like in appearance with a clipper bow, advertisements stated that her passenger facilities included 'Saloon amidships, electric light, bathroom, etc'. She could accommodate 20 first class and 1,000 steerage passengers. After a second and a third voyage she was joined by a sister ship, the 3,273 ton TROJAN PRINCE, a product of J. Readhead & Sons of South Shields.

Unfortunately, the United Kingdom–South American trade cannot have come up to expectation as in April 1897 both ships proceeded from the River Plate and Santos to New York. The TROJAN PRINCE then undertook a round voyage from New York to Buenos Aires before being despatched on 26 September 1897 from New York to Genoa. But the TARTAR PRINCE proceeded from New York to the Tyne, from where she made a round voyage via Antwerp to Vera Cruz and New Orleans. Upon return to the Tyne, she sailed to New York to join her sister ship in a regular line to Italy, to which was added the 3,299 ton SPARTAN PRINCE in January 1898.

Subsequently, there were Prince Line cargo sailings from British ports

338

to South America, but no further ones by multi-passenger ships.

At a later date, in 1929–30, the 10,900 ton motorships NORTHERN PRINCE, EASTERN PRINCE, SOUTHERN PRINCE and WESTERN PRINCE were built for service between New York and the River Plate, and had accommodation for 100 first class passengers. They became very popular, but it was necessary to close down the service soon after the outbreak of World War II in September 1939 and it was never re-instated.

The PRINCE LINE was acquired by the Furness Withy Group in 1916, retaining its name and independent existence. James Knott was created a baronet a year later. He died in Jersey on 8 June 1934.

1. 1895 TARTAR PRINCE
    3,272. 104,44 x 13,16. (342.7 x 43.2). C–1–2. S–T3–12. (I–20; III–1,000). Short Bros, Sunderland (engines Blair & Co Ltd, Stockton). 1895 (Jan) launched. 1895 (26/9) MV London–Montevideo–Rosario–Buenos Aires. 1897 (27/2) LV ditto, thence New York and Newcastle. 1897 (10/11) FV Newcastle–New York–Naples–Genoa–Leghorn. 1902 (Jly) transferred to New York–S. Africa service 1902 (25/11) destroyed by fire on voyage New York–S. Africa.

2. 1896 TROJAN PRINCE
    3,273. 107,10 x 13,59. (351.4 x 44.6). C–1–2. S–T3–12. (I–20; III–1,000). J. Readhead & Sons, South Shields. 1896 (14/5) launched. 1896 (30/7) MV London–Montevideo–Rosario–Buenos Aires. 1897 (16/2) LV London–Montevideo–Buenos Aires–New York. 1897 (26/9) FV New York–Naples–Genoa–Leghorn. 1917 (23/2) torpedoed and sunk by German submarine 5 miles NW of Port Shershel.

FUNNEL: Black; broad red band with white 'Prince of Wales feathers'.
FLAG: Red; large white 'Prince of Wales feathers'.

LIGURE BRASILIANA

1897. Ligure Brasiliana Società di Navigazione
1909. Società di Navigazione la Ligure Brasiliana

(Italian)

The LIGURE BRASILIANA SOCIETÀ DI NAVIGAZIONE was founded in Genoa by Giulio Gavotti on 29 November 1897 with a capital of 2½ million lire (£100,000). Three of its principal ships – the RE UMBERTO, MINAS and RIO AMAZONAS (ex-MARANHAO) – had been taken over from the defunct Ligure Romana, the remainder of its requirements being looked after by chartered tonnage.

The first Ligure Brasiliana sailing was undertaken by the 3,164 ton RE UMBERTO, which left Genoa on 15 December 1897 for Marseilles, Barcelona. Lisbon, Fayal (Azores), Para (Belem) and Manaos (Manaus). She had been built in 1892 by G. Ansaldo & Co of Sestri Ponente with a passenger complement of 34 first class and 925 third.

The second sailing was taken by the 2,964 ton MINAS from Genoa on 24 December 1897 for Rio de Janeiro and Santos. She, too, was a product of Ansaldo, built in 1891 as the MICHELE LAZZARONI for B. Mazzino of Genoa, and could carry 60 first class and about 900 third. In 1893 Mazzino renamed her REMO and a year later she became the PARA when, apparently, acquired by Ligure Romana.

A chartered steamer, the COLOMBO, was responsible for the third sailing on 6 January 1898 for Rio de Janeiro and Santos. At that time there were two Italian ships named COLOMBO, but it seems that the one in question was built by A. Leslie & Co of Hebburn-on-Tyne and had a tonnage of 2,408.

Next came the 2,532 ton chartered SAN GOTTARDO, another Ansaldo product, built in 1884 for Dufour & Bruzzo of Genoa. She left that port on 15 January 1898 for Rio de Janeiro and Santos.

The second sailing to the River Amazon was taken by the 3,171 ton RIO AMAZONAS, a sister ship of the RE UMBERTO, but built as the GIULIO CESARE. She was acquired by Ligure Romana about 1894 and renamed MARANHAO. The RIO AMAZONAS left Genoa about 20 January 1898 and Marseilles on 22 January for Para.

A sixth steamer was the 2,550 ton chartered AGORDAT, launched in

September 1883 by A. Leslie & Co as the Anglo–Australasian Steam Navigation Company's PORT JACKSON. She sailed on 15 February 1898 for Brazil and the River Plate.

Subsequent voyages of the MINAS until 1903, no fewer than 32 in number, were to Para and Manaos, and it is evident that she was well-patronised as she carried 32,000 outward passengers and 15,000 homeward, in addition to considerable quantities of cargo.

To begin with the North Brazil line was considered to be the principal one, on which the RE UMBERTO, RIO AMAZONAS and MINAS sailed. Usually the time taken from Genoa to Para was 17 days, and to Manaos 25 days. Sailings to South Brazil were taken by the chartered steamers until 1903, when they were returned to their owners. At the same time, the Amazon service was abandoned and the three ships owned by Ligure Brasiliana were transferred to the Brazil and River Plate service.

There was a greatly increased passenger demand to Argentina in the autumn of 1906, and the 11,494 ton Hamburg American Line twin-screw steamer BULGARIA was chartered by Ligure Brasiliana to make two round voyages from Genoa, her passenger capacity being no less than 300 second class and 2,400 third. She sailed from Hamburg for Genoa on 6 September, from Genoa for Buenos Aires on 4 October and left Genoa again for the same destination on 14 December. She carried on her two voyages a total of over 3,000 emigrants and some 6,000 tons of cargo. It has been said that a sister ship, the BATAVIA, made a voyage to South America but this is not correct.

There were financial changes at the end of 1908 and Angelo Parodi succeeded Giulio Gavotti as president of Ligure Brasiliana. The Company's name was changed on 18 March 1909 to SOCIETÀ DI NAVIGAZIONE LA LIGURE BRASILIANA.

By this time the RE UMBERTO, RIO AMAZONAS and MINAS were long past their prime, and in 1911 the 5,018 ton FLORIDA and the 5,181 ton VIRGINIA were bought from Lloyd Italiano (Chapter 50) to replace them. Twin-screw steamers built by the Società Esercizio Bacini of Riva Trigoso in 1905–06, their first class accommodation had been increased to 65 berths, and in addition they could cater for 1,600 third class. They were renamed CAVOUR and GARIBALDI, respectively. The latter was advertised to sail from Genoa for the River Plate on 18 August 1911, but had been taken up as an Italian Government troopship and her first South American sailing was postponed to 15 January 1912. The CAVOUR got away on 5 November 1911.

The three discarded South American ships were otherwise employed by Parodi, and all three were victims of World War I.

In 1913 the Hamburg American Line bought the entire share capital of

Ligure Brasiliana and 12 months later, on 28 July 1914, the Company's name was changed to TRANSATLANTICA ITALIANA SOCIETÀ ANONIMA DI NAVIGAZIONE. Details of the new concern's activities are in Chapter 58.

As World War I started only a few days later, it will be appropriate to add that the GARIBALDI survived until towards the end of World War II, but the CAVOUR was sunk in collision with the Italian auxiliary cruiser CAPRERA on 12 December 1917.

1. (1897) RE UMBERTO
    3,164. 101,03 x 12,25. (331.5 x 40.2). S–1–2. S–T3–12. (I–34; III–925). G. Ansaldo & Co, Sestri Ponente. 1891 launched for Ligure Romana. 1897 RE UMBERTO (Ligure Brasiliana). 1897 (15/12) FV Genoa–Lisbon–Manaos. 1903 transferred to R. Plate service. 1911 LV ditto. 1915 (2/12) sunk by mine near Sasseno (94).

2. (1897) MINAS
    2,964. 101,00 x 12,22 (331.4 x 40.1). S–1–2. S–T3–12. (I–60; III–900). G. Ansaldo & Co, Sestri Ponente. 1891 built as MICHELE LAZZARONI (It). 1893 REMO (It). 1894 PARA (Ligure Romana). 1897 MINAS (Ligure Brasiliana). 1897 (24/12) FV Genoa–Rio de Janeiro–Santos. 1911 (May) LV Genoa–R. Plate. 1916 (15/2) torpedoed and sunk by enemy submarine on voyage Taranto–Salonica (331).

2a. (1898) COLOMBO (c)
    2,408. 104,23 x 10,67. (342.0 x 35.0). 1–2. I–S–C2–10. A. Leslie & Co, Hebburn-on-Tyne. Built 1873 for G. Cresta, Genoa. 1898 (6/1) FV for Ligure Brasiliana (c), Genoa–Rio de Janeiro–Santos.

2b. (1898) SAN GOTTARDO (c)
    2,532. 105,00 x 11,61. (344.5 x 38.1). 1–2. I–S–T3–12. G. Ansaldo & Co, Sampierdarena. 1884 launched for Dufour & Bruzzo, Genoa. 1896 C2 became T3 by D. Torriani & Co, Sampierdarena. 1898 (15/1) FV for Ligure Brasiliana (c), Genoa–Rio de Janeiro–Santos. 1903 returned to owners.

3. (1898) RIO AMAZONAS
    3,171. 101,00 x 12,22. (331.4 x 40.1). 1–2. S–T3–12. (I–34; III–925). G. Ansaldo & Co, Sestri Ponente. 1891 launched as GIULIO CESARE (It). 1897 MARANHAO (Ligure Romana). 1897 RIO AMAZONAS (Ligure Brasiliana). 1898 (Jan) FV Genoa–Marseilles (22/1)–Para. 1903 transferred to R. Plate service. 1911 LV ditto. 1917 (13/5) sunk by gunfire from German submarine U.38, 70 miles from Benghazi.

3a. (1898) AGORDAT (c)
   2,550. 96,61 x 11,34. (317.0 x 37.2). 1–2. I–S–C2–10. A. Leslie &
   Co, Hebburn-on-Tyne (engines T. Clark & Co, Newcastle). 1883
   (Sep) launched as PORT JACKSON (Anglo-Australasian SN
   Co). 1898 (15/2) FV as AGORDAT (c) for Ligure Brasiliana,
   Genoa–Marseilles–Brazil–R. Plate. 1903 BEPPE (Italian). 1905
   JEANNE MARCELLE. 1910 scrapped in Italy.
3b. (1906) BULGARIA (c)
   11,494. 152,39 x 18,90. (500.0 x 62.0). 1–2. 2S–Q8–14. (II–300;
   III–2,400). Blohm & Voss, Hamburg. 1898 (5/2) launched for
   Hapag. 1898 (10/4) MV Hamburg–New York. 1906 (4/10) FV for
   Ligure Brasiliana (c), Genoa–Buenos Aires. 1906 (14/12) LV
   ditto (2 RV). 1913 CANADA (Unione Austriaca). 1913 BUL-
   GARIA (Hapag). 1917 (Apr) seized at Baltimore; became
   HERCULES (US Govt). 1919 PHILIPPINES (USSB). 1924
   scrapped at New York.
4. (1911) CAVOUR
   5,018. 116,24 x 14,66. (381.4 x 48.1). 2–2. 2S–T6–14. (I–65;
   III–1,600). Società Esercizio Bacini, Riva Trigoso. 1905 (22/6)
   launched as FLORIDA (Lloyd Italiano). 1905 (18/9) MV
   Genoa–Naples–Buenos Aires (1 RV). 1909 (23/1) collided with
   and sank REPUBLIC (White Star) off US coast. 1911 CAVOUR
   (Ligure Brasiliana). 1911 (5/11) FV Genoa–S. America. 1914
   CAVOUR (Transatlantica Italiana). 1917 (12/12) sunk in collision with Italian auxiliary cruiser CAPRERA near Armeville.
5. (1912) GARIBALDI
   5,181. 116,24 x 14,66. (381.4 x 48.1). 2–2. 2S–T6–14. (I–65;
   III–1,600). Società Esercizio Bacini, Riva Trigoso (engines G.
   Ansaldo, Armstrong & Co, Sampierdarena). 1906 (19/9) launched as VIRGINIA (Lloyd Italiano). 1906 (8/10) MV Genoa–
   Naples–New York. 1911 GARIBALDI (Ligure Brasiliana). 1912
   (15/1) FV Genoa–S. America. 1914 GARIBALDI (Transatlantica Italiana). 1925 ditto (Citra). 1932 ditto (Tirrenia). 1944
   (2/8) sunk during air attack on Genoa. 1946 refloated; scrapped.

FUNNEL: Red with white star; black top.

Chapter 47

(1900–34)

HAMBURG – AMERIKANISCHE PACKETFAHRT AKTIEN GESELLSCHAFT
('HAPAG')

(Hamburg–Amerika Linie – Hamburg American Line)

(German)

The HAMBURG – AMERIKANISCHE PACKETFAHRT AKTIEN GESELLSCHAFT or 'Hapag' (to quote the initial letters of its title), but best known in the English-speaking world as the HAMBURG AMERICAN LINE, was founded on 27 May 1847. It started operations with wooden sailing ships, and its first steamship did not leave Hamburg for New York until 1 June 1856.

Its chief competitor, Norddeutscher Lloyd of Bremen, entered the South American trade in 1876 (Chapter 29), but Hapag did not regularly follow suit until 1900, principally because the Hamburg – Südamerikanischen Dampfschiffahrts Gesellschaft (Hamburg–Süd) – (Chapter 26) – had been running an intensive service between Hamburg, Brazil and the River Plate since 1872.

Things changed because of events concerning another Hamburg line, de Freitas, which had run a service to the east coast of South America since 1892. During much of the time up to 1899 they had had a pooling arrangement with Hamburg–Süd but intense competition sprang up after this was allowed to lapse, and in 1900 the goodwill and 14 de Freitas steamers were sold to Hapag. It was announced on 15 November 1900 that Hamburg–Süd had come to terms with Hapag as regards services to Brazil and the River Plate, the basis of agreement being a one-third interest for Hapag and two-thirds for Hamburg–Süd.

The de Freitas steamers, most of which had accommodation for about 12 passengers, continued in service to South America, but it seems that the first sailing of Hapag cargo and multi-passengers ships, to Brazil, was taken by the 2,404 ton CANADIA from Hamburg on 14 July 1900. Built as the Hansa Line STEINHÖFT, she had been acquired in 1892 and renamed in 1894. Her complement was 10 first class and 550 steerage passengers.

Five 'PRINCE' class ships – the 4,650 ton single-screw PRINZ EITEL FRIEDRICH, PRINZ WALDEMAR and PRINZ SIGISMUND and

344

1900 CANADIA 2,404 tons
Undertook one of the first Hapag sailings to Brazil.

the 6,030 ton twin-screw PRINZ ADALBERT and PRINZ OSKAR –
were completed in 1902–03. The maiden voyage of the PRINZ EITEL
FRIEDRICH took place to the West Indies, but her second was to Rio
de Janeiro, as were the maiden voyages of the other four. The PRINZ
ADALBERT and PRINZ OSKAR had many changes of itinerary, and
in 1906 both were transferred for a time to the Hapag service from Genoa
to Buenos Aires, which had been started in 1904 by the ex-Hamburg–Süd
PATAGONIA, LA PLATA and ANTONINA. The ITAPARICA made
one similar voyage in 1905 after purchase from Hamburg–Süd. Later in
the same year she was renamed VIRGINIA, and detailed to Hapag's
West Indies service.

Also in 1905, the Hamburg–Süd RIO PARDO became temporarily
the DALMATIA of Hapag's Brazilian service, pending delivery of a
batch of new ships, but reverted to Hamburg–Süd and her original name
a year later.

1903 PRINZ OSKAR 6,026 tons
Ran to Buenos Aires from Hamburg and later from Genoa.

345

Steamers completed in 1905–06 and detailed to the Hapag South American line at once, or fairly soon afterwards, included the 6,600 ton RHAETIA, the 6,598 ton RUGIA, the 6,951 ton BORUSSIA and the 6,437 ton HABSBURG and HOHENSTAUFEN, all carrying large numbers of first and third class passengers. The BORUSSIA catered for second class as well, and was a twin-screw ship. She had a very short life as she foundered in 1907 when coaling at Lisbon, three lives being lost. The 5,779 ton NAVARRA and the 5,970 ton SALAMANCA both catered for a large number of third class only.

A much larger and more luxurious ship was launched on 4 July 1906. This was the 9,462 ton twin screw KÖNIG FRIEDRICH AUGUST, which started her maiden voyage from Hamburg to Buenos Aires on 26 October 1906. She was a product of Blohm & Voss of Hamburg, was fitted with two sets of quadruple-expansion engines giving a service speed of 15 knots and could accommodate 296 first, 56 second and 696 third class passengers. A similar ship, the 9,408 ton KÖNIG WILHEM II, followed her into service on 30 July 1907.

1907 KÖNIG WILHELM II 9,408 tons
Near sister of KÖNIG FRIEDRICH AUGUST.

The 8,103 ton YPIRANGA and the 8,099 ton CORCOVADO were completed for the Hamburg–Brazil service in 1908, but were transferred in 1911 to Hapag's Hamburg–Cuba–Mexico trade.

The next development was of a very different nature. In 1912 the 12,334 ton BLÜCHER, built in 1902 as a sister ship of the MOLTKE for service between Hamburg, Boulogne, Southampton and New York, was transferred to the Hamburg–Brazil–River Plate trade. She had luxurious accommodation for 390 first class passengers in addition to 230 second class and 1,550 third.

The 5,227 ton VALESIA and the 5,232 ton VALENCIA were completed in 1913, and could accommodate 60 first class and over 600 third.

By far the most imposing of all, however, were the 21,498 ton

346

TIRPITZ, launched on 20 December 1913 as the ADMIRAL VON TIRPITZ, the 19,582 ton JOHANN HEINRICH BURCHARD, launched on 10 February 1914 and the 19,653 ton WILLIAM O'SWALD, launched on 30 March 1914. These three were a match for the big new CAP TRAFALGAR and CAP POLONIO of Hamburg–Süd, but sadly the Hapag ships never entered the service for which they were built, and for a long time it looked as if none would ever run for Hapag at all. As it happened, the TIRPITZ never did as she was bought by Canadian Pacific in 1921 and commissioned as the EMPRESS OF AUSTRALIA.

The JOHANN HEINRICH BURCHARD and WILLIAM O'SWALD were secretly purchased by the Royal Holland Lloyd (Chapter 51) in 1916 and renamed LIMBURGIA and BRABANTIA. The Dutch Line ignored Allied demands after the 1918 Armistice to hand over the ships, which were placed in service between Amsterdam and South America in 1920. However, financial difficulties made it necessary for them to be sold in 1922, and they became the RELIANCE and RESOLUTE of United American Lines, running between New York, Cherbourg, Southampton and Hamburg. At long last, in 1926, Hapag bought them and retained them on the same route.

As was to be expected, Hapag lost virtually every worthwhile ship of their colossal 442-strong fleet during or after the war. Seven ships which had run on the South Atlantic were seized in North or South America during the war, including the BLÜCHER and VALESIA. One was captured, one torpedoed, one scuttled by the Germans and five surrendered after the war.

By 1921 the Allied regulations prohibiting the re-sale of ex-German ships to Germany were considerably relaxed, and two former Hapag steamers restarted the South American passenger service in that year – the 6,598 ton RUGIA built in 1905 and the 6,533 ton TEUTONIA, built as the HABSBURG in 1906. On 10 July 1923 the RUGIA stranded at Santa Rosa, Uruguay, and it was not until more than five months later, on 29 December, that she was refloated.

The first Hapag passenger sailing to the River Plate of a post-war steamer was undertaken by the 8,803 ton BADEN, a single-screw ship with triple-expansion engines, a service speed of 13 knots and accommodation for 17 first and 744 third class passengers. She was launched on 25 February 1922, and her maiden voyage started from Hamburg on 16 May. This ship was followed by the 8,109 ton SACHSEN, whose dimensions were very similar although her passenger accommodation was limited to 20 first class. She left Hamburg for Buenos Aires on 16 September 1922.

The 8,829 ton WÜRTTEMBERG was a sister ship of the BADEN, but made 10 round voyages from Hamburg to New York before sailing

1922 BADEN 8,803 tons
First Hapag passenger sailing to River Plate by post-World War I steamer.

for the River Plate on 31 January 1923. Similarly, the 8,116 ton
HESSEN, which also sailed in 1923, was a sister ship of the SACHSEN,
her passenger complement being 18 first class.

The 8,899 ton single-screw BAYERN, launched on 2 June 1921, had
been responsible for restarting sailings between Hamburg and New York
on 13 September 1921, but by 1924 Hapag had ample tonnage available
for this service and so the BAYERN was despatched from Hamburg to
the River Plate in March of that year. She had accommodation for 568
third class passengers.

Hamburg–Süd had commissioned the 10,121 ton twin-screw BAHIA
CASTILLO in 1913. She was surrendered to Britain in 1919, and in
September 1922 was sold to Hugo Stinnes of Hamburg, who renamed her
GENERAL SAN MARTIN, later changed to GENERAL BELGRA-
NO. In 1924 the Hugo Stinnes Linien got into financial difficulties and
was taken over by the Deutsch–Austral & Kosmos Linien, which in turn
was taken over by Hapag in 1926. Thus the GENERAL BELGRANO
became a Hapag ship and, as before, was placed in service between
Hamburg and the River Plate.

This acquisition increased the tonnage of the Hapag fleet to nearly
850,000 – a remarkable achievement in such a short space of time. Their
steamers had had buff funnels since 1909, whereas the Deutsch–Austral
& Kosmos ships had a black funnel with white and red bands. It was
decided in 1927 that the entire fleet should have buff funnels with narrow
black, white and red bands from the top downwards.

The 11,590 ton twin-screw motorship GENERAL OSORIO was
completed by Bremer Vulkan of Vegesack for the River Plate service in

348

1929 and shared with the pre-war BLÜCHER the distinction of having two funnels. Her passenger capacity was 228 cabin class and 752 third.

Two further ships were transferred to the South American service in 1930 – the 11,250 ton single-screw THURINGIA and WESTPHALIA, which had been built for the North Atlantic trade in 1923 and were renamed GENERAL SAN MARTIN and GENERAL ARTIGAS. They could accommodate 169 cabin and 650 third class passengers. This influx of tonnage enabled the 20 year old GENERAL BELGRANO to be scrapped at Hamburg in 1933.

1930 GENERAL ARTIGAS 11,254 tons
Built 1923 as WESTPHALIA for Hapag New York service.

The German Government announced in 1934 that Hamburg–Süd should have a monopoly of the German shipping activities to the east coast of South America, and in consequence both Hapag and Norddeutscher Lloyd chartered their South Atlantic fleets to their successor in 1934–5. Hapag's contribution consisted of the GENERAL OSORIO, GENERAL SAN MARTIN, GENERAL ARTIGAS, SACHSEN and 11 purely cargo steamers. All 15 were bought by Hamburg–Süd in 1936.

Looking back, Hapag was undoubtedly spared many headaches by the withdrawal of its South American service. Only one of the 15 transferred ships – the GENERAL SAN MARTIN – survived World War II, and even she was seized by Britain at Copenhagen in 1945.

1. (1900) CANADIA
    2,404. 91,86 x 11,52. (301.4 x 37.8). 1–2. S–T3–11. (I–10; III–550). Reiherstieg, Hamburg. 1889 (16/3) launched as STEINHÖFT (Hansa). 1892 STEINHÖFT (Hapag). 1894 CANADIA (Hapag). 1900 (4/7) FV Hamburg–Brazil. 1905 REVAL (Russian). 1905 CANADIA (Hapag). 1906 CANADIA (Furness). 1910 MYRTOON (Greek). 1914 GYPTIS (Fr). 1919 VILLE DE NANCY (Fr). 1924 scrapped in Italy.

2. (1902) PRINZ EITEL FRIEDRICH
    4,650. 113,07 x 13,80. (371.0 x 45.3). 1–2. S–Q4–12. (I–100;
    III–634). Reiherstieg, Hamburg. 1901 (21/12) launched. 1902
    (24/6) FV Hamburg–Rio de Janeiro. 1914 (6/8) laid up at New
    York. 1917 (6/4) seized by US Govt; renamed OTSEGO. 1924
    ditto (US). 1947 DOLINSK (USSR). 1955 scrapped at Vladivos-
    tock.
3. 1902 PRINZ WALDEMAR
    4,658. 113,10 x 13,71. (371.1 x 45.0). 1–2. S–Q4–12. (I–100;
    III–634). Reiherstieg, Hamburg. 1902 (7/5) launched. 1902 (10/9)
    MV Hamburg–Brazil. 1907 (14/1) wrecked near Kingston,
    Jamaica.
4. 1903 PRINZ ADALBERT
    6,030. 122,92 x 14,99. (403.3 x 49.2). 1–2. 2S–Q8–13. (I–124;
    III–1,033). Bremer Vulkan, Vegesack. 1902 (21/8) launched.
    1903 (20/1) MV Hamburg–Brazil (1 RV). 1906 FV Genoa–
    Buenos Aires. 1914 (4/8) seized at Falmouth. 1916 became
    H.M.S. PRINCETOWN. 1917 ALÉSIA (Fr). 1917 (6/9) torpe-
    doed and sunk by German submarine UC.50 40 miles from
    Ushant.
5. 1903 PRINZ OSKAR
    6,026. 122,95 x 14,99. (403.4 x 49.2). 1–2. 2S–Q8–13. (I–125;
    III–1,039). Bremer Vulkan, Vegesack. 1902 (15/12) launched.
    1903 (Jun) MV Hamburg–Brazil. 1906 (22/9) FV Genoa–Buenos
    Aires. 1917 (Apr) seized at Philadelphia; became ORION (US
    Govt). 1922–3 ORION (Black Star). 1929 scrapped at Baltimore.
6. 1903 PRINZ SIGISMUND
    4,689. 112,83 x 13,80. (370.2 x 45.3). 1–2. S–Q4–12. (I–100;
    III–708). AG Neptun, Rostock. 1902 (27–28/9) launched. 1903
    (Jul) MV Hamburg–Brazil. 1914 (Aug) sheltered at Colon.
    1917 (Apr) seized; renamed GENERAL W.C. GORGAS.
    1941 MIKHAIL LOMONOSOV (USSR). 1958 scrapped in
    Russia.
7. (1904) PATAGONIA
    2,975. 100,58 x 12,68. (330.0 x 41.6). 1–2. S–T3–12. (I–40;
    III–230). Reiherstieg, Hamburg. 1890 (6/9) launched for Ham-
    burg–Süd. 1904 PATAGONIA (Hapag). 1904 (5/5) FV Genoa–
    Buenos Aires. 1911 (19/1) sank during repairs by Blohm & Voss;
    refloated; recommissioned. 1914 interned at Bahia Blanca. 1921
    surrendered to Britain. 1923 VALPARAISO (Chilean). 1933
    (4/10) wrecked near Taital, Chile.
8. (1904) LA PLATA
    4,004. 110,10 x 13,60. (361.3 x 44.6). 1–2. S–T3–12. (I–54;

III–330). Reiherstieg, Hamburg. 1898 (15/6) launched as PELO-
TAS (Hamburg–Süd). 1901 LA PLATA (Italia (c)). 1901 (27/3)
FV Genoa–S. America. 1904 LA PLATA (Hapag) 1904 (28/5)
FV Genoa–Buenos Aires. 1914 (Aug) laid up at Hamburg. (See
Hamburg–Süd (26)).

9. (1904) ANTONINA
4,010. 110,10 x 13,60. (361.3 x 44.6). 1–2. S–T3–12. (I–52;
III–330). Blohm & Voss, Hamburg. 1898 (18/6) launched for
Hamburg–Süd. 1901 (17/4) FV for Italia (c), Genoa–S. America.
1904 (24/5) ANTONINA (Hapag). 1904 (16/7) FV Genoa–
Buenos Aires. 1905 (27/7) Genoa–Hamburg. 1905 (4/9) FV
Hamburg–Para. 1914 (Aug) interned at Tampico. (See Ham-
burg–Süd (26)).

10. (1904) AMAZONAS
2,950. 99,26 x 12,59. (325.7 x 41.3). 1–2. S–T3–12. (I–82;
III–228). Blohm & Voss, Hamburg. 1890 (26/7) launched for
Hamburg–Süd. 1903 RIO GALLEGOS (ditto but Argentine
flag). 1904 AMAZONAS (Hamburg–Süd). 1904 ditto (Hapag).
1904 (7/12) FV Hamburg–R. Plate. 1905 VENETIA (Hapag–
West Indies service). 1914 SPERRBRECHER 11 (German
navy). 1915 torpedoed by British submarine off Borkum;
beached but a constructive total loss.

11. (1905) ITAPARICA
2,543. 99,36 x 12,19. (326.0 x 40.0). 1–2. S–T3–11. (I–40;
III–246). Sir W.G. Armstrong, Mitchell & Co, Walker-on-Tyne
(engines Wallsend Slipway Co Ltd). 1889 (21/10) launched for
Hamburg–Süd. 1901 CHUBUT (ditto but Argentine flag). 1904
ITAPARICA (Hamburg–Süd). 1905 ITAPARICA (Hapag).
1905 (9/3) FV Genoa–Buenos Aires (1 RV). 1905 VIRGINIA
(Hapag–West Indies service). 1914 (Aug) interned at Cartagena,
Colombia. 1916 JASON (US). 1920 URALKER (Spanish). 1923
scrapped at Wilhelmshaven.

12. 1905 DALMATIA
4,588. 110,05 x 14,23. (361.1 x 46.7). 1–2. 2S–T6–11. (I–50;
III–230). J.C. Tecklenborg, Geestemünde. 1905 (20/5) launched
as RIO PARDO (Hamburg–Süd). 1905 DALMATIA (Hapag).
1905 (31/8) MV Hamburg–Brazil. 1906 RIO PARDO (Hamburg–Süd). 1914 SPERRBRECHER 11 (German Navy); later
SPERRBRECHER 4. 1919 surrendered to Britain. 1921 CITY
OF ALEXANDRIA (Ellerman). 1933 scrapped at Cobh.

13. (1905) RHAETIA
6,600. 124,81 x 16,06. (409.5 x 52.7). 1–2. S–Q4–13. (I–120;
III–706). Bremer Vulkan, Vegesack. 1904 (5/11) launched. 1905

(30/8) FV Hamburg–Brazil. 1914 (Aug) interned at Philadelphia. 1917 (Apr) seized by USA; renamed BLACK HAWK (US Govt). 1919 BLACK ARROW (USSB). 1920 ditto (New York & Cuba Mail SS Co). 1924 scrapped.

14. 1906 NAVARRA

5,779. 119,56 x 15,33. (392.3 x 50.3). 1–2. S–T3–12. (III–1,221). AG Vulcan, Stettin. 1905 (16/12) launched. 1906 (28/4) MV Hamburg–Buenos Aires. 1914 (Sep) sheltered at Punta Arenas. 1914 (Oct) rendezvous with commerce raider KRONPRINZ WILHELM. 1914 (Nov) intercepted by British auxiliary cruiser ORAMA; scuttled to avoid capture.

15. (1906) RUGIA

6,598. 124,78 x 16,06. (409.4 x 52.7). 1–2. S–Q4–13. (I–130; III–824). Bremer Vulkan, Vegesack. 1905 (17/5) launched. 1906 (13/5) FV Hamburg–Brazil. 1919 surrendered to Britain. 1921 RUGIA (Hapag); (I–75; III–66); resumed Hamburg–S. America. 1923 (10/7) stranded at Santa Rosa, Uruguay. 1923 (29/12) refloated. 1932 scrapped.

16. (1906) BORUSSIA

6,951. 128,40 x 16,50. (421.3 x 54.1). 1–2. 2S–Q8–13. (I–62; II–40; III–1,776). Germaniawerft (Fried Krupp AG), Kiel. 1905 (24/3) launched. 1906 (25/9) FV Hamburg–Brazil. 1907 (22/10) foundered when taking on coal at Lisbon (3).

17. 1906 KÖNIG FRIEDRICH AUGUST

9,462. 145,01 x 16,88. (475.8 x 55.4). 1–2. 2S–Q8–15. (I–296; II–56; III–696). Blohm & Voss, Hamburg. 1906 (4/7) launched. 1906 (26/10) MV Hamburg–Buenos Aires. 1914 (Aug) at Hamburg. 1919 surrendered to Britain. 1920 (6/11) to Canadian Pacific. 1921 (3/2) renamed MONTREAL. 1927 laid up at Southend. 1928 ALÉSIA (Fabre). 1933 scrapped at Genoa.

18. (1906) SALAMANCA

5,970. 119,47 x 15,30. (392.0 x 50.2). 1–2. S–T3–12. (III–976). Harland & Wolff, Belfast. 1906 (5/7) launched. 1906 (26/9) MV Hamburg–Newport News. 1906 (25/11) FV Hamburg–S. America. 1914 (Aug) interned at Cabedello, Brazil. 1917 (1/6) seized by Brazil; renamed CABEDELLO. 1926 ditto (Lloyd Brasileiro). 1942 (1/6) torpedoed and sunk by German submarine U.156 off Brazilian coast.

19. 1907 KÖNIG WILHELM II

9,408. 149,46 x 16,85. (490.4 x 55.3). 1–2. 2S–Q8–15. (I–326; II–44; III–655). AG Vulcan, Stettin. 1907 (23/3) launched. 1907 (30/7) MV Hamburg–Buenos Aires. 1914 (Aug) interned at New York. 1917 (Apr) seized by USA; renamed MADAWASKA.

1922 GRANT (US Navy). 1946 laid up at Seattle by US Army. 1947 scrapped.
20. 1908 CORCOVADO
8,099. 136,63 x 16,82. (448.3 x 55.2). 1–2. 2S–Q8–13. (I–136; III–1,126). Germaniawerft (Fried Krupp AG), Kiel. 1907 (21/12) launched. 1908 (Apr) MV Hamburg–Brazil. 1911 Hamburg–Cuba–Mexico. 1912 (19/10) FV Hamburg–New York. 1914 (15/4) FV New York–Mediterranean–Black Sea. 1914 (Aug) sheltered at Constantinople. 1918 (6/11) SUEH (Turkish). 1919 CORCO-VADO (Fr). 1920 GUGLIELMO PEIRCE (Sicula Americana). 1926 ditto (Cosulich). 1927 MARIA CRISTINA (Lloyd Sabaudo). 1930 MOUZINHO (Cia Colonial (Portuguese). 1954 scrapped at Savona.
21. 1908 YPIRANGA
8,103. 136,66 x 16,85. (448.4 x 55.3). 1–2. 2S–Q8–13. (I–136; III–1,049). Germaniawerft (Fried Krupp AG), Kiel. 1908 (3/5) launched. 1908 (14/10) MV Hamburg–Brazil. 1911 FV Hamburg–Cuba–Mexico. 1914 (Aug) at Hamburg. 1919 surrendered to Britain. 1921 ASSYRIA (Anchor). 1929 COLONIAL (Cia Colonial (Portuguese). 1950 BISCO 9 (British Iron & Steel Corporation). 1950 (17/9) stranded at Campbeltown, Kintyre; scrapped 'as lies'.
22. (1909) HABSBURG
(1921) TEUTONIA
6,437. 124,90 x 16,09. (409.8 x 52.8). 1–2. S–Q4–13. (I–62; III–900). Bremer Vulkan, Vegesack. 1906 (25/5) launched. 1906 (20/8) MV Hamburg–Far East. 1909 (24/8) FV Hamburg–Brazil. 1914 (Aug) laid up at Hamburg. 1918 (Oct) damaged by mine in Baltic; repaired at Reval and Hamburg. 1920 RENO (It). 1921 TEUTONIA (Hapag); 6,533 tons; (I–58; III–714). 1921 resumed Hamburg–S. America. 1933 scrapped at Hamburg.
23. (1909) HOHENSTAUFEN
6,437. 124,75 x 16,06. (409.3 x 52.7). 1–2. S–Q4–13. (I–64; III–1,100). Bremer Vulkan, Vegesack. 1906 (18/8) launched. 1906 (20/10) MV Hamburg–Far East. 1909 (13/7) FV Hamburg–Brazil. 1914 (Aug) interned at Rio de Janeiro. 1917 (1/6) seized by Brazil; renamed CUYABA. 1927 ditto (Lloyd Brasileiro). 1964 scrapped in Brazil.
24. (1912) BLÜCHER
12,334. 160,19 x 18,99. (525.6 x 62.3). 2–2. 2S–Q8–16. (I–390; II–230; III–1,550). Blohm & Voss, Hamburg. 1901 (23/11) launched. 1902 (7/6) MV Hamburg–New York. 1911 (30/12) LV ditto. 1912 (25/6) FV Hamburg–Brazil–R. Plate. 1914 (Aug)

interned at Pernambuco. 1917 (1/6) seized by Brazil; renamed LEOPOLDINA (Brazilian Govt). 1923 SUFFREN (CGT (Fr)). 1929 scrapped at Genoa.

25. 1913 VALESIA

5,227. 108,68 x 15,51. (356.6 x 50.9). 1–2. S–T3–12. (I–60; III–625). AG Neptun, Rostock. 1912 (26/9) launched. 1913 (Feb) MV Hamburg–Brazil. 1914 (Aug) sheltered at Santos. 1917 (Jun) seized by Brazil; renamed PALMARES. 1918 BELMONTE (Brazilian Navy). 1969 scrapped.

26. 1913 VALENCIA

5,232. 108,68 x 15,51. (356.6 x 50.9). 1–2. S–T3–12. (I–60; III–696). AG Neptun, Rostock. 1913 (13/4) launched. 1913 (Aug) MV Hamburg–Brazil. 1914 (Aug) at Hamburg. 1919 surrendered to Britain. 1920 HUGHLI (Br). 1928 TINHOW (Br). 1943 (11/4) torpedoed and sunk by German submarine U.181 on voyage Durban–Calcutta (75).

— —— TIRPITZ

21,498, 179,78 [187,44] x 22,92. (589.9 [615.0] x 75.2). 3–2. 2S–ST–17. (I–400; II–190; III–1,000). AG Vulcan, Stettin. 1913 (20/12) launched as ADMIRAL VON TIRPITZ (Hapag). 1914 (Jan) renamed TIRPITZ. 1920 (Nov) completed. 1921 (Jan) proceeded Swinemünde–Immingham; surrendered to Britain. 1921 (Jly) EMPRESS OF CHINA (Canadian Pacific). 1922 EMPRESS OF AUSTRALIA (ditto). 1939 (Sep) requisitioned as British troopship. 1952 scrapped at Inverkeithing.

— —— JOHANN HEINRICH BURCHARD

19,582, 179,94 [188,36] x 22,09. (590.4 [618.0] x 72.5). 3–2. 3S–T8&ST–17. (I–355; II–284; III–800). J.C. Tecklenborg, Geestemünde. 1914 (10/2) launched as JOHANN HEINRICH BURCHARD (Hapag). 1916 (31/5) secretly purchased by Royal Holland Lloyd; renamed LIMBURGIA. 1920 (14/4) MV Amsterdam–S. America. 1922 RELIANCE (United American Lines). 1926 ditto (Hapag). 1938 (7/8) gutted by fire at Hamburg. 1940 scrapped at Bremerhaven.

— —— WILLIAM O'SWALD

19,653. 179,94 [188,36] x 22.00. (590.4 [618.0] x 72.2). 3–2. 3S–T8&ST–17. (I–355; II–284; III–800). AG Weser, Bremen. 1914 (30/3) launched as WILLIAM O'SWALD (Hapag). 1916 (31/5) secretly purchased by Royal Holland Lloyd; renamed BRABANTIA. 1920 (1/9) MV Amsterdam–S. America. 1922 RESOLUTE (United American Lines). 1926 ditto (Hapag). 1935 LOMBARDIA (Italian transport). 1943 (4/8) damaged in air attack on Naples. 1947 scrapped at La Spezia.

27. 1922 BADEN

   8,803. 142,03 x 17,68. (466.0 x 58.0). 1–4. S–T3–13. (I–17;
   III–744). Bremer Vulkan, Vegesack. 1922 (25/2) launched. 1922
   (16/5) MV Hamburg–R. Plate. 1930 (24/10) at Rio de Janeiro
   during a revolution; ship disregarded an order to remain in port;
   coastal guns opened fire; many casualties. 1935 converted to a
   freighter (North American and Far East services). 1939 (Sept)
   took refuge at Santa Cruz. 1940 (25/12) intercepted by British
   cruiser BERWICK; scuttled to avoid capture.

28. 1922 SACHSEN

   8,109. 142,79 x 17,83. (468.5 x 58.5). 1–4. S–T3–13. (I–20).
   Bremer Vulkan, Vegesack. 1922 (3/6) launched. 1922 (16/9) MV
   Hamburg–R. Plate. 1935 SACHSEN (Hamburg–Süd (c)). 1936
   SACHSEN (Hamburg–Süd). 1937 LA PLATA (ditto). 1939
   (Sep) sheltered at Vigo. 1940 (Dec) returned to Germany. 1943
   (4/10) badly damaged by Allied air attack at Bodö, Norway;
   beached. 1949 scrapped.

29. (1923) WÜRTTEMBERG

   8,829. 142,03 x 17,68. (466.0 x 58.0). 1–4. S–T3–13. (I–17;
   III–751). Bremer Vulkan, Vegesack. 1921 (Aug) launched. 1921
   (14/11) MV Hamburg–New York (10 RV). 1923 (31/1) FV
   Hamburg–R. Plate. 1935 JAN WELLEM (German whaling
   ship); 11,767 tons. 1940 (13/4) sunk by British destroyers at
   Narvik; raised; towed to Kiel; repaired. 1947 scrapped at
   Blyth.

30. (1923) HESSEN

   8,116. 142,85 x 17,77. (468.7 x 58.3). 1–4. S–T3–13. (I–18).
   Bremer Vulkan, Vegesack. 1922 (18/11) launched. 1923 (16/2)
   MV Hamburg–New York. 1923 FV Hamburg–R. Plate. 1935
   FECHENHEIM (Ger). 1943 (12/2) torpedoed and sunk by
   Russian submarine K.3; subsequently refloated. 1946 (13/6)
   scuttled off Arendal with a cargo of poison gas.

31. (1924) BAYERN

   8,899. 142,03 x 17,68. (466.0 x 58.0). 1–4. S–T3–13. (III–568).
   Bremer Vulkan, Vegesack. 1921 (2/6) launched. 1921 (13/9) MV
   Hamburg–New York. 1924 (Mar) FV Hamburg–R. Plate. 1936
   SONTAY (Messageries Maritimes). 1955 SUNLOCK (Panama-
   nian). 1959 scrapped in Italy.

32. (1926) GENERAL BELGRANO

   10,121. 149,83 x 18,00. (491.6 x 59.1). 1–2. 2S–T6–13. (II–200;
   III–2,500). Reiherstieg, Hamburg. 1913 (4/1) launched as
   BAHIA CASTILLO (Hamburg–Süd). 1919 surrendered to
   Britain. 1922 GENERAL SAN MARTIN (Hugo Stinnes (Ger);

later GENERAL BELGRANO (ditto). 1926 ditto (Hapag). 1926 FV Hamburg–Buenos Aires. 1933 scrapped at Hamburg.

33. 1929 GENERAL OSORIO (M/S)

11,590. 151,93 x 20,11. (498.5 x 66.0). 2–2–C. 2S–2SC.DA–14. (cabin 228; III–752). Bremer Vulkan, Vegesack. 1929 (20/3) launched. 1929 (29/6) MV Hamburg–R. Plate. 1931 (8/8) rescued 88 passengers and crew of WESTERN WORLD (USA), stranded at San Sebastian. 1934 (1/11) GENERAL OSORIO (Hamburg–Süd (c)). 1936 (30/6) GENERAL OSORIO (Hamburg–Süd). 1940 accommodation ship at Kiel. 1944 (24/7) damaged by allied air attack at Kiel. 1944 temporarily repaired. 1945 (9/4) sunk by Allied air attack at Kiel. 1947 refloated; scrapped in Britain.

34. (1930) GENERAL SAN MARTIN

11,251. 144,34 x 18,50. (473.6 x 60.7). 1–2. S–ST(DR)–13. (cabin 169; III–650). Howaldtswerke, Kiel. 1917 planned as HAVEL-LAND (Hapag freighter). 1922 (12/8) launched as THURINGIA (Hapag). 1923 (22/1) MV Hamburg–New York. 1930 GENERAL SAN MARTIN (Hapag). 1930 FV Hamburg–R. Plate. 1934 GENERAL SAN MARTIN (Hamburg–Süd (c)). 1936 ditto (Hamburg–Süd). 1940 accommodation ship. 1945 (8/10) seized by Britain at Copenhagen. 1946 EMPIRE DEBEN (Shaw Savill (c)). 1949 scrapped at Newport, Mon.

35. (1930) GENERAL ARTIGAS

11,254. 144,34 x 18,50. (473.6 x 60.7). 1–2. S–ST(DR)–13. (cabin 169; III–650). Howaldtswerke, Kiel. 1917 planned as AMMER-LAND (Hapag freighter). 1923 (19/1) launched as WESTPHA-LIA (Hapag). 1923 (21/6) MV Hamburg–New York. 1930 GENERAL ARTIGAS (Hapag). 1930 FV Hamburg–R. Plate. 1934 GENERAL ARTIGAS (Hamburg–Süd (c)). 1935 ditto (Hamburg–Süd). 1940 accommodation ship at Hamburg. 1943 (25/7) burnt out in British air attack on Hamburg. 1946 scrapped.

FUNNEL: (a) 1900. Black.
(b) 1909. Buff.
(c) 1927. Buff; black-white-red top.

FLAG: Blue and white diagonally quartered; yellow shield in centre on black anchor and black 'HAPAG'.

ITALIA (I)

(Italia Società di Navigazione a Vapore)

(Italian)

ITALIA SOCIETÀ DI NAVIGAZIONE A VAPORE was founded in Genoa on 6 May 1899 with a capital of five million lire (£200,000) to run a passenger and cargo service between Italy, Brazil, Uruguay and Argentina. Although nominally an Italian concern, the Company was controlled by the Hamburg American Line, whose director-general, Albert Ballin, had played a prominent part in its formation.

Orders were placed with N. Odero & Co of Genoa for the 4,113 ton single-screw TOSCANA and the 4,101 ton RAVENNA, which started their maiden voyages from Genoa to Buenos Aires on 4 November 1900 and 5 June 1901, respectively. The TOSCANA, in particular, was launched in a fully completed condition and her maiden voyage started only nine days later. Each steamer could accommodate 42 first class and 1,320 steerage passengers.

1901 ANTONINA 4,010 tons
Chartered to Italia 1901–04.

It has often been said that the 4,000 ton LA PLATA (ex-PELOTAS) and ANTONINA were chartered from Hamburg–Süd (Chapter 26) to run until the TOSCANA and RAVENNA were delivered, but this is far from correct as the LA PLATA's first voyage for Italia did not take place until 27 March 1901 and the ANTONINA's until 17 April 1901. Moreover, each made 19 round voyages for Italia. Rather than being stopgaps for the TOSCANA and RAVENNA they, in fact, held the fort until the arrival of the 4,553 ton twin-screw SIENA, which was completed in May 1905 by N. Odero & Co, and the 4,680 ton BOLOGNA, completed a month later by Harland & Wolff of Belfast. The building of these two ships had been made possible by an increase of Italia's capital in 1904 to eight million lire.

Rather surprisingly, the RAVENNA made three round voyages in 1903 between Genoa, Naples and New York under charter to the Hamburg American Line when the LA PLATA and ANTONINA were still under charter to Italia. A ready explanation is that as Italia was then owned by Hapag they felt obliged to fall in with their wishes. The RAVENNA also made a round voyage in 1906 for Navigazione Generale Italiana (Chapter 36) between Genoa, Palermo and New York.

The activities of Italia did not produce the spectacular results Hapag had hoped for, and they decided in 1906 to accept an offer from NGI, which already controlled the La Veloce Line, to buy their shareholding, another justification of the German company's action being that their own recently-inaugurated service between the Mediterranean and South America was making very satisfactory progress. The outcome was that Italian directors replaced the Germans, and the paid up capital of Italia was increased to 12 million lire to enable three ships, the ANCONA, VERONA and TAORMINA, to be built for a new service from Genoa to New York and Philadelphia.

From 1908 onwards, sailings of NGI and its two subsidiaries, La Veloce and Italia, were co-ordinated on both North and South Atlantic.

The year 1908 was one of serious slump and the Company was unable to pay a dividend. However, conditions improved considerably in 1909, when six per cent was declared. Then in 1910 NGI obtained full control of Lloyd Italiano, a part interest in which they had acquired in 1907. A further co-ordination of sailings took place in 1912–13, and among several transfers of tonnage NGI passed to Italia for its South American service the 5,018 ton twin-screw ITALIA, which had reached them from La Veloce some months earlier. In addition, Italia received a sister ship, the 4,985 ton twin-screw BRASILE (ex-ARGENTINA) direct from La Veloce. They were joined briefly by the ex-NGI SAN PAULO. In exchange, Italia parted with the SIENA and BOLOGNA to La Veloce, who employed them on their Central American line.

1905 SIENA 4,553 tons
Sister ship of BOLOGNA.

Owing to competition from Sicula Americana (Chapter 57) on both North and South Atlantic, Italia decided at an extraordinary general meeting on 28 June 1913 to move its headquarters from Genoa to Naples.

The RAVENNA was torpedoed and sunk in the Gulf of Genoa on 4 April 1917, leaving the TOSCANA, BRASILE and ITALIA to take care of the South American service. Depletion of the Italia fleet on this as well as the North Atlantic run, combined with the exceptional conditions prevailing during the war, and above all the likelihood of increased competition from Sicula Americana after the war prompted NGI to arrange for the formation, on 19 August 1917, of TRANSOCEANICA SOCIETÀ ITALIANA DI NAVIGAZIONE (Chapter 59), which absorbed Italia, Sicula Americana and the latter's parent concern, the Peirce Line.

1. 1900 TOSCANA
     4,113. 110,69 x 13,25. (363.2 x 43.5). 1–2. S–T3–12. (I–42; III–1,320). N. Odero & Co, Genoa. 1900 (26/10) launched. 1900 (4/11) MV Genoa–S. America. 1917 TOSCANA (Transoceanica). 1918 (5/2) sunk near Gibraltar in collision with MOLIÈRE (Fr).
1a. (1901) LA PLATA (c)
     4,004. 110,10 x 13,60. (361.3 x 44.6). 1–2. S–T3–12. (I–54; III–330). Reiherstieg, Hamburg. 1898 (15/6) launched as PELOTAS (Hamburg–Süd). 1901 (27/3) FV as LA PLATA for Italia (c), Genoa–S. America. 1904 (Mar) LV ditto (19 RV). 1904 LA PLATA (Hapag). (See Hamburg–Süd (26)).
1b. (1901) ANTONINA (c)
     4,010. 110,10 x 13,60. (361.3 x 44.6). 1–2. S–T3–12. (I–52; III–330). Blohm & Voss, Hamburg. 1898 (18/6) launched for Hamburg–Süd. 1901 (17/4) FV for Italia (c), Genoa–S. America.

1904 (14/5) LV ditto (19 RV). 1904 ANTONINA (Hapag). (See Hamburg–Süd (26)).

2. 1901 RAVENNA
   4,101. 110,69 x 13,25. (363.2 x 43.5). 1–2. S–T3–12. (I–42; III–1,320). N. Odero & Co, Genoa. 1901 (2/3) launched. 1901 (5/6) MV Genoa–S. America. 1917 (4/4) torpedoed and sunk by German submarine U.52 in Gulf of Genoa.

3. 1905 SIENA
   4,553. 115,90 x 14,10. (380.3 x 46.3). 1–2. 2S–T6–14. (I–75; III–1,290). N. Odero & Co, Genoa. 1905 (Apr) launched. 1905 (20/5) MV Genoa–S. America. 1913 SIENA (La Veloce). 1916 (4/8) torpedoed and sunk by German submarine U.35 in Gulf of Lion (46).

4. 1905 BOLOGNA
   4,680. 115,90 x 14,10. (380.3 x 46.3). 1–2. 2S–T6–14. (I–75; III–1,290). Harland & Wolff Ltd, Belfast. 1905 (10/3) launched. 1905 (17/6) MV Genoa–S. America. 1913 BOLOGNA (La Veloce). 1928 scrapped in Italy.

5. (1913) SAN PAULO
   5,020. 122,32 x 14,20. (401.4 x 46.6). 1–2. S–Q4–14. (I–38; II–49; III–1,016). Fratelli Orlando, Leghorn. 1901 (8/8) launched as UMBRIA (NGI). 1902 (19/5) MV Genoa–Naples–New York. 1913 SAN PAULO (Italia). 1913 (10/1) FV Genoa–S. America. 1913 UMBRIA (Sitmar). 1932 scrapped.

6. (1913) BRASILE
   4,985. 120,11 x 14,53. (394.1 x 47.7). 2–2. 2S–T6–13. (I–61; II–56; III–950). Fratelli Orlando, Leghorn. 1905 (Jly) launched for La Veloce as ARGENTINA. 1912 BRASILE (La Veloce). 1913 BRASILE (Italia). 1917 BRASILE (Transoceanica). 1921 BRASILE (NGI). 1922 BRASILE (Sitmar).

7. (1913) ITALIA
   5,018. 119,99 x 14,56. (393.7 x 47.8). 2–2. 2S–T6–13. (I–61, II–56, III–980). N. Odero & Co, Genoa. 1905 (25/6) launched for La Veloce. 1905 (10/8) MV Genoa–Naples–S. America. 1912 ITALIA (NGI). 1913 ITALIA (Italia). 1917 ITALIA (Transoceanica). 1922 ITALIA (NGI). 1923 ITALIA (Sitmar). 1932 ITALIA (Lloyd Triestino). 1944 (6/7) sunk at Arsa (Trieste) by Allied bombers. 1950 refloated; scrapped.

Note: The 9,203 ton NAPOLI (ex-SANNIO) was acquired from NGI (Chapter 36) in 1912 and ran to New York.

FUNNEL: Yellow.
FLAG: Blue cross with white border; blue upper quarter at hoist, with red 'I' in a six-pointed white star; other quarters yellow.

Chapter 49

(1901–32)

NELSON LINE

(British)

The NELSON LINE can be traced back to 1889, when the firm of James Nelson & Sons bought the 3,060 ton steamer SPINDRIFT, which a year later was renamed HIGHLAND SCOT (I). The owners were registered as the HIGHLAND SCOT STEAMSHIP COMPANY LIMITED, the brothers Hugh & William Nelson being named as managers. The ship was fitted with refrigerating plant working on the cold-air system.

Hugh Nelson had recently established a flourishing meat factory at Zarate, not far from the mouth of the Parana River and fairly near to Buenos Aires. It was largely in order to have a ready and economical means of shipping the produce of this factory to England that the steamship business was started.

The HIGHLAND SCOT was an instant success, and orders were placed almost at once for the HIGHLAND CHIEF, HIGHLAND LASSIE, HIGHLAND MARY and HIGHLAND GLEN (I), two with Glasgow firms and two at Stockton-on-Tees, their tonnage varying between 2,488 and 2,974. Each ship was registered in her own name as a limited liability company. But this was only a temporary arrangement as the NELSON LINE (LIVERPOOL) LIMITED was formed in 1898 to take over the fleet of five ships, and three years later the firm of Hugh & William Nelson was converted into a limited liability company, H. & W. NELSON LIMITED.

First of the fleet to make provision for passengers was the 5,662 ton HIGHLAND BRIGADE, delivered by William Beardmore & Company Limited of Glasgow in March 1901. She carried a limited number of first class only passengers, and like all her predecessors had large cold storage facilities. By this time a regular service was in operation between Liverpool and Buenos Aires. General cargo was carried on the homeward voyage as well as the outward but, of course, homeward shipments depended to a considerable extent on Argentina meat.

The 5,150 ton HIGHLAND HOPE (I) and HIGHLAND ENTERPRISE followed the HIGHLAND BRIGADE in 1903 with similar facilities, and then in 1904 came the 6,000 ton HIGHLAND WATCH, HIGHLAND HARRIS and HIGHLAND HEATHER, all products of Russell & Co of Port Glasgow. A further development was, however, that they carried second as well as first class passengers. They became very popular, especially with people seeking less elaborate accommodation than that provided on the Royal Mail Steam Packet Company's ships from and to Southampton.

The Nelson Line's success was marred when the HIGHLAND LASSIE disappeared without trace after leaving Swansea for Buenos Aires on 10 December 1904. Happily, this was the only peacetime disaster experienced by the Company with loss of life.

The NELSON LINE (LONDON) LIMITED was established in 1910 preparatory to the building of 10 new steamers intended principally for the London–River Plate trade, a further concern, the NELSON STEAM NAVIGATION COMPANY LIMITED, being registered as owners of the new ships. Orders were shared equally between Russell & Co and Cammell, Laird & Company Limited of Birkenhead. The HIGHLAND BRAE, HIGHLAND CORRIE (II), HIGHLAND GLEN (II), HIGHLAND LADDIE, HIGHLAND PRIDE, HIGHLAND ROVER and

1910 HIGHLAND LADDIE 7,381 tons
One of 10 sister ships completed in 1910–11.

HIGHLAND SCOT (II) were delivered in 1910, and the HIGHLAND LOCH, HIGHLAND PIPER and HIGHLAND WARRIOR in 1911. Their tonnages varied between 7,381 and 7,634, and their single-screws were driven by three-cylinder triple-expansion engines giving them a service speed of 13 knots. Comfortable accommodation was provided for 80 first class, 40 second and 400 steerage passengers, and in addition they could carry 2,000 tons of refrigerated cargo. Their designer was the Nelson Line general manager, A. R. T. Woods, whose connection with the Company dated back to the acquisition of the pioneer HIGHLAND SCOT, which was scrapped in 1909 as was the HIGHLAND GLEN (I). The HIGHLAND MARY was sold to the Blue Star Line (Chapter 62) in 1911, the year of its foundation by the Vestey brothers, and was renamed BRODLAND.

It was rumoured, but denied, as early as 1911 that Royal Mail (Chapter 1) were trying to buy up the Nelson Line. Their first move, however, was to introduce a series of five 11,500 ton 'D' steamers in 1912. They sailed from and to Liverpool as did the Nelson Line secondary fleet.

But in 1913 Royal Mail decided to purchase the entire ordinary shares of the Nelson Steam Navigation Company Limited, Nelson Line (London) Limited and Nelson Line (Liverpool) Limited, and the Royal Mail chairman, Sir Owen Philipps (who in 1923 became Lord Kylsant) was appointed chairman of Nelson also. Nevertheless the line retained its separate identity, the ships their 'HIGHLAND' names and the funnels and flags their Nelson colours.

No fewer than seven Nelson Line ships were lost during World War I, and an eighth, the HIGHLAND HEATHER, managed to reach port after being torpedoed on 26 November 1916 in the Mediterranean when on war service. First of the lost ships was the HIGHLAND HOPE (I), which was captured in the Atlantic by the German cruiser KARLS-RUHE on 14 September 1914 and scuttled. The next loss, on 14 January 1915, had a certain similarity as the HIGHLAND BRAE was captured by the German merchant cruiser KRONPRINZ WILHELM and scuttled a few days later. The HIGHLAND CORRIE received mine damage on 14 August 1915 and although towed to Tilbury for repairs, was reprieved only temporarily as she was torpedoed and sunk by a German submarine on 16 May 1917, as were the HIGHLAND BRIGADE on 7 April 1918 and the HIGHLAND HARRIS on 6 August 1918. The other two ships were wrecked – the HIGHLAND WARRIOR on 3 October 1915 on the coast of Spain and the HIGHLAND SCOT (II) on 6 May 1918 on Maricas Island, Brazil. Rather surprisingly, only one ship – the 4,331 ton HIGHLAND STAR (ex-STAR OF IRELAND) – was acquired by the Company during the war, but the newly-built cargo carrier, the 8,442 ton HIGHLAND WARRIOR (II), joined the fleet in 1920.

Progress of the Blue Star Line since their purchase of the HIGH-LAND MARY in 1911 had been spectacular, and in February 1927 the first of their 'A' series of five steamers, the 12,848 ton ALMEDA (later renamed ALMEDA STAR) left London for Buenos Aires. Her passenger accommodation consisted of 162 first class berths. It was the Nelson Line rather than Royal Mail that was chosen to try to meet this new competition, and once again Mr. Woods, by this time a director of the Company, came to the rescue with excellent designs for five 14,100 ton twin-screw motorships, which were built by Harland & Wolff, four at Belfast and one at Glasgow. They were fitted with accommodation for 150 first class, 70 intermediate and 500 third class passengers. Insulated space amounted to over 12,500 tons measurement and the service speed of the ships was 15 knots. They were distinctive but not particularly good

1932 HIGHLAND PATRIOT 14,137 tons
Replacement for HIGHLAND HOPE, wrecked off Portugal in 1930.

looking, with two closely-spaced stumpy funnels and two masts. The first
to be launched was the HIGHLAND MONARCH on 3 May 1928,
followed by the HIGHLAND CHIEFTAIN on 21 June, HIGHLAND
BRIGADE on 1 November, HIGHLAND HOPE on 24 January 1929
and HIGHLAND PRINCESS on 11 April. The HIGHLAND HOPE
was the ship built at Glasgow, and was towed from the Clyde to Belfast
for her engines to be fitted.

Four of the six surviving ships of the 1910–11 series – the HIGHLAND
GLEN (II), HIGHLAND LADDIE, HIGHLAND LOCH and HIGH-
LAND PIPER – were sold in 1929 to Kaye, Son & Company Limited,
and were renamed JAMAICA PRODUCER, JAMAICA SETTLER,
JAMAICA PLANTER and JAMAICA MERCHANT of the newly-
formed Jamaica Banana Producers Company Limited. They ran between
London and Kingston, Jamaica, and were replaced by the 7,206 ton
ex-Lamport & Holt MURILLO, MEISSONIER and MOLIERE, which
retained their names and were thus the only Nelson Line ships lacking
the 'HIGHLAND' prefix. Twin-screw cargo steamers, they were fitted
with refrigerating apparatus.

During the same year, 1929, the HIGHLAND PRIDE was wrecked in
dense fog near Vigo, but worse was to follow as on 9 November 1930 the
HIGHLAND HOPE (II), less than a year old, was wrecked near Peniche
on the Portuguese coast. Fortunately, there were no casualties, but it was
a serious blow to the Company, which was already suffering from the
competition of the Blue Star Line. A replacement was launched on 10
December 1931 as the HIGHLAND PATRIOT, and started her maiden
voyage on 28 May 1932 from London to Buenos Aires.

The crash of the Royal Mail Steam Packet Company has already been
referred to in Chapter 1. A new company, ROYAL MAIL LINES
LIMITED, came into being on 4 August 1932 under the chairmanship of
Lord Essendon to take over the Royal Mail fleet in its entirety, together

with RMSP Meat Transports Ltd, the Nelson Steam Navigation Company Ltd and David MacIver & Company Ltd. The remaining entities of the once all-powerful Royal Mail group regained their independence.

The five 'HIGHLAND' motorships (including the HIGHLAND PATRIOT) were taken over by Royal Mail Lines Limited, together with the HIGHLAND WARRIOR (II) (renamed NAGOYA) and the MURILLO, MEISSONIER, and MOLIERE (renamed NALON, NASINA and NELA).

The 'HIGHLAND' motorships were allowed to retain their names, but their attractive grey hulls were changed to the sombre Royal Mail black, and their two red funnels with narrow white – black – white bands below a black top became a common or garden buff.

1. 1901 HIGHLAND BRIGADE (I)
    5,662. 117,24 x 15,30. (384.7 x 50.2). 1–2. S–T3–12. (I). Wm. Beardmore & Co Ltd, Glasgow. 1901 (5/2) launched. 1901 (13/4) MV Liverpool–R. Plate. 1918 (7/4) torpedoed and sunk 6 miles from St. Catherine's Point, Isle of Wight.
2. 1903 HIGHLAND HOPE (I)
    5,150. 117,15 x 15,54. (384.4 x 51.0). 1–2. S–T3–12. (I). Russell & Co, Port Glasgow (engines Rankin & Blackmore, Greenock). 1902 (13/11) launched. 1903 (Feb) MV Liverpool–R. Plate. 1914 (14/9) captured by German cruiser KARLSRUHE; scuttled.
3. 1903 HIGHLAND ENTERPRISE
    5,155. 117,34 x 15,54. (385.0 x 51.0). 1–2. S–T3–12. (I). Russell & Co, Port Glasgow (engines Rankin & Blackmore, Greenock). 1903 (27/1) launched. 1903 (14/3) MV Liverpool–R. Plate. 1930 NORTHLAND (Kaye, Son & Co). 1932 THORLAND (London Whaling Co). 1951 scrapped at Faslane.
4. 1904 HIGHLAND WATCH
    6,022. 118,86 x 16,00. (390.0 x 52.5). 1–2. S–T3–12. (I; II). Russell & Co, Port Glasgow (engines Rankin & Blackmore, Greenock). 1904 (3/2) launched. 1904 (9/4) MV Liverpool–R. Plate. 1930 scrapped at Inverkeithing.
5. 1904 HIGHLAND HARRIS
    6,023. 118,86 x 16,00. (390.0 x 52.5). 1–2. S–T3–12. (I; II). Russell & Co, Port Glasgow (engines Rankin & Blackmore, Greenock). 1904 (4/3) launched. 1904 (21/5) MV Liverpool–R. Plate. 1918 (6/8) torpedoed and sunk by German submarine.
6. 1904 HIGHLAND HEATHER
    6,027. 118,89 x 16,00. (390.1 x 52.5). 1–2. S–T3–12. (I; II).

Russell & Co, Port Glasgow (engines Rankin & Blackmore, Greenock). 1904 (20/4) launched. 1904 (4/7) MV Liverpool–R. Plate. 1916 (26/11) torpedoed in Mediterranean but reached port; repaired. 1930 scrapped at Hayle, Cornwall.

7. 1910 HIGHLAND ROVER
7,490. 123,44 x 17,13. (405.0 x 56.2). 1–2. S–T3–13. (I–80; II–40; III–400). Russell & Co, Port Glasgow (engines Rankin & Blackmore, Greenock). 1909 (28/10) launched. 1910 (6/2) MV Glasgow–R. Plate. 1932 scrapped at Grays, Essex.

8. 1910 HIGHLAND LADDIE
7,381. 123,68 x 17,10. (405.8 x 56.1). 1–2. S–T3–13. (I–80; II–40; III–400). Cammell, Laird & Co Ltd, Birkenhead. 1909 (30/10) launched. 1910 (16/3) MV Liverpool–R. Plate. 1929 JAMAICA SETTLER (Jamaica Banana Producers). 1935 scrapped at Dalmuir.

9. 1910 HIGHLAND PRIDE
7,469. 123,44 x 17,13. (405.0 x 56.2). 1–2. S–T3–13. (I–80; II–40; III–400). Russell & Co, Port Glasgow (engines Rankin & Blackmore, Greenock). 1910 (26/1) launched. 1910 (10/4) MV Glasgow–R. Plate. 1929 (9/9) wrecked near Vigo.

10. 1910 HIGHLAND CORRIE
7,583. 126,18 x 17,16. (414.0 x 56.3). 1–2. S–T3–13. (I–80; II–40; III–400). Russell & Co, Port Glasgow (engines Rankin & Blackmore, Greenock. 1910 (21/5) launched. 1910 (30/7) MV Liverpool–R. Plate. 1915 (14/8) mine damage off Elbow Buoy; towed to Tilbury; repaired. 1917 (16/5) torpedoed and sunk by German submarine near Owers Lightship.

11. 1910 HIGHLAND SCOT (II)
7,604. 126,18 x 17,16. (414.0 x 56.3). 1–2. S–T3–13. (I–80; II–40; III–400). Russell & Co, Port Glasgow (engines Rankin & Blackmore, Greenock). 1910 (11/6) launched. 1910 (6/9) MV Glasgow–R. Plate. 1918 (6/5) wrecked on Maricas Island, Brazil.

12. 1910 HIGHLAND BRAE
7,634. 126,12 x 17,13. (413.8 x 56.2). 1–2. S–T3–13. (I–80; II–40; III–400). Cammell, Laird & Co Ltd, Birkenhead. 1910 6/8) launched. 1910 (21/11) MV Liverpool–R. Plate. 1915 (14/1) captured by German merchant cruiser KRONPRINZ WILHELM. 1915 (31/1) scuttled by Germans.

13. 1910 HIGHLAND GLEN (II)
7,598. 126,18 x 17,16. (414.0 x 56.3). 1–2. S–T3–13. (I–80; II–40; III–400). Russell & Co, Port Glasgow (engines Rankin & Blackmore, Greenock). 1910 (23/7) launched. 1910 (20/12) MV London–R. Plate. 1929 JAMAICA PRODUCER (Jamaica

Banana Producers). 1933 (20/11) serious fire damage in East India Dock, London; scrapped at Rotterdam.

14. 1911 HIGHLAND LOCH
    7,493. 126,12 x 17,13. (413.8 x 56.2). 1–2. S–T3–13. (I–80; II–40; III–400). Cammell, Laird & Co Ltd, Birkenhead. 1911 (17/1) launched. 1911 (28/3) MV Liverpool–R. Plate. 1929 JAMAICA PLANTER (Jamaica Banana Producers). 1935 scrapped at Bo'ness.

15. 1911 HIGHLAND PIPER
    7,490. 126,12 x 17,13. (413.8 x 56.2). 1–2. S–T3–13. (I–80; II–40; III–400). Cammell, Laird & Co Ltd, Birkenhead. 1911 (18/3) launched. 1911 (11/7) MV Liverpool–R. Plate. 1929 JAMAICA MERCHANT (Jamaica Banana Producers). 1937 scrapped at Trieste.

16. 1911 HIGHLAND WARRIOR
    7,485. 126,12 x 17,13. (413.8 56.2). 1–2. S–T3–13. (I–80; II–40; III–400). Cammell, Laird & Co Ltd, Birkenhead. 1911 (13/5) launched. 1911 (28/8) MV Glasgow–R. Plate. 1915 (3/10) wrecked on NW coast of Spain.

17. 1928 HIGHLAND MONARCH (M/S)
    14,137. 159,52 [166,04] x 21,15. (523.4 [544.8] x 69.4). 2–2–C. 2S–4SC.DA–15. (I–150; intermediate 70; III–500). Harland & Wolff, Belfast. 1928 (3/5) launched. 1928 (18/10) MV London–R. Plate. 1932 HIGHLAND MONARCH (Royal Mail). 1932 (20/8) FV London–R. Plate. 1960 scrapped at Dalmuir.

18. 1929 HIGHLAND CHIEFTAIN (M/S)
    14,141. 159,52 [166,04] x 21,15. (523.4 [544.8] x 69.4). 2–2–C. 2S–4SC.DA–15. (I–150; intermediate 70; III–500). Harland & Wolff, Belfast. 1928 (21/6) launched. 1929 (21/2) MV London–R. Plate. 1932 HIGHLAND CHIEFTAIN (Royal Mail). 1932 (3/9) FV London–R. Plate. 1959 CALPEAN STAR (Calpe Shipping Co, Gibraltar). 1960 (1/6) wrecked at Montevideo.

19. 1929 HIGHLAND BRIGADE (II) (M/S)
    14,131. 159,52 [165,89] x 21,15. (523.4 [544.3] x 69.4). 2–2–C. 2S–4SC.DA–15. (I–150; intermediate 70; III–500). Harland & Wolff, Belfast. 1928 (1/11) launched. 1929 (May) MV London–R. Plate. 1932 HIGHLAND BRIGADE (Royal Mail). 1932 (23/7) FV London–R. Plate. 1940 British troop transport. 1946 (18/1) damaged by mine at Singapore. 1959 HENRIETTA (J.S. Latsis, Greek). 1960 MARIANNA (ditto). 1965 (29/6) arrived at Kaohsiung for demolition.

20. 1930 HIGHLAND HOPE (II) (M/S)
    14,129. 159,52 [166,04] x 21,15. (523.4 [544.8] x 69.4). 2–2–C.

2S–4SC.DA–15. (I–150; intermediate 70; III-500). Harland & Wolff, Glasgow. 1929 (24/1) launched. 1929 (5/2) towed Clyde–Belfast for fitting of engines. 1930 (6/2) MV London–R. Plate. 1930 (9/11) wrecked near Peniche, Portugal.

21. 1930 HIGHLAND PRINCESS (M/S)
14,128. 159,52 [166,04] x 21,15. (523.4 [544.8] x 69.4). 2–2–C. 2S–4SC.DA–15. (1–150; intermediate 70; III–500). Harland & Wolff, Belfast. 1929 (11/4) launched. 1930 (20/3) MV London–R. Plate. 1932 HIGHLAND PRINCESS (Royal Mail). 1932 (17/9) FV London–R. Plate. 1959 MARIANNA (Greek). 1960 SLAPY (Czechoslovak); 1960 GUANG HUA (Chinese). 1982 still listed.

22. 1932 HIGHLAND PATRIOT (M/S)
14,137. 159,52 [166,04] x 21,15. (523.4 [544.8] x 69.4). 2–2–C. 2S–4SC.DA–15. (I–150; intermediate 70; III–500). Harland & Wolff, Belfast. 1931 (10/12) launched. 1932 (28/5) MV London–R. Plate (1 RV). 1932 HIGHLAND PATRIOT (Royal Mail). 1932 (6/8) FV London–R. Plate. 1940 (1/10) torpedoed and sunk by German submarine in Atlantic.

FUNNEL: Red; narrow white-black-white bands; black top.
FLAG: Red burgee; in centre a white diamond with black 'N'.
HULL: Grey.

Chapter 50

1905–18

LLOYD ITALIANO

(Lloyd Italiano Società di Navigazione)

(Italian)

The LLOYD ITALIANO SOCIETÀ DI NAVIGAZIONE was founded in Genoa on 7 November 1904 with a capital of 12 million lire (£480,000) by Erasmo Piaggio, formerly general manager of Navigazione Generale Italiana. Passenger services were started in the following year on both North and South Atlantic.

1905 INDIANA 4,996 tons
Sister ship of FLORIDA, LUISIANA and VIRGINIA.

The 5,000 ton twin-screw FLORIDA, INDIANA, LUISIANA and VIRGINIA were ordered from the Società Esercizio Bacini of Riva Trigoso, Genoa, in which Piaggio had an interest. They had a speed of 14 knots and accommodation for 25 first class and 1,600 steerage passengers.

The FLORIDA's maiden voyage started from Genoa on 18 September 1905 and from Naples four days later for Buenos Aires. She was succeeded by the 6,847 ton MENDOZA, a product of Armstrong Whitworth of Walker-on-Tyne, built as the Bucknall Line MARITZ-BURG. First class accommodation was provided for 130 passengers and steerage for 1,500.

A third sailing was taken on 29 October by the INDIANA, but the

369

1907 PRINCIPESSA JOLANDA 9,200 tons
Shown as capsized during launching.

LUISIANA and VIRGINIA made their maiden voyages to New York. The former did not run to the River Plate until July 1913, while the VIRGINIA did not sail at all to South America for Lloyd Italiano. Meanwhile, a sixth steamer, the 4,933 ton CORDOVA, was bought on the stocks at Glasgow, where she was under construction for the Société Générale de Transports Maritimes (Chapter 17). She sailed from Genoa for Brazil and the Argentine on 1 May 1906.

On her second voyage, the FLORIDA inaugurated the North Atlantic service and the INDIANA, too, made only one South Atlantic voyage at this time.

The Company's first attempt to introduce a fast luxury service to South America met with disaster as, on 22 September 1907, the 9,000 ton PRINCIPESSA JOLANDA capsized at her launching and became a total loss. Fortunately, there were no casualties. A sister ship, the 9,210 ton PRINCIPESSA MAFALDA, was successfully launched by the same

1909 PRINCIPESSA MAFALDA 9,210 tons
Foundered off Brazil in 1927 with heavy loss of life.

370

firm, Società Esercizio Bacini, on 22 October 1908 and started her maiden voyage from Genoa to Buenos Aires on 30 March 1909. A two-funnelled twin-screw steamer, she was propelled by two sets of quadruple-expansion engines, her service speed being 16 knots. At a later date, in August 1914, shortly after the outbreak of World War I, she made a special voyage from Genoa to New York for the benefit of Americans stranded in Italy.

The Company was involved in a second disaster on 23 January 1909 when the FLORIDA collided with the White Star liner REPUBLIC in dense fog off the United States coast. The REPUBLIC sank after unsuccessful efforts to tow her to port, but although the FLORIDA's bows were badly damaged she managed to reach New York, where repairs were completed within a month.

Signor Piaggio retired from the chairmanship of Lloyd Italiano in March 1910. Navigazione Generale Italiana (Chapter 36) had already acquired a substantial interest in the Company in 1907, when its capital was increased to 20 million lire, and they obtained a majority holding in 1910. They had already become proprietors of La Veloce and Italia, and sailings of all four were co-ordinated. To make this feasible, there was a considerable exchange of tonnage within the group, although Lloyd Italiano was the least affected.

The 8,282 ton TAORMINA, acquired from Italia, sailed from Genoa for New York on 23 January 1912 on her first Lloyd Italiano voyage, and from July 1913 she and the MENDOZA, soon to be renamed CASERTA, were in sole charge of this service. The INDIANA and LUISIANA were transferred from the North to the South Atlantic; the FLORIDA and VIRGINIA were sold to the Ligure Brasiliana (Chapter 46).

The LUISIANA was torpedoed and sunk by a German submarine on 2 February 1917 near Almeria, Spain.

It was decided on 1 June 1918 that Lloyd Italiano would be absorbed by NGI, which thenceforth adopted the amended title of NAVIGA-ZIONE GENERALE ITALIANA – FLOTTE RIUNITE FLORIO – RUBATTINO & LLOYD ITALIANO. They acquired the Lloyd Italiano steamers CASERTA, CORDOVA, INDIANA, PRIN-CIPESSA MAFALDA and TAORMINA, but the CORDOVA was of very little use to them as she was torpedoed and sunk near Cape Armi, Italy, on 4 June 1918.

1. 1905 FLORIDA
      5,018. 116,24 x 14,66. (381.4 x 48.1). 2–2. 2S–T6–14. (I–25; III–1,600) Società Esercizio Bacini, Riva Trigoso. 1905 (22/6)

launched. 1905 (18/9) MV Genoa–Naples–Buenos Aires (1 RV). 1909 (23/1) collided off US coast with REPUBLIC (White Star), which sank. FLORIDA had crumpled bow. 1911 CAVOUR (Ligure Brasiliana (Italian)). 1914 ditto (Transatlantica Italiana). 1917 (12/12) sunk in collision with CAPRERA (Italian auxiliary cruiser) near Armeville.

2. 1905 MENDOZA

6,847. 128,01 x 15,72. (420.0 x 51.6). 1–2. 2S–T6–14. (I–130; III–1,500). Sir W.G. Armstrong, Whitworth & Co Ltd, Walker-on-Tyne. 1904 (16/5) launched as MARITZBURG (Bucknall). 1905 MENDOZA (Lloyd Italiano). 1905 (10/10) FV Genoa–Buenos Aires. 1914 renamed CASERTA (Lloyd Italiano). 1918 ditto (NGI). 1923 VENEZUELA (La Veloce). 1928 scrapped.

3. 1905 INDIANA

4,996. 119,99 x 14,66. (393.7 x 48.1). 2–2. 2S–T6–14. (I–25; III–1,600). Società Esercizio Bacini, Riva Trigoso. 1905 (10/10) launched. 1905 (29/10) MV Genoa–Naples–Buenos Aires (1 RV). 1913 (29/6) resumed Genoa–Naples–Buenos Aires. 1918 INDIANA (NGI). 1924 ROMANIA (Sitmar). 1928 scrapped.

4. 1906 CORDOVA

4,933. 125,39 x 14,38. (411.4 x 47.2). 1–2. 2S–T6–14. D. & W. Henderson Ltd, Glasgow. 1905 laid down as CORDOBA; bought on stocks from SGTM (Fr). 1905 (12/12) launched. 1906 (1/5) MV Genoa–Naples–Buenos Aires. 1912 renamed RIO DE JANEIRO. 1913 reverted to CORDOVA (Lloyd Italiano). 1918 (4/6) torpedoed and sunk near Cape Armi, Italy.

— —— PRINCIPESSA JOLANDA

9,000. Capsized 1907 (22/9) during launching at Riva Trigoso; total loss.

5. 1909 PRINCIPESSA MAFALDA

9,210. 147,88 x 16,94. (485.2 x 55.6). 2–2. 2S–Q8–16. Società Esercizio Bacini, Riva Trigoso. 1908 (22/10) launched. 1909 (30/3) MV Genoa–Naples–Buenos Aires. 1914–18 laid up at Taranto, Italy. 1918 PRINCIPESSA MAFALDA (NGI). 1927 (25/10) foundered off Bahia, Brazil (303).

6. (1913) LUISIANA

4,983. 119,99 x 14,66. (393.7 x 48.1). 2–2. 2S–T6–14. (I–25; III–1,600). Società Esercizio Bacini, Riva Trigoso. 1906 (18/3) launched. 1906 (5/4) MV Genoa–Naples–New York. 1913 (15/8) FV Genoa–Naples–Buenos Aires. 1917 (6/2) torpedoed and sunk by German submarine near Almeria, Spain.

Note: The 5,181 ton VIRGINIA did not run to South America for Lloyd Italiano. (See Chapter 46).

FUNNEL: Yellow with narrow black band; black top.
FLAG: Blue with large white diamond; in the diamond a yellow anchor with yellow 'LI' in a blue circle.

Chapter 51

(1906–36)

KONINKLIJKE HOLLANDSCHE LLOYD

(Royal Holland Lloyd)

(1906) Zuid Amerika Lijn
1908. Koninklijke Hollandsche Lloyd

(Dutch)

The KONINKLIJKE HOLLANDSCHE LLOYD, best-known in the English-speaking world as the ROYAL HOLLAND LLOYD, can be traced back to 10 July 1899 when the ZUID AMERIKA LIJN (South American Line) was founded in Amsterdam to run a cattle and cargo service between Amsterdam and South America. The 4,150 ton steamers AMSTELLAND, ZAANLAND and RIJNLAND were built by Russell & Co of Port Glasgow in 1900, their main objectives being to carry cattle from Argentina to Deptford (London) and Dutch stock cattle from Amsterdam to South America. The first sailing was taken by the AMSTELLAND, which was launched on 5 June 1900. The cattle trade came to an abrupt halt about the middle of 1903 when foot and mouth disease in Argentina made the British Government prohibit the importation of live cattle. The three steamers had to be converted for pure cargo carrying by closing the tonnage-openings in the cattle deck (the upper 'tweendeck), thus increasing their gross tonnage to 5,400.

However, from 1905 onwards there was considerable emigration from the Netherlands and adjacent countries to South America, and the three ships were fitted with accommodation for several hundred steerage passengers. The ZAANLAND started a regular monthly passenger service from Amsterdam on 23 September 1906, followed by the RIJNLAND on 23 October and the AMSTELLAND on 23 November.

By a decision made on 28 December 1907 the Zuid Amerika Lijn was reorganised and changed its name to KONINKLIJKE HOLLAND-SCHE LLOYD on 21 January 1908. Orders were placed almost at once with A. Stephen & Sons of Glasgow for the 7,291 ton HOLLANDIA and with Koninklijke Maatschappij de Schelde of Vlissingen (Flushing) for the 7,442 ton FRISIA, both of which had berths for 91 first class, 116 second and 1,000 steerage passengers. Twin-screw ships propelled by triple-expansion engines, their service speed was 13 knots. The HOL-

374

1910 ZEELANDIA 7,995 tons
Improved version of pioneer HOLLANDIA and FRISIA.

LANDIA's maiden voyage started from Amsterdam on 14 April 1909, followed by the FRISIA on 21 July. A third steamer, the 7,995 ton ZEELANDIA was completed by Stephen in time to sail on 21 July 1910. She had slightly larger dimensions, a service speed of 14 knots and could accommodate an additional 27 first class passengers. Ports of call between Amsterdam and Buenos Aires were Boulogne, Plymouth, Coruña, Lisbon, Las Palmas, Pernambuco, Bahia, Rio de Janeiro, Santos and Montevideo.

Completion of the passenger liners enabled the earlier trio to have their passenger accommodation removed, and they reverted purely to cargo carriers. Two were lost during World War I, but the RIJNLAND survived until 1933.

Two much larger passenger liners, the 13,868 ton GELRIA, whose maiden voyage started from Amsterdam on 5 November 1913, and the 14,061 ton TUBANTIA, which sailed on 8 April 1914, were delivered by Stephen. Their twin-screws were driven by quadruple-expansion engines giving them a service speed of 17½ knots, and they had greatly increased accommodation for 197 first class, 236 second, 136 intermediate and 854 third class passengers.

The outbreak of World War I in August 1914 was responsible for the withdrawal of German-flag services to South America, and for various curtailments in respect of British and French lines, leaving Koninklijke Hollandsche Lloyd with considerably reduced foreign competition. Unfortunately, however, their flagship TUBANTIA was torpedoed and sunk by German submarine UB.13 at 2.20 a.m. on 16 March 1916, despite having her name and home port, Amsterdam, painted in large white letters on her black hull amidships, and also her name, illuminated at night, in large block letters in a wooden casing. As a result of this unexpected disaster, it was decided to lay up the GELRIA, and she was not recommissioned until March 1919.

375

1914 TUBANTIA 14,061 tons
Sister ship of GELRIA. Torpedoed and sunk by German submarine in 1916.

The 3,935 ton, 28 passenger, DRECHTERLAND of 1903 vintage was bought by KHL in 1915. She sailed under the US flag in 1918–19, but then reverted to KHL until scrapped in 1933.

After making strong protests to Germany about the sinking of the TUBANTIA, the Company secretly bought the 19,600 ton WILLIAM O'SWALD and JOHANN HEINRICH BURCHARD, which had been launched for the Hamburg American Line (Chapter 47) early in 1914, and in due course they were renamed BRABANTIA and LIMBURGIA.

1920 BRABANTIA 19,653 tons
Proceeding from German builders to Amsterdam via North Sea Canal.

They were not completed until 1920 when the Allied authorities insisted that they be surrendered. However, Koninklijke Hollandsche Lloyd remained adamant and the pair duly entered the South American trade in April and September 1920. They were triple-screw ships driven by a combination of triple-expansion engines and a low-pressure steam turbine, could accommodate 290 first, 320 second and 400 third class passengers. The intakes of their first and second of three funnels were divided and carried down the sides of the superstructure, allowing an unrestricted vista through the principal public rooms.

Eventually, on 4 January 1922, the BRABANTIA and LIMBURGIA were sold to the United American Lines to become the RESOLUTE and RELIANCE, the reason being that the Company had grossly overspent their capital on these ships and two new ones they were about to place in commission. In fact, the financial position was so bad that, in addition, they were compelled to sell the HOLLANDIA and FRISIA, this time to Hapag, all four being disposed of at appreciably less than their book value.

A few months previously, in September 1921, the British port of call was changed from Plymouth to Southampton. Outward bound ships then proceeded to Las Palmas, Pernambuco, Bahia, Rio de Janeiro, Santos, Montevideo and, finally, Buenos Aires.

1922 ORANIA 9,763 tons
Rammed and sunk in Leixões harbour by Portuguese liner LOANDA in 1934.

The two newcomers were the 9,763 ton ORANIA and the 10,171 ton FLANDRIA, built by Workman Clark of Belfast and Barclay Curle of Glasgow, respectively. They were twin-screw ships propelled by two sets of double-reduction geared turbines, their service speed being 15 knots. Thus, the KHL passenger fleet was reduced from eight to four ships, the GELRIA and ZEELANDIA being the only running mates of the newcomers.

377

Owing to the worldwide depression, the GELRIA was laid up at Amsterdam in November 1931. During the second half of 1933 she was chartered by Argentine interests for conversion into an exhibition ship. However, the scheme fell through at the last minute and she returned from Buenos Aires to Amsterdam, there to be laid up again in 1934 until sold a year later to Lloyd Triestino, who renamed her GRADISCA.

The Company's passenger service would probably have remained in existence at least until Holland was invaded in 1940, and as likely as not would have been resumed after World War II had not the Portuguese liner LOANDA entered the small harbour of Leixões, the port of Oporto, on 19 December 1934 without permission from the harbour authorities. The ORANIA had just anchored inside the harbour when she was rammed by the LOANDA, took a decided list to port and it was soon evident that she was liable to capsize. Fortunately, she remained afloat just long enough for all her passengers and crew to be taken off. A British firm was employed to undertake her dismantling, which was not completed until 1936.

The 25 year old ZEELANDIA was laid up at Amsterdam in February 1935 preparatory to being scrapped. The Company was in no position to acquire new passenger tonnage, and as it had been proved time and time again that a one-ship service is seldom viable, the FLANDRIA was sold in 1936 to the Compagnie Générale Transatlantique, who renamed her BRETAGNE.

The Koninklijke Hollandsche Lloyd, which is now incorporated in the NEDLLOYD concern, continued to run a cargo service between Holland and South America, and from time to time employed ships carrying a maximum of 12 passengers.

1. (1906) ZAANLAND
   5,417. 118,68 x 15,57. (389.4 x 51.1). 1–2. S–T3–11. (III). Russell & Co, Port Glasgow. 1900 (7/9) launched. 1903 tonnage increased from 4,160. 1906 (23/9) FV Amsterdam–S. America with passengers. 1910 discontinued carrying passengers. 1918 (21/3) requisitioned by US Govt. at Newport News. 1918 (12/5) sunk in collision in North Atlantic.
2. (1906) RIJNLAND
   5,421, 118,68 x 15,60. (389.4 x 51.2). 1–2. S–T3–11. (III). Russell & Co, Port Glasgow. 1900 (24/10) launched. 1903 tonnage increased from 4,155. 1906 (23/10) FV Amsterdam–S. America with passengers. 1910 discontinued carrying passengers. 1933 scrapped at Genoa.

3. (1906) AMSTELLAND
    5,404. 118,74 x 15,57. (389.6 x 51.1). 1–2. S–T3–11. (III). Russell
    & Co, Port Glasgow. 1900 (5/6) launched. 1903 tonnage
    increased from 4,152. 1906 (23/11) FV Amsterdam–S. America
    with passengers. 1910 discontinued carrying passengers. 1917
    (1/7) torpedoed and sunk by German submarine south of Galley
    Head, Ireland, on voyage Buenos Aires–Belfast.
4. 1909 HOLLANDIA
    7,291. 127,91 x 16,52. (419.7 x 54.2). 1–2. 2S–T6–13. (I–91;
    II–116; III–1,000). A. Stephen & Sons, Glasgow. 1909 (23/1)
    launched. 1909 (14/4) MV Amsterdam–S. America. 1919 (Mar)
    trooping voyage Brest–New York, thence New York–S. Amer-
    ica. 1922 HAMMONIA (Hapag). 1922 (8/9) struck submerged
    object 75 miles W. of Vigo. 1922 (9/9) foundered.
5. 1909 FRISIA
    7,442. 128,31 x 16,49. (421.0 x 54.1). 1–2. 2S–T6–13. (I–91;
    II–116; III–1,000). Koninklijke Maatschappij de Schelde,
    Flushing. 1909 (6/3) launched. 1909 (21/7) MV Amsterdam–S.
    America. 1922 HOLSATIA (Hapag). 1928 scrapped at Ham-
    burg.
6. 1910 ZEELANDIA
    7,995. 134,10 x 16,97. (440.0 x 55.7). 1–2. 2S–T6–14. (I–118;
    II–114; III–998. A. Stephen & Sons, Glasgow. 1910 (26/4)
    launched. 1910 (21/7) MV Amsterdam–S. America. 1918 (21/3)
    requisitioned at New York by US Govt. 1919 returned to Dutch
    flag. 1934 or earlier Intermediate 194; III–710. 1935 (Feb) laid up
    at Amsterdam. 1936 scrapped at Hendrik-Ido-Ambacht.
7. 1913 GELRIA
    13,868. 164,92 [170,68] x 20,05. (541.1 [560.0] x 65.8). 2–2.
    2S–Q8–17½. (I–197; II–236; intermediate 136; III–854). A.
    Stephen & Sons, Glasgow. 1913 (20/5) launched. 1913 (5/11) MV
    Amsterdam–S. America. 1916 (Mar) laid up at Amsterdam. 1919
    (12/3) resumed Amsterdam–S. America. 1931 (Nov) laid up at
    Amsterdam. 1933 chartered by Argentinian interests as exhibi-
    tion ship; scheme fell through; returned Buenos Aires–Amster-
    dam; laid up. 1935 GRADISCA (Lloyd Triestino). 1946 (2/1)
    stranded at Gavdo Island. 1947 (Jun) refloated. 1947 (Sep) laid
    up at Venice. 1951 scrapped at Venice.
8. 1914 TUBANTIA
    14,061. 164,58 [170,68] x 20,02. (540.0 [560.0] x 65.7). 2–2.
    2S–Q8–17½. (I–197; II–236; intermediate 136; III–854). A.
    Stephen & Sons, Glasgow. 1913 (15/11) launched. 1914 (8/4) MV
    Amsterdam–S. America. 1916 (15/3) left Amsterdam on 11th

outward voyage. 1916 (16/3) torpedoed and sunk by German submarine UB.13 near Noord Hinder lightship; passengers and crew landed at Hook of Holland.

9. (1915) DRECHTERLAND
3,935. 111,55 x 14,26. (366.0 x 46.8). C–1–2. S–T3–10 (One-class 28). J. Laing & Sons, Sunderland. 1903 (28/4) launched as WENSLEYDALE. 1911 STEENBERGEN (Dutch Furness Co). 1915 DRECHTERLAND (KHL). 1918 (21/3)–1919 (9/7) under US flag. 1933 scrapped in Italy.

10. 1920 LIMBURGIA
19,582. 179,94 [188,36] x 22,09. (590.4 [618.0] x 72.5). 3–2. 3S–T8&ST–17. (I–290; II–320; III–400). J.C. Tecklenborg, Geestemünde. 1914 (10/2) launched as JOHANN HEINRICH BURCHARD (Hapag). 1916 (31/5) secretly purchased by KHL; renamed LIMBURGIA. 1920 (5/2) arr Amsterdam from Bremerhaven. 1920 (14/4) MV Amsterdam–S. America. 1922 RELIANCE (United American Lines). 1926 ditto (Hapag). 1938 (7/8) gutted by fire at Hamburg. 1940 (4/1) sold; scrapped at Bremerhaven.

11. 1920 BRABANTIA
19,653. 179,94 [188,36] x 22.00. (590.4 [618.0] x 72.2). 3–2. 3S–T8&ST–17. (I–290; II–320; III–400). AG Weser, Bremen. 1914 (30/3) launched as WILLIAM O'SWALD (Hapag). 1916 (31/5) secretly purchased by KHL; renamed BRABANTIA. 1920 (28/7) arr Amsterdam from Bremerhaven. 1920 (1/9) MV Amsterdam–S. America. 1922 RESOLUTE (United American Lines). 1926 ditto (Hapag). 1935 LOMBARDIA (Italian transport). 1943 (4/8) damaged in air attack on Naples. 1947 scrapped at La Spezia.

12. 1922 ORANIA
9,763. 137,24 x 18,10. (450.3 x 59.4). 2–2–C. 2S–ST(DR)–15. (I–154; II–68; intermediate 120; III–850). Workman, Clark & Co Ltd, Belfast. 1921 (1/10) launched. 1922 MV Amsterdam–S. America. 1934 (19/12) rammed and sunk in Leixões harbour by LOANDA (Cia Colonial (Portuguese)) (0). 1936 dismantling completed.

13. 1922 FLANDRIA
10,171. 137,18 x 18,04. (450.1 x 59.2). 2–2–C. 2S–ST(DR)–15. (I–215; II–110; intermediate 100; III–900. Barclay, Curle & Co Ltd, Glasgow. 1922 (2/6) launched. 1922 (Oct) MV Amsterdam–S. America. 1936 (May) BRETAGNE (CGT). 1936 (31/5) left Amsterdam for Havre under tow. 1939 (14/10) torpedoed and sunk by German submarine U.45 in Atlantic (7).

Note: The following ships had accommodation for 12 passengers:
1938 WESTLAND (ex-NANSENVILLE)1963 scrapped
1956 MONTFERLAND   1973 sold
1957 ZAANLAND   1972 sold

FUNNEL: Yellow; narrow blue-black band.
FLAG: White; horizontal red band at top, blue at bottom; golden
        ball in centre surmounted by golden crown; red lion within
        ball.

Chapter 52

1907–31

LLOYD SABAUDO

(Lloyd Sabaudo Società Anonima di Navigazione)

(Italian)

The LLOYD SABAUDO SOCIETÀ ANONIMA DI NAVIGAZIONE was founded in Turin on 21 June 1906 with a paid up capital of six million lire (£240,000), soon increased to 11,000,000. The port of registry of the ships was Genoa.

The Italian Royal Family took a great interest in the formation and running of Lloyd Sabaudo, so much so that at one time there were rumours that at least one royal personage had a financial interest in the line. In any event, the second word of the title indicated the close associations it had with the Royal House of Savoy, and regal names were chosen for the passenger ships.

1908 PRINCIPE DI UDINE 7,785 tons
Sister ship of TOMASO DI SAVOIA.

The 7,914 ton TOMASO DI SAVOIA and the 7,785 ton PRINCIPE DI UDINE were ordered from Barclay Curle of Glasgow for a service from Genoa to South America, but as they were not ready in time one of three smaller ships built for the New York line was transferred to make the first South Atlantic sailing. This was the 6,500 ton REGINA D'ITALIA, which left Genoa for Rio de Janeiro, Montevideo and

Buenos Aires on 6 October 1907, the TOMASO DI SAVOIA's maiden voyage starting on 11 November. After a second voyage by the REGINA D'ITALIA, the PRINCIPE DI UDINE entered the service on 31 March 1908.

At this time, five other Italian lines were operating on both North and South Atlantic. Partly for this reason and partly because of difficult trading conditions. no dividend was paid by the Company in 1908 and 1911, but a distribution of 5 per cent was made in 1909 and 1910 and 6¼ per cent in 1912. It had become evident by this time that five ships were more than sufficient for the two routes, and following the disastrous fire which destroyed the Uranium Line's VOLTURNO, one of the North Atlantic ships, the PRINCIPE DI PIEMONTE, became their PRIN-CIPELLO in January 1914. On a few occasions previously and subsequently both the TOMASO DI SAVOIA and PRINCIPE DI UDINE made a voyage to New York.

The sale of the PRINCIPE DI PIEMONTE helped to pave the way for placing an order with W. Beardmore & Co Ltd, of Glasgow, for the 16,500 ton quadruple-screw CONTE ROSSO for the New York service. William Beardmore, head of the firm, was appointed to the Lloyd Sabaudo board in return for his undertaking to help finance the new ship. Guglielmo Marconi, inventor of wireless telegraphy, became chairman at this time, a position he held until 1922. Unfortunately for the Company, the new ship was taken over by the British Admiralty when nearing completion and was commissioned as the aircraft carrier ARGUS.

At the first opportunity after the Armistice of November 1918, the 18,000 ton luxury liners CONTE ROSSO (II) and CONTE VERDE were ordered from Beardmore.

Meanwhile, the South American service was resumed by the TOMA-SO DI SAVOIA and PRINCIPE DI UDINE, both of which had been taken up by the Italian Government during the war.

The 18,017 ton CONTE ROSSO (II) was launched on 10 February 1921. The decoration of the first class public rooms was entrusted to a Florentine firm, results being described as 'extremely ornate, walls and ceilings alike being a mass of paintings, hand-carved wood, inlay, metal work, tapestry and stained glass.' Propelling machinery consisted of double-reduction geared turbines driving twin-screws, the service speed being 18 knots. She left Genoa on 29 March 1922 on her maiden voyage to South America, but subsequent voyages were to New York. Her introduction enabled the REGINA D'ITALIA, her sister ship RE D'ITALIA and the chartered 12,335 ton PESARO, formerly the Hamburg American MOLTKE, to be transferred to the South America trade.

The 18,383 ton CONTE VERDE was completed in 1923 and she, too,

1921 PESARO 12,335 tons
Built 1902 as Hapag MOLTKE.

was despatched on a round voyage to South America before being detailed to the New York run. The CONTE ROSSO had accommodation for 342 first, 214 second and 1,800 third class passengers, while the CONTE VERDE could carry 336 first, 198 second and 1,700 third.

Another Beardmore product, the 24,416 ton CONTE BIANCA-MANO, entered North Atlantic service in November 1925 and simultaneously the CONTE VERDE was transferred to the South Atlantic.

A further luxury liner was badly needed and was made possible by increasing the share capital and arranging a bank loan. The new ship, the 25,661 ton CONTE GRANDE, was laid down at Trieste in October 1926 and sailed for New York on 3 April 1928. The CONTE ROSSO was, thus, in a position to join the CONTE VERDE on the South American service, enabling the RE D'ITALIA, REGINA D'ITALIA, TOMASO DI SAVOIA and PRINCIPE DI UDINE to be scrapped. The PESARO had been similarly dealt with in 1925.

1923 CONTE VERDE 18,383 tons
Sister ship of CONTE ROSSO.

384

A report in April 1927 stated that Signor Mussolini was planning the merger of NGI, Lloyd Sabaudo and Cosulich. Well over two years later it was announced that Lloyd Sabaudo had signed a contract for a high-speed liner of over 45,000 tons, to be named the CONTE AZZURRO, with the likelihood of NGI ordering a sister ship. In due course, it was stated that the NGI ship (Chapter 36) would be named REX, and that the Lloyd Sabaudo ship was expected to be the DUX.

In 1929 the unsatisfactory financial position of Cosulich (Chapter 60) made it expedient for the Banca Commerciale Italiana to step in, and Cosulich was placed under the control of Lloyd Sabaudo, which at the same time took charge of Lloyd Triestino, Marittima Italiana and Adria. A subsidiary of Lloyd Sabaudo, La Polare, was wound up, with the result that the parent company's capital was reduced from 250 to 200 million lire.

The world depression of the early 1930s affected the Italian lines very seriously, and it was becoming increasingly obvious that a union between NGI, Lloyd Sabaudo and Cosulich could not be delayed much longer. In October 1931 the directorates of the three companies accepted the Banca Commerciale Italiana's invitation to attend a conference in Milan. The outcome was fair to all, and on 11 November 1931, the Italian Ministry of Communications announced that the fusion of the three lines would become effective on 2 January 1932 with the formation of a new company, ITALIA (FLOTTE RIUNITE COSULICH – LLOYD SABAUDO – NGI). Its activities are described in Chapter 65, which also deals with the CONTE DI SAVOIA, referred to above as the DUX and the CONTE AZZURRO. Lloyd Sabaudo received 640,000 shares in Italia to a nominal value of 320 million lire.

1. (1907) REGINA D'ITALIA
      6,560. 131,06 x 16,06. (430.0 x 52.7). 2–2. 2S–T6–14. (I–120; III–1,900). Sir J. Laing & Sons Ltd, Sunderland (engines G. Clark Ltd, Sunderland. 1906 laid down as SARDINIAN PRINCE (Prince). 1907 (20/1) launched as REGINA D'ITALIA. 1907 (15/5) MV Genoa–New York. 1907 (6/10) FV Genoa–S. America (2 RV). 1908 (Dec) hospital ship at Messina after earthquake. 1922 (Apr) transferred to Genoa–S. American service. 1928 (Oct) scrapped in Italy.
2. 1907 TOMASO DI SAVOIA
      7,914. 137,36 x 16,82. (450.7 x 55.2). 2–2. 2S–Q8–16. (I–150; II–150; III–1,200). Barclay, Curle & Co. Ltd, Glasgow. 1907 (15/9) launched. 1907 (11/11) MV Genoa–S. America. 1928 scrapped in Italy.

3. 1908 PRINCIPE DI UDINE
    7,785. 137,39 x 16,82. (450.8 x 55.2). 2–2. 2S–Q8–16. (I–150; II–150; III–1,200). Barclay, Curle & Co Ltd, Glasgow. 1907 (19/12) launched. 1908 (31/3) MV Genoa–S. America. 1929 scrapped in Italy.
4. (1921) RE D'ITALIA
    6,560. 131,06 x 16,06. (430.0 x 52.7). 2–2. 2S–T6–14. (I–120; III–1,900). Sir J. Laing & Sons Ltd, Sunderland (engines G. Clark Ltd, Sunderland). 1906 laid down as PIEDMONTESE PRINCE (Prince). 1906 (22/12) launched as RE D'ITALIA. 1907 (6/4) MV Genoa–New York. 1921 (10/4) LV Naples–New York; transferred to S. American service. 1929 scrapped at Genoa.
4a. (1921) PESARO (c)
    12,335. 160,19 x 18,99. (525.6 x 62.3). 2–2. 2S–Q8–15. (I–390; II–230; III–550). Blohm & Voss, Hamburg. 1901 (27/8) launched as MOLTKE (Hapag). 1902 (9/3) MV Hamburg–New York. 1915 (25/5) seized by Italy at Genoa; renamed PESARO. 1919 (23/4) FV for Lloyd Sabaudo (c), Genoa–New York. 1921 (3/7) LV ditto (12 RV); subsequently Genoa–Naples–S. America. 1925 scrapped in Italy.
5. 1922 CONTE ROSSO
    18,017. 173,78 [179,27] x 22,61. (570.2 [588.2] x 74.2) 2–2. 2S–ST(DR)–18. (I–342; II–214; III–1,800). W. Beardmore & Co Ltd, Glasgow. 1921 (10/2) launched. 1922 (29/3) MV Genoa–Naples–S. America. (1 RV). 1922 (15/5) FV Genoa–Naples–New York. 1928 (27/2) LV ditto; 1928 (19/4) resumed Genoa–Naples–S. America. 1932 CONTE ROSSO (Lloyd Triestino). 1941 (24/5) torpedoed and sunk by British submarine UPHOLDER 10 miles from Sicily (1,212).
6. 1923 CONTE VERDE
    18,383. 173,78 [180,52] x 22,61. (570.2 [592.3] x 74.2). 2–2. 2S–ST(DR)–18. (I–336; II–198; III–1,700). W. Beardmore & Co Ltd, Glasgow. 1922 (21/10) launched. 1923 (21/4) MV Genoa–Naples–S. America (1 RV). 1923 (13/6) FV Genoa–Naples–New York. 1925 (22/9) LV ditto; to S. America subsequently. 1932 CONTE VERDE (Lloyd Triestino). 1943 (9/9) scuttled at Shanghai to avoid capture by Japanese; later refloated; troopship KOTOBUKI MARU (Japanese). 1944 (Dec) bombed and sunk at Maiguru, near Kioto. 1949 (Jan) refloated; bought by Matsui Line. 1951 scrapped.

FUNNEL: (a) 1907. Yellow; white band with narrow green band on either side.

(b) 1914. Yellow; white band with narrow blue band on either side.

FLAG: (a) 1907. Square, divided into two triangles from upper left corner to lower right corner. Upper triangle green; lower white with 'LS' interposed in black.

(b) 1914. White; the eagle of Savoy in blue with golden crown.

Chapter 53

1907–42

COMPAGNIE DE NAVIGATION FRANCE – AMÉRIQUE

(French)

During the early years of the present century, the Spanish Government was not entirely satisfied with the arrangements made by foreign lines for carrying large numbers of emigrants from Spain to South America. The French-owned Société Générale de Transports Maritimes (Chapter 17) had been engaged in the trade since 1867, and anxious that the facilities they offered should meet with full approval they founded the COMPAGNIE DE NAVIGATION FRANCE – AMÉRIQUE in 1907, and transferred to it the 3,874 ton PROVENCE, the 3,952 ton ESPAGNE and the 3,864 ton LES ALPES, the last-named built by Harland & Wolff of Belfast in 1883 as the BRITISH PRINCESS. She was scrapped within three years of transfer, but business had been sufficiently brisk for the 3,161 ton AQUITAINE and the 3,966 ton ITALIE to replace her.

The usual itinerary was Marseilles–Genoa–Malaga or Valencia–Dakar–Buenos Aires, with a homeward call at Bahia or Rio de Janeiro, but other calls were inserted as and when required.

The AQUITAINE served as an ammunition depot ship at Salonica during much of the 1914–18 war, and after the Armistice had a thorough refit before returning to France–Amérique service. But the ITALIE in 1916 and the ESPAGNE in 1919 were returned in SGTM. Unfortunately, the PROVENCE was torpedoed on 13 April 1918 by a German submarine off the Spanish coast when on passage from Buenos Aires to Marseilles. She foundered at Palamos, but was later refloated and in due course returned to France–Amérique service.

The 4,282 ton single-screw GUARUJA and IPANEMA were completed for SGTM in 1921–2, and a year or so later were transferred to France–Amérique. Their propelling machinery consisted of two Ljunstrom turbines connected to two electric motors, and they had a service speed of 13 knots when both systems were in operation. But as SGTM did not repeat the arrangement it can hardly have been a great success.

The 6,375 ton twin-screw CORDOBA, built in 1903 as the German East African PRINZREGENT and handed to SGTM in 1919 as part compensation for war losses, was transferred to France–Amérique in 1925 and enabled the PROVENCE of 1884 and the AQUITAINE of

388

1891 to be scrapped. But the CORDOBA, also, was scrapped in 1932 and on 2 January 1938 the GUARUJA stranded near Almeria and broke her back, leaving the IPANEMA as the only survivor. In 1942, during World War II, she was seized by Italy, renamed VILLAROSA and in September 1943 was scuttled by the Germans at Naples.

France–Amérique was not revived after the war, but the VILLA-ROSA was refloated by the Italians, repaired and re-entered service as the Italian TAURINIA.

1. (1907) PROVENCE
   3,874. 117,98 x 12,89. (387.1 x 42.3). 1–3. S&I–S–C2–14. Forges & Chantiers de la Méditerranée, La Seyne. 1884 (1/4) launched for SGTM. 1884 (20/7) MV Marseilles–S. America. 1907 PROVENCE (France–Amérique). 1907 FV Marseilles–Spain–S. America. 1918 (13/4) torpedoed off Spanish coast on voyage Buenos Aires–Marseilles; foundered at Palamos; later refloated and returned to France–Amérique service. 1927 scrapped at La Seyne.

2. (1907) ESPAGNE
   3,952. 121,54 x 12,77. (398.8 x 41.9). 1–3. S–S–T3–14. (I–17; II–88; III–1,204). Forges & Chantiers de la Méditerranée, La Seyne. 1891 (8/3) launched for SGTM. 1891 (8/8) MV Genoa–Marseilles–S. America. 1907 ESPAGNE (France–Amérique). 1907 FV Marseilles–Spain–S. America. 1919 ESPAGNE (SGTM). 1934 scrapped in Italy.

3. (1907) LES ALPES
   3,864. 128,04 x 12,86. (420.1 x 42.2). 1–4. S–S–C2–12. (I; II; III–1,000). Harland & Wolff, Belfast. 1882 (Dec) launched as BRITISH PRINCESS (British Shipowners). 1883 (28/4) MV for American Line (c), Liverpool–Philadelphia. 1896 LES ALPES (SGTM). 1896 (24/3) FV Marseilles–S. America. 1907 LES ALPES (France–Amérique). 1907 FV Marseilles–Spain–S. America. 1910 scrapped at Marseilles.

4. (1908) AQUITAINE
   3,161, 106,82 x 12,98. (350.5 x 42.6). 1–2. S–S–T3–13. Sunderland Shipbuilding Co, Sunderland. 1890 (27/10) launched for SGTM. 1891 (Feb) MV Marseilles–S. America. 1908 AQUITAINE (France–Amérique). 1908 FV Marseilles–Spain–S. America. 1915–18 served as ammunition depot at Salonica. 1919 returned to France–Amérique service after a refit. 1927 scrapped at La Seyne.

5. (1908) ITALIE
   3,966. 121,73 x 12,80. (399.4 x 42.0). 1–3. S–S–T3–14. (I–17;

II–88; III–1,204). Forges & Chantiers de la Méditerranée, La Seyne. 1894 (18/9) launched for SGTM. 1895 (29/4) MV Marseilles–S. America. 1908 ITALIE (France–Amérique). 1908 FV Marseilles–Spain–S. America. 1916 ITALIE (SGTM). 1929 scrapped in Italy.

6. (1923) GUARUJA
   4,282. 110,39 x 13,98. (362.2 x 45.9). 1–2. S–ST&TE–13. Forges & Chantiers de la Méditerranée, La Seyne. 1921 launched for SGTM. 1923 GUARUJA (France–Amérique). 1923 FV Marseilles–Spain–S. America. 1938 (2/1) stranded near Almeria; broke her back.

7. (1923) IPANEMA
   4,282. 109,78 x 13,98. (360.2 x 45.9). 1–2. S–ST&TE–13. Forges & Chantiers de la Méditerranée, La Seyne. 1921 launched for SGTM. 1923 IPANEMA (France–Amérique). 1923 FV Marseilles–Spain–S. America. 1942 seized by Italy; renamed VILLAROSA. 1943 (Sep) scuttled by Germans at Naples. 1946 refloated by Italians; repaired; re-entered service as TAURINIA (It).

8. (1925) CORDOBA
   6,375. 127,10 x 15,30. (417.0 x 50.2). 1–2. 2S–T6–14. (I–115; II–84; III–80). Blohm & Voss, Hamburg. 1903 (10/1) launched as PRINZREGENT (German East African). 1919 CORDOBA (SGTM). 1925 CORDOBA (France–Amérique). 1932 scrapped at Savona.

Note: It seems that the Compagnie de Navigation France–Amérique ships, like those of the Société Générale de Transports Maritimes, sailed from Marseilles for the River Plate via one or more Spanish ports. It has not been found possible to ascertain when exactly they started running for France–Amérique, and in consequence they may not be shown above in strict chronological order.

FUNNEL: Black.

FLAG: Four triangles – blue at top with black 'S'; red at bottom with black 'G'; white at sides with blue 'T' on left and blue 'M' on right.

Chapter 54

(1907–14)

UNIONE AUSTRIACA

(Società Anonima Unione Austriaca di Navigazione)
(Austro–Americana)

(Austrian)

The SOCIETÀ ANONIMA UNIONE AUSTRIACA DI NAVIGA-
ZIONE (the Austrian Shipping Union) was founded in 1903 by Fratelli
Cosulich (Cosulich Brothers) of Trieste, managers of the AUSTRO–
AMERICANA fleet, which for some years previously had been
operating as a cargo service between ports in the Adriatic and the USA.

In the same year the Cunard Line concluded as agreement with the
Hungarian Government for a passenger service between Fiume and New
York, the first sailing taking place in November 1903. Fearing that much
of the rapidly expanding trade between Trieste and New York might be
lost to the faster and more regular passenger ships, Unione Austriaca
decided to set up its own passenger and cargo service in competition.

Passenger sailings began to New York with the 4,212 ton single-screw
GERTY, laid down as a purely cargo steamer, but completed with
accommodation for 30 first class and 1,400 steerage passengers. Four
other ships followed her, two being detailed to a new service to Central
America and Mexico.

With the aid of the Hamburg American Line and the Norddeutscher
Lloyd, the Unione Austriaca capital was increased from four to 16
million kroner, enabling the Company to buy the 13 Austro–Americana
cargo steamers, build further passenger ships, and in 1907 passenger
services were inaugurated to New Orleans and also to Brazil and
Argentina. The first departure to South America was undertaken by the
new 5,526 ton ARGENTINA, which left Trieste on 31 October. She was
followed by a sister ship, the OCEANIA, on 26 November, but after two
round voyages was herself transferred to the New York route, as was the
OCEANIA after three or four. The 4,946 ton FRANCESCA and the
5,491 ton SOFIA HOHENBERG, previously on the Trieste–New York
run, were detailed to the South Atlantic in 1908, as were the newly-built
5,452 ton COLUMBIA and the 4,897 ton ATLANTA in 1909. A year
later the FRANCESCA, SOFIA HOHENBERG and ATLANTA –
were fitted to carry refrigerated meat from Argentina.

1905 FRANCESCA 4,946 tons
Ran to River Plate from 1908.

In March 1911 the Austrian Government entered into a contract with the Company for a fortnightly service to Brazil and Argentina. The usual itinerary was Trieste, Patras, Naples, Barcelona, Las Palmas, Rio de Janeiro, Santos, Montevideo and Buenos Aires.

Callisto and Alberto Cosulich, managers of the Company, decided to extend their activities to include shipbuilding. With the aid of British technical experts the Cantiere Navale Triestino shipyard was built at Monfalcone, Trieste, its first steamer of 800 tons being launched in 1910. The yard was soon in a position to tackle large passenger liners, and the 12,567 ton KAISER FRANZ JOSEF I was launched for Unione Austriaca on 9 September 1911. Her maiden voyage, starting on 25 May 1912, was made to New York, but she sailed on 22 September on her one and only voyage to the River Plate. Pride of the Austrian merchant marine, she was propelled by two sets of quadruple-expansion engines supplied by D. Rowan & Co of Glasgow. She could accommodate 125 first class, 550 second and 1,230 steerage passengers. In April 1913 the same yard launched the 7,644 ton single-screw BELVEDERE for the South American service, but in the event she never took part in it.

However, the 4,835 ton EUGENIA and the 6,135 ton ALICE were transferred to the South Atlantic in 1913, as was the latter's sister ship LAURA on 24 June 1914.

In 1913, 10 years after its foundation, Unione Austriaca (still popularly known as Austro–Americana) had a fleet of 29 ocean-going steamers in commission and five more under construction. There were, however, many in Austria who believed that it suffered from one serious disadvantage – it was still largely controlled from Germany. In April 1914, therefore, and with the full approval of the Austrian Government, the foreign-owned shares were bought by a group of Austrian banks.

The outbreak of World War I in August 1914 brought an immediate cessation of the Company's services and resulted in the loss of a number

392

1909 ATLANTA 4,897 tons
After World War I ran for Cosulich Line.

of ships. The KAISER FRANZ JOSEF I was safely in her home port, but the ALICE and LAURA were interned in Brazil and seized in 1917, eventually becoming the Fabre Line ASIA and BRAGA. The OCEANIA was damaged by a mine during the closing stages of the war and a few days later was blown up by the Austrians to prevent her from falling into Italian hands.

After the war, following a change from Austrian to Italian rule, the Company was re-established in Trieste as the COSULICH LINE (Chapter 60).

1. 1907 ARGENTINA
   5,526. 118,86 x 14,63. (390.0 x 48.0). 1–2. 2S–T6–15. (I–45; II–75; III–1,230). Russell & Co, Port Glasgow (engines Dunsmuir & Jackson, Glasgow). 1907 (26/8) launched. 1907 (31/10) MV Trieste–S. America (2 RV); subsequently ran to New York. 1919 ARGENTINA (Cosulich). 1926 ditto (Florio). 1932 ditto (Tirrenia). 1960 scrapped.

2. 1907 OCEANIA
   5,497. 119,20 x 15,24. (391.1 x 50.0). 1–2. 2S–T6–15. (I–45; II–75; III–1,230). A. Stephen & Sons, Glasgow. 1907 (10/9) launched. 1907 (26/11) MV Trieste–S. America. 1908 (26/9) FV Trieste–New York. 1918 (3/10) mined and beached near Cape Rondoni. 1918 (15/10) blown up by Austrians to prevent her from falling into Italian hands.

3. (1908) FRANCESCA
   4,946. 109,65 x 14,63. (359.8 x 48.0). 1–2. S–T3–12. (I–30; II–50; III–1,500). Russell & Co, Port Glasgow (engines J.G. Kincaid & Co, Greenock). 1905 (2/6) launched. 1905 (17/8) MV Trieste–New York. 1908 (7/5) FV Trieste–S. America. 1910 fitted to carry

393

refrigerated meat from Argentina. 1919 FRANCESCA (Cosulich). 1926 scrapped.

4. (1908) SOFIA HOHENBERG
5,491. 109,72 x 14,63. (360.0 x 48.0). 1–2. S–T3–12. (I–30; II–50; III–1,550). Lloyd Austriaco, Trieste. 1905 (3/9) launched. 1905 (15/12) MV Trieste–New York. 1908 (6/6) FV Trieste–S. America. 1910 fitted to carry refrigerated meat from Argentina. 1919 SOFIA (Cosulich). 1929 scrapped.

5. (1909) COLUMBIA
5,452. 121,91 x 15,88. (400.0 x 52.1). 1–2. S–T3–14. (I–50; II–75; III–1,200). Russell & Co, Port Glasgow (engines J.G. Kincaid & Co, Glasgow. 1908 (2/4) launched. 1909 (24/3) MV Trieste–New York. 1909 (28/11) FV Trieste–S. America. 1919 COLUMBIA (Cosulich). 1931 ANNOULA (Greek). 1933 foundered off Cape Lookout.

6. (1909) ATLANTA
4,897. 117,34 x 15,17. (385.0 x 49.8). 1–2. S–T3–12. (I–30; II–50; III–1,200). Russell & Co, Port Glasgow (engines D. Rowan & Co, Glasgow). 1908 (7/2) launched. 1908 (1/4) MV Glasgow–New York in ballast. 1909 (31/12) FV Trieste–S. America. 1910 fitted to carry refrigerated meat from Argentina. 1919 ATLANTA (Cosulich). 1943 CHARLOTTE (Ger). 1945 (11/1) bombed and sunk by Allied air attack off Egersund, Norway.

7. (1912) KAISER FRANZ JOSEF I
12,567. 145,53 x 18,35. (477.5 x 60.2). 2–2. 2S–Q8–17. (I–125; II–550; III–1,230). Cantiere Navale Triestino, Monfalcone (engines D. Rowan & Co, Glasgow). 1911 (9/9) launched. 1912 (25/5) MV Trieste–New York. 1912 (22/9) FV Trieste–S. America (1 RV); subsequently ran to New York. 1919 handed to Cosulich; contemplated name GENERALE DIAZ; final choice PRESIDENTE WILSON: ran to New York. 1930 GANGE (Lloyd Triestino). 1936 MARCO POLO (Adriatica). 1944 scuttled by Germans at La Spezia. 1949–50 refloated; scrapped.

8. (1913) EUGENIA
4,835. 117,34 x 15,14. (385.0 x 49.7). 1–2. S–T3–12. (I–15; III–1,200). Russell & Co, Port Glasgow (engines D. Rowan & Co, Glasgow). 1906 (7/9) launched. 1913 (1/5) FV Trieste–S. America. 1917 (6/8) torpedoed and sunk by German submarine off SW Ireland.

9. (1913) ALICE
6,125. 126,58 x 15,11. (415.3 x 49.6). 1–2. 2S–T6–15. (I–50; II–75; III–1,500). Russell & Co, Port Glasgow (engines J.G. Kincaid & Co, Greenock). 1907 (29/5) launched. 1907 (28/8) MV Trieste–

New York. 1913 (9/10) FV Trieste–S. America. 1917 seized by Brazil; renamed ASIA. 1919 (Dec) handed to France as war reparations; sold to Fabre; name unchanged; ran Marseilles–New York. 1930 (21/5) destroyed by fire in Red Sea carrying pilgrims to Mecca.

10. (1914) LAURA

6,125. 126,58 x 15,11. (415.3 x 49.6). 1–2. 2S–T6–15. (I–50; II–75; III–1,500). Russell & Co, Port Glasgow (engines J.G. Kincaid & Co, Greenock). 1907 (15/2) launched. 1907 (11/5) MV Trieste–New York. 1914 (24/6) FV Trieste–Naples–S. America. 1914–17 sheltered at Bahia. 1917 (2/7) seized by Brazil; renamed EUROPA (Lloyd Nacional). 1919 handed to France as war reparations; sold to Fabre; renamed BRAGA; ran Marseilles–New York. 1926 (16/11) wrecked on Aspro Island, Greece.

–– ––– BELVEDERE

7,644. 127,40 x 16,46. (418.0 x 54.0). 1–2. S–T3–12. (I–12; II–140; III–1,274). Cantiere Navale Triestino, Monfalcone. 1913 (8/4) launched for S. American service but ran to New York 1913–14. 1919 BELVEDERE (Cosulich (60)); q.v.

FUNNEL: Red with broad white band; black top.
FLAG: Three red and white stripes at top and bottom; remainder red and white diagonal quarters; red 'A' 'A' on the white quarters at left and right.

Chapter 55

1908–25

PINILLOS LINE

(Pinillos, Izquierdo y Compañía)

(Spanish)

The PINILLOS LINE can be traced back to 1884, when Don Antonio Martinez de Pinillos e Izquierdo acquired the steamer APOLO. A year later he and a relative, Martin Saenz, founded the firm of PINILLOS, SAENZ Y COMPAÑÍA in Cadiz, and a number of steamers were built to run between Barcelona, Havana and New Orleans.

A significant move came in 1908 when the firm, which had changed its name in 1896 to PINILLOS, IZQUIERDO Y COMPAÑÍA, commissioned the 5,617 ton CADIZ and the 5,574 ton BARCELONA, both

1908 BARCELONA 5,574 tons
Sister ship of the CADIZ, which undertook the Company's maiden voyage to the River Plate.

built by C. Connell & Co of Glasgow, and placed them in service between Genoa, Barcelona, Cadiz, Las Palmas, Montevideo and Buenos Aires. They were single-screw steamers propelled by triple-expansion engines, and had accommodation for 60 first class, 80 second, 24 third and 1,000 fourth class passengers.

The old-established Compañía Trasatlántica Española (Chapter 36) had been running a parallel service, but had not built any new steamers for about 20 years and so the Pinillos newcomers attracted a considerable

396

amount of favourable attention – so much so that further tonnage was soon forthcoming.

In 1913 the Compañía Trasatlántica placed in service the 10,137 ton quadruple-screw REINA VICTORIA EUGENIA and the 10,348 ton triple-screw INFANTA ISABEL DE BORBON. However, Pinillos were prepared for this move, and although they did not have the resources to match it, the 8,182 ton INFANTA ISABEL was launched on 29 June 1912 and sailed from Barcelona on the very day, 28 September, that the INFANTA ISABEL DE BORBON was launched. There must frequently have been a good deal of confusion between these names!

The Pinillos ship had twin-screws, and was fitted with two sets of quadruple-expansion engines, giving a service speed of 15 knots. Her passenger capacity was 144 first, 150 second and 1,750 third class.

1914 PRINCIPE DE ASTURIAS 8,371 tons
Wrecked near Santos in March 1916 with loss of 415 lives.

A sister ship, the 8,371 ton PRINCIPE DE ASTURIAS, was launched at Port Glasgow on 29 April 1914, and began her maiden voyage from Barcelona on 16 August. She was lost during her sixth voyage on 3 March 1916 while carrying 558 passengers and crew, many of the passengers being of German nationality. For this reason, the captain was attempting to avoid interception by the British cruiser GLASGOW, when the PRINCIPE DE ASTURIAS struck the Pirassununga Point, near Santos, 'turned over, bottom ripped open, boilers exploded, vessel broken in two; lying in 22 fathoms water'. [1] No fewer than 415 lives were lost.

The INFANTA ISABEL had made a round voyage from Barcelona and Cadiz to New York in August 1914 to help repatriate Americans stranded in Europe. After the war, in 1919, she made two North Atlantic voyages as a troopship from Marseilles and Bordeaux, respectively. The CADIZ started a round voyage from Cadiz to New York, Havana and Galveston in November 1914, and another from Barcelona, Tarragona, Almeria, Malaga and Cadiz to New York and Havana in 1915, while the BARCELONA made a round voyage from Barcelona, Tarragona, Alicante, Malaga and Cadiz to New York in November 1914.

The 4,796 ton CATALINA, built by C. Connell & Co in 1893, ran between Spain and the Mexican Gulf until 1915. She left New Orleans for the last time on 3 December 1915 for Galveston and Barcelona and a few days later, on 15 January 1916, sailed on her first South American voyage via Las Palmas and Santos for Montevideo and Buenos Aires. As the PRINCIPE DE ASTURIAS was not wrecked until 3 March 1916 there was no connection between this calamity and the decision to transfer the CATALINA to the South Atlantic, on which she made many further voyages.

Two more disasters hit the Company. On 5 December 1916 the 4,029 ton PIO X foundered near the Canary Islands with a death roll of 40 when destined from New Orleans to Spain and, much worse, the 4,999 ton VALBANERA foundered on 9 September 1919 between Santiago de Cuba and Havana during a hurricane, fatal casualties numbering no fewer than 488.

The Company never recovered from these losses although the CATALINA was retained by them until scrapped in 1924 and the INFANTA ISABEL, CADIZ and BARCELONA ran until 1925, when they were bought by the Compañía Oceanica of Barcelona, which itself only survived until 1928.

[1] Lloyd's Weekly Index, quoting a message received from the Salvage Association. (A fathom equals six feet or 1,83 metres).

1. 1908 CADIZ
    5,617. 126,30 x 16,15. (414.4 x 53.0). 2–2. S–T3–14. (I–60; II–80; III–24; IV–1,000). C. Connell & Co, Glasgow (engines D. Rowan & Co, Glasgow). 1908 (3/2) launched. 1908 (30/3) MV Barcelona–Genoa–Barcelona (8/4)–Cadiz–Las Palmas–Montevideo–Buenos Aires. 1925 CADIZ (Compañía Oceanica, Barcelona). 1928 scrapped at Savona.
2. 1908 BARCELONA
    5,574. 126,49 x 16,15. (415.0 x 53.0). 2–2. S–T3–14. (I–60; II–80; III–24; IV–1,000). C. Connell & Co, Glasgow (engines D. Rowan & Co, Glasgow). 1908 (18/3) launched. 1908 (8/5) MV (Barcelona)–Genoa–Barcelona–Cadiz–Las Palmas–Montevideo–

Buenos Aires. 1925 BARCELONA (Compañía Oceania, Barcelona). 1927 scrapped at Baltimore.

3. 1912 INFANTA ISABEL
    8,182. 140,05 x 17,74. (459.5 x 58.2). 1–2. 2S–Q8–15. (I–144; II–150; III–1,750). Russell & Co, Port Glasgow (engines D. Rowan & Co, Glasgow). 1912 (29/6) launched. 1912 (28/9) MV Barcelona–Cadiz–Las Palmas–Montevideo–Buenos Aires. 1925 INFANTA ISABEL (Compañía Oceanica, Barcelona). 1926 MIDZUHO MARU (OSK). 1938 MIZUHO MARU (OSK). 1944 (21/9) torpedoed and sunk by US Submarine REDFISH north of Philippine Islands.

4. 1914 PRINCIPE DE ASTURIAS
    8,371. 140,05 x 17,74. (459.5 x 58.2). 1–2. 2S–Q8–15. (I–144; II–150; III–1,750). Russell & Co, Port Glasgow (engines D. Rowan & Co, Glasgow). 1914 (29/4) launched. 1914 (16/8) MV Barcelona–Buenos Aires. 1916 (17/2) sailed Barcelona on 6th RV. 1916 (3/3) wrecked on Pirassununga Point, near Santos (415).

5. (1916) CATALINA
    4,796. 126,49 x 14,63. (415.0 x 48.0). 1–2. S–S–T3–12. C. Connell & Co, Glasgow (engines Dunsmuir & Jackson, Glasgow). 1893 launched. 1893 MV Barcelona–Mexican Gulf. 1915 (3/12) LV New Orleans–Galveston–Barcelona. 1916 (15/1) FV Barcelona–Las Palmas–Santos–Montevideo–Buenos Aires. 1924 scrapped.

FUNNEL: Black; red St. George's cross on white background.
FLAG: Red St. George's cross on white background.

Chapter 56

1912–62

COMPAGNIE DE NAVIGATION SUD ATLANTIQUE

(French)

A concern entitled the SOCIÉTÉ D'ETUDES DE NAVIGATION was founded in 1910 by the French shipowners Cyprien Fabre, Fraissinet and the Société Générale de Transports Maritimes in conjunction with two French banks. On 27 May 1910 they submitted a request to the French Government to be allowed to undertake all the mail services then maintained by Messageries Maritimes (Chapter 12). In this connection, it may be mentioned that Messageries had done very little since 1904 to improve their South American service.

After the French authorities had had private discussions with both Messageries and the Société d'Etudes, contracts were signed on 11 July 1911 and were to be effective from 22 July 1912. Messageries were allowed to retain all their mail services except the one to South America, which was to be transferred to the Société d'Etudes. They, for their part, were required to build four 18 knot passenger liners with a minimum length of 175 metres (570 feet) and provide six *paquebots mixtes* in order not only to maintain a fortnightly mail service but also a fortnightly intermediate service between Bordeaux and Buenos Aires. However, these arrangements were not confirmed by the French Parliament until 31 December 1911, thus allowing an unreasonably short time for the appropriate ships to be acquired. Nevertheless, orders were placed next day with the Chantiers de l'Atlantique at St. Nazaire for the 14,000 ton LUTETIA and with Forges & Chantiers de la Méditerranée at La Seyne for a similar ship, the GALLIA, both to be delivered in 1913. The MASSILIA and GERGOVIA were due to follow from La Seyne and St. Nazaire, respectively.

Then on 8 February 1912 the Société d'Etudes de Navigation changed its name to COMPAGNIE DE NAVIGATION SUD ATLANTIQUE, its capital being 15 million francs (£600,000). Its board of directors consisted of prominent bankers and shipowners, among whom were André Berthelot, Cyprien Fabre, Alfred Fraissinet, Comte Armand, Pellerin de la Touche and Hubert Giraud.

The inaugural date of the service was, not surprisingly, postponed from 22 July to 22 September 1912 and, of course, a number of second-hand ships had to be acquired in order to open it. The market was at its lowest ebb, but there was one obvious possibility in the 12,480 ton KAISER FRIEDRICH, which had been completed in 1898 for Nord-deutscher Lloyd as a consort to the record-breaker KAISER WILHELM DER GROSSE. Returned to her builders after a handful of disappointingly slow voyages, she had been chartered to the Hamburg America Line in 1899 for about a year, but had been lying idle ever since. Negotiations that had been proceeding between the builders and the newly-founded Norwegian America Line for the purchase of the ship broke down, and it is evident, looking back, that this was fortunate for the well-being of the Norwegian concern. In fact, the KAISER FRIEDRICH was bought by Sud Atlantique on 1 May 1912 for four million francs (£160,000), a third of her original cost. She was renamed BURDIGALA and left for Havre for drydocking, thence to Bordeaux where, on 26 September, an invitation luncheon was held on board for 200 guests.

1912 BURDIGALA 12,480 tons
Built 1898 as NDL KAISER FRIEDRICH. Made one round voyage, Bordeaux to River Plate.

By that time no fewer than six other ships had been acquired. The first was the 6,405 ton Orient Line ORMUZ, completed in 1886 and renamed DIVONA. Six weeks later the 7,000 ton LA GASCOGNE and LA BRETAGNE, also dating from 1886, were bought from the Compagnie Générale Transatlantique, both retaining their names. The 5,500 ton TINTAGEL CASTLE and AVONDALE CASTLE of 1897 vintage came from the Union–Castle Line and were renamed LIGER and GARONNA, while the 6,007 ton STAFFORDSHIRE, a Bibby Line veteran of 1893, was renamed SAMARA. Finally, the 4,950 ton City Line CITY OF CORINTH, renamed SEQUANA, was bought in September 1912.

Unfortunately, none of them was ready to sail by the stipulated date of 22 September 1912, so the Company had to charter the 6,479 ton

1912 DIVONA 6,405 tons
Built 1887 as ORMUZ (Orient).

ATLANTIQUE from Messageries Maritimes to open the service. She made only the one round voyage from Bordeaux, which she left on the appointed date for Lisbon, Dakar, Rio de Janeiro, Montevideo and Buenos Aires.

The next sailing was taken by the BURDIGALA, the former KAISER FRIEDRICH, on 5 October from Bordeaux. She averaged 17½ knots from Bordeaux to the first port of call, Lisbon, and reached Buenos Aires in record time, the customary call at Dakar being omitted as it was decided that she was too large to enter the harbour there. At first sight, the trip was a very successful one, but the effort was too much for the BURDIGALA and she had to undergo extensive repairs upon return to Bordeaux.

The LIGER took the first of the intermediate sailings on 12 October from Bordeaux, followed a week later by the mail steamer DIVONA, which arrived at Dakar with rudder trouble and was detained there until 13 November with the result that many of her passengers were transferred to her successor, the intermediate steamer GARONNA.

The LA GASCOGNE and LA BRETAGNE were next on the list of mail sailings, with two more intermediate departures by the SAMARA and SEQUANA. The following mail sailing should have been taken by the BURDIGALA, but as she was still undergoing repairs the LA CHAMPAGNE, a sister ship of LA GASCOGNE and LA BRE-TAGNE, was chartered from CGT. She collided at Lisbon with the Royal Mail Steam Packet Company's DESNA and was delayed there for some days.

The BURDIGALA was unable to start her second voyage on 14 December 1912, so there was a gap until LA GASCOGNE left on the 28th. It was foggy and she stranded near Royan at the mouth of the Gironde.

Further difficulties arose on 13 January 1913 as the DIVONA was not yet ready, and the Company had to charter the 7,168 ton VALDIVIA from the Société Générale de Transports Maritimes to take her place. She was not returned to her owners until the following September.

The first of the new mail fleet, the 14,783 ton LUTETIA, was launched on 23 March 1913, closely followed by the 14,966 ton GALLIA on the 26th. Only one day later, the keel of the MASSILIA was laid at La Seyne, but the building of the GERGOVIA was postponed, and eventually cancelled altogether owing to the outbreak of World War I.

1920 MASSILIA 15,147 tons
Third of the three-funnellers built for the Company.

The LUTETIA was ready to start her maiden voyage on 1 November 1913, and was an impressive-looking ship with three funnels. Her quadruple screws were driven by a combination of triple-expansion engines and low-pressure steam turbines, and she could accommodate 462 first class, 130 second, 90 third and 450 fourth class passengers. She averaged 18.7 knots on her outward voyage. But the Company's misfortunes continued as, after leaving Lisbon on her homeward maiden voyage, she collided with and sank the Greek cargo steamer DIMIT-RIOS. The LUTETIA's bow was badly damaged, and as she was letting in water she was obliged to return to Lisbon, where her passengers disembarked and left for their destinations by train. After temporary repairs, she proceeded to St. Nazaire for further attention.

The GALLIA's maiden voyage started on 29 November after a shakedown cruise to the Balearic Islands and Corsica, and was completed without serious incident, although her engines were giving trouble. It was also decided that her first class capacity of 300 berths in comparison with the LUTETIA's 462 was insufficient, so she was sent to La Seyne at the end of January 1914 for both matters to be rectified. Unlike the LUTETIA, the GALLIA was a triple-screw steamer.

Bearing in mind the serious mishaps to no fewer than six ships and the

Company's consequent inability to adhere to its schedule, it is not surprising that, first, Sud Atlantique received official complaints about the unsatisfactory nature of the service and, second, that the Company found itself in serious financial difficulties. In December 1913 discussions took place with the Compagnie Générale Transatlantique, the Société Générale de Transports Maritimes and the Crédit Français, with the result that the Sud Atlantique capital was reduced from 15 to five million francs, and then increased in two stages to the original figure by the issue of new shares. The other important decision was that the Company was to be placed under the management of CGT, whose steamers FLANDRE, PÉROU, FLORIDE and GUADELOUPE were later chartered to Sud Atlantique.

The GALLIA returned to Bordeaux in time to take the 20 February 1914 sailing. Work on her engines had only been partially completed, so she ran at reduced speed but without further incident, and at the conclusion of that voyage she went back to La Seyne for final attention. The costly BURDIGALA was laid up indefinitely at Bordeaux, but fortunately the LUTETIA was ready to sail on 16 May and made a fast passage out and home. She left Bordeaux some hours in advance of Hamburg–Süd's CAP TRAFALGAR and arrived at Buenos Aires 36 hours before her.

On 14 August 1914, a few days after the outbreak of World War I, LA BRETAGNE was taken up as a hospital ship and served in this capacity throughout the war. The LA GASCOGNE served as an auxiliary cruiser for a short time, but was then returned to Sud Atlantique. She made three round voyages between Bordeaux and New York under charter to CGT, after which she was again requisitioned, serving as a depot ship at Salonica. The LUTETIA and GALLIA became troopships, but the BURDIGALA and later the LUTETIA were converted into auxiliary cruisers in 1915. The GALLIA was torpedoed on 4 October 1916 and sank in about 15 minutes when carrying 2,350 troops to Salonica, 600 of whom were rescued by the French cruiser CHATEAURENAULT, which passed the spot on the following day. The BURDIGALA was sunk in the Aegean Sea on 14 November 1916 by a mine laid by German submarine U.73. At the beginning of that year the DIVONA had become a hospital ship.

Two of the ships chartered from CGT were lost in quick succession in 1915 – the 7,029 ton FLANDRE was sunk on 19 February near Dakar by the German raider PRINZ EITEL FRIEDRICH, and on 25 February the 6,600 ton GUADELOUPE was captured by the German auxiliary cruiser KRONPRINZ WILHELM between Dakar and Brazil. She was scuttled by the Germans on 28 February, her passengers and crew being transferred to the British steamer CHASE MILL.

Without any prior notice, Chargeurs Réunis were substituted for CGT as managers of Sud Atlantique in April 1916. This came about by their having acquired a large batch of the Company's shares from the Crédit Français.

The Hamburg American passenger steamer PRINZ ADALBERT, seized at Falmouth in August 1914 and at a later date renamed PRINCETOWN, was bought by Sud Atlantique in January 1917, became the ALÉSIA and was reconditioned in England. But she was of little or no use to her new owners as she was torpedoed and sunk by the German submarine UC.50 on 6 September 1917 on voyage from Cardiff to Bordeaux, before sailing for South America. A few weeks previously, on 8 June, the intermediate steamer SEQUANA had been torpedoed and sunk near the Ile d'Yeu.

Towards the end of the war the LUTETIA carried American troops from New York to Brest, but a month or so after the Armistice of 11 November 1918 she made the first of two voyages from Rotterdam to Havre, carrying on each occasion about 2,400 French people who had taken refuge in Holland during the war. Soon afterwards, having undergone four years of arduous service, she went to La Seyne for an extensive overhaul lasting until well into 1920.

The LA GASCOGNE returned from her Salonica duties in very bad shape. To begin with she was laid up near Bordeaux, but was sold in June 1919 and sailed to Genoa to be scrapped. LA BRETAGNE also returned to Bordeaux in 1919, and the Company decided to put her back in service after a complete refit. In June 1919 she was renamed ALÉSIA, and work on her is believed to have started but to have stopped almost at once. She was laid up until 1923, when she was sold and left in tow for Holland to be scrapped. The tow parted near the Island of Texel, where she stranded and became a total loss. The hospital ship DIVONA was laid up at Marseilles until towards the end of 1922, when partial demolition took place. She was later towed to Genoa for it to be completed.

During 1919 the only units of the original fleet remaining in commission were the intermediate steamers LIGER, GARONNA and SAMARA, of which the GARONNA was scrapped in 1920, but in July of that year the Company received from the French Government the 8,324 ton twin-screw liner SIERRA VENTANA, formerly of Norddeutscher Lloyd's South American service, and renamed her ALBA.

A new mail contract signed on 24 June 1920 was responsible for a discontinuance of the call at Dakar.

The LUTETIA resumed service on 2 October 1920. She was soon joined by the third express steamer, the MASSILIA, which had been launched at La Seyne as long ago as 30 April 1914, but whose fitting out

405

had been delayed by the war. It was not until September 1920 that she undertook her trials, during which she recorded a mean speed of 20.97 knots. Her maiden voyage started on 30 October from Bordeaux, the transatlantic crossing from Lisbon to Rio de Janeiro being completed in the record time of 9 days 19 hours; she returned from Buenos Aires to Bordeaux in 17 days. She was very similar in appearance to the LUTETIA and GALLIA; like the former she had quadruple screws.

The 10,123 ton twin-screw MEDUANA and MOSELLA were launched on 30 September 1920 and 3 September 1921 by Swan, Hunter & Wigham Richardson of Tyneside for the intermediate service, enabling the LIGER and SAMARA to be scrapped. The ALBA was transferred to Chargeurs Réunis in July 1926, renamed AMÉRIQUE and detailed to their west coast of Africa service.

It was decided in 1928 that Chargeurs Réunis would take over Sud Atlantique's intermediate service, and in consequence the former acquired the MEDUANA and MOSELLA, which were renamed KERGUÉLEN and JAMAIQUE.

This left Sud Atlantique with only the MASSILIA and LUTETIA, which maintained a monthly service between Bordeaux and Buenos Aires. However, the keel of by far the largest and finest ship built for the South American passenger trade was laid on 28 November 1928 by Chantiers & Ateliers de St. Nazaire, and the 40,945 ton L'ATLANTI-QUE was launched for Sud Atlantique on 15 April 1930. She was propelled by four sets of single-reduction geared turbines connected to quadruple screws, and during her trials reached a maximum speed of 23.85 knots, which meant that she could easily maintain 21 knots in service. Her public rooms and passenger accommodation were of an exceptionally high standard, provision being made for 414 first class, 158 second and 584 third class passengers. A tennis court was laid out between the second and third funnels and a swimming pool forward of the mainmast. She had an impressive appearance with three funnels. the aftermost being a dummy, with the uptakes of the other two (as in the case of the BRABANTIA and LIMBURGIA (Chapter 51)) divided so as to give a long unrestricted vista through the centre of the ship. She had two masts, a cruiser stern and, surprisingly, luffing davits. Her cost was £3,200,000.

Owing to her vast size, it was found desirable for departures and arrivals to take place at Pauillac, some 30 miles downstream from Bordeaux, her maiden voyage starting on 29 September 1931 for Vigo, Lisbon, Rio de Janeiro, Santos, Montevideo and Buenos Aires. Soon after entering service her funnels were lengthened by about 5 metres (about 16½ feet), thereby improving her appearance. Her only consort

1931 L'ATLANTIQUE 40,945 tons

The lower view shows her funnels as soon lengthened.

1933 L'ATLANTIQUE 40,945 tons
On fire, January 1933, in English Channel.

was the MASSILIA as the LUTETIA arrived at Bordeaux for the last time on 31 July 1931 and was laid up.

One serious disadvantage of L'ATLANTIQUE's great size was that there was no dry dock nearer to Bordeaux than Havre able to accommodate her, and on 3 January 1933 she sailed light, without passengers, from Pauillac for Havre. All went well until 3.30 a.m. on the 4th, when a fire was discovered in a first class 'E' deck cabin, in which mattresses were being stored. Despite all possible precautions, the fire spread with amazing rapidity and at 6 a.m. orders were given to abandon the ship, 17 lives being lost. The survivors were taken aboard a ship that was standing by. And then for 2½ days the giant vessel was adrift in the English Channel, burning furiously and at the mercy of wind and tide. Eventually, on the 6th a Frenchman managed with almost superhuman difficulty to board the liner, and in due course four French tugs had tow ropes attached to her stern. They towed her slowly, stern first, to Cherbourg, where she arrived on the 7th with the blaze extinguished. It was a long time before discussions and arguments with the insurers of the ship and with her real owners, the French Government, produced the admission that she was beyond repair. It was not until 1936 that she was towed to Scotland to be scrapped at Port Glasgow.

Meanwhile, the MASSILIA had in theory to carry on the service unaided, but Sud Altantique and Chargeurs Réunis were, in fact, running a joint service. There was still an adequate number of sailings even if the other ships taking part were smaller and slower.

It was not until 1936 that an order was placed at St. Nazaire for the 29,253 ton PASTEUR, which was launched on 15 February 1938. She had an overall length of 212,40 metres (696.9 feet) and quadruple screws, driven by four sets of single-reduction geared turbines giving her a service speed of 25 knots. Outwardly, she was an ugly ship with one enormous funnel situated considerably forward of amidships, but her interior was but little inferior to that of L'ATLANTIQUE, accommodation being provided for 216 first class and 906 tourist passengers.

The PASTEUR's maiden voyage was scheduled for 14 September 1939 from Bordeaux for Lisbon, Rio de Janeiro, Santos, Montevideo and Buenos Aires, but the outbreak of World War II at the beginning of the month made it necessary to cancel the sailing. Eventually, she sailed from Brest on 2 June 1940, having loaded 300 tons of gold bars belonging to the Banque de France in the space of a few hours, and reached Halifax in five days at an average speed of 26 knots. In August 1940 she was taken over by the British Ministry of War Transport and placed under Cunard – White Star management. In June 1945 she returned to the French flag, but never subsequently got nearer than Dakar to the South American service for which she had been built. She was laid up at Brest

1939 PASTEUR 29,253 tons
As completed for maiden voyage to River Plate in September 1939. Owing to World War
II she never visited South America.

on 25 January 1957, and in the following September was sold to
Norddeutscher Lloyd, who renamed her BREMEN. She reappeared
nearly two years later with a greatly-improved appearance and many
other alterations, and ran on the North Atlantic for 12 years before being
sold to the Chandris Lines as the cruise ship REGINA MAGNA. In 1974
she was laid up at Piraeus, three years later became an accommodation
ship at Jeddah and finally, on 9 June 1980, foundered while under tow to
Kaohsiung for demolition.

The MASSILIA carried many French Members of Parliament to
Casablanca in June 1940 and soon afterwards repatriated them to France!
Later that month she proceeded to Liverpool to collect a number of
French soldiers who had escaped from Dunkirk, and landed them at
Toulon. She was then laid up at Marseilles and in due course became an
accommodation ship for the Germans, who scuttled her in August 1944.
She was refloated after the war and scrapped.

Chargeurs Réunis were fortunate that four of the six units of their
pre-war South American fleet survived, including the former Sud
Atlantique KERGUÉLEN and JAMAIQUE, both of which were
reconditioned in 1947 but were scrapped in 1954–5.

The 11,968 ton LAVOISIER and the 12,021 ton CLAUDE BER-
NARD, both twin-screw motorships, had been built for the Chargeurs
service in 1950, followed by the 12,358 ton LOUIS LUMIÈRE in 1952.
For their part, Sud Atlantique commissioned the 12,003 ton twin-screw
motorship LAËNNEC and the 12,006 ton CHARLES TELLIER in
1952.

Ten years later, both Chargeurs Réunis and Sud Atlantique withdrew

409

1952 LAËNNEC 12,003 tons
Ran for Sud Atlantique for 10 years before purchase by Messageries Maritimes.

their South American services. They were replaced by Messageries Maritimes, who had discontinued their own South American service just 50 years earlier to make way for Sud Atlantique. Messageries bought the LOUIS LUMIÈRE together with the LAËNNEC and CHARLES TELLIER, and with them ran a regular service from Havre to Rio de Janeiro, Santos, Montevideo and Buenos Aires until 1966, when the newly-completed 17,986 ton motorship PASTEUR replaced them. She only ran on the South Atlantic until 1972, and as the other major French passenger line to the River Plate, the Société Générale de Transports Maritimes, had also closed down in 1962, the departure of Messageries marked the end of French passenger services to South America.

It must be admitted that Sud Atlantique was a singularly unfortunate company. Much of the trouble was undoubtedly due to the fact that it had to start operations long before it had time to build a fleet of suitable ships, but many of those it did have specially built were singularly unlucky too.

a. (1912) ATLANTIQUE (c)
     6,479. 142,91 x 15,42. (468.9 x 50.6). 2–2. 2S–T6–16. Messageries Maritimes, La Ciotat. 1899 (5/11) launched for Messageries Maritimes. 1912 (22/9) FV for Sud Atlantique (c), Bordeaux–S. America (1 RV). 1921 ANGKOR (Messageries Maritimes). 1933 (Dec) sold; scrapped. (See Messageries Maritimes (12)).
1. (1912) BURDIGALA
     12,480. 177,29 [182,87] x 19,47. (581.7 [600.0] x 63.9). 3–2. 2S–Q(10)–20. (I–400; II–250; III–700). F. Schichau, Danzig. 1897 (5/10) launched as KAISER FRIEDRICH (NDL). 1900 (Nov) laid up. 1912 BURDIGALA (Sud Atlantique). 1912 (5/10) FV

Bordeaux–S. America (1 RV); laid up at Bordeaux. 1915 French auxiliary cruiser. 1916 (14/11) sunk in Aegean Sea by mine laid by German submarine U.73.

2. (1912) LIGER
5,562. 129,59 x 15,24. (425.2 x 50.0). 1–4. S–T3–13. Fairfield Shipbuilding Co, Glasgow. 1896 (12/9) launched as TINTAGEL CASTLE (Castle). 1912 LIGER (Sud Atlantique). 1912 (12/10) FV Bordeaux–S. America. 1923 scrapped in Italy.

3. (1912) DIVONA
6,405. 141,87 x 15,88. (465.5 x 52.1). 2–4. S–T3–17. (I–166; II–170; III). Fairfield Shipbuilding Co, Glasgow. 1886 (Sep) launched as ORMUZ (Orient). 1912 DIVONA (Sud Atlantique). 1912 (19/10) FV Bordeaux–S. America; rudder trouble; repaired at Dakar (dep 16/11). 1913 (22/3) 2nd voyage Bordeaux–S. America. 1916 French hospital ship, 1919 laid up at Marseilles. 1922 partially scrapped at Marseilles; finally at Genoa.

4. (1912) GARONNA
5,531. 129,59 x 15,24. (425.2 x 50.0). 1–4. S–T3–13. Fairfield Shipbuilding Co, Glasgow. 1896 (5/11) launched as AVON-DALE CASTLE (Castle). 1912 GARONNA (Sud Atlantique). 1912 (26/10) FV Bordeaux–S. America. 1920 scrapped.

5. (1912) LA GASCOGNE
7,395. 150,99 x 15,91. (495.4 x 52.2). 2–2. I&S–S–Q4–17. (I–390; II–65; III–1,500). Forges & Chantiers de la Méditerranée, La Seyne. Laid down as L'ALGERIE. 1886 (5/1) launched as LA GASCOGNE (CGT). 1894 engines Q4 instead of C6; masts reduced from 4 to 2. 1912 LA GASCOGNE (Sud Atlantique). 1912 (2/11) FV Bordeaux–S. America. 1914 (Aug) French auxiliary cruiser, but soon returned to Company. 1915 (26/2) FV for CGT (c), Bordeaux–New York (3 RV). 1915 again requisitioned; depot ship at Salonica. 1919 laid up at Bordeaux. 1919 (1/7) arr Genoa; scrapped.

6. (1912) SAMARA
6,007. 135,78 x 14,96. (445.5 x 49.1). 1–4. 2S–T6–13. Harland & Wolff, Belfast. 1893 (7/12) launched as STAFFORDSHIRE (Bibby). 1912 SAMARA (Sud Atlantique). 1912 (9/11) FV Bordeaux–S. America. 1915 (Jun) FV for CGT (c), St. Nazaire–Panama (1 RV). 1915 resumed Bordeaux–S. America. 1922 scrapped.

7. (1912) LA BRETAGNE
7,112. 150,99 x 15,78. (495.4 x 51.8). 2–2. S–Q4–17. (I–390; II–65; III–1500). CGT, St. Nazaire. 1885 (9/9) launched for CGT. 1895 engines Q4 instead of T6; masts reduced from 4 to 2. 1912

411

LA BRETAGNE (Sud Atlantique). 1912 (16/11) FV Bordeaux–
S. America. 1914 (Aug) French hospital ship. 1919 (Jun)
renamed ALÉSIA reconditioning started but soon stopped; laid
up. 1923 (Dec) sold to Dutch shipbreakers; broke her tow near
Texel Island; stranded; total loss.

8. (1912) SEQUANA

4,950. 131,06 x 15,30. (430.0 x 50.2). 1–2. S–T3–13. Workman,
Clark & Co Ltd, Belfast. 1898 (22/2) launched as CITY OF
CORINTH (City). 1912 SEQUANA (Sud Atlantique). 1912
(23/11) FV Bordeaux–S. America. 1917 (8/6) torpedoed and sunk
by German submarine near Ile d'Yeu.

8a. (1912) LA CHAMPAGNE (c)

7,087. 150,38 x 15,78. (493.4 x 51.8). 2–2. S–Q4–17. (I–390;
II–65; III–1,500). CGT, St. Nazaire. 1885 (15/5) launched for
CGT. 1887 (7/8) seriously damaged in collision with VILLE DE
RIO JANEIRO (Chargeurs Réunis); latter sunk. 1896 engines
Q4 instead of T6; masts reduced from 4 to 2. 1912 (30/11) FV for
Sud Atlantique (c), Bordeaux–S. America in place of BURDI-
GALA (under repair). 1912 (Dec) collision at Lisbon with
DESNA (RMSP); slight damage. 1915 (28/5) stranded at St.
Nazaire; broke her back.

8b. (1913) VALDIVIA (c)

7,168. 141,05 x 16,55. (462.8 x 54.3). 2–2. 2S–T6–16. (I–60; II–80;
III–79). Chantiers & Ateliers de Provence, Port de Bouc. 1911
(27/8) launched for SGTM. 1913 (13/1) FV for Sud Atlantique
(c), Bordeaux–S. America in place of DIVONA (under repair).
1913 (25/9) returned to SGTM. 1933 scrapped at Genoa. (See
SGTM (17)).

9. 1913 LUTETIA

14,783, 176,47 x 19,53. (579.0 x 64.1). 3–2. 4S–T8 & ST–20.
(I–462; II–130; III–90; IV–450). Chantiers de l'Atlantique, St.
Nazaire. 1913 (23/3) launched. 1913 (1/11) MV Bordeaux–S.
America. 1913 (Dec) collided with and sank DIMITRIOS
(Greek) after leaving Lisbon for Bordeaux; proceeded to St.
Nazaire after temporary repairs. 1914 (16/5) 2nd voyage Bor-
deaux–St. America. 1914 (Aug) French troopship. 1915 (Dec)
armed merchant cruiser; later hospital ship and then troopship.
1918 (Dec) Rotterdam–Havre with 2,400 French refugees from
Holland (2 voyages). 1919–20 refitted at La Seyne. 1920 (2/10)
resumed Bordeaux–S. America. 1927 converted to oil fuel at St.
Nazaire. 1927 (15–16/6) heeled over and sank in dock. 1927
(19/11) resumed service. 1928 (Mar) damaged in collision with
BALZAC (Lamport & Holt) at Buenos Aires. 1931 (31/7) arr

Bordeaux for the last time; laid up. 1938 (12/1) left Bordeaux under tow for Blyth, where scrapped.

10. 1913 GALLIA

14,966. 174,94 x 19,50. (574.0 x 64.0). 3–2. 3S–T8&ST–20. (I–300; II–106; III–80; IV–600). Forges & Chantiers de la Méditerranée, La Seyne. 1913 (26/3) launched. 1913 (29/11) MV Bordeaux–S. America. 1914 (Jan) returned to La Seyne for adjustments to engines and increased first class. 1914 (20/2) 2nd voyage, Bordeaux–S. America. 1915 troopship. 1916 (4/10) torpedoed and sunk by German submarine U.35 on voyage to Salonica with 2,350 troops (1,750).

10a. (1914) FLANDRE (c)

8,503. 141,54 x 17,37. (464.4 x 57.0). 2–2, 4S–C8&ST–17. Chantiers de l'Atlantique. St. Nazaire. 1913 (31/10) launched for CGT. 1914 (30/9) FV Bordeaux–S. America for Sud Atlantique (c). 1940 (14/9) sunk by magnetic mine at mouth of Gironde.

10b. (1914) PÉROU (c)

6,599. 131,82 x 15,94. (432.5 x 52.3). 2–2. 2S–T6–16. Chantiers de l'Atlantique, St. Nazaire. 1907 (1/3) launched for CGT. 1914 (15/11) FV Bordeaux–S. America for Sud Atlantique (c). 1934 scrapped.

10c. (1915) FLORIDE (c)

7,029. 125,94 x 15,91. (413.2 x 52.2). 1–2. S–T3–13. (I–125; III–785). Chantiers & Ateliers de Provence, Port de Bouc. 1907 (14/7) launched for CGT. 1915 (28/1) FV Havre–Bordeaux–S. America for Sud Atlantique (c). 1915 (19/2) sunk by German raider PRINZ EITEL FRIEDRICH near Dakar.

10d. (1915) GUADELOUPE (c)

6,600. 131,85 x 15,94. (432.6 x 52.3). 2–2. 2S–T6–16. Chantiers de l'Atlantique, St. Nazaire. 1906 (15/12) launched for CGT. 1915 (4/2) sailed Bordeaux–S. America for Sud Atlantique (c). 1915 (25/2) captured by German auxiliary cruiser KRONPRINZ WILHELM between Dakar and Brazil. 1915 (9/3) scuttled by Germans; crew transferred to CHASE MILL (Br).

—— ——— ALÉSIA

6,030. 122,92 x 14,99. (403.3 x 49.2). 1–2. 2S–Q8–13. (I–60; III–1,200). Bremer Vulkan, Vegesack. 1902 (21/8) launched as PRINZ ADALBERT (Hapag). 1914 (Aug) seized at Falmouth. 1916 PRINCETOWN (Br). 1917 ALÉSIA (Sud Atlantique); reconditioned in England. 1917 (6/9) torpedoed and sunk by German submarine UC.50 near Ushant on voyage Cardiff–Bordeaux to take up her new duties.

11. (1920) ALBA

8,324. 133,95 x 17,07. (439.5 x 56.0). 1–2. 2S–T6–12. (I–120;

III–80; IV–1,450). Bremer Vulkan, Vegesack. 1912 (12/10) launched as SIERRA VENTANA (NDL). 1920 ALBA (Sud Atlantique). 1920 FV Bordeaux–S. America. 1926 (Jly) AMÉRIQUE (Chargeurs Réunis). 1936 scrapped at Blyth.

12. 1920 MASSILIA
   15,147. 175,89 x 19,53. (577.1 x 64.1). 3–2. 4S–T6&ST–20). (I–464; II–129; III–98; IV–350). Forges & Chantiers de la Méditerranée, La Seyne. 1914 (30/4) launched. 1920 (30/10) MV Bordeaux–Vigo–Lisbon–Rio de Janeiro–Santos–Montevideo–Buenos Aires. 1928 converted to oil fuel. 1940 carried French members of Parliament from Bordeaux to Casablanca. Proceeded to Liverpool, and returned to Toulon (27/6) with French soldiers who had escaped from Dunkirk. 1940 laid up at Marseilles. 1942 accommodation ship for Germans. 1944 (Aug) scuttled by Germans at Marseilles; salvaged; scrapped.

13. 1922 MOSELLA
   10,123. 147,57 x 18,07. (484.2 x 59.3). 1–2. 2S–ST(DR)–15. (I–100; II–150; III–150; IV–400). Swan, Hunter & Wigham Richardson, Wallsend-on-Tyne (engines Wallsend Slipway Co. Ltd). 1921 (3/9) launched. 1922 MV Bordeaux–S. America. 1928 JAMAIQUE (Chargeurs Réunis). 1954 scrapped at Ghent.

14. 1923 MEDUANA
   10,123. 147,57 x 18,07. (484.2 x 59.3). 1–2. 2S–ST(DR)–15. (I–100; II–150; III–150; IV–400). Swan, Hunter & Wigham Richardson, Wallsend-on-Tyne (engines Wallsend Slipway Co Ltd). 1920 (30/9) launched. 1920 (23/11) caught fire and sank when fitting out. 1921 (Apr) salvaged. 1923 (Feb) MV Bordeaux–S. America. 1928 KERGUELEN (Chargeurs Réunis). 1940 (6/8) WINRICH VON KNIPRODE (German Navy). 1945 (Mar) damaged by Allied Bombers at Pillau. 1945 KERGUELEN (Chargeurs Réunis). 1947–8 rebuilt at Rotterdam and Bordeaux. 1948 (10/6) resumed Bordeaux–S. America. 1955 scrapped at Antwerp.

15. 1931 L'ATLANTIQUE
   40,945. 217,49 [226,15] x 27,97. (713.6 [742.0] x 91.8). 3–2–C. 4S–ST(SR)–21. (I–414; II–158; III–585). Chantiers & Ateliers de St. Nazaire. 1928 (28/11) keel laid. 1930 (15/4) launched. 1931 (29/9) MV Pauillac (Bordeaux)–Lisbon–Rio de Janeiro–Montevideo–Buenos Aires (arr 12/10). 1933 (3/1) left Pauillac for Havre for dry docking. 1933 (4/1) caught fire in English Channel and abandoned (17); adrift for 2½ days. 1933 (6/1) taken in tow – stern first – by four French tugs. 1933 (7/1) berthed at Cherbourg; declared beyond repair. 1936 scrapped at Port Glasgow.

— —— PASTEUR
    29,253. 204,96 [212,40] x 27,49. (672.5 [696.9] x 90.2). 1–2–C.
4S–ST(SR)–26. (I–216; tourist 906). Chantiers & Ateliers de St.
Nazaire. 1938 (15/2) launched. 1939 (Sep) scheduled MV,
Bordeaux–S. America, but cancelled by World War II. 1940 (2/6)
MV Brest–Halifax with 300 tons of gold. 1940 (Aug) placed under
Cunard–White Star management. 1945 (Jun) returned to French
flag – 5 RV France–Dakar; 8 RV France–Algeria; 1 RV to
Indo-China. 1957 (25/1) laid up at Brest. 1957 (Sep) BREMEN
(NDL); extensively rebuilt; new funnel. 1970 BREMEN (Hapag–
Lloyd). 1971 REGINA MAGNA (Chandris). 1977 SAUDI
PHIL I (Saudi Arabian); accommodation ship at Jeddah. 1978
SAUDI FILIPINAS I (ditto). 1980 (9/6) foundered while under
tow to Kaohsiung for demolition.

16. 1951 LAËNNEC (M/S)
    12,003. 157,14 [163,97] x 19,62. (515.6 [538.0] x 64.4). 1–2–C.
2S–2SC.SA–17. (I–94; III–230). Ateliers & Chantiers de la Loire,
St. Nazaire. 1951 (25/2) launched. 1952 (16/1) MV Havre–S.
America. 1962 (20/9) LAËNNEC (Messageries Maritimes); S.
American service. 1966 BELLE ABETO (Panamanian); became
a pilgrim ship. 1976 (30/7) severe fire damage as Sasebo. 1976
(31/7) sank in the harbour.

17. 1952 CHARLES TELLIER (M/S)
    12,006. 157,14 [163,97] x 19,62. (515.6 [538.0] x 64.4). 1–2–C.
2S–2SC.SA–17. (I–92; III–326). Ateliers & Chantiers de la Loire,
St. Nazaire. 1951 (2/12) launched. 1952 (2/8) MV Bordeaux–S.
America. 1962 (3/11) CHARLES TELLIER (Messageries Mari-
times); S. American service. 1967 LE HAVRE ABETO
(Panamanian); became a pilgrim ship.

FUNNEL: Buff with black top.*
FLAG: 1912. Blue with large white lozenge; red cock on the white.
        1938 (approx). Blue with large white lozenge; large red 'O'
        on the white.

* Before World War I the LUTETIA and GALLIA's funnels (but not
those of any other ships) had a red cockerel painted on them between the
black tops and a narrow band well down the funnel.

Chapter 57

(1912–14)

SICULA AMERICANA

(Sicula Americana Società di Navigazione)

(Italian)

Early in the present century the brothers Guglielmo and Giorgio Peirce took over the old-established Messina firm of Peirce, Becker & Ilardi, which they renamed FRATELLI PEIRCE. They believed there were favourable opportunities for a passenger and cargo service between Sicily, Southern Italy and New York, and founded the SICULA AMERICANA SOCIETÀ DI NAVIGAZIONE in Messina on 31 October 1906 with a capital of 2½ million lire (£100,000).

The 6,392 ton twin-screw SAN GIORGIO and the 6,592 ton SAN GIOVANNI, the latter 7,32 metres (24 feet) longer than her consort, and effectively a sister ship of the Lloyd Sabaudo RE D'ITALIA and REGINA D'ITALIA (Chapter 52), were built for this service by Sir James Laing & Sons Limited of Sunderland. Both were stated to have accommodation for 30 first class, 60 second and 1,800 steerage passengers, but in fact carried first and steerage only until 1912. The service was opened by the SAN GIORGIO, which left Naples on 19 July 1907 for New York via Messina and Palermo.

Giorgio Peirce was killed in the Messina earthquake of 28 December 1908. Owing to this disaster, the Sicula Americana head office (but not that of Fratelli Peirce) was transferred to Naples, and their ships omitted a Messina call until January 1911.

Guglielmo Peirce and his son Giorgio were largely responsible for increasing the Company's capital to six million lire, thus enabling the 8,341 ton SAN GUGLIELMO to be launched on 29 March 1911. She had a speed of 15 knots, one knot faster than her predecessors, and greatly improved accommodation for 50 first class passengers, 175 second and 2,200 steerage.

However, passenger demand was insufficient to keep three ships fully employed on the North Atlantic throughout the winter months, so the SAN GIOVANNI was despatched from Naples to Montevideo and Buenos Aires on 2 October 1912, calling at Genoa two days later. Between then and the outbreak of World War I in August 1914 she made a total of four voyages to the River Plate, the SAN GUGLIELMO made

416

1913 SAN GUGLIELMO 8,341 tons
Made one voyage from Genoa to Buenos Aires.

one and the SAN GIORGIO two, all between October and March.

Sicula Americana took advantage of the exceptional conditions due to the outbreak of World War I in August 1914 by despatching all three ships to New York within a few days of one another for the benefit of Americans in a hurry to return home. The first two sailings, in particular, attracted large complements of passengers. Subsequently, the SAN GIOVANNI made one further voyage to South America.

Having managed to buy the greater part of the share capital of Fratelli Peirce and Sicula Americana, Navigazione Generale Italiana (Chapter 36) founded the TRANSOCEANICA SOCIETÀ ITALIANA DI NAVIGAZIONE in Naples on 19 August 1917. The firm of Fratelli Peirce, the Sicula Americana and one of NGI's subsidiaries, Italia Società di Navigazione a Vapore, were absorbed. Further details will be found in Chapter 59.

1. (1912) SAN GIOVANNI
 6,592. 131,06 x 16,06. (430.0 x 52.7). 2–2. 2S–T6–14. (I–30; II–60; III–1,800). Sir J. Laing & Sons, Sunderland (engines G. Clark Ltd, Sunderland). 1907 (27/6) launched. 1907 (14/10) MV Naples–Messina–Palermo–New York. 1912 (2/10) FV Naples–Genoa (4/10)–Buenos Aires (5 RV). 1917 (Aug) SAN GIOVAN-NI (Transoceanica). 1921 (Aug) ditto (NGI). 1921 PALERMO (NGI). 1928 scrapped.

2. (1913) SAN GUGLIELMO
 8,341. 143,25 x 17,07. (470.0 x 56.0). 2–2. 2S–T6–15. (I–50;

II–175; III–2,200). D. & W. Henderson Ltd, Glasgow. 1911 (29/3) launched. 1911 (31/10) MV Naples–New York. 1913 (8/1) FV Genoa–Buenos Aires (1 RV). 1917 (Aug) SAN GUGLIEL-MO (Transoceanica). 1918 (8/1) gunned and sunk by German submarine U.63 near Loano, Gulf of Genoa.

3. (1913) SAN GIORGIO

6,392. 123,74 x 15,75. (406.0 x 51.7). 2–2. 2S–T6–14. (I–30; II–60; III–1,800). Sir J. Laing & Sons, Sunderland (engines G. Clark Ltd, Sunderland). 1907 (10/4) launched. 1907 (19/7) MV Naples–Messina–Palermo–New York. 1913 (29/11) FV Naples–Buenos Aires (2 RV). 1917 (Aug) SAN GIORGIO (Transoceanica). 1921 (Aug) ditto (NGI). 1921 NAPOLI (ditto). 1926 scrapped.

FUNNEL: Yellow with two narrow red bands.
FLAG: White; in the centre a yellow cross on a red shield (the Arms of Messina).

Chapter 58

1914–34

TRANSATLANTICA ITALIANA

(Transatlantica Italiana Società Anonima di Navigazione)

(Italian)

In 1913 the Hamburg American Line (Chapter 47) bought the entire share capital of the LIGURE BRASILIANA (Chapter 46), together with its two twin-screw steamers, the 5,018 ton CAVOUR and the 5,181 ton GARIBALDI, formerly the FLORIDA and VIRGINIA of Lloyd Italiano (Chapter 50). At an extraordinary general meeting on 28 July 1913 an Italian, Venceslao Carrara, was appointed chairman of Ligure Brasiliana and a German, Dr. Otto Ecker, managing director. Exactly a year later to the day, the Company's name was changed to TRANS-ATLANTICA ITALIANA SOCIETÀ ANONIMA DI NAVIGA-ZIONE. Its capital, all held by the Hamburg American Line, was increased from 1¼ to 5 million lire (£200,000) to enable two new ships to be built.

Following the entry of Italy into World War I in May 1915, an extraordinary general meeting of the Company was held in September, when an all-Italian board of directors was appointed. Venceslao Carrara was able to buy the vast majority of the German-held shares, but a year later resold them to the Società Nazionale di Navigazione of Genoa, a member of the Ansaldo group.

The Transatlantica Italiana service was opened by the GARIBALDI, which sailed from Genoa for Buenos Aires on 5 September 1914, followed by the CAVOUR on 3 October. Unfortunately, the CAVOUR was sunk in collision with the Italian auxiliary cruiser CAPRERA on 12 December 1917 near Armeville, leaving the GARIBALDI to sail as a lone ship to and from South America during the remainder of the war.

The two steamers under construction for the Company were the 9,750 ton twin-screw DANTE ALIGHIERI and GIUSEPPE VERDI, which successfully inaugurated a new route from Genoa to New York via Palermo and Naples. This remained in operation until 1927. [1]

In 1920 the PIETRO CALVI (formerly the PRINZREGENT LUIT-POLD of Norddeutscher Lloyd) (Chapter 29) was chartered for a few South American voyages to replace the CAVOUR.

Six twin-screw steamers were ordered for the River Plate service from

1914 GARIBALDI 5,181 tons
At Malta in 1930 when owned by Citra. Battleship in the background is H.M.S.
RAMILLIES, which entered the harbour too fast and ran aground.

the Ansaldo group in 1919. They were originally designed as cargo steamers, but it was decided later to fit them with extensive passenger accommodation. The orders were made possible by increasing the Company's share capital to 100 million lire.

The first newcomer, the 8,331 ton CESARE BATTISTI, was launched on 17 April 1920 and started her maiden voyage from Genoa to South America in September 1922. She was succeeded by the 8,150 ton NAZARIO SAURO, launched on 14 May 1921, but whose first voyage did not take place until February 1924, suggesting that building had been deliberately slowed down. Next came the 8,139 ton AMMIRAGLIO BETTOLO, launched on 24 May 1923 and despatched to Buenos Aires in August 1924. The fourth of the series, the 7,432 ton LEONARDO DA VINCI, was launched on 28 December 1924. She was completed less than five months later, but as there was little or no immediate demand for her services on the South Atlantic she started her career by undertaking two round voyages to New York. Her first South American sailing took place in November 1925.

A short while previously the Banca Italiana di Sconto had become bankrupt, thereby resulting in the collapse of the Società Nazionale di Navigazione and the entire Ansaldo group. From then onwards there was a succession of owners of Transatlantica Italiana, which finally passed to

420

1925 LEONARDO DA VINCI 7,432 tons
Sister ship of CESARE BATTISTI, NAZARIO SAURO and AMMIRAGLIO
BETTOLO.

the Credito Italiano. Meanwhile, efforts were made for the Company to obtain the concession for certain Italian subsidiary services, but on 22 December 1925 the Compagnia Italiana Transatlantica ('CITRA') was established in Rome. It not only took over the concessions in question, but acquired the Transatlantica Italiana liner GARIBALDI, together with the two final ships ordered in 1919, the FRANCESCO CRISPI and the GIUSEPPE MAZZINI, both of which were still on the stocks. The Transatlantica Italiana capital was reduced to 50 million lire.

The AMMIRAGLIO BETTOLO was sold in 1932 to the Egyptian-owned Misr Line, and two years later the CESARE BATTISTI, NAZARIO SAURO and LEONARDO DA VINCI were disposed of to the Tirrenia Line (Flotte Riunite Florio–Citra), to whom they had been under charter for some time previously. There was no alternative but to wind up TRANSATLANTICA ITALIANA.

[1] N.R.P. Bonsor, *North Atlantic Seaway*, Volume 4, Pages 1448–52.

1. (1914) GARIBALDI
    5,181. 116,24 x 14,66. (381.4 x 48.1). 2–2. 2S–T6–14. (I–65; III–1,600). Società Esercizio Bacini, Riva Trigoso (engines G. Ansaldo, Armstrong & Co, Sampierdarena). 1906 (19/9) launched as VIRGINIA (Lloyd Italiano). 1906 (8/10) MV Genoa–Naples–New York. 1911 GARIBALDI (Ligure Brasiliana). 1912 (15/1) FV Genoa–S. America. 1914 GARIBALDI (Transatlantica Italiana). 1914 (5/9) FV Genoa–S. America. 1925 GARIBALDI (Citra). 1932 ditto (Tirrenia), 1944 (2/8) sunk during air attack on Genoa. 1946 refloated; scrapped.
2. (1914) CAVOUR
    5,018. 116,24 x 14,66. (381.4 x 48.1). 2–2. 2S–T6–14. (I–65;

III–1,600). Società Esercizio Bacini, Riva Trigoso. 1905 (22/6) launched as FLORIDA (Lloyd Italiano). 1905 (18/9) MV Genoa–Naples–Buenos Aires (1 RV). 1909 (23/1) collided with and sank REPUBLIC (White Star) off U.S. coast. 1911 CAVOUR (Ligure Brasiliana). 1911 (5/11) FV Genoa–S. America. 1914 CAVOUR (Transatlantica Italiana). 1914 (3/10) FV Genoa–S. America. 1917 (12/12) sunk in collision with Italian auxiliary cruiser CAPRERA near Armeville.

2a. (1920) PIETRO CALVI (c)
6,595. 138,77 x 15,30. (455.3 x 50.2). 1–2. 2S–T6–14. (I–224; II–101; III–850). F. Schichau, Danzig. 1894 (20/3) launched as PRINZREGENT LUITPOLD (NDL). 1894 (29/8) MV Bremen–Suez Canal–Australia. 1914 (Aug) sheltered in Italy. 1915 (May) seized by Italy; PIETRO CALVI. 1920 FV for Transatlantica Italiana (c), Genoa–S. America. 1928 scrapped.

3. 1922 CESARE BATTISTI
8,331. 135,63 x 16,15. (445.0 x 53.0). 2–2. 2S–ST(DR)–15. G. Ansaldo & Co, Sestri Ponente. 1920 (17/4) launched. 1922 (Sep) MV Genoa–S. America. 1932 CESARE BATTISTI (Tirrenia (c)). 1934 CESARE BATTISTI (Tirrenia). 1936 destroyed by explosion at Massaua, Eritrea.

4. 1924 NAZARIO SAURO
8,150. 136,27 x 16,06. (447.1 x 52.7). 2–2. 2S–ST(DR)–15. G. Ansaldo & Co, Sestri Ponente. 1921 (14/5) launched. 1924 (Feb) MV Genoa–S. America. 1934 NAZARIO SAURO (Tirrenia). 1941 (6/4) World War II casualty.

5. 1923 AMMIRAGLIO BETTOLO
8,139. 130,87 x 16,03. (429.4 x 52.6). 2–2. 2S–ST(DR)–15. G. Ansaldo & Co, Sestri Ponente. 1923 (24/6) launched. 1924 (Aug) MV Genoa–S. America. 1932 KAWSAR (Misr (Egyptian)).

6. (1925) LEONARDO DA VINCI
7,432. 130,17 x 16,00. (427.1 x 52.5). 2–2. 2S–ST(DR)–15. Ansaldo San Giorgio, La Spezia (engines Ansaldo, Sampierdarena). 1924 (28/12) launched. 1925 (24/5) MV Naples–Palermo–Boston–New York (2 RV). 1925 (Nov) FV Genoa–S. America. 1934 LEONARDO DA VINCI (Tirrenia). 1937 ditto (Lloyd Triestino). 1941 (11/2) captured by British at Kisimaju; renamed EMPIRE CLYDE: later MAINE (hospital ship). 1954 scrapped at Hong Kong.

FUNNEL: Red with white star; black top.
FLAG: Red burgee; in centre, white star within golden oak wreath; 'T' and 'I' in black on either side.

TRANSOCEANICA

(Transoceanica Società Italiana di Navigazione)

(Italian)

TRANSOCEANICA SOCIETÀ ITALIANA DI NAVIGAZIONE was founded at Naples by Navigazione Generale Italiana (Chapter 36) on 19 August 1917 with a view to merging the Sicula Americana Società di Navigazione (Chapter 57) and its parent concern, Fratelli Peirce, with Italia Società di Navigazione a Vapore (Chapter 48).

NGI's action followed depletion of the Italia fleet by war losses, combined with the likelihood of increased competition from Sicula Americana after the war.

Transoceanica took over a fleet of 13 ships – the passenger steamers BRASILE, ITALIA, NAPOLI (ex-SANNIO) and TOSCANA of Italia; the Peirce cargo and emigrant steamer ITALIA, which owing to the duplication of this name became the MASANIELLO; the Peirce cargo steamers DINNAMARE, POSILLIPO and SICANIA; the NGI cargo steamers MILAZZO and VOLTURNO; and the Sicula Americana passenger steamers SAN GIORGIO, SAN GIOVANNI and SAN GUGLIELMO, which had been running to New York with occasional autumn and winter sailings to Buenos Aires, as well as the SAN GENNARO, which was delivered in October 1917 by Palmers of Tyneside, although without her passenger accommodation.

Owing to the fact that it was founded during World War I, available information about Transoceanica's early activities is strictly limited, but it is evident that the SAN GIORGIO, SAN GIOVANNI and SAN GUGLIELMO continued to run between Italy and New York, as did the NAPOLI. However, the SAN GUGLIELMO was sunk by a German submarine on 18 January 1918, and the NAPOLI was sunk in collision on 4 July 1918 when in convoy. The cargo steamers MILAZZO and VOLTURNO had been sunk in 1917, and were later replaced by the British-built standard cargo steamers WAR HOSTAGE and WAR VICEROY, which were renamed with the names of their two predecessors.

The remaining passenger ships – the ex-Italia BRASILE (ex-ARGENTINA), ITALIA and TOSCANA – should all, in theory, have been running to South America, but it seems that the BRASILE and ITALIA had been requisitioned by the Italian Government and undertook various duties in the Mediterranean. It was left to the TOSCANA to maintain for a time the South American passenger sailings, but unfortunately she was sunk in collision near Gibraltar on 5 February 1918. As far as can be ascertained, this disaster marked the conclusion of the Company's South American passenger trade.

After the war, NGI suffered from a serious shortage of tonnage, and as it already owned 85 per cent of the Transoceanica share capital it made arrangements to absorb that company on 20 August 1921, together with its then fleet of 11 ships. Included among these were the BRASILE and ITALIA, which were disposed of to the Sitmar Line a year later.

1. (1917) TOSCANA

> 4,113. 110,69 x 13,25. (363.2 x 43.5). 1–2. S–T3–12. (I–42; III–1,320). N. Odero & Co, Genoa. 1900 (26/10) launched for Italia. 1900 (Nov) MV Genoa–S. America. 1917 TOSCANA (Transoceanica). 1917 FV Genoa–Naples–S. America. 1918 (5/2) sunk near Gibraltar in collision with MOLIÈRE (French).

Chapter 60

1919–37

COSULICH LINE

(Cosulich Società Triestina di Navigazione)

(Italian)

The brothers Callisto and Alberto Cosulich had been responsible for the formation of the Unione Austriaca di Navigazione in 1903, so it was fitting that when the company was re-established in 1919 under Italian instead of Austrian management it was renamed COSULICH SOCIETÀ TRIESTINA DI NAVIGAZIONE, particularly as the Cosulich family was still represented on the board.

The Cosulich Line's existence began on 5 May 1919 – the very day its largest steamer, the 12,567 ton twin-screw PRESIDENTE WILSON (formerly the KAISER FRANZ JOSEF I) sailed from Genoa for Marseilles, Gibraltar and New York – but as had been the case with its predecessor, it had every intention of catering for the South American trade. It seems that the first passenger sailing on the South Atlantic run was taken by the 4,946 ton single-screw FRANCESCA from Trieste in July 1919 to Rio de Janeiro, Montevideo and Buenos Aires, followed by the 5,452 ton single-screw COLUMBIA about a month later.

The 5,491 ton single-screw SOFIA, formerly the SOFIA HOHEN-BERG, sailed to South America during the early months of 1921, but all three then discontinued carrying passengers and from the autumn of 1922 the 7,644 ton single-screw BELVEDERE, followed a few months later

1919 COLUMBIA 5,452 tons
Built 1908 for Unione Austriaca.

425

1927 SATURNIA 23,940 tons
Made two voyages from Trieste and Naples to the River Plate.

by the 5,526 ton twin-screw ARGENTINA, both formerly running to New York, took sole charge of the South Atlantic service.

By 1924 there were only three really important Italian transatlantic lines – Navigazione Generale Italiana and Lloyd Sabaudo based on Genoa and Cosulich based on Trieste. Each of the Genoa lines had commissioned two fast luxury liners of around 20,000 tons, and it was only to be expected that Cosulich would follow suit. In the event, the keel of the 23,940 ton motorship SATURNIA was laid at Monfalcone, Trieste, on 30 May 1925. She was launched on 29 December 1925 as the world's largest passenger motorship, and started her maiden voyage from Trieste on 21 September 1927. Although built for the North Atlantic, her first two round voyages were to Naples, Marseilles, Rio de Janeiro, Montevideo and Buenos Aires. A twin-screw ship driven by four-stroke double-acting engines giving a service speed of 19 knots, she had excellent accommodation for 305 first class, 460 second, 310 intermediate and 700 third class passengers. A sister ship, the VULCANIA, followed from the same builders in December 1928, but was detailed to the New York route from the first.

The commissioning of the SATURNIA enabled the 8,145 ton twin-screw MARTHA WASHINGTON, second largest of the pre-war Unione Austriaca fleet, to join the BELVEDERE on the South Atlantic in the autumn of 1927. The ARGENTINA had already been sold.

The ITALIA FLOTTE RIUNITE COSULICH–LLOYD SABAUDO–NGI came into existence on 2 January 1932 with the amalgamation of NGI and Lloyd Sabaudo and the co-ordination of Cosulich in the same financial group. However, Cosulich still maintained a separate management at Trieste.

The 19,475 ton quadruple-screw motorship NEPTUNIA was launched for Cosulich on 27 December 1931 – a few days before the formation of

1927 MARTHA WASHINGTON 8,145 tons
Built 1908 for Unione Austriaca.

Italia – and sailed from Trieste for South America on 5 October 1932, followed by the 19,507 ton OCEANIA on 21 September 1933. The first class passenger capacity of the OCEANIA was 300, but that of the NEPTUNIA only 175. Both ships could cater for 700 second, but third class figures were 500 and 650 respectively.

On 2 January 1937 Italia Flotte Riunite was replaced by ITALIA SOCIETÀ ANONIMA DI NAVIGAZIONE, which absorbed the Cosulich Line, whose activities since 1932 had been closely interwoven with those of Italia.

The MARTHA WASHINGTON became the Lloyd Triestino TEL AVIV in 1933, the BELVEDERE became a purely cargo steamer in 1936 and in 1941 was seized by the USA. In June 1944 she was scuttled off the Normandy coast as part of a breakwater ('Gooseberry No. 1') in connection with the Allied landings. The VULCANIA and SATURNIA of the New York service were, in turn, fitted with new diesel engines in

1932 NEPTUNIA 19,475 tons
Torpedoed and sunk in the Mediterranean in 1941 by British submarine UPHOLDER.

1935, thereby increasing their speed from 19 to 21 knots. The NEPTUNIA and OCEANIA continued to run from Trieste to South America for Italia.

Subsequent activities of the Cosulich fleet are dealt with in Chapter 65, devoted to ITALIA.

1. (1919) FRANCESCA

    4,946. 109,65 x 14,13. (359.8 x 48.0). 1–2. S–T3–12. (I–30; II–50; III–1,500). Russell & Co, Port Glasgow (engines J.G. Kincaid & Co, Greenock). 1905 (2/6) launched for Unione Austriaca. 1919 FRANCESCA (Cosulich). 1919 (22/5) FV Genoa–Naples–New York. 1919 (July) FV Trieste–R. Plate. 1922–3 cargo only. 1928 scrapped.

2. (1919) COLUMBIA

    5,452. 121,91 x 15,88. (400.0 x 52.1). 1–2. S–T3–14. (I–50; II–75; III–1,200). Russell & Co, Port Glasgow (engines J.G. Kincaid & Co, Greenock). 1908 (2/4) launched for Unione Austriaca. 1919 COLUMBIA (Cosulich). 1919 (Aug) FV Trieste–R. Plate. 1922–3 cargo only. 1931 ANNOULA (Greek). 1933 (7/10) foundered off Cape Lookout.

3. (1919) SOFIA

    5,491. 109,72 x 14,63. (360.0 x 48.0). 1–2. S–T3–12. (I–70; III–1,500). Lloyd Austriaco, Trieste. 1905 (3/9) launched as SOFIA HOHENBERG (Unione Austriaca). 1919 SOFIA (Cosulich). 1921 (Jan) LV Trieste–New York. 1921 (Feb or Mar) FV Trieste–Naples–R. Plate. 1922–3 cargo only. 1929 scrapped.

4. (1922) BELVEDERE

    7,644. 127,40 x 16,46. (418.0 x 54.0). 1–2. S–T3–12. (I–12; II–140; III–1,274). Cantiere Navale Triestino, Monfalcone. 1913 (8/4) launched for Unione Austriaca (South American service). 1913 (30/8) MV Trieste–New York. 1919 BELVEDERE (Cosulich). 1922 (Sep) LV Trieste–New York. 1922 (Oct or Nov) FV Trieste–Naples–R. Plate. 1936 cargo only. 1941 seized by USA at Philadelphia; renamed AUDACIOUS. 1944 (Jun) scuttled off Normandy as part of 'Gooseberry No. 1'.

5. (1923) ARGENTINA

    5,526. 118,86 x 14,63. (390.0 x 48.0). 1–2. 2S–T6–15. (I–45; II–175; III–1,230). Russell & Co, Port Glasgow (engines Dunsmuir & Jackson, Glasgow). 1907 (26/8) launched for Unione Austriaca. 1919 ARGENTINA (Cosulich). 1919 (15/5) FV Genoa–Marseilles–New York (with civilian passengers). 1923 (Sep) FV Trieste–Naples–R. Plate. 1926 ARGENTINA (Florio). 1932 ditto (Tirrenia). 1960 scrapped.

6. (1927) MARTHA WASHINGTON
    8,145. 140,20 x 17,07. (460.0 x 56.0). 2–2. 2S–T6–16. (I–60;
    II–130; III–2,000). Russell & Co, Port Glasgow (engines Rankin
    & Blackmore, Greenock). 1907 (7/12) launched for Unione
    Austriaca. 1914 (Aug) interned by USA at New York. 1917
    (Apr) seized by USA at New York; MARTHA WASHINGTON
    (US). 1922 ditto (Cosulich). 1922 (15/12) FV New York–Trieste;
    reconditioned. 1927 (20/9) LV Trieste–Naples–Boston–New
    York. 1927 (6/11) FV Trieste–S. America. 1933 TEL AVIV
    (Lloyd Triestino). 1934 scrapped at Trieste.
7. 1927 SATURNIA (M/S)
    23,940. 183,24 [192,04] x 24,32. (601.2 [630.1] x 79.8). 1–2.
    2S–4SC.DA–19. (I–305; II–460; intermediate 310; III–700).
    Cantiere Navale Triestino, Monfalcone (engines Cantieri Riuniti
    dell' Adriatico, Monfalcone). 1925 (30/5) keel laid. 1925 (29/12)
    launched. 1927 (21/9) MV Trieste–Naples–Marseilles–R. Plate (2
    RV). 1928 (1/2) FV Trieste–New York. 1935 new diesel engines
    (2SC.DA); 21 knots; 24,470 tons. 1937 (2/1) SATURNIA
    (Italia). 1940 (May) LV Italy–New York, where interned. 1941
    (Dec) seized by USA. 1945 FRANCES Y. SLANGER (hospital
    ship). 1946 SATURNIA (returned to Italian Govt). 1965
    scrapped at La Spezia.
8. 1932 NEPTUNIA (M/S)
    19,475. 179,72 x 23,31. (589.7 x 76.5). 1–2–C. 4S–2SC.SA–19.
    (I–175; II–700; III–650). Cantieri Riuniti dell' Adriatico, Monfal-
    cone. 1931 (27/12) launched. 1932 (5/10) MV Trieste–R. Plate.
    1937 NEPTUNIA (Italia). 1940 Italian troopship. 1941 (18/9)
    torpedoed and sunk in Mediterranean by British submarine
    UPHOLDER.
9. 1933 OCEANIA (M/S)
    19,507. 179,72 x 23,37. (589.7 x 76.7). 1–2–C. 4S–2SC.SA–19.
    (I–300; II–700; III–500). Cantieri Riunti dell' Adriatico, Monfal-
    cone (engines SA Fiat, Turin). 1932 (29/9) launched. 1933 (21/9)
    MV Trieste–R. Plate. 1937 OCEANIA (Italia). 1940 Italian
    troopship. 1941 (18/9) torpedoed and sunk in Mediterranean by
    British submarine UPHOLDER.

Note: The VULCANIA did not run to South America for Cosulich, but
made one such voyage for Italia in 1947 (see Chapter 65).

FUNNEL: Red with broad white band; narrow black top.
FLAG: White; two narrow red horizontal stripes at top and bottom;
         wide flattened 'X' in green with solid top and bottom; black
         'C' and 'L' on either side.

Chapter 61

(1921–77)

ROTTERDAM – ZUID AMERIKA LIJN

(Rotterdam South American Line)

(Dutch)

The firm of N.V. VAN NIEVELT, GOUDRIAAN & CO'S STOOM-VAART MAATSCHAPPIJ was founded in Rotterdam on 1 January 1905 to carry timber from the Baltic to Holland and elsewhere during the summer months, and for general tramping during the remainder of the year. By 1910 it owned six steamers varying in size between 3,300 and 5,200 tons.

During 1920 a regular service was started by cargo steamers from Hamburg, Rotterdam and Antwerp direct to Argentina, and although completely owned by van Nievelt, Goudriaan & Co it was invariably known in Holland as the ROTTERDAM – ZUID AMERIKA LIJN or RZAL, and in the English-speaking world as the ROTTERDAM SOUTH AMERICAN LINE.

In 1921 the Company started to introduce ships carrying 12 passengers, the first two of these sailings being taken by the 4,540 ton ALCYONE and the 4,938 ton ALDABI.

The 5,500 ton sister ships ALPHACCA and ALPHERAT were completed in 1928 to carry 12 passengers, but in 1938 their accommodation was increased to 24. Unfortunately, the ALPHACCA was torpedoed and sunk by a German submarine off the Ivory Coast on 4 April 1942, and the ALPHERAT was bombed and sunk east of Malta on 21 December 1943.

The 7,258 ton motorship ALTAIR was laid down before Holland was invaded in May 1940, and was intended to carry 34 passengers. Building was deliberately slowed down so that she was not launched until 18 July 1941, but she was seized by the Germans on completion and sunk in Norwegian waters on 4 April 1943 when sailing under their flag.

The ALTAIR's sister ships ALBIREO, ALGOL and ALDABI all survived the war after serving the German cause. The ALBIREO sailed for Germany on 29 January 1942 as the troopship WURI and was sunk by a mine in Aalborg Bay on 17 August 1942 with the loss of 1,200 German soldiers, but during salvage operations after the war the fore part of the ship was cut off and the remainder from the bridge aft arrived at the

Deutsche Werft, Hamburg, for a new fore part to be fitted. A virtually new ship was delivered to RZAL on 14 April 1949 under the name ALNATI, with accommodation for 54 first class passengers.

The ALGOL became a unit of the German Navy. She was recovered at Wilhelmshaven in October 1945, repaired at Rotterdam and on 26 April 1947 was handed over to RZAL as the ALHENA, her first class complement being 50. The ALDABI, renamed WOLTA, left for Germany on 12 December 1944, returned to the Dutch flag on 29 June 1945 and arrived at Rotterdam on 11 November 1945, having reverted to the name ALDABI and also been fitted to carry 50 passengers.

1947 ALHENA 7,289 tons
Could carry 50 first class passengers. Note deck cargo of railway carriages.

At the time of VE Day in 1945 the Company had no passenger ships in a serviceable state, but the ALDABI was ready, as stated, in November 1945, the ALHENA in April 1947 and three ex-VICTORY ships, the ALWAKI (II), ALPHACCA (II) and ALPHERAT (II) were also commissioned in 1947 with accommodation for 12 passengers. Then came the 14 passenger ALBIREO in 1948 and the 54 passenger ALNATI in April 1949.

The 6,410 ton motorship ALTAIR and the 5,675 ton ALIOTH followed in 1950, differing from any predecessors or successors in the fleet in having accommodation for 80 steerage as well as 12 first class. The ALTAIR was wrecked on 15 April 1956 at the entrance to the port of Vitoria, Brazil, while in 1963 the ALIOTH was taken over by van Nievelt, Goudriaan & Co of Hamburg.

Between 1956 and 1960 eight further motorships with accommodation for 12 passengers were launched for RZAL, five with machinery aft. A further ship was bought second-hand. But the greatly decreased demand for passenger accommodation is confirmed by the fact that the last multi-passenger ships, the ALHENA and ALNATI were sold in 1968. The last 'twelves', the ALGOL, ALKES and ALGORAB were disposed of in November and December 1977. This meant that RZAL had given up carrying passengers, but they added four large purely cargo ships of 14,700 tons deadweight in 1977, and these are still trading with South America in company with three smaller cargo ships.

During the Company's career nine ships carried more than 12 passengers and are adequate justification for this chapter and fleet list. In addition, 22 ships carried 12 passengers, and although not eligible for the fleet list proper it has been decided to devote one line of information to each of them.

Almost without exception, the RZAL passenger-carrying ships were named after stars, which is understandable since the RZAL funnel and houseflag – exactly the same as those of their parent company, Van Nievelt, Goudriaan & Co – both included a white star.

1. (1938) ALPHACCA (I)
    5,546. 124,90 x 17,13. (409.8 x 56.2) 1–2. S–T3–12. (I–12). Wm. Gray & Co, Sunderland. 1928 (17/5) launched. 1928 (4/7) trials. 1938 I increased to 24. 1942 (4/4) torpedoed and sunk by German submarine U.505 off Cape Palmas, Ivory Coast (15).
2. (1938) ALPHERAT (I)
    5,549. 124,90 x 17,13. (409.8 x 56.2). 1–2. S–T3–12. (I–12). Wm. Gray & Co, Sunderland. 1928 (5/7) launched. 1928 (24/8) trials. 1938 I increased to 24. 1943 (21/12) bombed and sunk east of Malta.
—— ——— ALTAIR (I) (M/S)
    7,258. Nederlandsche Scheepsbouw Maatschappij, Amsterdam. (I–34). 1941 (18/7) launched. Seized by Germany. 1943 (4/4) sunk in Norwegian waters when under German flag.
3. (1945) ALDABI (M/S)
    7,239. 137,33 x 18,38. (450.6 x 60.3). 1–2. S–2SC.SA–13. (I–45). Nederlandsche Dok Maatschappij, Amsterdam. 1940 (23/11) launched. 1942 (2/2) delivered. 1944 (12/12) left for Germany; renamed WOLTA. 1945 (29/6) returned to Dutch flag. 1945 (11/11) arr Rotterdam; reverted to ALDABI. (I–50). 1967 ALBA (Liberian). 1972 (9/5) arr Istanbul; scrapped.
4. (1947) ALHENA (M/S)
    7,289. 137,36 x 18,35. (450.7 x 60.2). 1–2. S–2SC.SA–13. (I–45). Nederlandsche Scheepsbouw Maatschappij, Amsterdam. 1940 (28/6) launched as ALGOL (RZAL). 1943 in German Navy;

damaged by air attacks. 1945 (Oct) recovered at Wilhelm-shaven; repaired at Rotterdam. 1947 (26/4) back in RZAL service as ALHENA. (I–50). 1968 ALDA (Cyprus). 1973 (15/7) arr Kaohsiung; scrapped.

5. (1949) ALNATI (M/S)
   7,368. 137,27 x 18,35. (450.4 x 60.2). 1–2. S–2SC.SA–14. (I–34). Nederlandsche Dok Maatschappij, Amsterdam. 1940 (31/5) launched as ALBIREO (RZAL). 1942 (29/1) sailed for Germany as troopship WURI. 1942 (17/8) sunk by mine in Aalborg Bay with loss of 1,200 German soldiers. After the war, fore part cut off; after part from bridge salved and rebuilt. 1948 rebought by RZAL. 1948 (31/5) arr Deutsche Werft, Hamburg, for fitting new forepart. 1949 (14/4) delivered to RZAL as ALNATI; extended superstructure. (I–54). 1968 ALFA (Cyprus). 1972 scrapped in Turkey.

6. (1948) ALBIREO (M/S)
   6,482. 133,98 x 18,38. (439.6 x 60.3). 1–2. S–2SC.SA–12. (I–14). Nederlandsche Dok en Scheepsbouw, Amsterdam. Laid down as FRANKENFELS (Hansa). 1948 (May) trials as ALBIREO (RZAL). 1963 PROCYON (van Nievelt, Goudriaan & Co, Hamburg). 1966 MINOUTSI (Liberian). 1978 LASIA (Cyprus). 1980 (Mar) scrapped at Kaohsiung.

7. 1950 ALTAIR (II) (M/S)
   6,410. 133,98 x 18,19. (439.6 x 59.7). 1–2. S–2SC.SA–12. (I–12; III–80). Wm. Gray & Co, West Hartlepool. 1950 (2/2) launched. 1956 (15/4) wrecked near entrance to Vitoria, Brazil, on voyage Rosario–Hamburg.

8. 1950 ALIOTH (I) (M/S)
   5,675. 123,74 x 17,31. (406.0 x 56.8). 1–2. S–2SC.SA–12. (I–12; III–80). Burntisland Shipbuilding Co, Burntisland. Laid down as ALSCHAIN. 1950 (3/4) launched as ALIOTH. 1963 YILDUN (van Nievelt, Goudriaan & Co, Hamburg). 1970 AGIOS SPYRIDON (Greek). 1974 ASPYR (Cyprus). 1979 scrapped at Kaohsiung.

The following ships had accommodation for 12 passengers:

Launched	Ship	Gross tons	Disposal or final fate	Note
1920 (26/6)	ALCHIBA (I)	4,429	1942 (8/7) torpedoed	
1921 (May)	ALCYONE	4,540	1942 (16/3) mined	
1921 (16/7)	ALDABI	4,938	1937 (9/12) wrecked	
1921 (13/8)	GEMMA	8,420	1942 (6/12) sunk	A
1921 (31/8)	ALGORAB (I)	4,979	1952 (Jly) scrapped	
1921 (26/10)	ALHENA	4,930	1942 (10/9) foundered	

1922 (Jan)	ALUDRA (I)	4,930	1943 (29/4) sunk	B
1922 (Apr)	ZOSMA	8,429	1931 (7/9) sold	C
1922 (Apr)	ALWAKI (I)	4,537	1940 (10/7) torpedoed	
1946 J	ALCHIBA (II)	6,596	1956 (9/4) sold	D
1947 J	ALWAKI (II)	7,650	1974 scrapped Kaohsiung	E
1947 J	ALPHACCA (II)	7,651	1964 (Jly) sold	F
1947 J	ALPHERAT (II)	7,650	1963 (Jly) sold	G
1956 (17/10)	ALCOR (M/S)	6,735	1976 (Nov) sold	
1957 (27/5)	ALGOL (M/S)	6,735	1977 (Dec) sold	
1957 (14/12)	ALKES (M/S)	6,735	1977 (Dec) sold	
1959 (3/1)	ALAMAK (M/S)	6,722	1969 (Aug) sold	H
1959 (22/7)	ALCHIBA (III) (M/S)	6,723	1969 (Sep) sold	H
1959 (10/10)	ALGORAB (II) (M/S)	6,722	1977 (Nov) sold	H
1960 (10/5)	ALUDRA (II) (M/S)	6,723	1969 (Nov) sold	H
1960 (4/6)	ALNITAK (M/S)	6,723	1969 (Nov) sold	H
1967 J	ALIOTH (II) (M/S)	5,123	1970 (Apr) sold	I

Notes:
A. Lost with all hands in convoy NE of Azores.
B. Sunk in North Sea off Vlieland when in German service.
C. Date of trials, not launch.
D. Built as EMPIRE RENNIE (trials 1941 (Dec)).
E. Ex-CHAPEL HILL VICTORY (trials 1944 (Dec)).
F. Ex-CHANUTE VICTORY (trials 1945 (Feb)).
G. Ex-WHEATON VICTORY (trials 1945 (Apr).
H. Engines aft.
I. Ex-BLACK HAWK (1950). Bought May 1967.
J. Year purchased.

FUNNEL: Yellow with broad blue band containing white star.
FLAG: Blue with white star in centre; white letters 'V' and 'N' (above) and 'G' and 'C' (below) in the four corners.

Chapter 62

1927–72

BLUE STAR LINE

(British)

The BLUE STAR LINE was founded by the Vestey Brothers of London, and acquired its first ship in 1911 by the purchase of the Nelson Line cargo steamer HIGHLAND MARY (Chapter 49), which was renamed BRODLAND. At the outbreak of World War I in August 1914 the Company owned five ships, all with a 'BROD' prefix and all engaged in carrying frozen meat from the River Plate and tributaries to London. By 1916, the fleet still consisted of 'BRODs', but the number had increased to 12. There was a considerable change after the Armistice of November 1918 as numbers soon increased to 15, and although there were still seven 'BRODs' the remainder included four ships with a 'STAR' suffix. Of these, the first acquired was apparently the 5,583 ton MAGICSTAR, built in 1893 as the BUTESHIRE, which had become the Houlder Line BOLLINGTON GRANGE as recently as 1915 (Chapter 43). The 7,900 ton freighters ALBIONSTAR and ROYAL-STAR were twin-screw ships with cruiser sterns, newly-built by Workman, Clark & Co Ltd of Belfast.

At this time, the Royal Mail Steam Packet Company (Chapter 1) had five 'A' steamers averaging 15,000 tons for their Southampton–River Plate passenger service, with two much larger motorships in the offing, in addition to four 11,500 ton 'D' steamers, which sailed from Liverpool. They also owned the Nelson Line, whose fleet of 7,500 tonners and of somewhat smaller ships was reduced to nine owing to wartime losses. This company ran from London as well as Liverpool. However, Blue Star had made such progress by the mid 1920s that they felt capable of entering the passenger business, and chose the London to River Plate trade, perhaps because it was the least likely to subject them to severe competition. A contributory reason for their desire to enter the passenger business was that at Buenos Aires large passenger liners had improved docking facilities, thereby speeding up their turn-round at the port.

Orders were placed for five 12,850 ton ships, three with Cammell, Laird & Co Ltd of Birkenhead and two with John Brown & Co Ltd of Clydebank, Glasgow. Twin-screw ships fitted with single-reduction geared turbines, they had a service speed of 16 knots, and were

1927 AVILA 12,872 tons
In 1929 renamed AVILA STAR. Forepart lengthened in 1935 and Maier bow fitted.

imposing-looking vessels with two funnels (at first fitted with 'Admiralty' cowls), two masts and cruiser sterns, with a capacity of 162 first class only passengers.

First to be launched was the Cammell Laird ALMEDA on 29 June 1926, and she opened the service on 16 February 1927 from London to Boulogne, Lisbon, Madeira, Tenerife, Rio de Janeiro, Santoa, Montevideo and Buenos Aires. In fact, her maiden voyage had twice been postponed, the first time from 24 December 1926, owing to delays in her completion.

Next came the maiden voyage of the John Brown AVILA on 25 March, followed by the Cammel Laird ANDALUCIA, the John Brown AVELONA and the Cammell Laird ARANDORA, the last-named on 22 June 1927. However, it was soon found that there was much confusion between the Blue Star passenger names and those of the RMSP 'A' ships, and in May 1929 the word 'STAR' was added to the former, this time as a separate word. It remained a suffix for the cargo steamers until 1929–30, when the TACOMA STAR appeared as two words, and by 1931–2 the entire fleet had followed suit. In addition, the worldwide depression made it desirable to withdraw at least one of the ships from the River Plate passenger trade, and the ARANDORA STAR was converted into a cruising liner, her first cruise taking place in June 1929. During the rebuilding her passenger accommodation was increased to 350 and two years later she was painted white. Further alterations, some of quite a drastic nature, took place in 1934, 1935 and 1936.

In 1934, owing to the continued depression, the AVELONA STAR was rebuilt as a cargo steamer. Her second funnel and the upper decks were removed, and, surprisingly, her tonnage was increased to 13,376. In 1935 the ALMEDA STAR and AVILA STAR were lengthened and given Maier bows, while in 1936 the ANDALUCIA STAR received

1929 ALMEDA STAR 12,838 tons
Built 1927 as ALMEDA. Lengthened in 1935 and Maier bow fitted.

1934 AVELONA STAR 13,376 tons
Built 1927 as AVELONA. Passenger accommodation and after funnel removed in 1934.

similar treatment and, unlike the others, lost her mainmast. The tonnage of the ALMEDA STAR and ANDALUCIA STAR became 14,935 and 14,943 respectively, while that of the somewhat shorter AVILA STAR became 14,443. Thus, five originally identical ships all developed noticeable differences.

Unfortunately, all five were torpedoed and sunk by German submarines during World War II, the ARANDORA STAR suffering by far the greatest loss of life. She was carrying German internees and prisoners and Italian internees to Canada when, on 3 July 1940, she was torpedoed by U.47 west of Ireland and no fewer than 805 lives were lost.

Four identical passenger ships were ordered from Cammel Laird at the first opportunity after the war. First to be completed was the 10,716 ton ARGENTINA STAR, which was launched on 26 September 1946 and started her maiden voyage from Liverpool to the River Plate on 14 June 1947, subsequent voyages starting from London. Post-war ports of call were Lisbon, Madeira, Las Palmas or Tenerife, Rio de Janeiro, Santos and Montevideo *en route* to Buenos Aires. The ARGENTINA STAR and her sisters were single-screw ships fitted with double-reduction geared turbines, had a speed somewhat in excess of 16 knots and were, therefore, slightly faster than the pre-war quintet when completed. Passenger accommodation was limited to 51 first class in the case of the ARGENTINA STAR and 53 in the case of her three consorts.

Succeeding ships were the BRASIL STAR, URUGUAY STAR and PARAGUAY STAR, the last-named being launched on 23 April 1948 and started her maiden voyage in the following October. She was the unlucky ship of the series as on 12 August 1969, while in dock in London, her engine room and refrigerating rooms were badly damaged by fire. It was soon evident that it would be too costly to repair her, and she arrived at Hamburg a month or so later to be scrapped.

1948 URUGUAY STAR 10,723 tons
Sister ship of ARGENTINA STAR, BRASIL STAR and PARAGUAY STAR.

It had been stated in August 1947 that Blue Star had placed contracts with the Fairfield Shipbuilding & Engineering Co Ltd of Govan for two further passenger ships so that when all six newcomers were in commission a sailing about every 10 days would be practicable [1]. In the light of later events, it was fortunate that these additions did not materialise.

The three remaining passenger ships did not survive for many years longer as the aeroplane was attracting the cream of the Europe–South American passenger traffic. In consequence, all three arrived at Kaohsiung in 1972 to be scrapped.

Blue Star can no longer be regarded as a passenger line, but is still one of the world's great cargo carriers, possessing many container and dry cargo ships, besides acting as managers for a number of other vessels.

[1] *The Times* 21/8/1947.

1. 1926 ALMEDA
   (1929) ALMEDA STAR
   12,838. 150,05 x 20,81. (512.0 x 68.3). 2–2–C. 2S–ST(SR)–16.
   (I–162). Cammell, Laird & Co Ltd, Birkenhead. 1926 (29/6)
   launched. 1926 (24/12) MV London–S. America. 1929 renamed
   ALMEDA STAR. 1935 lengthened to 176,43 [182,16] metres
   (578.9 [597.7] feet); Maier bow; 14,935 tons. 1941 (17/1)
   torpedoed and sunk by German submarine U.96 in North
   Atlantic (360).
2. 1927 AVILA
   (1929) AVILA STAR
   12,872. 150,05 x 20,78. (512.0 x 68.2). 2–2–C. 2S–ST(SR)–16.
   (I–162). John Brown & Co Ltd, Glasgow. 1926 (22/9) launched.
   1927 (25/3) MV London–S. America. 1929 renamed AVILA
   STAR. 1935 forepart lengthened – total 167,75 [173,48] metres
   (550.4 [569.2] feet; Maier bow; 14,443 tons. 1942 (5/7) torpedoed
   and sunk by German submarine U.201 near the Azores (62).
3. 1927 ANDALUCIA
   (1929) ANDALUCIA STAR
   12,848. 150,05 x 20,81. (512.0 x 68.3). 2–2–C. 2S–ST(SR)–16.
   (I–162). Cammell, Laird & Co Ltd, Birkenhead. 1926 (21/9)
   launched. 1927 (10/5) MV London–S. America. 1929 renamed
   ANDALUCIA STAR. 1936 lengthened to 176,43 [182.16]
   metres (578.9 [597.7] feet); Maier bow; 14,943 tons; one mast.
   1942 (6/10) torpedoed and sunk by German submarine U.107,
   130 miles SW of Freetown (4).
4. 1927 AVELONA
   (1929) AVELONA STAR
   12,858. 155,50 x 20,78. (510.2 x 68.2). 2–2–C. 2S–ST(SR)–16.
   (I–162). John Brown & Co Ltd, Glasgow. 1926 (6/12) launched.
   1927 (20/5) MV London–S. America. 1929 renamed AVELONA
   STAR. 1934 passenger accommodation and after funnel removed; tonnage 13,376. 1940 (30/6) torpedoed by German
   submarine U.43 in Bay of Biscay. 1940 (1/7) sank (4).
5. 1927 ARANDORA
   (1929) ARANDORA STAR
   12,847. 156,29 [163,06] x 20,81. (512.8 [535.0] x 68.3). 2–2–C.
   2S–ST(SR)–16. (I–162). Cammell, Laird & Co Ltd, Birkenhead.
   1927 (4/1) launched. 1927 (22/6) MV London–S. America. 1928–9
   refitted as cruise liner; 14,694 tons. 1929 renamed ARANDORA
   STAR. 1929 (15/6) first cruise, Immingham–Norway. 1931 white
   hull and refitted. 1934 refitted; 15,305 tons. 1935 refitted. 1936
   refitted; mainmast removed; 15,501 tons. 1940 (2/7) sailed

439

Liverpool for St. John's, NF, with 479 German internees; 86 prisoners and 734 Italian internees. 1940 (3/7) torpedoed and sunk by German submarine U.47 west of Bloody Foreland (805).

6. 1947 ARGENTINA STAR
    10,716. 145,69 [153,24] x 20,81. (478.0 [502.8] x 68.3). 1–1–C. S–ST(DR)–16. (I–51). Cammell, Laird & Co Ltd, Birkenhead. 1946 (26/9) launched. 1947 (4/6) MV Liverpool–S. America. 1947 (3/9) 2nd voyage London–S. America. 1972 (19/10) arr. Kaohsiung; scrapped.

7. 1947 BRASIL STAR
    10,716. 145,69 [153,24] x 20,81. (478.0 [502.8] x 68.3). 1–1–C. S–ST(DR)–16. (I–53). Cammell, Laird & Co Ltd, Birkenhead. 1947 (6/3) launched. 1947 (31/10) MV Liverpool–S. America. 1948 (24/1) 2nd voyage London–S. America. 1972 (10/10) arr Kaohsiung; scrapped.

8. 1948 URUGUAY STAR
    10,723. 145,69 [153,24] x 20,81. (478.0 [502.8] x 68.3). 1–1–C. S–ST(DR)–16. (I–53). Cammell, Laird & Co Ltd, Birkenhead. 1947 (15/10) launched. 1948 (22/5) MV Liverpool–S. America. 1948 (31/7) 2nd voyage London–S. America. 1972 (25/8) arr. Kaohsiung; scrapped.

9. 1948 PARAGUAY STAR
    10,722. 145,69 [153,24] x 20,81. (478.0 [502.8] x 68.3). 1–1–C. S–ST(DR)–16. (I–53). Cammell, Laird & Co Ltd, Birkenhead. 1948 (23/4) launched. 1948 (22/10) MV London–S. America. 1969 (12/8) badly damaged by fire in London dock. 1969 (19/9) arr. Hamburg to be scrapped.

10. (1963) IBERIA STAR (M/S)
    10,868. 145,99 [153,91] x 19,74. (479.0 [505.0] x 64.8). 1–2. 2S–2SC.DA–17. SA Cockerill, Hoboken (engines Burmeister & Wain, Copenhagen). 1950 (4/3) launched as BAUDOUIN-VILLE (Compagnie Maritime Belge). 1957 THYSVILLE (ditto). 1961 ANSELM (Booth); (I–135; tourist 101). 1963 IBERIA STAR (Blue Star); refitted by Bremer Vulkan, Vegesack for London–River Plate service. 1965 AUSTRALASIA (Austasia); ran Singapore–Melbourne. 1973 scrapped at Kaohsiung.

FUNNEL: Red with black top above narrow white and black bands; a large white ball on the red bearing a blue star.

FLAG: Red swallow-tailed pennant; large white ball bearing a blue star.

Chapter 63

1927–77

YBARRA Y COMPAÑÍA

(Spanish)

The old-established firm of YBARRA Y COMPAÑÍA (Ybarra & Co) acquired its first steamer, the 382 ton ITALICA, in 1860, and during the 100 years between then and 1959 commissioned no fewer than 79 steamships and motorships. With only one exception all ships subsequent to the 1,453 ton CABO ORTEGAL of 1885 bore names starting with CABO (Cape).

It was not until 1926 that Ybarra began to operate a service with multi-passenger ships. Their first such acquisition was the 5,724 ton Swedish motorship HEMLAND, built by Götaverken of Gothenburg in 1921. She was renamed CABO TORTOSA and left Genoa on 31 May 1926 for New York, to which she made a total of three voyages, leaving there for the last time on 19 December for Malaga and Genoa. She then entered the South American trade, leaving Genoa on 25 January 1927 for Montevideo and Buenos Aires via Cadiz.

The 6,342 ton motorships CABO PALOS and CABO QUILATES were launched in 1926 by the Compañia Euskalduna de Construcción of Bilbao. The maiden voyage of the former started from Genoa for Montevideo and Buenos Aires on 28 February 1927, a month after the CABO TORTOSA, while the CABO QUILATES followed on 26 March from Genoa and one day later from Barcelona. It is understood that the two sister ships had accommodation for 76 third class passengers, but as likely as not the number was often greatly increased.

The 12,275 ton motorship CABO SAN ANTONIO was launched at Bilbao on 16 December 1929, followed by the 11,868 ton CABO SAN AGUSTIN in May 1931 and the CABO SANTO TOMÉ of exactly the same tonnage on 15 August. The first of the trio was a single-funnelled ship, whereas the sister ships had two funnels. The CABO SAN ANTONIO, with accommodation for 200 second and 500 third class passengers, began her maiden voyage on 25 April 1930. The CABO SAN AGUSTIN and CABO SANTO TOMÉ, with berths for 12 second class and 500 third class, started theirs on 25 September 1931 and 24 January 1932, respectively, from Genoa for Marseilles, Montevideo and Buenos Aires. All three had similar lengths and beams, so the higher tonnage of the first ship was undoubtedly due to the increased super-

441

1931 CABO SAN AGUSTIN 11,868 tons
Sister ship of CABO SAN TOMÉ. The CABO SAN ANTONIO had similar dimensions
but increased accommodation.

structure needed to accommodate her large total of second class passengers. However, in 1934 the tonnage of the CABO SAN AGUSTIN and CABO SANTO TOMÉ was increased to 12,589, suggesting that their second class accommodation had been increased to 200 or more.

The CABO TORTOSA was again detailed to sail to New York in 1931, but was sold a year later. She survived until 1964.

The South American service was suspended when the Spanish Civil War broke out on 18 July 1936, and during or very soon after the end of the war Ybarra lost its entire passenger fleet. First to go was the CABO PALOS, which was torpedoed and sunk on 26 June 1937 on passage from Odessa to Valencia by the Nationalist submarine GENERAL NOVA. A few months later, on 10 October 1937, the CABO SANTO TOMÉ, was attacked and set on fire off the Algerian coast by the Nationalist warships DATO and CANOVAS. She was abandoned, exploded and sank, one life being lost. The CABO QUILATES and CABO SAN AGUSTIN both became Republican transports, the former being renamed IBAI. Both were seized by Russia after the conclusion of hostilities on 2 April 1939. No information is available about the war activities of the CABO SAN ANTONIO, but she caught fire near Dakar on 29 December 1939 and had to be abandoned. Two days later the wreck was sunk by a French destroyer.

Owing to the outbreak of World War II in September 1939 and with Spanish shipbuilding still in a disorganised state after the Civil War, the only likely country from which Spanish concerns could buy passenger tonnage was the USA. A Spanish firm, Berge y Compañía, acquired the 19 year old 12,600 ton American President Lines PRESIDENT WILSON and PRESIDENT LINCOLN, and the former, renamed MARIA PIPA, sailed from Seattle on 27 June 1940 via Los Angeles,

Balboa, Callao, Valparaiso and the Straits of Magellan for Buenos Aires, which she reached on 4 August. Between then and 15 August she was renamed CABO DE HORNOS, having been acquired by the Ybarra Line, but whether the purchase from Berge actually took place then or at an earlier date is not clear. The CABO DE HORNOS sailed from Buenos Aires on 15 August, reached Rio de Janeiro on the 19th, left on 3 September and proceeded to Cadiz and Bilbao. She sailed again from the latter on or about 1 October and from Cadiz on 6 October via Tenerife and Santos for Buenos Aires, where she arrived on 25 October.

The PRESIDENT LINCOLN was at San Francisco on 31 May 1940 and it was stated soon afterwards that she was to be renamed MARIA DEL CARMEN. She was lying in the Columbia River from 13–21 July, and it was probably during that time that Berge y Compañía made arrangements for the renaming to take place. At any rate, she left Los Angeles on 25 July, reached Balboa on 6 August, passed through the Panama Canal and left Havana on 18 August, when it was announced that she was to be renamed CABO DE BUENA ESPERANZA,

1940 CABO DE BUENA ESPERANZA 12,594 tons
Sister ship of CABO DE HORNOS.

indicating, supposedly, that she had been bought by Ybarra. It is not clear whether her voyage terminated at Cadiz or at Bilbao. However, she left Cadiz on 4 September under her 'CABO' name for Madeira, Pernambuco and Buenos Aires. For many years subsequently, she and the CABO DE HORNOS maintained a regular service between Bilbao and Buenos Aires, with variations from time to time in the ports of call.

The 14,491 ton twin-screw motorship CABO SAN ROQUE was launched at Bilbao on 23 April 1955 and had accommodation for 241 cabin and 582 tourist class passengers, her service speed being 21 knots. She sailed from Genoa on 5 September 1957 for Marseilles and Barcelona, from where her maiden voyage to Montevideo and Buenos

Aires started in earnest. A sister ship, the 14,569 ton CABO SAN VICENTE, had similar accommodation and speed and was launched on 6 October 1956. Her maiden voyage started from Bilbao on 12 April 1959, and she called at Coruña, Vigo, Lisbon, Tenerife and Montevideo *en route* to Buenos Aires. She returned to Barcelona and Genoa, her second voyage starting from the latter on 4 September 1959, subsequent voyages being similarly based.

By this time the CABO DE BUENA ESPERANZA and CABO DE HORNOS were considerably more than 30 years old, and were scrapped at Barcelona in 1958 and at Aviles in 1959, respectively.

All went well with the CABO SAN ROQUE and CABO SAN VICENTE until 1975, both of them making a number of pleasure cruises in addition to their European–South American sailings. Unfortunately, however, insufficient employment could be found for two ships, and in 1975 the newer, and presumably more valuable CABO SAN VICENTE was sold to the Mogul Line of Bombay, who renamed her NOOR JEHAN and employed her as a pilgrim ship.

On 24 January 1977 the CABO SAN ROQUE was lying off Ferrol, an important naval port close to Coruña, when fire broke out and serious damage was done to the bridge and passenger accommodation. It would seem that Ybarra had already realised that a single-ship service is seldom viable as, when she left Ferrol on 5 April 1977 under tow for repairs at Piraeus she had been renamed GOLDEN MOON, and was flying the flag of Cyprus. A year later she became the Cuban AFRICA–CUBA.

No further Ybarra multi-passenger sailings have taken place to South America, but the Company acquired the 12,500 ton car ferries CABO SAN SEBASTIAN and CABO SAN JORGE, and ran them on a variety of routes in the Mediterranean. They have since been withdrawn.

1959 CABO SAN VICENTE 14,569 tons
Sister ship of CABO SAN ROQUE.

444

1. (1926) CABO TORTOSA (M/S)
   5,724. 119,74 x 16,42. (392.9 x 53.9). 1–2. 2S–4SC.SA–14.
   Aktiebolaget Götaverken, Gothenburg. 1921 launched as HEM-
   LAND (Swedish). 1926 CABO TORTOSA (Ybarra). 1926
   (31/5) FV Genoa–New York. 1926 (19/12) LV New York–Genoa.
   1927 (25/1) FV Genoa–Cadiz–Montevideo–Buenos Aires. 1931
   resumed Genoa–New York. 1932 sold Spanish; proposed name
   ADELA but CABO TORTOSA retained; later renamed
   MOTOMAR. 1964 scrapped at Bilbao.
2. 1927 CABO PALOS (M/S)
   6,342. 125,27 x 16,15. (411.0 x 53.0). 1–2. S–4SC.SA–14.
   (III–76). Compañía Euskalduna de Construcción, Bilbao (engines Maschinenfabrik Augsburg-Nürnberg, Augsburg). 1926
   launched. 1927 (28/2) MV Genoa–Buenos Aires. 1937 (26/6)
   torpedoed and sunk 28 miles from Alicante on voyage Odessa–
   Valencia by Nationalist submarine GENERAL MOVA.
3. 1927 CABO QUILATES (M/S)
   6,342. 125,27 x 16,15. (411.0 x 53.0). 1–2. S–4SC.SA–14.
   (III–76). Cia Eusakalduna de Construcción, Bilbao (engines
   Maschinenfabrik Augsburg-Nürnberg, Augsburg). 1926 (20/11)
   launched. 1927 (26/3) MV Genoa–Barcelona (28/3)–Buenos
   Aires. 1937 renamed IBAI during Spanish Civil War. 1939 seized
   by Russians at Murmansk and probably renamed DVINA. 1948
   (Jan) lost in the Pacific.
4. 1930 CABO SAN ANTONIO (M/S)
   12,275. 147,05 x 19,32. (482.5 x 63.4). 1–2. 2S–4SC.DA–15.
   (II–200; III–500). Sociedad Española de Construcción Naval,
   Bilbao. 1929 (16/12) launched. 1930 (25/4) MV Genoa–Barcelona
   (26/4)–Montevideo–Buenos Aires. 1939 (29/12) caught fire near
   Dakar and abandoned (5). 1939 (31/12) wreck sunk by French
   destroyer CASSARD.
5. 1931 CABO SAN AGUSTIN (M/S)
   11,868. 147,05 x 19,32. (482.5 x 63.3). 2–2. 2S–2SC.DA–16.
   (II–12; III–500). Sociedad Española de Construcción Naval,
   Bilbao. 1931 (May) launched. 1931 (25/9) MV Genoa–Marseilles–Montevideo–Buenos Aires. 1934 tonnage 12,589. 1937 Republican transport during Spanish Civil War. 1939 seized by
   Russians at Feodosia; became DNEPR (Russian). 1941 (Oct)
   sunk in Black Sea by German aircraft.
6. 1932 CABO SANTO TOMÉ (M/S)
   11,868. 147,05 x 19,32. (482.5 x 63.3). 2–2. 2S–2SC.DA–16.
   (II–12; III–500). Sociedad Española de Construcción Naval,
   Bilbao. 1931 (15/8) launched. 1932 (24/1) MV Genoa–Marseilles–

Montevideo–Buenos Aires. 1934 tonnage 12,589. 1937 Republican transport during Spanish Civil War. 1937 (10/10) attacked and set on fire off Algerian coast by Nationalist warships DATO and CANOVAS; ship abandoned, exploded and sank (1).

7. (1940) CABO DE HORNOS

12,597. 157,42 x 22,00. (516.5 x 72.2). 1–2–C. 2S–ST(SR)–18. (I–262; III–134; steerage 454). New York Shipbuilding Corporation, Camden, NJ. 1920 (4/8) launched as EMPIRE STATE (US Shipping Board); 14,127 tons. 1921 ran San Francisco–Manila for Pacific Mail. 1922 PRESIDENT WILSON (Pacific Mail (c)). 1925 PRESIDENT WILSON (Dollar). 1938 ditto (American President Lines). 1940 MARIA PIPA (Berge y Cia (Sp)). 1940 (27/6) Seattle–Los Angeles–Balboa–Valparaiso–Straits of Magellan–Buenos Aires. 1940 CABO DE HORNOS (Ybarra). 1940 (15/8) FV Buenos Aires–Rio de Janeiro–Bilbao. 1959 scrapped at Aviles.

8. (1940) CABO DE BUENA ESPERANZA

12,594. 157,42 x 22,00. (516.5 x 72.2). 1–2–C. 2S–ST(SR)–18. (I–262; III–134; steerage 454). New York Shipbuilding Corporation, Camden, NJ. 1920 (23/10) launched as HOOSIER STATE (US Shipping Board); 14,187 tons. 1922 ran San Francisco–Manila for Pacific Mail. 1922 PRESIDENT LINCOLN (Pacific Mail (c)). 1925 ditto (Dollar). 1938 ditto (American President Lines). 1940 MARIA DEL CARMEN (Berge y Cia (Sp)). 1940 (21/7) Columbia River–Los Angeles–Balboa–Panama Canal–Havana (dep 18/8)–Cadiz. 1940 CABO DE BUENA ESPERANZA (Ybarra). 1940 (4/9) FV Cadiz–Pernambuco–Buenos Aires–(arr 26/9; dep 3/10)–Rio de Janeiro–Pernambuco–Bilbao (arr 24/10). 1958 scrapped at Barcelona.

9. 1957 CABO SAN ROQUE (M/S)

14,491. 169,55 x 21,09. (556.3 x 69.2). 1–1–C. 2S–2SC.SA–21. (Cabin 241; tourist 582). Sociedad Española de Construcción Naval, Bilbao. 1955 (24/4) launched. 1957 (5/9) MV Genoa–Marseilles–Barcelona–Montevideo–Buenos Aires. 1977 (24/1) fire damage to bridge and passenger accommodation when lying at Ferrol. 1977 GOLDEN MOON (Cyprus). 1977 (5/4) left Ferrol in tow for Piraeus for repairs. 1978 AFRICA–CUBA (Republica de Cuba).

10. 1959 CABO SAN VICENTE (M/S)

14,569. 169,55 x 21,09 (556.3 x 69.2). 1–1–C. 2S–2SC.SA–21. (Cabin 241; tourist 582). Sociedad Española de Construcción Naval, Bilbao. 1956 (6/10) launched. 1959 (12/4) MV Bilbao–Coruña–Vigo–Lisbon–Tenerife–Montevideo–Buenos Aires. 1959

(4/9) 2nd voyage Genoa–Marseilles–Barcelona–Cadiz–Montevideo–Buenos Aires. 1975 NOOR JEHAN (Mogul Line, Bombay; pilgrim ship).

FUNNEL: Black, with white 'VA' intertwined.
FLAG: Blue, with white 'VA' intertwined.

Chapter 64

(1929–32)
(1939–49)

COMPANHIA NACIONAL DE NAVEGAÇÃO

(Portuguese)

The COMPANHIA NACIONAL DE NAVEGAÇÃO came into being on 1 July 1918, when its name was changed from EMPRESA NACIONAL DE NAVEGAÇÃO A VAPOR. As before, its principal service was from Lisbon to ports in Angola, South Africa and Mozambique. But on 7 December 1929 the 8,980 ton twin-screw NYASSA, built in 1906 as the Noredeutscher Lloyd BÜLOW, inaugurated a new service from Lisbon to Santos, Rio de Janeiro and occasionally Pernambuco. The ships seem to have been well-patronised as three outward sailings averaged over 600 passengers and four homeward ones nearly 1,000.

The NYASSA was responsible for 14 round voyages to South America between December 1929 and August 1932. In addition, the 6,298 ton LOURENÇO MARQUES (formerly the German East African ADMIRAL; totalled six in 1930–1, the 6,636 ton QUANZA five in 1931, the 5,771 ton MOÇAMBIQUE (ex-BRUXELLESVILLE) one in December 1931 and the 7,745 ton ANGOLA (ex-ALBERTVILLE) one in January 1932. Despite apparently satisfactory passenger bookings, the

1929 NYASSA 8,980 tons
Built 1906 as BÜLOW (NDL).

448

last South American sailing for a number of years took place in August 1932 and subsequently the ships were largely employed on the Mozambique mail service.

The South American service was resumed a month after the outbreak of World War II by the ANGOLA, which left Lisbon on 4 October 1939 for Madeira, Rio de Janeiro and Santos. She started further voyages on 10 January 1940, 28 February, 20 April, 7 June, 20 July, 15 September, 20 October and 3 March 1941. The QUANZA made one more voyage starting from Lisbon on 23 December 1940.

Finally, the NYASSA made three more South American voyages, the first starting on 12 November 1941, when she continued from Brazilian ports to Buenos Aires, and the second on 22 September 1942, when she called at Casablanca, the Guianas, Brazil and Argentina, arriving back at Lisbon on 5 March 1943. She made 10 round voyages to New York, Baltimore or Philadelphia between 1940–4, her final arrival from the USA taking place at Lisbon on 31 October 1944. Subsequently, she made many voyages in the Mozambique mail run as well as to Mormogāo, Portuguese India. On her last South American voyage she arrived at Buenos Aires on 18 March 1949. In the following November she was laid up at Lisbon, and was scrapped at Blyth in 1951 at the ripe age of 45.

After the war, the Company introduced some fine new vessels into the Portugal–Angola–South Africa–Mozambique service, by far the most outstanding being the 20,000 ton twin-screw turbine PRINCIPE PER-FEITO, which undertook a cruise from Lisbon to Brazil during the summer of 1965. This was, in fact, the last appearance of a Companhia Nacional De Navegação passenger ship in South American waters.

1. (1929) NYASSA

   8,980. 140,93 x 17,55. (462.4 x 57.6). 1–2. 2S–Q8–14. J. C. Tecklenborg, Geestemünde. 1906 (21/4) launched as BÜLOW (NDL). 1916 seized by Portugal; renamed TRAS-OS-MONTES. 1921 ditto (Transportes Maritimos do Estado). 1921 Hamburg–Havre–Brazil–River Plate. 1924 NYASSA (Cia Nacional–Mozambique line). 1929 (7/12) FV Lisbon–Brazil. 1932 (Aug) LV ditto (14 RV). 1940–4 Lisbon–New York, Baltimore or Philadelphia (10 RV). 1941 (12/11) Lisbon–Buenos Aires–Rio de Janeiro–Lisbon (arr 1942 (7/1)) (1 RV). 1942 (22/9) Lisbon–South America–Lisbon (arr 1943 (5/3)) (1 RV). 1944 (31/10) arr Lisbon from USA. 1949 LV Genoa–Lisbon–Brazil–Buenos Aires (arr 18/3)–Lisbon. 1949 (Nov) laid up at Lisbon. 1951 scrapped at Blyth.

2. (1930) LOURENÇO MARQUES
    6,298. 128,01 x 15,30. (420.0 x 50.2). 1–2. 2S–T6–14. Blohm &
    Voss, Hamburg. 1905 (25/6) launched as ADMIRAL (German
    East Africa). 1916 (28/2) seized by Portugal at Lourenço Marques
    renamed LOURENÇO MARQUES (Portugues Govt). 1925
    ditto (Cia Nacional). 1930 (30/3) FV Lisbon–Brazil. 1931 (29/1)
    LV ditto (6 RV). 1950 (Jul) left Lisbon in tow of tug SALVEDA;
    scrapped at Faslane, River Clyde.
3. (1931) QUANZA
    6,636. 127,40 x 15,85. (418.0 x 52.0). 1–2. 2S–T6–14. (I–111;
    II–120; III–98). Blohm & Voss, Hamburg. 1929 (1/6) launched as
    PORTUGAL (Cia Nacional). 1929 renamed QUANZA before
    delivery. 1931 (9/4) FV Lisbon–Brazil. 1931 (18/10) LV ditto (5
    RV). 1940 (23/12) resumed Lisbon–Brazil (1 RV). 1968 scrapped
    in Spain.
4. (1931) MOÇAMBIQUE
    5,771. 121,91 x 15,85. (400.0 x 52.0). 1–2. 2S–T6–15. A. Stephen
    & Sons, Glasgow. Built 1908 as BRUXELLESVILLE (Cie
    Maritime Belge). 1912 MOÇAMBIQUE (Cia Nacional). 1931
    (9/12) FV Lisbon–Rio de Janeiro–Santos (1 RV). 1939 scrapped
    in Italy.
5. (1932) ANGOLA
    7,745. 133,80 x 16,76. (439.0 x 55.0). 1–2. 2S–T6–14. John
    Cockerill, Hoboken. Built 1912 as ALBERTVILLE (Cie Mari-
    time Belge). 1922 ANGOLA (Cia Nacional). 1932 (9/1) FV
    Lisbon–Rio de Janeiro–Santos (1 RV). 1939 (4/10) resumed
    ditto. 1941 (3/3) LV ditto (9 RV). 1946 (21/2) NOVA LISBOA
    (Cia Nacional); East Africa and Central American services. 1950
    scrapped.

FUNNEL: Black
FLAG: Two blue and two white quarters.

ITALIA (II)

1932. Italia Flotte Riunite Cosulich–Lloyd Sabaudo–NGI
1937. Italia Società Anonima di Navigazione
1952. Italia Società per Azione di Navigazione

(Italian)

On 1 January 1932 there were three principal Italian transatlantic lines in existence – the Navigazione Generale Italiana, Lloyd Sabaudo and Cosulich. One day later the ITALIA FLOTTE RIUNITE COSULICH – LLOYD SABAUDO – NGI was formed by the amalgamation of NGI and Lloyd Sabaudo and the inclusion of Cosulich in the same financial group. However, Cosulich still maintained a separate management at Trieste so the reader should continue to refer to Chapter 60 for details of its activities up to 1937.

It had been evident for some time that a new company would have to see the light of day. First and foremost, the Italian Government had, for prestige reasons, encouraged both NGI and Lloyd Sabaudo to lay down a mammoth ship of about 50,000 tons, which were launched in 1931 as the REX and CONTE DI SAVOIA. They were due to enter service in the autumn of 1932, so the need for action was becoming urgent. As the worldwide depression was affecting the Italian lines as much as any, strict economy was necessary and the operation of the two new ships under a single management was a matter of paramount importance.

Italia started operations with a capital of 720 million lire and a fleet of 22 ships totalling 400,476 tons gross. Former NGI ships already in commission included the AUGUSTUS (32,650 tons), ROMA (32,583), DUILIO (24,281) and GIULIO CESARE (21,657), while Lloyd Sabaudo contributed the CONTE GRANDE (25,661), CONTE BIANCAMANO (24,416), CONTE VERDE (18,765) and CONTE ROSSO (17,048), the first pair of each concern running between Genoa and New York and the second between Genoa and South America. Thus, NGI and Lloyd Sabaudo services were duplicated on both North and South Atlantic.

The CONTE VERDE made the first South American sailing of the new company from Genoa on 28 January 1932 via Naples for Rio de Janeiro, Montevideo and Buenos Aires. The DUILIO was next on 18

1932 DUILIO 24,281 tons
Launched January 1916 for NGI. First NGI voyage to River Plate 1928; first Italia voyage
1932.

February, followed by the GIULIO CESARE on 24 March. After three round voyages, the CONTE VERDE was taken over by Lloyd Triestino and placed in service between Trieste and the Far East, as was the CONTE ROSSO, which did not run for Italia.

The 51,062 ton REX started her maiden voyage to New York on 27 September 1932 and the 48,502 ton CONTE DI SAVOIA on 30 November. Their commissioning enabled the CONTE BIANCAMA-NO, which had made six round trips to New York, to be transferred to the River Plate trade. The CONTE GRANDE followed her on 28 September 1933 and the AUGUSTUS on 9 November 1933. By arrangement with the South African Government, the GIULIO CESARE and DUILIO inaugurated a new service between Genoa, Marseilles, Gibraltar, Dakar, Cape Town and Durban in February 1934.

The ROMA was transferred to the South American service in 1935 and soon afterwards the CONTE BIANCAMANO was sold to Lloyd Triestino.

1932 CONTE BIANCAMANO 24,416 tons
Shown above with raked bow fitted in 1949, when tonnage 23,562.

452

It was announced in 1936 that Italian shipping would be concentrated into four principal groups – one to include both North and South Atlantic, another to work the lines to Africa, Asia and Australia and two others the subsidised lines in the Mediterranean. The new arrangements came into operation on 2 January 1937. They provided for the liquidation of Italia Flotta Riunite and the creation of ITALIA SOCIETÀ ANONIMA DI NAVIGAZIONE. As the new company's resources were concentrated entirely on the North and South Atlantic it had to part with a number of ships. Equally important, Italia absorbed the Cosulich Line, which meant that this old family name disappeared from the seas.

The 24,470 ton ex-Cosulich SATURNIA and VULCANIA, built in 1927–8 and re-engined in 1935 with new diesel engines, which increased their service speed from 19 to 21 knots, continued to run between Trieste and New York, while the 19,475 ton NEPTUNIA and the 19,507 ton OCEANIA, completed in 1932 and 1933 respectively, ran from Trieste to South America. They were quadruple-screw motorships with accommodation for 700 second and 500 or more third class passengers. Rather surprisingly, the OCEANIA's first class complement was 300 and the NEPTUNIA's only 175.

For some months after the outbreak of World War II in September 1939 both the North and South Atlantic services continued much as usual, but it was announced in April 1940 that the ROMA and AUGUSTUS would shortly return to the North Atlantic to meet increased passenger demand. In the event, the AUGUSTUS failed to do so, but the ROMA completed one round voyage before the declaration of war by Italy on 10 June 1940 resulted in the cessation of all Italian long-distance services.

The CONTE BIANCAMANO had been chartered from Lloyd Triestino and on 23 April 1940 sailed from Genoa for Valparaiso via the Panama Canal. She took shelter at Cristobal on 10 June, while the CONTE GRANDE sheltered at Rio de Janeiro.

The war was responsible for the loss of the Company's four largest ships – the REX, CONTE DI SAVOIA, AUGUSTUS and ROMA – and also for the South American service OCEANIA and NEPTUNIA, which became troopships and were both torpedoed and sunk by the British submarine UPHOLDER in the Mediterranean on 18 September 1941. Four ex-Italia ships owned by Lloyd Triestino – the DUILIO, GIULIO CESARE, CONTE ROSSO and CONTE VERDE were also lost. At the end of the war the only surviving members of the Italia passenger fleet were the CONTE GRANDE, CONTE BIANCAMANO, SATURNIA, VULCANIA and the PRINCIPESSA GIOVANNA, all of which had been requisitioned, the first four by the Americans and the last by the British.

The 8,387 ton twin-screw PRINCIPESSA GIOVANNA was built for Lloyd Sabaudo in 1923 and was acquired by Italia at the time of the amalgamation. In due course, she received a second funnel, her deckhouses were extended considerably fore and aft and her tonnage became 8,959. She was fitted to carry 640 third class passengers. After a spell of war service for the Italian Government she was requisitioned by Britain in 1944 and ran under British India management, at first as a hospital ship and later as a troopship. She was returned to Italy late in 1946, sailed from Southampton to Genoa under Italia colours and upon arrival was renamed SAN GIORGIO. She left Genoa for Buenos Aires

1947 SAN GIORGIO 8,959 tons
Built 1923 as Lloyd Sabaudo PRINCIPESSA GIOVANNA.

on 29 January 1947, this being the first Italian passenger sailing to South America since the war. A few months later, on 15 July, the 24,469 ton motorship VULCANIA left Genoa on the one and only voyage she ever made to the River Plate, after which she joined the SATURNIA on the North Atlantic. It may be added that the latter's maiden voyage for Cosulich and the one which succeeded it were her only two to South America.

After further voyages by the SAN GIORGIO, the 15,511 ton twin-screw SANTA CRUZ was chartered by Italia, sailed from Genoa for the River Plate on 30 December 1947 and for the next 18 months these two ships were responsible for Italia's South American service. The SANTA CRUZ had had an extremely varied career. Laid down as the Atlantic Transport MINNEKAHDA, she was launched on 2 November 1903 as the Pacific Mail MANCHURIA, in 1915 passed to the Atlantic Transport Company of West Virginia without change of name and made nine round voyages between New York and London. After World War I she ran for the American Line between New York and Hamburg, and later for the Panama Pacific Line between New York and San Francisco

1947 SANTA CRUZ 15,511 tons
Built 1904 as MANCHURIA of Pacific Mail.

via the Panama Canal. In 1927 she became the Dollar Line PRESIDENT
JOHNSON and in 1938 the American President Line's ship of the same
name. Early in 1947 she sailed for the Tagus Navigation Company as the
SANTA CRUZ from Lisbon for South America. The SAN GIORGIO
ran to South America until 1952, when she was transferred to Lloyd
Triestino's Australian service.

The CONTE BIANCAMANO had been seized in December 1941 by
the USA at Cristobal, and the CONTE GRANDE in August 1941 by
Brazil, who sold her to the USA in the following April. They became the
US troopships HERMITAGE and MONTECELLO, respectively, but
were returned to the Italian Government in 1947, after which they
received extensive refits, including new rounded bows. They were
bought by the Società Marittima Finanziaria, who chartered them to
Italia for service under their original names between Genoa and Buenos
Aires, the CONTE GRANDE being responsible for the first sailing on
14 July 1949, followed by the CONTE BIANCAMANO on 15
November, but the latter was transferred to the New York service in
March 1950. In due course both ships were repurchased by Italia.

The keel of the 27,078 ton motorship GIULIO CESARE (II) was laid
at Monfalcone, Trieste, on 28 July 1949. She was launched for the South
American service on 18 May 1950 and started her maiden voyage from
Genoa on 27 October 1951, followed by the 27,090 ton AUGUSTUS (II)
on 4 March 1952. Twin-screw ships with a service speed of 21 knots, their
passenger complement was 178 first class, 288 cabin and 714 tourist.

It was now the turn of the Italia North Atlantic service to receive a pair
of new ships, the 29,082 ton ANDREA DORIA and the 29,191 ton
CRISTOFORO COLOMBO, which were completed in 1953–4. They
were twin-screw steamers with single-reduction geared-turbines, and had
a service speed of 23 knots. The tragic collision between the ANDREA
DORIA and the Swedish American Line's motorship STOCKHOLM

1951 GIULIO CESARE 27,078 tons
Built for Genoa–Naples–River Plate service.

about 60 miles from Nantucket on 25 July 1956, resulted in the loss of the Italian ship with a total death roll of 52.

In the autumn of 1955 the SATURNIA and VULCANIA were detailed to a revived service from Trieste and Venice to New York. During June 1956, well before the disaster to the ANDREA DORIA, the GIULIO CESARE sailed from Genoa to New York on the first of three round voyages.

Following the loss of the ANDREA DORIA, the CONTE GRANDE made two voyages to New York, her first for 21 years. The GIULIO CESARE returned to the North Atlantic in January 1957 and three weeks later was joined by the AUGUSTUS. The pair was actively engaged on this route for upwards of three years during the building of the 33,340 ton LEONARDO DA VINCI as a replacement for the lost ship. She entered the New York service on 30 June 1960. The GIULIO CESARE rejoined the South American trade during the summer of 1960, as did the AUGUSTUS in the autumn of 1961.

The CONTE BIANCAMANO was scrapped at La Spezia in August 1960 after an active life of nearly 35 years, and the CONTE GRANDE met her fate at the same yard in September 1962 after being laid up for many months.

In 1963 the 9,000 ton ANTONIOTTO USODIMARE, MARCO POLO and AMERIGO VESPUCCI, which had been running for Italia between Italy, the Panama Canal and the west coast of South America for a number of years, were replaced by the 13,000 ton VERDI, DONIZETTI and ROSSINI, formerly the Lloyd Triestino OCEANIA, AUSTRALIA and NEPTUNIA. All three of these 'Musicians' have since been scrapped at La Spezia.

The 45,900 ton MICHELANGELO and RAFFAELLO entered the Genoa–Cannes–Naples–New York service on 12 May and 25 July 1965,

456

allowing the CRISTOFORO COLOMBO to replace the SATURNIA and VULCANIA on the Trieste–New York route. The former was scrapped, but the VULCANIA became the Siosa Line CARIBIA and survived until 1974.

It was evident by the time the keels of the MICHELANGELO and RAFFAELLO were laid that the airlines were bound to divert an ever increasing volume of traffic from the transatlantic steamship lines, and there were many, both inside and outside Italy, who were of the opinion that the ships should never have been built. It was rumoured as early as 1969–70 that in view of the heavy losses incurred by Italia drastic changes were on the way, and it was even suggested that the South American service would be suspended and the AUGUSTUS and GIULIO CESARE laid up. At the beginning of 1971 it seemed likely that they would be sold and the RAFFAELLO and LEONARDO DA VINCI transferred to the South Atlantic. This would have left the MICHE-LANGELO and CRISTOFORO COLOMBO to cope with a gradually phased out North Atlantic service, with more and more attention paid to cruising.

To some extent fate stepped in as the GIULIO CESARE arrived at Naples on 14 January 1973 from South America with serious rudder trouble, was laid up and a few weeks later was sold for scrap, it having been decided that repairs would be too costly to contemplate. In consequence, the CRISTOFORO COLOMBO was withdrawn from the New York service and sailed on 1 February 1973 from Genoa for Naples, Cannes, Barcelona, Lisbon, Rio de Janeiro, Santos, Montevideo and Buenos Aires as a consort for the AUGUSTUS.

In February 1973 the Italian Council of Ministers submitted a Bill to Parliament authorising the withdrawal within five years of the State-subsidised passenger ships from the Mediterranean–New York, Mediterranean–South American and all other long-distance routes. In fact, it was widely believed that the RAFFAELLO and MICHE-LANGELO would discontinue transatlantic service much sooner, and this turned out to be correct as they left New York for the last time in April and June 1975. Both were sold to the Iranian Navy to act as accommodation ships.

The AUGUSTUS arrived at Naples from South America on 16 January 1976. She was laid up and replaced by the chartered 27,900 ton Lloyd Triestino GUGLIELMO MARCONI, whose funnels were painted in Italia colours.

The Italia North Atlantic passenger service may be said to have ended on 6 July 1976 with the LEONARDO DA VINCI's arrival at Naples from New York, but she made one further voyage to New York before undertaking a series of Caribbean cruises. Laid up upon return to

1976 GUGLIELMO MARCONI 27,905 tons
Built 1963 for Lloyd Triestino. Ran 1976–77 for Italia to River Plate.

Genoa, she was later detailed to a series of short cruises from Port Everglades to Nassau. Subsequently, she was chartered by the Costa Line for a similar purpose. She finally arrived at La Spezia on 23 September 1978 to be laid up. She was gutted by fire on 3 July 1980, sank, and has since been scrapped.

The CRISTOFORO COLOMBO and GUGLIELMO MARCONI sailed to South America until the middle of 1977, after which the service was withdrawn for the usual reason – air competition. The CRISTO-FORO COLOMBO was sold for use in the Orinoco estuary as an accommodation ship, but was scrapped in 1981. The GUGLIELMO MARCONI was acquired by Italia Crociere Internazionali as a cruise ship, and at the time of writing is still listed as such.

Looking back, it is evident that the MICHELANGELO and RAF-FAELLO could never have been a viable proposition, but judging by the experience of other lines of other nations on both North and South Atlantic, it seems pretty certain that, in any event, the Italia transatlantic passenger services would have found it necessary to close down just about when they did.

Thus, Italia has retired from the passenger business, but is running container ships, specialised cargo ships and dry cargo ships and seems likely to continue to do so for many years to come.

1. (1932) CONTE VERDE
18,383. 173,78 [180,52] x 22,61. (570.2 [592.3] x 74.2. 2–2. 2S–ST(DR)–18. (I–336; II–198; III–1,700). W. Beardmore & Co Ltd, Glasgow. 1922 (21/10) launched for Lloyd Sabaudo. 1923 (21/4) MV Genoa–Naples–S. America (1 RV). 1923 (13/6) FV Genoa–Naples–New York. 1925 resumed Genoa–Naples–S.

America. 1932 CONTE VERDE (Italia). 1932 (28/1) FV Genoa–Naples–S. America (3 RV). 1932 CONTE VERDE (Lloyd Triestino). 1943 (9/9) scuttled at Shanghai to avoid capture by Japanese; later refloated by Japanese; troopship KOTOBUKI MARU. 1944 (Dec) bombed and sunk at Maiguru, near Kioto. 1949 (Jan) refloated. 1951 scrapped.

2. (1932) DUILIO

24,281. 183,60 x 23,25. (602.4 x 76.3). 2–2–C. 4S–ST(SR)–19. (I–280; II–670; III–600). G. Ansaldo & Co, Sestri Ponente. 1914 (30/5) keel laid. 1916 (9/1) launched for NGI. 1923 (29/10) MV Genoa–Naples–New York. 1928 (Aug) FV Genoa–Naples–S. America. 1932 DUILIO (Italia). 1932 (18/2) FV Genoa–Naples–S. America. 1933 transferred to S. African service. 1937 DUILIO (Lloyd Triestino). 1944 (10/7) bombed and sunk at Trieste. 1948 refloated; scrapped.

3. (1932) GIULIO CESARE (I)

21,657. 183,60 x 23,31. (602.4 x 76.5). 2–2–C. 4S–ST(SR)–19. (I–256; II–306; III–1,800). Swan Hunter & Wigham Richardson, Wallsend-on-Tyne (engines Wallsend Slipway Co Ltd). 1913 (13/12) keel laid. 1920 (7/2) launched for NGI. 1922 (4/5) MV Genoa–Naples–S. America (2 RV). 1922 (11/8) FV Genoa–Naples–New York. 1925 resumed Genoa–Naples–S. America. 1932 GIULIO CESARE (Italia). 1932 (24/3) FV Genoa–Naples–S. America. 1933 transferred to S. African service. 1937 GIULIO CESARE (Lloyd Triestino). 1944 (11/9) bombed and sunk at Trieste. 1949 refloated; scrapped.

4. (1932) CONTE BIANCAMANO

24,416. 190,91 [198,38] x 23,19. (626.4 [650.9] x 76.1). 2–2. 2S–ST(DR)–19. (I–180; I or II–220; II–200; economic II–390; III–2,660). W. Beardmore & Co Ltd, Glasgow. 1925 (23/4) launched for Lloyd Sabaudo. 1925 (20/11) MV Genoa–Naples–New York. 1932 CONTE BIANCAMANO (Italia). 1932 (8/9) FV Genoa–Naples–S. America. 1936 CONTE BIANCAMANO (Lloyd Triestino). 1940 ditto (Italia (c)). 1940 (23/4) FV Genoa–Naples–Panama Canal–Valparaiso–Panama. 1940 (10/6) laid up at Cristobal when Italy entered World War II. 1941 (Dec) seized by USA; became HERMITAGE (US troopship). 1947 (May) returned to Italian Govt. as CONTE BIANCAMANO. 1948 reconditioned; new raked bow; 202,68 metres OA (665 feet); 23,562 tons; (I–252; cabin 455; tourist 893). CONTE BIANCAMANO (Società Marittima Finanziaria); later repurchased by Italia. 1949 (10/11) resumed Genoa–S. America. 1950 (21/3) resumed Genoa–Naples–New York. 1960 scrapped at La Spezia.

5. (1933) CONTE GRANDE
25,661. 190,36 [198,78] x 23,86. (624.6 [652.2] x 78.3). 2–2.
2S–ST(DR)–19. (I–578; II–256; economic II–164; III–720). Stabi-
limento Tecnico Triestino, Trieste. 1926 (24/10) keel laid. 1927
(29/6) launched for Lloyd Sabaudo. 1928 (3/4) MV Genoa–
Naples–New York. 1932 CONTE GRANDE (Italia). 1933 (28/9)
FV Genoa–Naples–S. America. 1940 (22/5) LV Genoa–S. America (Santos arr 7/6). 1940 (10/6) laid up at Rio de Janeiro when
Italy entered World War II. 1941 (22/8) seized by Brazil. 1942
(16/4) sold to USA; renamed MONTICELLO (troopship). 1947
returned to Italian Govt. as CONTE GRANDE; reconditioned;
new bow fitted; 195,00 [203,29] metres. (639.8 [667.0] feet;
23,842 tons; (I–215; cabin 333; tourist 950); CONTE GRANDE
(Società Marittima Finanziaria); later repurchased by Italia. 1949
(14/7) resumed Genoa–Buenos Aires. 1961 (2/2) laid up at Genoa
after 1 RV to Australia for Lloyd Triestino (c). 1962 (Sep)
scrapped at La Spezia.
6. (1933) AUGUSTUS (I) (M/S)
32,650. 203,07 [216,40] x 25,23. (666.3 [710.0] x 82.8). 2–2.
4S–2SC.DA–19. (I–375; II–300; intermediate 300; III–700). G.
Ansaldo & Co, Sestri Ponente. World's largest-ever passenger
motorship. 1926 (13/12) launched for NGI. 1927 (12/11) MV
Genoa–Naples–Buenos Aires. 1928 (28/8) FV Genoa–Naples–
New York. 1932 AUGUSTUS (Italia). 1933 (9/11) resumed
Genoa–Naples–Buenos Aires. 1943 SPARVIERO (Italian
Navy); converted to aircraft carrier. 1944 (Sep) scuttled by
Germans at Genoa. 1946 refloated; sold. 1951 scrapped.
7. (1935) ROMA
32,583. 202,58 [216,09] x 25,17. (664.7 [709.0] x 82.6). 2–2.
4S–ST(SR)–20. (I–375; II–300; intermediate 300; III–700). G.
Ansaldo & Co, Sestri Ponente. 1926 (26/2) launched for NGI.
1926 (21/9) MV Genoa–Naples–New York. 1932 ROMA (Italia).
1935 FV Genoa–Naples–S. America. 1940 (29/4) FV Trieste–
Venice–New York–Genoa (1 RV). 1943 AQUILA (Italian
Navy); converted to aircraft carrier. 1944 (16/6) damaged by
bombing at Genoa. 1945 (19/4) sunk by aerial torpedoes. 1946
wreck towed to La Spezia. 1951 scrapped at La Spezia.
8. (1937) OCEANIA (M/S)
19,507. 179,72 x 23,37. (589.7 x 76.7). 1–2–C. 4S–2SC.SA–19.
(I–300; II–700; III–500). Cantieri Riuniti dell' Adriatico, Monfalcone (engines SA Fiat, Turin). 1932 (29/9) launched for Cosulich.
1933 (21/9) MV Trieste–S. America. 1937 OCEANIA (Italia).
1937 (22/1) FV Trieste–S. America. 1940 (4/5) LV Buenos

Aires–Trieste. 1940 Italian troopship. 1941 (18/9) torpedoed and sunk in Mediterranean by British submarine UPHOLDER.

9. (1937) NEPTUNIA (M/S)

19,475. 179,72 x 23,31. (589.7 x 76.5). 1–2–C. 4S–2SC.SA–19. (I–175; II–700; III–650). Cantieri Riuniti dell' Adriatico, Monfalcone. 1931 (27/12) launched for Cosulich. 1932 (5/10) MV Trieste–S. America. 1937 NEPTUNIA (Italia). 1937 (20/2) FV Trieste–S. America. 1940 (30/3) LV Buenos Aires–Trieste. 1940 Italian troopship. 1941 (18/9) torpedoed and sunk in Mediterranean by British submarine UPHOLDER.

10. (1947) SAN GIORGIO

8,959. 134,59 x 18,00. (441.6 x 59.1). 2–2. 2S–ST(DR)–13. Cantieri Navale Franco Tosi, Taranto. 1923 (29/4) launched as PRINCIPESSA GIOVANNA (Lloyd Sabaudo); 8,389 tons. 1923 (Aug) MV Genoa–Suez Canal–Australia. 1932 PRINCIPESSA GIOVANNA (Italia); funnels increased from one to two; (III–640). 1944 requisitioned by Britain (hospital ship; later troopship). 1946 returned to Italy; sailed Southampton–Genoa under Italia colours. 1947 renamed SAN GIORGIO (Italia). 1947 (29/1) FV Genoa–Buenos Aires. 1952 SAN GIORGIO (Lloyd Triestino); Australian service. 1953 laid up at Trieste; sold; scrapped at Savona.

11. (1947) VULCANIA (M/S)

24,469. 183,24 [192,44] x 24,32. (601.2 [631.4] x 79.8). 1–2. 2S–2SC.DA–21. (I–240; cabin 270; tourist 860). Cantiere Navale Triestino, Monfalcone (engines SA Fiat, Turin). 1926 (18/12) launched for Cosulich. 1928 (19/12) MV Trieste–New York. 1935 new diesel engines replaced 4SC.SA type. 1937 VULCANIA (Italia). 1941 requisitioned by Italian Govt. 1943 (Oct) US troopship. 1946 (29/3) FV for American Export (c), New York–Naples–Alexandria. 1946 (15/11) returned to Italia; reconditioned at Genoa. 1947 (15/7) FV Genoa–Buenos Aires (1 RV). 1947 (4/9) FV Genoa–Naples–New York. 1965 CARIBIA (Siosa). 1974 (20/7) arr Kaohsiung for scrapping.

11a. (1947) SANTA CRUZ (c)

15,511. 182,87 x 19,90. (600.0 x 65.3). 1–4. 2S–Q8–16. (I–450). New York Shipbuilding Corporation, Camden, N.J. Laid down as MINNEKAHDA (ATL). 1903 (2/11) launched as MANCHURIA (Pacific Mail). 1915 MANCHURIA (Atlantic Transport Co. of West Virginia). 1919 ditto (American Line (c)). 1923 ditto (Panama Pacific). 1927 PRESIDENT JOHNSON (Dollar). 1938 ditto (American President). 1947 SANTA CRUZ (Tagus Navigation Co, Lisbon), sailed Lisbon–R. Plate. 1947 SANTA

CRUZ (Panamanian). 1947 ditto (Italia (c)). 1947 (30/12) FV Genoa–R. Plate. 1952 (4/3) laid up. 1952 scrapped at Savona.

12. 1951 GIULIO CESARE (II) (M/S)
27,078. 188,45 [207,43] x 26,66. (618.3 [680.6] x 87.5. 1–2–C. 2S–2SC.DA–21. (I–178; cabin 288; tourist 714). Cantieri Riuniti dell' Adriatico, Monfalcone (engines SA Fiat, Turin). 1950 (18/5) launched. 1951 (27/10) MV Genoa–Naples–S. America. 1956 (29/6) FV Genoa–Naples–New York (32 RV). 1960 reverted to Genoa–S. America. 1964 (I–180; tourist 1,000). 1973 (14/1) arr Naples from S. America with rudder trouble; laid up. 1973 (20/4) sailed Naples–La Spezia; scrapped.

13. 1952 AUGUSTUS (II) (M/S)
27,090. 188,45 [207,37] x 26,66. (618.3 [680.4] x 87.5). 1–2–C. 2S–2SC.DA–21. (I–178; cabin 288; tourist 714). Cantieri Riuniti dell' Adriatico, Monfalcone (engines SA Fiat, Turin). 1950 (19/11) launched. 1952 (4/3) MV Genoa–Naples–S. America. 1957 (7/2) FV Genoa–Naples–New York (40 RV). 1961 reverted to Genoa–S. America. 1964 (I–180; tourist 1,000). 1975 (8/12) LV Naples–Rio de Janeiro–Santos–Montevideo–Buenos Aires (arr Naples 1976 (16/1)); laid up. 1976 GREAT SEA (Great Shipping Investment, Hong Kong).

14. (1973) CRISTOFORO COLOMBO
29,429. 190,97 [213,59] x 27,39. (626.6 [700.8] x 89.9). 1–2–C. 2S–ST(DR)–23. (I–202; cabin 222; tourist 640). SA Ansaldo, Genoa. 1953 (10/5) launched. 1954 (15/7) MV Genoa–Naples–New York. 1963 tonnage increased from 29,191; stabilisers fitted. 1973 (1/2) FV Genoa–Naples–Cannes–Barcelona–Lisbon–Rio de Janeiro–Santos–Montevideo–Buenos Aires in place of GIULIO CESARE. 1977 sold; became accommodation ship in Orinoco Estuary, Venezuela. 1981 sold for scrap.

15. (1976) GUGLIELMO MARCONI (c)
27,905. 188,69 [213,62] x 28,71. (619.1 [700.9] x 94.2). 1–1–C. 2S–ST(DR)–24. (I–100; I or tourist 200; tourist 1,400). Cantieri Riuniti dell' Adriatico, Monfalcone. 1961 (24/9) launched for Lloyd Triestino. 1963 (Nov) MV Italy–Suez Canal–Australia. 1976 GUGLIELMO MARCONI (Italia (c)). 1976 (Jan) FV Naples–Buenos Aires. 1977 LV ditto. 1979 GUGLIELMO MARCONI (Italia Crociere Internazionali). 1983 still listed.

Note: CONTE ROSSO, REX, CONTE DI SAVOIA, SATURNIA, ANDREA DORIA, LEONARDO DA VINCI, MICHELANGELO and RAFFAELLO did not run for Italia to South America.
VULCANIA made one South American voyage for Italia, but none

for Cosulich (Chapter 60). SATURNIA made two South American voyages for Cosulich.

FUNNEL: White with narrow green band; red top with black lip.
FLAG: Left half, red cross on white; right half, white halberd on red.

Chapter 66

(1936–9)

GDYNIA – AMERIKA LINJE

(Gdynia–Amerika Linje Zeglugowe Spolka)
(Gdynia–America Shipping Line)
(Gdynia–America Line)

(Polish)

The 1919 Treaty of Versailles gave Poland 50 miles of the Baltic coast, consisting of barren waste stretches, sleepy summer resorts and fishing hamlets. The largest of these, Gdynia, had a population of only about 500, but in 1924 the Poles set to work feverishly to transform it into a new port and six years later, by which time the population had increased to 42,000, Gdynia despatched its first transatlantic steamship, the KOSCIUSZKO, to Copenhagen, Halifax and New York.

This was one of three steamers newly bought from the Danish-flag Baltic American Line by the Polish Government to establish the GDYNIA–AMERIKA LINJE ZEGLUGOWE SPOLKA (Gdynia America Shipping Line), more usually known as the GDYNIA– AMERIKA LINJE (Gdynia–America Line). It first made a handful of sailings from Danzig (Gdansk).

These vessels varied between 15 and 20 years old, and were replaced within six years by two 14,000 ton motorships, the PILSUDSKI and BATORY, built in Italy under a barter agreement which provided for a series of shipments of Polish coal.

1930 PULASKI 6,503 tons
Built 1912 as Russian American CZAR.

Some weeks before the BATORY joined the PILSUDSKI on the New York run, one of the original steamers, the 6,500 ton PULASKI was detailed to a new service from Gdynia to Rio de Janeiro, Santos, Montevideo and Buenos Aires. She made the first sailing on 28 February 1936 and was joined on 20 October by the KOSCIUSZKO, which had recently been tried on a run between Constanza, Istanbul and Haifa. Both had accommodation for 110 cabin, 180 tourist and 500 third class passengers and for more than two years maintained a regular service to Buenos Aires. Success was evident by the commissioning of the 11,030 ton motorship SOBIESKI, which had accommodation for 70 first class, 270 tourist and 600 third class passengers, her maiden voyage to Buenos Aires starting from Gdynia on 15 June 1939. She was a product of Swan, Hunter & Wigham Richardson of Tyneside but a sister ship, the 11,442 ton CHROBRY, which sailed on 29 July 1939, was built by Nakskov Skibswaerft.

The advent of these two fine newcomers resulted in the PULASKI and KOSCIUSZKO being laid up at Gdynia. Very sensibly, both were taken to Dartmouth, Devon, at the end of August, a few days before the outbreak of the Second World War and in due course undertook valuable work as troopships. The CHROBRY, meanwhile, had begun her maiden homeward voyage from Buenos Aires on 25 August 1939 and has been traced as far as Rio de Janeiro. Suffice it to say that she eventually reached a British port and became an Allied troopship in company with the SOBIESKI. Unfortunately, the CHROBRY was torpedoed and sunk near Narvik in 1940, following the German occupation of Norway, but the SOBIESKI, PULASKI and KOSCIUSZKO all survived the war, although the older pair had become the EMPIRE PENRYN and EMPIRE HELFORD.

However, although a North Atlantic service was eventually reopened and remains to this day, the South American passenger service was never resumed. The former PULASKI and KOSCIUSZKO were scrapped in 1949–50 and the SOBIESKI made 29 round voyages for Gdynia–America between Italy and New York during 1947–50 before becoming the Russian GRUZIYA. She survived until 1975, when she was scrapped at La Spezia.

1. (1936) PULASKI
    6,503. 129,53 x 16,21. (425.0 x 53.2). 2–2. 2S–Q8–15. (cabin 110, tourist 180; III–500). Barclay, Curle & Co Ltd, Glasgow. 1912 (23/2) launched as CZAR (Russian American). 1921 ESTONIA (Baltic American). 1930 PULASKI (Gdynia–America). 1930 (25/4) FV Danzig–Halifax–New York. 1936 (28/2) FV Gdynia–Buenos Aires. 1939 (21/4) LV ditto. 1939 (24/8) sailed Gdynia–

Dartmouth (arr 29/8). 1946 EMPIRE PENRYN (Br). 1949 scrapped at Blyth.

2. (1936) KOSCIUSZKO

6,598. 134,10 x 16,27. (440.0 x 53.4). 2–2. 2S–Q8–15. (cabin 110; tourist 180; III–500). Barclay, Curle & Co Ltd, Glasgow. 1915 (14/2) launched as CZARITZA (Russian American). 1921 LITUANIA (Baltic American). 1930 LITUANIA (Gdynia–America). 1930 KOSCIUSZKO (ditto). 1930 (10/5) FV Gdynia–Copenhagen–New York. 1935 ran Constanza–Istanbul–Haifa. 1936 (20/10) FV Gdynia–S. America. 1938 (19/11) LV Buenos Aires–Gdynia (arr 12/12); laid up. 1939 (28/8) sailed Gdynia–Dartmouth (arr 2/9). 1940 GDYNIA (Polish Navy). 1946 EMPIRE HELFORD (Br). 1950 scrapped at Blyth.

3. 1939 SOBIESKI (M/S)

11,030. 150,26 [155,80] x 20,51. (493.0 [511.2] x 67.3). 1–2–C. 2S–2SC.DA–17. (I–70; tourist 270; III–600). Swan, Hunter & Wigham Richardson, Wallsend-on-Tyne (engines J.G. Kincaid & Co Ltd, Greenock). 1938 (25/8) launched. 1939 (15/6) MV Gdynia–S. America. 1939 Allied troopship. 1947 returned to Gdynia–America. 1947 (14/5) FV Genoa–Cannes–New York (29 RV). 1950 (Mar) GRUZIYA (Russian). 1975 (14/4) arr La Spezia in tow from Odessa; scrapped.

4. 1939 CHROBRY (M/S)

11,442. 145,65 [154,19] x 20,32. (477.9 [505.9] x 66.7). 1–2–C. 2S–2SC.DA–17. (I–70; tourist 270; III–600). Nakskov Skibswaerft, Nakskov (engines Burmeister & Wain, Copenhagen). 1939 (24/2) launched. 1939 (29/7) MV Gdynia–Buenos Aires. 1939 (25/8) MV Buenos Aires–Rio de Janeiro; subsequent movements unknown. 1939 Allied troopship. 1940 (14/5) set on fire by German aircraft near Bodö, Norway. 1940 (15/5) foundered.

FUNNEL: Buff; red band with shield and trident device of houseflag.
FLAG: White-red-white horizontal stripes; on the red, blue trident on red pointed shield with white sides; white 'GA' and 'L'.

Chapter 67

(1940–60)

COMPANHIA COLONIAL DE NAVEGAÇÃO

(Portuguese)

The COMPANHIA COLONIAL DE NAVEGAÇÃO started operations in 1922 between Lisbon, St. Vincent, Portuguese Guinea and Angola. The itinerary was extended to Mozambique on 5 January 1930.

In 1929 the Company bought the 8,142 ton twin-screw Anchor Line ASSYRIA, launched on 3 May 1908 as the Hamburg American YPIRANGA. She was renamed COLONIAL, and until some months after the outbreak of World War II was detailed to the Mozambique service. On 22 June 1940 she sailed from Lisbon for Madeira, St. Vincent, Rio de Janeiro and Santos. She made a second South American voyage in 1944.

In 1940, CCN, as the Company was familiarly known, bought the 8,267 ton Yugoslavian PRINCESA OLGA, launched on 8 September 1914 as the Royal Mail Packet Company's EBRO. She was renamed SERPA PINTO and despatched from Lisbon on 4 August 1940 for Madeira, St. Vincent, Rio de Janeiro and Santos. Between then and 10 October 1945 she left Lisbon for South America 11 times, the voyage which started on 31 March 1942 being extended from Brazil to Buenos Aires. There were a good many gaps between South American sailings to enable the SERPA PINTO to sail from Lisbon to New York, and later to Baltimore or Philadelphia. She sailed regularly on one or other route until 9 August 1948, when she reached Lisbon from Brazil with serious engine trouble, which took until December to repair. She reverted to the South American service on 15 January 1949. Meanwhile, the 13,196 ton PATRIA and the 13,186 ton IMPÉRIO were, respectively, responsible for one and three South American voyages [1] in place of the damaged ship.

The 8,374 ton Hamburg American CORCOVADO, completed in 1908, became the Sicula Americana GUGLIELMO PEIRCE in 1920, the Lloyd Sabaudo MARIA CRISTINA in 1927 and the Companhia Colonial MOUZINHO in 1930. She started the first of 17 round voyages to Brazil on 15 November 1946 (one of them to Brazil and the River Plate) and began the last on 17 January 1952. She was scrapped two years later.

The first of two much larger ships, the 21,765 ton twin-screw turbine

467

steamer VERA CRUZ, launched by Cockerill of Hoboken on 2 June 1951 and despatched from Lisbon for Madeira, Rio de Janeiro, Santos and Buenos Aires on 20 March 1952, had a service speed of 20 knots and could accommodate 148 first class, 250 cabin and 844 tourist passengers. The 20,906 ton SANTA MARIA was launched by the same builders on 20 September 1952, was commissioned in November 1953 and both she and the VERA CRUZ operated for a time between Lisbon and Brazil and, not infrequently, the River Plate.

Having two brand new ships built for the South American service it was decided to start regular sailings to Central America and on 14 August 1953 the SERPA PINTO sailed from Lisbon for Madeira, La Guaira, Curaçao and Havana. She made 12 round voyages, the last ending at Lisbon on 11 July 1955, after which she was laid up and sold for scrap. It should be added that her final Brazil voyage had started on 9 July 1954.

The VERA CRUZ sailed to the River Plate, or at times no further than Brazil, until 19 July 1954 when she started the first of 13 trips to Central America. These took four years to complete as in between were many South American voyages. From 1955 to 1973 the SANTA MARIA sailed mainly to Central America, but paid a number of visits to South America, the last on 18 November 1957 from Lisbon.

The SANTA MARIA had an extraordinary experience in 1961. She left Lisbon on 9 January, and was hi-jacked by an armed band of Portuguese and Spanish insurgents, who went aboard at Curaçao posing as passengers. After 11 days of search by aircraft and other ships, she was intercepted and forced to put in at Recife (Pernambuco), where the hi-jackers were landed.

The Central American service continued regularly until 11 April 1973, when the SANTA MARIA was laid up at Lisbon with engine trouble.

1952 VERA CRUZ 21,765 tons
Made many voyages from Lisbon to South America between 1952 and 1960.

She left Lisbon on 1 June 1973 for Kaohsiung, where she arrived on 19 July and was scrapped.

The VERA CRUZ undertook six round voyages to Angola starting from Lisbon between 20 June 1959 and 11 December 1960. Her last voyage to Brazil took place on 28 March 1961, when she had a full complement of 1,300 passengers. It was at this time that the Colonial War started in Angola and there was an urgent need to carry large numbers of Portuguese troops. In consequence, the VERA CRUZ voyage to Brazil scheduled for 22 April 1961 was cancelled and the ship was requisitioned by the Portuguese Government as a troopship. Her last trooping voyage took place in January 1972, after which she was laid up at Lisbon and eventually arrived at Kaohsiung on 19 April 1973 to be scrapped.

Mention has already been made of a special voyage from Lisbon to Brazil by the PATRIA in 1948. In fact, she made a second voyage in August 1956, while the 10,001 ton single-screw motorship UIGE was responsible for one similar voyage in 1958. [2] Much more important, the 23,000 ton twin-screw turbine steamer INFANTE DOM HENRIQUE was launched by Cockerill–Ougree of Hoboken on 29 April 1960 for the African service. However, she was the last CCN passenger liner to visit Brazil as she left Lisbon on 21 August 1972 on a cruise which included calls at Recife (Pernambuco), Salvador (Bahia) and Rio de Janeiro.

In conclusion it will be appropriate to mention that the 9,824 ton twin-screw turbine steamer FUNCHAL was built in Denmark in 1961 for the Empresa Insulana de Navegação to run between Madeira, the Azores and the Canary Islands. In 1974 the Companhia Colonial de Navegação and the Empresa Insulana were amalgamated to form the COMPANHIA PORTUGUESA DE TRANSPORTES MARITIMOS. It is a sign of the times that the FUNCHAL is now the only Portuguese liner in service between Europe and Brazil. She has become, in fact, a cruise liner, and sails from Lisbon on 5 December each year to Rio de Janeiro, undertaking a series of cruises from that port until the following March or April, when she returns to Lisbon. She was rebuilt and re-engined at Amsterdam in 1972–3 to make her thoroughly suitable for these new duties.

[1] See *Addenda and Corrigenda* for details for PATRIA and IMPÉRIO, and voyages thereby.

[2] See *Addenda and Corrigenda* for details of UIGE, and voyages thereby.

1. (1940) COLONIAL
     8,142. 136,66 x 16,85. (448.4 x 55.3). 1–2. 2S–Q8–14. Germania

Werft, Kiel. 1908 (3/5) launched as YPIRANGA (Hapag). 1919 surrendered to Britain. 1921 ASSYRIA (Anchor); (cabin 241; III–140). 1929 COLONIAL (Cia Colonial). 1939 rebuilt; modern funnel fitted. 1940 (22/6) FV Lisbon–Madeira–St. Vincent–Rio de Janeiro–Santos. 1944 (27/4) 2nd and last voyage Lisbon–Rio de Janeiro–Buenos Aires. 1950 (Sep) BISCO 9 (British Iron & Steel Corporation); towed to Scotland. 1950 (17/9) stranded near Campbeltown, Kintyre; scrapped as lies.

2. (1940) SERPA PINTO
   8,267. 137,24 x 17,61. (450.3 x 57.8). 1–2. 2S–Q8–14. (I–278; III–328). Workman, Clark & Co Ltd, Belfast. 1914 (8/9) launched as EBRO (RMSP). 1915 armed merchant cruiser. 1919 converted to oil fuel. 1919 EBRO (PSN (c)). 1922 EBRO (PSN). 1935 PRINCESA OLGA (Yugoslavian). 1940 SERPA PINTO (Cia Colonial). 1940 (14/8) FV Lisbon–Madeira–St. Vincent–Rio de Janeiro–Santos. 1945 (10/10) LV Lisbon–Brazil (11 RV) – the 1942 (31/3) voyage terminated at Buenos Aires. There were intervening voyages Lisbon–New York, Baltimore or Philadelphia. 1953 (14/8) FV Lisbon–Madeira–La Guaira–Curaçao–Havana (12 RV). 1954 (9/7) LV Lisbon–St. Vincent–Rio de Janeiro–Santos (1 RV). 1955 (6/9) left Lisbon in tow for Belgian shipbreakers.

3. (1946) MOUZINHO
   8,374. 136,63 x 16,82. (448.3 x 55.2). 1–2. 2S–Q8–14. Germania Werft, (Krupp), Kiel. 1907 (21/12) launched as CORCOVADO (Hapag). 1920 GUGLIELMO PEIRCE (Sicula Americana). 1927 MARIA CRISTINA (Lloyd Sabaudo). 1930 MOUZINHO (Cia Colonial). 1946 (15/11) FV Lisbon–St. Vincent–Rio de Janeiro–Santos. 1952 (17/1) LV ditto (17 RV, of which one was extended to River Plate). 1954 (22/3) laid up at Lisbon. 1954 scrapped at Savona, Italy.

4. 1952 VERA CRUZ
   21,765. 171,35 [185,83] x 23,10. (562.2 [609.7] x 75.8). 1–1–C. 2S–ST(DR)–20. (I–148; cabin 250; tourist 844). John Cockerill, Hoboken. 1951 (2/6) launched. 1952 (20/3) MV Lisbon–Madeira–Rio de Janeiro–Santos–Buenos Aires. 1954 (19/7) FV Lisbon–Madeira–Tenerife–La Guaira–Curaçao–Havana. 1958 (9/8) LV ditto (13 RV). 1959–60 Lisbon–Angola (6 RV). 1961 (28/3) LV Lisbon–Brazil. 1961 (5/5). – 1972 (26/1) trooping voyages Lisbon–Loanda. 1972 (26/1) – 1973 (4/3) laid up at Lisbon. 1973 (19/4) arr Kaohsiung; scrapped.

5. 1953 SANTA MARIA
   20,906. 171,25 [185,58] x 23,10. (561.9 [608.9] x 75.8). 1–1–C.

2S–ST(DR)–20. (I–156; cabin 228; tourist 800). John Cockerill, Hoboken. 1952 (20/9) launched. 1953 (12/11) MV Lisbon–Madeira–Rio de Janeiro–Santos–Montevideo–Buenos Aires. 1954 (19/10) FV Lisbon–Madeira–Tenerife–La Guaira–Curaçao–Havana. 1957 (18/11) LV Lisbon–Brazil. 1961 (22/1) hi-jacked at sea by armed band of Portuguese and Spanish insurgents, who went aboard at Curaçao posing as passengers. 1961 (2/2) put in at Recife (Pernambuco), where hi-jackers were landed. 1973 (11/4) last arrival at Lisbon (with engine trouble). 1973 (19/7) arrived Kaohsiung; scrapped.

FUNNEL: Yellow; narrow green-broad white-narrow green bands.
FLAG: White with green 'C.C.N.'; broad green horizontal stripes at top and bottom.

Chapter 68

1947–9

HOME LINES

(Panamanian Lines Inc)
(South Atlantic Lines Inc)

(Panamanian)

The 11,015 ton Norwegian America Line BERGENSFJORD, completed by Cammell Laird of Birkenhead in 1913, was sold in the autumn of 1946 to Panamanian Lines Inc, of which Cosulich Brothers of Genoa were appointed managers. She was reconditioned at Genoa, renamed ARGENTINA and despatched from Genoa for Rio de Janeiro and Buenos Aires on 13 January 1947 under her owners' trade name of HOME LINES. She was manned by Italian officers and crew but flew the Panamanian flag; the president of the line was a Greek, Eugen Eugenides.

There was ample justification for this move as Italia Società Anonima di Navigazione, which had a monopoly of the Italian-flag passenger business to South America when World War II broke out in 1939, lost its four best ships during the war as well as two other large units, and was left with only the 8,556 ton SAN GIORGIO (formerly the PRINCIPESSA GIOVANNA), which sailed for the first time from Genoa for Buenos Aires in January 1947, the chartered SANTA CRUZ whose first Italia voyage took place from Genoa on 30 December 1947, plus one intervening voyage by the VULCANIA in July 1947. The 25,000 ton CONTE GRANDE and CONTE BIANCAMANO were in theory available for Italia, but although returned to Italy in 1947 they then received extensive refits lasting well into 1949.

Simultaneously with the transfer of the BERGENSFJORD to Panamanian Lines, the 11,055 ton Swedish American DROTTNING-HOLM, built in 1905 as the Allan Line VIRGINIAN, was sold to the South Atlantic Lines Inc, another Panamanian concern managed by Cosulich Brothers. Its president was Axel Johnson, president also of the Swedish American Line, which had a 55 per cent interest in the newcomer. As the DROTTNINGHOLM continued in service between Gothenburg and New York until February 1948, her first sailing from Genoa for South America under the Home Line's houseflag did not take place before 8 April 1948. She had been renamed BRASIL.

472

1948 BRASIL 11,055 tons
Built 1905 as Allan Line VIRGINIAN.

Meanwhile, the 21,532 ton United States-owned JOHN ERICSSON, formerly the Swedish American KUNGSHOLM, had been damaged by fire at New York on 7 March 1947. She was repurchased by Swedish American and refitted at Genoa, but instead of running from Gothenburg to New York, as originally intended, she was sold to South Atlantic Lines, renamed ITALIA and on 27 July 1948 sailed from Genoa for South America, her tonnage having been remeasured as 16,777.

Towards the end of 1948 Home Lines acquired a fourth ship through the medium of Panamanian Lines – the 17,232 ton Matson Line MATSONIA, built in 1927 as the same company's MALOLO. It was

1948 ITALIA 16,777 tons
Built 1928 as KUNGSHOLM (Swedish American).

473

announced that after being reconditioned at Genoa she would enter the South American trade as the ATLANTIC.

The boom in South American immigration began to wane in 1949, when also there were serious currency difficulties. In addition, the much larger and more luxurious CONTE GRANDE of Italia was ready to re-enter the South American trade from Genoa on 14 July 1949, followed by the CONTE BIANCAMANO on 10 November. It was decided, therefore, to extend the activities of Home Lines to the North Atlantic and, in fact, the ATLANTIC started her new career on 14 May 1949 by sailing from Genoa for Naples, Barcelona and New York. She was joined a month later by the ITALIA.

In September 1949 the ARGENTINA was transferred from the South American to the Central American trade, and the Company withdrew completely from South America in the spring of 1950, when the BRASIL left Genoa on the first of five voyages to Naples, Halifax and New York to cater for pilgrims to Rome during Holy Year.

Home Lines continued operations on the North Atlantic until 1963 [1], when only 6,118 westbound passengers were carried by the Company, whereas in 1952 the total had been 47,166.

Apart from an occasional positioning voyage their subsequent activities have been confined to cruising, and they were well-served in this respect by the 27,000 ton OCEANIC and the 25,000 ton DORIC, built in 1964 as the Zim Lines SHALOM, becoming the German Atlantic Line's HANSEATIC in 1967 and the DORIC in 1973. She remained with Home Lines until November 1981, when she was sold to Greek-flag operators and renamed ROYAL ODYSSEY. In her place, the 33,800 ton motorship ATLANTIC was built for Home Lines at La Seyne, Toulon. She was launched on 1 February 1981 and reached New York on 14 April 1982 in readiness for her first cruise to Bermuda, which started three days later. She has a service speed of 21 knots, eight decks, 14 public rooms, two swimming pools and 561 cabins for a total of over 1,000 passengers. Her cost was 120 million dollars.

[1] N.R.P. Bonsor, *North Atlantic Seaway,* Volume 4, pages 1692–1699.

1. (1947) ARGENTINA
   11,015. 156,17 [161,53] x 18,66. (512.4 [530.0] x 61.2). 2–2. 2S–Q8–15. (I–32; tourist 969). Cammell, Laird & Co Ltd, Birkenhead. 1913 (8/4) launched as BERGENSFJORD (Norwegian America), 10,666 tons. 1913 (25/9) MV Christiania (Oslo)–Christiansand–Stavanger–Bergen–New York. 1946 ARGENTINA (Home); 11,015 tons. 1947 (13/1) FV Genoa–Rio de

Janeiro–Buenos Aires. 1949 (Sep) FV Genoa–Central America. 1951 (13/7) FV New York–Naples–Genoa. 1953 JERUSALEM (Zim). 1957 ALIYA (Zim). 1959 scrapped at La Spezia.

2. (1948) BRASIL

11,055. 158,61 [163,97] x 18,38. (520.4 [538.0] x 60.3). 1–2. 3S–ST(SR)–18. (I–180; tourist 700). A. Stephen & Sons Ltd, Glasgow (engines Parsons Marine Steam Turbine Co, Newcastle). 1904 (22/11) launched as VIRGINIAN (Allan) – 10,754 tons. 1905 (6/4) MV Liverpool–St. John, N.B. 1917 VIRGINIAN (CPOS). 1920 DROTTNINGHOLM (Swedish American). 1922 single-reduction geared turbines by De Laval, Stockholm. 1948 BRASIL (Home) – 11,055 tons. 1948 (8/4) FV Genoa–S. America. 1950 (1/5) FV Genoa–Naples–Halifax–New York. 1951 HOMELAND (Home). 1955 scrapped at Trieste.

3. (1948) ITALIA (M/S)

16,777. 181,31 [185,67] x 23,83. (594.9 [609.2] x 78.2). 2–2. 2S–4SC.DA–17. (I–226; cabin 296; tourist 800). Blohm & Voss, Hamburg (engines Burmeister & Wain, Copenhagen). 1928 (17/3) launched as KUNGSHOLM (Swedish American); 21,532 tons. 1928 (24/11) MV Gothenburg–New York. 1942 JOHN ERICSSON (US). 1947 (7/3) damaged by fire at New York. 1947 repurchased by Swedish American. 1947 (21/11) sailed New York–Genoa; refitted. 1948 ITALIA (Home); 16,777 tons. 1948 (27/7) FV Genoa–S. America. 1949 (12/6) FV Genoa–Naples–New York. 1962 ran New York–Nassau. 1964 IMPERIAL BAHAMA HOTEL (moored at Freeport). 1965 scrapped at Bilbao.

—— ——— ATLANTIC

15,602. 1926 (26/6) lauched by W. Cramp & Sons, Philadelphia as MALOLO (Matson). 1937 MATSONIA (Matson). 1948 ATLANTIC (Home); refitted by Ansaldo, Genoa, for South American trade. Instead sailed 1949 (14/5) Genoa–Naples–New York. 1955 VASILISSA FREIDERIKI (QUEEN FREDERICA) (Greek). 1977 scrapped at Elefsis, Greece. 1978 (1/2) gutted by fire in breakers' yard.

FUNNEL: Yellow; blue ball with a golden turret (crown).
FLAG: White; blue ball with a golden turret. (A narrow blue top was added to the funnels after the South American service was withdrawn.)

Chapter 69

COSTA LINE

(Linea 'C')

Ditta Giacomo Costa fu Andrea
1967. Costa Armatori Società per Azioni

(Italian)

The COSTA ARMATORI SOCIETÀ PER AZIONI, best known as the COSTA LINE, can be traced back to 1860, when 24 year old Giacomo Costa started an edible oil business in Genoa. Upon his death in 1916 he left the business, known as the DITTA GIACOMO COSTA FU ANDREA, to his three sons, Eugenio, Enrico and Federico.

The firm started shipping operations in 1924 with the 1,148 ton freighter RAVENNA, built at Leith in 1888, carrying edible oil between Genoa and various ports in the Mediterranean. The 1,245 ton LANGANO followed in 1928 and six more ships were added before the outbreak of World War II in 1939. The Company lost a number of ships during the war.

In 1947 the WILLIAM LUCKENBACH, HORACE LUCKENBACH and ROBERT LUCKENBACH were bought from the American-owned Luckenbach Line, renamed MARIA C, GIOVANNA C and LUISA C, respectively, their tonnages varying between 6,475 and 6,939. They were fitted with accommodation for 25 first class passengers and inaugurated a regular service between Genoa, Montevideo and Buenos Aires.

Costa also acquired in 1947 the 10,917 ton motorship SOUTHERN PRINCE, one of four sister ships which had been running before the war for the Prince Line between New York and Buenos Aires. She was renamed ANNA C and her passenger accommodation was increased from 100 to 500. A further purchase at about the same time was the 8,603 ton motorship OCEAN VIRTUE, built by the Permanente Metals Corporation of Richmond, California, in 1942. Her passenger capacity was 200 first class and she was renamed ANDREA C.

The ANNA C and ANDREA C were detailed to run from Genoa to Buenos Aires in place of the three ex-Luckenbach ships, which were transferred to the Genoa–Philadelphia–Baltimore–New York trade.

1952 FRANCA C 6,822 tons
Built 1914 as cargo steamer, but later ran to River Plate as a passenger liner.

The 6,822 ton ROMA was bought by the Costa Line in 1951. She had been launched by the Newport News Shipbuilding & Dry Dock Company as long previously as 22 August 1914 as the cargo steamer MEDINA of the Clyde Mallory Line but in 1949 had been rebuilt at La Spezia as the Panamanian flag ROMA with accommodation for 925 one-class passengers. Costa renamed her FRANCA C and in 1952 she joined the ANNA C and ANDREA C in the River Plate service.

The 9,585 ton motorship ASSUNCION was bought in 1957. She had been built in 1925 as Rotterdam Lloyd's INDRAPOERA, when she carried no fewer than 141 first, 184 second and 68 third class passengers. In 1931 she was lengthened by the fitting of a new bow and received new diesel engines. During World War II she ran under the British flag. After the war her passenger accommodation was reduced to 96 first class and in 1956 she became the Panamanian ASSUNCION. Costa renamed her BIANCA C and placed her in service between Genoa and the River Plate.

The first passenger ship to be laid down for Costa was the 20,416 ton twin-screw FEDERICO C, which was fitted with double-reduction

1958 FEDERICO C 20,416 tons
Spends much time cruising, but makes occasional Italy–South America voyages.

geared turbines giving her a service speed of 22 knots. She could carry 264 first class, 202 cabin and 672 tourist passengers. Launched on 31 March 1957, she started her maiden voyage from Genoa to Buenos Aires on 22 May 1958 and enabled the BIANCA C to be chartered to Messageries Maritimes.

The ANNA C had received new diesel engines in 1952, increasing her speed to 18 knots. Additions were made to her passenger accommodation so that she could cater for 202 first class and 864 tourist, her revised tonnage being 12,030. She ran subsequently from Italy to Central America, but was scrapped in 1972.

The 15,889 ton twin-screw turbine steamer PROVENCE was launched by Swan, Hunter & Wigham Richardson of Tyneside on 15 August 1950 for the Société Générale de Transports Maritimes's Marseilles–Buenos Aires trade (Chapter 17). By 1962 she was the last passenger ship so employed, the outcome being that she participated in a joint service with Costa, who were responsible for running her from Genoa to Buenos Aires without change of name until 1965, when they bought her and renamed her ENRICO C. Before continuing the same service her passenger accommodation was amended to 218 first and 980 tourist class, and her tonnage became 13,607. She was converted to a one-class cruise liner in 1972, but still makes occasional voyages between Genoa and the River Plate.

One of the finest passenger ships ever completed for the South American trade was commissioned by Costa in 1966 as the 30,567 ton EUGENIO C, built by the Cantieri Riuniti dell' Adriatico of Monfalcone with twin-screws driven by geared turbines, which gave her a service speed of 26 knots. Unlike her predecessors, she had two funnels arranged athwartships and situated well aft, her passenger complement being 178 first class, 356 intermediate and 1,102 tourist. Fully air-conditioned, she was fitted with a double set of Denny-Brown stabilisers. Her maiden voyage from Genoa to Buenos Aires started on 31 August 1966. The FEDERICO C had already been withdrawn from the River Plate and was transferred to the Company's Central American service. She became a one-class cruise ship in 1971 as did the ANDREA C at about this time, but the FEDERICO C still makes occasional voyages to Central America. Sailings to South America have been greatly reduced, but at the time of writing there is still a skeleton service by the EUGENIO C and ENRICO C. This, in fact, is the only surviving multi–passenger service between Europe and the River Plate. The usual itinerary is Genoa–Cannes–Barcelona–Lisbon–Rio de Janeiro–Santos–Buenos Aires.

Other Costa ships which are still taking part in the Company's cruise programme are the 19,974 ton CARLA C (ex-Compagnie Générale

Transatlantique FLANDRE) and the 12,218 ton ITALIA, which from time to time have been joined by various chartered ships, but the 15,464 ton FLAVIA (ex-Cunard MEDIA) was sold in 1982. The BIANCA C (II) was bought in 1958 and ran from Italy to the West Indies and Central America until 1961 when, during a cruise from New York, she was destroyed at Grenada by an engine room explosion and fire. She had been launched in 1949 as LA MARSEILLAISE and in 1957 became the Arosa Line AROSA SKY.

It remains to add that the Company changed its official title in 1967 to COSTA ARMATORI SOCIETÀ PER AZIONI.

1. (1947) GIOVANNA C
   6,475. 135,63 x 17,68. (445.0 x 58.0). 1–2. 2S–T6–12. (I–25). Asano Shipbuilding Co, Tsurumi (Japan) (engines Kubota Iron Works, Osaka). 1919 launched as EASTERN TRADER (United States Shipping Board). 1923 HORACE LUCKENBACH (Luckenbach (US)). 1947 GIOVANNA C (Costa). 1947 FV Genoa–Buenos Aires. 1948 FV Genoa–Philadelphia–Baltimore– New York. 1953 scrapped at La Spezia.
2. (1947) MARIA C
   6,939. 143,76 x 18,04. (471.7 x 59.2). 1–2. S–T3–12. (I–25). Bremer Vulkan, Vegesack. 1913 launched as POMMERN (NDL). 1914 (Aug) interned at Honolulu. 1917 RAPPAHAN- NOCK (US Govt). 1919 ditto (US Shipping Board). 1934 WILLIAM LUCKENBACH (Luckenbach (US)). 1947 MARIA C (Costa). 1947 FV Genoa–Buenos Aires. 1948 FV Genoa– Philadelphia–Baltimore–New York. 1953 scrapped at Savona
3. (1947) LUISA C
   6,547. 135,63 x 17,68. (445.0 x 58.0). 1–2. 2S–T6–12. (I–25). Asano Shipbuilding Co, Tsurumi (engines Kubota Iron Works, Osaka). 1919 launched as EASTERN MERCHANT (US Ship- ping Board). 1922 ROBERT LUCKENBACH (Luckenbach (US)). 1947 LUISA C (Costa). 1947 FV Genoa–Buenos Aires. 1948 FV Genoa–Philadelphia–Baltimore–New York. 1955 SULA (Panamanian). 1959 scrapped in Japan.
4. (1948) ANNA C (M/S)
   11,736. 154,43 [161,00] x 19,74. (506.7 [528.3] x 64.8). 1–2–C. 2S–4SC.DA–16. Lithgows Ltd, Port Glasgow (engines J.G. Kincaid & Co Ltd, Greenock). 1929 (12/3) launched as SOUTH- ERN PRINCE (Prince); 10,917 tons; (I–102); ran New York– Buenos Aires. 1940–7 British troopship. 1947 ANNA C (Costa); lengthened from 151,23 [157,27] metres (496.2 [516.0] feet); 500

passengers. 1948 FV Genoa–Buenos Aires. 1952 new diesel engines; 18 knots; 12,030 tons; (I–202; tourist 864); ran Italy–Central America. 1972 scrapped at La Spezia.

5. (1948) ANDREA C (M/S)

8,603. 132,28 [136,24] x 17,37. (434.0 [447.0] x 57.0). 1–2–C. S–2SC.SA–15. (I–200). Permanente Metals Corporation, Richmond, Calif. (engines SA Fiat, Turin). 1942 launched as OCEAN VIRTUE (Br); 7,174 tons; 129,56 [134,56] metres (425.1 [441.5] feet); T3 by General Machinery Corporation, Hamilton. 1946 (9/8) sold 'as lies' to Costa. 1948 ANDREA C (Costa); lengthened; re-engined and passenger accommodation fitted. 1948 FV Genoa–Buenos Aires; later became a cruise ship. 1983 still in service.

6. (1952) FRANCA C (M/S)

6,822. 121,21 [130,35] x 16,55. (397.7 [427.7] x 54.3). 1–2. S–T3–14. Newport News Shipbuilding & Dry Dock Co, Newport News. 1914 (22/8) launched as cargo steamer MEDINA (Clyde Mallory). 1949 ROMA (Panamanian); rebuilt at La Spezia as passenger steamer (one class 925). 1951 FRANCA C (Costa); diesel engines. 1952 FV Genoa–Buenos Aires. 1970 again re-engined. 1977 DOULOS (Maltese).

7. (1957) BIANCA C (M/S)

9,585. 148,67 x 18,35. (487.8 x 60.2). 1–2–C. 2S–2SC.SA–15. (I–141; II–184; III–68). Koninklijke Maatschappij de Schelde, Flushing. 1925 (21/3) launched as INDRAPOERA (Rotterdam Lloyd); 10,772 tons. 1926 (10/2) MV Rotterdam–Batavia. 1931 new bow fitted; former length 146,14 metres (479.5 feet); new diesel engines (2SC.DA). 1933 (27/11) fire damage at Rotterdam. 1940–7 ran under British flag. 1949 9,585 tons; (I–96). 1956 ASSUNCION (Panamanian). 1957 BIANCA C (Costa). 1957 FV Genoa–Buenos Aires. 1958 MELANESIEN (Messageries Maritimes (c)). 1962 scrapped in Italy.

8. 1958 FEDERICO C

20,416. 160,60 [184,61] x 24,04. (533.5 [605.7] x 78.9). 1–1–C. 2S–ST(DR)–22. (I–264; cabin 202; tourist 672). Ansaldo SA, Sestri Ponente. 1957 (31/3) launched. 1958 (22/3) MV Genoa–Buenos Aires. 1966 (4/6) FV Naples–Central America. 1968 (I–186; tourist 1,450). Still undertakes occasional Central American voyages, but largely employed in cruising.

9. (1962) PROVENCE (c)

(1966) ENRICO C

15,889. 168,94 [176,77] x 22,31. (554.3 [580.0] x 73.2). 1–2–C. 2S–ST(SR)–18. (I–148; tourist 167; III–426; IV–736). Swan,

Hunter & Wigham Richardson, Tyneside (engines Parsons Marine Turbine Co, Wallsend-on-Tyne). 1950 (15/8) launched as PROVENCE (SGTM). 1954 (18/2) collision in R. Plate with SAXONSEA (Liberian tanker). 1955 (26/3) resumed Marseilles–S. America. 1962 FV as PROVENCE (Costa (c)), Genoa–Buenos Aires. 1965 ENRICO C (Costa); 13,607 tons; (I–218; tourist 980). 1966 FV Genoa–Buenos Aires. Still makes occasional Genoa-Buenos Aires voyages, but principally employed in cruising. (See SGTM (17)).

10. 1966 EUGENIO C

30,567. 188,36 [217,31] x 29,26. (618.0 [713.0] x 96.0). 2 (athwartships)–1–C. 2S–ST(DR)–26. (I–178; intermediate 356; tourist 1,102). Cantieri Riuniti dell' Adriatico, Monfalcone. 1964 (21/11) launched. 1966 (31/8) MV Genoa–Buenos Aires. Still makes a few Genoa–Buenos Aires voyages, but spends much time cruising.

FUNNEL: 1947. Black with broad yellow band containing blue 'C'.
        1950 Yellow with narrow black top; large blue 'C' (in inverted commas) on yellow.
        1960 Yellow with narrow blue top; large blue 'C' (in inverted commas) on yellow.

FLAG: 1950 Yellow pennant with blue border; large 'C' (in inverted commas) in blue.
        1960 Yellow flag with blue border; large 'C' (in inverted commas) in blue.

Note: 1950 and 1960 dates are approximate.

Chapter 70

1949–55

COMPAÑÍA ARGENTINA DE NAVEGACIÓN DODERO

(Dodero Line)

(Argentinian)

The COMPAÑÍA ARGENTINA DE NAVEGACIÓN DODERO, or DODERO LINE, placed orders with Vickers-Armstrongs Limited of Barrow-in-Furness shortly after World War II for three 19 knot twin-screw passenger liners for service between Buenos Aires and London. The first of them, the 12,459 ton PRESIDENTE PERON, was launched on 3 November 1948 and started her maiden voyage from London in the following July, calling at Havre, Lisbon, Rio de Janeiro and Montevideo.

The 12,627 ton EVA PERON, launched on 25 August 1949, began her maiden voyage from London on 9 May 1950, but differed from her consort by having accommodation for 96 first class passengers instead of only 74. The third ship, the 12,634 ton 17 DE OCTUBRE, [1] was launched on 4 April 1950 and also had accommodation for 96 passengers.

Another passenger service between Buenos Aires and Hamburg, with

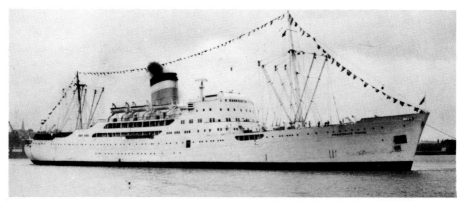

1949 PRESIDENTE PERON 12,459 tons
Maiden voyage of line July 1949, London to Buenos Aires. 1955 renamed
ARGENTINA.

calls at Vigo and Amsterdam, was begun by the Company with the 11,450 ton twin-screw motorship YAPEYU, launched by van der Giessen of Krimpen on 17 October 1950. She was followed by the 11,515 ton MAIPU, launched by Koninklijke Maastschappij de Schelde of Vlissingen (Flushing) on 20 January 1951 and the 11,521 ALBERTO DODERO, launched by the same firm on 30 June 1951. All three had accommodation for 13 first class passengers and 740 tourist.

1951 ALBERTO DODERO 11,521 tons
Ran Buenos Aires–Hamburg.

The MAIPU had a very short life as on 4 November 1951 she collided in fog at the mouth of the Elbe with the US transport GENERAL M.L. HERSEY, which was carrying 3,000 troops. The MAIPU was seriously damaged and sank three hours later, but her crew and over 100 passengers were taken off safely.

A third service was started between Buenos Aires, Rio de Janeiro, Las Palmas, Lisbon, Barcelona, Marseilles, Naples and Genoa, a further call being made at Montevideo on the southbound voyage. The ships employed were the 12,053 ton single-screw CORRIENTES and SALTA, which had been laid down by the Seattle-Tacoma Shipbuilding Corporation of Tacoma for the Moore-McCormack Line but launched as US aircraft carriers. In 1943 they were passed to the Royal Navy as H.M.S. TRACKER and H.M.S. SHAH, respectively. After the war they were handed back to the USA, who sold them to the Newport News Shipbuilding & Dry Dock Company. They, in turn, sold them to the Dodero Line for conversion into passenger ships, their complement being four first class and 1,338 tourist.

After the fall of the Peron Government in 1955, the Dodero Line ceased operations and the management of the ships passed to the FLOTA ARGENTINA DE NAVEGACIÓN DE ULTRAMAR (popularly abbreviated to FANU). The PRESIDENTE PERON was renamed ARGENTINA, the EVA PERON became the URUGUAY and the 17

1951 SALTA 12,053 tons
1942 launched as US aircraft carrier and completed 1943 as H.M.S. SHAH. Later rebuilt as passenger steamer.

DE OCTUBRE became the LIBERTAD. The same changes of management applied to the YAPEYÚ, ALBERTO DODERO, CORRIENTES and SALTA, but they retained their names.

In 1962 FANU and the Flota Merchante del Estado (the Argentinian State Line) amalgamated to form EMPRESA LINEAS MARITIMAS ARGENTINAS (ELMA) (Chapter 71).

The Flota Mercante had been running three passenger motorships, the RIO DE LA PLATA, the RIO JACHAL and the RIO TUNUYAN (for a time renamed EVITA) in a service between Buenos Aires and New York, which does not come within the scope of this volume, but it was decided in 1962 to refit them to run between Buenos Aires and Hamburg and two of them did so. This took place after the amalgamation, so there is no occasion to deal separately with Flota Mercante. The various activities of EMPRESA LINEAS MARITIMAS ARGENTINAS (ELMA) are dealt with in Chapter 71.

[1] The Spanish version of '17 October' is 'diez y siete de Octubre'.

1. 1949 PRESIDENTE PERON
   12,459. 155,13 [161,53] x 21,70. (509.0 [530.0] x 71.2). 1–2–C. 2S–ST(DR)–19. (I–74). Vickers-Armstrongs Ltd, Barrow. 1948 (3/11) launched. 1949 (Jly) MV London–Buenos Aires. 1955 ARGENTINA (Flota Argentina de Navegación de Ultramar). 1962 ditto (Empresa Lineas Maritimas Argentinas). 1966 employed as a cargo steamer. 1969 (31/7) laid up at Rosario. 1971 for sale.
2. 1950 EVA PERON
   12,627. 155,13 [161,53] x 21,70. (509.0 [530.0] x 71.2). 1–2–C.

2S–ST(DR)–19. (I–96). Vickers-Armstrongs Ltd, Barrow. 1949 (25/8) launched. 1950 (9/5) MV London–Buenos Aires. 1955 URUGUAY (Flota Argentina de Navegación de Ultramar. 1962 ditto (Empresa Lineas Maritimas Argentinas). 1967 employed as a cargo steamer. 1969 (21/10) laid up at Rosario. 1973 (16/1) arr San Pedro; scrapped.
3. 1950 17 DE OCTUBRE
    12,634. 155,13 [161,53] x 21,70. (509.0 [530.0] x 71.2). 1–2–C. 2S–ST(DR)–19. (I–96). Vickers-Armstrongs Ltd, Barrow. 1950 (4/4) launched. 1950 (Nov) MV London–Buenos Aires. 1955 LIBERTAD (Flota Argentina de Navegación de Ultramar. 1962 ditto (Empresa Lineas Maritimas Argentinas. 1964 one class (400 tourist). 1974 (15/1) laid up at Villa Constitucion. 1975 scrapped at Campana.
4. 1951 YAPEYÚ (M/S)
    11,450. 149,46 [159,36] x 19,56. (490.4 [522.9] x 64.2). 1–2–C. 2S–2SC.SA–18. (I–13; tourist 740). Van der Giessen, Krimpen. 1950 (17/10) launched. 1951 (May) MV Hamburg–Buenos Aires. 1955 YAPEYÚ (Flota Argentina de Navegación de Ultramar). 1962 ditto (Empresa Lineas Maritimas Argentinas). 1969 PETREL (Argentinian). 1974 CREMONA (Singapore). 1976 IRAN CREMONA (ditto).
5. 1951 MAIPU (M/S)
    11,515. 149,46 [159,36] x 19,56. (490.4 [522.9] x 64.2). 1–2–C. 2S–2SC.SA–18. (I–13; tourist 740). Koninklijke Maatschappij de Schelde, Flushing. 1951 (20/1) launched. 1951 (Jun) MV Hamburg–Buenos Aires. 1951 (4/11) collided with US transport GENERAL M.L. HERSEY near Weser Lightship. MAIPU sank 3 hours later (0).
6. 1951 ALBERTO DODERO (M/S)
    11,521. 149,46 [159,36] x 19,56. (490.4 [522.9] x 64.2). 1–2–C. 2S–2SC.SA–18. (I–13; tourist 740). Koninklijke Maatschappij de Schelde, Flushing. 1951 (30/6) launched. 1951 (Nov) MV Hamburg–Buenos Aires. 1955 ALBERTO DODERO (Flota Argentina de Navegación de Ultramar. 1962 ditto (Empresa Lineas Maritimas Argentinas). 1964 FV Buenos Aires–Genoa. 1969 CORMORAN (Argentinian). 1974 ditto (Singapore).
7. 1951 CORRIENTES
    12,053. 142,76 x 21,24. (468.4 x 69.7). 1–2–C. S–ST(DR)–16. (I–4; tourist 1,338). Seattle–Tacoma Shipbuilding Corporation, Tacoma. 1941 laid down as MORMACMAIL (Moore–McCormack). 1942 (7/3) launched for US Navy. 1943 H.M.S. TRACKER (British aircraft carrier). 1949 bought by Dodero; refitted as

passenger ship at Newport News; CORRIENTES. 1951 Buenos Aires–Genoa service. 1955 CORRIENTES (Flota Argentina de Navegación de Ultramar. 1962 ditto (Empresa Lineas Maritimas Argentinas). 1964 (1/8) arr. Lisbon with serious machinery damage. 1964 (14/9) arr. Antwerp; scrapped.

8. 1951 SALTA

12,053. 142,54 x 21,21. (467.7 x 69.6). 1–2–C. S–ST(DR)–16. (I–4; tourist 1,338). Seattle-Tacoma Shipbuilding Corporation, Tacoma. 1942 (20/7) launched as JAMAICA (US aircraft carrier). 1943 (27/9) H.M.S. SHAH (British aircraft carrier). 1949 bought by Dodero; refitted as passenger ship at Newport News; SALTA. 1951 Buenos Aires–Genoa service. 1955 SALTA (Flota Argentina de Navigación de Ultramar). 1962 ditto (Empresa Lineas Maritimas Argentinas. 1964 (Dec) laid up at Buenos Aires. 1966 scrapped at Buenos Aires.

FUNNEL: Blue with white band below black top.
FLAG: White semi-triangles at top and bottom; blue semi-triangles on each side; white oval with blue narrow surround in centre containing small black 'D'.

Chapter 71

(1962–74)

EMPRESA LINEAS MARITIMAS ARGENTINAS

(ELMA)

(Argentinian)

The EMPRESA LINEAS MARITIMAS ARGENTINAS, familiarly known as ELMA, was founded in Buenos Aires in 1962 by the amalgamation of the FLOTA ARGENTINA DE NAVEGACIÓN DE ULTRAMAR, or FANU, and the FLOTA MERCANTE DEL ESTADO (the Argentinian State Line).

ELMA took over the first class passenger service between Buenos Aires and London via Rio de Janeiro, Lisbon and Havre, which had been run by FANU and its predecessor, the Dodero Line (Chapter 70), using the 12,000 ton twin-screw steamers ARGENTINA (ex-PRESIDENTE PERON), URUGUAY (ex-EVA PERON) and LIBERTAD (ex-17 DE OCTUBRE). The ARGENTINA had a passenger complement of 74 and the other two of 96.

In 1963–4 the LIBERTAD was refitted to carry 400 tourist class passengers instead of first class, but it seems that the change was not very successful as in 1966 the ARGENTINA discontinued carrying any passengers at all, and the same happened to the URUGUAY in 1967. Worse was to follow as both were laid up at Rosario in 1969. The LIBERTAD survived a little longer as she was not laid up until 1974.

Two further ships taken over by ELMA in 1962 were the 12,053 ton single-screw CORRIENTES and SALTA, which had been commissioned by the Dodero Line in 1951–2 for service between Buenos Aires and Genoa. However, it is evident that by 1964 their condition must have deteriorated considerably as the CORRIENTES arrived at Lisbon on 1 August 1964 with serious machinery damage. This was considered beyond repair, and by the middle of the following month she turned up at Antwerp to be scrapped. In the following December the SALTA was laid up at Buenos Aires, and within two years she, too, was scrapped.

Their places on the Buenos Aires–Genoa service were taken by the 11,500 ton motorships YAPEYÚ and ALBERTO DODERO, which had been running between Buenos Aires and Hamburg since 1951. The Italian service was continued until 1969, when both ships were sold to

487

another Argentinian concern and renamed PETREL and CORMOR-AN, respectively.

The RIO DE LA PLATA, RIO TUNUYAN and RIO JACHAL of the Flota Mercante del Estado had been running from Buenos Aires to New York as first class carriers between 1950 and 1962, when the line was amalgamated with FANU to become ELMA. In 1963 the RIO DE LA PLATA was converted to carry 372 one-class (tourist) passengers, and was transferred to run between Buenos Aires and Hamburg. Unfortunately, she was destroyed by fire at Buenos Aires on 19 November 1964 and eventually scrapped.

The RIO TUNUYAN, also, was refitted to carry tourist only, and started running between Buenos Aires and Hamburg in 1964. She continued until 1972.

The RIO JACHAL was seriously damaged by fire at New York on 28 September 1962 before steps had been taken to convert her for one-class service between Buenos Aires and Hamburg. She was patched up, managed to reach Buenos Aires, laid up, had a further fire and was scrapped in 1970, so never ran to Hamburg.

Thus, the ELMA passenger ship LIBERTAD ran until 1974, the RIO TUNUYAN until 1972 and the YAPEYÚ and ALBERTO DODERO until 1969. Much of the blame for this early demise must be laid against competition by the air lines.

Meanwhile, the ARGENTINA was put up for sale in 1971 and her sister ship URUGUAY was scrapped in 1973. Only the LIBERTAD remained, although for little longer. Laid up in 1974, she was scrapped in the following year.

1. (1962) ARGENTINA (ex-PRESIDENTE PERON)
2. (1962) URUGUAY (ex-EVA PERON)
3. (1962) LIBERTAD (ex 17 DE OCTUBRE)
4. (1962) YAPEYÚ (M/S)
5. (1962) ALBERTO DODERO (M/S)
6. (1962) CORRIENTES
7. (1962) SALTA
(For full details of the above seven ships see COMPAÑÍA ARGENTI-NA DE NAVEGACIÓN DODERO (Chapter 70)).
8. (1963) RIO DE LA PLATA (M/S)
 11,317. 160,19 [167,53] x 20,08. (525.6 [549.7] x 65.9). 1–2–C. 2S–2SC.DA–18. (I–116). Ansaldo, Sestri Ponente. 1949 (6/3) launched for Flota Mercante del Estado. 1950 Buenos Aires–New York. 1962 RIO DE LA PLATA (ELMA). 1963 Buenos Aires–Hamburg service; (tourist 372). 1964 (19/11) destroyed by

fire when undergoing repairs at Buenos Aires. 1968 scrapped at Buenos Aires.
9. (1964) RIO TUNUYAN (M/S)
11,317. 160,19 [167,53] x 20,08. (525.6 [549.7] x 65.9). 1–2–C. 2S–2SC.DA–18. (I–116). Ansaldo, Sestri Ponente. 1949 (30/10) launched for Flota Mercante del Estado. 1951 Buenos Aires–New York. 1952 renamed EVITA. 1955 reverted to RIO TUNUYAN. 1962 RIO TUNUYAN (ELMA). 1963–4 373 tourist class only. 1964 FV Buenos Aires–Hamburg. 1972 laid up at Villa Constitucion.
— —— RIO JACHAL (M/S)
11,342. 160,19 [167,53] x 20,08. (525.6 [549.7] x 65.9). 1–2–C. 2S–2SC.DA–18. (I–116). Ansaldo, Sestri Ponente. 1949 (12/5) launched for Flota Mercante del Estado. 1950 Buenos Aires–New York. 1962 RIO JACHAL (ELMA). 1962 (28/9) badly damaged by fire at New York. 1964 temporary repairs; proceeded to Buenos Aires and laid up. (She had been intended to join the RIO DE LA PLATA and RIO TUNUYAN on the Buenos Aires–Hamburg service). 1968 (17/4) again badly damaged by fire. 1970 scrapped at Buenos Aires.

SUPPLEMENTARY LINES

It is confidently believed that the 71 chapters of this book include all the really important passenger services between Europe, Brazil, Uruguay and Argentina. Given unlimited space a number of additional lines could certainly have been added, but some of the more interesting are dealt with briefly in the following pages.

JOHNSON LINE (Swedish)

Axel Johnson opened an office in Stockholm in 1873, dealing principally with coal, iron and steel. Twelve years later he bought his first steamer, the 642 ton wooden screw W.T. MARSHALL, followed in 1890 by the 980 ton iron screw CYCLOP, built in 1873, which he renamed ANNIE THERESE.

Axel Johnson died in 1910 at the age of 66 and was succeeded by his son Axel Axelson Johnson, born in 1876. The Company's first motorship, the 3,730 ton SUECIA, was commissioned in 1912 and was so successful that all subsequent ships of the line had a similar form of propulsion.

By the 1960s the Company possessed a magnificent fleet of over 40 ships and was running a fast weekly service of cargo ships of over 8,000 tons from Sweden to Brazil, Uruguay and Argentina, as well as two services via the Panama Canal – one to North Pacific coast ports and the other to Peru and Chile.

The Company's principal shipping interest was the carriage of cargo, and few, if any, of their fleet carried more than 12 passengers.

LAURO LINES (Italian)

The 23,114 ton motorship WILLEM RUYS of the Koninklijke Rotterdamsche Lloyd (Royal Rotterdam Lloyd) and the 20,565 ton motorship ORANJE of the Stoomvaart Maatschappij Nederland (Nederland Line) were acquired by the Lauro Lines of Naples in 1964–5 and renamed ACHILLE LAURO and ANGELINA LAURO. Not only were both extensively rebuilt, but both were seriously damaged by fire before the alterations were completed. From 1966 they proceeded from Rotterdam or Bremen to Australia and New Zealand via the Suez Canal, while a year later they were routed via South Africa instead of Suez. From 1971 onwards some homeward voyages were made via east coast ports of South America, but the arrangement was discontinued in 1972–3, after which the two ships were employed exclusively in cruising.

The ANGELINA LAURO was destroyed by fire at St. Thomas, Virgin Islands, on 31 March 1979.

LLOYD BRASILEIRO (Brazilian)
The only available confirmation that this important line ever ran a passenger service between Brazil and Europe was an advertisement in *The Times* of 13 March 1922 stating that the 8,227 ton AVARE would sail from Southampton on 21 March for Leixões, Lisbon, Madeira, Pernambuco, Bahia, Rio de Janeiro and Santos, followed by the 8,235 ton BAGE on 21 April and the 6,456 ton CURVELLO on 21 May.

It seems likely that the Company had further sailings between Brazil and Hamburg or Bremen, but that very few of them called at a British port – hence the scarcity of available information.

NAVIERA AZNAR (Spanish)
Although the AZNAR LINE can be traced back to 1880, this title did not come into use until 1939, after which its ships had names prefixed with 'MONTE'.

The 6,500 ton passenger motorships MONTE UDALA (I) and MONTE UMBE (I) were commissioned in 1943, but much more important was the 10,170 ton motorship MONTE UDALA (II), which was launched on 1 May 1946 and completed in July 1948 to run between Genoa and Buenos Aires. She could accommodate 62 first, 40 second and 290 third class passengers. A sister ship proceeded to Vera Cruz. The 9,971 ton MONTE UMBE (II) was added in 1959 for the South American service.

The MONTE UDALA (II) sprang a leak on 8 September 1971 during a voyage from Buenos Aires to Genoa and had to be abandoned in a sinking condition. The MONTE UMBE (II) was sold in 1975 and the South American service withdrawn.

Between 1973 and 1977 passenger sailings took place between Santander and Southampton in summer, and the Company ran a series of cruises from Liverpool to the Canary Islands.

NEW ZEALAND SHIPPING COMPANY (British)
The 4,215 ton TONGARIRO sailed from London on 25 October 1883 for New Zealand via the Cape of Good Hope, and returned via Cape Horn, Montevideo, Rio de Janeiro and Tenerife. She had accommodation for 80 first, 80 second and 250 third class passengers. Subsequent sailings were undertaken from London by the AORANGI on 29 November 1883 and the RUAPEHU on 10 January 1884, followed by the chartered steamers BRITISH QUEEN, BRITISH KING, IONIC and

DORIC until 24 October 1884, when the KAIKOURA started regular sailings by the Company's own ships.

The Montevideo departures and Tenerife calls were made until late 1915, when homeward traffic was routed via the Cape of Good Hope. A further change took place in July 1916, when the ships started to use the Panama Canal.

SHAW, SAVILL & ALBION COMPANY (British)

After a few earlier sailings by chartered steamers, SHAW, SAVILL & ALBION and the WHITE STAR LINE started a joint four-weekly service with the departure from London of the 4,367 ton White Star COPTIC for New Zealand via the Cape of Good Hope. returning via Cape Horn with calls at Montevideo, Rio de Janeiro and Tenerife. All the ships were managed by Shaw Savill.

Subsequent sailings were undertaken by the ARAWA, IONIC, DORIC and TAINUI and, eventually, by their successors. The call at Rio de Janeiro was maintained until 1916, when the ships were routed homewards via the Panama Canal, but the Montevideo call had been abandoned some years previously.

SITMAR LINE (Italian)

During parts of 1953 and 1954 the SITMAR LINE's 12,150 ton twin-screw turbine steamer CASTEL FELICE, built in 1930 as the British India KENYA, made a few voyages from Genoa to Brazil and Argentina. She had been considerably rebuilt, and had accommodation for 1,500 one-class passengers, of whom about 950 were berthed in dormitories. The CASTEL FELICE was scrapped at Kaohsiung in 1970.

SOUTH AMERICAN SAINT LINE (British)

The Barry Shipping Company Limited, formed in the 1920s, changed its name in 1939 to the SOUTH AMERICAN SAINT LINE. In 1948 it commissioned the distinctive 6,855 ton motorships ST. ESSLYT and ST. THOMAS, which had accommodation for 12 passengers. Outward cargo was frequently loaded at Antwerp, Hamburg and Bremen before sailings took place from Cardiff for Brazil and the River Plate.

HUGO STINNES LINIEN (German)

Soon after World War I Hugh Stinnes, one of Germany's most famous industrial magnates, was determined to gain control of the Hamburg American Line (Hapag). He was unsuccessful and in consequence decided to start his own lines from Hamburg to Brazil and the River Plate, to Cuba and Mexico and to the Far East, to all of which destinations Hapag were closely involved.

One of the numerous vessels surrendered to Britain by Germany in 1919 was the 10,000 ton Hamburg–Süd BAHIA CASTILLO (Chapter 26), which was sold to Hugo Stinnes in September 1922. He renamed her GENERAL SAN MARTIN, soon changed to GENERAL BELGRANO, and placed her in service between Hamburg, Brazil and the River Plate. She was by far his most notable ship, with accommodation for 142 second and 542 third class passengers.

In 1924 the Stinnes group got into financial difficulties and sold their shipping interests to the Deutsch-Austral & Kosmos Linien, which in turn was taken over by Hapag in 1926. However, the name HUGO STINNES LINIEN remained in use for a good many months longer and the 7,879 ton GENERAL MITRE, built in 1920 for a Danzig firm as the ARTUS, was commissioned for the South American service. She had been fitted in 1924 to carry 700 third class passengers.

In addition, three Stinnes ships varying between 3,606 and 4,381 tons, and carrying between 14 and 22 first class passengers, were renamed ARTEMISIA, ALBINGIA and ARAGONIA by Hapag in 1927, and were interchangeable between South America and Cuba and Mexico.

A year or two later the names Hugo Stinnes Linien and Deutsch-Austral & Kosmos were things of the past, and Hapag's fleet increased to a grand total of nearly 850,000 tons, this within only a few years of being virtually nil.

TRANSPORTES MARITIMOS DO ESTADO (Portuguese)

Owing to the heavy demand for passages and freight after the Armistice of 11 November 1918, the Portuguese Government despatched steamers from Lisbon to both New York and South America under the description TRANSPORTES MARITIMOS DO ESTADO, which freely translated means 'Portuguese State Steamship Line'.

The 5,235 ton MORMUGÃO, the 5,605 ton GOA and the 5,055 ton SÃO VICENTE, formerly the German KOMMODORE (es-ESNE), LICHTENFELS and WÜRZBURG, respectively, made a total of 11 round voyages between Lisbon and New York in 1919–21.

In 1921 a service was started between Hamburg, Havre, Vigo, Leixões, Lisbon, Madeira, St. Vincent, Rio de Janeiro, Santos and Buenos Aires by the 6,636 ton twin-screw PORTO, formerly the Norddeutscher Lloyd PRINZ HEINRICH, which had accommodation for 136 first and 72 second class passengers, and the 8,980 ton twin-screw TRAS-OS-MONTES, formerly the NDL BÜLOW, which could accommodate 106 first, 113 second and 1,426 third class passengers.

It seems that this service only lasted for a year or two.

APPENDIX B

LARGEST PASSENGER LINERS

of 14,000 tons and over

Chapter No.	Ship	Line	Flag	Date	Gross tons
56	L'ATLANTIQUE	Sud Atlantique	Fr	1931	40,945
36	AUGUSTUS (I)	NGI	It	1927	32,650
36	ROMA	NGI	It	(1935)	32,583
69	EUGENIO C	Costa	It	1966	30,567
65	CRISTOFORO COLOMBO	Italia	It	(1973)	29,429
56	PASTEUR	Sud Atlantique	Fr	*	29,253
65	GUGLIELMO MARCONI	Italia (c)	It	(1976)	27,905
26	CAP ARCONA	Hamburg–Süd	Ger	1927	27,561
65	AUGUSTUS (II)	Italia	It	1952	27,090
65	GIULIO CESARE (II)	Italia	It	1951	27,078
65	CONTE GRANDE	Italia	It	(1933)	25,661
1	ANDES (II)	Royal Mail	Br	*	25,569
65	VULCANIA	Italia	It	(1947)	24,469
65	CONTE BIANCAMANO	Italia	It	(1932)	24,416
36	DUILIO	NGI	It	(1928)	24,281
60	SATURNIA	Cosulich	It	1927	23,940
1	ALCANTARA (II)	RMSP	Br	1927	22,181
1	ASTURIAS (II)	RMSP	Br	1926	22,071
36	GIULIO CESARE (I)	NGI	It	1932	21,657
26	CAP POLONIO	Hamburg–Süd	Ger	(1922)	20,576
69	FEDERICO C	Costa	It	1958	20,416
1	AMAZON	Royal Mail	Br	1960	20,368
1	ARAGON	Royal Mail	Br	1960	20,362
1	ARLANZA (II)	Royal Mail	Br	1960	20,362
51	BRABANTIA	Royal Holland Lloyd	Dut	1920	19,653
51	LIMBURGIA	Royal Holland Lloyd	Dut	1920	19,582
60	OCEANIA	Cosulich	It	1933	19,507
60	NEPTUNIA	Cosulich	It	1932	19,475
26	CAP TRAFALGAR	Hamburg–Süd	Ger	1914	18,710
52	CONTE VERDE	Lloyd Sabaudo	It	1923	18,383
52	CONTE ROSSO	Lloyd Sabaudo	It	1922	18,017
12	PASTEUR	Messageries Maritimes	Fr	1966	17,986
19	REINA DEL PACIFICO	PSN	Br	1931	17,702
1	MAGDALENA	Royal Mail	Br	1949	17,547
68	ITALIA	Home	Pan	(1948)	16,777
17	BRETAGNE	SGTM	Fr	1952	16,355
1	ALCANTARA (I)	RMSP	Br	1914	15,831
17	PROVENCE	SGTM	Fr	1951	15,719
1	ANDES (I)	RMSP	Br	1913	15,620
1	ALMANZORA	RMSP	Br	(1920)	15,551
19	ORDUÑA	PSN	Br	1914	15,507

19	ORBITA	PSN	Br	(1919)	15,495
56	MASSILIA	Sud Atlantique	Fr	1920	15,363
56	GALLIA	Sud Atlantique	Fr	1913	14,966
56	LUTETIA	Sud Atlantique	Fr	1913	14,783
63	CABO SAN VICENTE	Ybarra	Sp	1959	14,569
26	CAP FINISTERRE	Hamburg–Süd	Ger	1911	14,503
63	CABO SAN ROQUE	Ybarra	Sp	1957	14,491
49	HIGHLAND PRINCESS	Nelson	Br	1930	14,157
49	HIGHLAND PATRIOT	Nelson	Br	1932	14,157
49	HIGHLAND CHIEFTAIN	Nelson	Br	1929	14,141
49	HIGHLAND MONARCH	Nelson	Br	1928	14,137
49	HIGHLAND BRIGADE	Nelson	Br	1929	14,131
49	HIGHLAND HOPE	Nelson	Br	1930	14,129
19	OROPESA	PSN	Br	1920	14,118
51	TUBANTIA	Royal Holland Lloyd	Dut	1914	14,061

Note: Dates in brackets indicate when a ship first ran to South America if this date was different from that when she was built.
* Maiden voyage scheduled for September 1939, but postponed owing to outbreak of World War II.

APPENDIX C

SHIP LOSSES

Date	Ship	Line	Flag	From	To	How lost	Where	Lives lost
1854 (26/1)	OLINDA	S. Am & Gen	Br	Liverpool	Brazil	Wrecked	Holyhead	0
1856 (28/9)	FRANCE	Mixte	Fr			Fire	Bahia	
1865 (27/2)	BÉARN	Messageries	Fr	Bordeaux	Brazil	Wrecked	Brazil	0
1870 (4/5)	PARAENSE	Red X	Br	Liverpool	Maranham	Wrecked	Ceara	
1872 (24/4)	EVORA	Ryde	Br	R. Plate	London	Wrecked	Montevideo	0
1872 (28/10)	TACORA	PSN	Br	Liverpool	S. America	Wrecked	Montevideo	
1873 (13/4)	GAMBIE	Messageries	Fr	Rio de Janeiro	Bordeaux	Wrecked	Bahia	0
1873 (24/11)	FLAMSTEED	Lamport & Holt	Br	Liverpool	Brazil	Collision		
1874 (18/5)	BONITA	Ryde	Br	Brazil	Southampton	Wrecked	Vigo Island	
1874 (27/8)	LIFFEY	RMSP	Br	Southampton	Buenos Aires	Wrecked	Uruguay	
1874 (15/10)	MORENO	Ch. Réunis	Fr	Rio de Janeiro	Havre	Wrecked	Rio de Janeiro	
1875 (28/2)	MARALDI	Lamport & Holt	Br	Montevideo	Antwerp	Wrecked	Pernambuco	
1875 (12/8)	BOYNE	RMSP	Br	Buenos Aires	Southampton	Wrecked	Brest	0
1876 (10/8)	GERMANIA	Hamburg–Süd (c)	Ger	Hamburg	Brazil	Wrecked	Bahia	
1876 (23/12)	GOETHE	Hamburg–Süd (c)	Ger	Hamburg	Buenos Aires	Wrecked	R. Plate	
1877 (7/10)	PARANA	Messageries	Fr	Bordeaux	Buenos Aires	Wrecked	Bahia	
1878 (18/2)	ASTARTE	Donaldson	Br	Cardiff	Montevideo	Wrecked	Uruguay	
1878 (19/11)	HOOGLY	Messsageries	Fr	Bordeaux	Buenos Aires	Wrecked	Montevideo	0
1880 (20/8)	RIVADAVIA	Ch. Réunis	Fr	Havre	Brazil	Wrecked	Cape Villano	0
1881 (9/4)	NEWTON	Lamport & Holt	Br	Rio de Janeiro	London	Wrecked	Madeira	
1881 (16/4)	AMAZONENSE	Red X	Br	Liverpool	Para	Wrecked	Welsh coast	1
1882 (1/4)	DOURO	RMSP	Br	Buenos Aires	Southampton	Collision	Cape Finisterre	17
1882 (14/11)	NAVARRE	SGTM	Fr	Brazil	Marseilles	Wrecked	Marseilles	0
1883 (2/1)	NORD AMERICA	Lavarello	It	Buenos Aires	Genoa	Wrecked	Spain	0
1883 (26/2)	COPERNICUS	Lamport & Holt	Br	Liverpool	Brazil	Wrecked	Ponta de Pedras	0
1884 (11/9)	DART	RMSP	Br	Brazil	New York–London	Wrecked	Santos	1
1884 (11/10)	VILLE DE PARA	Ch. Réunis	Fr	Havre	Buenos Aires	Foundered	Brazil	
1885 (20/6)	GUADIANA	RMSP	Br	Brazil	New York–London	Wrecked	Morocco	2
1885 (1/12)	ABISSINIA	NGI	It	Genoa	Buenos Aires	Wrecked	Brazil	0
1886 (24/12)	VILLE DE VICTORIA	Ch. Réunis	Fr	Havre	Buenos Aires	Collision	Lisbon	32
1887 (28/2)	VALPARAISO	PSN	Br	Liverpool	Montevideo	Wrecked	Vigo Bay	0
1887 (7/5)	VILLE DE RIO DE JANEIRO	Ch. Réunis	Fr	Buenos Aires	Havre	Collision	French coast	0
1888 (13/9)	SUD AMERICA	La Veloce	It	Buenos Aires	Genoa	Collision	Las Palmas	87
1889 (4/9)	SAN MARTIN	Ch. Réunis	Fr	Havre	Buenos Aires	Wrecked	Montevideo	0
	LETTDAM	D…				Wrecked		0

Date	Ship	Line	Flag	From	To	Cause	Location	Lost
1892 (1/3)	PLATO	Lamport & Holt	Br	Liverpool	Brazil	Foundered	Scilly Isles	0
1892 (24/3)	DESTERRO	Hamburg–Süd	Ger	Rio de Janeiro	Hamburg	Collision	North Sea	0
1892 (19/5)	PARANA	Ch. Réunis	Fr	Buenos Aires	Havre	Wrecked	Rio de Janeiro	0
1893 (5/12)	NAPOLI	La Veloce	It	Genoa	Santos	Abandoned	Brazil	
1895 (24/5)	CIUDAD DE SANTANDER	Cia Tras	Sp	Barcelona	Buenos Aires	Wrecked	Lobos Island	103
1895 (27/5)	DOM PEDRO	Ch. Réunis	Fr	Havre	Buenos Aires	Wrecked	Galicia	0
1895 (22/6)	BESSEL	Lamport & Holt	Br	London	Brazil	Collision	British coast	
1895 (30/9)	URUGUAY	Hamburg–Süd	Ger	Buenos Aires	Hamburg	Wrecked	Cape Frio	
1896 (17/6)	SANTARENSE	Red X	Br	Liverpool	Para	Collision	North Atlantic	
1896 (7/12)	SALIER	NDL	Ger	Bremen	Buenos Aires	Wrecked	Spain	279
1899 (2/12)	MONTEVIDEO	La Veloce	It	Genoa	Buenos Aires	Wrecked	River Plate	
1900 (9/3)	CUVIER	Lamport & Holt	Br	Antwerp	Brazil	Collision	Goodwins	
1901 (11/7)	MEXICO	Cia Tras	Sp	Buenos Aires	Spain	Wrecked	Portugal	0
1903 (12/9)	BRETAGNE	SGTM	Fr	Santos	Marseilles	Wrecked	Bahia	0
1904 (10/12)	*HIGHLAND LASSIE	Nelson	Br	Swansea	Buenos Aires	Went missing		
1905 (5/9)	CYRIL	Booth	Br	Manaos	Liverpool	Collision	R. Amazon	0
1906 (4/8)	SIRIO	NGI	It	Genoa	Buenos Aires	Wrecked	Spain	442
1907 (7/5)	POITOU	SGTM	Fr	Marseilles	Buenos Aires	Wrecked	Uruguay	20
1907 (22/10)	BORUSSIA	Hapag	Ger	Hamburg	S. America	Foundered	Lisbon	3
1908 (30/8)	CAP FRIO	Hamburg–Süd	Ger	Bahia	Hamburg	Wrecked	Bahia	
1911 (15/6)	MILTON	Lamport & Holt	Br	London	Brazil	Wrecked	Portugal	
1912 (23/1)	CALDERON	Lamport & Holt	Br	Glasgow	Santos	Collision	R. Mersey	0
1912 (16/11)	ORAVIA	PSN	Br	Liverpool	S. America	Wrecked	Falkland Islands	
1913 (16/1)	VERONESE	Lamport & Holt	Br	Liverpool	Buenos Aires	Wrecked	Leixões	43
1915 (3/10)	HIGHLAND WARRIOR	Nelson	Br	London	Buenos Aires	Wrecked	Spain	0
1916 (3/3)	PRINCIPE DE ASTURIAS	Pinillos	Sp	Barcelona	Buenos Aires	Collision	Santos	415
1916 (5/2)	TOSCANA	Transoceanica	It	Genoa	Buenos Aires	Collision	Gibraltar	
1918 (6/5)	HIGHLAND SCOT	Nelson	Br	Buenos Aires	England	Wrecked	Brazil	
1927 (25/10)	PRINCIPESSA MAFALDA	NGI	It	Genoa	Buenos Aires	Foundered	Bahia	303
1929 (9/9)	HIGHLAND PRIDE	Nelson	Br	London	Buenos Aires	Wrecked	Vigo	0
1930 (9/11)	HIGHLAND HOPE	Nelson	Br	London	Buenos Aires	Wrecked	Portugal	0
1934 (19/12)	ORANIA	R.H. Lloyd	Dut	Buenos Aires	Amsterdam	Rammed	Leixões	0
1936 (16/8)	EUBÉE	Ch. Réunis	Fr	Bordeaux	Buenos Aires	Collision	S. Atlantic	0
1938 (2/1)	GUARUJA	France–Amérique	Fr	Genoa	Buenos Aires	Wrecked	Almeria	
1949 (26/4)	MAGDALENA	Royal Mail	Br	Buenos Aires	London	Foundered	Rio de Janeiro	0
1951 (4/11)	MAIPU	Dodero	Arg	Buenos Aires	Hamburg	Collision	Weser Lightship	
1956 (15/4)	ALTAIR	RZAL	Dut	Rosario	Hamburg	Wrecked	Brazil	0
1957 (25/9)	HILDEBRAND	Booth	Br	Liverpool	R. Amazon	Wrecked	Near Lisbon	0

* – date of sailing.
(c) – chartered.
Notes: Losses in the Pacific or the Straits of Magellan are not included.
War losses are not included.
Fuller details of individual losses will often be found in the relevant chapter or fleet list.

497

INDEX OF LINES

501

INDEX OF SHIPS

511

An alphabetical list of the ships illustrated will be found on pages x, xi, xii and xiii.
Note: The substitution of "A&C" for a page number denotes that details will be found in the Addenda and Corrigenda.

APPENDIX F

ADDENDA AND CORRIGENDA

Chapter	Page	
4	41–42	DONNA MARIA SEGONDA. Laid down as VICTORIA for unknown owners. 1859 (Sep) sold at Lisbon by public auction and bought by Mr. Burney of Lisbon on behalf of an unknown British company. 1859 (6/11) sailed as LIVERPOOL, Lisbon–Cape Raso (four miles from Tagus bar) for engine trials. 1859 (11/11) sailed Lisbon–Liverpool in ballast (B. H. Higgins, master). 1859 (14/11) registered at Liverpool as LIVERPOOL. 1860 (14/3) QUEEN OF ENGLAND (T. B. & A. B. Forwood, Liverpool). 1860 (24/7) ditto (F. W. Honischer, London). 1860 (Jly) sailed Liverpool–Messina. 1860 (23/8) sold at Messina; later details unknown.
12	75	32. 1967 MEI ABETO (Cie de Navigation Abeto (Panamanian)). 1977 (Jly) arr Jacarta; laid up until at least 1982–3.
12	75	33. 1967 LE HAVRE ABETO (Panamanian); became a pilgrim ship. 1978 (Mar) laid up off Jacarta, and so remained until at least 1982–3.
16	118	7. ANSELM (I). 1882 (11/11) launched.
16	121	25. GREGORY (II). 1891 (21/7) launched as CRESSWELL (Br).
16	121	27. LISBONENSE. 1928 (19/8) foundered.
28	233	43. (See Chapter 12, page 75, item 32 above.)
56	415	17. (See Chapter 12, page 75, item 33 above.)
67	470–1	4. 1952 VERA CRUZ transfer to item 6.

524

4. (1948) PATRIA.
13,196. 154,52 [161,87] x 20,84. (507.0 [531.1] x 68.4). 1–2–C. 2S–ST(DR)–17. (I–114; tourist 156; III–118; IV–384). John Brown & Co Ltd, Glasgow. 1947 (30/6) launched. 1948 (26/1) MV Lisbon–Mozambique. 1948 (5/8) FV Lisbon–Madeira–St. Vincent–Rio de Janeiro–Santos. 1956 (4/8) LV Lisbon–Brazil (2RV). 1973 scrapped at Kaohsiung.
5. 1953 SANTA MARIA transfer to item 7.
5. (1948) IMPÉRIO.
13,186. 154,52 [161,87] x 20,84. (507.0 [531.1] x 68.4). 1–2–C. 2S–ST(DR)–17. (I–114; tourist 156; III–118; IV–384. John Brown & Co Ltd, Glasgow. 1947 (27/12) launched. 1948 (20/7) MV Lisbon–Mozambique. 1948 (2/10) FV Lisbon–Brazil. 1948 (15/12) LV ditto (3 RV). 1974 scrapped at Kaohsiung.
8. (1958) UIGE (M/S).
10,001. 133,80 [145,50] x 19,14. (439.0 [477.4] x 62.8). 1–2–C. 1S–2SC.SA–16. (I–78; III–493). John Cockerill, Hoboken. 1954 (23/1) launched. 1954 (4/8) MV Lisbon–Angola. 1958 (15/7) FV Lisbon–Leixões–Madeira–St. Vincent–Recife (Pernambuco)–Salvador (Bahia)–Rio de Janeiro–Santos. 1974 UIGE (Cia Portuguesa de Transportes Maritimos). 1976 (26/1) laid up at Lisbon. 1979 (Mar) scrapped at Lisbon.

525

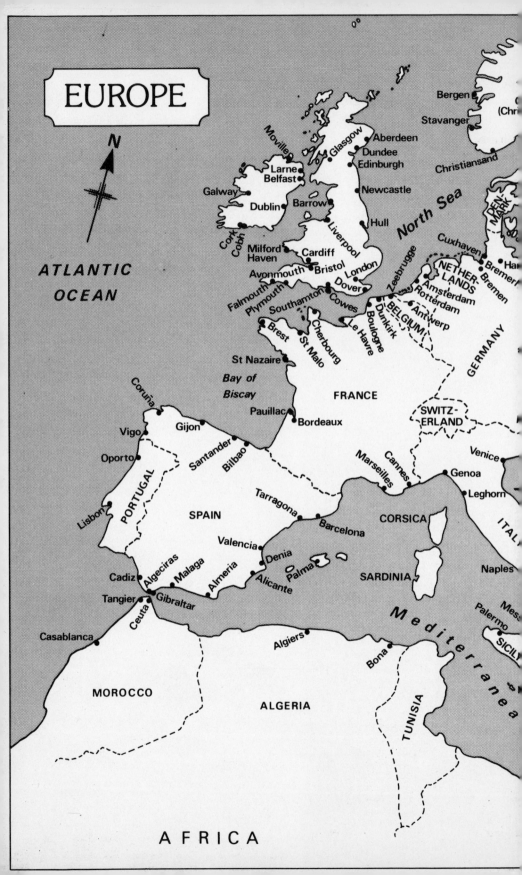